Contents

W9-BDN-544

Preface xix

Writing in Stages: The Process Approach 1

Introduction 1
    Learning by Doing 1
    Steps Make Writing Easier 1

CHAPTER 1 Writing a Paragraph 3

Beginning the Prewriting: Gathering Ideas 4
    Freewriting, Brainstorming, Keeping a Journal 4
    Finding Specific Ideas 6
    Selecting One Topic 7
    Adding Details to a Specific Topic 9

Focusing the Prewriting 12
    Listing Related Ideas 12
    Mapping 13
    Forming a Topic Sentence 13
    Writing Good Topic Sentences 13

    PLANNING **Devising a Plan for a Paragraph** 19
    Checking Your Details 19
    Adding Details When There Are Not Enough 20
    Eliminating Details That Do Not Relate to the Topic Sentence 21
    From List to Outline 21

Coherence: Putting Your Details in Proper Order 22

    DRAFTING **Drafting and Revising a Paragraph** 26
    Drafting a Paragraph 26
    Revising 27

    POLISHING **Polishing and Proofreading a Paragraph** 29
    Correcting the Last Draft of a Paragraph 30
    Giving Your Paragraph a Title 30
    The Final Version of a Paragraph 30
    Reviewing the Writing Process 31

Lines of Detail: A Walk-Through Assignment 32

Writing Your Own Paragraph 34

Peer Review Form for a Paragraph 38

CHAPTER 2   Illustration   **39**

What Is Illustration?   **39**
Hints for Writing an Illustration Paragraph   39
Knowing What Is Specific and What Is General   39

Writing the Illustration Paragraph in Steps   **42**
PREWRITING **Gathering Ideas: Illustration**   **42**
Adding Details to an Idea   43
Creating a Topic Sentence   44
PLANNING **Devising a Plan: Illustration**   **48**
DRAFTING **Drafting and Revising: Illustration**   **51**
Transitions   51
POLISHING **Polishing and Proofreading: Illustration**   **53**

Lines of Detail: A Walk-Through Assignment   **55**

Writing Your Own Illustration Paragraph   **55**

Peer Review for an Illustration Paragraph   **58**

CHAPTER 3   Description   **59**

What Is Description?   **59**
Hints for Writing a Descriptive Paragraph   59
Using Specific Words and Phrases   59
Using Sense Words in Your Descriptions   63

Writing the Descriptive Paragraph in Steps   **65**
PREWRITING **Gathering Ideas: Description**   **65**
The Dominant Impression   65
PLANNING **Devising a Plan: Description**   **67**
DRAFTING **Drafting and Revising: Description**   **72**
Transitions   74
POLISHING **Polishing and Proofreading: Description**   **76**

Lines of Detail: A Walk-Through Assignment   **78**

Writing Your Own Descriptive Paragraph   **78**

Peer Review Form for a Descriptive Paragraph   **81**

CHAPTER 4   Narration   **82**

What Is Narration?   **82**
Give the Narrative a Point   82
Hints for Writing a Narrative Paragraph   86
Using a Speaker's Exact Words in Narrative   88

Writing the Narrative Paragraph in Steps   **89**
PREWRITING **Gathering Ideas: Narration**   **89**
Freewriting for a Narrative Topic   90
Narrowing and Selecting a Suitable Narrative Topic   90
PLANNING **Devising a Plan: Narration**   **93**
DRAFTING **Drafting and Revising: Narration**   **96**
Revising for Sharper Details   97
Checking the Topic Sentence   97
Using Transitions Effectively in Narration   101
The Draft   101

POLISHING **Polishing and Proofreading: Narration   102**

Lines of Detail: A Walk-Through Assignment   104

Writing Your Own Narrative Paragraph   104

Peer Review Form for a Narrative Paragraph   107

CHAPTER 5   Process   108

What Is Process?   108
  A Process Involves Steps in Time Order   108
  Hints for Writing a Process Paragraph   109

Writing the Process Paragraph in Steps   111
  PREWRITING **Gathering Ideas: Process   111**
    Writing a Topic Sentence for a Process Paragraph   112

  PLANNING **Devising a Plan: Process   113**

  DRAFTING **Drafting and Revising: Process   118**
    Using the Same Grammatical Person   118
    Using Transitions Effectively   119
    The Draft   121

  POLISHING **Polishing and Proofreading: Process   122**

Lines of Detail: A Walk-Through Assignment   124

Writing Your Own Process Paragraph   125

Peer Review Form for a Process Paragraph   128

CHAPTER 6   Comparison and Contrast   129

What Is Comparison? What Is Contrast?   129
  Hints for Writing a Comparison or Contrast Paragraph   129
  Organizing Your Comparison or Contrast Paragraph   131
  Using Transitions Effectively for Comparison or Contrast   135

Writing the Comparison or Contrast Paragraph in Steps   137
  PREWRITING **Gathering Ideas: Comparison or Contrast   137**
    Getting Points of Comparison or Contrast   137
    Adding Details to Your Points   139

  PLANNING **Devising a Plan: Comparison or Contrast   141**

  DRAFTING **Drafting and Revising: Comparison or Contrast   146**
    The Draft   146

  POLISHING **Polishing and Proofreading: Comparison
      or Contrast   149**
    Contrast Paragraph: Point-by-Point Pattern   149
    The Same Contrast Paragraph: Subject-by-Subject   150

Lines of Detail: A Walk-Through Assignment   153

Writing Your Own Comparison or Contrast Paragraph   153

Peer Review Form for a Comparison or Contrast Paragraph   156

CHAPTER 7   Classification   157

What Is Classification?   157
  Hints for Writing a Classification Paragraph   157

Writing the Classification Paragraph in Steps   160

(PREWRITING) **Gathering Ideas: Classification**   160

Brainstorming a Basis for Classification   160

Matching the Points Within the Categories   161

Writing a Topic Sentence for a Classification Paragraph   162

(PLANNING) **Devising a Plan: Classification**   164

Effective Order in Classifying   164

(DRAFTING) **Drafting and Revising: Classification**   166

Transitions in Classification   166

(POLISHING) **Polishing and Proofreading: Classification**   169

Lines of Detail: A Walk-Through Assignment   171

Writing Your Own Classification Paragraph   172

Peer Review Form for a Classification Paragraph   174

CHAPTER 8   Definition   175

What Is Definition?   175

Hints for Writing a Definition Paragraph   175

Writing the Definition Paragraph in Steps   180

(PREWRITING) **Gathering Ideas: Definition**   180

Using Questions to Get Details   180

The Topic Sentence   181

(PLANNING) **Devising a Plan: Definition**   183

(DRAFTING) **Drafting and Revising: Definition**   185

Transitions   186

The Draft   186

(POLISHING) **Polishing and Proofreading: Definition**   190

Lines of Detail: A Walk-Through Assignment   192

Writing Your Own Definition Paragraph   193

Peer Review Form for a Definition Paragraph   195

CHAPTER 9   Cause and Effect   196

What Is Cause and Effect?   196

Hints for Writing a Cause or Effect Paragraph   196

Writing the Cause or Effect Paragraph in Steps   199

(PREWRITING) **Gathering Ideas: Cause or Effect**   199

Freewriting on a Topic   199

Devising a Topic Sentence   201

(PLANNING) **Devising a Plan: Cause or Effect**   204

The Order of Causes or Effects   204

(DRAFTING) **Drafting and Revising: Cause or Effect:**   207

Linking Ideas in Cause or Effect   208

Making the Links Clear   208

Revising the Draft   209

(POLISHING) **Polishing and Proofreading: Cause or Effect**   212

Lines of Detail: A Walk-Through Assignment   214

Writing Your Own Cause or Effect Paragraph   215

Peer Review Form for a Cause or Effect Paragraph   218

CHAPTER 10   Argument   219

What Is Argument?   219
  Hints for Writing an Argument Paragraph   219

Writing the Argument Paragraph in Steps   223
  PREWRITING **Gathering Ideas: Argument**   223
  Grouping Your Ideas   223

  PLANNING **Devising a Plan: Argument**   226
  The Order of Reasons in an Argument   226

  DRAFTING **Drafting and Revising: Argument:**   230
  Checking Your Reasons   230
  Explaining the Problem or Issue   231
  Transitions That Emphasize Your Reasons   231
  Revising a Draft   231

  POLISHING **Polishing and Proofreading: Argument**   234

Lines of Detail: A Walk-Through Assignment   236

Writing Your Own Argument Paragraph   236

Peer Review Form for an Argument Paragraph   239

CHAPTER 11   Writing an Essay   240

What Is an Essay?   240

Comparing the Single Paragraph and the Essay   240

Organizing an Essay   242

Writing the Thesis   242
  Hints for Writing a Thesis   243

Writing the Essay in Steps   245
  PREWRITING **Gathering Ideas: An Essay**   245
  Listing Ideas   245
  Clustering the Ideas   246

  PLANNING **Devising a Plan: An Outline for an Essay**   248
  Hints for Outlining   249
  Revisiting the Prewriting Stage   251

  DRAFTING **Drafting and Revising: An Essay**   254
  Writing the Introduction   254
  Where Does the Thesis Go?   254
  Hints for Writing the Introduction   254
  Writing the Body of the Essay   257
  How Long Are the Body Paragraphs?   257
  Developing the Body Paragraphs   257
  Writing the Conclusion   259
  Revising the Draft   260
  Transitions Within Paragraphs   261
  Transitions Between Paragraphs   262
  A Draft Essay   263

(POLISHING) **Polishing and Proofreading: An Essay   268**
Creating a Title   268
The Final Version of an Essay   268
Lines of Detail: A Walk-Through Assignment   271
Writing Your Own Essay   273
Peer Review Form for an Essay   276

CHAPTER 12   Different Essay Patterns   277

Illustration   277
Hints for Writing an Illustration Essay   277
Writing the Illustration Essay in Steps   278
(PREWRITING) **Gathering Ideas: Illustration Essay   278**
(PLANNING) **Devising a Plan: Illustration Essay   279**
(DRAFTING) **Drafting and Revising: Illustration Essay   280**
(POLISHING) **Polishing and Proofreading: Illustration Essay   281**
Topics for Writing an Illustration Essay   282
Description   283
Hints for Writing a Descriptive Essay   283
Writing the Descriptive Essay in Steps   283
(PREWRITING) **Gathering Ideas: Descriptive Essay   283**
(PLANNING) **Devising a Plan: Descriptive Essay   284**
(DRAFTING) **Drafting and Revising: Descriptive Essay   285**
(POLISHING) **Polishing and Proofreading: Descriptive Essay   285**
Topics for Writing a Descriptive Essay   287
Narration   287
Hints for Writing a Narrative Essay   287
Writing the Narrative Essay in Steps   288
(PREWRITING) **Gathering Ideas: Narrative Essay   288**
(PLANNING) **Devising a Plan: Narrative Essay   288**
(DRAFTING) **Drafting and Revising: Narrative Essay   289**
(POLISHING) **Polishing and Proofreading: Narrative Essay   290**
Topics for Writing a Narrative Essay   291
Process   292
Hints for Writing a Process Essay   292
Writing the Process Essay in Steps   292
(PREWRITING) **Gathering Ideas: Process   292**
(PLANNING) **Devising a Plan: Process Essay   293**
(DRAFTING) **Drafting and Revising: Process Essay   294**
(POLISHING) **Polishing and Proofreading: Process Essay   295**
Topics for Writing a Process Essay   296
Comparison and Contrast   297
Hints for Writing a Comparison or Contrast Essay   297
Writing the Comparison or Contrast Essay in Steps   298

PREWRITING **Gathering Ideas: Comparison or Contrast Essay   298**

Getting Points of Comparison or Contrast   298

PLANNING **Devising a Plan: Contrast Essay   299**

DRAFTING **Drafting and Revising: Contrast Essay   301**

POLISHING **Polishing and Proofreading: Contrast Essay   302**

Topics for Writing a Comparison or Contrast Essay   303

Classification   304

Hints for Writing a Classification Essay   304

Writing the Classification Essay in Steps   304

PREWRITING **Gathering Ideas: Classification Essay   304**

PLANNING **Devising a Plan: Classification Essay   305**

DRAFTING **Drafting and Revising: Classification Essay   306**

POLISHING **Polishing and Proofreading: Classification Essay   307**

Topics for Writing a Classification Essay   308

Definition   309

Hints for Writing a Definition Essay   309

Writing the Definition Essay in Steps   310

PREWRITING **Gathering Ideas: Definition Essay   310**

PLANNING **Devising a Plan: Definition Essay   311**

DRAFTING **Drafting and Revising: Definition Essay   312**

POLISHING **Polishing and Proofreading: Definition Essay   313**

Topics for Writing a Definition Essay   314

Cause and Effect   315

Hints for Writing a Cause or Effect Essay   315

Writing the Cause or Effect Essay in Steps   315

PREWRITING **Gathering Ideas: Cause or Effect Essay   315**

PLANNING **Devising a Plan: Effects Essay   317**

DRAFTING **Drafting and Revising: Effects Essay   318**

POLISHING **Polishing and Proofreading: Effects Essay   319**

Topics for Writing a Cause or Effect Essay   320

Argument   320

Hints for Writing an Argument Essay   320

Writing the Argument Essay in Steps   321

PREWRITING **Gathering Ideas: Argument Essay   321**

PLANNING **Devising a Plan: Argument Essay   322**

DRAFTING **Drafting and Revising: Argument Essay   324**

POLISHING **Polishing and Proofreading: Argument Essay   325**

Topics for Writing an Argument Essay   326

CHAPTER 13   Writing from Reading   327

What Is Writing from Reading?   327

An Approach to Writing from Reading   327

Attitude   327

Prereading   328

Why Preread? 328
Forming Questions Before You Read 329
An Example of the Prereading Step 329
"A Ridiculous Addiction" by Gwinn Owens 329
Reading 332
An Example of the Reading Step 332
Rereading with Pen or Pencil 332
An Example of Rereading with Pen or Pencil 333
What the Notes Mean 335

Writing a Summary of a Reading 336
PREWRITING **Gathering Ideas: Summary 336**
Marking a List of Ideas 336
Selecting a Main Idea 338

PLANNING **Devising a Plan: Summary 339**
DRAFTING **Drafting and Revising: Summary 340**
Attributing Ideas in a Summary 340

POLISHING **Polishing and Proofreading: Summary 341**

Writing a Reaction to a Reading 341
Writing on a Related Idea 341

PREWRITING **Gathering Ideas: Reaction 341**
Freewriting 341
Brainstorming 342
Developing Points of Agreement or Disagreement 343

PLANNING **Devising a Plan: Agree or Disagree 343**
DRAFTING **Drafting and Revising: Agree or Disagree 343**
POLISHING **Polishing and Proofreading: Agree or Disagree 344**

Writing for an Essay Test 344
Before the Test: The Steps of Reading 345
During the Test: The Stages of Writing 345

Prewriting 345
Planning 345
Drafting 345
Polishing 346
Organize Your Time 346

Lines of Detail: A Walk-Through Assignment 346

Writing from Reading: "A Ridiculous Addiction" 347

Peer Review Form for Writing from Reading 349

The Bottom Line: Grammar for Writers 351

Introduction 351
Overview 351
Using "The Bottom Line" 351

CHAPTER 14 The Simple Sentence 353

Recognizing a Sentence 353

Recognizing Verbs 354
More on Verbs 354

Recognizing Subjects   355
More About Recognizing Subjects and Verbs   356

Prepositions and Prepositional Phrases   356

Word Order   359
More on Word Order   360
Word Order in Questions   361
Words That Cannot Be Verbs   362
Recognizing Main Verbs   362
Verb Forms That Cannot Be Main Verbs   362

Chapter Test: The Simple Sentence   368

**CHAPTER 15   Beyond the Simple Sentence:
Coordination   370**

Options for Combining Simple Sentences   370

Option 1: Using a Comma with a Coordinating Conjunction   371
Where Does the Comma Go?   372
Placing the Comma by Using Subject-Verb (S-V) Patterns   372

Option 2: Using a Semicolon Between Two Simple Sentences   376

Option 3: Using a Semicolon and a Conjunctive Adverb   377
Punctuating After a Conjunctive Adverb   377

Chapter Test: Beyond the Simple Sentence: Coordination   383

**CHAPTER 16   Avoiding Run-On Sentences
and Comma Splices   384**

Run-On Sentences   384

Steps for Correcting Run-On Sentences   384

Comma Splices   387

Correcting Comma Splices   388

Chapter Test: Avoiding Run-On Sentences and Comma Splices   392

**CHAPTER 17   Beyond the Simple Sentence:
Subordination   393**

More on Combining Simple Sentences   393

Option 4: Using a Dependent Clause to Begin a Sentence   393

Option 5: Using a Dependent Clause to End a Sentence   394
Using Subordinating Conjunctions   394
Punctuating Complex Sentences   395

Combining Sentences: A Review of Your Options   397

Chapter Test: Coordination and Subordination   404

CHAPTER 18   Avoiding Sentence Fragments   405

Recognizing Fragments: Step 1   406

Recognizing Fragments: Step 2   407

Correcting Fragments   410
Chapter Test: Avoiding Sentence Fragments   415

CHAPTER 19   Using Parallelism in Sentences   417

Achieving Parallelism   418
Chapter Test: Using Parallelism in Sentences   425

CHAPTER 20   Using Adjectives and Adverbs   427

What Are Adjectives?   427
Adjectives: Comparative and Superlative Forms   428
What Are Adverbs?   430
Hints About Adjectives and Adverbs   431
Don't Confuse *Good* and *Well,* or *Bad* and *Badly*   432
Not *More* + *-er,* or *Most* + *-est*   433
Use *Than,* not *Then,* in Comparisons   433
When Do I Need a Comma Between Adjectives?   433
Chapter Test: Using Adjectives and Adverbs   435

CHAPTER 21   Correcting Problems with Modifiers   437

Correcting Modifier Problems   438
Correcting Dangling Modifiers   440
Reviewing the Steps and the Solutions   442
Chapter Test: Correcting Problems with Modifiers   445

CHAPTER 22   Using Verbs Correctly   447

Using Standard Verb Forms   447
The Present Tense   448
The Past Tense   449
The Four Main Forms of a Verb: Present, Past, Present Participle, and Past Participle   450
Irregular Verbs   451
The Past Tense of *be, have, do*   453
More Irregular Verb Forms   454
Chapter Test: Using Verbs Correctly   460

CHAPTER 23   More on Verbs: Consistency and Voice   461

Consistent Verb Tenses   461
The Present Perfect Tense   464
The Past Perfect Tense   465
Passive and Active Voice   466
Avoiding Unnecessary Shifts in Voice   468
A Few Tips About Verbs   470
Chapter Test: More on Verbs: Consistency and Voice   473

CHAPTER 24   Making Subjects and Verbs Agree   474

Pronouns as Subjects   476

Special Problems with Agreement   476
Finding the Subject   476
Changed Word Order   479

Compound Subjects   480

Indefinite Pronouns   482

Collective Nouns   484

Making Subjects and Verbs Agree: The Bottom Line   485

Chapter Test: Making Subjects and Verbs Agree   490

CHAPTER 25   Using Pronouns Correctly: Agreement and Reference   491

Nouns and Pronouns   491

Agreement of a Pronoun and Its Antecedent   492

Indefinite Pronouns   492
Avoiding Sexism   493

Collective Nouns   495

Pronouns and Their Antecedents: Being Clear   498

Chapter Test: Using Pronouns Correctly: Agreement
and Reference   502

CHAPTER 26   Using Pronouns Correctly: Consistency and Case   503

Choosing the Case of Pronouns   506
Pronoun Case in a Related Group of Words   507

Common Errors with Case of Pronouns   507

Chapter Test: Using Pronouns Correctly: Consistency and Case   512

CHAPTER 27   Punctuation: The Period and the Question Mark   513

The Period   513

The Question Mark   514

CHAPTER 28   Punctuation: The Comma   517

Use a Comma as a Lister   517

Use a Comma as a Linker   518

Use a Commas as an Introducer   519

Use a Comma as an Inserter   520
Other Ways to Use a Comma   522

CHAPTER 29   Punctuation: The Semicolon
                  and the Colon   526

The Semicolon   526
The Colon   527

CHAPTER 30   Punctuation: The Apostrophe   531

CHAPTER 31   Other Punctuation and Mechanics   536

The Exclamation Mark   536
The Dash   536
Parentheses   537
The Hyphen   537
Quotation Marks   537
Capital Letters   539
Numbers   541
Abbreviations   541

CHAPTER 32   Spelling   546

Vowels and Consonants   546
Spelling Rule 1: Doubling a Final Consonant   546
Spelling Rule 2: Dropping the Final *e*   547
Spelling Rule 3: Changing the Final *y* to *i*   548
Spelling Rule 4: Adding *-s* or *-es*   549
Spelling Rule 5: Using *ie* or *ei*   549
Do You Spell It As One Word or Two?   551
    Words Whose Spelling Depends on Their Meaning   551
A List of Commonly Misspelled Words   554

CHAPTER 33   Words That Sound Alike/Look Alike   557

Words That Sound Alike/Look Alike   557
More Words That Sound Alike/Look Alike   563

CHAPTER 34   Word Choice   572

Precise Language   572
Wordiness   573
Cliches   575
Slang   578

CHAPTER 35 Sentence Variety   580

Balancing Long and Short Sentences   580

Using Different Ways to Begin Sentences   582
Begin with an Adverb   583
Begin with a Prepositional Phrase   584

Using Different Ways to Join Ideas   585
Use an *-ing* Modifier   585
Use an *-ed* Modifier   587
Use an Appositive   588
Use a *Who, Which,* or *That* Clause   590

Readings to Accompany the Writing Chapters   593

The Writing Process   593
"Sticky Stuff" by Kendall Hamilton and Tessa Namuth   593

Illustration   596
"Spanglish," by Janice Castro, with Dan Cook and Cristina Garcia   596

Description   599
"A Present for Popo" by Elizabeth Wong   599

Narration   603
"The Good Father" by Alisa Valdes-Rodriguez   603

Process   606
"How to Write a Personal Letter" by Garrison Keillor   606

Comparison or Contrast   610
"Beautiful Daughter" by Carolyn Mason   610

Classification   613
"Three Disciplines for Children" by John Holt   613

Definition   616
"Breaking the Bonds of Hate" by Virak Khiev   616

Cause and Effect   620
"Students in Shock" by John Kellmayer   620

Argument   624
"Why Is Geezer-Bashing Acceptable?" by Abigail Trafford   624

"A Cell Phone? Never for Me." by Robert J. Samuelson   627

The Essay   630
"Eleven" by Sandra Cisneros   630

"A Brother's Murder" by Brent Staples   633

"Navajo Code Talkers: The Century's Best Kept Secret" by Jack Hitt   637

Writing from Reading   640
"My Daughter Smokes" by Alice Walker   640

"Parental Discretion" by Dennis Hevesi   645

Appendix A   Grammar Practice for ESL Students   **650**

Nouns and Articles   **650**
Using Articles with Nouns   651

Nouns or Pronouns Used as Subjects   **653**

Verbs   **654**
Necessary Verbs   654
-s Endings   654
-ed Endings   655
Two-Word Verbs   656
Contractions and Verbs   658

Prepositions   **659**
Prepositions That Show Time   659
Prepositions That Show Place   660

Appendix B   The Research Process   **662**

Research in Daily Life   **662**

Using Research to Strengthen Essays   **662**

An Example of an Essay Without Research   **663**
An Outline Without Research   663
An Essay Without Research   664

Finding Research to Strengthen Essays   **665**
Locating Material in Your College Library   665
The Online Catalog   665
Popular Periodical Indexes   666
Internet Search Engines   666
Checking for Validity of Sources   666

Incorporating and Acknowledging Your Sources   **667**
Gathering and Organizing Sources   667
Taking Notes and Acknowledging Your Sources   667
Avoiding Plagiarism   668
Options for Acknowledging Your Sources   668
The Modern Language Association (MLA) System
    of Documentation   668
MLA Internal ("In-text") Citation   668
Signal Phrases   669
Documenting Information from a Source with an Unknown Author   670
Works Cited Entries: MLA Format   670
Books   670
Periodicals   671
Electronic Sources   672
Other Sources: Non-Print   673
Incorporating Research into Your Outline   674
A Draft of an Essay with Research   675

Preparing the Final Version of an Essay with Research   **677**
Making Final Changes and Refinements   677
The Final Version of a Research Essay   678

Credits   **683**

Index   **685**

Photo Assignments to Accompany the Writing Chapters

Writing a Paragraph   36, 37

Illustration   56, 57

Description   79, 80

Narration   105, 106

Process   126, 127

Comparison and Contrast   154, 155

Classification   173

Definition   194

Cause and Effect   216, 217

Argument   238

Writing an Essay   274, 275

Preface

TO INSTRUCTORS

Over the years, we have been both gratified and encouraged by the positive reception the *Along These Lines* series has generated. This fourth edition of *Along These Lines: Writing Paragraphs and Essays* provides even more opportunities for students to prewrite, plan, draft, revise, and polish their work. Additionally, we have retooled many of the collaborative and independent activities to include computer-related assignments.

Whether working within the constraints of state-mandated objectives, evaluating the merits of the latest trend in computer-assisted instruction, or seeking a balance between traditionally graded essays and holistically scored portfolios, today's writing instructors employ a variety of teaching strategies. Similarly, student populations reflect a diversity of learning styles, abilities, and backgrounds. We trust you will find that *Along These Lines* continues to respect the challenges of this unique tapestry.

THE WRITING CHAPTERS

We have retained the intensive coverage of the writing process. Each writing chapter continues to trace the stages of writing, from generating ideas, to planning and focusing, to drafting and revising, and, finally, to polishing and proofreading. Each writing chapter covering a rhetorical pattern remains filled with exercises and activities—both individual and collaborative—because we believe that beginning writers are more motivated and learn more easily when they are *actively* involved with individual or collaborative tasks. In keeping with these beliefs and with the emphasis on process, *Along These Lines* offers instructors more options than ever.

New Features

In response to suggestions from current users and new reviewers, we have made the following additions:

- Writing assignments that now include suggested Web-based activities and computer-related topics
- New full-color photographs with accompanying writing prompts
- A new appendix, "The Research Process," introducing students to the basics of research and MLA documentation, includes a sample essay with clear examples of direct quotations, paraphrasing, online and traditional source documentation, and a Works Cited page
- New exercises throughout the writing chapters that maintain our coverage of every step in the writing process

Additional Features

Along These Lines continues to include these distinctive features:

- A lively conversational tone, including question-and-answer formats and dialogues
- Visually appealing lists, charts, and "Infoboxes"

- Boxed examples of an outline, draft, and final version of a writing assignment in each chapter
- Exercises throughout each chapter, not merely at the end, so that each concept is reinforced as soon as it is introduced
- Exercises that are not merely fill-in-the-blanks, but collaborative ones that have students writing with peers, interviewing classmates, reacting to others' suggestions, and building on others' ideas
- Numerous writing topics and activities in each chapter, providing more flexibility for instructors
- A "Walk-Through" writing assignment at the end of each chapter that guides students, step-by-step, through the stages of the writing process
- A Peer Review Form in each chapter so students can benefit from a classmate's reaction to their drafts

THE GRAMMAR CHAPTERS

New Features

- Grammar chapters now include three types of exercises: **Practice** (simple reinforcement), **Collaborate** (partner or group work), and **Connect** (application of the grammar principle to paragraphs) exercises
- A Chapter Test at the end of each grammar chapter, ideal for class review or quick quizzes
- Twice the number of proofreading/editing exercises in each chapter
- More exercises on coordinating conjunctions and conjunctive adverbs
- More exercises on sentence combining
- More coverage on avoiding slang

Additional Features

Because reviewers praised the scope of the grammar chapters and welcomed the variety of exercises, *Along These Lines* continues to include these popular features:

- Grammar concepts taught step-by-step, as in "Two Steps to Check for Fragments"
- Separate chapters on the comma and the apostrophe
- Paragraph-editing exercises at the end of each grammar chapter to connect the grammar principle to writing assignments
- An ESL grammar appendix with exercises that focus on common trouble spots for non-native speakers

THE READING SECTIONS

New Features

- Professional reading selections now grouped in one place for easy reference
- New format of Comprehension Check, Discussion Prompts, and Writing Options accompany each selection

- New, appealing, and accessible readings covering a wide range of subjects, including parental stress, cell phone mania, brotherly love and loss, and Navajo heroes of World War II; diverse writers include Brent Staples, Alicia Valdez-Rodriguez, and Robert Samuelson (*Newsweek* columnist)

Additional Features

The reading sections continue to include these popular features:

- A separate and detailed chapter, "Writing from Reading," explaining and illustrating the steps of prereading, annotating, summarizing, and reacting (in writing) to an author's ideas
- Readings that are relevant to today's diverse students, including selections on generational differences, family role models, peer pressure, racism, and overcoming adversity
- Vocabulary definitions based on the specific context of the writer's intent
- Writing options sparked by a selection's content and designed to elicit thinking, not rote replication of a model

OUR PHILOSOPHY

The basic premise of our work has always been that an effective text should respect students' individuality and their innate desire to learn and succeed. We trust that the *Along These Lines* series will continue to help students flourish within a framework of respect, encouragement, and meaningful interaction as they work through the writing process.

ACKNOWLEDGMENTS

Many individuals have helped us refine the *Along These Lines* series, and we are indebted to the following professionals for their collective wisdom, practical suggestions, and comprehensive reviews:

Sara Blake	El Camino College
Zoe Ann Cerny	Horry-Georgetown Technical College
Frieda Campbell-Peltier	Portland Community College
Neomi Daniels	West Hills College
Curt Duffy	Los Angeles Pierce College
Meg Files	Pima Community College
Eric P. Hibbison	J. Sargeant Reynolds Community College
Heather Jeddy	Northern Virginia Community College
Billy Jones	Miami Dade College
Dimitri Keriotis	Modesto Junior College
Deonne Kunkel	Diablo Valley College
Joan Maudlin	San Jacinto College
Dara Perales	Palomar College
Jessica Rabin	Anne Arundel Community College
Marcia A. Rogers	Orange Coast College
Harvey Rubenstein	Hudson County Community College
Jeff Torricelli	St. Clair County Community College
Stephanie Woods	Hinds Community College
Lynn Wright	Pasadena City College

Joan Polk, editorial assistant, coordinated these reviews with her customary meticulous attention to detail. She also searched Pearson Education's vast photo archives to find exactly what we requested. Thanks again, Joan, for the many favors, kind words, and quick wit.

Craig Campanella, executive editor, continued to impress us with his energy, humor, focus, and commitment. Despite his demanding travel schedule and constant juggling of deadlines, he stays current with all developmental English trends and still manages to alleviate authors' fears. Craig's insight, guidance, and friendship have been invaluable over the years, and he has rightfully earned the M.E. (Multitasker Extraordinaire) degree.

We were also fortunate to work with Karen Berry and Bruce Hobart of Pine Tree Composition; their production talents kept the *Along These Lines* series on track and our minds intact as deadlines loomed. Additionally, we extend many thanks and well-deserved kudos to Lori Bradshaw, permissions editor; Carol Lallier, copy editor; Jonathan Boylan, designer; Leslie Osher, creative design director; art director, Nancy Wells; Ann Marie McCarthy, executive managing editor; Fran Russello, production liaison; Cindy Gierhart, proofreader; and Sherri Dietrich, indexer. We are also very grateful to Kate Mitchell, marketing manager, not only for coordinating detailed promotions but also for her unwavering and enthusiastic support of our series.

Finally, and most importantly, we thank the many students who, for over three decades, constantly intrigued, impressed, and inspired us. You made our journey extraordinary along *all* lines.

John Sheridan Biays
Carol Wershoven

Writing in Stages
The Process Approach

INTRODUCTION

Learning By Doing

Writing is a skill, and like any skill, writing improves with practice. This book provides you with the practice to improve your writing through several activities. Some activities can be done by yourself, some will ask you to work with a partner or a group, some can be done in the classroom, and some can be done at home. The important thing to remember is that *good writing takes practice:* you can learn to write well by writing.

Steps Make Writing Easier

Writing is easier if you *do not try to do too much at once.* Producing a piece of effective writing requires that you think, plan, draft, rethink, focus, revise, edit, and proofread. You can become frustrated if you try to do all these things at the same time.

To make the task of writing easier, *Along These Lines* breaks the process into stages. Throughout this book, the writing process is divided into four major parts:

PREWRITING

In this stage, you think about your topic, and you *gather ideas.* You *react* to your own ideas and add more ideas to your first thoughts. You can also react to other people's ideas as a way of generating your own writing material.

PLANNING

In this stage, you *examine your ideas* and begin to *focus* them around one main idea. Planning involves combining, dividing, and even eliminating the ideas you started with. It involves more thinking about the point you want to make and the order of details that can best express your point. Placing your specific details in a logical order often involves *outlining.*

1

DRAFTING

In this stage, the thinking and planning begin to shape themselves into a piece of writing. You complete a draft of your work, a *rough version* of the finished product. Then you think again as you examine the draft and check it. Checking it begins the process of *revision*, or "fixing" the draft, so that it takes the shape you want and expresses your ideas clearly. Several drafts may be necessary before you are satisfied with your work.

POLISHING

In this stage, the final version of your writing gets one last, careful *review*. When you prepare the final copy of your work, you *proofread* and concentrate on identifying and correcting any mistakes in spelling, mechanics, or punctuation you may have overlooked. This stage is the *final check* of your work to make your writing the best it can be.

These four stages in the writing process—*prewriting, planning, drafting,* and *polishing*—may overlap. You may be changing your plan even as you work on the draft of your paper; there is no rule that prevents you from moving back to an earlier stage. Thinking of writing as a series of stages helps you see the process as a *manageable task*, for it helps you *avoid doing everything at once* and becoming overwhelmed by the challenge.

Throughout the chapters of this text, you will have many opportunities to become familiar with the stages of effective writing. Working individually and with your classmates, you can become a better writer along *all* lines.

CHAPTER 1
Writing a Paragraph

Usually, students write because they have a writing assignment requiring them to write on some topic or choice of topics, and the writing is due by a certain day. So assume that you get such an assignment and it calls for one paragraph. You might wonder, "Why a paragraph? Why not something large, like a two- or three-page paper? After all, many classes ask for papers, not just paragraphs."

For one thing, all essays are a series of paragraphs. If you can write one good paragraph, you can write more than one. The **paragraph** is the basic building block of any essay. It is a group of sentences focusing on *one idea* or one point. Keep this concept in mind: *one idea to a paragraph*. Focusing on one idea or one point gives a paragraph **unity.** If you have a new point, start a new paragraph.

You may ask, "Doesn't this mean a paragraph will be short? How long should a paragraph be, anyway?" To persuade a reader of one main point, you need to make it, support it, develop it, explain it, and describe it. There will be shorter and longer paragraphs, but for now, you can assume your paragraph will be somewhere between seven and twelve sentences long.

This chapter guides you through each stage of the writing process:

- **Prewriting**—how to generate and develop ideas for your paragraph
- **Planning**—how to organize your ideas
- **Drafting**—how to create and revise rough drafts
- **Polishing**—how to proofread and make one final check

We give extra emphasis to the prewriting stage in this chapter to give you some extra help in getting started.

BEGINNING THE PREWRITING: GATHERING IDEAS

Suppose your instructor asks you to write a paragraph about your favorite city or town. Writing about your favorite city or town is your general **topic,** but you must choose one city or town to make the topic more specific. With this topic, you already know your **purpose**—to write a paragraph that makes some point about the city or town. You have an **audience** because you are writing this paragraph for your instructor and classmates. Often, your purpose is to write a specific kind of paper for a class. Occasionally, you may have to write with a different purpose or for a different audience, such as writing instructions for a new employee at your workplace, or a letter of complaint to a manufacturer, or a short biographical essay for a scholarship application. Knowing your audience and purpose is important in writing effectively.

Freewriting, Brainstorming, Keeping a Journal

Once you have identified your purpose and audience, you can begin by finding some way to *think on paper.* You can use the techniques of freewriting, brainstorming, or keeping a journal to gather ideas and potential details.

Freewriting Give yourself fifteen minutes to write whatever comes into your mind on your subject. If your mind is a blank, write, "My mind's a blank. My mind's a blank," over and over until you think of something else. The main goal here is to *write without stopping.* Do not stop to tell yourself, "This is stupid" or "I can't use any of this in a paper." Do not stop to correct your spelling or punctuation. Just write. Let your ideas flow. Write *freely.* Here is an example:

Freewriting About a Favorite City or Town

Favorite city or town. City? I like New York. It's so big and exciting. Haven't been there much, though. Only once. My home town. I like it. It's just another town but comfortable and friendly. Maybe St. Augustine. Lots of fun visits there. Grandparents there. Hard to pick a favorite. Different places are good for different reasons.

Brainstorming This technique is like freewriting because you write whatever comes into your head, but it is a little different because you can pause *to ask yourself questions* that will lead to new ideas. When you brainstorm alone, you "interview" yourself about a subject. You can also brainstorm and ask questions within a group.

Brainstorming About a Favorite City or Town

Favorite place.

City or town.

What's the difference between a city and a town?
Doesn't matter. Just pick one. Cities bigger.

How is city life different from town life?
Cities are bigger. More crowded, like Atlanta.

Which do you like better, a city or a town?
Sometimes I like cities.

Why?
There is more to do.

So, what city do you like?
I like New York. St. Augustine.

Is St. Augustine a city?
Yes. A small one.

Do you like towns?
I loved this little town in Mexico.

If you feel like you are running out of ideas in brainstorming, try to form a question out of what you've just written. *Go where your questions and answers lead you.* For example, if you write, "There is more to do in cities," you could form these questions:

> What is there to do? Sports? Entertainment? Outdoor exercise? Meeting people?

You could also make a list of your brainstorming ideas, but remember to *do only one step at a time.*

Keeping a Journal A **journal** is a notebook of your personal writing, a notebook in which you write *regularly and often. It is not a diary, but it is a place to record your experiences, reactions, and observations.* In it, you can write about what you have done, heard, seen, read, or remembered. You can include sayings that you would like to remember, news clippings, snapshots—anything that you would like to recall or consider. A journal provides an enjoyable way to practice your writing, and it is a great source of ideas for writing.

Journal Entry About a Favorite City or Town

I'm not going south to see my grandparents this winter. They're coming here instead of me going to St. Augustine. I'd really like to go there. I like the warm weather. It's better than months of snow, ice, and rain here in Easthampton. I'll miss going there. I've been so many times that it's like a second home. St. Augustine is great around Christmas time.

Finding Specific Ideas

Whether you freewrite, brainstorm, or consult your journal, you end up with something on paper. Follow those first ideas; see where they can take you. You are looking for specific ideas, each of which can focus the general topic you started with. At this point, you do not have to decide which specific idea you want to write about. You just want to *narrow your range* of ideas.

You might think, "Why should I narrow my ideas? Won't I have more to say if I keep my topic big?" But remember that a paragraph has one idea; you want to state it clearly and with convincing details for support. If you try to write one paragraph on city life versus town life, for example, you will probably make so many general statements that you will say very little, or you will bore your reader with big, sweeping statements. General ideas are big, broad ones. Specific ideas are smaller, narrower. If you scanned the freewriting example on a favorite city or town, you might underline many specific ideas as possible topics:

> Favorite city or town. City? I like <u>New York</u>. It's so big and exciting. Haven't been there much, though. Only once. <u>My home town</u>. I like it. It's just another town but comfortable and friendly. Maybe <u>St. Augustine</u>. Lots of fun visits there. Grandparents there. Hard to pick a favorite. Different places are good for different reasons.

Consider the underlined terms. They are specific places. You could write a paragraph about any one of these places. Or you could underline specific places in your brainstorming questions and answers:

> Favorite place.
> City or town.
>
> **What's the difference between a city and a town?**
> Doesn't matter. Just pick one. Cities bigger.
>
> **How is city life different from town life?**
> Cities are bigger. More crowded, like <u>Atlanta</u>.
>
> **Which do you like better, a city or a town?**
> Sometimes I like cities.
>
> **Why?**
> There is more to do.
>
> **So, what city do you like?**
> I like <u>New York</u>. <u>St. Augustine</u>.
>
> **Is St. Augustine a city?**
> Yes. A small one.
>
> **Do you like towns?**
> I loved this <u>little town in Mexico</u>.

Each of these specific places could be a topic for your paragraph.

If you reviewed the journal entry on a favorite city or town, you would be also be able to underline specific places:

> I'm not going south to see my grandparents this winter. They're coming here instead of me going to <u>St. Augustine</u>. I'd really like to go there. I like the

warm weather. It's better than months of snow, ice, and rain here in <u>East-hampton</u>. I'll miss going there. I've been so many times that it's like a second home. St. Augustine is great around Christmas time.

Remember that if you follow the steps, they can lead you to specific ideas.

Selecting One Topic

Once you have a list of specific ideas that can lead you to a specific topic, you can pick one topic. Let's say you decided to work with the list of places you gathered through brainstorming:

Atlanta
New York
St. Augustine
a little town in Mexico

Looking at this list, you decide you want to write about St. Augustine as your favorite city.

Exercise 1   **Creating Questions for Brainstorming**

Following are several topics. For each one, brainstorm by writing at least six questions that are related to the topic and could lead you to further ideas. The first topic is done for you:

1. topic: dogs

Question 1. <u>Why are dogs such popular pets?</u>

Question 2. <u>What kind of dog is a favorite pet in America?</u>

Question 3. <u>Are dogs hard to train?</u>

Question 4. <u>What dog, in your life, do you remember best?</u>

Question 5. <u>What's the most famous dog on television?</u>

Question 6. <u>Are there dogs as cartoon characters?</u>

2. topic: talking

Question 1. Why do people talk about?

Question 2. What language do to talk?

Question 3. When is it foolish to talk?

Question 4. Why do girls talk a lot?

Question 5. Why do people have diffent accepts?

Question 6. Why are some people not talkative?

3. topic: deadlines

Question 1. *What are deadlines?*

Question 2. *Why do we have deadlines?*

Question 3. *Do you like deadlines?*

Question 4. *Do you hate deadlines?*

Question 5. *Have you never made a deadline?*

Question 6. *Do you have a deadline?*

> Exercise 2 **Finding Specific Details in Freewriting**

Below are two samples of freewriting. Each is a written response to a different topic. Read each sample, and then underline any words and phrases that could become the focus of a paragraph.

Freewriting Reaction to the Topic of Nature

I live in the city, so what do I know about nature? There are no mountains or oceans or lakes here. Can barely see a sunset here. Just some grass in the park. Also some squirrels. They're funny and bold, too. Come right up to you for food. Squirrels are like rats, but cuter because they have fluffy tails. No one likes rats in this city. I see pigeons too.

Freewriting Reaction to the Topic of Health

Lucky people have good health. What is good health? I'm a healthy person. So is my father. He doesn't smoke or drink. He works on staying healthy. Healthy people don't have operations or have to go to the hospital much. Health insurance costs so much you have to stay healthy.

> Exercise 3 **Finding Specific Details in a List**

Following are several lists of words and phrases. In each list, one item is a general term; the others are more specific. Underline the words or phrases that are more specific. The first list is done for you:

1. apple pie
   ice cream
   desserts
   butterscotch pudding
   jello
   chocolate brownies

2. space explorers
   soldiers
   detectives
   cartoon heroes
   television heroes

3. street racing
   racing
   racing movies
   NASCAR
   horse racing
   customized cars

4. boxing glove
   tennis racket
   golf club
   sports equipment
   catcher's mitt
   football helmet

5. braids
   curls
   hair styles
   frizz
   pony tail

6. costs of college
   parking stickers
   student activities fees
   lab fees
   tuition
   art supplies

Exercise 4 **Finding Topics Through Freewriting**

◀ COLLABORATE 👥

The following exercise must be completed with a partner or a group. Pick one of the following topics and freewrite on it for ten minutes. Then read your freewriting to your partner or group. Ask your listener(s) to jot down any words or phrases from your writing that could lead to a specific topic for a paragraph.

   Your listener(s) should read the jotted-down words or phrases to you. You will be hearing a collection of specific ideas that came from *your* writing. As you listen, underline the words in your freewriting.

   Freewriting topics (pick one):

   1. a happy surprise

   2. a misunderstanding

   3. a childhood tradition

   Freewriting on (name of topic chosen): _____

   _____

   _____

   _____

   _____

   _____

   _____

   _____

Adding Details to a Specific Topic

You can develop the specific topic you picked in a number of ways:

   1. *Check your list* for other ideas that seem to fit with the specific topic you've picked.
   2. *Brainstorm*—ask yourself more questions about your topic, and use the answers as detail.
   3. *List* any new ideas you have that may be connected to your topic.

One way to add details is to go back and check your brainstorming for other ideas about St. Augustine:

   I like St. Augustine.
   a small city

Now you can **brainstorm** some questions that will lead you to more details. The questions do not have to be connected to each other; they are just questions that could lead you to ideas and details:

What's a small city?

It doesn't have skyscrapers or freeways or millions of people.

So, what makes it a city?

Thousands of visitors come there every day.

What's so great about St. Augustine?

You can go to the beach nearby.

Is it a clean, big beach?

Sure. And the water is a clear blue.

What else can you do in St. Augustine?

There's lots of history.

Like what?

A fort. The oldest schoolhouse. Old houses.

Another way to add details is to list any ideas that may be connected to your topic. The list might give you more specific details:

grandparents live there
warm in winter
grandparents feed me
I use their car

If you tried all three ways of adding detail, you would end up with this list of details connected to the topic of a favorite city or town:

a small city	clear blue water
no freeways	lots of history
no sky scrapers	a fort
not millions of people	oldest schoolhouse
thousands of visitors every day	grandparents live there
can always visit family for free	warm in winter
beach nearby	grandparents feed me
clean, big beach	I use their car

INFO BOX: Beginning the Prewriting: A Summary

The prewriting stage of writing a paragraph enables you to gather ideas. This process begins with several steps:

1. *Think on paper and write down any ideas that you have about a topic.* You can do this by freewriting, brainstorming, or keeping a journal.

2. *Scan your writing for specific ideas that come from your first efforts.* List these specific ideas.

3. *Pick one specific idea.* Then, by reviewing your early writing, by questioning, and by thinking further, you can add details to the one specific idea.

This process may seem long, but once you have worked through it several times, it will become nearly automatic. When you think about ideas before you try to shape them into a paragraph, you are off to a good start. Confidence comes from having something to say, and once you have a specific idea, you will be ready to begin shaping and developing details that support your idea.

Exercise 5   Adding Details to a Topic by Brainstorming

Below are two topics. Each is followed by two or three details. Brainstorm more questions, based on the existing details, that can lead to more details.

1. **topic:** advantages of going to a college near home
   details: saves money
           comfortable environment

Question 1: How does it save you money?

Question 2: What makes the environment comfortable?

Question 3: Can you save money on trips home?

Question 4: Can you get more in an emergency?

Question 5: Can your parents help you easier?

Question 6: Can you walk to school?

2. **topic:** getting a speeding ticket
   details: frightening experience
           humiliating moment
           can be expensive

Question 1: What is frightening about the experience?

Question 2: Why is it humiliating?

Question 3: How did you feel after?

Question 4: What could you do to make it better?

Question 5: What did you do?

Question 6: When did it happen?

Exercise 6   Adding Details By Listing

Following are three topics for paragraphs. For each topic, list details that seem to fit the topic.

1. **topic:** e-mail
   details: a. computer   c. letter
             b. Sent Items   d. In Box

2. **topic:** a bad day at work
   details: a. Depressed   c. Sad
             b. Mad   d. Quit

3. topic: nosy neighbors

details: a. Angry c. rude

b. loud d. impolite

FOCUSING THE PREWRITING

The next step of writing is to *focus your ideas around some point.* Your ideas will begin to take a focus if you re-examine them, looking for *related ideas.* Two techniques that you can use are

- marking a list of related ideas
- mapping related ideas

Listing Related Ideas

To develop a marked list, take another look at the list we developed under the topic of a favorite city or town. The same list is shown below, but you will notice some of the items have been marked with symbols that show related ideas:

N marks ideas about St. Augustine's natural good points

H marks ideas about St. Augustine's history

F marks ideas about family in St. Augustine

Here is the marked list of ideas related to the topic of a favorite city or town:

	a small city	**N**	clear blue water
	no freeways	**H**	lots of history
	no sky scrapers	**H**	a fort
	not millions of people	**H**	oldest schoolhouse
	thousands of visitors every day	**F**	grandparents live there
F	can always visit family for free	**N**	warm in winter
N	beach nearby	**F**	grandparents feed me
N	clean, big beach	**F**	I use their car

You have probably noticed that some items are not marked: a small city, no freeways, no sky scrapers, not millions of people, thousands of visitors every day. Perhaps you can come back to them later, or you may decide you do not need them in your paragraph.

To make it easier to see what ideas you have and how they are related, try *grouping related ideas,* giving each list a title, like this:

Natural Good Points of St. Augustine

beach nearby
clean, big beach
clear blue water
warm in winter

History in St. Augustine

lots of history
a fort
oldest schoolhouse

Family in St. Augustine

can always visit family for free
grandparents feed me
grandparents live there
I use their car

Mapping

Another way to focus your ideas is to mark your first list of ideas, and then cluster the related ideas into separate lists. You can **map** your ideas, like this:

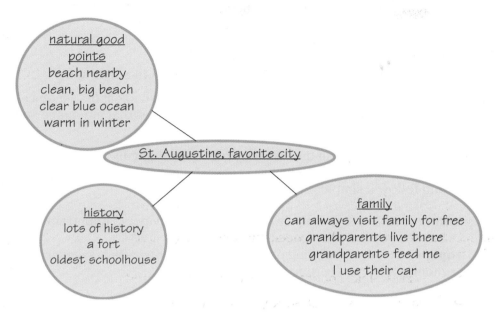

Whatever way you choose to examine and group your details, you are working toward a *focus*, a *point*. You are asking and beginning to answer the question, "Where do the details lead?" The answer will be the **topic sentence** of your paragraph. It will be the *main idea* of your paragraph.

Forming a Topic Sentence

To form a topic sentence, you can do the following:

1. Review your details and see if you can form some general idea that can summarize the details.
2. Write that general idea as one sentence.

Your sentence that summarizes the details is the **topic sentence.** It makes a general point, and the more specific details you have gathered will support this point.

   To form a topic sentence about your favorite city, St. Augustine, review the many details you have listed about the city. It is time to ask questions about those details. You could ask yourself, "What kind of details do I have? Can I summarize them?" You might then write the summary as the topic sentence:

   I love St. Augustine because it has sun and sea, history, and family.

Check the sentence against your details. Does it cover the natural good points of St. Augustine? Yes. The topic sentence sums them up as *sun and sea*. Does it cover history and family? Yes. The topic sentence says the place has *history and family*.

Writing Good Topic Sentences

Be careful. *Topics are not the same as topic sentences. Topics are the subjects you will write about.* A topic sentence states the **main idea** you have developed on a topic. Consider the differences between the topics and the topic sentences below:

>   **topic:** Why courtesy is important
>   **topic sentence:** Courtesy takes the conflict out of unpleasant encounters.

>   **topic:** Dogs and their owners
>   **topic sentence:** Many dog owners begin to look like their pets.

Topic sentences *do not announce—they make a point.* Look at the sentences below, and notice the differences between the sentences that announce and the topic sentences.

>   **announcement:** I will discuss the process of changing a tire.
>   **topic sentence:** Changing a tire is easy if you have the right tools and follow a simple process.

>   **announcement:** An analysis of why recycling paper is important will be the subject of this paper.
>   **topic sentence:** Recycling paper is important because it saves trees, money, and even certain animals.

Topic sentences can be too big to develop in one paragraph. A topic sentence that is *too broad* may take many paragraphs, even pages of writing, to develop. Look at the very broad sentences below, and then notice how they can be narrowed.

>   **too broad:** Athletes get paid too much money. (This sentence is too broad because the term "athletes" could mean anything from professional boxers to college football players to neighborhood softball teams; "too much money" could mean any fee that basketball players receive for endorsing products or bonuses that professional football players get if they make the Super Bowl. The sentence could also refer to all athletes in the world at any time in history.)
>   **a narrower, better topic sentence:** Last year, several professional baseball players negotiated high but fair salaries.

>   **too broad:** I changed a great deal in my last year of high school. (The phrase "changed a great deal" could refer to physical changes, intellectual changes, emotional changes, changes in attitude, changes in goals, or just about any other change you can think of.)
>   **a narrower, better topic sentence:** In my last year of high school, I overcame my shyness.

Topic sentences can also be too small to develop in one paragraph. A topic sentence that is *too narrow* cannot be supported by details. It may be a fact, which cannot be developed. A topic sentence that is too narrow leaves you with nothing more to say.

>   **too narrow:** I hate broccoli.
>   **an expanded topic sentence:** I hate broccoli for two reasons.

>   **too narrow:** It takes twenty minutes to get out of the airport parking lot.
>   **an expanded topic sentence:** Congestion at the airport parking lot is causing problems for travelers.

The prewriting stage begins with free, unstructured thinking and writing. As you work through the prewriting process, your thinking and writing will become more focused.

INFO BOX: **Focusing the Prewriting: A Summary**

The prewriting stage of writing a paragraph enables you to develop an idea into a topic sentence and related details. You can focus your thinking by working in steps.

1. Try marking a list of related details, or try mapping to group your ideas.

2. Write a topic sentence that summarizes your details.

3. Check that your topic sentence is a sentence, not a topic. Make sure that it is not too broad or too narrow, and that it is not an announcement. Check that it makes a point and focuses the details you have developed.

Exercise 7 **Grouping Related Items in Lists of Details**

Below are lists of details. In each list, circle the items that seem to fit into one group; then underline the items that seem to belong to a second group. Some items may not belong in either group. The first list is done for you.

1. **topic:** blizzards

   power outages   freedom from school
   sit by a warm fire   snows most in February
   drink hot chocolate   travel is hazardous
   snuggle up with loved ones   build a snowman
   weather reports   damage to trees

2. **topic:** cartoon characters

   Mickey Mouse   Spiderman
   Bambi   Nemo
   Superman   Homer Simpson
   Batman   Scooby-Doo
   Cinderella   The Hulk

3. **topic:** ending a relationship

   loss of security   failure to communicate
   facing the rumors   newfound freedom
   chance to meet others memories
   sense of relief   pain of familiar places
   expert advice   haunting loneliness

Exercise 8 **Writing Topic Sentences for Lists of Details**

Below are lists of details that have no topic sentence. Write an appropriate topic sentence for each one.

1. **topic sentence:** _Winter Holidays of different Heritages._

Some people think of Christmas as the only winter holiday.
Yet many African Americans celebrate Kwanza.
Those of Hispanic heritage may celebrate January 6, the feast of the Three Kings.
Hanukkah, a Jewish-American holiday, is also celebrated in the winter.
Americans with Northern European roots celebrate December 6, the feast of St. Nicholas.
People with a British heritage celebrate December 26 as Boxing Day.

2. topic sentence: _____

_____

Mr. Lin never bends the rules at Eagle High School.
As principal, he feels he has to keep the school in order and the students safe.
He patrols the halls like a military general.
He even checks the cafeteria and roams the parking lots at lunch time.
He never misses a pep rally.
He supports every football game and attends every social function.
His door is always open to a student with a question or problem.

3. topic sentence: _____

_____

My roommate Etienne is Haitian, so at first I had a hard time understanding his English.
He also seemed very shy.
I didn't see him much, so I figured he was socializing with his own friends and didn't like me.
Then one night I had an important algebra test to study for.
I went to the Tutoring Center to get some help with my math.
Etienne was there, wrapped up in books.
Later, I learned he was there every night, studying English, but also tutoring other people in math.
Etienne and I are good friends now; I help him with English, and he teaches me algebra.

Exercise 9 **Turning Topics into Topic Sentences**

Some of the items in the following list are topic sentences, but some are topics. Put an *X* by the items that are topics. On the lines below the list, rewrite the topics into topic sentences.

1. __X__ Three ways to save money.

2. __X__ Deciding on the right college major.

3. _____ My most serious mistake was quitting my last job.

4. __X__ Playing golf is expensive and boring.

5. __ _X_ __ How I got my car.

6. _____ My mother knows how to win an argument.

7. _____ Childhood dreams can come true.

8. _____ Why divorced parents should remain friendly.

9. _____ I go to a gym for my health and appearance.

10. _____ College students' greatest problem is lack of sleep.

Rewrite the topics. Make each one into a topic sentence:

Here are three wacts to Save Money,
Three Ways to help you Decide on
the right college major. These are
Some wats you can make Golf fun,
not ~~boooooo~~ boring. How I found and
Bought my Car.

_____

_____

[Exercise 10]   **Revising Topic Sentences That Are Too Broad**

Below is a list of topic sentences. Some of them are too broad to support in
one paragraph. Put an X by the ones that are too broad. Then, on the lines
below the list, rewrite those sentences, focusing on a limited idea, a topic
sentence that could be supported in one paragraph.

1. _____ Marriage can be stressful.

2. _____ The most difficult part of working on a lawn crew was the
summer heat.

3. _____ Houses are too expensive for many people.

4. _____ Christina Gomez knows how to teach shy preschoolers.

5. _____ Emilio believes in freedom and the right to live as he pleases.

6. _____ Relationships can be ruined by poor communication.

7. _____ My girlfriend and I are constantly fighting over money.

8. _____ In my neighborhood, old people are afraid to go out after
dark.

9. _____ Crime is destroying this country.

10. _____ Ivan lost his way in college.

Rewrite the broad sentences. Make each one more limited.

_____

_____

_____

_____

_____

_____

_____

Exercise 11   **Making Announcements into Topic Sentences**

Below is a list of sentences. Some are topic sentences. Some are announcements. Put an *X* by the announcements. Then, on the lines below the list, rewrite the announcements, making them into topic sentences.

1. _____ Living with diabetes is easier than it used to be.

2. _____ The importance of changing the oil in your car will be the subject of this paper.

3. _____ The uses of a microwave oven will be explained.

4. _____ A daily walk can be a way to better health.

5. _____ This essay concerns the parking situation on campus.

6. _____ Valentine's Day has become another day when spending money is connected to love.

7. _____ Why Fullerton Mall needs renovation is the area to be discussed.

8. _____ A new baseball field should be a priority for Bell High School.

9. _____ I have three reasons for not wearing a watch.

10. _____ This paper will be about the Food for Families Program.

Rewrite the announcements. Make each one a topic sentence.

_____

_____

_____

_____

_____

_____

Exercise 12   **Revising Topic Sentences That Are Too Narrow**

Below is a list of topic sentences. Some of them are topics that are too narrow; they cannot be developed with details. Put an *X* by the ones that are
too narrow. Then, on the lines below, rewrite those sentences as broader
topic sentences that could be developed in one paragraph.

   1. _____ My last day of high school was an emotional one.

   2. _____ I got my diploma last June.

   3. _____ It rained all day yesterday.

   4. _____ Ice on the runways caused turmoil at the airport.

   5. _____ The Coffee Corner is popular with all age groups.

   6. _____ Shop-Mart is the nearest mall.

   7. _____ Dr. Martinez has a Ph.D. in physics.

   8. _____ Linda Chao's fierce determination enabled her to finish college.

   9. _____ My sister reads the newspaper every day.

  10. _____ The house on the corner is fifty years old.

   Rewrite the narrow sentences. Make each one broader.

   _____

   _____

   _____

   _____

   _____

   _____

PLANNING   **Devising a Plan for a Paragraph**

Checking Your Details

Once you have a topic sentence, you can begin working on an **outline** for
your paragraph. The outline is a plan that helps you stay focused in your
writing. The outline begins to form when you write your topic sentence and
write your list of details beneath the topic sentence. You can now look at
your list and ask yourself an important question: "Do I have **enough details**

to **support** my topic sentence?" Remember, your goal is to write a paragraph of seven to twelve sentences.

Consider this topic sentence and list of details:

    topic sentence: People can be very rude when they shop in super-
                        markets.

        details: push in line
                express lane
                too many items

Does the list contain enough details for a paragraph of seven to twelve sentences? Probably not.

Adding Details When There Are Not Enough

To add details, try brainstorming. Ask yourself some questions like these:

    Where else in supermarkets are people rude?
    Are they rude in other lanes besides the express lane?
    Are they rude in the aisles? How?
    Is there crowding anywhere? Where?

By brainstorming, you might come up with this detail:

    topic sentence: People can be very rude when they shop in super-
                        markets.

        details: push in line
                express lane
                too many items
                hit my cart with theirs in aisles
                block aisles while they decide
                push ahead in deli area
                will not take a number
                argue with cashier over prices
                yell at the bagger

Keep brainstorming until you feel you have enough details for a paragraph of seven to twelve sentences. Remember that it is better to have too many details than too few, for you can always edit the extra details later.

If you try brainstorming and still do not have many details, you can refer to your original ideas—your freewriting or journal—for other details.

Eliminating Details That Do Not Relate to the Topic Sentence

Sometimes, what you thought were good details do not relate to the topic sentence because they do not fit or support your point. Eliminate details that do not relate to the topic sentence. For example, the following list contains details that really do not relate to the topic sentence. Those details are crossed out.

    topic sentence: Waiters have to be very patient in dealing with their
                        customers.

        details: customers take a long time ordering
                ~~waiter's salary is low~~
                waiters have to explain specials twice
                customers send orders back
                customers blame waiters for any delays

customers want food instantly
waiters can't react to sarcasm of customers
waiters can't get angry if customer does
~~waiters work long shifts~~
customers change their mind after ordering

From List to Outline

Take another look at the topic sentence and list of details on a favorite city or town:

topic sentence: I love St. Augustine because it has sun and sea, history, and family

details:
a small city	clear blue water
no freeways	lots of history
no sky scrapers	a fort
not millions of people	oldest schoolhouse
thousands of visitors every day	grandparents live there
can always visit family for free	warm in winter
beach nearby	grandparents feed me
clean, big beach	I use their car

After you scan that list, you are ready to develop the outline of the paragraph.

An outline is a plan for writing, and it can be a type of draft in list form. It sketches what you want to write and the order in which you want to present it. *An organized, logical list will make your writing unified because each item on the list will relate to your topic sentence.*

When you plan, keep your topic sentence in mind:

I love St. Augustine because it has <u>sun</u> and <u>sea</u>, <u>history</u>, and <u>family</u>.

Notice the underlined key words, which lead to three key parts of your outline:

sun and sea
history
family

You can put the details on your list together so that they connect to one of these parts:

sun and sea

beach nearby, clean, big beach, clear blue water, warm in winter

history

lots of history, a fort, oldest schoolhouse

family

can always visit family for free, grandparents live there, grandparents feed me, I drive their car

With this kind of grouping, you have a clearer idea of how to organize a paragraph.

Now that you have grouped your ideas with key words and details, you can write an outline.

An Outline for a Paragraph

topic sentence:	I love St. Augustine because it has sun and sea, history, and family.
details:	
sun and sea	It is warm in the winter. There is a beach nearby. It is big and clean. The water is clear blue.
history	It has lots of history. There is a fort. The oldest schoolhouse is there.
family	My grandparents live in St. Augustine. I stay at their house. They feed me. I use their car.

As you can see, the outline combines some of the details from the list. Even with these combinations, the details are very rough in style. As you reread the list of details, you will notice places that need more combination, places where ideas need more explaining, and places that are repetitive. Keep in mind that an outline is merely a very rough organization of your paragraph.

As you work through the steps of devising an outline, you can check for the following:

CHECKLIST **A Checklist for an Outline**

✔ **Unity:** Do all the details relate to the topic sentence? If they do, the paragraph will be unified.

✔ **Support:** Do you have enough supporting ideas? Can you add to these ideas with even more specific details?

✔ **Coherence:** Are the details listed in the right order? If the order of points is logical, the paragraph will be coherent.

COHERENCE: PUTTING YOUR DETAILS IN PROPER ORDER

Check the sample outline again, and you will notice that the details are grouped in the same order as the topic sentence: first, details about sun and sea; next, details about history; last, details about family in St. Augustine. Putting the details in an order that matches the topic sentence is a logical order for this paragraph.

Putting the details in logical order makes the ideas in your paragraph easy to follow. The most logical order for a paragraph depends on the subject of the paragraph. If you are writing about an event, you might use **time order** (such as telling what happened first, second, and so forth); if you are arguing some point, you might use **emphatic order** (such as saving your most convincing idea for last); if you are describing a room, you might use **space order** (such as from left to right or from top to bottom).

The format of the outline helps to organize your ideas. The topic sentence is written above the list of details. This position helps you to remember that the topic sentence is the *main idea*, and the details that support it are written under it. The topic sentence is the most important sentence of the paragraph. You can easily check the items on your list, one by one, against your main idea. You can also develop the *unity* (relevance) and *coherence* (logical order) of your details.

When you actually write a paragraph, the topic sentence does not necessarily have to be the first sentence in the paragraph. Read the paragraphs below, and notice where each topic sentence is placed.

Topic Sentence at the Beginning of the Paragraph

<u>Watching a horror movie on the late show can keep me up all night</u>. The movie itself scares me to death, especially if it involves a creepy character sneaking up on someone in the dark. After the movie, I'm afraid to turn out all the lights and be alone in the dark. Then every little noise seems like the sound of a sinister intruder. Strange shapes seem to appear in the shadows. My closet becomes a place where someone could be hiding. There might even be a creature under the bed! And if I go to sleep, these strange invaders might appear from under the bed or in the closet.

Topic Sentence in the Middle of the Paragraph

The kitchen counters gleamed. In the spice rack, every jar was organized neatly. The sink was polished, and not one spot marred its surface. The stove burners were surrounded by dazzling stainless steel rings. <u>The chef kept an immaculate kitchen.</u> There were no finger marks on the refrigerator door. No sticky spots dirtied the floor. No crumbs hid behind the toaster.

Topic Sentence at the End of the Paragraph

On long summer evenings, we would play softball in the street. Sometimes we'd play until it was so dark we could barely see the ball. Then our mothers would come to the front steps of the row houses and call us in, telling us to stop our play. But we'd pretend we couldn't hear them. If they insisted, we'd beg for a few minutes more or for just one more game. It was so good to be outdoors with our friends. It was warm, and we knew we had weeks of summer vacation ahead. There was no school in the morning; there would be more games to play. <u>We loved those street games on summer nights.</u>

Since many of your paragraph assignments will require a clear topic sentence, be sure you follow your own instructor's directions about placement of the topic sentence.

Exercise 13   **Adding Details to Support a Topic Sentence**

The topic sentences below have some—but not enough—details. Write sentences to add details to the list below each topic sentence.

1. topic sentence: My coworker is making my job unbearable.

a. When he is late for work, he expects me to cover up for him.

b. He also sneaks out early at least twice a week and asks me to lie for him.

c. I get stuck doing all the work he avoids by being absent.

d. _____

e. _____

f. _____

g. _____

2. topic sentence: Caring for a toddler can be stressful.

a. Toddlers like to explore and get into dangerous places.

b. _____

c. _____

d. _____

e. _____

f. _____

g. _____

3. topic sentence: Moving to a new house or apartment is a challenge.

a. Packing means sorting through all a person's belongings.

b. It is difficult to decide what to throw out.

c. A person goes on an endless search for more boxes for all his or her possessions.

d. _____

e. _____

f. _____

g. _____

Exercise 14 **Eliminating Details That Do Not Fit**

Below are topic sentences and lists of supporting details. Cross out the details that do not fit the topic sentence.

1. topic sentence: Cell phones offer many distractions.

details: When people are bored, standing in line, they use their cell phones to call a friend.

Some scientists say cell phones are dangerous to a person's health.

Students who are not interested in class send text messages on their cell phones.

In some cases, students attending lectures play games on their cell phones.

Today cell phones offer many kinds of musical rings.

People stuck in traffic make calls on their cell phones to make the time go faster.

Sometimes, people at a dull meeting use their cell phones to check their e-mail.

2. topic sentence: Everywhere I look, I see how sports influence fashion.

details: Men who have never played basketball wear shirts printed with a team's name and a superstar's number.

It seems as if half the world is wearing some form of baseball cap.

Even elderly men and women love sweat pants and hooded jackets.

There are sports restaurants and bars in many towns.

Superstar pro athletes are used to endorse and sell clothes and shoes.

Retired athletes often become sports commentators.

Star tennis players can design, wear, and sell their own line of fashions.

For a while, even bowling shirts became fashionable.

Exercise 15 **Coherence: Putting Details in the Right Order**

These outlines have details that are in the wrong order. In the space provided, number the sentences in the right order: 1 would be the number for the first sentence, and so on.

1. topic sentence: A short trip to pick up my mother at the airport turned into four frustrating hours.

_____ After an hour of circling the pick-up area, I still had not seen my mother.

_____ As soon as I got off the freeway, I raced to the airport terminal, expecting to find my mother at the pick-up area.

_____ But once I got to the pick-up area, she was nowhere to be seen.

_____ Forty minutes later, I was stuck in freeway traffic because of a bad accident half a mile ahead.

_____ A police officer soon told me I could not park at the pick-up area and ordered me to move on.

_____ Sick of circling, I decided to get a long-term parking space and wait inside the terminal.

_____ Finally, four hours after I left home, I greeted my tired and frustrated mother with a hug.

_____ I left my house at noon, expecting the usual thirty-minute ride to the airport.

_____ Once inside the terminal, I checked the flight schedule.

_____ The schedule indicated my mother's plane had been delayed and would be another two hours late.

2. topic sentence: Paying bills is an unpleasant chore for me.

_____ After I gather all the bills, I sort them into the ones I have to pay immediately and the ones I can avoid a little longer.

_____ Once I have all the bills sorted, I reluctantly pull out my checkbook.

_____ It starts when I gather all the bills I have scattered in my house.

_____ Depression leads to determination as I write a check for each urgent bill and put the others aside.

_____ As I sort, I feel depressed about the money I owe.

_____ Once the checks and bills are in their envelopes, I search the house for stamps.

_____ Eventually, I manage to find enough postage to send all the bills.

_____ As I walk to the mailbox, I congratulate myself on surviving another round of bill-paying.

DRAFTING Drafting and Revising a Paragraph

Drafting

The outline is a draft in list form. You are now ready to write the list in paragraph form, to "rough out" a draft of your assignment. This stage of writing is the time to draft, revise, edit, and draft again. You may write several drafts in this stage, but don't think of this as an unnecessary chore or a punishment. It is a way of taking the pressure off yourself. By revising in steps, you are reminding yourself that the first try does not have to be perfect.

Review the outline on a favorite city or town on page 22. You can create a first draft of this outline in the form of a paragraph. (Remember that the first line of each paragraph is indented). In the draft of the paragraph below, the first sentence of the paragraph is the topic sentence.

A First Draft of a Paragraph

      I love St. Augustine because it has sun and sea, history, and family. St. Augustine is warm in the winter. There is a beach nearby. It is clean and big. The water is clear blue. St. Augustine has lots of history. There is an old stone fort. The oldest schoolhouse is there. I can always visit my family for free. My grandparents live in St. Augustine. They feed me. I use their car.

Revising

Once you have a first draft, you can begin to think about revising and editing it. **Revising** means rewriting the draft by making changes in the structure, in the order of the sentences, and in the content. **Editing** includes making changes in the choice of words, in the selection of details, in punctuation, and in the pattern and kinds of sentences. It may also include **adding transitions,** which are words, phrases, or sentences that link ideas.

      One way to begin revising and editing is to read your work aloud to yourself. Listen to your words, and consider the following questions.

CHECKLIST **A Checklist for Revising the Draft of a Paragraph (with key terms)**

✔ Am I staying on my point? (unity)

✔ Should I take out any ideas that do not relate? (unity)

✔ Do I have enough to say about my point? (support)

✔ Should I add any details? (support)

✔ Should I change the order of my sentences? (coherence)

✔ Is my choice of words appropriate? (style)

✔ Is my choice of words repetitive? (style)

✔ Are my sentences too long? Too short? (style)

✔ Should I combine any sentences? (style)

✔ Am I running sentences together? (grammar)

✔ Am I writing complete sentences? (grammar)

✔ Can I link my ideas more smoothly? (transitions)

If you apply the checklist to the draft of the paragraph on a favorite city or town, you will probably find these rough spots:

- The sentences are very short and choppy.
- Some sentences could be combined.
- Some words are repeated often.
- Some ideas would be more effective if they were supported by more details.
- The paragraph could use a few transitions.

Consider the following revised draft of the paragraph, and notice the changes, underlined, that have been made in the draft:

A Revised Draft of a Paragraph

topic sentence	I love St. Augustine, <u>Florida</u>, because it has
sentences combined	sun and sea, history, and family. <u>St. Augustine</u>
	<u>is warm in the winter and a big, clean beach</u>
transition added	<u>with clear blue water is nearby. In addition,</u>
sentences combined	<u>St. Augustine has lots of history, including an</u>
transition added	<u>old stone fort that looks out on the water.</u> It
details added	<u>also</u> has the oldest schoolhouse <u>in America, a</u>
transition added	<u>tiny wooden building. Best of all</u>, my grand-
details added	parents live in St. Augustine. They are <u>my</u>
sentences combined	<u>favorite relatives</u>, and <u>they make me feel very</u>
	<u>welcome. When I am in St. Augustine, I stay</u>
	<u>with them, enjoy their food, and use their</u>
	<u>car</u>.

When you are revising your own paragraph, you can use the checklist to help you. Read the checklist several times; then reread your draft, looking for answers to the questions on the list. If your instructor agrees, you can work with your classmates. You can read your draft to a partner or a group. Your listener(s) can react to your draft by applying the questions on the checklist and by making notes about your draft as you read. When you are finished reading aloud, your partner(s) can discuss the notes about your work.

Exercise 16 **Revising a Draft by Combining Sentences**

The paragraph below has many short, choppy sentences, which are underlined. Wherever you see two or more underlined sentences clustered next to each other, combine the clustered sentences into one clear, smooth sentence. Write your revised version of the paragraph in the spaces above the lines.

Paragraph to be revised:

My brother is a souvenir collector who is becoming overwhelmed by his collection. One of his problems is that he defines a souvenir as almost anything connected to a special event. <u>This event can be a visit to a new place. Maybe it is a party. It can also be a sports event. Sometimes it is a family gathering.</u> Since his definition of a souvenir is so wide, he collects hundreds of souvenirs. <u>His closet is full of postcards, mugs, and photo booklets from places. These are places he visited on vacation.</u> He has so many refrigerator magnets that there is not enough room for them on the refrigerator. <u>Bobble-head sports figures cover every surface</u> <u>of his car's dashboard. Also, they hang from the rear-view mirror.</u> Strings of Mardi-Gras beads from several parties are looped around his bedposts. <u>My brother has</u> <u>to dump some of his collection. His other choice is to open a souvenir store.</u>

Exercise 17   **Adding Details to a Draft**

Complete this exercise with a partner or a group. The paragraph below lacks the kind of details that would make it more interesting. Working with a partner or a group, add the details to the blank spaces provided. When you are finished with the additions, read the revised paragraph to the class.

Paragraph to be revised:

While many college students say they are too busy to watch television, most have one or two programs they tune into frequently. These programs can be real-ity shows such as _____ and _____, which have many loyal viewers. Other students are fans of sports programs and will stay up late to watch _____ games or _____ tournaments. When it comes to music programming, shows featuring performers like _____ and _____ appeal to many viewers age eighteen to twenty-five, while older viewers may turn to programs with stars such as _____ and _____. Everyone has his or her favorite comedians, and college stu-dents may tune into comedians like _____ or _____ on pro-grams such as _____ and _____. Clearly, television may not be a constant source of entertainment for students, but it offers some escape from the studying, jobs, and other responsibilities of college life.

POLISHING **Polishing and Proofreading a Paragraph**

The final version of your paragraph is the result of careful thinking, plan-ning, and revising. After as many drafts as it takes, you read to polish and proofread. You can avoid too many last-minute corrections if you check your last draft carefully. Check that draft for the following:

- spelling errors
- punctuation errors
- word choice
- a final statement

Take a look at the last draft of the paragraph on a favorite city or town. Wherever something is crossed out, the draft has been corrected directly above the crossed out material. At the end of the paragraph, you will notice a concluding sentence has been added to unify the paragraph.

Correcting the Last Draft of a Paragraph

I love St. Augustine, ~~Fla.,~~ *Florida* because it has sun and sea, history, and family. St. Augustine is warm in the ~~Winter,~~ *winter* and a large, clean beach with clear ~~blew~~ *blue* water is nearby. In addition, St. Augustine has ~~lot's~~ *lots* of history, including an old stone fort that looks out on the water. It also ~~have~~ *has* the oldest schoolhouse in America, a tiny wooden building. Best of all, my grandparents live in St. Augustine. They are my favorite relatives, and they make me ~~fell~~ *feel* very welcome. When I am in St. Augustine, I stay with them, enjoy their food, and use ~~there~~ *their* car. St. Augustine has the perfect natural advantages, history, and family ~~connection~~ *connections* to make it my favorite city.

Giving Your Paragraph a Title

When you prepare the final version of your paragraph, you may be asked to give it a title. The title should be short and should fit the subject of the paragraph. For example, an appropriate title for the paragraph on a favorite city or town could be "My Favorite City" or "The City I Love." Check with your instructor to see if your paragraph needs a title. In this book, the paragraphs do not have titles.

The Final Version of a Paragraph

Following is the final version of the paragraph on a favorite city or town. As you read it, you will notice a few more changes. Even though the paragraph went through several drafts and many revisions, the final copy still reflects some additional polishing: some details have been added, some have been made more specific, and some words have been changed. These changes were made as the final version was prepared. (They are underlined for your reference.)

A Final Version of a Paragraph

(Changes from the previous draft are underlined.)

I love St. Augustine, Florida, because it has sun and sea, history, and family. St. Augustine is warm in the winter, and a <u>wide</u>, clean beach with clear blue water is <u>ten minutes away</u>. In addition, St. Augustine is <u>filled with</u> history, including an old stone fort that looks out on the water. It also has the oldest schoolhouse in America, a tiny wooden building <u>smaller than a two-car garage</u>. Best of all, my grandparents live in St. Augustine. They are my favorite relatives, and they make me feel very welcome. When I am in St. Augustine, I stay with them, enjoy their <u>delicious Spanish</u> food, and use their car. St. Augustine has the natural advantages, history, and family connections to make it my favorite city.

Reviewing the Writing Process

This chapter has taken you through four important stages in writing. As you become more comfortable with them, you will be able to work through them more quickly. For now, try to remember the four stages.

INFO BOX: **The Stages of the Writing Process**

Prewriting: gathering and developing ideas, thinking on paper through freewriting, brainstorming, mapping, or keeping a journal.

Planning: planning the paragraph by combining and dividing details, focusing the details with a topic sentence, listing the supporting details in proper order, and devising an outline.

Drafting: writing a rough draft of the paragraph, then revising and editing it several times.

Polishing: preparing the final version of the paragraph, with one last proofreading check for errors in preparation, punctuation, and spelling.

Exercise 18   **Proofreading to Prepare the Final Version**

Following are two paragraphs with the kinds of errors it is easy to overlook when you prepare the final version of an assignment. Correct the errors by writing above the lines. There are twelve errors in the first paragraph and eleven errors in the second paragraph.

1. My night class is different from my day class in both length and atmos-

phere. For on thing, its three hour's long, which is a long time to sit and lissen to a

teacher talk Most of my day classes last an hour and fifteen minutes. Fortunatly,

my night instructor gives us a break after the first half of class and in the second

half of the class, we do group work. The group activitys are more interesting then

the lecture. The second difference between my night and day classes is the stu-

dents. The night students are older, than the day students and more serious. These

older students don't fool aroun in class; instead, they want to get the job done. I

like the studious environment in my night class, but I think it is hard to stay allert

for three hours.

2. Taking a walk around campus can be an eye-opener for many students.

Since most students today do not live in dormitorys, the tend to arrive at school

for their classes, grab a snack at a vending machine, rush to class, and leave for work or home as soon as their class is over. As a result, most student the know

very little about their college. They know, the closest parking lot and the way to

their classrooms. They may also know the locations of the bookstore and the reg-

istration area. most likely, they never visit the other places their tuition and fees

pay for, such as the athletic facilities where students can work out, the libary and

media center where students have acess to book, computers, CDs, and videos, and

the student center where students can eat, talk, study, join clubs, and make

friends. A walk might also introduce students to campus gardens and quiet places

to study. A few minutes spend touring the cite can introduce students to the best-

kept secrets, of any school.

Lines of Detail: A Walk-Through Assignment

This assignment involves working within a group to write a paragraph.

> **Step 1:** Read the three sentences below. Pick the one sentence you
> prefer as a possible topic sentence for a paragraph. Fill in the
> blank for the sentence you chose.
>
> **a.** The most frightening movie I've ever seen was _____
>
> _____ (fill in the title).
>
> **b.** If money were no problem, the car I'd buy is _____
>
> _____ (fill in the name of the car).
>
> **c.** The one food I refuse to eat is _____ (fill in
>
> the name of the food).

 COLLABORATE ▶

> **Step 2:** Join a group composed of other students who picked the
> same topic sentence you picked. In your class, you'll have
> "movie" people, "car" people, and "food" people. Brainstorm
> in a group. Discuss questions that could be used to get ideas
> for your paragraph.
>
> For the movie topic, sample questions could include,
> "What was the most frightening part of the movie?" or "What
> kind of movie was it—a ghost story, a horror movie, etc.?" For
> the car topic, sample questions could include, "Have you ever
> driven this kind of car?" or "Do you know anyone who has
> one?" For the food topic, sample questions could include, "Did
> you hate this food when you were a child?" or "Where has this
> food been served to you?"

As you discuss your topic, write the questions, not the answers, below. Keep the questions flowing. Do not stop to say, "That's silly," or "I can't answer that." Try to devise **at least ten questions.**

Ten Brainstorming Questions

1. _____

2. _____

3. _____

4. _____

5. _____

6. _____

7. _____

8. _____

9. _____

10. _____

Step 3: Split up. Alone, begin to think on paper. Answer as many questions as you can, or add more questions and answers, or freewrite.

Step 4: Draft an outline of the paragraph. You will probably have to change the topic sentence to fit the details you have gathered. For example, your new topic sentence might be something like

_____ was the most frightening movie I have

ever seen; it creates fear by using _____,

_____, and _____.

or

If money were no problem, I would buy a _____ for

its performance, _____, and _____.

or

I refuse to eat _____ because _____.
Remember to look at your details to see where they lead you. The details will help you to refine your topic sentence.

Step 5: Prepare the first draft of the paragraph.

Step 6: Read the draft aloud to your writing group, the same people who met to brainstorm. Ask each member of your group to make at least one positive comment and one suggestion for revision.

Step 7: Revise and edit your draft, considering the group's ideas and your own ideas for improvement.

Step 8: Prepare a final version of the paragraph.

Writing Your Own Paragraph

When you write on any of these topics, follow the four basic stages of the writing process in preparing your paragraph.

 COLLABORATE ▶

1. Begin this assignment with a partner. The assignment requires an interview. Your final goal is to write a paragraph that will introduce a class member, your partner, to the rest of the class. In the final paragraph, you may design your own topic sentence or use one of the topic sentences below, filling in the blanks with the material you have discovered:

There are several details you should know about _____

(fill in your partner's name).

or

Three unusual events have happened to _____ (fill in

your partner's name).

Before you write the paragraph, follow these steps:

Step 1: Prepare to interview a classmate. Make a list of six questions you might want to ask. They can be questions like, "Where are you from?" or "Have you ever done anything unusual?" Write *at least six questions* before you start the interview. List the questions on the following interview form, leaving room to fill in short answers later.

Interview Form

Question 1: _____

Answer: _____

Question 2: _____

Answer: _____

Question 3: _____

Answer: _____

Question 4: _____

Answer: _____

Question 5: _____

Answer: _____

Question 6: _____

Answer: _____

Additional questions and answers: _____

_____

_____

_____

Step 2: Meet and interview your partner. Ask the questions on your list. Jot down brief answers. Ask *any other questions* you think of as you are talking; write down the answers on the additional lines at the end of the interview form.

Step 3: Change places. Let your partner interview you.

Step 4: Split up. Use the list of questions and answers about your partner as the prewriting part of your assignment. Work on the outline and draft steps.

Step 5: Ask your partner to read the draft version of your paragraph, to write any comments or suggestions for improvement below the paragraph, and to mark any spelling or grammar errors in the paragraph itself.

Step 6: When you have completed a final version of the paragraph, read the paragraph to the class.

2. Below are some topic sentences. Select one and use it to write a paragraph.

I am easily irritated by _____.

My first experience with college registration was _____.

High school students should never forget that _____.

3. Write a paragraph on one of the topics below. Create your own topic sentence; explain and support it with specific details.

a favorite activity	a dreaded chore	a challenging class
a special song	a treasured toy	a patriotic moment

4. Examine the two photographs of families above. After you have looked at them carefully, write a paragraph with this topic sentence:

Families can be as varied as their members.

You can write about many kinds of families, not just the kinds shown in the photographs.

5. Examine the photograph of the dog below. After you have looked at it carefully, write a paragraph with this topic sentence:

Some owners treat their pets like people.

The details of the photograph can provide you with some details, but come up with other details on your own.

Note: Additional writing options can be found after the professional reading, "Sticky Stuff," which begins on page 593.

Name: _____   **Section:** _____

PEER REVIEW FORM FOR A PARAGRAPH

After you have written a draft of your paragraph, let a writing partner read it. When your partner has completed the form below, discuss the comments. Then repeat the same process for your partner's paragraph.

The topic sentence of this paragraph is _____

_____

_____

The detail that I liked best begins with the words _____

_____

The paragraph has _____ (enough, too many, too few) details to support the topic sentence.

A particularly good part of the paragraph begins with the words

_____

I have questions about or would like to know more about _____

_____

_____

_____

Other comments on the paragraph: _____

_____

_____

_____

_____

_____

_____

_____

_____

_____

_____

_____

Reviewer's Name: _____

CHAPTER 2
Illustration

WHAT IS ILLUSTRATION?

Illustration uses specific examples to support a general point. In your writing, you often use illustration because you frequently want to explain a point with a specific example.

Hints for Writing an Illustration Paragraph

Knowing What Is Specific and What Is General A *general* statement is a broad point. The following statements are general:

Traffic can be bad on Hamilton Boulevard.
Car insurance costs more today than it did last year.
It is difficult to meet people at my college.

You can support a general statement with specific examples:

general statement: Traffic can be bad on Hamilton Boulevard.
 specific examples: During the morning rush hour, the exit to First Avenue is jammed.
If there is an accident, cars can be backed up for a mile.

general statement: Car insurance costs more today than it did last year.

specific examples: Last year I paid $150 a month; this year I pay $200 a month.

My mother, who has never had a traffic ticket, has seen her insurance premium rise fifty percent.

general statement: It is difficult to meet people at my college.

specific examples: After class, most students rush to their jobs.

There are very few places to sit and talk between classes.

When you write an illustration paragraph, be careful to support a general statement with specific examples, not with more general statements:

not this: general statement: College is harder than I thought it would be.

~~**more general statements:** It is tough to be a college student.~~
~~Studying takes a lot of my time.~~

but this: general statement: College is harder than I thought it would be.

specific examples: I cannot afford to miss any classes.

I have to study at least two hours a day.

If you remember to illustrate a broad statement with specific examples, you will have the key to this kind of paragraph.

 **Exercise 1** **Recognizing Broad Statements**

Each of the following lists below contains one broad statement and three specific examples. Underline the broad statement.

1. My car broke down on the highway last week.
My car is not reliable transportation.
Yesterday the car overheated in traffic.
The battery has been dead twice this month.

2. Davis Elementary School offers adult education classes in the evening.
The school auditorium is used for community events.
On weekends, the Police Athletic League sponsors teams on the playing fields of Davis Elementary School.
Davis Elementary School does more than teach schoolchildren.

3. Photographs can provoke powerful emotions.
My grandmother came across an old photograph of my grandfather, and the pain of losing him returned.
My cousin, who is a soldier far from home, was comforted by a photograph of his new baby girl.
Our community was shocked by newspaper pictures of a local murder.

4. Young adults work to pay off their college loans.
   Students face increases in college tuition.
   <u>Everybody seems to be short of money these days</u>.
   Families struggle to pay their credit card debt.

Exercise 2   **Distinguishing the General Statement
From the Specific Example**

Each general statement below is supported by three items. Two of these
items are specific examples; one is too general to be effective. Underline the
one that is too general.

   1. **general statement:** Toys are not just for children anymore.
      support: Many women have doll collections.
      <u>Adults today are drawn to various kinds of toys</u>.
      Adult males love their computer games.

   2. **general statement:** Asian food is becoming increasingly popular.
      support: Prepackaged sushi is available at the supermarket.
      <u>Everybody likes some form of Asian food</u>.
      Noodles (from noodle shops or in instant packets) are as
      popular as spaghetti.

   3. **general statement:** Children love cartoon characters.
      support: Cartoon characters are printed on children's backpacks.
      Many stuffed animals are the animal characters from car-
      toons.
      <u>Cartoon characters are what children adore</u>.

   4. **general statement:** Shopping can be a good way to meet new
      people.
      support: Pet lovers can bring their dogs and meet other dogs and
      their owners at stores like Petsmart.
      <u>You can make friends while you are shopping</u>.
      Bookstores have reading groups where book discussions
      can lead to friendships.

Exercise 3   **Adding Specific Examples to a General Statement**   ◀ COLLABORATE

With a partner or group, add four specific examples to each of the following
general statements.

   1. **general statement:** Summer brings outdoor and indoor insects.

      examples: _____

      _____

_____

_____

2. **general statement:** These days, pizza toppings can include almost anything.

examples: _____

_____

_____

_____

3. **general statement:** People have a number of ways of saying "I'm
sorry" without actually saying those words.

examples: _____

_____

_____

_____

4. **general statement:** Although jewelry is often associated with
women, many men also wear it.

examples: _____

_____

_____

_____

WRITING THE ILLUSTRATION
PARAGRAPH IN STEPS

PREWRITING Gathering Ideas: Illustration

Suppose your instructor asks you to write a paragraph about some aspect of
clothes. You can begin by thinking about your subject to gather ideas and to
find a focus for your paragraph.

Looking through entries in your journal might lead you to the following
underlined entry:

Journal Entry About Clothes

I went to the mall yesterday to look for some <u>good shoes</u>. What a crowd! Some big sale was going on, and the stores were packed. Everybody was pushing and shoving. I just left. I'll go when it's not so crowded. I hate <u>buying clothes and shoes</u>. Wish I could just wear <u>jeans and tee shirts</u> all the time. But even then, the <u>jeans have to have the right label</u>, or you're looked down on. There are <u>status labels on the tee shirts</u>, too. Not to mention <u>expensive athletic shoes</u>.

The underlined terms can lead you to a list:

good shoes	jeans have to have the right label
buying clothes and shoes	status labels on tee shirts
jeans and tee shirts	expensive athletic shoes

Consider the underlined terms. Many of them are specific ideas about clothes. You could write a paragraph about one item or about several related items on the list.

Adding Details to an Idea

Looking at this list, you might decide you want to write something about this topic: tee shirts. To add details, you decide to brainstorm:

Who wears tee shirts?

Athletes, children, teens, movie stars, musicians, parents, old people, restaurant workers.

How much do they cost?

Some are cheap, but some are expensive.

What kinds of tees are there?

Sports tees, concert tees, college names on tees, designer tees, ads on tees.

Why do people wear tees?

They're comfortable and fashionable.

What ads are on tees?

Beer, sporting goods.

What else do you see on tees?

Mickey Mouse, seascapes, political slogans, souvenir pictures or sayings.

You now have this list of ideas connected to the topic of tee shirts:

status labels on tees	concert tees
athletes	college names on tees
children	designer tees
teens	ads on tees
movie stars	comfortable
musicians	fashionable

parents	beer
old people	sporting goods
restaurant workers	Mickey Mouse
cheap	seascapes
expensive	political slogans
sports tees	souvenir pictures or sayings

Creating a Topic Sentence

If you examine this list, looking for *related ideas*, you can create a topic sentence. The ideas on the list include (1) details about the kinds of people who wear tee shirts, (2) details about the cost of tee shirts, and (3) details about what is pictured or written on tee shirts. Not all the details fit into these three categories, but many do.

Grouping the related ideas into the three categories can help you focus your ideas into a topic sentence.

Kinds of People Who Wear Tee Shirts

athletes	movie stars	old people
children	musicians	restaurant workers
teens	parents	

The Cost of Tee Shirts

cheap	some expensive

What Is Pictured or Written on Tee Shirts

ads on tees	beer ads	seascapes
concert tees	sporting goods	political slogans
college names	Mickey Mouse	souvenir pictures or sayings

You can summarize these related ideas in a topic sentence:

People of various backgrounds and ages wear all kinds of tee shirts.

Check the sentence against your details. Does it cover the people who wear tees? Does it cover what is on the shirts?

Yes. The topic sentence says, "*People of various backgrounds and ages wear all kinds of tee shirts.*" The topic sentence has given you a focus for your illustration paragraph.

Exercise 4 **Finding Specific Ideas in Freewriting**

Following are two samples of freewriting. Each is a response to a broad topic. Read each sample, and then underline any words that could become a more specific topic for a paragraph.

Freewriting Reaction to the Topic of Transportation

What does transportation mean? Am I supposed to write about planes, or trains, or what? There's public transportation, like the bus I take to college. I wish I had my own car so I could just get in the car and go whenever I wanted. Instead of waiting at the bus stop. Still, it's not so bad. And I use my father's car on weekends. Car payments. There's no way I could afford them.

DRAFTING   ## Drafting and Revising: Illustration

Review the outline on tee shirts on page 48. You can create a first draft of this outline in the form of a paragraph. At this point, you can combine some of the short, choppy sentences of the outline, add details, and add transitions to link your ideas. You can revise your draft using the following checklist.

CHECKLIST: A Checklist for Revising an Illustration Paragraph

✔ Should some of the sentences be combined?

✔ Do I need more or better transitions?

✔ Should I add more details to support my points?

✔ Should some of the details be more specific?

Transitions

As you revise your illustration paragraph, you may find places where one idea ends and another begins abruptly. This problem occurs when you forget to add **transitions,** which are words, phrases, or sentences that connect one idea to another. Using transitions effectively makes your writing clear and smooth. When you write an illustration paragraph, you need some transitions that link one example to another and other transitions to link one section of your paragraph to another section. Here are some transitions you may want to use in writing an illustration paragraph.

INFO BOX: Transitions for an Illustration Paragraph

another example	one instance
a second example	other examples
for example	other kinds
for instance	such as
in addition	the first instance
in the case of	another instance
like	to illustrate
one example	

Look carefully at the following draft of the paragraph on tee shirts, and note how it combines sentences, adds details, and uses transitions to transform the outline into a clear and developed paragraph.

A Draft of an Illustration Paragraph

topic sentence	<u>People of various backgrounds and ages wear all kinds of tee shirts</u>. <u>Athletes and movie</u>
sentences combined	<u>stars are seen in them</u>. <u>Musicians often</u>

sentences combined	<u>perform in them, and restaurant workers some-times work in tee shirts marked with the</u>
details added	
sentences combined	<u>name of the restaurant. Children, teens, their parents, and older people all wear tee shirts.</u>
transition sentence added	<u>Almost anything can be printed or pictured on a tee shirt. At concerts, fans can buy tee</u>
details added	<u>shirts stamped with the name of the group on stage.</u> College students can wear the name of their college on a shirt. Some shirts
details added	advertise a brand of beer, <u>like Bud</u>, or a
details added	sporting goods company, <u>like Nike</u>. Mickey Mouse is a favorite character on tee shirts.
transition added	<u>Other kinds of shirts include shirts with</u>
sentences combined	<u>seascapes on them, and souvenir shirts, like the ones that say, "My folks visited Philadel-</u>
details added	<u>phia, and all I got was this lousy tee shirt."</u>
transition	<u>Other shirts</u> have political slogans, <u>like "Save</u>
details added	<u>the Whales."</u>

Exercise 11 **Revising a Draft by Combining Sentences**

The following paragraph has many short, choppy sentences, which are un-derlined. Wherever you see two or more underlined sentences clustered next to each other, combine them into one clear, smooth sentence. Write your re-vised version of the paragraph in the spaces above the lines.

Sometimes I think my dog has a split personality. <u>At night I see her sleeping.</u>

<u>She is sweet and adorable. She is like an angel.</u> Her little face seems to be smiling

as she dreams happy dreams. <u>Then she wakes up. She is instantly ready to go.</u>

Begging for a walk, she jumps on me. She wants that walk immediately. As soon

as I get her on her leash, she becomes a wild dog. <u>She leaps ahead of me. She pulls</u>

<u>on the leash. She lurches at every squirrel. She lurches at every cat.</u> This crazy dog

has a completely different nature from the calm dog I see sleeping so peacefully.

Exercise 12 **Revising a Draft by Adding Transitions**

The following paragraph needs some transitions. Add appropriate transitions (words or phrases) to the blanks.

Mr. Rubenstein, my high school coach, was a generous person. _____

_____ he always stayed late after practice to give advice to any player who

wanted help with a personal question. He would offer his thoughts on any subject

from how to treat a backache to how to deal with family problems. He was more than a coach because he cared about all his players. _____ he once vis-

ited my father at home to discuss my chances of getting into college. _____

_____ Mr. Rubenstein lent money to a player who needed to pay a

school lab fee. _____ the coach stayed all night beside the hospital bed

of an injured athlete. I learned about sports from Mr. Rubenstein, but I also

learned about giving to others.

Exercise 13   **Adding Details to a Draft**   ◀ COLLABORATE 👥

The following paragraph lacks the kind of details that would make it more
interesting. Working with a partner or group, add details to the blank
spaces provided. When you are finished, read the revised paragraph to the
class.

   The clothes people wear to work depend on their positions. The average col-

lege student who works at a restaurant is likely to wear _Black pants_ or

Apron on the job. Men who work behind the counter of an expensive

men's clothing store may be required to dress in _Expensive clothes_, while women

who sell makeup in department stores often have to wear _their makeup_ and

perfect makeup. If a person works as a teller in a bank, he or she cannot come to

work in _Jeans_. Instead, appropriate dress is _Cackies_ and

Blouse. Executives in financial corporations are often expected to dress

in _Dress_, _Skirt_, and _Suit_. On the other hand,

people in creative fields such as music or film production can wear almost any-

thing from _ragy Jeans_ to _Skates shirts_ when they work.

POLISHING   **Polishing and Proofreading: Illustration**

As you prepare the final version of your illustration paragraph, make any
changes in word choice or transitions that can refine your writing. Following is the final version of the paragraph on tee shirts. As you read it, you will
notice a few more changes: some details have been added, some have been
made more specific, and a transition has been added. In addition, a concluding sentence has been added to unify the paragraph. These changes were
made as the final version was prepared. (They are underlined for your
reference.)

A Final Version of an Illustration Paragraph

(Changes from the draft are underlined.)

People of various backgrounds and ages wear all kinds of tee shirts. Athletes and movie stars are seen in them. Musicians often perform in <u>ragged tees</u>, and restaurant workers sometimes work in tee shirts marked with the name of the restaurant. Children, teens, their parents, and <u>elderly</u> people all wear tee shirts. Almost anything can be painted or pictured on a tee shirt. At concerts, <u>for example</u>, fans can buy tee shirts stamped with the name of the group on stage. College students can wear the name of their college on a shirt. Some <u>popular</u> shirts advertise a brand of beer, like Bud, or a sporting goods company, like Nike. Mickey Mouse is a favorite character on tee shirts. Other kinds of tee shirts include <u>surfer</u> shirts with seascapes on them and souvenir shirts, like the <u>surly</u> ones that say, "My folks visited Philadelphia, and all I got was this lousy tee shirt." Other shirts have political slogans, like "Save the Whales." <u>What is written or pictured on tee shirts is as varied as the people who wear them.</u>

Before you prepare the final version of your illustration paragraph, check your latest draft for errors in spelling, punctuation, typing, and copying.

Note: A sample illustration essay based on the same topic and following the same writing steps can be found in Chapter 12 on page 278–282.

Exercise 14   **Proofreading to Prepare the Final Version**

Following are two illustration paragraphs with the kinds of errors it is easy to overlook when you prepare the final version of an assignment. Correct the errors by writing above the lines. There are twelve errors in the first paragraph and ten errors in the second paragraph.

1. Today, when people say they want a drink of water, they could be axsing for a number of drinks. Of coarse, there is water right from the faucet, but manny people drink bottle water. There are dozens of brands of bottled water and there are also two basic kind of water in bottles. One kind is fizzy, and one kind is flat. In edition, there are many new types of water, such as water with vitamins, water with caffeine, and Flavored water. These days, a whole row in the suppermarket can be filled with ten or twenty variety of water, and restaurants may offer a choice of water, from free tap water to expensive kins of bottled water. As a result a person who asks for a glass of water has to be very specific.

2. Every member of my family has a peculiar driving habit. My Father, for example, always drives with the windows open even if it is freezing outside.

Riding with him, I have saw ice crystles forming on the car seats. My mother also has a strange driving habit, but her's is more dangerous. She never looks into her rear-view mirror. Instead, she just changes lane's whenever she feels like it. I always say my prayers when I get into a car with her. Unlike my mother, my brother is a very cautious driver. He was in a accident, and it scared him so much that he drives very slowly and does'nt change lanes unless he has to. I am too impatient to ride with him. Finally, my habit is quiet dramatic I blast the radio so that it can be heard a block away. My parents wont even ride with me because they are afraid they will burst their eardrums. In our family, every driver, because of some personal driving weirdness, tends to drive alone.

Lines of Detail: A Walk-Through Assignment

Your assignment is to write an illustration paragraph about music.

Step 1: Freewrite or brainstorm on this broad topic for ten minutes.

Step 2: Review your freewriting or brainstorming. Underline any parts that are a specific idea related to the broad topic, music.

Step 3: List all the specific ideas. Choose one as the narrowed topic for your paragraph.

Step 4: Add related ideas to your chosen, narrowed topic. Do this by reviewing your list for related ideas and by brainstorming for more related ideas.

Step 5: List all your related ideas and review their connection to your narrowed topic. Then write a topic sentence for your paragraph.

Step 6: Write a first draft of your paragraph.

Step 7: Revise your first draft. Be sure it has enough details and clear transitions. Combine any choppy sentences.

Step 8: After a final check for any errors in punctuation, spelling, and word choice, prepare the final version of the paragraph.

Writing Your Own Illustration Paragraph

When you write on any of these topics, follow the four basic stages of the writing process in preparing your illustration paragraph.

1. Begin this assignment with a partner or group. Together, write down as many old sayings as you can. (Old sayings include statements like, "It's not whether you win or lose; it's how you play the game that's important," or "Money can't buy happiness.") If anyone in your group speaks a second language, ask him or her to translate

◀ COLLABORATE

 COMPUTER ▶

and explain any old sayings from that language. To review quotations categorized by topics, visit http://www.quoteland.com.

Once you have a long list of sayings, split up. Pick one saying; then write a paragraph on that saying. Your paragraph should give several examples that prove the truth of the saying.

2. Select one of the following topic sentences and use it to write a paragraph in which you use examples to support (illustrate) the topic sentence.

_____ makes me nervous.

_____ takes great courage.

A snowstorm forces me to _____.

A rainy day is a good day to catch up on indoor chores.

The friendliest store in my neighborhood is _____.

3. Select one of the topics listed below. Write a paragraph on some narrowed part of the topic. If you choose the topic of jobs, for example, you might narrow the topic to illustrate the benefits or drawbacks of your job.

jobs	fears	dreams	mistakes
stress	money	television	mysteries
computers	children	celebrities	surprises
fashion	challenges	memories	holidays

4. Examine the photograph below. After you have looked at it carefully, write a paragraph using the following topic sentence:

Major malls appeal to a variety of ages and tastes. (The photograph may help you think of examples to support the topic sentence.)

5. Examine the photograph below. After you have looked at it carefully, write a paragraph with this topic sentence:

Whenever I am delayed by a traffic jam, I have several ways to cope with the irritation.

Note: Additional writing options suitable for illustration-related assignments can be found after the professional reading, "Spanglish," which begins on page 596.

Name: _____ Section: _____

PEER REVIEW FORM FOR AN ILLUSTRATION PARAGRAPH

After you have written a draft of your illustration paragraph, let a writing partner read it. When your partner has completed the form below, discuss the comments. Then repeat the same process for your partner's paragraph.

The examples in this paragraph relate to this topic sentence: _____

_____

_____

The paragraph has _____ (enough, too many, too few) details to support the topic sentence.

The most effective example is the one about _____

_____

Three words or phrases of specific detail in the paragraph are _____

_____

Two transitions (words or phrases) in the paragraph are _____

_____

I have questions about or would like to know more about _____

_____

Other comments: _____

_____

_____

_____

_____

_____

_____

_____

_____

_____

_____

_____

Reviewer's Name: _____

CHAPTER 3
Description

WHAT IS DESCRIPTION?

Description shows a reader what a person, place, thing, or situation is like. When you write description, you try to *show*, not *tell*, about something. You want to make the reader see that person, place, or situation, and then, perhaps, to make the reader think about or act on what you have shown.

Hints for Writing a Descriptive Paragraph

Using Specific Words and Phrases Your description will help the reader see if it uses specific words and phrases. If a word or phrase is *specific*, it is *exact and precise*. The opposite of specific language is language that is vague, general, or fuzzy. Think of the difference between specific and general in this way:

Imagine that you are browsing through a used-car lot. A salesman approaches you.

"Can I help you?" the salesman asks.
"I'm looking for a good, reliable car," you say.
"Well, what kind of car did you have in mind?" asks the salesman.
"Not too old," you say.
"A sports car?" asks the salesman.
"Maybe," you say.

The conversation could go on and on. You are being very general in saying that you want a "good, reliable" car. The salesman is looking for specific details: How old a car do you want? What model of car?

In writing, if you use words like "good" or "nice" or "bad" or "interesting," you will not have a specific description or a very effective piece of writing. Whenever you can, try to use a more precise word instead of a general term. To find a more explicit term, ask yourself such questions as, "What type?" or "How?" The examples below show how a general term can be replaced by a more specific one.

> **general word:** hat (Ask "What type?")
> **more specific words:** beret, fishing hat, baseball cap

> **general word:** lettuce (Ask "What type?")
> **more specific words:** iceberg lettuce, Romaine, arugula

> **general word:** ran (Ask "How?")
> **more specific words:** raced, sprinted, loped

> **general word:** nice (Ask "How?")
> **more specific words:** friendly, outgoing, courteous

Exercise 1   **Identifying General and Specific Words**

Below are lists of words. Put an *X* by the one term in each list that is a more general term than the others. The first one is done for you.

List 1

___X___ science

_____ botany

_____ biology

_____ astronomy

_____ geology

List 3

_____ jazz

___X___ music

_____ reggae

_____ hip-hop

_____ rock 'n' roll

List 2

___X___ medical worker

_____ surgeon

_____ nurse

_____ physical therapist

_____ radiologist

List 4

_____ preschoolers

_____ kindergartners

_____ toddlers

_____ babies

___X___ children

Exercise 2   **Ranking General and Specific Items**

Following are lists of items. In each list, rank the items from the most general (1) to the most specific (4).

furniture
{
There were lots of books about science fiction in two
bookcases.
I remember <u>Fahrenheit 451</u> and <u>The War of the Worlds</u>.
Old videos like <u>Raiders of the Lost Ark</u> were also
stacked on the bookshelves.
The bed was piled high with <u>Star Trek</u> pillows.
}

You probably noticed that the outline has more details than the original list. These details help to make the descriptions more specific. You can add them to the outline and to the drafts of your paragraph.

Once you have a list of details focused on a topic sentence and arranged in some logical order, you can begin writing a draft of your description paragraph.

Exercise 10 **Finding Details That Do Not Relate**

Survey the following lists. Each includes a topic sentence and several details. In each list, cross out the details that do not relate to the topic sentence.

1. **topic sentence:** I felt trapped in my cousin's living room.
   details: Every inch of the walls was covered in a flowery pink wallpaper.
   There were peach-colored shades on the windows, and heavy, stiff curtains at the sides and top of the window frames.
   Furniture crammed all four sides of the room.
   Huge lavender sofas were wedged against enormous side tables and giant chairs.
   There was no recliner.
   Even the carpet fought for space.
   It was covered by two smaller pink and purple rugs.
   Most people today like tile or wood floors.
   Walking on the rugs and carpet, I felt like I was sinking into a mattress.
   Worst of all, an enormous ceiling fan hung down into the room, threatening to cut off my head.
   My cousin loves that room.

2. **topic sentence:** My sister Briana has been a screamer since the day she was born.
   details: My mother says Briana was born kicking and crying so loudly the doctor was surprised.
   When she learned to talk, Briana shouted her words.
   On the other hand, I have a soft voice.
   She never raised her hand in first grade but just yelled at the teacher.
   She startled the teacher and scared the children.
   By the time she was ten, Briana could frighten grown men with her loud voice.

In a crowd of noisy people, Briana could always be heard.
She was a small girl with big eyes and long, thin legs.
When Briana was fourteen, her voice became her biggest asset.
She became a singer in a girl group.
Today, her powerful voice is heard on the radio.

3. topic sentence: Mr. Havel's backyard was a perfect playground.
   details: The large yard was bordered by tall, thick trees.
   They were perfect for climbing.
   Beneath the trees was soft grass.
   Children could lie on the grass in the shade and try to catch the flying insects.
   My brother once caught a small snake in our basement.
   The center of Mr. Havel's yard was an open area.
   It was worn down to dirt because the neighborhood children used it to play soccer and softball.
   Mr. Havel saved his flowers and bushes for his front yard.

Exercise 11   **Putting Details in Order**

Following are lists that start with a topic sentence. The details under each topic sentence are not in the right order. Put the details in logical order by labeling them, with 1 being the first detail, 2 the second, and so forth.

1. topic sentence: My little sister had obviously gotten into my closet. (Arrange the details from head to foot.)

   details: _____ She had my crystal beads around her neck.

   _____ My new lace blouse looked like a nightgown on her six-year-old's body.

   _____ My floppy hat nearly covered her face.

   _____ My ankle socks drooped around her ankles.

   _____ She tottered in my new pink high heels.

2. topic sentence: The thrift shop looked like a perfect place for treasures. (Arrange the details from outside to inside.)

   details: _____ Wind chimes tinkled as we opened the door.

   _____ Beyond the door we saw shadowy shapes.

   _____ A gold-lettered sign painted on the window said, "Hidden Beauties Thrift Shop."

   _____ In the window display were a child's wooden rocking horse, six brass candlesticks, and a table topped with tiles.

   _____ As we walked farther into the store, we saw lamps, china, clothing, and paintings.

3. topic sentence: Meeting my girlfriend's parents at dinner was an ordeal for me.

details: _____ As we sat down to eat dinner, I couldn't get my chair close enough to the table.

_____ My girlfriend's mother served spaghetti, and I panicked about strands hanging out of my mouth.

_____ When I finally got my chair under the table, I knocked over a glass of water.

_____ I left half the spaghetti on my plate because I ran out of ways to twirl it onto my fork.

_____ I ate all of my dessert, chocolate cake, so fast that everyone stared at me.

Exercise 12 **Creating Details Using a Logical Order**

The following lists include a topic sentence and indicate a required order for the details. Write five sentences of details in the required order.

1. topic sentence: The club was strange, but the people were stranger. (Describe the club; then describe the people.)

   a. _____

   b. _____

   c. _____

      _____

   d. _____

   e. _____

2. topic sentence: The restaurant was a pleasant surprise. (Arrange the details from outside to inside.)

   a. _____

   b. _____

   c. _____

   d. _____

      _____

   e. _____

3. topic sentence: Our drive to Arborville was boring. (Describe the drive from beginning to end.)

   a.

      _____

   b. _____

   c. _____

d. _____

_____

e. _____

DRAFTING Drafting and Revising: Description

After you have an outline, the next step is creating a first rough draft of the paragraph. At this point, you can begin combining some of the ideas in your outline, making two or more short sentences into one longer one. You can also write your first draft in short sentences and combine the sentences later. Your goal is simply to put your ideas in paragraph form so that you can see how they look and you can check them to see what needs to be improved.

The first draft of a paragraph will not be perfect. If it were perfect, it wouldn't be a first draft. Once you have the first draft, check it, using the following list:

CHECKLIST: A Checklist for Revising a Descriptive Paragraph

✔ Are there enough details?

✔ Are the details specific?

✔ Do the details use sense words?

✔ Are the details in order?

✔ Is there a dominant impression?

✔ Do the details connect to the dominant impression?

✔ Have I made my point?

A common problem in writing description is creating a fuzzy, vague description. Take a look at the following fuzzy description:

> The football fans were rowdy and excited. They shouted when their team scored. Some people jumped up. The fans showed their support by cheering and stomping. They were enjoying every minute of the game.

The description could be revised so that it is more specific and vivid:

> The football fans were rowdy and excited. When their team scored, they yelled, "Way to go!" or "Stomp 'em! Crush 'em!" until they were hoarse. Three fans, wearing the team colors of blue and white on their shirts, shorts, and socks, jumped up, spilling their drinks on the teenagers seated below them. During time-outs, the fans chanted rhythmically, and throughout the game they stomped their feet in a steady beat against the wooden bleachers. As people chanted, whooped, and woofed, they turned to grin at each other and thrust their clenched fists into the air.

The vivid description meets the requirements of the checklist. It has sufficient specific details. The details use sense words to describe what the fans looked and sounded like. The details also support a dominant impression of rowdy, excited fans. The vivid, specific details make the point.

Exercise 13   **Revising a Paragraph, Finding Irrelevant Sentences**

Following are two descriptive paragraphs. In each, there are sentences that are irrelevant, meaning they do not have anything to do with the first sentence, the topic sentence. Cross out the irrelevant sentences in the paragraphs below.

1. I remember Antonio as a good-natured person. The rest of his family was nasty, but Antonio was different. He never argued with me; instead, he always said, "You may be right." Then he changed the subject. When my brother and I raised our voices or snapped at each other, Antonio was the one to calm us down with a soft voice and a humorous remark. Whenever I needed a ride to work, I knew Antonio would drive me in his beat-up old truck. I didn't have a car in the days when I knew him. "We'll ask Antonio," was what all his friends would say when they needed money, or a meal, or a place to stay. He would even take care of his landlady's children if she had to work late. Antonio had a kind and generous heart.

2. The student cafeteria is not a place to study. It is always crowded, so it is impossible to find a quiet nook for reading. The noise level is high. People blast their music, shout to one another across the tables, and fight over their games of cards and dominoes. There is a patio outside, but nobody ever uses it. Students bump into one another and jostle the tables as they try to make their way through the crowds. In addition, there is always some special activity going on. For instance, one club sells flowers on Valentine's Day, and several student organizations sell candy. I think all those sales belong in high school. Anyone who wants to do homework or cram for a test will find it hard to concentrate in the cafeteria.

Exercise 14   **Revising a Paragraph for More Specific Details**

In the following paragraphs, the details that are underlined are not specific. Change the underlined sentences to a more specific description. Write the changes in the lines below each paragraph.

1. The Caribbean Festival ended with a delicious island dinner. To begin, banana bread and spicy conch fritters were served. The main course included snapper marinated in lime juice and broiled golden on the outside and tender white on the inside. Crispy coconut shrimp, pigeon peas and rice, and mango relish completed this course. <u>The meal ended with a great dessert.</u>

revisions: _____

_____

2. David transformed the old car into his most treasured possession. Inside, he covered the torn vinyl upholstery with dark leather seat covers. He bought expensive new floor mats with deep-pile carpet. The smell of polish on the gleaming dashboard and leather steering-wheel cover permeated the car. Outside, the car was as shiny as a new one. David had refinished, resurfaced, and repainted the auto. <u>Then he had done something to the wheels.</u> Tinted windows gave the car an updated look.

revisions: _____

_____

Transitions

As you revise your description paragraph, you may notice places in the paragraph that seem choppy or abrupt. That is, one sentence may end, and another may start, but the two sentences don't seem to be connected. Reading your paragraph aloud, you may sense that it is not very smooth.

You can make the writing smoother and make the content clearer by using **transitions,** which are words or phrases that link one idea to another idea. They tell the reader what he or she has just read and what is coming next. Here are some transitions you may want to use in writing a description:

INFO BOX: **Transitions for a Descriptive Paragraph**

To show ideas brought together:

and	also	in addition	next

To show a contrast:

although	however	on the contrary	unlike
but	in contrast	on the other hand	yet

To show a similarity:

all	each	like	similarly
both			

To show a time sequence:

after	first, second (etc.)	often	when
always	meanwhile	soon	while
before	next	then	

To show a position in space:

above	beside	in front of	over
ahead of	between	inside	there
alongside	beyond	near	toward
among	by	nearby	under
around	close	next to	underneath
away	down	on	up
below	far	on top of	where
beneath	here	outside	

There are many other transitions you can use, depending on what you need to link your ideas. Take a look at a draft of the description paragraph of a bedroom. Compare it to the outline on pages 68–69. You will notice that more sense details have been added. Transitions have been added, too. Pay particular attention to the transitions in this draft.

Before you prepare the final copy of your own descriptive paragraph, check your last draft for errors in spelling, punctuation, typing, and copying.

For your information: A sample descriptive essay based on the same topic and following the same writing steps can be found in Chapter 12, on pages 283–286.

Exercise 17 **Proofreading to Prepare the Final Version**

Following are two descriptive paragraphs with the kinds of errors it is easy to overlook when you write the final version of an assignment. Correct the errors, writing above the lines. There are nine errors in the first paragraph and twelve errors in the second.

1. My most comfortable shoes are dilapidated and disgracefull. They are sneakers that are so old I cannot remember when I bought them? The stiching around the top of each shoe is gone, and every day I expect one of my toe's to pop out. The leather is all cracked and dirty, but to me, the leather is soft and flexable. The souls of the shoes is worn down about three layers. The soles are so thin that walking in puddles wets my feet all the way through. However, those soles have been shaped to fit my feet, and I like them. My friends say, "When are you going to get rid of those shoes"? I just say, "Never." They don't realize that, it would take years to break in another pair of sneakers and make them as comfortable as my old ones.

2. The College library might frighten a newcomer. The entrance to the building is a tall wall of glass bricks and the first floor has high cielings. The space seems overwhelming. The quite in the room is also a little threatening at first. A stranger, is afraid to make a noise and annoy all the students. Worse of all, the people in the libray all seem to know what they are doing. They are sitting confidently infront of computer screens they are walking intelligently thru the stacks of book. A visitor to the library might feel lost but be afraid to ask for help. He or she might not want to look stupid when everyone else seems so smart. However, strangers to the library needs to know that everyone was a newcomer once.

Lines of Detail: A Walk-Through Assignment

Your assignment is to write a paragraph describing a popular place for socializing. Follow these steps:

Step 1: To begin, freewrite about a place where people socialize. For example, you could write about a place where people go to eat, or dance, or swim, or just "hang out."

Step 2: Read your freewriting. Underline all the words, phrases, and sentences of description.

Step 3: List everything you underlined, grouping the ideas in some order. Maybe the details can be listed from inside to outside, or maybe they can be put into categories, like walls, floor, and furniture, or scenery and people.

Step 4: After you've surveyed the list, write a sentence about the dominant impression of the details.

Step 5: Using the dominant impression as your topic sentence, write an outline. Add specific details where you need them. Concentrate on details that appeal to the senses.

Step 6: Write a first draft of your paragraph. Be sure to check the order of your details. Combine short sentences and add transitions.

Step 7: Revise your first draft, paying particular attention to order, specific details, and transitions.

Step 8: After a final check for punctuation, spelling, and word choice, prepare the final version of the paragraph.

Writing Your Own Descriptive Paragraph

When you write on any of the following topics, work through the stages of the writing process in preparing your descriptive paragraph. Be sure that your paragraph is based on a dominant impression, and put the dominant impression into your topic sentence.

1. Write a paragraph that describes one of the items below:

a favorite piece of clothing	a hospital waiting room
a perfect meal	an eccentric friend
a favorite relative	a messy car
a very young baby	an irritating customer

   the contents of your top bureau drawer
   the contents of your top kitchen drawer
   the contents of your purse or wallet
   your first impression of a school
   a person who was a positive influence in your life

2. Describe a place that creates one of these impressions:

peace	tension	friendliness
cheerfulness	danger	safety

3. Describe a person who conveys one of these impressions:

confidence	warmth	pride
fear	style	shyness
intelligence	conformity	strength

4. Visit the Web site of your local newspaper, and find a photograph of a local event involving two or more individuals. Describe where the people are, what the event is, what the people are doing, what their expressions suggest, and anything you find unique about the setting. You may have to look through the archives of the Web site until you find a photograph that prompts such details. Be sure your details relate to a dominant impression of the scene, and be sure to select a photograph that you find interesting or unique. Attach the photograph to the completed paragraph.

◄ COMPUTER

5. Look carefully at the face in the photograph below. Write a description that focuses on the aura of the face. Does the face give an impression of wisdom? Pain? Sorrow? Peace? Strength? You decide, and support your decision by describing the details of the photograph.

6. Interview a partner so that you and your partner can gather details, and then write a description paragraph with the title, "My Perfect Room."

◄ COLLABORATE

First, prepare a list of at least six questions to ask your partner. Write down the answers your partner gives and use those answers to form more questions. For example, if your partner says her dream room would be a game room, ask her what games she'd like to have in it. If your partner says his perfect room would be a workshop, ask him what kind of workshop.

When you've finished the interview, switch roles. Let your partner interview you. Feel free to add more questions or to follow up on previous ones.

Give your partner his or her interview responses. Take your own responses and use them as the basis for gathering as many details as you can on your perfect room. Then go on to the outline, draft, and final version of your paragraph. Be prepared to read your completed paragraph to your partner.

7. Study the photograph below. Then write a paragraph that describes and explains the dominant impression of this scene.

Note: Additional writing options suitable for description-related assignments can be found after the professional reading, "A Present for Popo," which begins on page 599.

Name _____ Section: _____

PEER REVIEW FORM FOR A DESCRIPTIVE PARAGRAPH

After you've written a draft of your descriptive paragraph, let a writing partner read it. When your partner has completed the form below, discuss the comments. Then repeat the same process for your partner's paragraph.

The dominant impression of the paragraph is this sentence: _____

_____

The details of the description are in a specific order. That order is (for example, top to bottom, time order, etc.) _____

_____

The part of the description I liked best begins with the words _____

_____

The part that could use more or better details begins with the words _____

_____

I have questions about or would like to know more about _____

_____

I noticed these transitions: _____

_____

A place where transitions could be added or improved is right before the words _____

_____

Other comments on the paragraph: _____

_____

_____

_____

_____

_____

_____

_____

_____

Reviewer's Name: _____

CHAPTER 4
Narration

WHAT IS NARRATION?

Narration means telling a story. Everybody tells stories; some people are better storytellers than others. When you write a **narrative** paragraph, you can tell a story about something that happened to you or to someone else, or about something that you saw or read.

A narrative, like a description, relies on specific details, but it is also different from a description because it covers events in a time sequence. While a description can be about a person, a place, or an object, a narrative is always about happenings: events, actions, incidents.

Interesting narratives do more than just tell what happened. They help the reader become involved in the story by providing vivid details. These details come from your memory, your observation, or your reading. Using good details, you don't just tell the story; you *show* it.

Give the Narrative a Point

We all know people who tell long stories that seem to lead nowhere. These people talk on and on; they recite an endless list of activities and soon become boring. Their narratives have no point.

The difficult part of writing a narrative is making sure that it has a point. That point will be included in the topic sentence. The point of a narrative is the meaning of the incident or incidents you are writing about. To get to the point of your narrative, ask yourself questions like these:

What did I learn?

What is the meaning of this story?

What is my attitude toward what happened?

Did it change me?

What emotion did it make me feel?

Was the experience a good example of something (such as unfairness, kindness, generosity, or some other quality)?

The answers to such questions can lead you to a point. An effective topic sentence for a narrative is

not this: I'm going to tell you about the time I flunked my driving test. (This is an announcement; it does not make a point.)

but this: When I failed my driving test, I learned not to be overconfident.

not this: Yesterday my car stalled in rush-hour traffic. (This identifies the incident but does not make a point. It is also too narrow to be a good topic sentence.)

but this: When my car stalled in rush-hour traffic, I was annoyed and embarrassed.

The topic sentence, stating the point of your narrative paragraph, can be placed in the beginning or middle or end of the paragraph. You may want to start your story with the point so that the reader knows exactly where your story is headed, or you may want to conclude your story by leaving the point until last. Sometimes the point can even fit smoothly into the middle of your paragraph.

Consider the narrative paragraphs below. The topic sentences are in various places.

Topic Sentence at the Beginning

<u>When I was five, I learned how serious it is to tell a lie.</u> One afternoon, my seven-year-old friend Tina asked me if I wanted to walk down the block to play ball in an empty lot. When I asked my mother, she said I couldn't go because it was too near dinner time. I don't know why I lied, but when Tina asked me if my mother had said yes, I nodded my head in a lie. I wanted to go play, and I did. Yet as I played in the dusty lot, a dull buzz of guilt or fear distracted me. As soon as I got home, my mother confronted me. She asked me whether I had gone to the sandlot and whether I had lied to Tina about getting permission. This time, I told the truth. Something about my mother's tone of voice made me feel very dirty and ashamed. I had let her down.

Topic Sentence in the Middle

When I was little, I was afraid of diving into water. I thought I would go down and never come back up. Then one day, my father took me to a pool where we swam and fooled around, but he never forced me to try a dive. After about an hour of playing, I walked round and round the edge of the pool, trying to get the courage to dive in. Finally, I did it. <u>When I made that first dive, I felt blissful because I had done something I had been</u>

<u>afraid to do</u>. As I came to the surface, I wiped the water from my eyes and looked around. The sun seemed more dazzling, and the water sparkled. Best of all, I saw my father looking at me with a smile. "You did it," he said. "Good for you! I'm proud of you."

Topic Sentence at the End

It seemed like I'd been in love with Reeza for years. Unfortunately, Reeza was always in love with someone else. Finally, she broke up with her boyfriend Nelson. I saw my chance. I asked Reeza out. After dinner, we talked and talked. Reeza told me all about her hopes and dreams. She told me about her family and her job, and I felt very close to her. We talked late into the night. When she left, Reeza kissed me. "Thanks for listening," she said. "You're like a brother to me." <u>Reeza meant to be kind, but she shattered my hopes and dreams.</u>

 **Finding the Topic Sentence in a Narrative Paragraph**

Underline the topic sentence in each of the following narrative paragraphs.

Paragraph 1

When my family gathers for dinner, the meal usually turns into a series of arguments. My mother and her sister remember grudges from their teenage years; my father and my uncles argue about politics. My grandparents then begin complaining about their children's constant fighting. Last Sunday, however, was different. Our traditional dinner found unity and peace with one small announcement. After an hour of listening to the relatives grumble and snarl, my sister Melanie stood up. "Joaquin and I are having a baby," she said. The room was suddenly silent. Then there were cries of happiness. The baby would be the first grandchild for my parents and the first great-grandchild for my grandparents. The joy of this announcement spread as everyone pictured a bright and innocent addition to the family.

Paragraph 2

When the police showed up at our party, we knew the fun had gone too far. My parents had gone away for the weekend, so my brother and I told a few friends to come over on Saturday night for a get-together. Unfortunately, those friends must have told other friends because our house was full of people by 10:00 p.m. Meanwhile, cars full of strangers kept circling the block, looking for places to park. I tried to keep the noise down, but each car arrived with speakers blasting. By midnight, trash covered the front yard, and cars blocked all the driveways on the street. Within minutes, two officers arrived and told us our neighbors had complained. We were actually relieved because the arrival of the police gave us an excuse to get rid of some of the weird people who had invaded our space.

Paragraph 3

There is a couple that own a deli near my apartment. The place is always busy, and customers are always lined up, waiting for their numbers to be called. The wife, Mrs. Ling, is about thirty-five, small, plump, and very efficient. She takes the orders at the counter while two assistants prepare the sandwiches, salads, and platters. Meanwhile, Mr. Ling, a thin and quiet man of forty, handles the cash register. The couple work in different parts of the room, and they run a very successful business. Yet until yesterday, I had never seen them together or even make eye contact. Then, late last night, I ran into the deli as it was about to close. As I waited for my sandwich, I saw Mrs. Ling lower the window shades. Mr. Ling was wiping the tables. Suddenly, he came behind Mrs. Ling, bent his head, and kissed the back of her neck. She turned her head and smiled. At that moment, I realized the Lings have what I would like to have: a marriage with shared goals, love, and support.

| Exercise 2 | **Writing the Missing Topic Sentences in Narrative Paragraphs** |

Following are three paragraphs. If the paragraph already has a topic sentence, write it in the lines provided. If it does not have a topic sentence, create one. (Two of the paragraphs have no topic sentence.)

Paragraph 1

Once I joined the computer club, I felt like a part of the college. I am a basically shy person, and my first months at college were unhappy ones. I went to class and went home again, never talking to anyone. Then, one day, I saw a notice posted about the computer club. I love my computer and am fascinated by anything online or digital. Gathering up my courage, I went to the next meeting of the club. As I entered the room, I felt like running out immediately. Everyone seemed to know everyone else, and I didn't know where to sit. I decided to sit next to two people who were talking about laptops and notebooks. I became so interested in the conversation that I was drawn into it. By the end of the first meeting, I had met five people and had arranged to get together for coffee with three of them. Suddenly, school did not seem like such a lonely place.

If the paragraph already has a topic sentence, write it here. If it does not

have a topic sentence, create one. _____

_____

_____

Paragraph 2

Last Saturday, I woke up feeling feverish. My face was flushed, and my hair was damp with sweat. One look at my air conditioner told me why I was so warm. The machine was pumping hot air. I pushed all the buttons and played with the thermostat, but nothing worked. To cool off, I took my breakfast out onto my tiny screened patio. Unfortunately, I could not enjoy myself since I saw two large gashes my curious cat had created in the screening. After a few minutes, I went back indoors, hoping to soothe my spirit and cool my body in a lukewarm bath. As I soaked in the tub, I noticed a slow "drip, drip" sound. I reached to tighten the faucet. However, it was not the faucet causing the drip. It was a steady trickle of water from a ceiling panel. Finally, I got out of the water, reached for the yellow pages, and began searching for a plumber, an air-conditioning repair service, and a screening company.

If the paragraph already has a topic sentence, write it here. If it does not

have a topic sentence, create one. _____

_____

_____

Paragraph 3

A few days ago, I was driving down the highway when I saw a car pulled over on the shoulder of the road. There was an elderly couple standing by their car and the trunk of the car was open. "Somebody will stop," I told myself as I passed the couple. However, something made me get off at the next exit and head back toward the disabled car. When I got to it, nobody was helping the old people. I pulled over and helped the gentleman change his tire. It was quick and easy, yet the couple treated me like a hero. The man wanted to give me money, and his wife said, "We'll never forget you." I didn't take any money and just drove away, feeling happy with myself. I was surprised a week later when I found out that the lady in the car wrote a letter to the local newspaper, thanking me. I have never felt so honored.

If the paragraph already has a topic sentence, write it here. if it does not

have a topic sentence, create one. _____

_____

_____

Hints for Writing a Narrative Paragraph

Everyone tells stories, but some people tell stories better than others. When you write a story, be sure to follow these rules:

- Be clear.
- Be interesting.
- Stay in order.
- Pick a topic that is not too big.

1. Be clear. Put in all the information the reader needs to follow your story. Sometimes you need to explain the time or place or the relationships of the people in your story to make the story clear. Sometimes you need to explain how much time has elapsed between one action and another. This paragraph is not clear:

> I've never felt so stupid as I did on my first day of work. I was stocking the shelves when Mr. Cimino came up to me and said, "You're doing it wrong." Then he showed me how to do it. An hour later, he told me to call the produce supplier and check on the order for grapefruit. Well, I didn't know how to tell Mr. Cimino that I didn't know what phone to use or how to get an outside line. I also didn't know how to get the phone number of the produce supplier, or what the order for the grapefruit was supposed to be and when it was supposed to arrive. I felt really stupid asking these questions.

What is wrong with the paragraph? It lacks all kinds of information. Who is Mr. Cimino? Is he the boss? Is he a produce supervisor? And, more importantly, what kind of place is the writer's workplace? The reader knows the place has something to do with food, but is it a supermarket, a fruit market, or a warehouse?

2. Be interesting. A boring narrative can make the greatest adventure sound dull. Here is a dull narrative:

> I had a wonderful time on prom night. First, we went out to dinner. The meal was excellent. Then we went to the dance and saw all our friends. Everyone was dressed up great. We stayed until late. Then we went out to breakfast. After breakfast we watched the sun come up.

Good specific details are the difference between an interesting story and a dull one.

3. Stay in order. Put the details in a clear order so that the reader can follow your story. Usually, time order is the order you follow in narration. This narrative has a confusing order:

> My impatience cost me twenty dollars last week. There was a pair of shoes I really wanted. I had wanted them for weeks. So, when payday came around, I went to the mall and checked the price on the shoes. I had been checking the price for weeks before. The shoes were expensive, but I really wanted them. On payday, my friend, who works at the shoe store, told me the shoes were about to go on sale. But I was impatient. I bought them at full price, and three days later, the shoes were marked down twenty dollars.

There's something wrong with the order of events here. Tell the story in the order it happened: first, I saw the shoes and wanted them; second, the shoes were expensive; third, I checked the price for several weeks; fourth, I got paid; fifth, I checked the price again; sixth, my friend told me the shoes were about to go on sale; seventh, I paid full price right away; eighth, the shoes went on sale. A clear time sequence helps the reader follow your narrative.

4. Pick a topic that is not too big. If you try to write about too many events in a short space, you run the risk of being superficial. You cannot describe anything well if you cover too much. This paragraph covers too much:

> Starting my sophomore year at a new high school was a difficult experience. Because my family had just moved to town, I didn't know anybody at school. On the first day of school, I sat by myself at lunch. Finally, two students at another table started a conversation with me. I thought they were just feeling sorry for me. At the end of the first week, it seemed like the whole school was talking about exciting plans for the weekend. I spent Friday and Saturday night at home, doing all kinds of things to keep my mind off my loneliness. On Monday, people casually asked, "Have a good weekend?" I lied and said, "Of course."

This paragraph would be better if it discussed one shorter time period in greater depth and detail. It could cover the first day at school, or the first lunch at school, or the first Saturday night at home alone, when the writer was doing "all kinds of things" to keep from feeling lonely.

Using a Speaker's Exact Words in Narrative

Some of the examples of narrative that you have already seen have included the exact words someone said. You may want to include part of a conversation in your narrative. To do so, you need to know how to punctuate speech.

A person's exact words get quotation marks around them. If you change the words, you do not use quotation marks.

> **exact words:** "You're being silly," he told me.
> **not exact words:** He told me that I was being silly.

> **exact words:** My sister said, "I'd love to go to the party."
> **not exact words:** My sister said she would love to go to the party.

There are a few other points to remember about punctuating a person's exact words. Once you've started quoting a person's exact words, periods and commas generally go inside the quotation marks. Here are two examples:

> Richard said, "Nothing can be done."
> "Be careful," my mother warned us.

When you introduce a person's exact words with phrases like "She said," or "The teacher told us," put a comma before the quotation marks. Here are two examples:

> She said, "You'd better watch out."
> The teacher told us, "This will be a challenging class."

If you are using a person's exact words and have other questions about punctuation, read about the use of quotation marks in Chapter 31 of the grammar section of this book.

WRITING THE NARRATIVE PARAGRAPH IN STEPS

PREWRITING Gathering Ideas: Narration

Finding something to write about can be the hardest part of writing a narrative paragraph because it is usually difficult to think of anything interesting or significant that you have experienced. By answering the questions in Exercise 3, you can gather topics for your paragraph.

Exercise 3 **Questionnaire for Gathering Narrative Topics** ◀ COLLABORATE 👥

Answer the following questions as best you can. Then read your answers to a group. The members of the group should then ask you follow-up questions. Write your answers on the lines provided; the answers will add details to your list.

   Finally, ask each member of your group to circle one topic or detail on your questionnaire that could be developed into a narrative paragraph. Discuss the suggestions. Repeat this process for each member of the group.

Narrative Questionnaire

1. Did you ever have a close call? When?_____

   Write four details you remember about it:

   a. _____

   b. _____

   c. _____

   d. _____

   Additional details, to be added after working with the group:

   _____

   _____

2. Have you ever lost an item that was important to you? Write four details about what happened before, during, and after:

   a. _Set them down some where_

   b. _woke up couldn't find them_

   c. _was late for school_

   d. _found them in car cul_

   Additional details, to be added after working with the group:

   _____

   _____

3. Have you ever had a day when everything went wrong? Write four details about that day:

a. _____

b. _____

c. _____

d. _____

Additional details, to be added after working with the group:

_____

_____

Freewriting for a Narrative Topic

One good way to discover something to write about is to freewrite. For example, if your instructor asks you to write a narrative paragraph about something that changed you, you might begin by freewriting.

Freewriting for a Narrative Paragraph

Topic: Something That Changed Me

Something that changed me. I don't know. What changed me? Lots of things happened to me, but I can't find one that changed me. Graduating from high school? Everybody will write about that, how boring, and anyway, what was the big deal? I haven't gotten married. No big change there. Divorce. My parents' divorce really changed the whole family. A big shock to me. I couldn't believe it was happening. I was really scared. Who would I live with? They were real calm when they told me. I've never been so scared. I was too young to understand. Kept thinking they'd just get back together. They didn't. Then I got a stepmother. The year of the divorce a hard time for me. Kids suffer in divorce.

Narrowing and Selecting a Suitable Narrative Topic

After you freewrite, you can assess your writing, looking for words, phrases, or sentences that you could expand into a paragraph. The sample writing has several ideas for a narrative:

> high school graduation
> learning about my parents' divorce
> adjusting to a stepmother
> the year of my parents' divorce

Looking for a topic that is not too big, you could use

> high school graduation
> learning about my parents' divorce

Because the freewriting has already called graduation a boring topic, the divorce seems to be a more attractive subject. In the freewriting, you already have some details related to the divorce; add to these details by brainstorming. Follow-up questions and answers might include the following:

Revising for Sharper Details

A good idea for a narrative can be made better if you revise for sharper details. In the paragraph below, the underlined words and phrases could be revised to create better details. In the following example, see how the second draft has more vivid details than the first draft.

First Draft: Details Are Dull

A woman at the movies showed me just how rude and selfish people can be. It all started when I was in line with <u>a lot</u> of other people. We had been waiting <u>a long time</u> to buy our tickets. We were outside, and it <u>wasn't pleasant</u>. We were impatient because time was running out and the movie was about to start. Some people were <u>making remarks</u>, and <u>others were pushing</u>. Then <u>a woman</u> <u>cut to</u> the front of the line. The cashier at the ticket window <u>told</u> the woman there was a line and she would have to go to the end of it. The woman <u>said she didn't want to</u> <u>wait because her son didn't want to miss the beginning of the</u> <u>movie.</u>

Second Draft: Better Details

A woman at the movies showed me just how rude and selfish people can be. It all started when I was in line with <u>forty or fifty</u> <u>other people</u>. We had been waiting to buy our tickets for <u>twenty</u> <u>minutes</u>. We were outside, <u>where the temperature was about 90</u> <u>degrees, and it looked like rain</u>. We were all getting impatient because time was running out and the movie was about to start. <u>I heard two people mutter about how ridiculous the wait was,</u> <u>and someone else kept saying, "Let's go!" The man directly be-</u> <u>hind me kept pushing me, and each new person at the end of the</u> <u>line pushed the whole line forward, against the ticket window.</u> Then a woman <u>with a loud voice and a large purse thrust her</u> <u>purse and her body in front of the ticket window</u>. The cashier <u>politely</u> told the woman there was a line and she had to go to the end of it. But the woman answered <u>indignantly</u>. "Oh no," she said. "I'm with my son Mickey. And Mickey really wants to see this martial arts movie. And he hates to miss the first part of any movie. So I can't wait. I've got to have those tickets now."

Checking the Topic Sentence

Sometimes you think you have a good idea, a good topic sentence and specific details, but when you write the draft of the paragraph, you realize the topic sentence does not quite fit all the details. When that happens, you can either revise the detail or *rewrite the topic sentence.*

In the following paragraph, the topic sentence (underlined) does not quite fit all the details, so the topic sentence should be rewritten.

<u>I didn't know what to do when a crime occurred in front of</u> <u>my house.</u> At nine p.m. I was sitting in my living room, watching

television, when I heard what sounded like a crash outside. At first I thought it was a garbage can that had fallen over. Then I heard another crash and a shout. I ran to the window, and I looked out into the dark. I couldn't see anything because the street light in front of my house was broken. But I heard at least two voices, and they sounded angry and threatening. I heard another voice, and it sounded like someone moaning. I was afraid. I ran to the telephone. I was going to call 911, but then I froze in fear. What if the police came, and people got arrested? Would the suspects find out I was the one who had called the police? Would they come after <u>me</u>? Would I be a witness at a trial? I didn't want to get involved. So I just stood behind the curtain, peeking out and listening. Pretty soon the shouting stopped, but I still heard sounds like hitting. I couldn't stand it anymore. I called the police. When they came, they found a young teenager, badly beaten, in the street. They said my call may have saved his life.

The preceding paragraph has good details, but the story has more of a point than "I didn't know what to do." The person telling the story did, finally, do something. Following is a better topic sentence that covers the whole story.

topic sentence rewritten: I finally found the courage to take the proper action when a crime occurred in front of my house.

Exercise 8   **Combining Sentences in a Draft of a Narrative**

The following paragraph contains some short, choppy sentences, which are underlined. Wherever you see two or more underlined sentences clustered next to each other, combine them into one clear, smooth sentence. Write your revised version of the paragraph in the spaces above the lines.

A sad incident led me to an important decision. <u>It began one afternoon. It was summer. I was playing with my dog, Jesse. We were outside.</u> I was throwing a tennis ball for him to fetch. <u>After one catch, Jesse got excited. He didn't return the ball. He ran away with it in his mouth.</u> Unfortunately, he ran into the street. <u>A car was going by. It was going slowly. It couldn't stop in time to avoid Jesse.</u> He lay in the street, bleeding. <u>I wrapped him in a blanket. At the same time, my mother started the car.</u> We raced to our veterinarian's office. The veterinarian's assistant was calm and gentle as she took my dog to the examining room. <u>Then the doctor came and examined Jesse. The doctor was slow and careful in his examination.</u> Jesse looked at him with trusting eyes. "Jesse is cut and bruised, and we'll keep him here for a while. But I don't see any broken bones," he said. "I want to watch for internal injuries." <u>The next day, the veterinarian called. He wanted to let us</u>

<u>know Jesse was going to make it.</u> I was relieved and grateful. <u>In addition, I had</u>

<u>one other feeling. It was a feeling of certainty.</u> At that moment, I knew that I

wanted to work in the veterinary field so I could help suffering animals like Jesse.

Exercise 9   **Adding Better Details to a Draft of a Narrative**

The following paragraph has some details that could be more vivid. Rewrite
the paragraph on the lines provided, replacing the underlined details with
more vivid words, phrases, or sentences.

　　　　Fareed supported me when no one else would. Fareed and I share an
apartment with two other <u>guys</u>, Joe and Tyrone. Last week, I was the only
one in the apartment on Saturday night. The other three went out to <u>do some</u>
<u>stuff</u> while I just <u>sat around</u>. The next morning, Joe said he had left twenty
dollars in his top drawer, for emergency money, and now it was gone. The
next thing I knew, Joe was <u>looking at me</u> and <u>being mean</u>. Soon Tyrone was
<u>acting nasty</u>. Only Fareed tried to be reasonable, saying, "Did you look every-
where, Joe? Maybe you misplaced it." By the next day, Joe had spread the
story to his friends. When I returned to the apartment after class, somebody
had <u>messed up my dresser and closet</u>. When Fareed saw the mess, he confronted Joe and Tyrone. <u>He said things to defend me, but they were not lis-</u>
<u>tening</u>. By Friday, I felt like such an outcast that I was thinking of finding a
new place to live. Then, on Friday night, Joe found his twenty dollars. It had
slipped through a crack in the top drawer and fallen into the second drawer.
"I told you so," Fareed said to Joe.

Rewrite: _____

_____

_____

_____

_____

_____

_____

_____

_____

_____

_____

_____

_____

_____

_____

_____

_____

_____

Exercise 10   **Writing a Better Topic Sentence for a Narrative**

The paragraphs below could use better topic sentences. (In each paragraph, the current topic sentence is underlined.) Read each paragraph carefully, then write a new topic sentence for it on the lines provided.

1. <u>My old boyfriend called me last week.</u> I had not seen him in three years. At our last meeting, he had left me feeling hurt and worthless. I felt that I had lost my only chance at love and that he had rejected me because I just wasn't good enough to meet his standards. Now, I suddenly heard his voice and froze. I was not prepared to speak to him. He filled up the blank spaces, however. He told me of his accomplishments: his great new job and his new apartment. He never asked how I was or what I had been doing. Instead, he went on and on, telling me of his travels to Mexico and Arizona, his sports car, and his flat-screen television. His bragging was empty and sad. Suddenly, I was grateful that I had never become one of that man's possessions. "You sound like you have everything you want," I said, and I knew that he had nothing I wanted.

New topic sentence:_____

_____

2. <u>I visited my old school yesterday.</u> I was there to attend my niece's class play. The kindergartners were giving a short entertainment with costumes, music, and dance. First, a little boy dressed as a teddy bear came out from behind the curtains. He was so serious and proud of himself that I couldn't help smiling. Then six or seven other children, dressed to look like trees, surrounded him and began to dance. One of the trees bumped into the other trees, and the audience tried not to laugh. Soon other children, dressed as flowers, appeared. Their faces gleamed with joy as they recognized their families in the audience. Suddenly, my niece Kayla appeared, wearing a pink, spangled princess dress. The sight of her and of all the children, so trusting and happy, was a gift to all the adults who loved them.

New topic sentence:_____

_____

Using Transitions Effectively in Narration

When you tell a story, you have to be sure that your reader can follow you as you move through the steps of your story. One way to make your story easier to follow is to use transitions. Most of the transitions in narration have to do with time. Below is a list of transitions writers often use in writing narration.

INFO BOX: Transitions for a Narrative Paragraph

after	before	later	still
again	during	later on	suddenly
always	finally	meanwhile	then
at first	first, second, (etc.)	next	until
at last	frequently	now	when
at once	immediately	soon	while
at the same time	in the meantime	soon after	

The Draft

Below is a draft of the paragraph on divorce. As you read it, you will notice that some ideas from the outline on pages 93–94 have been combined, the details have been put in order, and transitions have been added. Exact words of dialogue have been used to add vivid details.

A Draft of a Narrative Paragraph

(Transitions are underlined.)

When my parents announced that they were divorcing, I felt confused by all my emotions. At the time of their announcement, I was seven and my sister was ten. Both my folks were there to tell us. They told us at breakfast, in the kitchen. I was eating toast, but I remember I couldn't eat anything when they started talking. I remember a piece of toast with one bite taken out of it. My parents were very calm when they told us. "We love both you kids very much," my dad said, "but your mother and I aren't getting along." They said they would always love us. The announcement was such a shock to me that I couldn't believe it was happening. At first, I just thought they were having another fight. Because I was too young to understand, I didn't cry. Suddenly, my sister started to cry, and then I knew it was serious. I kept thinking I would have to choose which parent to live with. I knew I'd really hurt the one I didn't choose, so I felt so much guilt about hurting one of them. I felt ripped apart.

Exercise 11   **Recognizing Transitions in a Narrative Paragraph**

Underline the transitions in the following paragraph.

A serious accident brought out the worst in drivers this morning. When I turned south onto Fifth Street at 8:00 a.m., I noticed the traffic had slowed down. Soon, it had slowed to a crawl. While I inched forward, I noticed the flashing of blue lights and saw two emergency vehicles and several police cars ahead, on the side of the road, and at the median. Then, as I moved closer to the emergency vehicles, I saw two wrecked cars blocking one of the northbound lanes. <u>At the same time</u> that I saw the accident, I noticed all the traffic going north merging into one lane. This merger was chaotic because impatient drivers sped to the front of the line, cutting off other cars. <u>Meanwhile</u>, horns blared and some desperate drivers tried to escape the scene by driving on the sidewalk. <u>Suddenly</u>, a driver in a hurry attempted to make a U-turn into the southbound lanes. I heard brakes squeal and metal crunch. The crazy U-turn had turned into another accident, this one directly in front of my car.

> **Exercise 12**   **Adding the Right Transitions to a Narrative Paragraph**

In the following paragraph, circle the correct transition in each of the pairs.

I struggled to find the right gift for my father last week; later /at once I followed my instincts. I was in the mall looking for the right Father's Day gift last Wednesday, but nothing seemed right. At first, /Soon after, the items I considered were too expensive, for I could never afford a good camera or a satellite radio system for my father's car. Again/Then I began to look at some of the displays labeled "For Father's Day," but they included the same old sport shirts, ties, and cologne that all fathers get every year. I began to feel hopeless when /still I realized I had no idea how to find an appropriate gift. Before/ Suddenly, a thought hit me: I should focus on what makes my father happy. What he likes, I soon /still realized, is spending time with me. He likes to fish, drive, or watch a baseball game with me, but I never seem to have the time. Now /Frequently, I knew what to give my father. This Father's Day, he and I will spend a day together, driving to the lake and fishing. Maybe we'll even watch a baseball game on television.

> **POLISHING**   **Polishing and Proofreading: Narration**

As you prepare the final version of the narration paragraph, make any minor changes in word choice or transitions that can refine your writing. Below is the final copy of the narrative paragraph on divorce. Notice these changes in the final version:

- The draft version used both formal and informal words such as "folks" and "parents" and "dad." The final version uses only "parents" and "father."
- A few details have been added.
- A few details have been changed.
- A transition has been added.

A Final Version of a Narrative Paragraph

(Changes from the draft are underlined.)

When my parents announced that they were divorcing, I felt confused by all my emotions. At the time of the announcement, I was seven, and my sister was ten. Both <u>my parents</u> were there to tell us. They told us at breakfast, in the kitchen. I was eating toast, but I remember I couldn't eat anything when they started talking. <u>In fact,</u> I remember <u>staring at</u> a piece of toast with one bite taken out of it. My parents were very calm when they told us. "We both love you very much," my <u>father</u> said. "But your mother and I aren't getting along." They said they would always love us. The announcement was such a shock to me that I couldn't believe it was happening. At first, I just thought they were having another fight. Because I was too young to understand, I didn't cry. Suddenly, my sister started to cry, and then I knew it was serious. I kept thinking I would have to choose which parent to live with. I knew I'd really hurt the one I didn't choose, so I felt <u>terrible</u> guilt about hurting one of them. I felt ripped apart.

Before you prepare the final version of your narrative paragraph, check your latest draft for errors in spelling, punctuation, typing, and copying.

For your information: A sample narrative essay based on this topic and following the same writing steps can be found in Chapter 12, on pages 288–291.

Exercise 13 **Proofreading to Prepare the Final Version**

Following are two narrative paragraphs with the kinds of errors it is easy to overlook when you prepare the final version of an assignment. Correct the errors, writing above the lines. There are thirteen errors in the first paragraph and thirteen in the second.

1. Last week in my painting Class, I received a wonderfull gift. I took the

class only because I needed an art, music, or theater class in order to graduate.

Art seemed easier then singing, dancing, or acting, so I signed up for a painting

class. I was really self-conscience at first, for I hated the idea of some one watch-

ing over my shoulder while I tryed to paint. After a few days, I calmed down a lit-

tle because the teacher was helpful, not critical. At the same time, I developed a

real fear of the other students They seemed so talented and confident as they

laughed and talked. I hunched over my painting and worried. "Your not an artist," I

told myself, "and You've never been good at anything." I imagined the other stu-

dents feeling sorry for me, the poor untalented loser. Then, last Tuesday, the

teacher said he had a announcement. Two paintings from our art class had been

selected for a local exhibition. Immediately, I stopped listening. I wondered who

the lucky students would be but I never thought I had a chance. Suddenly, I heard

my name called. When I realized there was no mistake, I feel shocked by my hap-

piness. At last, I knew I could be good at something.

2. My coworker crossed the line yesterday and I finally stood up to him. Eddie is a talkative young man who works at the workstation next to mine. Since we both work in phone sale's, we are expected to spend most of our time on the phone. On the day Eddie began his job. He asked me many questions about the procedures to follow. I tried to help him because I felt sorry for him. "I really need this job", he told me. I want to do well," he added. I figured that he would soon learn his job, and leave me alone. However, after weeks on the job, Eddie was still nagging me, and he had started interupting me when I was on my phone line. Because our calls are monitored, I was afraid I wood get in trouble. Soon the supervisor called me over. He was concern that I had not reached my calling goals for four days in a row. Upset, I returned to my workstation and went back to my call list. Just as I had a contact on the phone, Eddie cut off my connection. "What happened with the supervisor? Are You in trouble?" he demanded. Finely, I turned to him. "Leave me alone," I said, "or you'll be in big trouble."

Lines of Detail: A Walk-Through Assignment

Write a paragraph about an incident in your life that embarrassed, amused, frightened, saddened, or angered you. In writing the paragraph, follow these steps:

Step 1: Begin by freewriting. Then read your freewriting, looking for both the details and focus of your paragraph.

Step 2: Brainstorm for more details. Then write all the freewriting and brainstorming as a list.

Step 3: Survey your list. Write a topic sentence that makes a point about the details.

Step 4: Write an outline. As you write the outline, check that your details fit the topic sentence and are in clear order. As you revise your outline, add details where they are needed.

Step 5: Write and revise a draft of your paragraph. Revise until your details are specific and in a clear order, and your transitions are smooth. Combine any sentences that are short and choppy. Add a speaker's exact words if they will make the details more specific.

Step 6: In preparing the final version, check for punctuation, spelling, and word choice.

Writing Your Own Narrative Paragraph

When you write on any of the following topics, be sure to work through the stages of the writing process in preparing your narrative paragraph.

1. Write about some surprising event you saw that you will never forget. Begin by freewriting. Then read your freewriting, looking for both the details and the focus of your paragraph.

   If your instructor agrees, ask a writing partner or group to (a) listen to you read your freewriting, (b) help you focus it, and (c) help you add details by asking questions.

2. Write a narrative paragraph about a mistake you made at your first job. Include how that mistake proved to be a valuable lesson.

3. Have you ever been judged unfairly because of your age, race, or appearance? Write a narrative about the incident and include the emotions you experienced at the time.

4. Write a narrative paragraph about the couple below. Look carefully at their expressions and body language and write about events you imagine happened before, during, and after this scene. You may want to include some dialogue in your paragraph.

5. Visit the Web site of your local newspaper, and find a news article about a crime that involved a sequence of events leading to a confrontation, arrest, or escape. Write the details of the story in time order, and be sure to use effective transitions. Your topic sentence

◀ COMPUTER

should state what type of crime occurred as well as the outcome of it. (As you take notes from the article, be aware that newspaper accounts are not written in time order, so you will do some reordering of events.) Include a copy of the article with your paragraph.

6. Interview an older family member or friend. Ask him or her to tell you an interesting story about his or her past. Ask questions as the person speaks. Take notes. If you have a tape recorder, you can tape the interview, but take notes as well.

   When you've finished the interview, review the information with the person you interviewed. Ask the person if he or she would like to add anything. If you wish, ask follow-up questions.

   Next, on your own, find a point to the story. Work through the stages of the writing process to turn the interview into a narrative paragraph.

7. Write a narrative about the hurricane in the photograph below. You can include events you imagine happened to the family before, during, and after the dramatic scene in the photograph.

Note: Additional writing options suitable for narrative-related assignments can be found after the professional reading, "The Good Father," which begins on page 603.

Name: _____ **Section:** _____

PEER REVIEW FORM FOR A NARRATIVE PARAGRAPH

After you have written a draft of your narrative paragraph, let a writing partner read it. When your partner has completed the form below, discuss the responses. Repeat the same process for your partner's paragraph.

I think the topic sentence of this paragraph is _____.

_____

_____ (Write the sentence.)

I think the topic sentence (a) states the point well, (b) could be revised. (Choose one.)

The part of the narrative I liked best begins with the words _____

_____

The part that could use more or better details begins with the words _____

_____

An effective transition was _____

_____ (Write the words of a good transition.)

I have questions about or would like to know more about _____

_____

_____

I would like to take out the part about _____

I think the narrative is (a) easy to follow, (b) a little confusing. (Choose one.)

Other comments: _____

_____

_____

_____

_____

_____

_____

_____

_____

Reviewer's Name: _____

CHAPTER 5
Process

WHAT IS PROCESS?

A **process** writing explains how to do something or describes how something happens or is done. When you tell the reader how to do something (a **directional process**), you speak directly to the reader, giving clear, specific instructions about performing some activity. Your purpose is to explain an activity so that a reader can do it. For example, you may have to leave instructions telling a new employee how to close the cash register or use the copy machine.

When you describe how something happens or is done (an **informational process**), your purpose is to explain an activity without telling a reader how to do it. For example, you can explain how a boxer trains for a fight or how the special effects for a movie were created. Instead of speaking directly to the reader, an informational process speaks about "I," "he," "she," "we," "they," or about a person by his or her name. A directional process uses "you" or, in the way it gives directions, the word "you" is understood.

A Process Involves Steps in Time Order

Whether a process is directional or informational, it describes something that is done in steps, and these steps are in a specific order: a **time order.** The process can involve steps that are followed in minutes, hours, days, weeks, months, or even years. For example, the steps in changing a tire may take minutes, whereas the steps taken to lose ten pounds may take months.

You should keep in mind that a process involves steps that *must follow a certain order*, not just a range of activities that can be placed in any order. This sentence *signals a process:*

Learning to search the Internet is easy if you follow a few simple directions. (Using the Internet involves following steps in order; that is, you cannot search before you turn on the computer.)

This sentence *does not signal a process:*

There are several ways to get a person to like you. (Each way is separate; there is no time sequence here.)

Telling a person, in a conversation, how to do something or how something is done gives you the opportunity to add important points you may have overlooked or to throw in details you may have skipped at first. Your listener can ask questions if he or she does not understand you. Writing a process, however, is more difficult. Your reader is not there to stop you, to ask you to explain further, or to question you. In writing a process, you must be organized and clear.

Hints for Writing a Process Paragraph

1. **In choosing a topic, find an activity you know well.** If you write about something familiar to you, you will have a clearer paragraph.

2. **Choose a topic that includes steps that must be done in a specific time sequence.**

   not this: I find lots of things to do on a rainy day.
   but this: I have a plan for cleaning the garage.

3. **Choose a topic that is fairly small.** A complicated process cannot be covered well in one paragraph. If your topic is too big, the paragraph can become vague, incomplete, or boring.

   too big: There are many stages in the process of a bill before Congress becoming a law.
   smaller and manageable: Will power and support were the most important elements in my struggle to quit smoking.

4. **Write a topic sentence that makes a point.** Your topic sentence should do more than announce. Like the topic sentence for any paragraph, it should have a point. As you plan the steps of your process and gather details, ask yourself some questions: What point do I want to make about this process? Is the process hard? Is it easy? Does the process require certain tools? Does the process require certain skills such as organization, patience, endurance?

   an announcement: This paragraph is about how to change the oil in your car.
   a topic sentence: You do not have to be a mechanic to change the oil in your car, but you do have to take a few simple precautions.

5. **Include all of the steps.** If you are explaining a process, you are writing for someone who does not know the process as well as you do. Keep in mind that what seems clear or simple to you may not be clear or simple to the reader, and be sure to tell what is needed before the process starts. For instance, what ingredients are needed to cook the dish? Or what tools are needed to assemble the toy?

6. **Put the steps in the right order.** Nothing is more irritating to a reader than trying to follow directions that skip back and forth. Careful planning, drafting, and revision can help you get the time sequence right.

7. **Be specific in the details and steps.** To be sure you have sufficient details and clear steps, keep your reader in mind. Put yourself in the reader's place. Could you follow your own directions or understand your steps?

   If you remember that a process explains, you will focus on being clear. Now that you know the purpose and strategies of writing a process, you can begin the prewriting stage of writing one.

Exercise 1 **Recognizing Good Topic Sentences for Process Paragraphs**

If a sentence is a good topic sentence for a process paragraph, put OK on the line provided. If a sentence has a problem, label that sentence with one of these letters:

A This is an **announcement;** it makes no point.

B This sentence covers a topic that is **too big** for one paragraph.

S This sentence describes a topic that does **not require steps.**

1. _____ There is a simple plan for finding the best deals on car insurance.

2. _____ How I learned to clean fish is the subject of this paragraph.

3. _____ There are several reasons to cut your own hair.

4. _____ The process of building a house is challenging.

5. _____ Selling your car for the best price means knowing how to clean it to look its best.

6. _____ This paper shows the method of barbecuing on a gas grill.

7. _____ Space exploration in America evolved in several stages.

8. _____ There are many things to remember when you start your first job.

9. _____ My brother learned the right way to repair a leaky faucet.

10. _____ I discovered a simple way to turn a thrift shop chair into a classic piece of furniture.

COLLABORATE ▶ **Exercise 2** **Including Necessary Materials in a Process**

Following are three possible topics for a process paragraph. For each topic, work with a partner or a group and list the items (materials, ingredients, tools, utensils, supplies) the reader would have to gather before he or she began the process. When you finish the exercise, check your lists with another group to see if you missed any items.

1. topic: cleaning the inside of a car

needed items: _____

_____

_____

2. topic: doing laundry

needed items: _____

_____

_____

3. topic: painting a room

needed items: _____

_____

_____

WRITING THE PROCESS PARAGRAPH IN STEPS

PREWRITING Gathering Ideas: Process

The easiest way to start writing a process paragraph is to pick a small topic, one that you can cover well in one paragraph. Then you can gather ideas by listing or freewriting or both.

If you decided to write about how to find the right apartment, you might begin by freewriting. Then you might check your freewriting, looking for details that have to do with the process of finding an apartment. You can underline those details, as in the example that follows.

Freewriting for a Process Paragraph

Topic: Finding the right apartment

You have to <u>look around</u>. <u>Don't pick the first apartment you see</u>. Sean did that, and he wound up with a dump. <u>Look at a bunch</u>. But <u>not too many</u>, or you'll get confused. <u>The lease</u>, too. <u>Check it carefully</u>. <u>How much is the security deposit?</u> <u>Do you want a one bedroom?</u> <u>Friends can help</u> if they know of any nice apartments. I found my place that way. Maybe somebody you know lives in <u>a good neighborhood</u>. <u>A convenient location can be more expensive</u>. But <u>can save you money on transportation</u>.

Next, you can put what you've underlined into a list in correct time sequence:

before the search

Do you want a one bedroom?
Friends can help
a good neighborhood
A convenient location can be more expensive
can save you money on transportation

during the search

look around
Don't pick the first apartment you see.
Look at a bunch.
But not too many

after the search

Check the lease carefully.
How much is the security deposit?

Check the list. Are some details missing? Yes. A reader might ask, "What other ways (besides asking friends) can help you find apartments? What else should you do before you search? When you're looking at apartments, what should you be looking for? What questions should you ask? After the search, how do you decide which apartment is best? And what, besides the security deposit, should you check on the lease?" Answers to questions like these can give you the details needed to write a clear and interesting directional process.

Writing a Topic Sentence for a Process Paragraph

Freewriting and a list can now help you focus your paragraph by identifying the point of your process. You already know what the subject of your paragraph is: finding the right apartment. But what's the point? Is it easy to find the right apartment? Is it difficult? What does it take to find the right apartment?

Maybe a topic sentence could be as follows:

Finding the right apartment takes planning and careful investigation.

Once you have a topic sentence, you can think about adding details that explain your topic sentence, and you can begin the planning stage of writing.

Exercise 3   **Finding the Steps of a Process in Freewriting**

Read the following freewriting, then reread it, looking for all the words, phrases, or sentences that have to do with steps. Underline all those items. Once you've underlined the freewriting, put what you've underlined into a list in a correct time sequence.

How to Wrap a Gift: Freewriting

Gifts are hard to wrap. The size of the gift can be a problem, and so can a weirdly shaped gift. The best thing is to find a box big enough to hold the gift. Get wire ribbon; it's great. You can tie wire ribbon around the wrapped box, and the ribbon stays in place better than ordinary ribbon. Of course, you also need wrapping paper, scissors, tissue paper, and cellophane tape before you do anything. Use the tissue paper inside the gift box so the gift fits snugly inside. Then cut enough wrapping paper to cover the box. Place the box upside down on the cut paper and join the paper at the center, using tape to hold it. Then fold the two ends neatly and tape them shut. This is kind of tough because the ends crumple easily.

Your List of Steps in Time Sequence

1. _____

2. _____

3. _____

   _____

4. _____

5. _____

6. _____

7. _____

8. _____

9. _____

PLANNING **Devising a Plan: Process**

Using the freewriting and topic sentence on finding an apartment, you can make an outline. Then you can revise it, checking the topic sentence and the list of details, improving them where you think they could be better. A revised outline on finding the right apartment follows.

An Outline for a Process Paragraph

topic sentence: Finding the apartment you want takes planning and careful investigation.

details:
Decide what you want.
Ask yourself, "Do I want a one bedroom?" "What can I afford?"
A convenient location can be expensive.
It can also save you money on transportation.

before the search
Friends can help you with names of nice apartments.
Maybe somebody you know lives in a good neighborhood.
Check the classified advertisements in the newspapers.
Look around.

during the search
Don't pick the first apartment you see.
Look at several.
But don't look at too many.
Check the cleanness, safety, plumbing, and appliances of each one.
Ask the manager about the laundry room, additional storage, parking facilities, and maintenance policies.

after the search

Compare the two best places you saw.
Consider the price, location, and condition of the apartments.
Check the leases carefully.
Check the amount of the security deposit.
Check the requirements for first and last months' rent deposits.

The following checklist may help you revise an outline for your own process paragraph.

CHECKLIST: **A Checklist for Revising a Process Outline**

✔ Is my topic sentence focused on some point about the process?

✔ Does it cover the whole process?

✔ Do I have all the steps?

✔ Are they in the right order?

✔ Have I explained clearly?

✔ Do I need better details?

Exercise 4   **Revising the Topic Sentence in a Process Outline**

The topic sentence below doesn't cover all the steps of the process. Read the outline several times; then write a topic sentence that covers all the steps of the process and has a point.

topic sentence: If you want to clean out a closet, get some boxes.

details: First, get three large boxes.
Mark each one: 1. "To Keep," 2. "To Give Away," and 3. "To Throw Away."
Survey your closet.
Pull out each item.
Examine it carefully and ruthlessly.
Be honest about the clothes and shoes you never wear.
Put each item into one of your boxes.
Continue until the closet is empty.
Then put the items in the "To Keep" box back into your closet.
Immediately get rid of the box of things labeled "To Throw Away."
Take the "To Give Away" box to your favorite charity.
Now you have a clutter-free closet.

Revised Topic Sentence: _____

_____

_____

Exercise 5   **Revising the Order of Steps in a Process Outline**

The steps in each of these outlines are out of order. Put numbers in the spaces provided, indicating what step should be first, second, and so on.

1. topic sentence: My roommate has the same wake-up routine every morning.

details: _____ Once he has his coffee, he drags himself to the bathroom.

_____ Finally, he returns to the bedroom, scoops some clothes off the floor, and puts them on.

_____ He is too impatient to wait for the kettle to boil, so he just pours some of its warm water into his mug.

_____ He turns on the kettle.

_____ As soon as the alarm goes off, he knocks it onto the floor.

_____ Fifteen minutes after the alarm rings, he stumbles out of bed.

_____ With his eyes shut, he staggers from the bedroom to the kitchen.

_____ He stirs the mess with his finger and gulps.

_____ In the bathroom, he brushes his teeth, then combs his hair with his fingers.

_____ In the kitchen, he grabs the jar of instant coffee and shakes about three tablespoons of coffee powder into a dirty mug.

2. topic sentence: Mrs. Fernandez has a system for watering her hanging plants.

details: _____ After a few minutes, she replaces each potted plant on its hook.

_____ She reaches high and lifts each potted plant from its hook.

_____ After she has all the plants in one area of the lawn, she turns on the hose.

_____ Once the water begins running, she adjusts the nozzle to a light sprinkle.

_____ She places each plant on the lawn, near the garden hose.

_____ She waters all the plants, moving in a circle from one plant to another several times.

_____ Having turned off the water, she waits a few minutes so that any extra water in the pots can seep into the grass.

_____ When the soil in each pot is moist, she turns off the hose.

3. topic sentence: Ken has a perfect system for getting out of work early.

details: _____ Ken's excuse always gets him out of work early because our boss thinks Ken has done so much extra work all day.

_____ He starts by getting to work earlier than our boss does.

_____ By the time our boss arrives, Ken looks as if he is hard at work.

_____ He makes sure she notices him as soon as she arrives because he immediately asks her a question or strolls by her work area.

_____ Ken acts busy all morning and most of the afternoon.

_____ Then, about an hour before his shift is over, he comes up with an excuse.

_____ As he acts busy, he calls attention to himself by sighing or racing around.

_____ His excuse can be a headache, or a dentist's appointment, or a sudden need to buy more fax paper or other office supplies.

Exercise 6   **Listing All of the Steps in an Outline**

Following are three topic sentences for process paragraphs. Write all the steps needed to complete an outline for each sentence. After you list all the steps, number them in the correct time order.

1. topic sentence: There are a few simple steps for cooking a hamburger.

steps: _____

_____

_____

_____

_____

_____

_____

_____

_____

_____

_____

_____

2. topic sentence: You can devise a plan for saving money on your credit card bills.

steps: _____

_____

_____

_____

_____

_____

_____

3. topic sentence: Anyone can create his or her own exercise plan.

steps: _____

_____

_____

_____

_____

_____

_____

_____

_____

DRAFTING Drafting and Revising: Process

You can take the outline and write it in paragraph form, and you'll have a first draft of the process paragraph. As you write the first draft, you can combine some of the short sentences from the outline. Then you can review your draft and revise it for organization, details, clarity, grammar, style, and word choice.

Using the Same Grammatical Person

Remember that the *directional* process speaks directly to the reader, calling him or her "you." Sentences in a directional process use the word "you," or they imply "you."

> **directional:** *You* need a good paint brush to get started.
> Begin by making a list. ("You" is implied.)

Remember that the *informational* process involves somebody doing the process. Sentences in an informational process use words such as "I," "we," "he," "she," or "they," or a person's name.

> **informational:** *Chip* needed a good paint brush to get started.
> First, *I* can make a list.

One problem in writing a process is shifting from describing how somebody did something to telling the reader how to do an activity. When that shift happens, the two kinds of processes get mixed. That shift is called a **shift in person.** In grammar, the words "I" and "we" are considered to be in the first person, "you" is the second person," and "he," "she," "it," and "they" are in the third person.

If these words refer to one, they are *singular;* if they refer to more than one, they are *plural.* The following list may help.

INFO BOX: **A List of Persons**

1st person singular:	I
2nd person singular:	you
3rd person singular:	he, she, it, or a person's name
1st person plural:	we
2nd person plural:	you
3rd person plural:	they, or the names of more than one person

---

In writing your process paragraph, decide whether your process will be directional or informational, and stay with one kind.

Following are two examples of a shift in person. Look at them carefully and study how the shift is corrected.

> **shift in person:** After *I* preheat the oven to 350 degrees, *I* mix the egg whites and sugar with an electric mixer set at high speed. *Mix* until stiff peaks form. Then *I* put the mixture in small mounds on an ungreased

cookie sheet. ("Mix until stiff peaks form" is a shift to the "you" person.)

shift corrected: After *I* preheat the oven to 350 degrees, *I* mix the egg whites and sugar with an electric mixer set at high speed. *I* mix until stiff peaks form. Then *I* put the mixture in small mounds on an ungreased cookie sheet.

shift in person: *A salesperson* has to be very careful when a customer tries on clothes. *The clerk* can't hint that a suit may be a size too small. *You* can insult a customer with a hint like that. (The sentences shifted from "salesperson" and "clerk" to "you.")

shift corrected: *A salesperson* has to be very careful when customers try on clothes. *The clerk* can't hint that a suit may be a size too small. *He or she* can insult a customer with a hint like that.

Using Transitions Effectively

As you revise your draft, you can add transitions. Transitions are particularly important in a process paragraph because you are trying to show the steps in a *specific sequence*, and you are trying to show the *connections* between steps. Effective transitions will also keep your paragraph from sounding like a choppy, boring list.

Following is a list of some of the transitions you can use in writing a process paragraph. Be sure that you use transitional words and phrases only when it is logical to do so, and try not to overuse the same transitions in a paragraph.

INFO BOX: **Transitions for a Process Paragraph**

after	during	later	then
afterward	eventually	meanwhile	to begin
as	finally	next	to start
as he/she is	first, second, etc.	now	until
as soon as	first of all	quickly	when
as you are	gradually	sometimes	whenever
at last	in the beginning	soon	while
at the same time	immediately	suddenly	while I am . . .
before	initially	the first step,	
begin by	last	the second step, etc.	

When you write a process paragraph, you must pay particular attention to clarity. As you revise, keep thinking about your audience to be sure your steps are easy to follow. The following can help you revise your draft.

> **CHECKLIST:** **A Checklist for Revising a Process Paragraph**
> ✔ Does the topic sentence cover the whole paragraph?
> ✔ Does the topic sentence make a point about the process?
> ✔ Is any important step left out?
> ✔ Should any step be explained further?
> ✔ Are the steps in the right order?
> ✔ Should any sentences be combined?
> ✔ Have I used the same person throughout the paragraph to describe the process?
> ✔ Have I used transitions effectively?

Exercise 7 **Correcting Shifts in Person in a Process Paragraph**

Below is a paragraph that shifts from an informational to a directional process in several places. Those places are underlined. Rewrite the underlined parts directly above the underlining so that the whole paragraph is an informational process.

Simon found a stress-free system of studying for his psychology tests. A week before each test, <u>make</u> a list of all the terms <u>you need</u> to know. Then he writes each term at the top of a large index card. As soon as he has completed this task, he reviews his class notes and textbook for the definition of each term and for any important explanation or example. For example, if the term is "defense mechanism," <u>you</u> can look up its definition and an example of how defense mechanisms work. Next, <u>put</u> that information on the card labeled "defense mechanism." Simon continues this process until he has a definition, example, or explanation for each term. By preparing these cards, he reviews all the key points of his material and condenses them on a set of note cards. Then, with several days left before the test, he can simply carry the cards everywhere and review one or two whenever <u>you have</u> a free minute between classes, at lunch, or waiting in a traffic jam.

Exercise 8 **Revising Transitions in a Process Paragraph**

The transitions in this paragraph could be better. Rewrite the underlined transitions directly above each one so that the transitions are smoother.

In a few simple steps, you can make a delicious ice cream sundae. <u>First,</u> gather a deep bowl or sundae glass, one large and one small spoon, ice cream, chocolate syrup, nuts, and a spray can of whipped cream. <u>Second,</u> use the large spoon to put mounds of ice cream into the glass or bowl. <u>Third,</u> cover the ice cream with the chocolate syrup. <u>Fourth,</u> sprinkle the ice cream with nuts. <u>Sixth,</u> spray the whipped cream to form a peak at the top of the ice cream. <u>Seventh,</u> dip the small spoon into the sundae and enjoy the treat.

> **Exercise 9** **Combining Sentences in a Process Paragraph**
>
> The following paragraph has many short, choppy sentences, which are underlined. Wherever you see two or more underlined sentences clustered next to each other, combine them into one clear, smooth sentence. Write your revised version of the paragraph in the spaces above the lines.

My father has a nightly routine for recovering from his stressful job. <u>Each weekday, when he walks in the door, he is tired. He is cranky. He is also depressed.</u> His first stop is the bedroom, where he changes out of his work clothes. <u>He puts on shorts and a tee shirt. Then he grabs his sneakers. He walks outside. He is silent.</u> For the next thirty minutes, my father runs. He follows the same route through the neighborhood every night. <u>He runs down the bare streets for fifteen minutes. After that, he turns around and runs home. The run back takes fifteen minutes.</u> Once he re-enters the house, he is worn out, but he is less stressed. <u>Now he is ready. He is ready to help out with dinner. He is ready to make conversation. He is ready to be a part of the family again.</u> Running has cleared his mind of the worries of work.

The Draft

Following is a draft of the process paragraph on finding an apartment. This draft has more details than the outline on pages 113–114. Some short sentences have been combined, and transitions have been added.

A Draft of a Process Paragraph

Finding the apartment you want takes planning and investigation. First of all, you must decide what you want. Ask yourself, "Do I want a one bedroom apartment?" or "Do I want a studio apartment?" Most important, ask yourself, "What can I afford?"

A convenient location can be expensive; on the other hand, that location can save you money in transportation. Before you start looking for a place, do some research. Friends can help you with the names of nice apartments. Be sure to check the classified advertisements in the newspaper. Once you begin your search, don't pick the first place you see. You should look at several places, but looking at too many can make your search confusing. Just be sure to check each apartment's cleanness, safety, plumbing, and appliances. Then ask the manager about the laundry room, additional storage, parking facilities, and maintenance policies. After you've completed your search, compare the two best places you saw. Consider each one's price, location, and condition. Carefully check each lease, studying the amount of the security deposit and deposit for first and last months' rent.

POLISHING Polishing and Proofreading: Process

Before you prepare the final copy of your process paragraph, you can check your latest draft for any places in grammar, word choice, and style that need revision.

Following is the final version of the process paragraph on finding the apartment you want. You'll notice that it contains several changes from the previous draft.

- The word "nice" has been changed to "suitable" to make the description more specific.
- The sentence that began, "You should look" has been rewritten so that it follows the pattern of the preceding sentences. Three sentences in a row now include the parallel pattern of "Be sure," "don't pick," and "Look at."
- The second use of "be sure" has been changed to "remember" to avoid repetition.
- New details about what to check for in the leases have been added.
- A final sentence that relates to the topic of the paragraph has been added.

A Final Version of a Process Paragraph
(Changes from the draft are underlined.)

Finding the apartment you want takes planning and investigation. First of all, you must decide what you want. Ask yourself, "Do I want a one-bedroom apartment?" or "Do I want a studio apartment?" Most important, ask yourself, "What can I afford?" A convenient location can be expensive; on the other hand, that location can save you money in transportation. Before you start looking for a place, do some research. Friends can help you with the names of <u>suitable</u> apartments. Be sure to check the classified advertisements in the newspaper. Once you begin your search, don't pick the first place you see. <u>Look at</u> several places, but <u>be aware that</u> looking at too many can make your search confusing. <u>Just remember</u> to check each apartment's cleanness, safety, plumbing, and appliances. Then ask the manager about the laundry room, additional storage, parking facilities, and maintenance policies. After you've completed your search, compare the two best places you saw. Consider each one's price, location, and condition. Carefully check each lease, studying the amount of the security deposit, the deposit for first and last months' rent, <u>and the rules for tenants. When you've completed your comparison, you're ready to choose the apartment you want.</u>

Before you prepare the final copy of your process paragraph, check your latest draft for errors in spelling, punctuation, typing, and copying.

For your information: A sample process essay based on this topic and following the same writing steps can be found in Chapter 12, pp. 292–296.

Exercise 10   **Proofreading to Prepare the Final Paragraph**

Following are two process paragraphs with the kinds of errors it is easy to overlook when you prepare the final version of an assignment. Correct the errors, writing above the lines. There are twelve errors in the first paragraph and fourteen in the second paragraph.

1. The best way to deal with cockroaches is never to give up. Let's say you get up in the nite for a glass on water. Suddenly, when you turn on the light, an enormous roach skitters across you're bear feet. Of course, the first thing you do is scream, as if an ax murderer were at the window. Next, you begin to plan an extermination You grab a newspaper and swat at the insect just as the ugly bug slips between the sink and the kitchen counter. You've missed it. Immediately, you begin a search for the can of insect spray that You keep for emergencies. Eventually you find it, and spray the entire kitchen. You spray so much that every roach within twenny mile should be dead. Unfortunately, you don't know if youv'e killed the roach that crossed your toes in your kitchen. Now is the time to persevere. Never go back to bed in defeat. Instead, stand guard in the kitchen until one big roach staggers out in to the open.

2. Furnishing my first apartmen led me to an easy and cheap way to make a bookcase. When I moved into my studio apartment, I had only a bed, a table, and three chairs. I needed cheap furniture, specially a piece that would feel up much of the empty space. I decided that a bookcase was the best choice. Suddenly, I remembered a bookcase my older brother had made when he went away to college. It was made of bricks and boards, and I decided to make one for myself. First, I considered the dimensions of the bookcase. I wanted a low, bookcase, about three feet high, five feet long, and one foot deep. Once I had the measurements, I visited a big Home Improvement wearhouse. I bought three boards, 5 feet long and one foot wide. Then I bought some bricks, enough to create three stacks reaching three feet. Next, I piled my purchases into my friend Jims' truck and returned home for the best part of my project. once I had unloaded my supplies, I made tree stacks of bricks, each about a foot high, against the bare wall of my apartment. Then I covered the bricks with a board so that the board reached passed the ends of the outer stacks. This was one shelf of my bookcase. I piled and covered bricks two more times, making three shelves. Soon I had an inexpensive and usefull edition to my new home.

Lines of Detail: A Walk-Through Assignment

Your assignment is to write a paragraph on how to plan a special day. Follow these steps:

Step 1: Focus on one special day. If you want to, you can begin by using your own experience. Ask yourself such questions as, "Have I ever planned a birthday party? A baby or wedding shower? A surprise party? A picnic? A reunion? A barbecue? A celebration of a religious holiday? Have I ever seen anyone else plan such a day? If so, how should I teach a reader about planning for such a day?"

Step 2: Once you have picked the day, freewrite. Write anything you can remember about the day and how you or someone else planned it.

Step 3: When you've completed the freewriting, read it. Underline all the details that refer to steps in planning that event. List the underlined details in time order.

Step 4: Add to the list by brainstorming. Ask yourself questions that can lead to more details. For example, if an item on your list is, "Send out invitations early," ask questions like, "How early?" and "How do you decide whom to invite?"

Step 5: Survey your expanded list. Then write a topic sentence that makes some point about your planning for this special day. To reach a point, think of questions like these: "What makes a plan successful?" or "If you are planning for a special day (birthday, barbecue, surprise party, and so forth), what must you remember?"

Step 6: Use the topic sentence to prepare an outline. Be sure that the steps in the outline are in the correct time order.

Step 7: Write a first draft of the paragraph, adding details and combining short sentences.

Step 8: Revise your draft. Be careful to use smooth transitions, and check that you have included all the necessary steps.

Step 9: Prepare and proofread the final version of your paragraph.

Writing Your Own Process Paragraph

When you write on one of these topics, be sure to work through the stages of the writing process in preparing your process paragraph.

1. Write a **directional or informational process** about one of these topics:

packing a suitcase	fixing a clogged drain
preparing for a garage sale	changing the oil in a car
painting a room	washing and waxing a car
taking a test	breaking a specific habit
losing weight	gaining weight
training a roommate	giving a pet a bath
coping with rejection	walking for better health
doing holiday shopping early	getting up in the morning

breaking up with a boyfriend or girlfriend

getting good tips while working as a waiter or waitress

getting ready to go out for a special occasion

sizing up a new acquaintance

2. Write about the wrong way to do something or the wrong way you (or someone else) did it. You can use any of the topics in the list above, or you can choose your own topic.

3. Imagine that a relative who has never been to your state is coming to visit. This relative will arrive at the nearest airport, rent a car, and drive to your house. Write a paragraph giving your relative clear directions for getting from the airport to your house. Be sure to have an appropriate topic sentence.

4. Interview one of the counselors at your college. Ask the counselor to tell you the steps for applying for financial aid. Take notes or tape the interview, get copies of any forms that are included in the application process, and ask questions about these forms.

   After the interview, write a paragraph explaining the process of applying for financial aid. Your explanation is directed at a high school senior who has never applied for aid.

5. Interview someone whose cooking you admire. Ask that person to tell you the steps involved in making a certain dish. Take notes or tape the interview. After the interview, write a paragraph, *not* a recipe, explaining how to prepare the dish. Your paragraph will explain the process to someone who is a beginner at cooking.

◄ COLLABORATE

6. Brainstorm about a particular task or function of a word-processing program that took considerable practice for you to master. (For

◄ COMPUTER

example, you could write about moving text, highlighting, finding or creating a file, and so forth.) Write a paragraph that explains how to master this specific skill. Conclude your paragraph by stressing the benefits and/or practical uses of this skill.

 COMPUTER ▶

7. Visit your college's Web site, and follow any links that are associated with your campus bookstore. After reviewing the information about shopping for books and supplies, and based on your own experience, write a paragraph that explains the most efficient way to avoid long lines and waiting periods. If your college bookstore offers online purchasing, be sure to include the steps involved in this option.

8. Study the photograph below, and notice the connection between the dog and the man. Then write a process paragraph on how to train a dog to walk on a leash without pulling away.

9. Examine the photograph below, and then write a paragraph on how an athlete can focus his or her concentration for maximum benefit.

Note: Additional writing options suitable for process-related assignments can be found after the professional reading, "How to Write a Personal Letter," which begins on page 606.

Name: _____ **Section:** _____

PEER REVIEW FORM FOR A PROCESS PARAGRAPH

After you've written a draft of your process paragraph, let a writing partner read it. When your partner has completed the form below, discuss your draft. Repeat the same process for your partner's paragraph.

The steps that are most clearly described are _____

_____

_____

I'd like more explanation about this step: _____

_____

Some details could be added to the part that begins with the words _____

A transition could be added to the part that begins with the words _____

I have questions about _____

_____

The best part of this paragraph is _____

_____

Other comments: _____

_____

_____

_____

_____

_____

_____

_____

_____

_____

_____

_____

Reviewer's Name: _____

CHAPTER 6
Comparison and Contrast

WHAT IS COMPARISON?
WHAT IS CONTRAST?

To **compare** means to point out *similarities*. To **contrast** means to point out *differences*. **When you compare or contrast, you need to come to some conclusion.** It's not enough to say, "These two things are similar" or "They are different." Your reader will be asking, "So what? What's your point?" You may be showing the differences between two restaurants to explain which is the better buy:

> If you like Mexican food, you can go to either Café Mexicana or Juanita's, but Juanita's has lower prices.

Or you may be explaining the similarities between two family members to explain how people with similar personalities can clash.

> My cousin Bill and my brother Karram are both so stubborn they can't get along.

Hints for Writing a Comparison or Contrast Paragraph

1. Limit your topic. When you write a comparison or contrast paragraph, you might think that the easiest topics to write about are broad ones with many similarities or differences. However, if you make your topic too large, you will not be able to cover it well, and your paragraph will be full of very large, boring statements.

Here are some topics that are too large for a comparison or contrast paragraph: two countries, two periods in history, two kinds of addiction, two wars, two economic or political systems, two presidents.

2. Avoid the obvious topic. Some people think it is easier to write about two items if the similarities or differences between them are obvious, but with an obvious topic, you will have nothing new to say, and you will risk writing a boring paragraph.

Here are some obvious topics: the differences between high school and college, the similarities between *Men in Black* and *Men in Black 2*. If you are drawn to an obvious topic, *try a new angle* on the topic. Write about the unexpected, using the same topic. Write about the similarities between high school and college, or the differences between *Men in Black* and *Men in Black 2*. You may have to do more thinking before you come up with ideas, but your ideas may be more interesting to write about and to read.

3. Make your point in the topic sentence of your comparison or contrast paragraph. Indicate whether the paragraph is about similarities or differences in a topic sentence like this:

> Because he is so reliable and loyal, Michael is a much better friend to me than Stefan. (The phrase "much better" indicates differences.)
> My two botany teachers share a love of the environment and a passion for protecting it. (The word "share" indicates similarities.)

4. Do not announce in the topic sentence. The sentences below are announcements, not topic sentences:

> This paper will explain the similarities between my two botany teachers.
> Let me tell you about why Michael is a different kind of friend than Stefan.

5. Make sure your topic sentence has a focus. It should indicate similarities or differences; it should focus on the specific kind of comparison or contrast you will make.

> **not focused:** My old house and my new one are different.
> **focused:** My new home is bigger, brighter, and more comfortable than my old one.

6. In the topic sentence, cover both subjects to be compared or contrasted.

> **covers only one subject:** The beach at Santa Lucia was dirty and crowded.
> **covers both subjects:** The beach at Santa Lucia was dirty and crowded, but the beach at Fisher Bay was clean and private.

Be careful. It is easy to get so carried away by the details of your paragraph that you forget to put both subjects into one sentence.

Exercise 1 **Identifying Suitable Topic Sentences for a Comparison or Contrast Paragraph**

Following is a list of possible topic sentences for a comparison or contrast paragraph. Some would make good topic sentences. The ones that wouldn't make good topic sentences have one or more of these problems: they are announcements, they don't indicate whether the paragraph will be about similarities or differences, they don't focus on the specific kind of comparison or contrast to be made, they cover subjects that are too big to write about in one paragraph, or they don't cover both subjects.

Mark the problem sentences with an *X*. If a sentence would make a good topic sentence for a comparison or contrast paragraph, mark it *OK*.

1. _____ My children, Hector and Jacob, are very different.

2. _____ I get all my clothes at two stores, Fashions Unlimited and Style Mart.

3. _____ My children, Hector and Jacob, are different in their athletic ability and interest in school.

4. _____ Philadelphia and Boston are similar in their British heritage, revolutionary power, and cultural growth.

5. _____ Car Cavern has better prices and a wider choice of car accessories.

6. _____ This essay will discuss the similarities between tea and Coca-Cola.

7. _____ Boys and girls have different interests, physical abilities, and emotional needs.

8. _____ On the one hand, there is Mexico City, and on the other hand, there is Tijuana.

9. _____ Fashions Unlimited has more original and youth-oriented clothes than Style Mart.

10. _____ My second semester in college was a big improvement over my first.

Organizing Your Comparison or Contrast Paragraph

Whether you decide to write about similarities (to compare) or differences (to contrast), you will have to decide how to organize your paragraph. You can choose between two patterns of organization: subject-by-subject or point-by-point.

Subject-by-Subject Organization   In the subject-by-subject pattern, you support and explain your topic sentence by first writing all of your details on one subject and then writing all of your details on the other subject. If you choose a subject-by-subject pattern, be sure to discuss the points for your second subject *in the same order* as you did for the first subject. For example, if your first subject is an amusement park, and you cover (1) the price of admission, (2) the long lines at rides, and (3) the quality of the rides, when you discuss the second subject, another amusement park, you should write about its prices, lines, and quality of rides *in the same order*.

Look carefully at the outline and comparison paragraph below for a subject-by-subject pattern.

A Comparison Outline: Subject-by-Subject Pattern
   topic sentence: Once I realized that my brother and my mother are very much alike in temperament, I realized why they don't get along.

details:

subject 1, James—temper	My brother James is a hot-tempered person. It is easy for him to lose control of his temper.
unkind words	When he does, he often says things he later regrets.
stubbornness	James is also very stubborn. In an argument, he will never admit he is wrong. Once we were arguing about baseball scores. Even when I showed him the right score, printed in the paper, he wouldn't admit he was wrong. He said the newspaper had made a mistake. James' stubbornness overtakes his common sense.
subject 2, mother—	James has inherited many of his character traits from our mother.
temper	She has a quick temper, and anything can provoke it. Once, she got angry because she had to wait too long at a traffic light.
unkind words	She also has a tendency to use unkind words when she's mad.
stubbornness	She never backs down from a disagreement or concedes she is wrong. My mother even quit a job because she refused to admit she'd made a mistake in taking inventory. Her pride can lead her into foolish acts. After I realized how similar my brother and mother are, I understood how such inflexible people are likely to clash.

A Comparison Paragraph: Subject-by-Subject Pattern

subject 1, James—temper	Once I realized that my brother and my mother are very much alike in temperament, I realized why they don't get along. My brother James is a hot-tempered person. It is easy for him to lose control of his temper, and when he does, he often
unkind words stubbornness	says things he regrets. James is also very stubborn. In an argument, he will never admit he is wrong. I remember one time when we were arguing about baseball scores. Even when I showed him the right score, printed in the newspaper, he wouldn't admit he was wrong. James insisted that that the newspaper must have made a mistake in printing the score. As this example shows, sometimes James' stubbornness overtakes James' common sense. It took me a while to realize that my stubborn brother James has inherited many
subject 2, mother—temper	of his traits from our mother. Like James, she has a quick temper, and almost anything can provoke it. She once got angry because she had to wait
temper unkind words	too long at a traffic light. She also shares James' habit of saying unkind things when she's angry.

stubbornness

And just as James refuses to back down when he's wrong, my mother will never back down from a disagreement or concede she's wrong. In fact, my mother once quit a job because she refused to admit she'd made a mistake in taking inventory. Her pride is as powerful as James' pride, and it can be just as foolish. After I realized how similar my mother and brother are, I understood how such inflexible people are likely to clash.

Look carefully at the paragraph in the subject-by-subject pattern, and you'll note that it

- begins with a topic sentence about both subjects—James and his mother
- gives all the details about one subject—James
- then gives all the details about the second subject—his mother—in the same order

Point-by-Point Organization In the point-by-point pattern, you support and explain your topic sentence by discussing each point of comparison or contrast, switching back and forth between your subjects. You explain one point for each subject, then explain another point for each subject, and so on.

Look carefully at the outline and the comparison paragraph below for the point-by-point pattern.

A Comparison Outline: Point-by-Point Pattern

topic sentence: Once I realized that my brother and my mother are very much alike in temperament, I realized why they don't get along.

details:

point 1, temper James and mother	My brother James is a hot-tempered person. It is easy for him to lose control of his temper. My mother has a quick temper, and anything can provoke it. Once she got angry because she had to wait too long at a traffic light.
point 2, unkind words James and mother	When my brother gets mad, he often says things he regrets. My mother has a tendency to use unkind words when she's mad.
point 3, stubbornness James and mother	James is very stubborn. In an argument, he will never admit he is wrong. Once we were arguing about baseball scores. Even when I showed him the right score, printed in the paper, he wouldn't admit he was wrong. He said the newspaper had made a mistake. James' stubbornness overtakes his common sense. My mother will never back down from a disagreement or admit she is wrong. She even quit a job because she refused to admit she'd made a mistake in taking inventory.

She was foolish in her stubbornness.
After I realized how similar my mother and brother are, I understood how such inflexible people are likely to clash.

A Comparison Paragraph: Point-by-Point Pattern

point 1,
James and mother

point 2,
James and mother

point 3,
James and mother

Once I realized that my brother and my mother are very much alike in temperament, I realized why they don't get along. My brother is a hot-tempered person, and it is easy for him to lose control of his temper. My mother shares James' quick temper, and anything can provoke her anger. Once, she got angry because she had to wait too long at a traffic light. When my brother gets mad, he often says things he regrets. Similarly, my mother is known for the unkind things she's said in anger. James is a very stubborn person. In an argument, he will never admit he's wrong. I can remember one argument we were having over baseball scores. Even when I showed him the right score, printed in the newspaper, he wouldn't admit he had been wrong. He simply insisted the paper had made a mistake. At times like that, James' stubbornness overtakes his common sense. Like her son, my mother will never back down from an argument or admit she was wrong. She even quit a job because she refused to admit she'd made a mistake in taking inventory. In that case, her stubbornness was as foolish as James'. It took me a while to see the similarities between my brother and mother. Yet after I realized how similar these two people are, I understood how two inflexible people are likely to clash.

Look carefully at the paragraph in the point-by-point pattern, and you'll note that it

- begins with a topic sentence about both subjects—James and his mother
- discusses how both James and his mother are alike in these points: their quick tempers, the unkind remarks they make when angry, their often foolish stubbornness
- switches back and forth between the two subjects

The subject-by-subject and point-by-point patterns can be used for either a comparison or contrast paragraph. But whatever pattern you choose, remember these hints:

1. Be sure to use the same points to compare or contrast two subjects. If you are contrasting two cars, you can't discuss the price and safety features of one, then the styling and speed of the other. You must discuss the price of both, or the safety features, styling, or speed of both.

You don't have to list the points in your topic sentence, but you can include them, like this: "My old Celica turned out to be a cheaper, safer, and faster car than my boyfriend's new Mazda."

2. Be sure to give roughly equal space to both subjects. This rule doesn't mean you must write the same number of words—or even sentences—on both subjects. It does mean you should be giving fairly equal attention to the details of both subjects.

Since you will be writing about two subjects, this type of paragraph can involve more details than other paragraph formats. Thus, a comparison or contrast paragraph may be longer than twelve sentences.

Using Transitions Effectively for Comparison or Contrast

Transitions in a comparison or contrast paragraph depend on the answers to two questions:

1. Are you writing a comparison or contrast paragraph?
   - When you choose to write a *comparison* paragraph, you use transitional words, phrases, or sentences that point out *similarities*.
   - When you choose to write a *contrast* paragraph, you use transitional words, phrases, or sentences that point out *differences*.
2. Are you organizing your paragraph in the point-by-point or subject-by-subject pattern?
   - When you choose to organize your paragraph in the *point-by-point* pattern, you need transitions *within* each point and *between points*.
   - When you choose to organize in the *subject-by-subject* pattern, you need *most of your transitions* in the *second half* of the paragraph to remind the reader of the points you made in the first half.

Here are some transitions you can use in writing comparison or contrast paragraphs. You may think of others that will be appropriate for your ideas.

INFO BOX: Transitions for a Comparison or Contrast Paragraph

To show similarities:

additionally	both	in the same way	similarly
again	each of	just like	similar to
also	equally	like	too
and	furthermore	likewise	so
as well as	in addition		

To show differences:

although	even though	in spite of	though
but	except	nevertheless	unlike
conversely	however	on the other hand	whereas
different from	in contrast to	otherwise	while
despite	instead of	still	yet

Writing a comparison or contrast paragraph challenges you to make decisions: Will I compare or contrast? Will I use a point-by-point or a subject-by-subject pattern? Those decisions will determine what kind of transitions you will use and where you will use them.

> **Exercise 2** **Writing Appropriate Transitions for a Comparison or Contrast Paragraph**

Below are pairs of sentences. First, decide whether each pair shows a comparison or contrast. Then combine the two sentences into one, using an appropriate transition (either a word or a phrase). You may have to rewrite parts of the original sentences to create one smooth sentence. The first pair is done for you.

1. My mother is a late sleeper.
My father always wakes up at dawn.

combined: <u>My mother is a late sleeper; on the other hand, my father</u>

<u>always wakes up at dawn.</u>

2. Midnight was an affectionate cat who loved to snuggle.
Puff-Kitty, our orange cat, liked her privacy.

combined: _____

_____

3. Talking to a therapist can help people fight depression.
Doctors can prescribe medication for depression.

combined: _____

_____

4. Sandra Tomasso is a singer with a popular band.
Her brother Nick can't sing a note.

combined: _____

_____

5. Professor Wu challenged me to think before I wrote my essays.
Professor Farrell urged me to use my head in solving math problems.

combined: _____

_____

_____

2. topic sentence: _____

_____

List of Details

rain	**snow**
relation to sports—no sports require rain	winter sports like skiing and snowboarding require snow
relation to seasons—it can rain in any season	snow falls mostly in winter
relation to nature—rain is needed for plants and crops to grow	plants and crops do not grow in the snow

3. topic sentence: _____

_____

List of Details

motorcycles	**motor scooters**
size—smaller than the smallest car	smallest engine-powered vehicle
appeal—to everyone who likes the freedom of the ride	to all who enjoy the maneuverability and fresh air
safety—little defense against auto drivers	vulnerable in crashes with cars

4. topic sentence: _____

_____

List of Details

motorcycles	**motor scooters**
price—can be expensive	more reasonably priced
power—powerful engine, suitable for racing	minimal engine power, suitable for riding around town
size—large and heavy	small and light

PLANNING Devising a Plan: Comparison or Contrast

With a topic sentence, you can begin to draft an outline. Before you can write an outline, however, you have to make a decision: What pattern do you want to use in organizing your paragraph? Do you want to use the subject-by-subject or the point-by-point pattern?

The following is an outline of a contrast paragraph in point-by-point form.

An Outline of a Contrast Paragraph: Point-by-Point

topic sentence:	Some people would rather eat at The Garden than at Victor's because The Garden offers better, cheaper food in a more casual environment.
details:	Food at Victor's is bland-tasting and traditional.
	The menu has broiled fish, chicken, traditional steaks.
	The spices used are mostly parsley and salt.
	The food is the usual American food, with a little French food on the list.
	Appetizers are the usual things like shrimp cocktail or onion soup.
point 1, food	Food at The Garden is more spicy and adventurous.
	There are many pasta dishes in tomato sauce.
	There is garlic in just about everything.
	The Garden serves four different curry dishes.
	It has all kinds of ethnic food.
	Appetizers include items like tiny tortillas and hot, honey-mustard ribs.
point 2, prices	The prices of the two restaurants differ.
	Victor's is expensive.
	Everything you order costs extra.
	An appetizer and a salad costs extra.
	Food at The Garden is moderately priced.
	The price of a dinner includes an appetizer and a salad.
point 3, environment	Certain diners may feel uncomfortable in Victor's, which has a formal environment.
	Everyone is dressed up, the men in jackets and ties and the women in dresses.
	Less formal diners would rather eat in a more casual place.
	People don't dress up to go to The Garden; they wear jeans.
conclusion	Many people prefer a place where they can relax, with reasonable prices and unusual food, to a place that's a little stuffy, with a traditional and expensive menu.

Once you've drafted an outline, check it. Use the following checklist to help you review and revise your outline.

CHECKLIST: **A Checklist for an Outline of a Comparison or Contrast Paragraph**

✔ Do I have enough details?

✔ Are all my details relevant?

✔ Have I covered all the points on both sides?

✔ If I'm using a subject-by-subject pattern, have I covered the points in the same order on both sides?

✔ Have I tried to cover too many points?

✔ Have I made my main idea clear?

There is also a possible loss of self-esteem because this business is a part of one's identity.

A failed business can make a person appear foolish or reckless.

Effort has to be invested in a new business.

No one must work longer hours and make harder decisions than the owner.

A business is not a hobby; it is a full-time commitment.

Starting a business has its rewards.

A person gets to see a dream become reality.

The sense of possibility, of satisfaction to come, is a great motivator.

Starting a relationship has its rewards.

Everyone dreams of finding the perfect partner, and beginning a relationship offers the chance to fulfill a dream.

The hope of a great future also motivates the couple.

Starting a relationship has its risks.

There is the risk of investing too much emotion in the wrong connection.

A person's painfully gained confidence and trust can be wasted in a bad choice.

In addition, self-esteem can be lost if a person feels foolish or impulsive.

A new relationship takes work.

The only people who can work at learning about each other are the partners.

If the relationship is to grow, the partners must be fully committed.

Rewritten order: _____

_____

_____

_____

_____

_____

_____

_____

_____

_____

_____

_____

DRAFTING Drafting and Revising: Comparison or Contrast

When you've revised your outline, you can write the first draft of the restaurant paragraph. After making a first draft, you may want to combine more sentences, rearrange your points, fix your topic sentence, or add vivid details. You may also need to add transitions.

The Draft

Here is a draft version of the paragraph on contrasting two restaurants. As you read it, notice the changes from the outline on page 142: the order of some details in the outline has been changed, sentences have been combined, and transitional devices have been added.

A Draft of a Contrast Paragraph, Point-by-Point

(Transitions are underlined.)

Some people would rather eat at The Garden than at Victor's because The Garden offers better and cheaper food in a more casual environment. The food at Victor's is bland-tasting and traditional. The menu has broiled fish, chicken, and traditional steaks. The food is the usual American food with a little French food on the list. Appetizers are the usual things like shrimp cocktail and onion soup. The spices used are mainly parsley and salt. Food at The Garden, <u>however,</u> is more spicy and adventurous. The restaurant has all kinds of ethnic food. There are many pasta dishes with tomato sauce. The menu has four kinds of curry on it. The appetizers include items like tiny tortillas and hot, honey-mustard ribs. <u>And if parsley is the spice of choice at Victor's,</u> garlic is the favorite spice at The Garden. The prices at the restaurants differ, <u>too.</u> Victor's is expensive because everything you order costs extra. An appetizer or a salad costs extra. Food at The Garden, <u>in contrast,</u> is more moderately priced because the price of a dinner includes an appetizer and a salad. <u>Price and menu are important, but the most important difference between the restaurants has to do with environment</u>. Certain diners may feel uncomfortable at Victor's, which has a formal kind of atmosphere. Everyone is dressed up, the men in jackets and ties and the women in dresses. The less formal diners would rather eat in a more casual place like The Garden, where everyone wears jeans. Many people prefer a place where they can relax, with reasonable prices and unusual food, to a place that is a little stuffy, with a traditional and expensive menu.

The checklist below may help you to revise your own draft.

CHECKLIST: A Checklist for Revising the Draft of a Comparison or Contrast Paragraph

✔ Did I include a topic sentence that covers both subjects?

✔ Is the paragraph in a clear order?

✔ Does it stick to one pattern, either subject-by-subject or point-by-point?

✔ Are both subjects given roughly the same amount of space?

✔ Does all the detail fit?

✔ Are the details specific and vivid?

✔ Do I need to combine any sentences?

✔ Are transitions used effectively?

✔ Have I made my point?

Exercise 10   **Revising the Draft of a Comparison or Contrast Paragraph by Adding Vivid Details**

You can do this exercise alone, with a writing partner, or with a group. The following contrast paragraph lacks the vivid details that could make it interesting. Read it; then rewrite the underlined parts in the space above the underlining. Replace the original words with more vivid details.

My two attempts at passing Introduction to Algebra were different in three ways. The instructor in my first class was very <u>nice</u>. He had no absence policy, used humor in class, and allowed students to ask as many questions as they wanted. He gave <u>some</u> tests and <u>some</u> optional homework assignments. The textbook we used was confusing; it had <u>lots of examples</u>, but they weren't explained very clearly. Frustrated with the book, I stopped reading it and began to <u>slack off</u>. I skipped all the homework and didn't come to class as often. I figured I could always ask questions when I did come, and the instructor would help me out. Unfortunately, I failed the class and had to repeat it the following semester. The second time around, my instructor was tough. She allowed only three absences, rarely smiled, and limited class questions to new material. She left <u>some time</u> at the end of class to answer other, individual questions. Unlike my first instructor, this one gave seven tests, assigned homework for every class, and checked it. We used the same <u>stupid</u> textbook I had used in the first class. However, this time I read all the assignments because I had to turn in the homework. Because I was determined to pass the course and my teacher was so strict, I <u>had better attendance</u>. Even though I preferred my first teacher, I learned more the second time I took the class. I learned to concentrate on the reading assignments, do the homework, and attend class regularly. As a result, I passed Introduction to Algebra on my second try.

Exercise 11   **Revising a Draft by Combining Sentences**

The paragraph below has many short, choppy sentences, which are underlined. Whenever you see two or more underlined sentences clustered next to each other, combine them into one smooth, clear sentence.

Although I am twenty-one, I still behave like a five-year-old in my relationship to my parents. Five-year-olds depend on their parents to feed them. <u>I can remember coming home from kindergarten. I went directly to the refrigerator.</u> I was starving after a long day of lessons and play. <u>I searched the shelves for comfort food like cookies. I also wanted chocolate pudding. Ice cream sandwiches were another favorite.</u> Today, when I visit my parents, I quickly greet them and head straight for the refrigerator. I expect it to be full of the same childhood treats I craved in kindergarten. Somehow, no matter how old they are, children look to their parents for comfort food. At age five, I depended on my parents for money as well as for food. That is, my parents paid for all my needs, such as clothing and shelter, and for my desires, such as toys. <u>I am an adult today. I confess to acting like a child. I do this when I beg my parents to help out with my rent. Sometimes I ask them to lend me some cash for my phone bill.</u> Children are also known for throwing tantrums. When I was five, I used to kick and scream as my father dragged me off to bed. I also protested when I was denied a toy in the toy store or a candy bar right before dinner. I can be equally stubborn today. <u>I don't kick and scream any more. I lose control of myself.</u> I have stormed out of my parents' house when they have disapproved of my behavior. I have sulked by refusing to call them for weeks at a time. Most of the time, I think of myself as a grown up.

However, I know there is another part of me. It is the part of me that wants to be a

child.

 **Polishing and Proofreading: Comparison or Contrast**

Contrast Paragraph: Point-by-Point Pattern

Following is the final version of the paragraph contrasting restaurants, using a point-by-point pattern. When you read it, you'll notice several changes from the draft on page 146:

- "Usual" or "usually" was used too often, so synonyms were substituted.
- "Onion soup" became "*French* onion soup" to polish the detail.
- "Everything *you* order" was changed to "everything *a person* orders, to avoid sounding as if the reader is ordering food at Victor's.
- "A formal *kind of atmosphere*" became "a formal *environment*" to eliminate extra words.

A Final Version of a Contrast Paragraph: Point-by-Point
(Changes from the draft are underlined.)

Some people would rather eat at The Garden than at Victor's because The Garden gives offers better and cheaper food in a more casual environment. The food at Victor's is bland-tasting and traditional. The menu has broiled fish, chicken, and traditional steaks. The food is typical American food with a little French food on the list. Appetizers are standard things like shrimp cocktail and French onion soup. The spices are mostly parsley and salt. Food at The Garden, however, is more spicy and adventurous. The restaurant has all kinds of ethnic food. There are many pasta dishes with tomato sauce. The menu has four kinds of curry on it. The appetizers include items like tiny tortillas and hot, honey-mustard ribs. And if parsley is the spice of choice at Victor's, garlic is the favorite spice at The Garden. The prices at the restaurants differ, too. Victor's is expensive because everything a person orders costs extra. An appetizer or a salad costs extra. Food at The Garden, in contrast, is more moderately priced because the price of a dinner includes an appetizer and a salad. Price and menu are important, but the most important difference between the two restaurants has to do with environment. Certain diners may feel uncomfortable at Victor's, which has a formal environment. Everyone is dressed up, the men in jackets and ties and the women in dresses. Less formal diners would rather eat in a more casual place like The Garden, where everyone wears jeans. Many people prefer a place where they can relax, with reasonable prices and unusual food, to a place that is a little stuffy, with a traditional and expensive menu.

Before you prepare the final copy of your comparison or contrast paragraph, check your latest draft for errors in spelling, punctuation, typing, and copying.

For your information: A sample point-by-point contrast essay based on this topic and following the same writing steps can be found in Chapter 12, pp. 298–303.

The Same Contrast Paragraph: Subject-by-Subject

To show you what the same paragraph contrasting restaurants would look like in a subject-by-subject pattern, the outline, draft, and final version are shown below.

An Outline: Subject-by-Subject

topic sentence:	Some people would rather eat at The Garden than at Victor's because The Garden offers better, cheaper food in a more casual environment.
details:	Food at Victor's is bland-tasting and traditional.
	The menu has broiled fish, chicken, and traditional steaks.
	The spices used are mostly parsley and salt.
	The food is the usual American food, with a little French food on the list.
	Appetizers are the usual things like shrimp cocktail and onion soup.
subject 1, Victor's	Victor's is expensive.
	Everything you order costs extra.
	An appetizer or salad costs extra.
	Certain diners may feel uncomfortable at Victor's, which has a formal environment.
	Everyone is dressed up, the men in jackets and ties and the women in dresses.
	Food at The Garden is more spicy and adventurous.
	There are many pasta dishes in tomato sauce.
	There is garlic in just about everything.
	The Garden serves four different curry dishes.
	It has all kinds of ethnic food.
subject 2, The Garden	Appetizers include items like tiny tortillas and hot, honey-mustard ribs.
	Food at The Garden is moderately priced.
	The price of a dinner includes an appetizer and a salad.
	The Garden is casual.
	People don't dress up to go there; they wear jeans.
conclusion	Many people prefer a place where they can relax, with reasonable prices and unusual food, to a place that's a little stuffy, with a traditional and expensive menu.

A Draft: Subject-by-Subject

(Transitions are underlined.)

Some people would rather eat at The Garden than at Victor's because The Garden offers better, cheaper food in a more casual environment. The food at Victor's is bland-tasting and traditional. The menu has broiled fish, chicken, and traditional steaks on it. The food is the usual American food, with a little French food on the list. Appetizers are the usual things like shrimp cocktail and onion soup. At Victor's, the spices are mostly parsley and salt. Eating traditional food at Victor's is expensive, because everything you order costs extra. An appetizer or a salad, for instance, costs extra. Victor's prices make some people nervous, and the restaurant's formal environment makes them uncomfortable. At Victor's, everyone is dressed up, the men in jackets and ties and the women in dresses. <u>The formal atmosphere, the food, and the prices attract some diners, but others would rather go to The Garden for a meal.</u> The food at The Garden is more spicy and adventurous <u>than the offerings at Victor's.</u> The place has all kinds of ethnic food. There are many pasta dishes in tomato sauce, and The Garden serves four different curry dishes. Appetizers include items like tiny tortillas and hot, honey-mustard ribs. <u>If Victor's relies on parsley and salt to flavor its food</u>, The Garden sticks to garlic, which is in just about everything. Prices are lower at The Garden <u>than they are at Victor's</u>. The Garden's meals are more moderately priced because, <u>unlike Victor's</u>, The Garden includes an appetizer and a salad in the price of a dinner. <u>And in contrast to Victor's</u>, The Garden is a casual restaurant. People don't dress up to go to The Garden; everyone wears jeans. Many people prefer a place where they can relax, with unusual food at reasonable prices, to a place that's a little stuffy, with a traditional and expensive menu.

A Final Version: Subject-by-Subject
(Changes from the draft are underlined.)

Some people would rather eat at The Garden than at Victor's because The Garden offers better, cheaper food in a more casual environment. The food at Victor's is bland-tasting and traditional. The menu has broiled fish, chicken, and traditional steaks on it. The food is typical American food, with a little French food on the list. Appetizers are the <u>standard</u> things like shrimp cocktail and <u>French</u> onion soup. At Victor's, the spices are mostly parsley and salt. Eating traditional food at Victor's is expensive, because everything <u>a person</u> orders costs extra. An appetizer or a salad, for instance, costs extra. Victor's prices make some people nervous, and the restaurant's formal environment makes them uncomfortable. At Victor's, everyone is dressed up, the men in jackets and ties and the women in dresses. The formal <u>environment</u> and the prices attract some diners, but others would rather go to The Garden for a meal. The food at The Garden is more spicy and adventurous than the offerings at Victor's. The place has all kinds of ethnic food. There are many pasta dishes in tomato sauce, and The Garden serves four different curry dishes. Appetizers include items like tiny tortillas and hot, honey-mustard ribs. If Victor's relies on parsley and salt to flavor its food, The Garden sticks to garlic, which is in just about everything. Prices are lower at The Garden than they are at Victor's. The Garden's meals are moderately priced because, unlike Victor's, The Garden includes an appetizer and a salad in the price of a dinner. And in contrast to Victor's, The Garden is a casual restaurant. People don't dress up to go to The Garden; everyone wears jeans. Many people prefer place where they can relax, with unusual food at reasonable prices, to a place that's a little stuffy, with a traditional and expensive menu.

Exercise 12   **Proofreading to Prepare the Final Version**

Following are two comparison or contrast paragraphs with the kinds of errors it is easy to overlook in a final copy of an assignment. Correct the errors, writing your corrections above the lines. There are nine errors in the first paragraph and fifteen in the second.

1. Anyone who regularly drinks iced tea can tell the difference between real iced tea and Instant iced tea. The real tea is hot tea brewed with a tea bag and cooled. Instant tea is cold water mix with a spoonful of iced tea powder. The first differance is in the taste. Real iced tea taste light and soft. It is obviously tea, but it is not strong tea. Instant tea is strong, harsh, and biter. The texture of the two kinds of tea are another contrast. While brewed iced tea is smooth and even silky, powdered tea never mixes right There is a gritty texture to it as if the powder has never really dissolved. Another contrast, is the appearance of the tea. Real tea is a clear golden-brown. Instant tea on the other hand, is often a dull color. Sometimes it is even cloudy. As all iced tea drinkers know, instant tea is acceptable, but real iced tea is preferable.

2. My current girlfriend is turning out to be a copy of my last girlfriend. My last girlfriend, Dina, was deeply in love with me for about a month. She tought everything I did or say was great, and she loved to sit at home with me and watch television. But after about six weeks, I noticed Dina was complaining more and more. She say she di'nt want to set around the house anymore; she wanted to go out to club and attend partys. I got sick of her complaining, so I stopped seeing her as much. I went out with my friends instead. One night at a party, I met a beautiful women named Cherisse. When Dina found out, she gave me a choice: I could see her, or I could see Cherisse. That is how I wound up with my current girlfriend, Cherisse. Like Dina, Cherisse was sweet and lovley for a while. She said, she was happy to spend privite time with me, watching television and talking. Then, in the same way Dina did, Cherisse started to wine. She said I never took her anywhere. She claim I must be ashamed of her. She insisted she wanted to meet my friends.

When I brought some friends over, she didn't like them. As a result, I started socializing with my friends more. Cherisse was even angrier that I wasnt taking her out. One day she discovered, that I had been seen at a club with another woman. The next day, just like Dina, she gave me a choice. I don't know what I'll do this time because I don't seem to have much luck with women!

Lines of Detail: A Walk-Through Assignment

Write a paragraph that compares or contrasts any experience you've heard about with the same experience as you lived it. For example, you could compare or contrast what you heard about starting college with your actual experience of starting college. You could compare or contrast what you heard about falling in love with your experience of falling in love, or what you heard about playing a sport with your own experience playing that sport. To write your paragraph, follow these steps:

Step 1: Choose the experience you will write about; then list all the similarities and differences between the experience as you heard about it and the experience as you lived it.

Step 2: To decide whether to write a comparison or contrast paragraph, survey your list to see which has more details, the similarities or the differences.

Step 3: Add details to your comparison or contrast list. Survey your list again, and group the details into points of comparison or contrast.

Step 4: Write a topic sentence that includes both subjects, focuses on comparison or contrast, and makes a point.

Step 5: Decide whether your paragraph will be in the subject-by-subject or point-by-point pattern. Write your outline in the pattern you choose.

Step 6: Write a draft of your paragraph. Revise your draft, checking the transitions, the order of the points and the space given to each subject, and the relevance and vividness of details. Combine any short, choppy sentences.

Step 7: Before you prepare the final copy of your paragraph, edit for word choice, spelling, punctuation, and transitions.

Writing Your Own Comparison or Contrast Paragraph

When you write on one of these topics, be sure to follow the stages of the writing process in preparing your comparison or contrast paragraph.

1. Compare or contrast what is most important in your life now to what was most important to you as a child. You might want to brainstorm about your values then and now before narrowing your focus to specific similarities or differences.

2. Compare or contrast any of the following:

two pets	two relatives	two college Web sites
two gifts	two jobs	two family traditions

| two supervisors | two role models | two discount stores |
| two clubs | two talk shows | two athletic teams |

If your instructor agrees, you may want to brainstorm points of comparison or contrast with a writing partner or a group.

3. Imagine that you are a reporter who specializes in helping consumers get the best for their money and you are asked to rate two brands of the same supermarket item. Write a paragraph advising your readers which is the better buy. You can rate two brands of cola, or yogurt, or potato chips, or toothpaste, or ice cream, or chocolate chip cookies, or paper towels—any item you can get in a supermarket.

    Be sure to devise *enough* points to contrast. You can't, for example, do a well-developed paragraph on just the taste of two cookies. But you can also discuss texture, color, smell, price, fat content, calories, number of chocolate chips, and so on. If your instructor agrees, you may want to brainstorm topics or points of contrast with a group as a way of beginning the writing process. Then work on your own on the outline, drafts, and final version.

4. Compare or contrast your taste in music, or dress, or ways of spending leisure time, with that of another generation.

5. Examine the photograph of the two tall buildings. Then write a paragraph contrasting them. You can start by asking such questions as, Which seems more impressive? Is more inviting? Is more modern? Use the details of the photograph to support your topic sentence.

6. Interview a person of your age group who comes from a different part of the country. (Note: There may be quite a few people from different parts of the country in your class.) Ask him or her about similarities or differences between his or her former home and this part of the country. You could ask about similarities or differences in dress, music, dating, nightlife, ways to spend leisure time, favorite entertainers, or anything else that you like.

   After the interview, write a paragraph showing either that people of the same age group, but from different parts of the country, have different tastes in something like music or dress or that they share the same tastes in music, dress, and so on. Whichever approach you use, use details you collected in the interview.

7. If you have ever shopped online for sales or bargains offered by your favorite department store, contrast this experience with shopping inside the store itself. Select one specific store for this assignment, but be sure to contrast the specific differences between the two shopping choices. You should include three points of contrast in your paragraph.

◀ COLLABORATE 👥

8. Look carefully at the photograph of the two boys. Write a paragraph contrasting the mood of the boys with the atmosphere of the background.

Note: Additional writing options suitable for comparison or contrast-related assignments can be found after the professional reading, "Beautiful Daughter," which begins on page 610.

Name: _____ Section: _____

PEER REVIEW FORM FOR A COMPARISON OR CONTRAST PARAGRAPH

After you've written a draft of your paragraph, let a writing partner read it. When your partner has completed the form below, discuss the comments. Then repeat the same process for your partner's paragraph.

I think the topic sentence of this paragraph is _____

_____

_____

The pattern of this paragraph is (a) subject-by-subject or (b) point-by-point. (Choose one.)

The points used to compare or contrast are _____

_____

_____

The part of the paragraph I liked best is about _____

_____

The comparison or contrast is (a) easy to follow or (b) a little confusing. (Choose one.)

I have questions about or would like to know more about _____

_____

I would like to see a few more details about _____

I would like to take out the part about _____

I would like to add or change a transition in front of the words _____

_____

Other comments: _____

_____

_____

_____

_____

_____

_____

_____

Reviewer's Name: _____

CHAPTER 7
Classification

WHAT IS CLASSIFICATION?

When you **classify,** you divide something into different categories, and you do it according to some basis. For example, you may classify the people in your neighborhood into three types: those you know well, those you know slightly, and those you don't know at all. Although you may not be aware of it, you have chosen a basis for this classification. You are classifying the people in your neighborhood according to *how well you know them.*

Hints for Writing a Classification Paragraph

1. Divide your subject into three or more categories or types. If you are thinking about classifying DVD players, for instance, you might think about dividing them into cheap players and expensive players. Your basis for classification would be the price of DVD players. But you would need at least one more type—moderately priced players. Using at least three types helps you to be reasonably complete in your classification.

2. Pick one basis for classification and stick with it. If you are classifying DVD players by price, you cannot divide them into cheap, expensive, and Japanese. Two of the categories relate to price, but "Japanese" does not.

In the following examples, notice how one item does not fit its classification and has been crossed out.

fishermen

fishermen who fish every day
weekend fishermen
~~fishermen who own their own boat~~

(If you are classifying fishermen on the basis of how often they fish, "fishermen who own their own boat" does not fit.)

tests

essay tests
objective tests
~~math tests~~
combination essay and objective tests

(If you are classifying tests on the basis of the type of questions they ask, "math tests" does not fit, because it describes the subject being tested.)

3. Be creative in your classification. While it is easy to classify drivers according to their age, your paragraph will be more interesting if you choose another basis for comparison, such as how drivers react to a very slow driver in front of them.

4. Have a reason for your classification. You may be classifying to help a reader understand a topic or to help a reader choose something, or you may be trying to prove a point, to criticize, or to attack.

A classification paragraph must have a unifying reason behind it, and the detail for each type should be as descriptive and specific as possible. Determining your audience and deciding why you are classifying can help you stay focused and make your paragraph more interesting.

Exercise 1 **Finding a Basis for Classifying**

Write three bases for classifying each of the following topics. The first topic is done for you.

1. **topic to classify:** cats
   You can classify cats on the basis of

   a. their age _____

   b. their color _____

   c. how friendly they are _____

2. **topic to classify:** trucks
   You can classify trucks on the basis of

   a. _____

   b. _____

   c. _____

3. **topic to classify:** war movies
   You can classify war movies on the basis of

   a. _____

   b. _____

   c. _____

4. topic to classify: lakes

You can classify lakes on the basis of

a. _____

b. _____

c. _____

Exercise 2 **Identifying What Does Not Fit the Classification**

In each list below, one item does not fit because it is not classified on the same basis as the others on the list. First, determine the basis for the classification. Then cross out the one item on each list that does not fit.

1. topic: fish

basis for classification: _____

list: broiled fish
frozen fish
fried fish
baked fish

2. topic: rings

basis for classification: _____

list: earring
nose ring
toe ring
gold ring

3. topic: liars

basis for classification: _____

list: constant liars
frequent liars
occasional liars
vicious liars

4. topic: soldiers

basis for classification: _____

list: captain
sergeant
infantry
lieutenant

Exercise 3 **Finding Categories That Fit One Basis for Classification**

In the lines under each topic, write three categories that fit the basis of classification that is given. The first one is done for you.

1. **topic:** cartoons on television
   basis for classification: when they are shown
   categories:

   a. Saturday morning cartoons

   b. weekly cartoon series shown in the evening

   c. cartoons that are holiday specials

2. **topic:** snow
   basis for classification: its texture
   categories:

   a. _____

   b. _____

   c. _____

3. **topic:** doctors
   basis for classification: their specialty
   categories:

   a. _____

   b. _____

   c. _____

4. **topic:** computers
   basis for classification: price
   categories:

   a. _____

   b. _____

   c. _____

WRITING THE CLASSIFICATION PARAGRAPH IN STEPS

PREWRITING Gathering Ideas: Classification

First, pick a topic for your classification. The next step is to choose some basis for your classification.

Brainstorming a Basis for Classification

Sometimes the easiest way to choose one basis is to brainstorm about different types related to your topic and see where your brainstorming leads you. For example, if you were to write a paragraph classifying phone calls, you could begin by listing anything about phone calls that occurs to you:

Phone Calls

sales calls at dinner time   people who talk too long
short calls   calls I hate getting

calls in middle of night   wrong numbers
long-distance calls   waiting for a call

The next step is to survey your list. See where it is leading you. The list on phone calls seems to have a few items about *unpleasant phone calls:*

sales calls at dinner time
wrong numbers
calls in middle of night

Maybe you can label these "Calls I Do Not Want," and that will lead you toward a basis for classification. You might think about calls you *do not* want and calls you *do* want. You think further and realize that you want or do not want certain calls because of their effect on you.

You decide to use the effect of the calls on you as the basis for classification. Remember, however, that you need at least three categories. If you stick with this basis for classification, you can come up with three categories:

calls that please me
calls that irritate me
calls that frighten me

By brainstorming, you can then gather details about your three categories:

Added Details for Three Categories

calls that please me
from boyfriend

good friends

catch-up calls—someone I haven't talked to for a while

make me feel close

calls that irritate me
sales calls at dinner time

wrong numbers

calls that interrupt

invade privacy

calls that frighten me
emergency call in middle of night

"let's break up" call from boyfriend

change my life, indicate some bad change

Matching the Points Within the Categories

As you begin thinking about details for each of your categories, try to write about the same points in each type. For instance, in the list on phone calls, each category includes some details about who made the call:

calls that please me—from good friends, my boyfriend
calls that irritate me—from salespeople, unknown callers
calls that frighten me—from the emergency room, my boyfriend

Each category also includes some details about why you react to them in a specific way:

calls that please me—make me feel close
calls that irritate me—invade privacy
calls that frighten me—indicate some bad change

You achieve unity by covering the same points for each category.

Writing a Topic Sentence for a Classification Paragraph

The topic sentence for a classification paragraph should do two things:

1. It should mention what you are classifying.
2. It should indicate the basis for your classification by stating the basis or listing your categories, or both.

Consider the details on phone calls. To write a topic sentence about the details, you

1. mention what you are classifying: phone calls.
2. indicate the basis for classifying by (a) stating the basis (their effect on me) or (b) listing the categories (calls that please me, calls that irritate me, and calls that frighten me). You may also state both the basis and the categories in the topic sentence.

Following these guidelines, you can write a topic sentence like this:

I can classify phone calls according to their effect on me.

or

Phone calls can be grouped into the ones that please me, the ones that irritate me, and the ones that frighten me.

Both of these topic sentences state what you're classifying and give some indication of the basis for the classification. Once you have a topic sentence, you are ready to begin the planning stage of writing the classification paragraph.

 COLLABORATE ▶   (Exercise 4) **Creating Questions to Get Details for a Classification Paragraph**

Do this exercise with a partner or group. Each list below includes a topic, the basis for classifying that topic, and three categories. For each list, think of three questions that you could ask to get more details about the types. The first list is done for you.

1. **topic:** moviegoers
   basis for classification: how they behave during the movie
   categories: the quiet moviegoers, the irritating moviegoers, the obnoxious moviegoers
   questions you can ask:

   a. Does each type use a cell phone?

   b. Does each type talk during the movie?

   c. Does each type come and go during the movie?

2. **topic:** sports fans watching a televised game at home
basis for classification: how interested they are in the game
categories: fascinated fans, interested fans, bored fans
questions you can ask:

   a. _____

   b. _____

   c. _____

3. **topic:** people in line at the supermarket
basis for classification: their reason for shopping
categories: the party planners, the responsible parents, the healthy dieters
questions you can ask:

   a. _____

   b. _____

   c. _____

4. **topic:** people who send flowers
basis for classification: their motives for sending flowers
categories: the romantic, the thoughtful, the guilty
questions you can ask:

   a. _____

   b. _____

   c. _____

Exercise 5 **Writing Topic Sentences for a Classification Paragraph**

Review the topics, bases for classification, and categories in Exercise 4. Then, using that material, write a good topic sentence for each topic.

Topic Sentences

for topic 1: _____

_____

_____

for topic 2: _____

_____

_____

for topic 3: _____

_____

_____

for topic 4: _____

_____

_____

PLANNING Devising a Plan: Classification

Effective Order in Classifying

After you have a topic sentence and a list of details, you can create an outline. Think about which category you want to write about first, second, and so on. The order of your categories will depend on what you're writing about. If you're classifying ways to meet people, you can save the best for last. If you're classifying three habits that are bad for your health, you can save the worst one for last.

If you list your categories in the topic sentence, list them in the same order you will use to explain them in the paragraph.

Following is an outline for a paragraph classifying phone calls. The details have been put into categories. The underlined sentences have been added to clearly define each category before the details are given.

An Outline for a Classification Paragraph

topic sentence: Phone calls can be grouped into the ones that please me, the ones that irritate me, and the ones that frighten me.

category 1, details
There are some calls that please me.
They make me feel close to someone.
I like calls from my boyfriend, especially when he calls just to say he is thinking of me.
I like to hear from good friends.
I like catch-up calls.
These are calls from people I haven't talked to in a while.

category 2, details
There are some calls that irritate me.
These calls invade my privacy.
Sales calls always come at dinner time.
They offer me newspaper subscriptions or "free" vacations.
I get at least four wrong-number calls each week.
All of these calls irritate me, and I have to interrupt what I'm doing to answer them.

category 3, details
There are some calls that frighten me.
They are the calls that tell me about some bad change in my life.
I once got a call in the middle of the night.
It was from a hospital emergency room.
The nurse said my brother had been in an accident.
I once got a call from a boyfriend.
He said he wanted to break up.

You can use the following checklist to help you revise your own classification outline.

CHECKLIST: **A Checklist for Revising the Classification Outline**

✔ Do I have a consistent basis for classifying?

✔ Does my topic sentence mention what I am classifying and indicate the basis for classification?

✔ Do I have enough to say about each category in my classification?

✔ Are the categories presented in the most effective order?

✔ Am I using clear and specific details?

With a revised outline, you can begin writing your draft.

Exercise 6   **Recognizing the Basis for Classification Within the Topic Sentence**

The topic sentences below do not state a basis for classification, but you can recognize the basis nevertheless. After you've read each topic sentence, write the basis for classification on the lines provided. The first one is done for you.

1. topic sentence: Neighbors can be classified into complete strangers, acquaintances, and buddies.

   basis for classification: _how well you know them_

2. topic sentence: When it comes to car owners, there are those who never clean their cars; those who occasionally use the drive-through car wash; and those who wash, wax, and polish their cars every weekend.

   basis for classification: _____

3. topic sentence: Neighbors can be grouped into hostile, distant, and friendly.

   basis for classification: _____

4. topic sentence: Children fall into three types: the ones who willingly go to bed on a schedule, the ones who plead for more time, and the ones who refuse to go to bed at all.

   basis for classification: _____

Exercise 7   **Adding Details to a Classification Outline**   ◀ COLLABORATE

Do this exercise with a partner or group. In this outline, add details where the blank lines indicate. Match the points covered in the other categories.

> **topic sentence:** My jobs can be categorized into pleasant jobs, acceptable jobs, and unbearable jobs.
>
> **details:** My first job was a pleasant job.
> I worked at a small coffee shop.
> I worked behind the take-out counter.
> Business was steady but never hectic.
> The staff was friendly and helpful to new employees.
> The customers were regulars who enjoyed visiting the café.
> Another job was an acceptable job.
> I worked in the library at college.
> I worked at the book check-out and return counter.
> Sometimes there was no one in the library, and the job was boring.
>
> _____
>
> The library users sometimes got upset about overdue or missing books and library fines.
> My last job was an unbearable job.
> I worked at a movie theater.
> I sold tickets.
>
> _____
>
> There were very few staff members, so it was lonely.
>
> _____

DRAFTING Drafting and Revising: Classification

You can transform your outline into a first draft of a paragraph by writing the topic sentence and the details in paragraph form. As you write, you can begin combining some of the short sentences, adding details, and inserting transitions.

Transitions in Classification

Various transitions can be used in a classification paragraph. The transitions you select will depend on what you are classifying and the basis you choose for classifying. For example, if you are classifying roses according to how pretty they are, you can use transitions like "*one lovely kind* of rose," and "*another, more beautiful kind*," and "*the most beautiful kind*." In other classifications, you can use transitions like "the first type," "another type," or "the final type." In revising your classification paragraph, use the transitions that most clearly connect your ideas.

As you write your own paragraph, you may want to refer to a "kind" or a "type." For variety, try other words like "class," "group," "species," "form," or "version" if it is logical to do so.

After you have a draft of your paragraph, you can revise and review it. The following checklist may help you with your revisions.

CHECKLIST: **A Checklist for Revising the Draft of a Classification Paragraph**

✔ Does my topic sentence state what I am classifying?

✔ Does it indicate the basis of my classification?

✔ Should any of my sentences be combined?

✔ Do my transitions clearly connect my ideas?

✔ Should I add more details to any of the categories?

✔ Are the categories presented in the most effective order?

Following is a draft of the classification paragraph on phone calls. Compare these changes to the outline on page 164:

- An introduction has been added in front of the topic sentence to make the paragraph smoother.
- Some sentences have been combined.
- Some details have been added.
- Transitions have been added.
- A final sentence has been added so that the paragraph makes a stronger point.

A Draft of a Classification Paragraph

I get many phone calls, but they fit into three types. Phone calls can be grouped into the ones that please me, the ones that irritate me, and the ones that frighten me. There are some calls that please me because they make me feel close to someone. I like calls from my boyfriend, especially when he calls just to say he is thinking of me. I like to hear from my good friends. I like catch-up calls, the calls from people I haven't talked to in a while that fill me in on what friends have been doing. There are also calls that irritate me because they invade my privacy. Sales calls, offering me newspaper subscriptions and "free" vacations, always come at dinner time. In addition, I get at least four wrong-number calls each week. All these calls irritate me, and I have to interrupt what I'm doing to answer them. The more serious calls are the ones that frighten me. They are the calls that tell me about some bad change in my life. Once, in the middle of the night, a call from a hospital emergency room told me my brother had been in an accident. Another time, a boyfriend called to tell me he wanted to break up. When I get bad news by phone, I realize that the telephone can bring frightening calls as well as friendly or irritating ones.

Exercise 8 **Combining Sentences for a Better Classification Paragraph**

The paragraph below has some short sentences that would be more effective if they were combined. Combine each pair of underlined sentences into one sentence. Write the new sentence in the space above the old ones.

In the cat world, there are cozy cats, tolerant cats, and independent cats.

Cozy cats are devoted to their people. <u>A cozy cat sleeps in its owner's bed. It does</u>

it every night. <u>It curls up as close as possible to its favorite person.</u> A cozy cat usually greets its owner at the door. <u>It rubs against its owner's legs. It purrs. It is thrilled to be reunited with its loved one.</u> A cozy cat sits in people's laps. <u>It naps on the couch. It does this while people are watching television.</u> Tolerant cats are somewhat like cozy cats, but they are not so clingy. On cold nights, a tolerant cat may sleep in its owner's bed, yet it may also choose to spend many nights in other places. A tolerant cat may look up when its owner comes home. It will not, however, bother to get up from its nap unless it is hungry. If its owner is watching television, a tolerant cat may allow itself to be petted. <u>*Unfortunately*, this kind of cat may suddenly leap out of petting mode. It may then grab a person's fingers and nip.</u> The third kind of cat is an independent cat. An independent cat never sleeps with people. <u>It likes to sleep in its own space. It sleeps under the bed. Sometimes it sleeps at the top of a high bookcase. Sometimes it sleeps in the closet.</u> When its owner returns home, an independent cat does not seem to notice. If its loved one greets an independent cat, the cat will allow itself to be petted. The independent cat is not a lap cat. While its owner is watching television, an independent cat is exploring the house or looking out the window. <u>Cats are like people. They come with different personalities.</u> Cat owners find something to love in each type of cat.

Exercise 9   **Identifying Transitions in a Classification Paragraph**

Underline all the transitions in the paragraph below. The transitions may be words or groups of words.

In my family, I can classify my relatives according to how long they like to talk on the phone. First, there are those who will talk forever if I allow them. This class of talker includes my mother and my sister. My mother has been known to carry on one long phone conversation while she prepares and cooks a three-course dinner. My sister had to take a second job to pay her phone bill. Both women will talk to me about anything from the song they just heard on the radio to my cousin's divorce. Another kind of talker likes to chat but not to talk for hours. My brother is this type of talker. His calls are frequent but short. He may

call me several times a day, when he gets out of work and wants to tell me about

his day, when he needs a ride to college, or when he wants to talk about his girl-

friend. Each time, he sticks to his subject and talks no more than ten minutes. The

final type of caller in my family is the rapid responder. My father and my uncle are

members of this group. They never call unless they are returning my call. When

they do call, they spend as little time as possible on the phone. They give one-

word answers to my questions or tell me dinner will be "six o'clock at Aunt Con-

nie's house. Good bye." To them, a phone is used only to convey essential

information. Family members like my mother, father, and brother are different in

their phone habits, and these differences reveal the varieties of personality within

one family.

POLISHING Polishing and Proofreading: Classification

Following is the final version of the classification paragraph on phone calls.
Compare the draft of the paragraph on page 167 to the final version and you'll
notice these changes:

- The first sentence has been rewritten so that it is less choppy, and
  a word of transition, "My," links the second sentence to the first.
- Some words have been eliminated and sentences rewritten so that
  they are not too wordy.
- The word choice has been refined: "bad change" has been replaced
  by "crisis," "someone" has been changed to "a person I care about"
  to make the detail more precise, and "irritate" has been changed to
  "annoy" to avoid repetition.

A Final Version of a Classification Paragraph
(Changes from the draft are underlined.)

   <u>I get many phone calls, but most of them fall into one of three types.</u> My phone
calls can be grouped into the ones that please me, the ones that irritate me, and the
ones that frighten me. There are some calls I want to receive because they make me
feel close to <u>a person I care about</u>. I like calls from my boyfriend, especially when he
calls just to say he is thinking of me. I like to hear from my good friends. I like catch-
up calls from <u>friends</u> I haven't talked to in a while. There are also calls I don't want
because they invade my privacy. Sales calls, offering me newspaper subscriptions
and "free" vacations, always come at dinner time. In addition, I get at least four
wrong number calls each week. All these calls <u>annoy</u> me, and I have to interrupt
what I'm doing to answer them. The more serious calls are the ones I really don't
want to receive. They are the calls that tell me about some <u>crisis</u> in my life. <u>I once got</u>

a midnight call from a hospital emergency room, informing me my brother had been in an accident. Another time, a boyfriend called to tell me he wanted to break up. When I get bad news by phone, I realize that the telephone can bring frightening calls as well as friendly or irritating ones.

Before you prepare the final version of your own classification paragraph, check your latest draft for errors in spelling, punctuation, typing, and copying.

For your information: A sample classification essay based on this topic and following the same writing steps can be found in Chapter 12, pp. 304–308.

Exercise 10   **Proofreading to Prepare the Final Version**

Following are two classification paragraphs with the kinds of errors it is easy to overlook when you prepare the final version of an assignment. Correct the errors, writing above the lines. The first paragraph has thirteen errors; the second has eleven errors.

1. Sleepers fall into three categories and they are the light sleepers, the average sleepers, and the heavy sleepers. Light sleepers have a hard time falling asleep and staying asleep. My mother is a light sleeper, and she cant fall asleep unless the room is totaly quite and completely dark. She have a sleep mask and earplugs to help her get to sleep. Even after she falls asleep, she does not sleep soundly. She swears she can hear me tiptoe acrost the living room when she is wearing her earplugs in bed. She wakes up and reads, raids the refridgerator, or turns on the television at least twice each night. Unlike my mother, I am a average sleeper. I fall asleep fairly easily, unless I have a problem on my mind. Even if I toss and turn until I get to sleep, I tend to sleep through the night. Loud noises like car alarms or sirens can wake me, but I am usually deep in sleep until my clock radio blasts me awake. My roommate is a much deeper sleeper then I am. He falls into the class of sleeper who can fall asleep in an instant. He can climb into bed and be unconscience in a minute. I may come in late, slam the door, and bump into a chair, but my roommate won't wake up. A car wreck outside the window doesn't disturb him. He sleeps trough the alarm clock, every morning until I shake him into awareness. He has a gift for sleeping that I wish he could share with my mother.

2. For those who love chocolate treats, there are three kinds of deserts: mildly chocolate, real chocolate, and extreme chocolate. Mildly choclate desserts have a chocolate flavor, but they are lite on satisfaction. Such desserts include chocolate Popsicles or chocolate-covered marshmallow cookies. These desserts, are not rich enough in deep chocolate flavor. Real chocolate desserts have more of that essential ingredient In this category, there are chocolate layer cakes, fudge brownies, and chocolate cream pies. These goodies offer a more, chocolate experience. For those who can never have enough chocolate, there is a third type of dessert, in the extreme chocolate class. Extreme chocolate desserts come with names like Death by Chocolate or Chocolate Overload. They contain multiple forms of chocolate such as, layers of cake, chocolate chips, chocolate icing, bits of fudge, chunks of brownies, chocolate ice cream, chocolate pudding, and chocolate-cover nuts. The names of these desserts says it all. These goodies must be eaten in small portions because chocolate lovers could die of happiness if they ate to much

Lines of Detail: A Walk-Through Assignment

Write a paragraph that classifies bosses on the basis of how they treat their employees. To write the paragraph, follow these steps.

Step 1: List all of the details you can remember about bosses you have worked for or known.

Step 2: Survey your list. Then list three categories of bosses, based on how they treat their employees.

Step 3: Now that you have three categories, study your list again, looking for matching points for all three categories. For example, all three categories could be described by this matching point: where the boss works.

Step 4: Write a topic sentence that (a) names what you are classifying and (b) states the basis for classification or names all three categories.

Step 5: Write an outline. Check that your outline defines each category, uses matching points for each category, and puts the categories in an effective order.

Step 6: Write a draft of the classification paragraph. Check the draft, revising it until it has specific details, smooth transitions, and effective word choice.

Step 7: Before you prepare the final copy of your paragraph, check your last draft for any errors in punctuation, spelling, word choice, or mechanics.

Writing Your Own Classification Paragraph

When you write on any of these topics, be sure to work through the stages of the writing process in preparing your classification paragraph.

 COLLABORATE ▶

1. Write a classification paragraph on any of the topics below. As a first step, you will need to narrow the topic. For example, instead of classifying all cars, you can narrow the topic to *sports cars*, or fears to *irrational* fears. If your instructor agrees, brainstorm with a partner or a group to come up with (a) a basis for your classification, (b) categories related to the basis, and (c) points you can make to give details about each of the categories.

horror movies	drivers	restaurants
romantic movies	birthdays	dates
children	cars	scams
parents	cell phone options	salespeople
students	fans at a concert	fears
professors	fans at a sports event	weddings
coaches	drivers	excuses

 COLLABORATE ▶

2. Below are some topics. Each one already has a basis for classification. Write a classification paragraph on one of these choices. If your instructor agrees, work with a partner or group to brainstorm categories, matching points and details for the categories.

Classify
   a. exams on the basis of how *difficult* they are.
   b. weekends on the basis of how *busy* they are.
   c. Valentines on the basis of how *romantic* they are.
   d. breakfasts on the basis of how *healthy* they are.
   e. skin divers (or some other recreational athletes) on the basis of how *experienced* they are.
   f. singers on the basis of the *kind of audience* they appeal to.
   g. television commercials on the basis of what *time of day or night* they are broadcast.
   h. radio stations on the basis of what *kind of music* they play.
   i. urban legends on the basis of how *illogical* they are.

3. Look carefully at the photograph on the next page. Then use its details to write a classification paragraph with this topic sentence:

College students can be classified according to the way they react to a professor's explanation of a concept.

Note: Additional writing options suitable for classification-related assignments can be found after the professional reading, "Three Disciplines for Children," which begins on page 613.

Name: _____ **Section:** _____

PEER REVIEW FORM FOR CLASSIFICATION PARAGRAPH

After you've written a draft of your classification paragraph, let a writing partner read it. When your partner has completed the form below, discuss his or her comments. Then repeat the same process for your partner's paragraph.

This paragraph classifies _____ (write the topic).

The basis for the classification is

_____

_____

The matching points are

_____

_____

_____

A part that could use more or better details is _____

_____

I have questions about or would like to know more about _____

_____

I would like to see more specifics about

_____

_____

I would like to take out the part about _____

_____

The part of this paragraph I like best is _____

_____

Additional comments: _____

_____

_____

_____

_____

_____

_____

Reviewer's Name: _____

CHAPTER 8
Definition

1 term 2 classification — 3 distinguishing
category(?) characteristics

WHAT IS DEFINITION?

A **definition** paragraph is one that explains *what a term means to you*. You can begin thinking about what a term means by consulting the dictionary, but your paragraph will include much more than a dictionary definition. It will include a personal definition.

You can select several ways to explain the meaning of a term. You can give examples, you can tell a story, or you can contrast your term with another term. If you were writing a definition of perseverance, for example, you could do one or more of the following: you could give examples of people you know who have persevered, you could tell a story about someone who persevered, or you could contrast perseverance with another quality, like impatience. You could also write about times when perseverance is most needed or about the rewards of perseverance.

Hints for Writing a Definition Paragraph

1. Pick a word or phrase that has a personal meaning for you and that allows you room to develop your idea. Remember that you will be writing a full paragraph on this term. Therefore, a term that can be defined quickly, in only one way, is not a good choice. For example, you would not have much to say about terms like "cauliflower" or "dental floss" unless you have strong personal feelings about cauliflower or dental floss. If you don't have such feelings, your paragraph will be very short.

When you think about a term to define, you might think about some personal quality you admire or dislike. If some quality provokes a strong reaction in you, you will probably have something to write about that term.

2. The topic sentence should have three parts. Include these items:

- the *term* you are defining
- the broad *class* or *category* into which your term fits
- the specific *distinguishing characteristics* that make the term different from all the others in the class or category

Each of the following topic sentences could be a topic sentence for a definition paragraph because it has the three parts.

Resentment is the *feeling* that *life has been unfair.*

A *clock-watcher* is a *worker* who *is just putting in time, not effort.*

3. Select an appropriate class or category when you write your topic sentence.

not this: Resentment is a thing that makes you feel life has been unfair. (Resentment is a feeling or an attitude. Say so.)

not this: Resentment is when you feel life has been unfair. ("When" is a word that refers to a time, like noon or 7:00 p.m. Resentment is a feeling, not a time.)

not this: Resentment is where a person feels life has been unfair. ("Where" is a word that refers to a place, like a kitchen or a beach. Resentment is not a place; it is a feeling.)

but this: Resentment is the feeling that life has been unfair.

4. Express your attitude toward the term you are defining in the "distinguishing characteristics" part of the topic sentence. Make that attitude clear and specific.

not this: Resentment is the feeling that can be bad for a person. (Many feelings can be bad for a person. Hate, envy, anger, and impatience, for instance, can all be bad. What is special about resentment?)

not this: Resentment is an attitude of resenting another person or a circumstance. (Do not define a word with another form of the word.)

but this: Resentment is the feeling that life has been unfair.

5. Use specific and concrete examples to explain your definition. *Concrete* terms refer to things you can see, touch, taste, smell, or hear. Using concrete terms and specific examples will make your definition interesting and clear.

You may be asked to define an *abstract* idea like happiness. Even though an abstract idea cannot be seen, touched, tasted, smelled, or heard directly, you can give a personal definition of it by using concrete terms and specific examples:

not this: Happiness takes place when you feel the joy of reaching a special goal. ("Joy" and "special goal" are abstract terms. Avoid defining one abstract term by using other abstract terms.)

but this: I felt happiness when I saw my name at the top of the list of athletes picked for the team. Three months of daily, six-hour practices had paid off, and I had achieved more than I had set out to do. (The abstract idea of happiness is linked to a specific idea of feeling happiness.)

If you remember to show, not tell, your reader what your term means, you'll have a better definition. Be especially careful not to define a term with another form of that term.

Exercise 1   **Recognizing Abstract and Concrete Words**

In the list below, put an *A* by the abstract words and a *C* by the concrete words.

1. _____ ignorance   11. _____ cruelty
2. _____ automobile   12. _____ lightning
3. _____ liberty   13. _____ morality
4. _____ laughter   14. _____ skyscraper
5. _____ window   15. _____ health
6. _____ personality   16. _____ trust
7. _____ stadium   17. _____ optimism
8. _____ confidence   18. _____ magazine
9. _____ security   19. _____ generosity
10. _____ loyalty   20. _____ imagination

Exercise 2   **Completing a Topic Sentence for a Definition**

Following are unfinished topic sentences for definition paragraphs. Finish each sentence so that the sentence expresses a personal definition of the term and has the three requirements for a definition's topic sentence.

1. A peacemaker is a person who *makes peace with people*

2. A road hog is a driver who *is all over the road & dont give others room*

3. A bargain is an item *something that ya get a good deal on.*

4. A trendsetter is a person who *sets an thread of stylish clothing for ext*

_____

5. The teacher's pet is the student who *sucks up to teacher*

6. A phony is a person who *fake*

7. A role model is a person who *others look up to*

_____

8. A starter home is a residence that _____

_____

9. The head of the family is the relative who _____

_____

10. A pack rat is a person who _____

_____

Exercise 3   **Recognizing Problems in Topic Sentences**
              for Definition Paragraphs

Review the three components that should be included in the topic sentence
for a definition paragraph. Then read the topic sentences below, put an X
next to each sentence that has a problem, and underline the part of the sentence that is faulty.

1. _____ Stamina is the ability to remain strong for long periods.

2. ___X___ Aggression is the habit of being aggressive to others.

3. _____ Stubbornness is where a person refuses to change his or
           her mind.

4. _____ Concentration is the ability to focus on one idea.

5. _____ Maturity is the stage at which people take responsibility for
           their own choices.

6. _____ A brat is a child who insists on having his or her own way.

7. _____ Happiness is when a person feels uplifted.

8. _____ Pessimism is a tendency to expect the worst.

9. _____ Faith is a thing that helps people get by.

10. _____ Financial security is the position of being financially secure.

COLLABORATE ▶   Exercise 4   **Writing Examples for Definition Paragraphs**

Below are incomplete statements from definition paragraphs. Complete them
in the spaces provided by writing specific examples. When you have completed the statements, share your work with a group. After each group member has read his or her examples aloud, discuss the examples. Which examples
did you like best? Which are the clearest and most specific? Do some examples lead to a different definition of a term than other examples do?
   The first part of each sentence has been started for you.

1. I first saw betrayal in action when _____

_____

_____

_____

Another example of betrayal was my experience with _____

_____

_____

_____

_____

2. The cruelest comment I ever heard was _____

_____

_____

It was cruel because _____

_____

_____

A person in the news who I think is cruel is_____

_____

because he/she _____

_____

3. The person who represents kindness to me is _____

because this person _____

_____

I was called on to show kindness when _____

_____

_____

4. A situation when a person must be tactful is _____

_____

_____

I saw tact in action when _____

_____

_____

WRITING THE DEFINITION PARAGRAPH IN STEPS

PREWRITING Gathering Ideas: Definition

To pick a topic for your definition paragraph, begin with some personality trait or type of person. For instance, you might define "the insecure person." If you listed your first thoughts, your list might look like this:

> the insecure person
> someone who is not emotionally secure
> wants (needs?) other people to make him or her feel good
> no self-respect

Using Questions to Get Details

Often, when you look for ideas to define a term, you get stuck with big, general statements or abstract words, or you simply cannot come up with enough to say. If you are having trouble getting ideas, think of questions about your term. Jot these questions down without stopping to answer them. One question can lead you to another question. Once you have five or more questions, you can answer them, and the answers will provide details for your definition paragraph.

If you were writing about the insecure person, for example, you could begin with questions like these:

> What are insecure people like?
> What behavior shows a person is insecure?
> How do insecure people dress or talk?
> What makes a person insecure?
> Why is insecurity a bad trait?
> How do insecure people relate to others?
> Does insecurity hurt the insecure person? If so, how?
> Does the insecure person hurt others? If so, how?

By scanning the questions and answering as many as you can, you can add details to your list. Once you have a longer list, you can review it and begin to group the items on the list. Following is a list of grouped details on the insecure person.

Grouped Details on the Insecure Person

wants (needs?) other people to make him or her feel important

no self-respect

insecure people have to brag about everything

a friend who brags about his car

they tell you the price of everything

they put others down

saying bad things about other people makes insecure people feel better

insecure people can never relax inside

can never enjoy being with other people

other people are always their competitors

must always worry about what others think of them

The Topic Sentence

Grouping the details can help you arrive at several main ideas. Can they be combined and revised to create a topic sentence? Following is a topic sentence on the insecure person that meets the requirements of naming the term, placing it in a category, and distinguishing the term from others in the category:

The *insecure person* is a *person* who *needs other people to make him or her feel respected and important.*

Once you have a topic sentence, you can begin working on the planning stage of the paragraph.

Exercise 5   **Designing Questions to Gather Details**

Following are terms that could be defined in a paragraph. For each term, write five questions that could lead you to details for the definition. The first one has been done for you, as an example.

1. **term:** arrogance

   questions: a.   Do I know anyone who displays arrogance?

   b.   Is there any celebrity I think is arrogant?

   c.   What is an arrogant action?

   d.   What kind of remark is an example of arrogance?

   e.   Why are people arrogant?

2. **term:** the life of the party

   questions: a.   Who is the life of the party.

   b.   What is the life of the party.

   c.   Why are people life of the party.

   d.   Does the party depend on it.

   e.   Could you learn to be the life of the party.

3. **term:** foolishness

   questions: a.   What is foolishness

   b.   Why are people foolish

c. _Have bod done any thing that was foolish,_
d. _Can foolishness hurt bu._
e. _is foolishness fun._

4. **term:** insight

   questions: a. _____

   b. _____

   c. _____

   d. _____

   e. _____

Exercise 6   **Grouping Related Ideas for a Definition Paragraph**

Following is a list of ideas for a definition paragraph. Read the list several times; then group all of the ideas on the list into one of the three categories below. Put the letter of the category next to each idea.

Categories:

   G = how thrift can be **good**

   B = how thrift can be **bad**

   W = **why** thrift isn't valued today

List

1. _____ Most people today buy disposable items like razors, paper towels, and dustcloths and are not used to saving and reusing.

2. _____ A person who is thrifty in small ways can save money for big-budget items.

3. _____ Some thrifty people become hoarders of useless items like newspapers.

4. _____ Thrift can lead to stinginess toward others in need.

5. _____ If people learned thrift, they would recycle more.

6. _____ Easily available credit cards discourage thrift.

7. _____ Being thrifty can lead to creative ways to manage money and live simply.

8. _____ People who shop less have more time to spend with friends, family, and nature.

9. _____ It's fun to find bargains instead of paying full price.

10. _____ People who overdo thriftiness can become money-obsessed.

PLANNING **Devising a Plan: Definition**

To make an outline for a definition paragraph, start with the topic sentence and list the grouped details. Often, a first outline does not have many examples or concrete, specific details. A good way to be sure you put specific details and concrete examples into your paragraph is to put some shortened version of them into your revised outline. If you compare the following outline with the grouped list of details on pages 180–181, you will see how specific details and concrete examples have been added.

An Outline for a Definition Paragraph

topic sentence:	The insecure person is a person who needs other people to make him or her feel respected and important.
details:	Insecure people have to brag about everything.
	An insecure friend may brag about his car.
added detail	Insecure people wear expensive jewelry and tell you what it costs.
added detail	They brag about their expensive clothes.
added detail	They make sure they wear clothes with trendy labels, another kind of bragging.
	Insecure people put others down.
	Saying bad things about others makes insecure people feel better.
added example	When some friends were talking about Susan's great new job, Jill had to make mean remarks about Susan.
	Jill hated having Susan look like a winner.
	Insecure people can never relax inside.
	They can never enjoy being with other people.
	Other people are always their competitors.
added example	Luke can't enjoy any game of basketball unless he is the star.
	Insecure people must always worry about what others think of them.

When you prepare your own definition outline, use the following checklist to help you revise.

CHECKLIST: A Checklist for Revising a Definition Outline

✔ Does my topic sentence include a category and the characteristics that show how my term is different from others in the category?

✔ Have I defined my term so that it is different from any other term?

✔ Am I being concrete and specific in the details?

✔ Do I have enough examples?

✔ Do my examples relate to the topic sentence?

✔ Are my details in the most effective order?

With a revised outline, you are ready to begin writing a rough draft of your definition paragraph.

> **Exercise 7** **Rewriting a Topic Sentence for a Definition Paragraph**

Below is an outline in which the topic sentence does not make the same point as the rest of the outline. Rewrite the topic sentence so that it relates to the details.

topic sentence: Buyer's remorse is a sadness that comes after shopping.

details: When I was twelve, I wanted a new game.
My parents said it was too expensive, so I saved my allowance for months.
I also earned money working on my uncle's garden.
Finally, I was able to buy the game.
As soon as I left the store with the game in my hand, I began to feel let down.
By the time I played the game at home, it seemed stupid and boring.
I experienced a bad case of buyer's remorse last year.
I bought my first car.
It was five years old, and it was sold "as is."
I desperately wanted my own transportation, so I ignored its flaws and signed a loan agreement.
Within a week, I was experiencing buyer's remorse.
I realized that the car needed a new battery, a new radiator, and work on the electrical system.
I have felt less intense remorse over smaller purchases like clothes that didn't fit or a bargain camera that didn't work right.
Each time I suffer from buyer's remorse, I swear to be more rational in my buying habits.

Rewrite the topic sentence: _____

_____

> **Exercise 8** **Revising an Example to Make It More Concrete and Specific**

The following outline contains one example that is too abstract. In the lines provided, rewrite the example that is too abstract, using more specific, concrete details.

topic sentence: Intuition is knowledge that cannot be explained by thinking.

details:

example 1   My grandmother has a strong intuition.
As a sixteen-year-old in Mexico, she met a young man who drove a moving van.
"That's the man I'm going to marry," she proclaimed, but she never became friends with him.

Thirty years, two husbands, and two children later, she was a widow living in San Diego.

The man who came to move her furniture to a new apartment looked familiar.

He was the truck driver she had met in Mexico.

They were married a year later.

example 2   My father has inherited my grandmother's gift of intuition.

Last summer he had to fly somewhere.

But two days before the flight, he got a funny feeling.

He decided to change his reservation.

My mother said something.

But he insisted.

It turns out that the flight he had originally scheduled got into trouble.

example 3   Occasionally, I have little flashes of intuition.

Once, for example, my friends were all excited about a new player on our basketball team.

He was confident, outgoing, and smart.

He would come home with us, charm our mothers, help us out, and make us laugh.

Yet some inner voice told me he was not right.

Somehow, I was not totally surprised when he committed an armed robbery and disappeared.

There are things we can know without knowing how we know them.

The revised example: _____

_____

_____

_____

_____

_____

_____

_____

_____

_____

DRAFTING Drafting and Revising: Definition

To write the first draft of your definition paragraph, you can rewrite the outline in paragraph form, combining some of the short sentences and adding more details. Remember that your purpose in this definition paragraph is to explain your personal understanding of a term. Therefore, you want to be sure that your topic sentence is clear and that your explanation connects your details to the topic sentence. A careful use of transitions will link your details to your topic sentence.

Transitions

Because you can define a term in many ways, you can also use many transitions. If you are listing several examples in your paragraph, you can use transitions like "first," "second," and "finally." If you are contrasting your term with another, you can use transitions like "on the other hand" or "in contrast." You may want to alert or remind the reader that you are writing a definition paragraph by using phrases like "can be defined as," "can be considered as," "means that," or "implies that."

Because many definitions rely on examples, the transitions below are ones you may want to use.

INFO BOX: **Transitions for a Definition Paragraph**

a classic case of _____ is _____	in fact	another time
another case	in one case	sometimes
for example	in one instance	specifically
for instance	one time	

The Draft

Following is a draft of the definition paragraph on the insecure person. When you read it, you'll notice several changes from the outline on page 183.

- Transitions have been added in several places. Some transitions let the reader know an example is coming, some transitions link one point about the topic to another point, and other transitions connect an example to the topic sentence.
- Examples have been made concrete and specific.
- The word choice has been improved.

A Draft of a Definition Paragraph

(Transitions are underlined.)

The insecure person is a person who needs other people to make him or her feel respected and important. The insecure person loves to brag about everything. For instance, a friend may brag about his car. He tells everyone he meets that he drives a Corvette. An insecure person tells you the price of everything. He wears expensive jewelry and tells you what it costs, like the person who always flashes his Rolex watch. Another insecure person will brag about her expensive clothes or make sure she always wears clothes with trendy labels, another kind of bragging. Bragging is not the only way an insecure person tries to look good; he or she may put other people down. Saying bad things about other people can put the insecure person on top. For instance, some friends were recently talking about another friend, Susan, who had just started a great new job. Jill had to add some mean remarks about how lucky Susan had been to get the job because Susan really wasn't qualified for it. Jill hated having Susan look like a winner. The insecure person can hurt others <u>but also</u> suffers inside. <u>Such a person</u> can never relax because he or she always sees other people as competitors. <u>An example of this attitude is</u> seen in Luke, a college acquaintance who always plays pickup basketball games. Even though the games are just for fun, Luke can't enjoy any game unless he is the star. Luke is a typically insecure person, for he must always worry about what others think of him.

The following checklist may help you to revise the draft of your own definition paragraph.

CHECKLIST: **A Checklist for Revising the Draft of a Definition Paragraph**

✔ Is my topic sentence clear?

✔ Have I written enough to define my term clearly?

✔ Is my definition interesting?

✔ Could it use another example?

✔ Could it use more details?

✔ Do I need to combine any sentences?

✔ Do I need any words, phrases, or sentences to link the examples or details to the topic sentence?

✔ Do I need any words, phrases, or sentences to reinforce the topic sentence?

Exercise 9 **Adding Examples to a Draft of a Definition Paragraph**

Two of the following paragraphs need examples with concrete, specific details to explain their points. Where the lines indicate, write an example with concrete, specific details. Each example should be at least two sentences long. The first paragraph is done for you.

1. Listlessness is the feeling that nothing is worth starting. After a hectic week, I often wake up on Saturday morning feeling listless. I just do not have the energy to do the things I intended to do. <u>I may have planned to wash my car, for example, but I cannot bring myself to get going. I cannot put together the bucket, detergent, brushes, and window cleaner I need to start the process. I tell myself, "Why wash the car? It will probably rain anyway."</u> Another time I feel listless is when I am faced with a big assignment. <u>For instance, I hate to start a term paper because there is so much to do. I have to think of a topic, do research, read, take notes, plan, write, and revise. When I am faced with so</u>

many things to do, I don't do anything. I tell myself it is not worth starting because I will probably get a bad grade on the paper anyway. I put off getting started. I let listlessness get the better of me.

    2. Strivers are people who constantly work to improve themselves or their situation. There is a striver in every school. _____

_____

_____

_____ The workplace is another spot for recognizing strivers.

_____

_____

_____ Many successful

athletes are strivers. _____

_____

_____ Strivers

have the stamina to keep working and the drive to hold on to their goals.

    3. Road rage is a dangerous expression of the frustrations of driving. Crowded roads, long commutes, and personal stress can provoke a person to ex-press road rage. Common expressions of road rage involve language or car signal-ing. _____

_____

_____ Some road rage gets more

personal. _____

_____

_____ Road rage can even become deadly.

_____

_____

_____

_____ Then the foolishness of road rage becomes tragic.

Exercise 10   **Identifying the Words That Need Revision in a Definition Paragraph**

The following paragraph has too many vague, abstract words. Underline the words that you think should be replaced with more specific or concrete words or examples.

Courage is the ability to face fear. Some people show physical courage when they risk their lives to save children from burning buildings or other things like that. Explorers show courage when they face unknown territory. Astronauts are brave explorers; so are researchers in arctic stations. They face dangers no person has ever experienced, yet they go for it. There is another kind of courage that faces inner fear. A person may be terrified of flying, for instance. That person may simply decide never to fly. If a time comes when the person has to fly, to get to the deathbed of a loved one or for whatever other reason, he or she needs inner courage. In another case, a family may be living with a member who has something wrong with him or her. This member, who drinks too much or uses drugs, may be hurting the entire family as well as doing dangerous things to himself or herself. The family may be trying to survive by denying the problem. It takes inner courage for all of the family members to admit one of their own needs help.

Exercise 11   **Combining Sentences in a Definition Paragraph**

The following definition paragraph has some short, choppy sentences that could be combined. These pairs or clusters of sentences are underlined. Combine each pair or cluster into one smooth sentence, and write the new sentence in the lines above the old ones.

A sense of humor is a gift for seeing the funny side of almost any situation. My best friend has a sense of humor. He works at a service station. It is a boring job. He sits in a glass booth for hours, yet he always manages to find something that amuses him. It can be a poodle dressed in a pink sweater. The poodle was sitting in a pink convertible. It can be a car with a strange bumper sticker or a carload of teens dancing to the music of the car stereo. Even rude customers make him laugh. He is learning to do comic imitations of their insults. Another person with a sense of humor is my girlfriend. Her attitude has brightened up many stressful occasions. <u>One day she and I were stuck on an interstate highway. We had a flat tire. We had no spare tire.</u> It was about ninety degrees outside, cars were whizzing by, and our cell phone was dead. "Oh well," said my girlfriend, "at least I can get a tan while we wait for help. Where's the sunscreen?" <u>Drivers on that highway must have been surprised to see us. We were camped out on the roadside. We were laughing.</u>

> **Exercise 12** **Adding the Right Transitions to a Definition Paragraph**

In the following paragraph, circle the correct transition in each of the pairs.

Calmness is a sense of accepting one's situation. A woman who faces surgery in the morning may spend the night tossing and turning. On the other hand/ Specifically, another woman facing the same surgery may sleep soundly because she knows she cannot control her operation and must rely on her doctor. The second woman is calm. Sometimes/ For example, a person feels calm because of his or her own skills. A driver in a snowstorm can handle the weather calmly because he has driven in snow many times. One time/ Another example of calm behavior based on confidence is some students taking a final examination. All students would like to skip the examination, but some can accept the challenge calmly if they feel prepared. Finally/ Another case, there are people whose careers demand calmness. Firefighters, law enforcement officers, and emergency medical workers know that every day can be dangerous for them, yet they accept that danger and calmly do their jobs. Clearly/ In fact, the ability to remain calm takes strength and understanding.

> **POLISHING** Polishing and Proofreading: Definition

Before you prepare the final version of your definition paragraph, check your latest draft to see if it needs a few changes. You may want to check for good transitions, appropriate word choice, and effective details. If you compare the draft on pages 186–187 to the following final version of the paragraph on the insecure person, you will see a few more revisions:

- The wording has been improved so that it is more precise.
- Transitions have been added to reinforce the topic sentence.
- The word "you" has been taken out so that the paragraph is consistent in person.

A Final Version of a Definition Paragraph

(Changes from the draft are underlined.)

The insecure person is a person who needs other people to make him or her feel respected and important. <u>To get respect</u>, the insecure person loves to brag about everything. For instance, a friend may brag about his car. He tells everyone he meets that he drives a Corvette. An insecure person tells <u>people</u> the price of everything. He wears expensive jewelry and tells <u>people</u> what it costs, like the man who always flashes his Rolex watch. Another insecure person will brag about her expensive clothes or make sure she wears clothes with trendy labels, another kind of bragging. Bragging isn't the only way an insecure person tries to look good; he or she may also <u>criticize</u> other people. <u>Criticizing</u> others can put the insecure person on top. For instance, some friends were recently talking about another friend, Susan, who had just started a great new job. Jill had to add some mean remarks about how lucky Susan had been to get the job because Susan really wasn't qualified for it. Jill couldn't stand to have Susan look like a winner. The insecure person <u>like Jill</u> can hurt others but also suffers inside. Such a person can never relax because he or she always sees other people as competitors. An example of this attitude can be seen in Luke, a college acquaintance who always plays pickup basketball games. Even though the games are just for fun, Luke can't enjoy any game unless he is the star. Luke is a typically insecure person, for he must always worry about what others think of him.

As you prepare the final version of your definition paragraph, check your latest draft for any errors in spelling, punctuation, typing, and copying.

For your information: A sample definition essay based on this topic and following the same writing steps can be found in Chapter 12, pp. 309–314.

Exercise 13   **Correcting Errors in the Final Version of a Definition Paragraph**

Below are two definition paragraphs with the kinds of errors it is easy to overlook in a final version. Correct the errors by writing above the lines. There are twelve errors in the first paragraph and nine in the second paragraph.

1. Anticipation is the excited feeling a person experences before a happy event. The best example, of anticipation is the jittery joy of a child about to celebrate his or her birthday. People who's jobs require a traditional Monday-through-Friday schedule experience anticipation on Friday morning and it builds during the rest of the day. Students are fill with expectation weeks before summer vacation begins, and High School seniors anticipate graduation for nearly a year. Anticipation can make events better, for instance, Halloween would not be as much fun without the planning of extravagant custumes and buying of special candy. There are even occassions that are so exciting they include lively preliminary events. For example, people have baby showers before the birth of a baby and hold family dinners the nite before a wedding. Every one likes to look foreward to life's high points; therefore, anticipation can brighten many dull days.

2. A doubter is a person who questions the truth of statements he or she hears or reads. A doubter can be a valueable person to have aroun. A doubter wont sign a lease or a contract for a loan without studying it carefully Doubters are not likely to become the victims of fraud or Internet swindles. On the other hand, a person who constantly challenges the truth can make other people irritated or depressed. Even if the weather forcast is for sun the doubter sees clouds gathering at the horizon and tells her boyfriend she doesn't want to go to the beach. If three of his friends praise the latest blockbuster movie, a doubter will say, "It can't be that good." Doubters tend to expect the worst. If a doubter won the lottery, he wouldnt believe it, until he had the check in his hand or, even better, deposited it in a bank. If you tell a doubter she looks beautiful, she might frown and say, "Really?" Doubters may say they are just being realistic, or they may claim to think more deeply than others. However even doubters need to trust sometime.

Lines of Detail: A Walk-Through Assignment

Write a paragraph that gives a personal definition of a secure person. To write the paragraph, follow these steps:

Step 1: List all your ideas about a secure person.

Step 2: Write at least five questions that can add details about a secure person. Answer the questions as a way of adding details to your list.

Step 3: Group your details; then survey your groups.

Step 4: Write a topic sentence that includes the term you are defining, puts the term into a category, and distinguishes the term from others in the category.

Step 5: Write an outline. Begin by writing the topic sentence and the groups of details. Then add more details and specific examples.

Step 6: Write a draft of your paragraph. To revise, check that you have enough examples, that your examples fit your definition, and that the examples are in an effective order. Combine any choppy sentences, and add transitions.

Step 7: Before you prepare the final version of your definition paragraph, check the punctuation, word choice, transitions, and grammar of your latest draft.

Writing Your Own Definition Paragraph

When you write on any of these topics, be sure to work through the stages of the writing process in preparing your definition paragraph.

1. Define an abstract term using concrete, specific details. Choose from the following list. You can begin by looking up the term in a dictionary to be sure you understand the dictionary meaning. Then write a personal definition.

◄ COLLABORATE

   You can begin by freewriting. If your instructor agrees, you can read your freewriting to a group for reactions and suggestions. If you prefer, you can begin by brainstorming a list of questions to help you define the term. Again, if your instructor agrees, you can work with a group to develop brainstorming questions. Here is the list of abstract terms:

loyalty	generosity	bliss
charm	style	patience
boredom	charisma	persistence
initiative	consideration	prejudice
ambition	selfishness	envy
suspicion	fear	loneliness
failure	shame	irritation
anger	self-deception	self-discipline

2. Write a definition of a type of person. Develop your personal definition with specific, concrete details. You can choose one of the following types or choose your own type.

◄ COLLABORATE

   Freewriting on the topic is one way to begin. If your instructor agrees, you can read your freewriting to a group for reactions and suggestions. You can also begin by brainstorming a list of questions to help you define your term. If your instructor agrees, you can work with a group to develop brainstorming questions. Following is the list of types.

the procrastinator	the bully	the daredevil
the braggart	the bodybuilder	the jock
the chocaholic	the neatness fanatic	the apologizer
the organizer	the fitness fanatic	the joker
the inventor	the manipulator	the dreamer
the worrywart	the whiner	the buddy
the workaholic	the old reliable friend	the fan
the compulsive liar	the Mr./Ms. Fixit	the achiever

3. Think of one word that best defines you. In a paragraph, define that word, using yourself as a source of examples and details. To begin, you may want to freewrite about several words that define you; then you can select the most appropriate one.

 COMPUTER ▶

4. Using Google or a similar search engine, type in the words "Web log" and "blog." Investigate as many definitions as you can of the term "blog." Based on this information, write a definition of this term and assume your audience is a group of adults who have never read or written a blog. Your definition may include examples of blogs from the fields of politics, entertainment, news, business, and education.

5. Study the photograph below. Then write a paragraph that defines the emotion you see in the picture. Be sure you first have a word to identify the emotion before continuing with your planning.

Note: Additional writing options suitable for definition-related assignments can be found after the professional reading, "Breaking the Bonds of Hate," which begins on page 616.

Name: _____   **Section:** _____

PEER REVIEW FORM FOR A DEFINITION PARAGRAPH

After you've written a draft of your definition paragraph, let a writing partner read it. When your partner has completed the form below, discuss the comments. Then repeat the same process for your partner's paragraph.

In the topic sentence, the term being defined is placed in this category or class: _____

In the topic sentence, the characteristic(s) that make(s) the term different from others in its class or category is/are _____

_____

_____

The most enjoyable or interesting part of this definition starts with the words _____

_____

The part that could use a clear example or more details starts with the words _____

_____

I have questions about or would like to know more about _____

_____

I would like to take out the part about _____

_____

Other comments: _____

_____

_____

_____

_____

_____

_____

_____

_____

_____

Reviewer's Name: _____

CHAPTER 9
Cause and Effect

WHAT IS CAUSE AND EFFECT?

Almost every day, you consider the causes or effects of events so that you can make choices and take action. In writing a paragraph, when you explain the **reasons** for something, you are writing about **causes.** When you write about the **results** of something, you are writing about **effects.** Often in writing, you consider both the causes and effects of a decision, an event, a change in your life, or change in society, but in this chapter, you will be asked to *concentrate on either causes (reasons) or effects (results)*.

Hints for Writing a Cause or Effect Paragraph

1. Pick a topic you can handle in one paragraph. A topic you can handle in one paragraph is one that is not too big and doesn't require research.

Some topics are so large that you probably can't cover them in one paragraph. Topics that are too big include ones such as

Why People Get Angry
Effects of Unemployment on My Family

Other topics require you to research the facts and to include the opinions of experts. They would be good topics for a research paper, but not for a one-paragraph assignment. Topics that require research include ones such as

The Causes of Divorce
The Effects of Television Viewing on Children

When you write a cause or effect paragraph, choose a topic you can write about by using what you already know. That is, make your topic smaller and more personal. Topics that use what you already know are ones such as

Why Children Love Video Games
The Causes of My Divorce
What Enlistment in the Navy Did for My Brother
How Alcoholics Anonymous Changed My Life

2. Try to have at least three causes or effects in your paragraph. Be sure you consider immediate and remote causes or immediate and remote effects. Think about your topic and gather as many causes or effects as you can *before* you start drafting your paragraph.

An event usually has more than one cause. Think beyond the obvious, the **immediate cause,** to more **remote causes.** For example, the immediate cause of your car accident might be the other driver who hit the rear end of your car. But more remote causes might include the weather conditions or the condition of the road.

Situations can have more than one result, too. If you take Algebra I for the second time and you pass the course with a C, an **immediate result** is that you fulfill the requirements for graduation. But there may be other, **more remote results.** Your success in Algebra I may help to change your attitude toward mathematics courses, or may build your confidence in your ability to handle college work, or may lead you to sign up for another course taught by the same teacher.

3. Make your causes and effects clear and specific. If you are writing about why short haircuts are popular, don't write, "Short haircuts are popular because everybody is getting one" or "Short haircuts are popular because they are a trend." If you write either of those statements, you have really said, "Short haircuts are popular because they are popular."

Think further. Have any celebrities been seen with this haircut? Write the names of actors, athletes, or musicians who have the haircut, or the name of the movie and the actor who started the trend. By giving specific details that explain, illustrate, or describe a cause or effect, you help the reader understand your point.

4. Write a topic sentence that indicates whether your paragraph is about causes or effects. You should not announce, but you can *indicate.*

not this: The effects of my winning the scholarship are going to be discussed. (an announcement)
but this: Winning the scholarship changed my plans for college. (indicates effects will be discussed)

You can *list* a short version of all your causes or effects in your topic sentence, like this:

The high price of concert tickets has enriched a few performers and promoters, excluded many fans, and threatened the future of live entertainment.

You can just *hint* at your points by summarizing them, like this:

> The high price of concert tickets has brought riches to a few but hurt many others.

Or you can use words that *signal* causes or effects.

> **words that signal causes:** reasons, why, because, motives, intentions
> **words that signal effects:** results, impact, consequences, changed, threatened, improved

Exercise 1 **Selecting a Suitable Topic for a Cause or Effect Paragraph**

Below is a list of topics. Some are suitable for a cause or effect paragraph. Some are too large to handle in one paragraph, some would require research, and some are both too large and would require research. Put an *X* next to any topic that is not suitable.

1. _____ Why My Child Loves Sugary Sweets

2. _____ Effects of Cosmetic Surgery

3. _____ Reasons I Chose a Community College

4. _____ The Impact of Technology on the Workplace

5. _____ The Causes of Violent Crime

6. _____ The Effects of Welfare on Our Society

7. _____ How Drug Dealing Changed My Neighborhood

8. _____ Why the Number of Single-Parent Families Is Increasing

9. _____ The Causes of Rising Oil Prices

10. _____ The Impact of the Internet on Children

Exercise 2 **Recognizing Cause and Effect in Topic Sentences**

In the following list, if the topic sentence is for a cause paragraph, put *C* next to it. If the sentence is for an effect paragraph, put *E* next to it.

1. _____ A visit to Ecuador had surprising consequences for me.

2. _____ I took a job on a fishing boat for a chance to work outdoors, to do physically demanding work, and to take a break from my life as a student.

3. _____ The mayor has three motives for supporting the new park.

4. _____ Until I joined one, I never knew how a gym can change a a person's body and attitudes.

5. _____ My daughter's cell phone has created conflicts over her social life and family responsibilities.

6. _____ College students need their families because home provides meals, sympathy, and a place to do laundry.

7. _____ People shop online because it is easy, it is quick, and it offers bargains.

8. _____ My father's remarriage had a deep impact on my younger brother.

9. _____ My husband's background is the key to why he struggled with depression.

10. _____ Vegetarians are changing the restaurant industry.

WRITING THE CAUSE OR EFFECT PARAGRAPH IN STEPS

PREWRITING Gathering Ideas: Cause or Effect

Once you've picked a topic, the next—and very important—step is getting ideas. Because this paragraph will contain only causes *or* effects and details about them, you must be sure you have enough causes or effects to write a developed paragraph.

Freewriting on a Topic

One way to get ideas is to freewrite on your topic. Because causes and effects are so clearly connected, you can begin by freewriting about both and then choose one, causes or effects, later.

If you were thinking about writing a cause or effect paragraph on owning a car, you could begin by freewriting something like this:

Freewriting on Owning a Car

A car of my own. Why? I needed it. Couldn't get a part time job without one. Because I couldn't get to work. Needed it to get to school. Of course I could have taken the bus to school. But I didn't want to. Feel like a grown-up when you have a car of your own. Freedom to come and go. I was the last of my friends to have a car. Couldn't wait. An old Camaro. But I fixed it up nicely. Costs a lot to maintain. Car payments, car loan. Car insurance.

Now you can review the freewriting and make separate lists of causes and effects you wrote down:

causes (reasons)

needed to get a part time job
needed to get to school
my friends had cars

effects (results)

feel like a grown-up
freedom to come and go
costs a lot to maintain
car payments
car loan
car insurance

Because you have more details on the effects of owning a car, you decide to write an effects paragraph.

Your list of effects can be used several ways. You can add to it if you think of ideas as you are reviewing your list. You can begin to group ideas in your list and then add to it. Following is a grouping of the list of effects; grouping helps you see how many effects and details you have.

effects of getting my own car

effect 1:   I had to pay for the car and related expenses
details: costs a lot to maintain
          car payments
          car loan
          car insurance

effect 2:   I had the freedom to come and go.
details: none

effect 3:   I felt like a grown-up.
details: none

Will these effects work in a paragraph? One way to decide is to try to add details to the ones that have no details. Ask questions to get those details.

effect 2:   I had the freedom to come and go.

What do you mean?

Well, I didn't have to beg my father for his truck anymore. I didn't have to get rides from friends. I could go to the city when I wanted. I could ride around just for fun.

effect 3:   I felt like a grown up.

What do you mean, "like a grown up"?

Adults can go where they want, when they want. They drive themselves.

If you look carefully at the answers to the questions above, you'll find that the two effects are really *the same.* By adding details to both effects, you'll find that both are saying that owning a car gives you the adult freedom to come and go.

So the list needs another effect of owning a car. What else happened? How else did things change when you got your car? You might answer:

I worried about someone hitting my car.
I worried about bad drivers.
I wanted to avoid the scratches you get in parking lots.

With answers like these, your third effect could be

I became a more careful driver.

Now that you have three effects and some details, you can rewrite your list. You can add details as you rewrite.

List of Effects of Getting My Own Car

effect 1:   I had to pay for the car and related expenses.
details: costs a lot to maintain
            car payments
            car loans
            car insurance

effect 2:   I had the adult freedom to come and go.
details: didn't have to beg my father for his truck
              didn't have to get rides from friends
              could go to the city when I wanted
              could ride around for fun
effect 3:   I became a more careful driver.
details: worried about someone hitting the car
              worried about bad drivers
              wanted to avoid the scratches cars get in parking lots

Designing a Topic Sentence

With at least three effects and some details for each effect, you can create a topic sentence. The topic sentence for this paragraph should indicate that the subject is the *effects* of getting a car. You can summarize all three effects in your topic sentence, or you can just hint at them. A possible topic sentence for the paragraph can be

> Owning my own car cost me money, gave me freedom, and made me more careful about how I drive.

or

> Once I got a car of my own, I realized the good and bad sides of ownership.

With a topic sentence and a fairly extensive list of details, you are ready to begin the planning step in preparing your paragraph.

Exercise 3 **Devising Questions for a Cause or Effect Paragraph**   ◀ COLLABORATE

Following are four topics for cause or effect paragraphs. For each topic, write five questions that could lead you to ideas on the topic. (The first one is completed for you.) After you've written five questions for each topic, give your list to a member of your writing group. Ask him or her to add one question to each topic and then to pass the exercise on to the next member of the group. Repeat the process so that each group member adds to the lists of all the other members.

Later, if your instructor agrees, you can answer the questions (and add more questions and answers) as a way to begin writing a cause or effect paragraph.

1. **topic:** the effects of camera phones on crime
   questions that can lead to ideas and details:
   a. Are unsuspecting people photographed and blackmailed?
   b. Can the cameras be used to photograph confidential documents?
   c. Are the cameras being used by Peeping Toms?
   d. Can criminals use the camera phones to photograph banks?

e. *Can citizens photograph a crime in progress?* _____

additional questions: *Can citizens photograph a suspect or* _____

perpetrator? _____

Can police use the cameras in surveillance? _____

2. **topic:** the effects of e-mail on the workplace
   questions that can lead to ideas and details:

   a. _____

   b. _____

   c. _____

   d. _____

   e. _____

   additional questions: _____

   _____

   _____

3. **topic:** the effects of high gas prices on drivers
   questions that can lead to ideas and details:

   a. _____

   b. _____

   c. _____

   d. _____

   e. _____

   additional questions: _____

   _____

   _____

4. **topic:** why Americans want DVD players in their cars
   questions that could lead to ideas and details:

   a. _____

   b. _____

   c. _____

   d. _____

   e. _____

   additional questions: _____

   _____

   _____

Exercise 4 **Creating Causes or Effects for Topic Sentences**

For each of the following topic sentences, create three causes or effects, depending on what the topic sentence requires. The first one is completed for you.

1. **topic sentence:** Sticking to an exercise routine has both improved and complicated my life.

    a. I am in better physical shape than I have been in years.

    _____

    b. The physical exercise also gives me a mental boost.

    _____

    c. I now have to find time to fit my routine into my busy schedule.

2. **topic sentence:** There are several reasons why some elderly people may seem unfriendly to young people.

    a. _____

    _____

    b. _____

    _____

    c. _____

    _____

3. **topic sentence:** Computers can have negative effects on those who use them for entertainment.

    a. _____

    _____

    b. _____

    _____

    c. _____

    _____

4. **topic sentence:** Taking a course or two in a short summer term can be rewarding for college students.

    a. _____

    _____

    b. _____

    _____

    c. _____

    _____

PLANNING Devising a Plan: Cause or Effect

With a topic sentence and a list of causes (or effects) and details, you can draft an outline of your paragraph. Once you have a rough outline, you can work on revising it. You may want to add to it, to take out certain ideas, to rewrite the topic sentence, or to change the order of the ideas. The following checklist may help you revise your outline.

CHECKLIST: A Checklist for Revising the Outline of a Cause or Effect Paragraph

✔ Does my topic sentence make my point?

✔ Does it indicate whether my paragraph is about causes or effects?

✔ Does the topic sentence fit the rest of the outline?

✔ Have I included enough causes or effects to make my point?

✔ Have I included enough details?

✔ Should I eliminate any ideas?

✔ Is the order of my causes or effects clear and logical?

The Order of Causes or Effects

Looking at a draft outline can help you decide on the best order for your reasons or results. There is no single rule for organizing reasons or results. Instead, you should think about the ideas you are presenting and decide on the most logical and effective order.

For example, if you are writing about some immediate and some long-range effects, you might want to discuss the effects in a **time order.** You might begin with the immediate effect, then discuss what happens later, and end with what happens last of all. If you are discussing three or four effects that are not in any particular time order, you might save the most important effect for last, for an **emphatic order.** If one cause leads to another, then use the **logical order** of discussing the causes.

Compare the following outline on owning a car with the list of effects on pages 200–201. Notice that in the outline, the carefree side of owning a car comes first, and the cares of owning a car, the expense and the worry, come later. The topic sentence follows the same order.

An Outline for an Effects Paragraph

revised topic sentence:	Owning my own car gave me freedom, cost me money, and made me careful about how I drive.
effect 1	I had the adult freedom to come and go.
	I didn't have to beg my father for his truck.
details	I didn't have to get rides from my friends.
	I could go to the city when I wanted.
	I could ride around for fun.

effect 2	⎰ I had to pay for the car and related expenses.
	⎱ A car costs a lot to maintain.
details	⎰ I had car payments.
	⎱ I had a car loan to pay.
	⎱ I had car insurance.
effect 3	⎰ I became a more careful driver.
	⎱ I worried about someone hitting the car.
details	⎰ I worried about bad drivers.
	⎱ I wanted to avoid the scratches cars can get in a parking lot.

Once you have a revised outline of your cause or effect paragraph, you are ready to begin writing your draft.

Exercise 5 **Writing Topic Sentences for Cause or Effect Outlines**

Following are two outlines. They have no topic sentences. Read the outlines carefully several times. Then write a topic sentence for each.

1. topic sentence: _____

_____

_____

details: After I am stuck working overtime, I don't want to talk to anybody when I get home.
I ignore my wife when she asks me questions.
I ignore my daughter, who wants attention.
When I am overworked, I also refuse to do any family chores.
I pile all the dirty dishes in the sink for someone else to do.
I leave the garbage for someone else to take out.
I let my wife put my daughter to bed.
Long working hours can make me impatient and irritable.
I can't stand waiting for my dinner to heat.
I snap at my daughter if she jumps on the furniture.
I am likely to quarrel with my wife.

2. topic sentence: _____

_____

_____

details: Alan was extremely good-looking.
He had thick, dark hair and deep brown eyes.
He was tall and muscular.
Alan had a good job and could support me.
He worked as a manager at an athletic store.
He owned his own sports car.
He rented an apartment in a complex with a gym and a pool.
The main reason I married Alan was to get away from home.

I couldn't stand my mother's rules any more.
I wanted more freedom to come and go.
I wanted to be treated like an adult.

Exercise 6 **Revising the Order of Causes or Effects**

Below are topic sentences and lists of causes or effects. Re-order each list according the directions given at the end of the list. Put *1* by the item that would come first, and so forth.

1. **topic sentence:** Miriam moved out of state for several reasons.

    _____ She was offered a better job.

    _____ She wanted a warmer climate.

    _____ She wanted to get away from her ex-boyfriend, who was stalking her.

    Use this order: From least important to most important.

2. **topic sentence:** A focus on auto safety has changed the standard equipment on cars.

    _____ Front air bags cushion the shock of head-on collisions.

    _____ Shoulder harnesses held people more tightly and safely in place than lap belts.

    _____ Lap belts were a way to prevent people from being ejected from or thrown against the windows of a car.

    Use this order: Time order.

3. **topic sentence:** Living on my own has had negative and positive effects on me.

    _____ I missed my family and always having someone to talk to.

    _____ I eventually began to enjoy my own privacy.

    _____ I gradually learned to depend on my own inner resources.

    Use this order: The order indicated by the topic sentence, from bad to good.

Exercise 7 **Developing an Outline**

The following outlines need one more cause or effect and details for that cause or effect. Fill in the missing parts.

1. **topic sentence:** Falling in love can be both wonderful and terrifying.
    effect 1: The moment I fell in love for the first time, the rush of my emotions made the world seem a better place.
    details: Even if it was raining, the weather seemed perfect.
    Strangers seemed friendly and approving.
    Every pleasant sensation, like warmth or comfort, seemed magnified.

effect 2: Being in love seems to give a person a purpose in life.
details: My brother thought about his girlfriend day and night.
He kept planning their future.
He would replay every encounter with her and enjoy every detail.

effect 3: _____

_____

details (at least two sentences): _____

_____

_____

_____

_____

2. **topic sentence:** People give many reasons for waiting until the last minute to file their income tax returns.
   cause 1: Some complain that it takes longer to complete than they expected.
   details: They may say they couldn't find all the receipts and documents they needed.
They may argue that the tax forms are too complicated.
   cause 2: Others complain they forgot about the deadline.
   details: Some say that the tax forms came so early they put them aside and lost track of the deadline.
Others say they had so many other obligations that the income tax forms slipped their mind.
A few say they got sick and forgot the due date until friends started talking about filing the returns.

   cause 3: _____

_____

   details (at least two sentences): _____

_____

_____

_____

_____

DRAFTING **Drafting and Revising: Cause or Effect**

Once you have an outline in good order, with a sufficient number of causes or effects and a fair amount of detail, you can write a first draft of the paragraph. When the first draft is complete, you can read and reread it, deciding how you'd like to improve it. The following checklist may help you revise.

> **CHECKLIST:** **A Checklist for Revising the Draft of a Cause or Effect Paragraph**
>
> ✔ Does my topic sentence indicate cause or effect?
>
> ✔ Does it fit the rest of the paragraph?
>
> ✔ Do I have enough causes or effects to make my point?
>
> ✔ Do I have enough details for each cause or effect?
>
> ✔ Are my causes or effects explained clearly?
>
> ✔ Is there a clear connection between my ideas?
>
> ✔ Have I shown the links between my ideas?
>
> ✔ Do I need to combine sentences?
>
> ✔ Do I need an opening or closing sentence?

Linking Ideas in Cause or Effect

When you write about how one event or situation causes another, or about how one result leads to another, you have to be very clear in showing the connections between events, situations, or effects. One way to be clear is to rely on transitions. Some transitions are particularly helpful in writing cause and effect paragraphs.

> **INFO BOX:** **Transitions for a Cause or Effect Paragraph**
>
> **For cause paragraphs:**
>
> | | | | |
> |---|---|---|---|
> | because | for | for this reason | since |
> | due to | | | |
>
> **For effect paragraphs:**
>
> | | | | |
> |---|---|---|---|
> | as a result | hence | then | thus |
> | consequently | in consequence | therefore | so |

Making the Links Clear

Using the right transition is not always enough to make your point. Sometimes you have to write the missing link in your line of thinking so that the reader can understand your point. To write the missing link means writing phrases, clauses, or sentences that help the reader follow your point.

> **not this:** Many mothers are working outside the home. Consequently, microwave ovens are popular.
>
> **but this:** Many mothers are working outside the home and have less time to cook. Consequently, microwave ovens, which can cook food in minutes, are popular.

The hard part of making clear links between ideas is that you have to put yourself in your reader's place. Remember that your reader cannot read your mind, only your paper. Connections between ideas may be very clear in your mind, but you must spell them out on paper.

Revising the Draft

Below is a draft of the paragraph on owning a car. When you read it, you'll notice many changes from the planning stage on pages 204–205:

- The details on "car payments" and "a car loan" said the same thing, so the repetition has been cut.
- Some details about the costs of maintaining a car and about parking have been added.
- The order of the details about the costs of a car has been changed. Now, paying for a car comes first; maintaining it comes after.
- Sentences have been combined.
- Transitions have been added.

A Draft of an Effects Paragraph

(**Transitions are underlined.**)

      Owning my own car gave me freedom, cost me money, and made me more careful about how I drive. <u>First of all</u>, my car gave me the adult freedom to come and go. I didn't have to beg my father for his truck or get rides from my friends any more. I could go to the city or even ride around for fun when I wanted. <u>On the negative side,</u> I had to pay for the car and related expenses. I had to pay for the car loan. I also paid for car insurance. <u>A car costs a lot to maintain, too.</u> I paid for oil changes, tune-ups, tires, belts, and filters. <u>With so much of my money put into my car,</u> I became a more careful driver. I worried about someone hitting the car and watched out for bad drivers. <u>In addition,</u> I wanted to avoid the scratches a car can get in a parking lot, so I always parked far away from other cars.

Exercise 8   **Making the Links Clear**

Following are ideas that are linked, but their connection is not clearly explained. Rewrite each pair of ideas, making the connection clear.

1. It was raining outside. Therefore, I didn't go to Wellington Market.

Rewritten: _____

_____

_____

_____

(**Hint:** Is it an outdoor market?)

2. Young teens see musicians and actors with elaborate tattoos. These celebrities seem cool, so the young teens want to get tattoos.

Rewritten: _____

_____

_____

_____

(**Hint:** Do the young teens want to look cool?)

3. I shouldn't have watched that horror movie last night. I couldn't get to sleep until 3:00 a.m.

Rewritten: _____

_____

_____

(**Hint:** Did the frightening parts of the movie make you anxious?)

4. Some cities are facing massive traffic jams on the highways. As a result, the cities have created carpool-only lanes.

Rewritten: _____

_____

_____

_____

(**Hint:** Are the carpool-only lanes designed to attract drivers to share rides? What makes the lanes attractive?)

Exercise 9 **Revising a Paragraph by Adding Details**

Each of the following paragraphs is missing details. Add details, at least two sentences, to each paragraph.

1. I have decided to study nursing because the field can offer me job security, mobility, and meaningful work. I come from a family in which both parents had to struggle to find steady work. As a result, job security is important to me. There is a great demand for nurses, not only in hospitals, but in clinics, rehabilitation centers, retirement homes, and the military. I want to know that years of education will lead me to a growing profession. Another reason that I find nursing attractive is that the field is open anywhere in the country. If I want to start my career at home, I can. On the other hand, if I decide to move to California or Chicago, I can be confident that I will find work in my field. My most important reason for choosing nursing is that the field helps others. _____

_____

_____

_____

_____

When I become a nurse, I hope to find a job I can work in for a long time, in many places, and with self-respect.

2. Surviving a hurricane has had a great impact on me. When a major hurricane devastated my community, it first brought me stunned horror. My apartment was blown apart, my car was crushed, and my neighborhood was without power or water for weeks. I couldn't even call my family because my cell phone wasn't working. Gradually, I felt myself becoming stronger and more determined. Government relief workers and volunteers arrived, and weeks turned into months of slow recovery. I drew hope from small incidents like the volunteer who distributed bags of ice in the searing heat, and later from large events like the reconstruction of my apartment building. However, the most important and lasting effect of the hurricane was my new gratitude for the simple joys of being alive.

_____

_____

_____

Living through a hurricane was horrible, but it taught me how to appreciate daily life.

Exercise 10   Revising a Draft by Combining Sentences

Combine the underlined sentences in the following paragraph. Write your combinations in the space above the original sentences.

There are three good reasons why television advertisers put children in food commercials. One reason is that the commercials appeal to anxious parents. <u>One particular kind of commercial appeals to these parents. It is the cereal commercial. This commercial has happy children.</u> Cereal is usually eaten at breakfast, when most parents are in a hurry to get to work and get their children to day care or school on time. <u>Unfortunately, children tend to be slow on workday mornings.</u>

<u>They resist getting dressed. They play with their food. Other times they refuse to eat it.</u> When parents see television children eating their cereal or even offering it to their brother or sister, the parents feel hope. Maybe their child will rush to eat this brand of cereal. Then everyone can get to work or school on time. Another group that is attracted to commercials featuring children and food is the children themselves. <u>The children in food advertisements are adorable. They are adorable as they eat their burgers. They are adorable when they drink their juice.</u> Not only are these children cute, they are also popular. In food commercials, children eat potato chips with friends and munch on pizza with their Little League team. Lastly, they are loved. In the advertisements, a grandfather smiles as he shares milk and cookies with a little boy, and a mother beams at her children as she serves them steamy mugs of soup. <u>All children want to be adorable. All children want to be popular. All children want to be loved. They learn lessons from the commercials.</u> They learn to link the food products with their emotional needs. Finally, adults who are not parents are drawn to these commercials. Everyone was a child once, and an advertisement with a little boy and an ice cream cone dripping all over his clothes can make adults smile. <u>It might even make someone think. It might get someone to think about how much fun it would be to be a child again.</u> Of course, no advertisement can offer a return to childhood, but it can link an ice cream cone to a pleasant feeling.

POLISHING Polishing and Proofreading: Cause or Effect

Following is the final version of the paragraph on owning a car. When you contrast the final version with the draft on page 209, you'll notice several changes:

- An introductory sentence has been added.
- Some sentences have been combined.
- Transitions have been revised.
- Some words have been changed so that the language is more precise.

Changes in style, word choice, sentence variety, and transitions can all be made before you decide on the final version of your paragraph. You may also want to add an opening or closing sentence to your paragraph.

A Final Version of an Effects Paragraph
(Changes from the draft are underlined.)

<u>When I bought my first car, I wasn't prepared for all the changes it made in my life.</u> Owning my own car gave me freedom, cost me money, and made me careful about how I drive. First of all, my car gave me the adult freedom to come and go. I didn't have to beg my father for his truck or get rides from my friends anymore. I could go to the city or even ride around for fun when I wanted. On the negative side, I had to pay for the car and related expenses. <u>I had to pay for both the car loan and car insurance</u>. A car costs <u>money</u> to maintain, too. I paid for oil changes, tune-ups, tires, belts, and filters. With so much of my money put into my car, I became a more careful driver. I worried about someone hitting the car and watched out for bad drivers. <u>To avoid dangers in the parking lot as well as on the road</u>, I always parked <u>my car far</u> away from other cars, <u>keeping my car safe from scratches</u>.

Before you prepare the final version of your cause or effect paragraph, check your latest draft for errors in spelling, punctuation, typing, and copying.

For your information: A sample effects essay based on this topic and following the same writing steps can be found in Chapter 12, pp. 315–319.

Exercise 11   **Correcting a Final Copy of a Cause or Effect Paragraph**

Following are one cause and one effects paragraph with the kinds of errors it is easy to overlook when you prepare the final version of an assignment. Correct the errors, writing above the lines. There are thirteen errors in the first (effects) paragraph and twelve errors in the second (cause) paragraph.

1. Studying a forine language taught me more than I expected. The first thing I learned was enough spanish to help me fullfil a college language requirement. It wasn't easy to grasp this new language and I struggled to learn all the vocabulary we were assign. The grammer was even harder; because I am not to good with grammar in English. One lesson I learned from the coarse was sympathy for all the people who come to this country and have to learn English. I now realize how difficult it is to grasp a new language. I was lucky to learn the new language in my own land, but I cant imagine having to learn one in a new land where every sign, every newspaper, and every set of directions is in strange words. Finely, my Spanish class made me eager to visit a Spanish-speaking country. My teacher made the language come alive by teaching us about the customs, culture, and even the food of Spanish-speaking people in different countries. Althogh I am not ready to speak Spanish like a native, I would love to try out my few words in a place like Mexico or Costa Rica. It would be a wonderful way to keep learning about the language and the people who speak it

2. I gave my grandmother a cat for tree reasons. The first reason was necessity. I found a poor, thin kitten in an alley near my school last week and I couldn't leave her there. On the other hand, I couldn't bring her home. My apartment manager don't allow pets. As I searched for a home for the cat, I thought of my grandmother. My Grandmother recently lost my grandfather, and she has been filling very depress. It was hard for her to get out of bed and face the day alone. I wanted to help her, and to cheer her up. If she had a cat to feed, she would have to get up in the mourning, I thought. In addition, a curious kitten wood give my grandmother someone to play with and even to talk to. My final reason was selfish. I loved that kitten. I couldn't take it to a shelter and never know its fate. With the kitten in my grandmother house, I could visit often and all 3 of us (my grandmother, the cat, and I) would be happy.

Lines of Detail: A Walk-Through Assignment

Write a paragraph on this topic: The Effects of High Gas Prices on Drivers. To write your paragraph, follow these steps:

Step 1: Go back to Exercise 3 on page 201. Topic 3 is the same topic as this assignment. If you have already done that exercise, you have five or more questions that can lead you to ideas and details. If you haven't done the exercise, do Topic 3 now.

Step 2: Use the answers to your questions to prepare a list of ideas and details. Put the items on your list into groups of effects and related details. Add to the groups until you have at least three effects (and related details) of high gas prices on drivers.

Step 3: Write a topic sentence that fits your effects.

Step 4: Write an outline. Check that your outline has sufficient details and that you have put the effects in the best order.

Step 5: Write a rough draft of your paragraph. Revise it until you have enough specific details to explain each effect and the links between your ideas are smooth and clear. Check whether any sentences should be combined and whether your paragraph could use an opening sentence or a concluding one.

Step 6: Before you prepare the final lines copy of your paragraph, check your latest draft for word choice, punctuation, transitions, and spelling.

Writing Your Own Cause or Effect Paragraph

When you write on any of the following topics, be sure to work through the stages of the writing process in preparing your cause or effect paragraph.

1. Write a cause paragraph on one of the following topics. You can create the topic by filling in the blanks.

   Why I Chose _____

   Why I Stopped _____

   Why I Enjoy _____

   Why I Started _____

   Why I Bought _____

2. Write a one-paragraph letter of complaint to the manufacturers of a product you bought or to the company that owns a hotel, restaurant, airline, or some other service you used. In your letter, write at least three reasons why you (a) want your money refunded or (b) want the product replaced. Be clear and specific about your reasons. Be sure your letter has a topic sentence.

   ◄ COLLABORATE

   If your instructor agrees, read a draft of your letter to a writing partner, and ask your partner to pretend to be the manufacturer or the head of the company. Ask your partner to point out where your ideas are not clear or convincing and where you make your point effectively.

3. Think of a current fad or trend. The fad can be a popular style of clothing, kind of movie, kind of music, a sport, a pastime, an actor, an athlete, a gadget, an invention, an appliance, and so on. Write a paragraph on the causes of this fad or trend or the effects of it.

   ◄ COLLABORATE

   If your instructor agrees, begin by brainstorming with a group. Create a list of three or four fads or trends. Then create a list of questions to ask (and answer) about each fad or trend. If you are going to write about causes, for example, you might ask questions like these:

   What changes in society have encouraged this trend?
   Have changes in the economy helped to make it popular?
   Does it appeal to a specific age group? Why?
   Does it meet any hidden emotional needs? For instance, is it a way to gain status or to feel safe or powerful?

   If you are going to write about effects, you might ask questions like these:

   Will this trend last?
   Has it affected competitors?
   Is it spreading?
   Is the fad changing business, or education, or the family?
   Has it improved daily life?

4. If you have a vivid memory of one of the following experiences, write a paragraph about the experience's effects on you.

moving to a new place   losing a friend
losing a job   starting a job
being a victim of a crime   breaking a bad habit
winning a contest   entering a relationship
undergoing surgery   ending a relationship

 **COMPUTER ▶**

5. If you currently use a computer for drafting your writing assignments, write a paragraph that summarizes the effects of relying on the computer for composing most, if not all, of your writing assignments. Remember that the effects may be both positive and negative, so you will need to brainstorm or freewrite first. Be sure your final version of the paragraph reflects logical organization of details and appropriate transitions.

6. After looking at the photograph below, write a paragraph on why joining an exercise group can have social benefits.

7. After looking at the photograph below, write a paragraph on the positive effects of the very young and the old creating a bond.

Note: Additional writing options suitable for cause or effect–related assignments can be found after the professional reading, "Students in Shock," which begins on page 620.

Name: _____ Section: _____

PEER REVIEW FORM FOR A CAUSE OR EFFECT PARAGRAPH

After you've written a draft of your cause or effect paragraph, let a writing partner read it. When your partner has completed the form below, discuss the comments. Then repeat the same process for your partner's paragraph.

This is a cause paragraph/an effect paragraph. (Circle one.)

In this paragraph, the causes or effects are (briefly list all of them) _____

_____

_____

_____

The topic sentence uses these words to indicate cause or effect:_____

_____

_____ (Write the exact words.)

The cause or effect that is most clearly explained is _____

_____

I would like to see more details added to _____

_____

I have questions about _____

I would like to take out the part about _____

Other comments on the paragraph: _____

_____

_____

_____

_____

_____

_____

_____

_____

_____

Reviewer's Name: _____

CHAPTER 10
Argument

WHAT IS ARGUMENT?

A written **argument** is an attempt to *persuade* a reader to think or act in a certain way. When you write an argument paragraph, your goal is to get people to see your point so that they are persuaded to accept it and perhaps to act on it.

In an argument paragraph, you take a stand. Then you support your stand with reasons. In addition, you give details for each reason. Your goal is to persuade your reader by making a point that has convincing reasons and details.

Hints for Writing an Argument Paragraph

1. Pick a topic you can handle. Your topic should be small enough to be covered in one paragraph. For instance, you can't argue effectively for world peace in just one paragraph.

2. Pick a topic you can handle based on your own experience and observation. Topics such as legalizing drugs, gun control, capital punishment, or air pollution require research into facts, figures, and expert opinions to make a complete argument. They are topics you can write about convincingly in a longer research paper, but for a one-paragraph argument, pick a topic based on what you've experienced yourself.

not this topic: Organized Crime

but this topic: Starting a Crime Watch Program in My Neighborhood

3. Do two things in your topic sentence: name the subject of your argument, and take a stand. The following topic sentences do both.

The college cafeteria should serve more healthy snacks.

High school athletes who fail a course should not be allowed to play on a school team.

You should take a stand, but *don't* announce it:

not this: This paragraph will explain why Springfield needs a teen center.

but this: Springfield should open a teen center. (This is a topic sentence with a subject and a stand.)

4. Consider your audience. Consider why these people should support your points. How will they be likely to object? How will you get around these objections? For instance, you might want to argue to the residents of your community that the intersection of Hawthorne Road and Sheridan Street needs a traffic light. Would anyone object?

At first, you might think, "No. Why would anyone object? The intersection is dangerous. There's too much traffic there. People risk major accidents getting across the intersection." However, if you think further about your audience, which is the people in your community, you might identify these objections: (1) Some town residents may not want to pay for a traffic signal, and (2) some drivers may not want to spend extra time waiting for a light to change.

There are several ways to handle objections:

You can *refute* an objection. To refute it means to prove it isn't valid; it isn't true. For instance, if someone says that a light wouldn't do any good, you might say that a new light has already worked in a nearby neighborhood.

Sometimes it's best to admit the other side has a point. You have to *concede* that point. For instance, traffic lights do cost money, and waiting for a light to change does take time.

Sometimes you can *turn an objection into an advantage.* When you acknowledge the objection and yet use it to make your own point, you show that you've considered both sides of the argument. For instance, you might say that the price of a traffic signal at the intersection is well worth it because that light will buy safety for all the drivers who try to cross Hawthorne Road and Sheridan Street. As an alternative, you might say that waiting a few moments for the light to change is better than waiting many minutes for an opening in the heavy traffic of the intersection.

5. Be specific, clear, and logical in your reasons. As always, think before you write. Think about your point and your audience. Try to come up with at least three reasons for your position.

Be careful that your reasons do not overlap. For instance, you might write the following:

_____ Physical exercise can keep students alert.

_____ There is less restlessness and fidgeting in class when students know they will have a break.

2. **topic sentence:** The entrance to River Rock badly needs improvement.

_____ The sign is hard to read.

_____ "Welcome to River Rock: The Best Little City in The World" is no longer accurate because River Rock has many problems.

_____ The landscaping gives a bad first impression.

_____ The sign has faded blue letters on a chipped and cracked tan background.

_____ Three dead trees welcome the visitor to River Rock.

_____ The slogan is out of date.

_____ River Rock has lost half its population since the slogan was created, so it isn't a city any longer.

_____ There is one dim light bulb focused on the sign at night.

_____ A pile of rocks near a dried-out fountain is depressing.

_____ A few scraggly chrysanthemums fight among the weeds.

Exercise 4 **Finding Reasons to Support an Argument**

Give three reasons that support each point. In each case, the readers of your local newspaper will be the audience for an argument paragraph.

1. **point:** Bus stops in Garfield should be transformed into bus shelters.

   reasons: a. _____

   _____

   b. _____

   _____

   c. _____

   _____

2. **point:** Sansbury needs a twenty-four-hour pharmacy.

   reasons: a. _____

   _____

   b. _____

   _____

c. _____

_____

3. **point:** Public elementary schools should offer low-cost day care during all school vacations and holidays.

reasons: a. _____

_____

b. _____

_____

c. _____

_____

PLANNING Devising a Plan: Argument

With a topic sentence and a list of reasons and details, you can draft an outline. Then you can review it, making whatever changes you think it needs. The checklist below may help you review and revise your outline.

CHECKLIST: A Checklist for Revising an Argument Outline

✔ Does my topic sentence make my point? Does it state a subject and take a stand?

✔ Have I considered the objections to my argument so that I am arguing intelligently?

✔ Do I have all the reasons I need to make my point?

✔ Do any reasons overlap?

✔ Are my reasons specific?

✔ Do I have enough details for each reason?

✔ Are my reasons in the best order?

The Order of Reasons in an Argument

When you are giving several reasons, it is a good idea to keep the most convincing or most important reason for last. Saving the best for last is called using **emphatic order.** For example, you might have these three reasons to tear down an abandoned building in your neighborhood: (1) The building is ugly. (2) Drug dealers are using the building. (3) The building is infested with rats. The most important reason, the drug dealing, should be used last for an emphatic order.

Following is an outline on improving Roberts Park. When you look at the outline, you'll notice several changes from the list on page 224:

- Because the safety of children at play is important, it is put as the last detail.
- Some details have been added.
- A sentence has been added to the end of the outline. It explains why improving the park is a good idea even to people who will never use the park themselves. It is a way of answering these people's objections.

An Outline for an Argument Paragraph

topic sentence:	Roberts Park should be cleaned up and improved.
reason:	Improving the park would make the downtown area more attractive to shoppers.
details:	Shoppers could stroll through the park or rest there after shopping. Friends could meet at the park for a day of shopping and lunch.
reason:	Workers from nearby offices and stores could eat lunch outdoors.
details:	Several office complexes are nearby. An hour outdoors is a pleasant break from work.
reason:	City children could play there.
details:	They would get fresh air. They would play on grass, not on asphalt. They would not have to play near traffic.
final idea:	An attractive park improves the city, and all residents benefit when the community is beautified.

Exercise 5   **Working with the Order of Reasons in an Argument Outline**

Below are topic sentences and lists of reasons. For each list, put an *X* by the reason that is the most significant, the reason you would save for last in an argument paragraph.

1. **topic sentence:** Parents should limit their children's intake of soft drinks to an occasional treat.

   reason 1: _____ Even one or two sodas per week can increase the risk of adult diabetes.

   reason 2: _____ Sugary soft drinks lack nutritional value.

   reason 3: _____ The soft drinks are full of calories.

2. **topic sentence:** Anderson Hospital needs to expand its emergency room services.

   reason 1: _____ Waiting time in the emergency room can be as long as three hours.

   reason 2: _____ More and more uninsured, sick people choose the emergency room as their only source of health care.

   reason 3: _____ Last month, an elderly man who got lost in the crowd at the Anderson emergency room nearly died there.

3. **topic sentence:** College students should receive free annual flu shots at their colleges.

   reason 1: _____ Flu keeps people of all ages from work or school.

reason 2: _____ Classrooms, lecture halls, or labs are perfect
places for the flu to spread.

reason 3: _____ People die of the flu every year.

Exercise 6   Recognizing Reasons That Overlap

Below are topic sentences and lists of reasons. In each list, two reasons overlap. Put an *X* by the two reasons that overlap.

1. topic sentence: Chili Haven needs to expand its menu.

a. _____ The restaurant needs a few low-fat and low-carbohy-
drate appetizers and entrees for dieters.

b. _____ Chili Haven needs a few more Mexican entrees; for
example, it currently serves no chili.

c. _____ People trying to lose weight may find the current menu
inadequate.

d. _____ Adding desserts would please many people, especially
children.

2. topic sentence: The college bookstore should sell blank diskettes
and CDs.

a. _____ Everyone who uses the writing lab needs CDs or
diskettes.

b. _____ Students in the library who do research use diskettes to
copy the articles available online.

c. _____ The bookstore could save students time and effort and
could make money by selling these essential CDs and
diskettes.

d. _____ Students who write their papers in the writing lab save
their drafts on diskettes.

3. topic sentence: The new classroom building at the college should
put benches in the halls.

a. _____ Students who come early to class need a place to sit
while the previous class ends.

b. _____ On cold and rainy days, students and teachers need shelter indoors between classes.

c. _____ Benches would make the wide hallways more people-
friendly.

d. _____ Benches would welcome students who come inside in
bad weather.

Exercise 7   **Identifying a Reason That Is Not Specific**

For each of the following lists, put an *X* by the reason that is not specific.

1. **topic sentence:** The advanced swimming class should hold a swim party for disabled children.

   a. _____ Water is good for many disabled children.

   b. _____ Exercise in water is an important part of rehabilitation for many disabled children.

   c. _____ Members of the swim class are skilled enough to assist children in the water.

   d. _____ The children would enjoy a place where they could be themselves, make new friends, and splash their old friends.

2. **topic sentence:** Residents of the Parkview Seniors' Residence should invite the children at the Children's Society Day Care Center to a weekly party.

   a. _____ Many small children do not have grandparents nearby and would love the attention.

   b. _____ Many older people miss seeing their own grandchildren who are far away.

   c. _____ A weekly get-together would break the monotony of the institutional routine at both places.

   d. _____ Everyone should get together and show love.

3. **topic sentence:** Woodvale Apartments needs more outdoor lighting.

   a. _____ People can stumble and fall because the sidewalk outside of each apartment is not lighted.

   b. _____ Dark buildings and a dimly lit parking lot are dangerous.

   c. _____ Lack of lighting makes it difficult for visitors to see the apartment numbers.

   d. _____ Several break-ins have occurred lately; the lack of lighting invites crime.

Exercise 8   **Adding Details to an Outline**

Following is part of an outline. It includes a topic sentence and three reasons. Add at least two sentences of details to each reason. Your details may be examples or description.

topic sentence: Food Festival Supermarket should sell all of its fruit and vegetables loose instead of packaged.

    reason: Packaged fruit or vegetables often conceal spoiled pieces.

    details: _____

    _____

    details: _____

    _____

    reason: Some customers want very small portions of the fruit or vegetables.

    details: _____

    _____

    details: _____

    _____

    reason: Customers enjoy picking through a selection of produce to find what they most desire.

    details: _____

    _____

    details: _____

    _____

DRAFTING Drafting and Revising: Argument

Once you are satisfied with your outline, you can write the first draft of your paragraph. When you have completed it, you can begin revising the draft so that your argument is as clear, smooth, and convincing as it can be. The checklist below may help you with your revisions.

CHECKLIST: A Checklist for Revising a Draft of an Argument Paragraph

✔ Do any of my sentences need combining?

✔ Have I left out a serious or obvious reason?

✔ Should I change the order of my reasons?

✔ Do I have enough details?

✔ Are my details specific?

✔ Do I need to explain the problem or issue I am writing about?

✔ Do I need to link my ideas more clearly?

✔ Do I need a final sentence to stress my point?

Checking Your Reasons

Be sure that your argument has covered all the serious or obvious reasons. Sometimes writers get so caught up in drafting their ideas they forget to mention something very basic to the argument. For instance, if you were arguing for a leash law for your community, you might state that dogs who run free

    d. a tax on all dog or cat owners who do not have their animals neutered, to be used to support animal shelters

2. In a paragraph, argue one of the following topics to the audience specified. If your instructor agrees, brainstorm your topic with a group before you start writing. Ask the group to "play audience," reacting to your reasons, raising objections, asking questions.

◀ COLLABORATE 👥

    topic a. Early-morning classes should be abolished at your college.
    audience: the dean of academic affairs

    topic b. College students should get discounts at movie theaters.
    audience: the owner of your local movie theater

    topic c. Your college should provide a day-care facility for students with children.
    audience: the president of your college

    topic d. Businesses should hire more student interns.
    audience: the president of a company (name it) you'd like to work for

3. Write a paragraph for or against any of the following topics. Your audience for the argument is your classmates and your instructor.

    For or Against
    a. seat belt laws
    b. hidden cameras to catch drivers who run red lights
    c. dress codes in high school
    d. uniforms in elementary schools
    e. mandatory student activities fees for commuter students at colleges and universities
    f. a law requiring a month waiting period between buying a marriage license and getting married
    g. a higher tax on cigarettes to be used to pay the health costs of smokers with smoking-related illnesses

4. Visit your state's department of motor vehicles Web site. Review the penalties for DUI (Driving Under the Influence of Alcohol) or DWI (Driving While Intoxicated). Argue for or against one of these penalties, and be sure to be as logical as possible. As an alternative, argue in favor of stricter penalties for either DUI or DWI in your city or state.

◀ COMPUTER 🖱

5. Some educators and parents are very concerned about the potentially harmful effects of violent video games on children. Using a search engine such as Google or Alta Vista, type in the words "video games" and "action." See if you can find manufacturers' descriptions of a video game you have played, and find the targeted age range. Using this information, argue for or against this point: (<u>Name of the video game</u>) is suitable for children ages _____ to _____.

◀ COMPUTER 🖱

6. Study the photograph at the top of the next page. Then argue for some way to solve this congestion. You may want to argue for widening the road, better public transportation, carpooling, staggered work hours, or another solution.

7. Study the photograph below. Pretend this alley is near your home, and argue for a way to keep it clean.

Note: Additional writing options suitable for argument-related assignments can be found after each of these professional readings: "Why Is Geezer-Bashing Acceptable?" which begins on page 624, and "A Cell Phone? Never for Me," which begins on page 627.

Name: _____   **Section:** _____

PEER REVIEW FORM FOR AN ARGUMENT PARAGRAPH

After you've written a draft of your argument paragraph, let a writing partner read it. When your partner has completed the form below, discuss the comments. Then repeat the same process for your partner's paragraph.

The topic sentence has this subject: _____

It takes this stand: _____

The most convincing part of the paragraph started with the words _____

and ended with the words _____

After reading this paragraph, I can think of an objection to this argument. The objection is _____

_____

The paragraph has/has not handled this objection. (Choose one.)

The part of the argument with the best details is the part about _____

_____

The part that could use more or better details is the part about _____

_____

The order of the reasons (a) is effective (b) could be better. (Choose one.)

I have questions about _____

_____

Other comments: _____

_____

_____

_____

_____

_____

_____

_____

_____

_____

_____

_____

Reviewer's Name: _____

CHAPTER 11
Writing an Essay

WHAT IS AN ESSAY?

You write an essay when you have more to say than can be covered in one paragraph. An **essay** can consist of one paragraph, but in this book, we take it to mean a writing of more than one paragraph. An essay has a main point, called a *thesis*, supported by subpoints. The subpoints are the *topic sentences*. Each paragraph in the *body*, or main part, of the essay has a topic sentence. In fact, each paragraph in the body of the essay is like the paragraphs you've already written because each one makes a point and then supports it.

Comparing the Single Paragraph and the Essay

Read the paragraph and the essay that follow, both about Bob, the writer's brother. You will notice many similarities.

A Single Paragraph

I think I'm lucky to have a brother who is two years older than I am. For one thing, my brother Bob fought all the typical child-parent battles, and I was the real winner. Bob was the one who made my parents understand that seventeen-year-olds shouldn't have an 11:00 p.m. curfew on weekends. He fought for his rights. By the time I turned seventeen, my parents had accepted the later curfew, and I didn't have to fight for it. Bob also paved the way for me at school. He was such a great athlete that I benefited from his reputation. When I tried out for the basketball team, I had an advantage before I hit the court. I was Bob Cruz's younger brother, so the coach thought I had to be pretty good. At home and at school, my big brother was a big help to me.

An Essay

Some people complain about being the youngest child or the middle child in the family. These people believe older children get all the attention and grab all the power. I'm the younger brother in my family, and I disagree with the complainers. I think I'm lucky to have a brother who is two years older than I am.

For one thing, my brother Bob fought all the typical child-parent battles, and I was the real winner. Bob was the one who made my parents understand that seventeen-year-olds shouldn't have an 11:00 p.m. curfew on weekends. He fought for his rights, and the fighting wasn't easy. I remember months of arguments between Bob and my parents as Bob tried to explain that not all teens on the street at 11:30 are punks or criminals. Bob was the one who suffered from being grounded or who lost the use of my father's car. By the time I turned seventeen, my parents had accepted the later curfew, and I didn't have to fight for it.

Bob also paved the way for me at school. Because he was so popular with the other students and the teachers, he created a positive image of what the boys in our family were like. When I started school, I walked into a place where people were ready to like me, just as they liked Bob. I remember the first day of class, when the teachers read the new class rolls. When they got to my name, they asked, "Are you Bob Cruz's brother?" When I said yes, they smiled. Bob's success opened doors for me in school sports, too. He was such a great athlete that I benefited from his reputation. When I tried out for the basketball team, I had an advantage before I hit the court. I was Bob Cruz's younger brother, so the coach thought I had to be pretty good.

I had many battles to fight as I grew up. Like all children, I had to struggle to gain independence and respect. In my struggles at home and at school, my big brother was a big help to me.

If you read the two selections carefully, you noticed that they make the same main point, and they support that point with two subpoints.

main point: I think I'm lucky to have a brother who is two years older than I am.

> **subpoints:** 1. My brother Bob fought all the typical child-parent battles, and I was the real winner.
> 2. Bob also paved the way at school.

You noticed that the essay is longer because it has more details and examples to support the points.

ORGANIZING AN ESSAY

When you write an essay of more than one paragraph, the **thesis** is the focus of your entire essay; it is the major point of your essay. The other important points that relate to the thesis are in topic sentences.

Thesis: Working as a salesperson has changed my character.

    Topic sentence: I have had to learn patience.

    Topic sentence: I have developed the ability to listen.

    Topic sentence: I have become more tactful.

Notice that the thesis expresses a bigger idea than the topic sentences below it, and it is supported by the topic sentences. The essay has an introduction, a body, and a conclusion.

1. **Introduction:** The first paragraph is usually the introduction. The thesis is included in this paragraph.

2. **Body:** This central part of the essay is the part where you support your main point (the thesis). Each paragraph in the body of the essay has its own topic sentence.

3. **Conclusion:** Usually one paragraph long, the conclusion reminds the reader of the thesis.

Writing the Thesis

There are several characteristics of a thesis:

1. It is expressed in a sentence. A thesis is *not* the same as the topic of the essay or as the title of the essay:

   topic: quitting smoking
   title: Why I Quit Smoking
   thesis: I quit smoking because I was concerned for my health, and I wanted to prove to myself that I could break the habit.

2. A thesis *does not announce*; it makes a point about the subject.

   announcement: This essay will explain the reasons why young adults should watch what they eat.
   thesis: Young adults should watch what they eat so they can live healthy lives today and prevent future health problems.

3. A thesis *is not too broad.* Some ideas are just too big to cover well in an essay. A thesis that tries to cover too much can lead to a superficial or boring essay.

   too broad: People all over the world should work on solving their interpersonal communications problems.
   acceptable thesis: As a Southerner, I had a hard time understanding that some New Yorkers think slow speech is ignorant speech.

4. A thesis *is not too narrow*. Sometimes, writers start with a thesis that looks good because it seems specific and precise. Later, when they try to support such a thesis, they can't find anything to say.

> **too narrow:** My sister pays forty dollars a week for a special formula for her baby.
> **acceptable thesis:** My sister had no idea what it would cost to care for a baby.

Hints for Writing a Thesis

1. Your thesis can **mention the specific subpoints** of your essay. For example, your thesis might be as follows:

> I hated *Alien vs. Predator* because the film's plot was disorganized, its conflict was unrealistic, and its scenes were overly violent.

With this thesis, you have indicated the three subpoints of your essay: *Alien vs. Predator* had a disorganized plot, it had an unrealistic conflict, and it had overly violent scenes.

2. You can **make a point** without listing your subpoints. For example, you can write a thesis like this:

> I hated *Alien vs. Predator* because it was a bloody mess.

With this thesis, you can still use the subpoints stating that the movie had a disorganized plot, an unrealistic conflict, and overly violent scenes. You just don't have to mention all your subpoints in the thesis.

Exercise 1   **Recognizing Good Thesis Sentences**

Following is a list of thesis statements. Some are acceptable, but others are too broad or too narrow. Some are announcements; others are topics, not sentences. Put a *G* next to the good thesis sentences.

1. _____ How parents can find bargains on children's clothing will be discussed in this essay.

2. _____ The company I work for is laying off fifty workers.

3. _____ Immigration is an issue in our country today.

4. _____ Why flu shots are not widely available in this community.

5. _____ Global warming concerns many nations.

6. _____ New rules will make it hard for me, a foreign student, to finish college in America.

7. _____ I have discovered three ways to save money on gas.

8. _____ A solid family foundation can help in child development.

9. _____ The reasons for developing public transportation.

10. _____ My mother grew up poor, but a loving foster family sustained her.

Exercise 2 **Selecting a Good Thesis Sentence**

In each pair of thesis statements below, put a *G* next to the good topic sentence.

1. a. _____ Social anxiety and the likelihood of acceptance by peers.

    b. _____ People with social anxiety should not give up on acceptance by peers.

2. a. _____ Before they eat fish, people in our county need to read the local warnings about poisoned fish species.

    b. _____ The oceans, rivers, and lakes of the world are becoming dangerously polluted.

3. a. _____ The challenges of getting financial aid will be discussed in this essay.

    b. _____ Students who want financial aid must be ready to face the paperwork, find the necessary documents, and research possible sources of aid.

4. a. _____ Alan got a divorce last month.

    b. _____ Alan's divorce was a result of immaturity and mistrust on both sides.

5. a. _____ Flea markets and thrift shops often sell unusual furniture.

    b. _____ Where to look for unusual furniture is the subject of this essay.

Exercise 3 **Writing a Thesis That Relates to the Subpoints**

Following are lists of subpoints that could be discussed in an essay. Write a thesis for each list. Remember that there are two ways to write a thesis: you can write a thesis that includes the specific subpoints, or you can write one that makes a point without listing the subpoints. As an example, the first one is done for you, using both kinds of topic sentences.

1. **one kind of thesis:** If you want a pet, a cat is easier to care for than a dog.

    another kind of thesis: Cats make better pets than dogs because cats don't need to be walked, don't mind being alone, and don't make any noise.

    subpoints: a. Cats don't have to be walked and exercised, like dogs do.
    b. Cats are independent and don't mind being home alone, but a dog gets lonely.
    c. Cats are quieter than dogs.

2. **thesis:** _____

    _____

subpoints: a. A tough boss can be overly demanding.
        b. A tough boss can be extremely critical.

3. thesis: _____

_____

subpoints: a. A tough boss can be overly demanding.
        b. A tough boss can be extremely critical.
        c. Working for a tough boss can motivate you to do your best work.
        d. Working for a tough boss can make you less sensitive to criticism.

4. thesis: _____

_____

subpoints: a. For an only child, cousins can take the place of sisters or brothers.
        b. Older cousins can play the role of parents.
        c. Cousins can also become best friends.

WRITING THE ESSAY IN STEPS

In an essay, you follow the same steps you learned in writing a paragraph—prewriting, planning, drafting, and polishing—but you adapt them to the longer essay form.

PREWRITING Gathering Ideas: An Essay

Often, you begin by *narrowing a topic*. Your instructor may give you a large topic so that you can find something smaller, within the broad one, that you would like to write about.

Some students think that because they have several paragraphs to write, they should pick a big topic, one that will give them enough to say. But big topics can lead to boring, superficial, general essays. A smaller topic can challenge you to find the specific, concrete examples and details that make an essay effective.

If your instructor asked you to write about college, for instance, you might *freewrite* some ideas as you narrow the topic:

narrowing the topic of college

what college means to me—too big, and it could be boring
college vs. high school—everyone might choose this topic
college students—too big
college students who have jobs—better!
problems of working and going to college—OK!

In your freewriting, you can consider your *purpose*—to write an essay about some aspect of college—and *audience*—your instructor and classmates. Your narrowed topic will appeal to this audience because many students hold jobs and instructors are familiar with the problems of working students.

Listing Ideas

Once you have a narrow topic, you can use whatever process works for you. You can brainstorm by writing a series of questions and answers about your topic, you can freewrite on the topic, you can list ideas on the topic, or you can do any combination of these processes.

Following is a sample listing of ideas on the topic of the problems of working and going to college.

problems of working and going to college

early classes	weekends only time to study
too tired to pay attention	no social life
tried to study at work	apartment a mess
got caught	missed work for make-up test
got reprimanded	got behind in school
slept in class	need salary for tuition
constantly racing around	rude to customers
no sleep	girlfriend ready to kill me
little time to do homework	

Clustering the Ideas

By clustering related items on the list, you'll find it easier to see the connections between ideas. The following items have been clustered (grouped), and they have been listed under a subtitle.

Problems of Working and Going to College: Ideas in Clusters

problems at school	**problems at work**
early classes	tried to study at work
too tired to pay attention	got caught
slept in class	got reprimanded
little time to do homework	missed work for make-up test
got behind in school	rude to customers

problems outside of work and school

weekends only time to study

no social life

apartment a mess

girlfriend ready to kill me

When you surveyed the clusters, you probably noticed that some of the ideas from the original list were left out. These ideas—on racing around, not getting enough sleep, and needing tuition money—could fit into more than one place and might not fit anywhere. You might come back to them later.

When you name each cluster by giving it a subtitle, you move toward a focus for each body paragraph of your essay. And by beginning to focus the body paragraphs, you start thinking about the main point, the thesis of the essay. Concentrating on the thesis and on focused paragraphs helps you to *unify* your essay.

Reread the clustered ideas. When you do so, you'll notice that each cluster is about problems at a different place. You can incorporate that concept into a thesis with a sentence like this:

Students who work while they attend college face problems at school, at work, and at home.

Once you have a thesis and a list of details, you can begin working on the planning part of your essay.

Exercise 4 **Narrowing Topics**

◀ COLLABORATE 👥

Working with a partner or a group, narrow these topics so that the new topics are related but smaller and suitable for short essays between four and six paragraphs long. The first topic is narrowed for you.

1. **topic:** summer vacation
   smaller, related topics:

   a. _a car trip with children_

   b. _finding the cheapest flight to Mexico_

   c. _my vacation job_

2. **topic:** entertainment
   smaller, related topics:

   a. _____

   b. _____

   c. _____

3. **topic:** emotions
   smaller, related topics:

   a. _____

   b. _____

   c. _____

4. **topic:** work
   smaller, related topics:

   a. _____

   b. _____

   c. _____

Exercise 5 **Clustering Related Ideas**

Following are two topics, each with a list of ideas. Mark all the related items on the list with the same number (*1*, *2*, or *3*). Some items might not get any number. When you've finished marking the list, write a title for each number that explains the cluster of ideas.

1. topic: a sleepless night

_____ a loud party going on in the apartment upstairs

_____ I lay there and thought about my early morning math exam

_____ became stressed about sleeping through the alarm

_____ car horns blared all night

_____ saw car lights coming through the window

_____ my air conditioner broke down

_____ started obsessing about my grades

_____ doors slammed and car alarms screamed

_____ I was sweating into a damp pillow

_____ the sheets stuck to my clammy skin

The ideas marked *1* can be titled _____

The ideas marked *2* can be titled _____

The ideas marked *3* can be titled _____

2. topic: why I miss my home town

_____ it is nearly always sunny

_____ people were not pushy

_____ everyone said "hello"

_____ a great football team

_____ dozens of local softball and soccer teams

_____ temperature never went below 60 degrees

_____ great public transportation

_____ neighbors helped each other

_____ many trails for cycling

_____ very few storms

_____ good schools

The items marked *1* can be titled _____

The items marked *2* can be titled _____

The items marked *3* can be titled _____

PLANNING   Devising a Plan: An Outline for an Essay

In the next stage of writing your essay, draft an outline. Use the thesis to focus your ideas. There are many kinds of outlines, but all are used to help a writer organize ideas. When you use a **formal outline,** you show the difference between a main idea and its supporting detail by *indenting* the supporting detail. In a formal outline, Roman numerals (numbers I, II, III, and so on) and capital letters are used. Each Roman numeral represents a paragraph, and the letters beneath the numeral represent supporting details.

The Structure of a Formal Outline

first paragraph	I. Thesis
second paragraph	II. Topic sentence
	A.
	B.
details	C.
	D.
	E.
third paragraph	III. Topic sentence
	A.
	B.
details	C.
	D.
	E.
fourth paragraph	IV. Topic sentence
	A.
	B.
details	C.
	D.
	E.
fifth paragraph	V. Conclusion

Hints for Outlining

Developing a good, clear outline now can save you hours of confused, disorganized writing later. The extra time you spend to make sure your outline has sufficient details and that *each paragraph stays on one point* will pay off in the long run.

1. Check the topic sentences. Keep in mind that each topic sentence in each body paragraph should support the thesis sentence. If a topic sentence is not carefully connected to the thesis, the structure of the essay will be confusing. Here are a thesis and a list of topic sentences; the topic sentence that does not fit is crossed out:

thesis: I. A home-cooked dinner can be a rewarding experience for the cook and the guests.

topic sentences: II. Preparing a meal is a satisfying activity.
III. It is a pleasure for the cook to see guests enjoy the meal.
IV. ~~Many recipes are handed down through generations.~~
V. Dinner guests are flattered that someone cooked for them.
VI. Dining at home is a treat for everyone at the table or in the kitchen.

Because the thesis of this outline is about the pleasure of dining at home, for the cook and the guests, topic sentence IV doesn't fit: it isn't about the joy of cooking *or* of being a dinner guest. It takes the essay off track. A careful check of the links between the thesis and the topic sentences will help keep your essay focused.

2. Include enough details. Some writers believe that they don't need many details in the outline. They feel they can fill in the details later, when they actually write the essay. Even though some writers do manage to add details later, others who are in a hurry or who run out of ideas will have problems. For example, imagine that a writer has included very few details in an outline, like this outline for a paragraph:

> II. A burglary makes the victim feel unsafe.
>   A. The person has lost property.
>   B. The person's home territory has been invaded.

The paragraph created from that outline might be too short, lack specific details, and look like this:

> A burglary makes the victim feel unsafe. First of all, the victim has lost property. Second, a person's home territory has been invaded.

If you have difficulty thinking of ideas when you write, try to tackle the problem in the outline. The more details you put into your outline, the more detailed and effective your draft essay will be. For example, suppose the same outline on the burglary topic had more details, like this:

> II. A burglary makes the victim feel unsafe.
>   A. The person has lost property.
>   B. The property could be worth hundreds of dollars.
>   C. The victim can lose a television or camera or DVD player.
>   D. The burglars may take cash.
>   E. Worse, items with personal value, like family jewelry or heirlooms, can be stolen.
>   F. Even worse, a person's territory has been invaded.
>   G. People who thought they were safe know they are not safe.
>   H. The fear is that the invasion can happen again.

more details about burglary corresponds to A–E, and *more details about safety concerns* corresponds to F–H.

You will probably agree that the paragraph will be more detailed, too.

3. Stay on one point. It is a good idea to check the outline of each body paragraph to see if each paragraph stays on one point. Compare each topic sentence, which is at the top of the list for the paragraph, against the details indented under it. Staying on one point gives each paragraph unity.

Below is the outline for a paragraph that has problems staying on one point. See if you can spot the problem areas.

> III. Sonya is a generous person.
>   A. I remember how freely she gave her time when our club had a car wash.
>   B. She is always willing to share her lecture notes with me.
>   C. Sonya gives ten percent of her salary to her church.

  D. She is a member of Big Sisters and spends every Saturday with
    a disadvantaged child.
  E. She can read people's minds when they are in trouble.
  F. She knows what they are feeling.

The topic sentence of the paragraph is about generosity. However, sentences
E and F talk about Sonya's insight, not her generosity.

When you have a problem staying on one point, you can solve the problem two ways:

1. Eliminate details that do not fit your main point.
2. Change the topic sentence to cover all the ideas in the paragraph.

For example, you could cut out sentences E and F about Sonya's generosity,
getting rid of the details that do not fit. As an alternative, you could change
the topic sentence in the paragraph so that it relates to all the ideas in the
paragraph. A better topic sentence is "Sonya is a generous and insightful
person."

Revisiting the Prewriting Stage

Writing an outline can help you identify undeveloped places in your plan,
places where your paragraphs will need more details. You can get these details in two ways:

1. Go back to the writing you did in the prewriting stage. Check whether
   items on a list or ideas from prewriting can lead you to more details
   for your outline.
2. Brainstorm for more details by a question-and-answer approach. For
   example, if the outline includes "My apartment is a mess," you might
   ask, "Why? How messy?" Or if the outline includes "I have no social
   life," you might ask, "What do you mean? No friends? No activities?
   What about school organizations?"

The time you spend writing and revising your outline will make it easier for
you to write an essay that is well developed, unified, and coherently struc-
tured. The checklist below may help you to revise.

CHECKLIST: A Checklist for Revising the Outline of an Essay

✔ **Unity:** Do the thesis and topic sentences all lead to the same point? Does
  each paragraph make one, and only one, point? Do the details in each
  paragraph support the topic sentence? Does the conclusion unify the
  essay?

✔ **Support:** Do the body paragraphs have enough supporting details?

✔ **Coherence:** Are the paragraphs in the most effective order? Are the details
  in each paragraph arranged in the most effective order?

A sentence outline on the problems of working and going to college follows.
It includes the thesis in the first paragraph. The topic sentences have been
created from the titles of the ideas clustered earlier. The details have been
drawn from ideas in the clusters and from further brainstorming. The conclusion has just one sentence that unifies the essay.

An Outline for an Essay

paragraph 1	I. Thesis: Students who work while going to college face problems at school, at work, and at home.
paragraph 2 topic sentence details	II. Trying to juggle job and school responsibilities creates problems at school. A. Early classes are difficult. B. I am too tired to pay attention. C. Once I slept in class. D. I have little time to do homework. E. I get behind in school assignments.
paragraph 3 topic sentence details	III. Work can suffer when workers attend college. A. I tried to study at work. B. I got caught by my boss. C. I was reprimanded. D. Sometimes I come to work very tired. E. When I don't have enough sleep, I can be rude to customers. F. Rudeness gets me in trouble. G. Another time, I had to cut work to take a make-up test.
paragraph 4 topic sentence details	IV. Working students suffer outside of classes and the workplace. A. I work nights during the week. B. The weekends are the only time I can study. C. My apartment is a mess since I have no time to clean it. D. Worse, my girlfriend is ready to kill me because I have no social life. E. We never even go to the movies anymore. F. When she comes over, I am busy studying.
paragraph 5 conclusion	V. I have learned that working students have to be very organized to cope with their responsibilities at college, work, and home.

Exercise 6   **Completing an Outline for an Essay**

Following is part of an outline that has a thesis and topic sentences, but no details. Add the details and write in complete sentences. Write one sentence for each capital letter. Be sure that the details are connected to the topic sentence.

    I. Thesis: Products that were once designed for adults have become a part of many children's lives.

    II. Children routinely use technology once restricted to adults.

        A. _____

        B. _____

        C. _____

D. _____

E. _____

III. Cosmetics and cosmetic surgery are not just for grown-ups anymore.

A. _____

B. _____

C. _____

D. _____

E. _____

IV. Years ago, children's personal transportation was limited to bicycles and little red wagons, but today's children have new "toys" to help them get around.

A. _____

B. _____

C. _____

D. _____

E. _____

V. Children today are linked to the latest technology, turned on to the latest in self-improvement, and transported by the best in motorized toys.

Exercise 7 **Focusing an Outline for an Essay**

The outline below has a thesis and details, but it has no topic sentences for the body paragraphs. Write the topic sentences.

I. Thesis: Yesterday's visit to the Lucky Seven Supermarket will be my last.

II. _____

_____

A. The "fresh" bread was so stale I could feel its stiffness through the plastic wrapper.
B. There were three crumbling cookies on a shelf in the glass display case.
C. One cake had mold on it.
D. The rolls were as hard as tennis balls.
E. The icing had melted off the cupcakes.
F. The apples in the apple pies were a strange brown color.

III. _____

_____

A. When I picked up a banana, it was so overripe that it split at the top.

    B. A head of lettuce showed brown leaves beneath its wrapping.
    C. The red peppers looked as if they had been smashed by a hammer.
    D. A cucumber was soft.
    E. A bag of onions included several rotten ones.
    F. A pile of peaches was full of bruised fruit.

    IV. The Lucky Seven Supermarket was not lucky for me.

DRAFTING Drafting and Revising: An Essay

When you are satisfied with your outline, you can begin drafting and revising the essay. Start by writing a first draft of the essay, which includes these parts: introduction, body paragraphs, and conclusion.

WRITING THE INTRODUCTION

Where Does the Thesis Go?

The **thesis** should appear in the introduction of the essay, in the first paragraph. But most of the time, it should not be the first sentence. In front of the thesis, write a few (three or more) sentences of introduction. Generally, the thesis is the *last sentence* in the introductory paragraph.

Why put the thesis at the end of the first paragraph? First of all, writing several sentences in front of your main idea gives you a chance to lead into it, gradually and smoothly. This will help you build interest and gain the reader's attention. Also, by placing the thesis after a few sentences of introduction, you will not startle the reader with your main point.

Finally, if your thesis is at the end of the introduction, it states the main point of the essay just before that point is supported in the body paragraphs. Putting the thesis at the end of the introduction is like putting an arrow pointing to the supporting ideas in the essay.

Hints for Writing the Introduction

There are a number of ways to write an introduction.

    1. You can begin with some general statements that gradually lead to your thesis:

general statements

    Students face all kinds of problems when they start college. Some students struggle with a lack of basic math skills; others have never learned to write a term paper. Students who were stars in high school have to cope with being just another social security number at a large institution. Students with small children have to find a way to be good parents and good students, too. Although all these problems are common, I found an even more typical conflict. <u>My biggest problem in college was learning to organize my time.</u>

thesis at end

2. You can begin with a quotation that smoothly leads to your thesis. The quotation can be from someone famous, or it can be an old saying. It can be something your mother always told you, or it can be a slogan from an advertisement or the words of a song.

quotation

Everybody has heard the old saying, "Time flies," but I never really thought about that statement until I started college. I expected college to challenge me with demanding coursework. I expected it to excite me with the range of people I would meet. I even thought it might amuse me with the fun and intrigue of dating and romance. But I never expected college to exhaust me. I was surprised to discover that <u>my biggest problem in college was learning to</u>

thesis at end

<u>organize my time.</u>

(**Note:** You can add transition words or phrases to your thesis, as in the sample above.)

3. You can tell a story as a way of leading into your thesis. You can open with the story of something that happened to you or to someone you know, a story you read about or heard on the news.

story

My friend Phyllis is two years older than I am, and so she started college before I did. When Phyllis came home from college for the Thanksgiving weekend, I called her with plans for fun, but Phyllis told me she planned to spend most of the weekend sleeping. I didn't understand her when she told me she was worn out. When I started college myself, I understood her perfectly. Phyllis was a victim of that old college ailment: not knowing how to handle time. I developed the same disease. <u>My</u>

thesis at end

<u>biggest problem in college was learning to organize my time.</u>

4. You can explain why this topic is worth writing about. Explaining could mean giving some background on the topic, or it could mean discussing why the topic is an important one.

explain

I do not remember a word of what was said during my freshman orientation, and I wish I did. I am sure somebody somewhere warned me about the problems I would face in college. I am sure somebody talked about getting organized. Unfortunately, I didn't listen, and I had to learn the hard way. I hope other students will listen and learn and be spared my hard lesson and my big problem. <u>My</u>

thesis at end

<u>biggest problem in college was learning to organize my time.</u>

5. You can use one or more questions to lead into your thesis. You can open with a question or questions that will be answered by your thesis. Or you can open with a question or questions that catch the reader's attention and move toward your thesis.

question

Have you ever stayed up all night to study for an exam, then fallen asleep at dawn and slept right through the time of the exam? If you have, then you were probably the same kind of college student I was. I was the student who always ran into class three minutes late, the one who begged for an extension on the term paper, the one who pleaded with the teacher to postpone the test. I just could

thesis at end

not get things done on schedule. <u>My biggest problem in college was learning to organize my time.</u>

6. You can open with a contradiction of your main point as a way of attracting the reader's interest and leading to your thesis. You can begin with an idea that is the opposite of what you will say in your thesis. The opposition of your opening and your thesis creates interest.

contradiction

People who knew me in my freshman year probably felt really sorry for me. They saw a girl with dark circles under her bloodshot eyes, a girl who was always racing from one place to another. Those people probably thought I was exhausted from overwork. But they were wrong. My problem in college was definitely not too much work; it was the

thesis at end

way I handled my work. <u>My biggest problem in college was learning to organize my time.</u>

Exercise 8 Writing an Introduction

Below are five thesis sentences. Pick one. Then write an introductory paragraph on the lines provided. Your last sentence should be the thesis sentence. If your instructor agrees, read your introduction to others in the class who wrote an introduction to the same thesis, or read your introduction to the entire class.

Thesis Sentences:

1. Television should focus on how young adults really live.
2. Credit cards can be dangerous.
3. My best friend has saved my life twice.
4. Three sports heroes represent what it means to be a true winner.
5. Often, violence seems to be a person's first choice for handling a difficult situation.

(Write an introduction) _____

_____

_____

_____

_____

_____

_____

_____

WRITING THE BODY OF THE ESSAY

In the body of the essay, the paragraphs *explain, support, and develop* your thesis. In this part of the essay, each paragraph has its own topic sentence. The topic sentence in each paragraph does two things:

1. It focuses the sentences in the paragraph.
2. It makes a point connected to the thesis.

The thesis and the topic sentences are ideas that need to be supported by details, explanations, and examples. You can visualize the connections among the parts of an essay like this:

Introduction with Thesis

Body
- Topic Sentence
  Details
- Topic Sentence
  Details
- Topic Sentence
  Details

Conclusion

When you write topic sentences, you can help to organize your essay by referring to the checklist below.

CHECKLIST: A Checklist for the Topic Sentences of an Essay

✔ Does the topic sentence give the point of the paragraph?

✔ Does the topic sentence connect to the thesis of the essay?

How Long Are the Body Paragraphs?

Remember that the body paragraphs of an essay are the place where you explain and develop your thesis. Those paragraphs should be long enough to explain your points, not just list them. To do this well, try to make your body paragraphs *at least seven sentences* long. As you develop your writing skills, you may find that you can support your ideas in fewer than seven sentences.

Developing the Body Paragraphs

You can write well-developed body paragraphs by following the same steps you used in writing single paragraphs for the earlier assignments in this course. By working through the stages of gathering ideas, planning, drafting, revising, editing, and proofreading, you can create clear, effective paragraphs.

To focus and develop the body paragraphs, ask the questions below as you revise:

CHECKLIST: A Checklist for Developing Body Paragraphs for an Essay

✔ Does the topic sentence cover everything in the paragraph?

✔ Do I have enough details to explain the topic sentence?

✔ Do all the details in the paragraph support, develop, or illustrate the topic sentence?

Exercise 9 Creating Topic Sentences

Following are thesis sentences. For each thesis, write topic sentences (as many as indicated by the numbered blanks). The first one is done for you.

1. **thesis:** Cats make good pets.

   topic sentence 1: _Cats are independent and don't mind being home_

   alone.

   topic sentence 2: _Cats are easy to litter-train._

   _____

   topic sentence 3: _Cats are fun to play with._

   _____

2. **thesis:** My brother is a caring father and a loyal son.

   topic sentence 1: _____

   _____

   topic sentence 2: _____

   _____

3. **thesis:** Students who are frequently absent from class can find themselves in academic trouble.

   topic sentence 1: _____

   _____

   topic sentence 2: _____

   _____

   topic sentence 3: _____

   _____

4. **thesis:** Joining the military can offer opportunities, but it can also present challenges.

   topic sentence 1: _____

   _____

   topic sentence 2: _____

   _____

   topic sentence 3: _____

   _____

topic sentence 4: _____

_____

WRITING THE CONCLUSION

The last paragraph in the essay is the **conclusion.** It does not have to be as long as a body paragraph, but it should be long enough to unify the essay and remind the reader of the thesis. You can use any of these strategies in writing the conclusion:

1. You can restate the thesis in new words. Go back to the first paragraph of your essay and reread it. For example, this could be the first paragraph of an essay:

introduction

> Even when I was a child, I did not like being told what to do. I wanted to be my own boss. When I grew up, I figured that the best way to be my own boss was to own my own business. I thought that being in charge would be easy. I now know how difficult being an independent businessperson can be.

thesis at end

> Independent business owners have to be smart, highly motivated, and hard-working.

The thesis, underlined above, is the sentence that you can restate in your conclusion. Your task is to *keep the point but put it in different words.* Then work that restatement into a short paragraph, like this:

restating the thesis

> People who own their own business have to be harder on themselves than any employer would ever be. Their success is their own responsibility; they cannot blame company policy or rules because they set the policy and make the rules. If the business is to succeed, their intelligence, drive, and effort are essential.

2. You can make a judgment, valuation, or recommendation. Instead of simply restating your point, you can end by making some comment on the issue you've described or the problem you've illustrated. If you were looking for another way to end the essay on owning one's own business, for example, you could end with a recommendation.

ending with a recommendation

> People often dream of owning their own business. Dreaming is easy, but the reality is tough. Those who want to succeed in their own venture should find a role model. Studying a role model would teach them how know-how, ambition, and constant effort lead to success.

3. You can conclude by framing your essay. You can tie your essay together neatly by *using something from your introduction* as a way of concluding. When you take an example, or a question, or even a quotation from your first paragraph and refer to it in your last paragraph, you are "framing" the essay. Take another look at the introduction to the essay on owning your own business. The writer talks about not liking to be told what to do, being one's own boss, and believing that being in charge would be easy. The writer also mentions the need to be smart, highly motivated, and hard-working. Now consider how the ideas of the introduction are used in this conclusion:

frame	Children <u>who do not like to take directions</u> may
frame	think that <u>being their own boss will be easy.</u> Adults who try to start a business soon discover that they must be totally self-directed; that is, they must be
frame	strong enough to <u>keep learning</u>, to <u>keep pushing</u>
frame	<u>forward</u>, and to <u>keep working</u>.

Exercise 10 **Choosing a Better Way to Restate the Thesis**

Following are five clusters. Each cluster consists of a thesis sentence and two sentences that try to restate the thesis. Each restated sentence could be used as part of the conclusion to an essay. Put *B* next to the sentence in each pair that is a better restatement. Remember that the better choice repeats the same idea as the thesis but does not rely on too many of the same words.

1. thesis: Students who want to save money should bring their own snacks to school, use the campus computers, and take advantage of low-cost student activities.

restatement 1: _____ If students come to school with their own snacks, use the campus computers, and take advantage of cheap student activities, they can save money.

restatement 2: _____ Students can cut costs by packing their own snacks, spending time in the computer labs, and relaxing at inexpensive campus activities.

2. thesis: Volunteer work is a great way for people to get more than they give.

restatement 1: _____ The rewards of volunteering are much greater than the sacrifices.

restatement 2: _____ People who volunteer get more than they give.

3. thesis: Learning to box gave me a new confidence.

restatement 1: _____ Boxing lessons made me self-assured.
restatement 2: _____ By learning to box, I got a new confidence.

4. thesis: Most young people long to be free of their parents' rules and family rituals.

restatement 1: _____ Most young people desire to be free of their parents' rules and family rituals.

restatement 2: _____ Most young adults dream of escaping their parents' restrictions and customs.

Revising the Draft

Once you have a rough draft of your essay, you can begin revising it. The following checklist may help you to make the necessary changes in your draft.

CHECKLIST: Checklist for Revising the Draft of an Essay

✔ Does the essay have a clear, unifying thesis?

✔ Does the thesis make a point?

✔ Does each body paragraph have a topic sentence?

✔ Is each body paragraph focused on its topic sentence?

✔ Are the body paragraphs roughly the same size?

✔ Do any of the sentences need combining?

✔ Do any of the words need to be changed?

✔ Do the ideas seem to be smoothly linked?

✔ Does the introduction catch the reader's interest?

✔ Is there a definite conclusion?

✔ Does the conclusion remind the reader of the thesis?

Transitions Within Paragraphs

In an essay, you can use two kinds of transitions: those within a paragraph and those between paragraphs.

Transitions that link ideas *within a paragraph* are the same kinds you've used earlier. Your choice of words, phrases, or even sentences depends on the kind of connection you want to make. Here is a list of some common transitions and the kind of connection they express.

INFO BOX: Common Transitions Within a Paragraph

To join two ideas:

again	another	in addition	moreover
also	besides	likewise	similarly
and	furthermore		

To show a contrast or a different opinion:

but	instead	on the other hand	still
however	nevertheless	or	yet
in contrast	on the contrary	otherwise	

To show a cause-and-effect connection:

accordingly	because	for	therefore
as a result	consequently	so	thus

To give an example:

for example	in the case of	such as	to illustrate
for instance	like		

To show time:

after	first	recently	subsequently
at the same time	meanwhile	shortly	then
before	next	soon	until
finally			

Transitions Between Paragraphs

When you write something that is more than one paragraph long, you need transitions that link each paragraph to the others. There are several effective ways to link paragraphs and remind the reader of your main idea and of how the smaller points connect to it. Restatement and repetition are two ways:

1. Restate an idea from the preceding paragraph at the start of a new paragraph. Look closely at the two paragraphs below and notice how the second paragraph repeats an idea from the first paragraph and provides a link.

If people were more patient, driving would be less of an ordeal. If, for instance, the driver behind me didn't honk his horn as soon as the traffic light turned green, both he and I would probably have lower blood pressure. He wouldn't be irritating himself by pushing so hard. And I wouldn't be reacting by slowing down, trying to irritate him even more, and getting angry at him. When I get impatient in heavy traffic, I just make a bad situation worse. My hurry doesn't get me to my destination any faster; it just stresses me out.

transition
restating an idea

<u>The impatient driver doesn't get anywhere; neither does the</u> impatient customer at a restaurant. Impatience at restaurants doesn't pay. I work as a hostess at a restaurant, and I know that the customer who moans and complains about waiting for a table won't get one any faster than the person who makes the best of the wait. In fact, if a customer is too aggressive or obnoxious, the restaurant staff may actually slow down the process of getting that customer a table.

2. Use synonyms and repetition as a way of reminding the reader of an important point. For example, in the two paragraphs below, notice how certain repeated words, phrases, and synonyms all remind the reader of a point about facing fear. The repeated words and synonyms are underlined.

Some people just <u>avoid</u> whatever they <u>fear</u>. I have an uncle who is <u>afraid</u> to fly. Whenever he has to go on a trip, he does anything he can to <u>avoid</u> getting on an airplane. He will drive for days, travel by train, take a bus trip. Because he is so <u>terrified</u> of flying, he lives with <u>constant anxiety</u> that some day he may have to fly. He is always thinking of the one emergency that could force him to <u>confront what he most dreads.</u> Instead of <u>dealing directly with his fear</u>, he lets it <u>haunt</u> him.

Other people are even worse than my uncle. He won't <u>attack his fear</u> of something external. But there are people who won't <u>deal with their fear</u> of themselves. My friend Sam is a good example of this kind of person. Sam has a serious drinking problem. All Sam's friends know he is an alcoholic. But Sam <u>will not admit</u> his addiction. I think he is <u>afraid to face</u> that part of himself. So he <u>denies</u> his problem, saying he can stop drinking any time he wants to. Of course, until Sam has the courage to <u>admit what he is most afraid of</u>, his alcoholism, he won't be able to change.

A Draft Essay

Below is a draft of the essay on working and going to college. As you read it, you'll notice many changes from the outline on page 252:

- An introduction has been added, written in the first person, "I," to unify the essay.
- Transitions have been added within and between paragraphs.
- General statements have been replaced by more specific ones.
- Word choice has been improved.
- A conclusion has been added. Some of the ideas added to the conclusion came from the original list of ideas about the topic of work and school. They are ideas that do not belong in the body paragraphs but are useful in the conclusion.

A Draft of an Essay

(Thesis and topic sentences are underlined.)

I work thirty hours a week at the front desk of a motel in Riverside. When I first signed up for college classes, I figured college would be fairly easy to fit into my schedule. After all, college students are not in class all day, as high school students are. So I thought the twelve hours a week I'd spend in class wouldn't be too much of a load. But I was in for a big surprise. <u>My first semester at college showed me that students who work while going to school face problems at school, at work, and at home.</u>

<u>First of all, trying to juggle job and school responsibilities creates problems at school.</u> Early morning classes, for example, are particularly difficult for me. Because I work every weeknight from six to midnight, I don't get home until 1:00 a.m., and I can't fall asleep until 2:00 a.m. or later. I am too tired to pay attention in my 8:00 a.m. class. Once, I even fell asleep in that class. My work hours create other conflicts. They cut into my study time, so I have little time to do all the assigned reading and papers. I get behind in these assignments, and I never seem to have enough time to catch up. Consequently, my grades are not as good as they could be.

Because I both work and go to school, I have problems doing well at school. But <u>work can also suffer when workers attend college.</u> Students can bring school into the workplace. One night I tried to study at work, but my boss caught me reading my biology textbook at the front desk. I was reprimanded, and now my boss doesn't trust me. Sometimes I come to work very tired. When I don't get enough sleep, I can be rude to motel guests who give me a hard time. Then the rudeness can get me into trouble. I remember one particular guest who reported me because I was sarcastic to her. She had spent a half hour complaining about her bill, and I had been too tired to be patient. Once again, my boss reprimanded me. Another time, school interfered with my job when I had to cut work to take a make-up test at school. I know my boss was unhappy with me then, too.

As a working student, I run into trouble on the job and at college. <u>Working students also suffer outside of college and the workplace.</u> Since I work nights during the week, the weekends are the only time I can study. Because I have to use my weekends to do schoolwork, I can't do other things. My apartment is a mess since I have no time to clean it. Worse, my girlfriend is ready to kill me because I have no social life. We never even go to the movies anymore. When she comes over, I am busy studying.

With responsibilities at home, work, and college, I face a cycle of stress. I am constantly racing around, and I can't break the cycle. I want a college education, and I must have a job to pay my tuition. The only way I can manage is to learn to manage my time. <u>I have learned that working students have to be very organized to cope with their responsibilities at college, work, and home.</u>

Exercise 11 **Identifying the Main Points in the Draft of an Essay**

Below is the draft of a five-paragraph essay. Read it, then reread it and underline the thesis and the topic sentences in each body paragraph and in the conclusion.

Until this year, I had never considered spending my free time helping others in my community. Volunteer work, I thought, was something retired folks and rich people did to fill their days. Just by chance, I became a volunteer for the public library's Classic Connection, a group that arranges read-a-thons and special programs for elementary schoolchildren. Although I don't receive a salary, working with some perceptive and entertaining third-graders has been very rewarding in other ways.

Currently, I meet with my small group of four girls and three boys each Saturday morning from ten to eleven o'clock, and they have actually taught me more than I ever thought possible. I usually assign the children various passages in an illustrated children's classic like <u>The Little Prince</u>, and I help them with the difficult words as they read aloud. When I occasionally read to them, they follow right along, but when it's their turn, they happily go off track. I've learned that each child has a mind of his or her own, and I now have much more respect for day care workers and elementary school teachers who must teach, entertain, and discipline thirty rowdy children all day long. I'm tired after one hour with just seven children.

I have also learned the value of careful planning. I arrive at each session with a tape recorder and have them record a sound effect related to the story we'll be reading. At certain points during the session, we stop to hear the sound effects. They love to hear themselves and seem more focused on reading when I use this method. I feel more relaxed when I am well prepared and the sessions go smoothly.

I have enjoyed making several new friends and contacts through the Classic Connection. I've become friendly with the parents of the kids in my reading group, and one of the fathers has offered me a good-paying job at his printing business. He even mentioned he could be flexible about my schedule. I asked him if he could help me put a collection together of the group's most outrageous original stories, and he said he'd be glad to do it in <u>his</u> free time. I've thus learned that the spirit of volunteerism is indeed contagious.

I plan to keep volunteering for the Classic Connection's programs and look forward to a new group that should be starting soon. I don't know if I'm ready to graduate to an older group. After all, third-graders still have much to teach me.

Exercise 12   **Adding Transitions to an Essay**

The following essay needs transitions. Add the transitions where indicated, and add the kind of transition—word, phrase, or sentence—indicated.

I was an average student in high school. That is, I did not receive any outstanding grades, nor did I fail any courses. When I entered college, I expected to be an average student once again. I was surprised to find that college challenges me more than high school ever did. After some thought, I identified several reasons why college is more difficult than I anticipated.

_____ (add a word or phrase), I didn't study much in high school. I avoided the demanding courses that would require me to read, write, and think beyond my comfort zone. _____ (add a word or phrase), I never stretched myself and developed my abilities. _____ (add a word or phrase), I settled for the classes everyone knew were "fun" or "easy," where the teachers were called "nice" or "easygoing." In these classes, I could skim the reading assignments, show up for class, and slide through with a passing grade. _____ (add a word or phrase), my lazy brain never got a workout. Now that I am in college, I have to put my brain through basic training.

_____

_____ (add a sentence). Another problem is learning to handle the freedom of college. _____ (add a phrase), some of my instructors do not take attendance. I am often tempted to skip class, especially when a class is large and I am hardly noticed. _____ (add a word or phrase), one of my teachers has a very kind policy about make-up tests. Students can take a make-up test whenever they are ready. I have turned this teacher's kindness into my excuse to procrastinate about taking a test. College policies allow students to make their own decisions; however, they tempt me to avoid my responsibilities. Sometimes these responsibilities build up until the missed tests or classes overwhelm me.

_____

_____ (add a sentence). Yet my most important challenge is re-entering the academic world. After high school, I worked full-time for five years, married, and became a parent. _____ (add a word or phrase), I have forgotten much of what I learned in high school. _____ (add a word or phrase), mathematics is like a foreign language to me now, and I get lost when my professor refers to a term and says, "You should have learned this in high school." _____ (add a word or phrase), I haven't written an essay in years and feel insecure about my spelling and grammar. _____ (add a word or phrase), I sometimes feel so inadequate that I believe everyone in class except me knows what is going on. At times like that, I have to be very determined and positive.

There are many times when I feel overwhelmed by the challenges of college. _____ (add a word or phrase), there are also times when I earn a "B" on a test and congratulate myself on studying hard. I know that college tests my

strength, my intelligence, and my perseverance in ways that high school never did,

but I am determined to do my best.

Exercise 13 **Recognizing Synonyms and Repetition**
Used to Link Ideas in an Essay

In the following essay, underline all the synonyms and repetition (of words
or phrases) that help remind the reader of the thesis sentence. (To help you,
the thesis is underlined.)

Every boy has his heroes. Some boys look up to sports figures; others ad-

mire the stars of action movies. When I was eight, I found a hero closer to home.

He was Nate Almander, a twelve-year-old boy who lived on my block. To me, Nate

represented the confidence and freedom I wanted.

Nate never seemed to be afraid. His walk was a manly swagger, as if he

owned the neighborhood. He was usually accompanied by two or three younger

boys of ten or eleven who relied on Nate's cool leadership. If Nate and his buddies

visited the local convenience store, Nate would stare down the disapproving clerk

and lead his friends right up to the counter. My hero acted as if he had a hundred

dollars in his pocket instead of some spare change. In his self-assured manner, he

would keep other customers waiting while he debated which candy bar to buy. At

eight, I respected and even feared adults, teens, and older boys. I was afraid of

being scolded, threatened, or—worst of all—ridiculed. Nate never seemed to

worry about such possibilities. I wished I could be more like Nate.

I envied Nate's self-assurance, but I longed for his freedom. I would look out

my bedroom window and see him playing on the street late at night. No parent or

grandparent ever seemed to call him in to dinner or to bed. Sometimes, on my way

to school, I would run into Nate, who would tease me as I climbed onto the school

bus. "I'm not going to school today," he would laugh. "I've had enough of school." I

craved the liberty of one day's release from school, but even when I played sick,

my mother hustled me onto the school bus. My mother also controlled what I wore; it had to be clean and suitable for the occasion. Yet Nate could wear the same tee shirt and pants for a week and go barefoot in the summer.

Today, when I think of Nate Almander, I wonder if he had anyone to care for him. I wonder if he would have liked someone to call him in to meals or tell him how to behave. But when I was eight, Nate was everything I wanted to be: independent and bold.

POLISHING Polishing and Proofreading: An Essay

Creating a Title

When you are satisfied with the final version of your essay, you can begin preparing a good copy. Your essay will need a title. Try to think of a short title that is connected to your thesis. Since the title is the reader's first contact with your essay, an imaginative title can create a good first impression. If you can't think of anything clever, try using a key phrase from your essay.

The title is placed at the top of your essay, about an inch above the first paragraph. Always capitalize the first word of the title and all other words *except* "the," "an," "a," or prepositions (like "of," "in," "with") that are under five letters. *Do not* underline or put quotation marks around your title.

The Final Version of an Essay

Following is the final version of the essay on working and going to college. When you compare it to the draft on page 263–264, you will notice some changes:

- In the first paragraph, the words "I thought" have been added to make it clear that the statement is the writer's opinion.
- One topic sentence, in paragraph two, has been revised so that it includes the word "students" and the meaning is more precise.
- Words have been changed to sharpen the meaning.
- Transitions have been added.

A Final Version of an Essay

(Changes from the draft are underlined.)

Problems of the Working College Student

I work thirty hours a week at the front desk of a motel in Riverside. When I first underline{registered} for college classes, I figured college would be fairly easy to fit into my schedule. After all, underline{I thought,} college students are not in class all day, like high school students are. So I underline{assumed} the twelve hours a week I'd spend in class wouldn't be too much of a load. But I was in for a big surprise. My first semester at college showed me that students who work while going to college face problems at school, at work, and at home.

First of all, <u>students who try</u> to juggle job and school responsibilities <u>find trouble at school.</u> Early morning classes, for example, are particularly difficult for me. Because I work every week night from six to midnight, I don't get home until 1:00 a.m., and I can't fall asleep until 2:00 a.m. or later. <u>Consequently,</u> I am too tired to pay attention in my <u>eight o'clock class.</u> Once, I even fell asleep in that class. My work hours create other conflicts. They cut into my study time, so I have little time to do all the assigned reading and papers. I get behind in the assignments, and I never seem to have enough time to catch up. <u>As a result,</u> my grades are not as good as they could be.

Because I both work and go to school, I have problems doing well at school. But work can also suffer when workers attend college. Students can bring school into the workplace. <u>I've been guilty of this practice and have paid the price.</u> One night I tried to study at work, but my boss caught me reading my biology textbook at the front desk. I was reprimanded, and now my boss doesn't trust me. Sometimes I come to work very tired, <u>another problem.</u> When I don't get enough sleep, I can be rude to <u>motel</u> guests who give me a hard time. Then the rudeness can get me into trouble. I remember one particular guest who reported me because I was sarcastic to her. She had spent a half hour complaining about her bill, and I had been too tired to be patient. Once again, my boss reprimanded me. Another time, school interfered with my job when I had to cut work to take a make-up test at school. I know my boss was unhappy with me then, too.

As a working student, I run into trouble on the job and at college. Working students also suffer outside of classes and the workplace. <u>My schedule illustrates the conflicts of trying to juggle too many duties.</u> Since I work nights during the week, the weekends are the only time I can study. Because I have to use my weekends to do schoolwork, I can't do other things. My apartment is a mess since I have no time to clean it. Worse, my girlfriend is ready to kill me because I have no social life. We never even go to the movies anymore. When she comes over, I am busy studying.

With responsibilities at home, work, and college, I face a cycle of stress. I am constantly racing around, and I can't break the cycle. I want a college education, and I must have a job to pay my tuition. The only way I can manage is to learn to manage my time. <u>In my first semester at college, I've realized</u> that working students have to be very organized to cope with the responsibilities of college, work, and home.

Before you prepare the final copy of your essay, check your latest draft for errors in spelling, punctuation, typing, and copying.

Exercise 14   **Proofreading to Prepare the Final Version**

Following are two essays with the kinds of errors it is easy to overlook when you prepare the final version of an assignment. Correct the errors, writing above the lines. There are fourteen errors in the first essay and sixteen in the second.

"The Best Times of My Day"

Most of my life is routine. I go to work, I go to school, and I come home. This

is my schedule for most of the week. Even on weekends, I go to work and find my-

self back at school, studying in the library. Even though, routines can be boring,

there are certain times of each day that I enjoy.

One of the best parts of my day occur right after my alarm goes off. At that moment, I feel wonderful. My bed is warm, and I am resting my head on soft pillows and my body on a firm mattress. I am coming out of the deepest sleep of the night. Some times, I am half inside a terrific dream Unfortunately, this part of my day is short since I have to get up.

Another part of the day that I enjoy is my ten-minute break. I buy a large cup of coffee and relax. For 10 minutes, I don't study I don't call anyone on my cell phone, and I don't even talk to anyone. I find a quiet corner at school, or work and tune out the world. Concentrating on the taste and warmth of the coffee, I recharge my batteries for the rest of the day.

The end of my day is my favorite time. Once again, I am alone. I stretch out on the couch and listen to music. Sometimes my cat joins me curling up against my leg and purring like a motor cycle. I look back on my day and fill that I have accomplished what I set out to do. At last, I can let go of my responsibilities and worries.

Everybody long for those special holidays, vacations, or celebrations that are never forgotten. I want them, too, but I have realized that even the most ordinary day has it's pleasure's. In fact, I can find three of these moments every day.

The Place and the Food.

People tend to connect certain foods to certain countries. Spaghetti, for examples, makes people think of Italy. Japan is connected to sushi, and England is famous for its tea. However, certain foods have a different link. They are connected to popular places, not to countries.

As soon as most people pay for their movie tickets, they head to the enormous refreshment counter. Most of them buy Popcorn, the special kind of movie popcorn saturated in liquid butter and sprinkled with salt. Movie popcorn comes in cardboard tubs big enough to hold three chihuahuas. Another popular by at the movies is beverages. They, too, come in huge cups filled to overflowing. Moviegoers have to be careful not to tilt there cups as they search for seats. A tilted cup will spill over the side of the plastic lid.

Fairs and carnivales also have their own food. Where else are corn dogs sold. This combination of a hot dog rapped in cornbread and speared on a stick is loved by children and adults. Generations of children have been fascinated by the mysterious cotton candy machines. In fact, watching cotton candy form itself as it spin's maybe more fun than eating it. The whirring of the bright pink, blue, or purple fuzz promises an exotic treat.

Another treat is connected with summer places. Wherever there is a beach, river, or lake and people can sun bathe or swim, there is sure to be ice cream. Sometimes ice cream comes on a truck that sells soft, swirling ice cream in cones or cups, Popsicles, and ice cream sandwiches. Near a boardwalk or peer, an ice cream parlor may offer dozens of flavors of ice cream, frozen yogurt, sundaes, and shakes. People who love the sun and water always eats ice cream, and some poor child always drop the ice cream out of their cone.

Beaches, boardwalks, fairs, and movies are all places that offer pleasure. That pleasure is increased when people enjoy certain foods. As a result, their happy memories of a carnival may be mixed with visions of coton candy, or a sunny day may make them hungry for a Popsicle.

Lines of Detail: A Walk-Through Assignment

Choose two radio stations popular with people your age. They can be two stations that broadcast music or two stations that broadcast talk programs. Write a four-paragraph essay describing who listens to each station. To write the essay, follow these steps:

Step 1: Begin with some investigation. Listen to two stations, talk or music, popular with your age group. Before you listen, prepare a list of at least six questions. The questions will help you gather details for your essay. For any radio station, you can ask:

What kinds of products, restaurants, or services are advertised?
Does the station offer any contests?
Does the station sponsor any events?

For two music stations, your questions might include these:

> What groups or individuals does the station play?
> What kind of music does it play?

For two talk-radio stations, your questions might include these:

> What are the talk-show hosts like? Are they funny or insulting or serious?
> What topics are discussed?
> What kind of people call in?

Listen to the stations you chose, and as you listen, take notes. Answer your own questions, and write down anything about each station that catches your interest or that seems relevant.

Step 2: Survey your notes. Mark the related ideas with the same number. Then cluster the information you have gathered, and give each cluster a title.

Step 3: Focus all your clusters around one point. To find a focus, ask yourself whether the listeners of the two stations are people of the same social class, with the same interests, the same educational background, the same ethnic or racial background.

Try to focus your information with a thesis like one of these:

_____ (station name) and _____

(station name) appeal to the same audience.

_____ (station name) and _____

(station name) appeal to different audiences.

_____ (station name) and _____

(station name) use different strategies to appeal to the same

kind of listeners.

_____ (station name) appeals to young people

who _____, but _____ (station name)

appeals to young people who _____.

While _____ (station name) is popular with

middle-aged listeners interested in _____,

_____ (station name) appeals to middle-aged

listeners who like _____.

Step 4: Once you have a thesis and clustered details, draft an outline. Revise your draft outline until it is unified, expresses the ideas in a clear order, and has enough supporting details.

Step 5: Write a draft of your essay. Revise the draft, checking it for balanced paragraphs, relevant and specific details, a strong conclusion, and smooth transitions.

Step 6: Before you prepare the final version of your essay, check for spelling, word choice, punctuation, and mechanical errors. Also, give your essay a title.

Writing Your Own Essay

When you write on any of these topics, be sure to work through the stages of the writing process in preparing your essay.

1. Take any paragraph you have already written for this class and develop it into an essay of four or five paragraphs. If your instructor agrees, read the paragraph to a partner or group, and ask your listener(s) to suggest points inside the paragraph that could be developed into paragraphs of their own.   ◀ COLLABORATE

2. Write an essay using one of the following thesis statements:

   If I won a million dollars, I know what I would do with it.
   Most families waste our natural resources every day, simply by going through their daily routines.
   Television's coverage of football [or basketball, or tennis, or any other sport you choose] could be improved by a few changes.
   All bad romances share certain characteristics.
   If I could be someone else, I'd like to be _____ for several reasons.

3. Write an essay on earliest childhood memories. Interview three classmates to gather details and to focus your essay. Ask each one to tell you about the earliest memory he or she has of childhood. Before you begin interviewing, make a list of questions, like these: What is your earliest memory? How old were you at the time of that recollection? What were you doing? Do you remember other people or events in that scene? If so, what were the others doing? Were you indoors? Outdoors? Is this a pleasant memory? Why do you think this memory has stayed with you? Use the details collected at the interviews to write a five-paragraph essay with a thesis sentence like one of the following: ◀ COLLABORATE

   Childhood memories vary a great deal from person to person.
   The childhood memories of different people are surprisingly similar.
   Although some people's first memories are painful, others remember a happy time.
   Some people claim to remember events from their infancy, but others can't remember anything before their third (or fourth, fifth, etc.) birthday.

4. Freewrite for ten minutes on the two best days of your life. After you've completed the freewriting, review it. Do the two days have

much in commmon? Or were they very different? Write a four-paragraph essay based on their similarities or differences, with a thesis like one of these:

The two best days of my life were both _____. (Focus on similarities.)

While one of the best days of my life was _____, the other great day was _____. (Fill in with differences.)

5. Write a five-paragraph essay on one of the following topics:

Three Careers for Me   The Three Worst Jobs
Three Workplace Hazards   Three Workplace Friends
Three Lucky People   Three Wishes
Three Family Traditions   Three Decisions for Me

6. Look closely at the photograph below. Write a five-paragraph essay in which you describe a situation that the picture may represent. In one body paragraph, you can write about how these two people met and decided to head for New York; in another paragraph, about what they are hoping for as they stand together hitchhiking; and in another paragraph, about what may happen to them next.

 COMPUTER ▶

7. Many people are turning to online dating services as a way to meet people and potential partners. Find an online dating service and investigate its methods, claims, and fees. Based on your research,

write an essay that takes a stand on the following statement: _____, an online dating service, is ethical/unethical (choose one) in its promises.

If you or someone you know has ever used an online dating service, write an essay based on the following statement:

Finding a suitable mate through an online dating service can be a _____ experience.

8. Narrow one of the following topics and then write an essay on it. Remember that brainstorming and freewriting can help you narrow your focus.

nature	dreams	crime	music	celebrities
fears	family	lies	health	romance
habits	books	money	animals	travel
students	teachers	games	secrets	fashion

9. Look closely at the photograph below. Write a four-paragraph essay in which you describe the relationship between the people in the photograph. You can use your imagination, but try to base your imaginings on the facial expressions and body language of the people.

Note: Additional writing options suitable for essay assignments can be found after three professional readings: "Eleven," which begins on page 630, "A Brother's Murder," which begins on page 633, and "Navajo Code Talkers: The Century's Best Kept Secret," which begins on page 637.

Name: _____ **Section:** _____

PEER REVIEW FORM FOR AN ESSAY

After you've written a draft of your essay, let a writing partner read it. When your partner has completed the form below, discuss the comments. Then repeat the same process for your partner's paragraph.

The thesis of this essay is _____

_____

The topic sentences for the body paragraphs are _____

_____

_____

_____

_____

The topic sentence in the conclusion is _____

_____

The best part of the essay is the _____ (first, second, third, etc.) paragraph.

I would like to see details added to the part about _____

_____

I would take out the part about _____

The introduction is (a) good or (b) could be better. (Choose one.)

The conclusion is (a) good or (b) could be better. (Choose one.)

I have questions about _____

Additional comments: _____

_____

_____

_____

_____

_____

_____

_____

Reviewer's Name: _____

CHAPTER 12
Different Essay Patterns

You can write essays in a number of patterns, but any pattern will develop more successfully if you follow the writing steps in preparing your essay. The following examples take you through the steps of preparing an essay in each pattern. Each essay expands on its related paragraph pattern in an earlier chapter of this book.

ILLUSTRATION

Hints for Writing an Illustration Essay

1. Use specific examples to support a general point. Remember that a *general* statement is a broad point, and a *specific* example is narrow.

general statement: The weather was terrible yesterday.
specific example: It rained for six hours.

general statement: I am having trouble in my math class.
specific example: I can't understand the problems in Chapter 12.

2. Be sure that you support a general statement by using specific examples instead of merely writing another general statement.

not this: general statement: The weather was terrible yesterday.
more general statements: ~~It was awful outside. Yesterday brought nasty weather.~~

but this: general statement: The weather was terrible yesterday.
specific examples: It rained for six hours.
                      Several highways were flooded.

3. Be sure that you have sufficient examples and that you develop them well. If you use one or two examples and do not development them effectively, you will have a skimpy paragraph. You can use fewer examples and develop each one, or you can use more examples and develop them less extensively.

not this: a skimpy paragraph:

The weather was terrible yesterday. It rained for six hours. Several highways were flooded.

but this: a paragraph with few examples, each one well developed:

The weather was terrible yesterday. It rained for six hours. The rain was heavy and harsh, accompanied by high winds that lashed the trees and signs on stores and restaurants. The downpour was so heavy that several highways were flooded. Drivers who usually take the Collins Road Expressway were diverted to a narrow city street and crawled home at 30 m.p.h. Additionally, traffic on the interstate highway was at a standstill because drivers slowed to gawk at the numerous accidents caused by the lack of visibility and water-slicked roads.

or this: a paragraph developed with more examples:

The weather was terrible yesterday. It rained for six hours, and several highways were flooded. Cedar Forest Elementary School closed early because of a leak in the auditorium's roof. The standing water also collected in low-lying residential areas where some children put on their swimsuits and splashed in four to six inches of water. Their parents, meanwhile, were trying to sweep the water out of porches and patios and praying that more rain would not seep into their houses. The high winds that accompanied the rain snapped tree branches and littered the area with debris. Two small "For Sale" signs were blown into the drive-through window at Burger King.

WRITING THE ILLUSTRATION ESSAY IN STEPS

PREWRITING Gathering Ideas: Illustration Essay

If you were asked to write an illustration essay about some aspect of clothes, you might first freewrite to narrow the topic and then decide to write about *tee shirts*. Brainstorming and listing your ideas about tee shirts might lead you to group your ideas into three categories:

Listing and Grouping Ideas for an Illustration Paragraph
Topic: Tee Shirts

Kinds of People Who Wear Tee Shirts

athletes	movie stars	old people
children	musicians	restaurant workers
teens	parents	

The Cost of Tee Shirts

cheap   some expensive

What Is Pictured or Written on Tee Shirts

ads on tees   beer ads   seascapes

concert tees   sporting goods   political slogans

college names   Mickey Mouse   souvenir pictures or sayings

You can summarize these ideas in a thesis sentence:

People of various backgrounds and ages wear all kinds of tee shirts.

This thesis sentence contains three parts: (1) people of various backgrounds, (2) people of all ages, and (3) all kinds of tee shirts. The part about the cost of tee shirts has been left out of the thesis. As you work toward a thesis, you can decide what to include and what to leave out. The three parts of the thesis may lead you to topic sentences for your outline.

With a thesis sentence and a list of ideas, you are now ready to write an outline for your essay.

PLANNING Devising a Plan: Illustration Essay

Following is an outline for an illustration essay on tee shirts.

An Outline for an Illustration Essay

paragraph 1

I. Thesis: People of various backgrounds and ages wear all kinds of tee shirts.

paragraph 2
topic sentence
and details
people of
various
backgrounds

II. The rich and poor, famous and unknown, all wear tee shirts.
   A. Famous athletes can be seen in tee shirts, signing autographs after a game.
   B. Members of the local Little League team wear tees.
   C. Movie stars are seen in them.
   D. Musicians perform in tee shirts.
   E. Restaurant workers wear tee shirts.
   F. Famous political leaders work out in tee shirts.

paragraph 3
topic sentence
and details
people of all ages

III. Every age group feels comfortable in tee shirts.
   A. Mothers dress their babies in soft, washable little tees.
   B. Older children wear a favorite tee shirt until it falls apart.
   C. A teen wardrobe would not be complete without the latest style in tee shirts.
   D. Parents wear them to clean and do chores.
   E. Old people can be seen jogging or gardening in tees.

paragraph 4
topic sentence
and details
all kinds of
tee shirts

IV. Almost anything can be printed or pictured on a tee shirt.
   A. There are tees sold at concerts.
   B. Some shirts have the names of colleges on them.

C. Others advertise a brand of beer or sporting
    goods.
D. Mickey Mouse is a favorite character on them.
E. Surfers' tee shirts have seascapes on them.
F. Some shirts are souvenirs.
G. Others have political slogans.

paragraph 5
conclusion

V. Anyone can find a tee shirt suited to his or her age
    and lifestyle, and that shirt can carry almost any
    message.

The outline combined some of the details from the list with new details gathered during the outlining process. As you write and revise your draft, you can continue to add details. You can also combine sentences, add transitions, and work on word choice.

DRAFTING Drafting and Revising: Illustration Essay

Following is a revised draft of the essay on tee shirts. As you read it, you'll notice many changes from the outline on pages 279–280.

- An introduction has been added.
- Transitions have been added within and between paragraphs.
- Details have been added.
- Sentences have been combined.
- A concluding paragraph has been added.

A Draft of an Illustration Essay

(Thesis and topic sentences are underlined.)

Fashion fads come and go. One year, everyone wears ripped jeans, and another year, striped soccer shirts are in. Whatever is most popular this year will most likely be out of style by next year. However, there is one piece of clothing that never goes out of style: the tee shirt. <u>People of various backgrounds and ages wear all kinds of tee shirts.</u>

<u>The rich and poor, famous and unknown all wear tee shirts.</u> While famous athletes dressed in tees sign autographs after a big game, children of the local Little League proudly sport their team shirts. Movie stars wear tees to their movie premieres. Musicians, both famous and struggling, perform in tee shirts. Meanwhile, many restaurant workers wear the restaurant's name or logo on their uniform tee. Even famous politicians have been photographed jogging or working out in tee shirts.

Tees appeal to all classes, and they also appeal to all generations. <u>Every age group feels comfortable in tee shirts.</u> Mothers dress their babies in soft little tee shirts. Older children often become so attached to a favorite tee that they wear it until it falls apart. In addition, a teen wardrobe would not be complete without the latest style in tee shirts. Parents wear them to clean the house, do the shopping, and wash the car. Older people in tees can be see jogging through the neighborhood or gardening in their front yard.

All kinds of people wear tees, just as the shirts themselves come in all varieties. <u>Almost anything can be pictured or printed on a tee shirt.</u> At concerts, tee shirts with the performer's name on them cost a lot of money. Another popular kind of tee carries the name of a college. Other tees advertise a brand of beer, like Bud, or a sporting goods company, like Nike. Mickey Mouse is a favorite character on tee shirts, and not just on children's tees. Still other kinds of shirts include surfer tee shirts with seascapes on them and souvenir tees, like the ones that say, "My folks visited Philadelphia, and all I got was this lousy tee shirt." Some shirts have political slogans, like "Save the Whales."

Fads can fade, but the tee shirt is everywhere. It has become so popular that it is almost a uniform. Its popularity is connected to its variety. <u>Anyone can find a tee shirt suited to his or her age and lifestyle, and that shirt can carry almost any message.</u>

POLISHING   Polishing and Proofreading: Illustration Essay

Following is the final version of the essay on tee shirts. When you compare it to the draft on pages 280–281, you will notice some changes:

- Some of the word choice has been polished to make a description more precise or to eliminate an awkward phrase.
- One phrase, "cost a lot of money," was changed to "can be expensive" to eliminate the use of "a lot," a phrase that some writers rely on too heavily.
- A transition was added to the conclusion.
- The conclusion includes a new, final sentence to stress the link between tee shirts' popularity and their variety.
- A title has been added.

A Final Version of an Illustration Essay
(Changes from the draft are underlined.)

Tee Shirts Galore

Fashion fads come and go. One year, everyone wears ripped jeans, and another year, striped soccer shirts are in. Whatever is most popular this year will most likely be out of style by next year. However, there is one piece of clothing that never goes out of style: the tee shirt. People of various backgrounds and ages wear all kinds of tee shirts.

The rich and poor, famous and unknown all wear tee shirts. While famous athletes dressed in tees sign autographs after a big game, children of the local Little League proudly sport their team shirts. Movie stars wear tees to their <u>glamorous</u> movie premieres. Musicians, both famous and struggling, perform in tee shirts. Meanwhile, many restaurant workers wear the restaurant's name or logo on their uniform tee. Even famous politicians have been photographed jogging or working out in tee shirts.

Tees appeal to all classes, and they also appeal to all generations. Every age group feels comfortable in tee shirts. Mothers dress their babies in soft little tee shirts. Older children often become so attached to a favorite tee that they wear it until it falls apart. In addition, a teen wardrobe would not be complete without the latest style in tee shirts. Parents wear them to clean the house, do the shopping, and wash the car. Older people in tees can be see jogging through the neighborhood or gardening in their front yard.

All kinds of people wear tees, just as the shirts themselves come in all varieties. Almost anything can be pictured or printed on a tee shirt. At concerts, tee shirts with the performer's name on them <u>can be expensive</u>. Another popular kind of tee carries the name of a college. Other tees advertise a brand of beer, like Bud, or a sporting goods company, like Nike. Mickey Mouse is a favorite character on tee shirts <u>for all ages</u>. Still other kinds of shirts include surfer tee shirts with seascapes on them and souvenir tees, like the ones that say, "My folks visited Philadelphia, and all I got was this lousy tee shirt." Some shirts have political slogans, like "Save the Whales."

Fads can fade, but the tee shirt is everywhere. It has become so popular that it is <u>like a uniform</u>. <u>Yet</u> its <u>universal appeal</u> is connected to its variety. Anyone can find a tee shirt suited to his or her age and lifestyle, and that shirt can carry almost any message. <u>Therefore, each tee shirt is a uniform that reflects the person who wears it.</u>

TOPICS FOR WRITING AN ILLUSTRATION ESSAY

When you write on any of these topics, work through the stages of the writing process in preparing your essay.

1. Complete one of the following statements and use it as the thesis for an illustration essay.

Finding a job can be _____.

People in love often _____.

Students under pressure sometimes _____.

A sense of humor can _____.

Fitting in is _____.

In a crisis, there are always people who _____.

2. Choose one of the following topics. Narrow it to a more specific topic and then write a thesis statement about it. Use that thesis to write an illustration essay.

families	loneliness	nature
weddings	babies	adolescents
young adults	laws	crime
change	technology	health

 COLLABORATE ▶ **3.** To begin this assignment, work with two or three classmates. Brainstorm as many typical, general statements as you can. You are looking for the kinds of generalizations we have all heard or even said—for example, "Your college years are the best years of your life" or "Old people are the worst drivers on the road." List as many as you can. Then split up. Pick one of the general statements and write a thesis that challenges the truth of the statement. For example, your thesis could be, "The college years are not the best of a person's life" or "Old people are not always bad drivers." Use the thesis for an illustration essay.

4. To begin this assignment, look around your classroom. Now, write a general statement about some aspect of the classroom: the furniture, the colors used to decorate, the condition of the room, what the students carry to class, the students' footwear, facial expressions, hairstyles, and so forth. Write a five-paragraph essay using that general statement as your thesis and supporting it with specific examples from your observation.

DESCRIPTION

Hints for Writing a Descriptive Essay

1. Use many specific details. Because an essay is usually longer than one paragraph, you will need to develop an essay with more details. To ensure that your details create an effective description, make them specific.

2. Decide on a clear order. Without a clear order, a descriptive essay will become a jumble of details spread over several paragraphs. Decide on a clear order (from inside to outside, from top to bottom, and so forth) and stick to it. Each body paragraph can focus on one part of that order.

WRITING THE DESCRIPTIVE ESSAY IN STEPS

PREWRITING Gathering Ideas: Descriptive Essay

If you were going to write an essay describing your brother's bedroom, you might first brainstorm a list.

Brainstorming a List for a Descriptive Essay

Topic: My Brother's Bedroom

- older brother Michael—got a big bedroom
- I shared with my little brother
- stars pasted on the ceiling
- took a long time to fix it up the way he wanted it
- lots of books about science fiction in two bookcases
- movie posters of <u>AI: Artificial Intelligence</u> and <u>The Matrix</u>
- old videos like <u>Raiders of the Lost Ark</u> in bookcases
- his bed had no headboard, made to look like a couch
- <u>Star Trek</u> pillows on the bed

After surveying the list, you want to think about what point it makes. The main point of the list is the *dominant impression*. For this list, the dominant impression could be this sentence:

> My brother's bedroom reflected his fascination with fantasy and science fiction.

This sentence could be the thesis sentence of the descriptive essay.

PLANNING Devising a Plan: Descriptive Essay

Following is an outline for a descriptive essay on a brother's bedroom.

An Outline for a Descriptive Essay

paragraph 1 | I. Thesis: My brother's bedroom reflected his fascination with fantasy and science fiction.

paragraph 2
topic sentence
and details
the ceiling

II. The ceiling created a fantasy.
  A. Stars were pasted on the ceiling.
  B. In the daylight, they were nearly invisible.
  C. At night, they glowed in the dark.
  D. The room appeared to be covered by a starry sky.
  E. On many nights, my brother and I would lie on the floor.
  F. We would pretend his room was a spaceship and the stars were the planets.

paragraph 3
topic sentence
and details
the walls

III. The walls were the most obvious sign of my brother's interests.
  A. They were covered in movie posters from fantasy or science fiction films.
  B. There was a poster of Steven Spielberg's film <u>AI: Artificial Intelligence</u>.
  C. My brother had seen the movie five times.
  D. At a garage sale, he had found an old poster of <u>E.T. the Extra-Terrestrial</u>.
  E. It was also on the wall.
  F. Another poster, of <u>The Matrix</u>, was framed.
  G. The walls made me feel as if I were in the lobby of a movie theater.

paragraph 4
topic sentence
and details
the furniture

IV. The furniture was ordinary, but it had some fantastic touches.
  A. There were two battered old bookcases ready for the junk pile.
  B. They were full of books about science fiction.
  C. I remember <u>Fahrenheit 451</u> and <u>The War of the Worlds</u>.
  D. Old videos like <u>Raiders of the Lost Ark</u> were also stacked on the bookshelves.
  E. My brother had the same standard single bed that I had.
  F. His was piled high with <u>Star Trek</u> pillows.

paragraph 5 conclusion

V. My brother created his own fantastic world in his room.

The outline combined some of the details from the list with new details gathered during the outlining process. As you write and revise your draft, you can continue to add details. You can also combine sentences, add transitions, and work on word choice.

 **DRAFTING** Drafting and Revising: Descriptive Essay

Following is a revised draft of the essay on a brother's bedroom. As you read it, you'll notice many changes from the outline on page 284.

- An introduction has been added.
- Transitions have been added within and between paragraphs.
- Details have been added.
- Sentences have been combined.
- A concluding paragraph has been written.

A Draft of a Descriptive Essay

(Thesis and topic sentences are underlined.)

Whenever my older brother and I would watch television, we would fight over what to watch. I always wanted to watch wrestling, but my brother was bigger than I was, so we ended up watching <u>Deep Space Nine</u> or <u>Alien 2</u>. He would watch even the oldest reruns of <u>The Twilight Zone</u> because he loved the strange, the unreal, and the scientific. Even <u>my brother's bedroom reflected his fascination with fantasy and science fiction.</u>

<u>The ceiling of his room created a fantasy.</u> Stars were pasted on the ceiling. In the daylight, they were nearly invisible. In the night, they glowed in the dark so that the room appeared to be covered by a starry sky. On many nights, my brother and I would lie on the floor. We would pretend his room was a spaceship and the stars were the planets.

Although the ceiling gave a hint of my brother's dreams, and that hint was visible at night, there was another hint. <u>The walls were the most visible sign of my brother's interests.</u> They were covered in movie posters from fantasy or science fiction films. There was a poster of Steven Spielberg's film <u>AI: Artificial Intelligence</u>. My brother had seen the movie five times, and the poster hung over his bed. At a garage sale, he found an old poster of <u>E.T. the Extra-Terrestrial</u>. It and the <u>AI</u> poster hung over his bed. Another poster, of <u>The Matrix</u>, was framed and covered the opposite wall. The posters made me feel as if I were in the lobby of a movie theater.

Unlike the wall decorations, <u>the furniture was ordinary, but my brother had given it some fantastic touches.</u> He had two battered old bookcases ready for the junk pile. They were like any other boy's furniture except that they were full of books about science fiction. I particularly remember <u>Fahrenheit 451</u> and <u>The War of the Worlds</u>. Old videos like <u>Raiders of the Lost Ark</u> were also stacked on the bookshelves. And even though my brother had the same standard single bed that I had, his was different. It was piled high with <u>Star Trek</u> pillows.

Any boy's room reveals his interests. However, few boys are as determined as my brother was in transforming his room into something else. <u>My brother created his own fantastic world in his room.</u>

 **POLISHING** Polishing and Proofreading: Descriptive Essay

Following is a final version of the essay on a brother's bedroom. When you compare it to the draft above, you will notice some changes:

- The introduction used the word "even" twice, an awkward repetition. A change in word choice and a new transition to the thesis statement eliminated the repetition.

- A final sentence was added to the second paragraph. The paragraph needed a few more details, and the new sentence helped to reinforce the thesis, too.
- A change in word choice in the third paragraph eliminates the repetition of "visible."
- The third paragraph also repeated the detail that the <u>AI</u> poster hung over the bed. The repetition was cut.
- New details were added to the third paragraph.
- A sentence of specific details was added to the conclusion; so were other details.
- A title has been added.

A Final Version of a Descriptive Essay

(Changes from the draft are underlined.)

My Brother's Heavenly Bedroom

Whenever my older brother and I would watch television, we would fight over what to watch. I always wanted to watch wrestling, but my brother was bigger than I was, so we ended up watching <u>Deep Space Nine</u> or <u>Alien 2</u>. He would watch the oldest reruns of <u>The Twilight Zone</u> because he loved the strange, the unreal, and the scientific. <u>This love was so strong that</u> even my brother's bedroom reflected his fascination with fantasy and science fiction.

The ceiling of his room created a fantasy. Stars were pasted on the ceiling. In the daylight, they were nearly invisible. In the night, they glowed in the dark so that the room appeared to be covered by a starry sky. On many nights, my brother and I would lie on the floor. We would pretend his room was a spaceship and the stars were the planets. <u>At these moments, I became a partner in his imaginary world</u>.

Although the ceiling gave a hint of my brother's dreams, and that hint was <u>apparent</u> at night, there was another, <u>stronger</u> hint. The walls were the most visible sign of my brother's interests. They were covered in movie posters from fantasy or science fiction films. There was a poster of Steven Spielberg's film <u>AI: Artificial Intelligence</u>. My brother had seen the movie five times. At a garage sale, he found an old, ragged poster of <u>E.T. the Extra-Terrestrial. He cut the poster's ragged edges and covered it in plastic.</u> It and the <u>AI</u> poster hung over his bed. Another poster, <u>a dark vision</u> of <u>The Matrix</u>, was framed and covered the opposite wall. The posters made me feel as if I were in the lobby of a movie theater.

Unlike the wall decorations, the furniture was ordinary, but my brother had given it some fantastic touches. He had two battered old bookcases ready for the junk pile. They were like any other boy's furniture except that they were full of books about science fiction. I particularly remember <u>Fahrenheit 451</u> and <u>The War of the Worlds</u>. Old videos like <u>Raiders of the Lost Ark</u> were also stacked on the bookshelves. And even though my brother had the same standard single bed that I had, his was different. It was piled high with <u>Star Trek</u> pillows.

Any boy's room reveals his interests. <u>There may be a basketball, some video games, and a poster or two.</u> However, few boys are as determined as my brother was in transforming his room into <u>his private space</u>. My brother created his own fantastic world in his room.

TOPICS FOR WRITING A DESCRIPTIVE ESSAY

When you write on any of these topics, work through the stages of the writing process in preparing your essay.

1. Begin this essay with a partner. Describe your ideal man or woman to your partner. Ask your partner to (1) jot down the details of your description and (2) help you come up with specific details by asking you follow-up questions each time you run out of ideas. Work together for at least ten minutes. Then change roles. Let your partner describe his or her ideal man or woman to you and take notes for your partner. Then split up and use the details you collected to write an essay.

◀ COLLABORATE 👥

2. Describe a place you would never want to return to. Be sure to use specific details that explain why this place is terrible, unpleasant, or unattractive.

3. If you were allowed to take only three items (furniture, pictures, photographs, jewelry, and so forth) from your home, what would these things be? Write an essay describing them and their importance to you.

4. Describe one of the following:

> a place that you loved when you were a child
> a room that makes you feel comfortable
> a place you go to when you feel stressed
> a favorite pet
> your workplace
> your favorite place outdoors
> the place you go to study

5. Describe someone you know well and who has two sides to him or her. These sides may be the private and the public sides, the happy and sad sides, the calm and angry sides, and so forth. Give specific details for both sides of this person.

6. We all associate certain people with certain rooms. For instance, you may associate your mother with her kitchen or her home office, or your brother with the garage, where he works on his car. You may picture your father in the den, where he likes to relax. Choose a person you know well, and then decide which room you associate with this person. Then write an essay showing how the details of that room relate to the person's personality, interests, and goals.

NARRATION

Hints for Writing a Narrative Essay

1. Give the essay a point and stick to it. A narrative essay tells a story. A story without a point becomes a list of moments that lead nowhere. Once you have your point, check that your use of details does not lead you away from the point.

2. Divide your narrative into clear stages. In an essay, you divide your narrative into several paragraphs. Check that each body paragraph has a clear focus (in the topic sentence) and that you have a clear reason for your division. You may decide to divide your body paragraphs into (a) before, during, and after, or (b) the first part of the story, the middle part, the ending.

WRITING THE NARRATIVE ESSAY IN STEPS

PREWRITING Gathering Ideas: Narrative Essay

If you were asked to write a narrative essay about something that changed you, you might begin by freewriting.

Freewriting for a Narrative Essay

Topic: Something That Changed Me

Something that changed me. I don't know. What changed me? Lots of things happened to me, but I can't find one that changed me. Graduating from high school? Everybody will write about that, how boring, and anyway, what was the big deal? I haven't gotten married. No big change there. Divorce. My parents' divorce really changed the whole family. A big shock to me. I couldn't believe it was happening. I was really scared. Who would I live with? They were real calm when they told me. I've never been so scared. I was too young to understand. Kept thinking they'd just get back together. They didn't. Then I got a stepmother. The year of the divorce a hard time for me. Kids suffer in divorce.

Reviewing your freewriting, you decide to write on the topic of your parents' divorce. Once you have this topic, you begin to brainstorm about your topic, asking yourself questions that can lead to further details about the divorce.

With more details, you can decide that your essay will focus on the announcement of your parents' divorce and the emotions you felt. You devise the following topic sentence:

When my parents announced that they were divorcing, I felt confused by all my emotions.

POLISHING Devising a Plan: Narrative Essay

Following is an outline for a narrative essay on the announcement of your parents' divorce and the emotions you felt. As you read it, note how it divides the announcement into three parts: (1) the background of the announcement, (2) the story of the divorce announcement, and (3) the emotions connected to the announcement.

An Outline for a Narrative Essay

paragraph 1	I. Thesis: When my parents announced that they were divorcing, I felt confused by all my emotions.
paragraph 2	II. I will never forget how one ordinary day suddenly
topic sentence	became a terrible one.
and details	A. I was seven when my mom and dad divorced.

background of
the announcement

    B. My sister was ten.
    C. Both of my parents were there.
    D. They told us at breakfast, in the kitchen.
    E. I was eating toast.
    F. I remember I couldn't eat anything after they started talking.
    G. I remember a piece of toast with one bite out of it.

paragraph 3
topic sentence
and details
story of the
announcement

III. When my parents first spoke, I was in shock.
    A. They were very calm when they told us.
    B. They said they loved us, but they couldn't get along.
    C. They said they would always love us kids.
    D. It was an unreal moment to me.
    E. I couldn't believe it was happening.
    F. At first I just thought they were having another fight.
    G. I was too young to understand.
    H. I didn't cry.

paragraph 4
topic sentence
and details
my emotions

IV. When the reality hit me, my emotions overwhelmed me.
    A. My sister cried.
    B. Then I knew it was serious.
    C. I kept thinking I would have to choose which parent to live with.
    D. I knew I would really hurt the one I didn't choose.
    E. I loved them both.
    F. I felt so much guilt about leaving one of them.
    G. I also needed both of them.
    H. I felt ripped apart.

paragraph 5
conclusion

V. When my parents' marriage fell apart, so did I.

The outline combined some of the details from the freewriting with other details gathering through brainstorming and during the outlining process. As you write and revise your draft, you can continue to add details. You can also combine sentences, add transitions, and work on word choice.

DRAFTING   Drafting and Revising: Narrative Essay

Following is a revised draft of the essay on an announcement of divorce. As you read it, you'll notice many changes from the outline on pages 288–289.

- An introduction has been added.
- Transitions within the paragraphs have been added.
- Details have been added.
- Some dialogue has been added.
- A concluding paragraph has been added.

A Draft of a Narrative Essay

(Thesis and topic sentences are underlined.)

Divorce can be really hard on children. <u>When my parents announced that they were divorcing, I felt confused by all my emotions.</u>

<u>I will never forget how one ordinary day suddenly became a terrible one</u>. I was seven, and my sister was ten on that day. Both of my parents told us at breakfast, in the kitchen. I clearly remember that I was eating toast, but once they started talking, I couldn't eat anything. I can still recall holding a piece of toast with one bite out of it. I stared at the toast stupidly as I listened to what they had to say.

<u>When my parents first spoke, I was in shock</u>. They were very calm when they told us. "We love both of you very much," my dad said, "but your mother and I aren't getting along." "But we will always love you," my mother added. The announcement was such an unreal moment that I couldn't believe it was happening. My parents used to fight a lot, so at first I just thought they were having another fight. I was too young to understand. In fact, I didn't even cry.

<u>When the reality hit me, my emotions overwhelmed me</u>. My sister began to cry, and I suddenly knew it was serious. I kept thinking I would have to choose which parent to live with, and I knew I would really hurt the one I didn't choose. I loved them both. I was filled with guilt about hurting one. I also needed both parents so much that I dreaded separating from one of them. I believed that the one I didn't choose would hate me. I felt ripped apart.

In one morning, my world changed. One minute, I was an ordinary seven-year-old having breakfast with his family. The next, I was experiencing powerful emotions no child should feel. <u>When my parents' marriage fell apart, so did I.</u>

POLISHING

Polishing and Proofreading: Narrative Essay

Following is the final version of the essay on an announcement of divorce. When you compare it to the draft above, you will notice some changes:

- The introduction has been developed and improved.
- More specific details have been added.
- The word "dad" has been replaced with "father" so that the language is more formal.
- The phrase "a lot" was changed to "often" because "a lot" is an overused phrase.
- The word "fight" was replaced by "argument" so that "fight" does not appear twice in one sentence.
- The first word in paragraph 4 has been changed from "When" to "Then" so that the openings of paragraphs 3 and 4 are not repetitive.
- The word "it" in paragraph 4 has been replaced by "the situation" so that the sentence is clearer.
- To improve the style in paragraph 4, some sentences have been combined.
- A title has been added.

A Final Version of a Narrative Essay

(Changes from the draft are underlined.)

An Emotional Morning

<u>No childhood is perfect, and part of growing up is facing disappointment, change, and loss. However, there is one loss that can be overwhelming.</u> Divorce can be really hard on children. When my parents announced that they were divorcing, I felt confused by all my emotions.

I will never forget how one ordinary day suddenly became a terrible one. I was seven, and my sister was ten on that day. Both of my parents told us at breakfast, in the kitchen. I clearly remember that I was eating toast, but once they started talking, I couldn't eat anything. I can still recall holding a piece of <u>whole wheat</u> toast with one bite out of it. I stared at the toast stupidly as I listened to what they had to say.

When my parents first spoke, I was in shock. They were very calm when they told us. "We love both of you very much," my <u>father</u> said, "but your mother and I aren't getting along." "But we will always love you," my mother added. The announcement was such an unreal moment that I couldn't believe it was happening. My parents used to fight <u>often</u>, so at first I just thought they were having another <u>argument</u>. I was too young to understand. In fact, I didn't even cry.

<u>Then</u> the reality hit me, and my emotions overwhelmed me. My sister began to cry, and I suddenly knew <u>the situation</u> was serious. I kept thinking I would have to choose which parent to live with, and I knew I would really hurt the one I didn't choose. Because I loved them both, I was filled with guilt about hurting one. I also needed both parents so much that I dreaded separating from one of them. I believed that the one I didn't choose would hate me. I felt ripped apart.

In one morning, my world changed. One minute, I was an ordinary seven-year-old having breakfast with his family. The next, I was experiencing powerful emotions no child should feel. When my parents' marriage fell apart, so did I.

TOPICS FOR WRITING A NARRATIVE ESSAY

When you write on any of these topics, work through the stages of the writing process in preparing your essay.

1. This assignment begins with an interview. Ask one (or both) of your parents to tell you about the day you were born. Be prepared to ask questions. (For example, were you expected that day, or did you surprise your family? Was there a rush to the hospital?) Get as many details as you can. Then write a narrative essay about that day.

2. Write about a time you learned an important lesson. Use the events of the time to explain how you learned the lesson.

3. Write the story of an argument (one you were involved in or one you observed) and its consequences.

4. Write about a crime you witnessed or were a victim of. Be sure to include details about what happened after the crime was committed.

5. Write about an incident in your life that seemed to be fate (that is, meant to happen).

6. Write the story of an accident. The accident can be one you were involved in or one you observed. It can be any kind of accident: a car accident, a sports injury, and so forth.

7. Write on any of the following topics:

your first day at work	your first day at school
the best day of your life	the worst day of your life
the day you witnessed a victory	a day you made a friend
a day you lost a friend	a day with a pleasant surprise

PROCESS

Hints for Writing a Process Essay

1. Remember that there are two kinds of process essays: a **directional** process essay tells the reader how to do something; an **informational** process essay explains an activity without telling the reader how to do it. Whether you write a directional or process essay, be sure to make a point. That point is expressed in your thesis.

When you write a process essay, it is easy to confuse a topic with a thesis.

> **topic:** How to change the oil in your car.
> **thesis:** You don't have to be an expert to learn how to change the oil in your car.

> **topic:** How gardeners squirrel-proof their backyards.
> **thesis:** Gardeners have to think like squirrels to keep the critters away from plants and trees.

2. Find some logical way to divide the steps into paragraphs. If you have seven steps, you probably don't want to put each one into a separate paragraph, especially if they are short steps. You would run the risk of having a list instead of a well-developed essay. To avoid writing a list, try to cluster your steps according to some logical division.

For instance, if you are writing about how to prepare for a successful party, you could divide your steps into groups like (1) what to do a week before the party, (2) what to do the day before the party, and (3) what to do the day of the party. Or if you are writing about how to make a carrot cake, you could divide the steps into (1) assembling the ingredients, (2) making the cake, and (3) baking and frosting the cake.

3. Develop your paragraphs by explaining each step thoroughly and by using details. If you are explaining how to make a cake, you can't simply tell the reader to mix the combined ingredients well. You need to explain how long to mix and whether to mix with a fork, spoon, spatula, or electric mixer. Fortunately, an essay gives you the time and space to be clear. And you will be clear if you put yourself in the reader's place and anticipate his or her questions.

WRITING THE PROCESS ESSAY IN STEPS

PREWRITING Gathering Ideas: Process

If you were writing a process essay about finding an apartment, you might first freewrite your ideas on the topic. Brainstorming and listing your ideas might lead you to group your ideas into three categories, organized in time order:

Listing and Grouping Ideas for a Process Essay

Topic: Finding an Apartment

before the search
Do you want a one bedroom?

Friends can help.

A good neighborhood

A convenient location can be more expensive

Can save you money on transportation

during the search
Look around

Don't pick the first apartment you see.

Look at a bunch.

But not too many

after the search
Check the lease carefully.

How much is the security deposit?

After some more thinking, you could summarize these ideas in a thesis:

> Finding the apartment you want takes planning and careful investigation.

With a thesis sentence and some ideas clustered in categories, you can write an outline for your essay.

PLANNING Devising a Plan: Process Essay

Following is an outline for a process essay on finding an apartment.

An Outline for a Process Essay

paragraph 1

I. Thesis: Finding the apartment you want takes planning and careful investigation.

paragraph 2
topic sentence
and details
before the search

II. You can save yourself stress by doing some preliminary work.
 A. Decide what you want.
 B. Ask yourself, "Do I want a one bedroom?" and "What can I afford?"
 C. Weigh the pros and cons of your wishes.
 D. A convenient location can be expensive.
 E. It can also save you money on transportation.
 F. Friends can help you with the names of nice apartments.
 G. Maybe somebody you know lives in a good neighborhood.
 H. Check the classified advertisements in the newspapers.

<table>
<tr><td>paragraph 3
topic sentence
and details
during the search</td><td>III.</td><td colspan="2">On your search, be patient, look carefully, and ask questions.</td></tr>
<tr><td></td><td></td><td>A.</td><td>Look around.</td></tr>
<tr><td></td><td></td><td>B.</td><td>Don't pick the first apartment you see.</td></tr>
<tr><td></td><td></td><td>C.</td><td>Look at several.</td></tr>
<tr><td></td><td></td><td>D.</td><td>But don't look at too many.</td></tr>
<tr><td></td><td></td><td>E.</td><td>Check the cleanness, safety, plumbing, and appliances of each one.</td></tr>
<tr><td></td><td></td><td>F.</td><td>Ask the manager about the laundry room, additional storage, parking facilities, and maintenance policies.</td></tr>
<tr><td>paragraph 4
topic sentence
and details
after the search</td><td>IV.</td><td colspan="2">When you've seen enough apartments, take time to examine your options.</td></tr>
<tr><td></td><td></td><td>A.</td><td>Compare the two best places you saw.</td></tr>
<tr><td></td><td></td><td>B.</td><td>Consider the price, locations, and condition of the apartments.</td></tr>
<tr><td></td><td></td><td>C.</td><td>Check the leases carefully.</td></tr>
<tr><td></td><td></td><td>D.</td><td>Are pets allowed?</td></tr>
<tr><td></td><td></td><td>E.</td><td>Are there rules about getting roommates?</td></tr>
<tr><td></td><td></td><td>F.</td><td>Check the amount of the security deposit.</td></tr>
<tr><td></td><td></td><td>G.</td><td>Check the requirements for the first and last months' rent deposit.</td></tr>
<tr><td>paragraph 5
conclusion</td><td>V.</td><td colspan="2">With the right strategies and a thorough search, you can get the apartment that suits you.</td></tr>
</table>

The outline used each cluster of steps as one body paragraph. A topic sentence for each body paragraph made some point about that group of steps. It also added many new details gathered during the outlining process. As you write and revise your draft, you can continue to add details. You can also combine sentences, add transitions, and work on word choice.

DRAFTING Drafting and Revising: Process Essay

Following is a revised draft of the essay on finding an apartment. As you read it, you'll notice many changes from the outline on pages 293–294.

- An introduction has been added.
- Transitions have been added within and between paragraphs.
- Details have been added.
- Sentences have been combined.
- A concluding paragraph has been added.

A Draft of a Process Essay

(Thesis and topic sentences are underlined.)

Some people drive around a neighborhood until they see an apartment complex with a "Vacancy" sign. They talk to the building manager, visit the apartment, and sign a lease. Soon they are residents of their new apartment, and often they are unhappy with their home. These people went about their search the wrong way. <u>They did not realize that finding the apartment you want takes planning and careful investigation.</u>

<u>You can save yourself stress by doing some preliminary work.</u> First of all, decide what you want. Ask yourself, "Do I want a one-bedroom apartment?" and "What can I afford?" Weigh the pros and cons of your wishes. You may want a convenient location, but that can be expensive. On the other hand, that location can save you money on transportation. When you've decided what you want, rely on friends to help you with your search. They can help you with the names of nice apartments. Maybe somebody you know lives in a good neighborhood and can help you find an apartment. In addition, check the classified advertisements in the newspapers. They are full of possibilities.

<u>In your search, be patient, look carefully, and ask questions.</u> It's important to look around and not to pick the first apartment you see. Look at several so that you can get a sense of your options. However, don't look at so many apartments that they all become a blur in your memory. As you visit each apartment, check its cleanness, safety, plumbing, and appliances. You don't want an apartment that opens onto a bad area or one with a leaky refrigerator. Be sure to ask the apartment manager whether there are a laundry room, storage area, and sufficient assigned parking and guest parking. Check to see if a maintenance person lives on the premises.

<u>When you've seen enough apartments, take the time to examine your options.</u> First, compare the two best places you saw. Now that you have narrowed your search, consider the price, location, and condition of each apartment. Check the leases carefully. If you have or are thinking of getting a pet, check to see if pets are allowed. Check the rules about roommates, too. Next, check to see how much money you will have to put up initially. Does the lease specify the amount of the security deposit? Does it require a payment of first and last months' rent? The answers to these questions can help you reach a decision.

Once you have followed the steps of the process, you are ready to make your choice. While these steps take more time than simply picking the first place you see on the street, they are worth it. <u>With the right strategies and a thorough search, you can get the apartment that suits your needs.</u> All that remains is to settle into your new home.

POLISHING Polishing and Proofreading: Process Essay

Following is the final version of the essay on finding an apartment. When you compare it to the draft on pages 294–295, you will notice some changes:

- A transition has been added to the beginning of paragraph 2 so that there is a smoother movement from the thesis at the end of paragraph 1 and the topic sentence of paragraph 2.
- The words "nice," "good," and "bad" have been changed to more specific ones.
- More details have been added to the end of paragraph 3.
- A title has been added.

A Final Version of a Process Essay
(Changes from the draft are underlined.)

How to Find a Suitable Apartment

Some people drive around a neighborhood until they see an apartment complex with a "Vacancy" sign. They talk to the building manager, visit the apartment, and sign a lease. Soon they are residents of their new apartment, and often they are unhappy with their home. These people went about their search the wrong way. They did not realize that finding the apartment you want takes planning and careful investigation.

When it comes to choosing an apartment, you can save yourself stress by doing some preliminary work. First of all, decide what you want. Ask yourself, "Do I want a one-bedroom apartment?" and "What can I afford?" Weigh the pros and cons of your wishes. You may want a convenient location, but that can be expensive. On the other hand, that location can save you money on transportation. When you've decided what you want, rely on friends to help you with your search. They can help you with the names of suitable apartments. Maybe somebody you know lives in an attractive neighborhood and can help you find an apartment. In addition, check the classified advertisements in the newspapers. They are full of possibilities.

In your search, be patient, look carefully, and ask questions. It's important to look around and not to pick the first apartment you see. Look at several so that you can get a sense of your options. However, don't look at so many apartments that they all become a blur in your memory. As you visit each apartment, check its cleanness, safety, plumbing, and appliances. You don't want an apartment that opens onto a dark and deserted area or one with a leaky refrigerator. Be sure to ask the apartment manager whether there are a laundry room, storage area, and sufficient assigned parking and guest parking. Check to see if a maintenance person lives on the premises or if a rental agency handles emergencies and repairs.

When you've seen enough apartments, take the time to examine your options. First, compare the two best places you saw. Now that you have narrowed your search, consider the price, location, and condition of each apartment. Check the leases carefully. If you have or are thinking of getting a pet, check to see if pets are allowed. Check the rules about roommates, too. Next, check to see how much money you will have to put up initially. Does the lease specify the amount of the security deposit? Does it require a payment of first and last months' rent? The answers to these questions can help you reach a decision.

Once you have followed the steps of the process, you are ready to make your choice. While these steps take more time than simply picking the first place you see on the street, they are worth it. With the right strategies and a thorough search, you can get the apartment that suits your needs. All that remains is to settle into your new home.

TOPICS FOR WRITING A PROCESS ESSAY

When you write on any of these topics, work through the stages of the writing process in preparing your essay.

1. Write a directional or informational process essay about one of these topics:

trying out for a team	childproofing a room
finding the best airfare	painting a room
setting up a new computer	teaching someone to drive
finding a roommate	applying for a loan
selling a car	proposing marriage
getting a good night's sleep	cutting and styling hair
giving yourself a manicure	learning to ski
learning to surf	learning to skateboard
learning to dance	overcoming shyness
installing a car's sound system	writing a thank-you note
having a pleasant first date	registering for class

2. You may follow some process at work. For example, you may have to open or close a store, clean a piece of machinery, fill out a report, use a specific computer program, or follow a process in making telemarketing calls. You may have to maintain the appearance of a work area (such as aisles in a super-market) or follow a procedure in dealing with complaints. If you follow a process at work, write an essay that teaches the process to a new employee.

3. Think of a time when you had to make an important decision. Write an essay about how you reached that decision. You can write about the circumstances that led to your having to make a choice and about the steps you took to come to a decision. That is, what did you consider first? Did you weigh the good and bad points of your options? What was your first choice? Did you stick with that decision or change your mind? Trace the steps of your thought process.

4. Is there someone you know who has an irritating habit or is hard to live with? For instance, you may be living with someone who leaves the kitchen a mess or working with someone who always loses items (staplers, pens) and borrows yours. Write an essay in which you teach this person the steps to breaking the bad habit or changing the annoying behavior.

COMPARISON AND CONTRAST

Hints for Writing a Comparison or Contrast Essay

1. Use the thesis of your comparison or contrast to make a statement. Your essay must do more than explain the similarities or differences of two people, places, or things. It must make some statement about the two. For instance, if you are writing about the differences between your first and second semester of college, your thesis may be that a person can change radically in a short time.

2. Use your points of comparison or contrast as a way to organize your body paragraphs. A comparison or contrast essay needs points; each point focuses on a specific similarity or difference. For example, you might use three points to compare two dogs: their appearance, their temperament, and their abilities. You can write one body paragraph on each of these points of comparison.

3. Use a point-by-point pattern. That is, each body paragraph can explain one point of comparison or contrast. The topic sentence can summarize the point, and the details about the two subjects (people, places, or things you are comparing) can support the topic sentence. These details can be grouped so that you first discuss one subject and then discuss the other. You might, for example, compare the appearance of two dogs. An outline for one body paragraph might look like the following:

topic sentence	II. My German shepherd and my border collie are similar in appearance.
point: appearance	
subject 1:	A. Max, my shepherd, has long, shiny black and brown hair.
my German shepherd	
	B. His ears stand up as if he is always alert.
	C. His eyes are dark and intelligent.

subject 2:
my border collie

   D. Sheba, my collie, has glossy black and white hair.
   E. Her pointed ears make it seem as if she is always listening to something.
   F. Her black eyes are knowing and wise.

WRITING THE COMPARISON OR CONTRAST ESSAY IN STEPS

 **Gathering Ideas: Comparison or Contrast Essay**

One way to get started on a comparison or contrast paragraph is to list as many differences or similarities as you can on one topic. Then you can see whether you have more similarities (comparisons) or differences (contrasts) and decide which approach to use. For example, if you decide to compare or contrast two restaurants, you could begin with a list like this:

Listing Ideas for a Comparison or Contrast Essay

Topic: Two restaurants: Victor's and The Garden

similarities

both offer lunch and dinner

very popular

nearby

differences

Victor's	The Garden
formal dress	informal dress
tablecloths	placemats
food is bland	spicy food
expensive	moderate
statues, fountains, fresh flowers	dark wood, hanging plants

Getting Points of Comparison or Contrast

Whether you compare or contrast, you are looking for points of comparison or contrast, items you can discuss about both subjects.

If you surveyed the list on the two restaurants and decided you wanted to contrast the two restaurants, you'd see that you already have these points of contrast:

     dress   food
     decor   prices

To write your essay, start with several points of comparison or contrast. As you work through the stages of writing, you may decide you don't need all the points you've jotted down, but it is better to start with too many points than with too few.

Once you have some points, you can begin adding details to them. The details may lead you to more points. If they do not, they will still help you develop the ideas of your paragraph. If you were to write about the differences in restaurants, for example, your new list with added details might look like this:

Listing Ideas for a Contrast Essay

Topic: Two Restaurants

Victor's	The Garden
dress—formal	informal dress
men in jackets, women in dresses	all in jeans
decor—pretty, elegant	place mats, on table is a card
statues, fountains	listing specials, lots of
fresh flowers on tables	dark wood, brass, green
tablecloths	hanging plants
food—bland tasting	spicy and adventurous
traditional, broiled fish or	pasta in tomato sauces, garlic
chicken, traditional steaks,	in everything, curry,
appetizers like shrimp cocktail,	appetizers like tiny
onion soup	tortillas, ribs in honey-mustard sauce
price—expensive	moderate
everything costs extra,	price of dinner includes
like appetizer, salad	appetizer and salad

Reading the list about restaurants, you might conclude that some people may prefer The Garden to Victor's. Why? There are several hints in your list. The Garden has cheaper food, better food, and a more casual atmosphere. Now that you have a point, you can put it into a topic sentence. A topic sentence contrasting the restaurants could be as follows:

> Some people would rather eat at The Garden than at Victor's because The Garden offers better, cheaper food in a more casual environment.

Once you have a possible topic sentence, you can begin working on the planning stage of your paragraph.

PLANNING   Devising a Plan: Contrast Essay

Following is an outline for an contrast essay on two restaurants.

An Outline for a Contrast Essay

paragraph 1

I.   Thesis: Some people would rather eat at The Garden than at Victor's because The Garden offers better, cheaper food in a more casual environment.

paragraph 2	II. The menus at the two restaurants reveal significant differences.
topic sentence	
and details	A. Food at Victor's is bland-tasting and traditional.
food	B. The menu has broiled fish, chicken, and traditional steaks.
Victor's	C. The spices used are mostly parsley and salt.
	D. The food is the usual American food, with a little French food on the list.
The Garden	E. Food at The Garden is more spicy and adventurous.
	F. There are many pasta dishes in tomato sauce.
	G. There is garlic in just about everything.
	H. The Garden serves four different curry dishes.
	I. It has all kinds of ethnic food.
	J. Appetizers include items like tiny tortillas and hot honey-mustard ribs.
paragraph 3	III. There is a contrast in prices at the two restaurants.
topic sentence	A. Victor's is expensive.
and details	B. Everything you order costs extra.
price	C. An appetizer or a salad costs extra.
Victor's	D. Even a potato costs extra.
The Garden	E. Food at The Garden is more moderately priced.
	F. The price of a dinner includes an appetizer and a salad.
	G. All meals come with a potato, pasta, or rice.
paragraph 4	IV. At Victor's and The Garden, meals are served in opposing environments.
topic sentence	A. Certain diners may feel uncomfortable in Victor's, which has a formal atmosphere.
and details	
environment	B. Everyone is dressed up, the men in jackets and ties and the women in dresses.
Victor's	C. Even the children in the restaurant are in their best clothes and sit up straight.
	D. Less formal diners would rather eat in a more casual place.
The Garden	E. People don't dress up to go to The Garden; they wear jeans.
	F. Some come in shorts and sandals.
	G. The children often wear sneakers and caps.
	H. They wriggle in their seats and even crawl under the table.
paragraph 5	V. Many people prefer a place where they can relax, with reasonable prices and unusual food, or to a place that's a little stuffy, with a traditional and expensive menu.
conclusion	

The outline added some new details gathered during the outlining process. The topic sentences of the body paragraphs are based on the points of contrast on the earlier list. One point of contrast, the decor of the restaurants, has been omitted. The details about decor may be useful in the introduction or conclusion of the essay.

As you write and revise your draft, you can continue to add details. You can also combine sentences, add transitions, and work on word choice.

DRAFTING Drafting and Revising: Contrast Essay

Following is a revised draft of the essay on two restaurants. As you read it, you'll notice many changes from the outline on pages 299–300.

- An introduction has been added, and it contains some of the details on decor gathered earlier.
- Transitions have been added within and between paragraphs.
- Details have been added.
- Sentences have been combined.
- The word choice has been improved.
- A concluding paragraph has been added.

A Draft of a Contrast Essay

(Thesis and topic sentences are underlined.)

There are two well-known restaurants in town. One, Victor's, is an elegant place with white linen tablecloths and fresh flowers on each table. The other, The Garden, has paper place mats on the tables. The only other item on the tables is a small card listing the day's specials. While it might seem that Victor's is a more attractive setting for a meal, The Garden has its advantages. <u>Some people would rather eat at The Garden than at Victor's because The Garden offers better, cheaper food in a more casual environment.</u>

<u>The menus at the two restaurants reveal significant differences.</u> Food at Victor's is bland-tasting and traditional. The menu offers broiled fish, baked chicken, and typical steaks like T-bone and sirloin. The spices used are mostly parsley and salt. Victor's cooks standard American food with a little French food on the list; for example, the appetizers include an American favorite, shrimp cocktail, and a French onion soup. While food at Victor's relies on old, safe choices, food at The Garden is more spicy and adventurous. There are many pasta dishes in tomato sauce. Garlic appears in just about everything from mashed potatoes to pork roasts. The Garden serves four different curry dishes. In fact, it has all kinds of ethnic food; tiny tortillas and ribs dipped in honey and hot Chinese mustard are the most popular appetizers.

Food choices are not the only difference between Victor's and The Garden; <u>there is also a contrast in prices at the two restaurants.</u> Victor's is expensive. Everything you order, such as an appetizer or a salad, costs extra. Even a baked potato costs extra. An entree like a steak, for example, comes on a platter with a sprig of parsley. If you want a potato or a vegetable, you have to pay extra for it. Food at The Garden is more moderately priced. The price of a dinner includes an appetizer and a salad; in addition, all meals come with a potato, pasta, or rice, so there are few pricey extras to pay for.

The cost of a meal at Victor's is different from one at The Garden, and the atmosphere in which the meal is enjoyed is different, too. <u>At the two places, meals are served in opposing settings.</u> Certain diners may feel uncomfortable in Victor's, which has a formal atmosphere. Everyone is dressed up, the men in jackets and ties and the women in dresses. Even the children at Victor's are dressed in their best and sit straight up in their chairs. Less formal diners would rather eat in a more casual place, like The Garden. People don't dress up to go to The Garden; they wear jeans or shorts and sandals. The children often wear sneakers and baseball caps. They wriggle in their seats and even explore under the table.

Sometimes adults want to let go, just as children do. They want to sit back, not up; stretch their legs in casual clothes, not jackets and ties or dresses; and explore new food choices, not the same old standards. The Garden appeals to that childlike need for physical comfort and adventurous dining, at a moderate cost. <u>People</u> choose it over Victor's because they <u>prefer a place where they can relax, with reasonable prices and unusual food, to a place that's a little stuffy, with a traditional and expensive menu.</u>

(POLISHING) **Polishing and Proofreading: Contrast Essay**

Following is a final version of the essay on two restaurants. When you compare it to the draft on pages 301–302, you will notice some changes:

- More specific details have been added.
- Two sentences in paragraph 3 have been revised so that the shift to "you" is eliminated.
- The phrase "explore under the table" in paragraph 4 has been changed to "explore the spaces under the table" for clarity.
- One sentence in the conclusion has been revised so that it has a stronger parallel structure.
- A title has been added.

A Final Version of A Contrast Essay

(Changes from the draft are underlined.)

Victor's and The Garden: Two Contrasting Restaurants

There are two well-known restaurants in town. One, Victor's, is an elegant place with white linen tablecloths and fresh flowers on each table. The other, The Garden, has paper place mats on the tables. The only other item on the tables is a small card listing the day's specials. While it might seem that Victor's is a more attractive setting for a meal, The Garden has its advantages. Some people would rather eat at The Garden than at Victor's because The Garden offers better, cheaper food in a more casual environment.

The menus at the two restaurants reveal significant differences. Food at Victor's is bland-tasting and traditional. The menu offers broiled fish, baked chicken, and typical steaks like T-bone and sirloin. The spices used are mostly parsley and salt; <u>pepper, garlic, and curry are nowhere to be found.</u> Victor's cooks standard American food with a little French food on the list; for example, the appetizers include an American favorite, shrimp cocktail, and a French onion soup. While food at Victor's relies on old, safe choices, food at The Garden is more spicy and adventurous. There are many pasta dishes, <u>from linguini to lasagna,</u> in <u>a rich</u> tomato sauce. Garlic appears in just about everything from mashed potatoes to pork roasts. The Garden serves four different curry dishes. In fact, it has all kinds of ethnic food; tiny tortillas and ribs dipped in honey and hot Chinese mustard are the most popular appetizers.

Food choices are not the only difference at Victor's and The Garden; there is also a contrast in prices at the two restaurants. Victor's is expensive. Everything <u>a person orders,</u> such as an appetizer or a salad, costs extra. Even a baked potato costs extra. An entree like a steak, for example, comes on a platter with a sprig of parsley. <u>Anyone who wants</u> a potato or a vegetable has to pay extra for it. Food at The Garden is more moderately priced. The price of a dinner includes an appetizer and a salad; in addition, all meals come with a potato, pasta, or rice, so there are few pricey extras to pay for.

The cost of a meal at Victor's is different from one at The Garden, and the atmosphere in which the meal is enjoyed is different, too. At the two places, meals are served in opposing settings. Certain diners may feel uncomfortable in Victor's, which has a formal atmosphere. Everyone is dressed up, the men in jackets and ties and the women in <u>fancy</u> dresses. Even the children at Victor's are dressed in their best and sit straight up in their chairs. Less formal diners would rather eat in a more casual place, like The Garden. People don't dress up to go to The Garden; they wear jeans or shorts and sandals. The children often wear sneakers and baseball caps. They wriggle in their seats and even explore <u>the spaces</u> under the table.

Sometimes adults want to let go, just as children do. They want to sit back, not up; stretch their legs in casual clothes, <u>not hold their breath in tight ties or fancy dresses;</u> and explore new food choices, not <u>settle for</u> the same old standards. The Garden appeals to that childlike need for physical comfort and adventurous dining, at a moderate cost. People choose it over Victor's because they prefer a place where they can relax, with reasonable prices and unusual food, to a place that's a little stuffy, with a traditional and expensive menu.

TOPICS FOR WRITING A COMPARISON OR CONTRAST ESSAY

When you write on any of these topics, work through the stages of the writing process in preparing your essay.

1. Compare or contrast any of the following:

two holidays	satellite and cable television
two video games	two Internet providers
two personal goals	two clothing styles
two weddings	two surprises
two movie theaters	two role models
two expensive purchases	two houses you've lived in
two coworkers	two assignments

2. Find a baby picture of yourself. Study it carefully; then write an essay about the similarities between the baby and the adult you are today. You can use physical similarities or similarities in personality or attitude (as expressed in the photo). If your instructor agrees, you can ask a classmate to help you find physical resemblances between you as you are today and the baby in the picture.

3. Compare or contrast the person you were two years ago to the person you are today. You might consider such points of comparison as your worries, fears, hopes, goals, or relationships.

4. Begin this assignment by working with a partner or group. Brainstorm to make a list of four or five top performers (singers, actors, comedians) popular with one age group (young teens, high school students, college students, people in their twenties, thirties, and so forth—your group can decide on the age group). Once you have the list, write individual essays comparing or contrasting two of the people on the list.

◀ COLLABORATE

5. Compare or contrast the way you spend a weekday with the way you spend a day off. You can consider what you do in the morning, afternoon, and evening as points of comparison or contrast.

CLASSIFICATION

Hints for Writing a Classification Essay

1. Be sure to have a point in your classification. Remember that you need to do more than divide something into three or more types, according to some basis, and explain and describe these types. You must have a reason for your classification. For example, if you write about three types of digital cameras, you may be writing to evaluate them, and your point may state which type is the best buy. If you are classifying weight-loss programs, you may be studying each type so that you can prove that two types are dangerous.

2. A simple way to structure your classification essay is to explain each type in a separate body paragraph. Then use the same kind of details to describe each type. For instance, if you describe the medical principles, food restrictions, and results of one type of weight-loss program, describe the medical principles, food restrictions, and results of the other types of weight-loss programs.

WRITING THE CLASSIFICATION ESSAY IN STEPS

PREWRITING Gathering Ideas: Classification Essay

First, pick a topic for your classification. The next step is to choose some basis for your classification. For example, if you were to write a paragraph classifying phone calls, you could write about phone calls on the basis of their effect on you. With this basis for classification, you can come up with three categories:

calls that please me
calls that irritate me
calls that frighten me

By brainstorming, you can then gather details about your three categories:

Added Details for Three Categories of a Classification Essay

Topic: Phone Calls

calls that please me

from boyfriend

good friends

catch-up calls—someone I haven't talked to for a while

make me feel close

calls that irritate me

sales calls at dinner time

wrong numbers

calls that interrupt

invade privacy

calls that frighten me

emergency call in middle of night

"let's break up" call from boyfriend

change my life, indicate some bad change

With these categories and details, you can write a thesis that (1) mentions what you are classifying and (2) indicates the basis for your classification by listing all three categories or by stating the basis, or both. Here is a thesis that follows the guidelines:

Phone calls can be grouped into the ones that please me, the ones that irritate me, and the ones that frighten me.

This thesis mentions what you are classifying, *phone calls*. It indicates the basis for classification, the effect of the phone calls, by listing the types: *the ones that please me, the ones that irritate me, and the ones that frighten me.* Here is another thesis that follows the guidelines:

I can classify phone calls according to their effect on me.

This thesis also mentions what you are classifying, *phone calls*, but it mentions the basis for classification, *their effect on me*, instead of listing the types.

Once you have a thesis sentence and a list of ideas, you are ready to begin the planning stage of writing the classification essay.

PLANNING   Devising a Plan: Classification Essay

Following is an outline for a classification essay on phone calls.

An Outline for a Classification Essay

paragraph 1	I. Thesis: Phone calls can be grouped into the ones that please me, the ones that irritate me, and the ones that frighten me.
paragraph 2 topic sentence and details pleasing calls	II. Calls that please me make me feel close to someone. A. I like calls from my boyfriend, especially when he calls to say he is thinking of me. B. I like to hear from good friends. C. My two best friends call me at least twice a day. D. I like catch-up calls. E. These are calls from people I haven't talked to in a while.

F.   A friend I hadn't seen in a year called me from Ecuador to say "Happy Birthday."

G.   We talked for a long time.

paragraph 3
topic sentence
and details
irritating calls

III.   Some calls irritate me because they invade my privacy.

A.   Sales calls always come at dinner time.

B.   They offer me newspaper subscriptions or "free" vacations.

C.   The calls start with a friendly voice, talking fast.

D.   By the time I find out what the caller is selling, my dinner is cold.

E.   I get at least four wrong number calls each week.

F.   Some of the callers don't even apologize.

G.   These calls annoy me because I have to interrupt what I'm doing to answer them.

paragraph 4
topic sentence
and details
frightening calls

IV.   The calls that tell me about some bad change in my life frighten me.

A.   I once got a call in the middle of the night.

B.   It was from a hospital emergency room.

C.   The nurse said my brother had been in an accident.

D.   That was the most terrifying call of my life.

E.   I once got a call from a boyfriend.

F.   He said he wanted to break up.

G.   His words hurt me.

paragraph 5

V.   A phone is just an instrument; its effect on the person who receives a call makes it a good or bad instrument.

The outline combined some of the details from the list with new details gathered during the writing process. It used the three categories as the basis for the topic sentences for the body paragraphs. Each topic sentence has two parts: (1) the name of the category, like pleasing calls, and (2) the effect of calls in this category. For example, here is one topic sentence:

Calls that please me make me feel close to someone.

Because the point of the essay is to show the effect of different kinds of calls, this topic sentence is effective.

As you write and revise your draft, you can continue to add details. You can also combine sentences, add transitions, and work on word choice.

 **Drafting and Revising:**
Classification Essay

Following is a revised draft of the essay on phone calls. As you read it, you'll notice many changes from the outline on pages 305–306.

- An introduction has been added.
- Transitions have been added within and between paragraphs.
- Details have been added.

- Sentences have been combined.
- A concluding paragraph has been added.

A Draft of a Classification Essay

(Thesis and topic sentences are underlined.)

I am lost without a phone. My friends swear that I must have been born holding a tiny phone to my ear. Although I am constantly talking on the phone, I am not always enjoying the process. Not all my phone calls are enjoyable. In fact, <u>the calls can be grouped into the ones that please me, the ones that irritate me, and the ones that frighten me.</u>

<u>Calls that please me make me feel close to someone.</u> For example, I like calls from my boyfriend, especially when he calls to say that he is thinking of me. I also like to hear from good friends. My two best friends call me at least twice a day, and it is amazing that we can always find something to talk about. Catch-up calls, calls from people I haven't seen in a while, are another kind of call I enjoy. Recently, a friend I hadn't seen in a year called me from Ecuador to say "Happy Birthday." It was so good to hear from her that we talked for a long time.

The ring of a phone can bring me warm feelings, but it can sometimes bring irritation. <u>Calls that irritate me invade my privacy.</u> Sales calls, for instance, always come at dinnertime. They offer me newspaper subscriptions or "free" vacations that always have a hidden cost. This kind of call always starts with a friendly voice, talking fast. By the time I figure out what the caller is selling, my dinner is cold. Also in this category are wrong-number calls. I get at least four of these a week, and some of the callers don't even apologize for bothering me. These calls annoy me because I have to interrupt what I'm doing to answer them.

Finally, there are the worst calls of all. <u>The calls that frighten me tell me about some bad change in my life.</u> I once got a call in the middle of the night. It was from a hospital emergency room; the nurse told me my brother had been in an accident. That was the most terrifying call of my life. Another time, a boyfriend called to say he wanted to break up. His cold words surprised and hurt me.

I rely on the telephone, but it is not always good to me. Ever since I received the call about my brother's accident, I tremble when the phone rings late at night. However, I have come to realize that <u>a phone is just an instrument; its effect on the person who receives a call makes it a good or bad instrument.</u>

 ## Polishing and Proofreading: Classification Essay

Following is the final version of the essay on phone calls. When you compare it to the draft above, you will notice some changes:

- Some of the word choice has been polished to make a detail more specific, to eliminate repetition, or to eliminate an awkward phrase.
- A final sentence has been added to paragraph 4 to reinforce the point that both examples in the paragraph are about a life-changing phone call.
- The last sentence in the concluding paragraph has been revised to make a more precise statement about the basis for the classification: the effect of each type of phone call.
- A title has been added.

A Final Version of a Classification Essay
(Changes from the draft are underlined.)

Phone Calls: The Good, The Bad, and The Ugly

I am lost without a phone. My friends swear that I must have been born holding a tiny phone to my ear. Although I am constantly talking on the phone, I am not always enjoying the process. Not all <u>the conversations</u> are <u>pleasant</u>. In fact, the calls can be grouped into the ones that please me, the ones that irritate me, and the ones that frighten me.

Calls that please me make me feel close to someone. For example, I like calls from my boyfriend, especially when he calls to say that he is thinking of me. I also like to hear from good friends. My two best friends call me at least twice a day, and it is amazing that we can always find something to talk about. Catch-up calls, calls from people I haven't seen in a while, are another kind of call I enjoy. Recently, a friend I hadn't seen in a year called me from Ecuador to say "Happy Birthday." It was so good to hear from her that we talked for <u>an hour</u>.

The ring of a phone can bring me warm feelings, but it can sometimes bring irritation. Calls that irritate me invade my privacy. Sales calls, for instance, always come at dinnertime. They offer me newspaper subscriptions or "free" vacations that always have a hidden cost. This kind of call always starts with a friendly voice, talking fast. By the time I figure out what the caller is selling, my dinner is cold. Also in this category are wrong-number calls. I get at least four of these a week, and some of the callers don't even apologize for bothering me. These calls annoy me because I have to interrupt what I'm doing to answer them.

Finally, there are the worst calls of all. The calls that frighten me tell me about some <u>crisis</u> in my life. I once got a call in the middle of the night. It was from a hospital emergency room; the nurse told me my brother had been in an accident. That was the most terrifying call of my life. Another time, a boyfriend called to say he wanted to break up. His cold words surprised and hurt me. <u>Both of these calls brought me news that changed my life, and the news was totally unexpected.</u>

I rely on the telephone, but it is not always good to me. Ever since I received the call about my brother's accident, I tremble when the phone rings late at night. However, I have come to realize that a phone is just an instrument; <u>it conveys a message</u>. Its effect on the person who <u>receives that message</u> makes it a <u>welcome, annoying, or dreaded</u> instrument.

TOPICS FOR WRITING A CLASSIFICATION ESSAY

When you write on any of these topics, work through the stages of the writing process in preparing your essay.

 COLLABORATE ▶ **1.** Write a classification essay on any of the following topics. If your instructor agrees, brainstorm with a partner or group to come up with a basis for your classification and categories related to the basis.

your clothes	your dreams	your mistakes
your relatives	your coworkers	your travels
photographs	discount stores	snacks
cartoon heroes	Web sites	workouts
ghost stories	bargains	gossip

recipes	talk shows	music videos
visits to the dentist	war movies	teen idols

2. You may not know it, but you are probably an expert on something. For example, you may work in a jewelry store and know all about diamonds. You may be a paramedic and know about medical emergencies. If you are a veterinarian's assistant, you know about cats and dogs. If you collect Barbie dolls, you are an expert on these toys. Consider what you know best, through your work, hobbies, education, or leisure activities, and write a classification essay about a subject in that area. If you know about diamonds, you can classify engagement rings. If you work at a veterinarian's office, you can classify pet owners or poodles.

3. Below are some topics. Each one already has a basis for classification. Write a classification essay on one of the choices.

Classify

    a. baby-sitters on the basis of how competent they are
    b. small children on the basis of their behavior in a restaurant
    c. teenage boys on the basis of their favorite sport
    d. government offices (such as the driver's license office, courthouse) on the basis of how efficient they are
    e. roads on the basis of how safe they are
    f. fads on the basis of how long they last
    g. auto repair shops on the basis of their reliability
    h. classrooms on the basis of how comfortable they are
    i. uniforms on the basis of how attractive they are
    j. uniforms on the basis of how comfortable they are

4. This assignment requires a little research. Write an essay that classifies some product according to price. That is, you can classify home computers (or hair dryers, bookbags, hiking boots, motorcycles, and so forth) according to their cost. Pretend that you are writing to advise readers who may want to buy this product and want the best deal for their money. Research the details of this product in different price ranges; for example, explain what the most expensive computer includes and how useful these features are, and then explain what mid-priced and low-priced computers offer for their price. Use your essay to recommend the best deal for the money.

DEFINITION

Hints for Writing a Definition Essay

1. Write a personal definition, not a dictionary definition. To develop a definition essay, you need to define a term that can be explained by more than the words in the dictionary. You can develop your essay with concrete terms and specific examples that help define the term.

    terms that won't work in a personal definition:
    photosynthesis, DNA, the Colt Revolver, the Renaissance

    terms that will work in a personal definition:
    self-pity, patience, the team player, the pessimist

2. Include in your thesis (1) the term you are defining, (2) the broad class or category into which your term fits, and (3) the specific distinguishing characteristics that make the term different from all others in the class or category. Each of the following sentences could be the thesis for a definition essay.

Envy is the desire for what others have.

A nit-picker is a person who worries excessively about minor details.

3. Form your body paragraphs from different aspects of your term. For example, if you define patience, you might write one paragraph on the times when patience is necessary and another on the times when people need to stop being patient and take action. If you write about temptation, you might write one paragraph on how to resist temptation and another on when to give in to temptation.

WRITING THE DEFINITION ESSAY IN STEPS

PREWRITING Gathering Ideas: Definition Essay

To pick a topic for your definition essay, you can begin with some personality trait or type of person. For instance, you might define "the insecure person." If you listed your first thoughts, your list might look like this:

the insecure person
someone who is not emotionally secure
wants (needs?) other people to make him or her feel good
no self-respect

Often, when you look for ideas to define a term, you get stuck with big, general statements or abstract words, or you simply cannot come up with enough to say. If you are having trouble getting ideas, think of questions about your term. Jot these questions down without stopping to answer them. One question can lead you to another question. Once you have five or more questions, you can answer them, and the answers will provide details for your definition paragraph.

If you were writing about the insecure person, for example, you could begin with questions like these:

What are insecure people like?
What behavior shows a person is insecure?
How do insecure people dress or talk?
What makes a person insecure?
Why is insecurity a bad trait?
How do insecure people relate to others?
Does insecurity hurt the insecure person? If so, how?
Does the insecure person hurt others? If so, how?

By scanning the questions and answering as many as you can, you can add details to your list. Once you have a longer list, you can review it and begin to group the items on the list. Following is a list of grouped details on the insecure person.

Grouped Details for a Definition Essay

Topic: The Insecure Person

wants (needs?) other people to make him or her feel important
 no self-respect

insecure people have to brag about everything
 a friend who brags about his car
 they tell you the price of everything

they put others down
 saying bad things about other people makes insecure people feel better

insecure people can never relax inside
 can never enjoy being with other people
 other people are always their competitors
 must always worry about what others think of them

Grouping the details can help you arrive at several main ideas. Can they be combined and revised to create a topic sentence? Following is a thesis on the insecure person that meets the requirements of naming the term, placing it in a category, and distinguishing the term from others in the category:

> The insecure person is a person who needs other people to make him or her feel respected and important.

Once you have a thesis sentence, you can begin working on the planning stage of the paragraph.

PLANNING Devising a Plan: Definition Essay

Following is an outline for a definition essay on the insecure person.

An Outline for a Definition Essay

paragraph 1   I.   Thesis: The insecure person is a person who needs other people to make him or her feel respected and important.

paragraph 2   II.   Insecure people have to brag about everything.
topic sentence   A.   An insecure friend may have to brag about his car.
and details   B.   He is sure to tell you how fast it can go.
bragging   C.   Insecure people wear expensive jewelry and tell you what it cost.
                        D.   A man will tell you what his ring cost; a woman will tell you what her boyfriend paid for her ring.
                        E.   They make sure they wear clothes with trendy labels.

F. They have to have shirts with the designer's logo on the pocket and jackets with the designer's name spread across the front.

G. This is another kind of bragging.

paragraph 3

topic sentence

and details

putting others

down

III. Insecure people put others down.

A. They make mean remarks about other people's looks, clothes, or style.

B. Saying bad things about others makes insecure people feel better.

C. When some friends were talking about Susan's great new job, Jill had to make mean remarks about Susan.

D. Jill hated having Susan look like a winner.

E. Jill wanted all the attention and admiration for herself.

F. I work with a man who is always spreading cruel gossip.

G. His attacks on others are a cowardly way of making himself look good.

paragraph 4

topic sentence

and details

never relaxing

IV. Insecure people can never relax inside.

A. They can never enjoy being with other people.

B. Other people are always their competition.

C. Luke plays pickup basketball games.

D. He can't enjoy any game of basketball unless he is the star.

E. When someone on his team scores, he is not pleased.

F. Instead, he becomes aggressive and selfish.

G. Another person I know is always loud and crude at parties.

H. He is so desperate to be liked that he turns himself into an obnoxious character that he thinks is the life of the party.

paragraph 5

conclusion

V. Insecure people must always worry about what others think about them.

The outline combined some of the details from the list with new details and examples gathered during the outlining process. As you write and revise your draft, you can continue to add details. You can also combine sentences, add transitions, and work on word choice.

DRAFTING Drafting and Revising: Definition Essay

Following is a revised draft of the essay on the insecure person. As you read it, you'll notice many changes from the outline on pages 311–312.

- An introduction has been added.
- Transitions have been added within and between paragraphs.
- Details have been added.
- Sentences have been combined.
- A concluding paragraph has been added.

A Draft of a Definition Essay

(Thesis and topic sentences are underlined.)

Everybody knows at least one person who seems to feel so superior that no one could ever reach his or her status. Sometimes this person annoys others; at other times, this person hurts them. While it seems to be pride that motivates this person to irritate and belittle others, it is really insecurity disguised as ego. <u>The insecure person is a person who needs other people to make him or her feel respected and important.</u>

One sign of the insecure person is bragging. <u>Insecure people have to brag about everything.</u> An insecure friend may have to brag about his car and will be sure to tell everyone how fast it can go. Some insecure people wear expensive jewelry and tell you what it cost. A man may boast about what his ring cost; a woman will mention to you what her boyfriend paid for her ring. Others filled with insecurity brag about their expensive clothes. They make sure they wear clothes with trendy labels. They have to have shirts with the designer's logo on the pocket or jackets with the designer's name spread across the front. This is another kind of bragging.

<u>Insecure people</u> not only like to build themselves up, but they also <u>have to put others down</u>. They make mean remarks about other people's looks, clothes, and style. Saying bad things about others makes insecure people feel better. Recently, some friends were talking about our classmate Susan's great new job. While most of us were happy for Susan, Jill had to add some comments about how lucky Susan had been to get the job because Susan was not qualified for it. Because she wants all the attention and admiration for herself, Jill hated having Susan looking like a winner. Another insecure person is a man I work with who is always spreading cruel gossip. His attacks on others are his cowardly way of making himself look good.

The constant need to shine in other people's opinion means that <u>insecure people can never relax inside.</u> Other people are always their competition for attention or approval. One such person is Luke, a college acquaintance who always plays on our pickup basketball games. Even though the games are just for fun, Luke can't enjoy any game of basketball unless he is the star. When someone on his team scores, he isn't pleased. Instead, he becomes aggressive and selfish. He wants to win every game singlehandedly. Another person who is eager to shine is always loud and crude at parties. He is so desperate to be liked that he turns himself into an obnoxious character that he thinks is the life of the party.

Insecure people can be mean and obnoxious, but they are mainly sad. <u>Insecure people must always worry about what others think of them.</u> Because they care so much about others' opinions, they cannot be spontaneous or open. They must get very tired of hiding their fears behind their bragging and criticizing. They must also be very lonely.

Polishing and Proofreading: Definition Essay

Following is the final version of the essay on the insecure person. When you compare it to the draft above, you will notice some changes:

- Sentences in paragraph 2 have been combined for a smoother style.
- The word "this" in the last sentence of paragraph 2 has been replaced with a more specific phrase: "This obsession with designer clothes."
- Some of the word choice has been polished to avoid repetition or to be precise.
- A title has been added.

A Final Version of a Definition Essay
(Changes from the draft are underlined.)

The Insecure Person

Everybody knows at least one person who seems to feel so superior that no one could ever reach his or her status. Sometimes this person annoys others; at other times, this person hurts them. While it seems to be pride that motivates this person to irritate and belittle others, it is really insecurity disguised as ego. The insecure person is a person who needs other people to make him or her feel respected and important.

<u>One sign of the insecure person is bragging, for insecure people have to brag about everything.</u> An insecure friend may have to brag about his car and will be sure to tell you about <u>its powerful engine</u>. Some insecure people wear expensive jewelry and brag about what it cost. A man may boast about what his ring cost; a woman will mention what her boyfriend paid for her ring. Others filled with insecurity <u>show off</u> their expensive clothes. They make sure they wear clothes with trendy labels. They have to have shirts with the designer's logo on the pocket or jackets with the designer's name spread across the front. This <u>obsession with designer clothes</u> is another kind of bragging.

Insecure people not only like to build themselves up, but they also have to put others down. They make mean remarks about other people's looks, clothes, and style. <u>Making nasty comments</u> about others makes insecure people feel better. Recently, some friends were talking about our classmate Susan's great new job. While most of us were happy for Susan, Jill had to add some comments about how lucky Susan had been to get the job because Susan was not qualified for it. Because she wants all the attention and admiration for herself, Jill hated having Susan looking like a winner. Another insecure person is a man I work with who is always spreading cruel gossip. His attacks on others are his cowardly way of making himself look good.

The constant need to shine in other people's opinion means that insecure people can never relax inside. Other people are always their competition for attention or approval. One such person is Luke, a college acquaintance who always plays on our pickup basketball games. Even though the games are just for fun, Luke can't enjoy any game of basketball unless he is the star. When someone on his team scores, he isn't pleased. Instead, he becomes aggressive and selfish. He wants to win every game singlehandedly. Another person who is eager to shine is <u>my cousin Jamie, a generally good-natured person who</u> is always loud and crude at parties. He is so desperate to be liked that he turns himself into an obnoxious character that he thinks is the life of the party.

Insecure people can be mean and obnoxious, but they are mainly sad. Insecure people must always worry about what others think of them. Because they care so much about others' opinions, they cannot be spontaneous or open. They must get very tired of hiding their fears behind their bragging and criticizing. They must also be very lonely.

TOPICS FOR WRITING A DEFINITION ESSAY

When you write on any of these topics, work through the stages of the writing process in preparing your essay.

1. What is the one quality you most admire in other people? Is it courage, kindness, drive, or another character trait? Decide on that quality and write an essay defining it.

2. Define any of the terms below, using specific details and examples. You can begin by looking up the term in a dictionary to be sure you understand the dictionary meaning. Then write a personal definition.

guilt	satisfaction	longing
worry	stress	contentment
paranoia	trust	shyness
boldness	confidence	will power
sympathy	brotherhood	compassion
nerve	perseverance	generosity

3. Write a definition of a specific type of person. Develop your definition by using specific details and examples. Following is a list of types.

the tattletale	the guardian angel	the loner
the natural athlete	the ideal mate	the planner
the big brother/sister	the computer geek	the nagger
the control freak	the hypochondriac	the sneak
the good sport	the lost soul	the patriot
the rebel	the tightwad	the critic

4. We often use terms that we understand and that we assume everyone knows, but that may not have a clear definition. Write your definition of such a term. Examples of these terms are listed below, but you can also choose your own terms.

street smarts	a people person	fashion sense
people skills	negative vibes	personal issues

CAUSE AND EFFECT

Hints for Writing a Cause or Effect Essay

1. Choose either causes or effects. If you try to do both in a short essay, you will make your task more difficult. In addition, you need a longer and more complex essay to cover both causes and effects adequately.

2. You can use each cause or effect as the focus of one body paragraph. You can develop the paragraph by explaining and describing that cause or effect.

WRITING THE CAUSE OR EFFECT ESSAY IN STEPS

 **Gathering Ideas:
Cause or Effect Essay**

If you were thinking about writing a cause or effect paragraph on owning a car, you could begin by freewriting something like this:

Freewriting for a Cause or Effect Essay

Topic: Owning a Car

A car of my own. Why? I needed it. Couldn't get a part-time job without one. Because I couldn't get to work. Needed it to get to school. Of course I could have taken the bus to school. But I didn't want to. Feel like a grown-up when you have a car of your own. Freedom to come and go. I was the last of my friends to have a car. Couldn't wait. An old Camaro. But I fixed it up nicely. Costs a lot to maintain. Car payments, car loan. Car insurance.

Now you can review the freewriting and make separate lists of causes and effects you wrote down:

causes (reasons)

needed to get a part-time job
needed to get to school
my friends had cars

effects (results)

feel like a grown-up
freedom to come and go
costs a lot to maintain
car payments
car loan
car insurance

Because you have more details on the effects of owning a car, you decide to write an effects paragraph.

After brainstorming questions to help you gather more effects and details, you are ready to write another list:

List of Effects for an Effect Essay

Topic: Owning a Car

effect 1: I had to pay for the car and related expenses.

details: costs a lot to maintain

car payments

car loans

car insurance

effect 2: I had the adult freedom to come and go.

details: didn't have to beg my father for his truck

didn't have to get rides from friends

could go to the city when I wanted

could ride around for fun

effect 3:   I became a more careful driver.

details: worried about someone hitting the car

worried about bad drivers

wanted to avoid the scratches cars get in parking lots

With at least three effects and some details for each effect, you can create a thesis. The thesis for this paragraph should indicate that the subject is the *effects* of getting a car. You can summarize all three effects in your thesis, or you can just hint at them. A possible thesis sentence for the paragraph can be

> Owning my own car cost me money, gave me freedom, and made me more careful about how I drive.

The thesis summarizes all three effects. Another possible thesis hints at the effects:

> Once I got a car, I realized the good and bad sides of ownership.

With a thesis sentence, three effects, and a list of details, you are ready to write an outline for your essay.

PLANNING Devising a Plan: Effects Essay
Following is an outline for an effects essay on owning a car.

An Outline for an Effects Essay

paragraph 1	I.	Thesis: Owning my own car gave me freedom, cost me money, and made me a more careful driver.
paragraph 2	II.	The wonderful part of owning a car was the adult freedom it gave me.
topic sentence		
and details	A.	I didn't have to beg my father for his truck.
effect 1	B.	Every time I asked him, he seemed reluctant to lend it to me.
freedom	C.	He was always worried that I would get the interior dirty.
	D.	I didn't have to get rides from my friends.
	E.	I was really tired of begging rides from my buddies, and I am sure they were sick of driving me around.
	F.	I could go to the city whenever I wanted.
	G.	I could even ride around for fun.
paragraph 3	III.	I had to pay for the car and related expenses.
topic sentence	A.	A car costs a lot to maintain.
and details	B.	There are oil changes and tune-ups.
effect 2	C.	My car needed new tires.
costs	D.	I had car payments.
	E.	I had a car loan to pay.
	F.	I had car insurance.
	G.	I had to work overtime to pay the insurance bills.
paragraph 4	IV.	I became a more careful driver.
topic sentence	A.	I worried about someone hitting the car.
effect 3	B.	I could see my beautiful car dented and dinged.
cautiousness	C.	I began to worry about bad drivers.
	D.	I became more nervous on the road.
	E.	I worried about parking lots.
	F.	I wanted to avoid the scratches cars can get in parking lots.
	G.	I parked at the end of the row, away from other cars.

paragraph 5
conclusion

V. Owning a car gave me adult freedom, but it gave me adult responsibilities and worries, too.

The outline put each effect into a separate body paragraph. It combined some of the details from the list with details gathered during the outlining process. As you write and revise your draft, you can continue to add details. You can also combine sentences, add transitions, and work on word choice.

DRAFTING Drafting and Revising: Effects Essay

Following is a revised draft of the essay on owning a car. As you read it, you'll notice many changes from the outline on pages 317–318.

- An introduction has been added.
- Transitions have been added within and between paragraphs.
- Details have been added.
- Sentences have been combined.
- A concluding paragraph has been added.

A Draft of an Effects Essay

(Thesis and topic sentences are underlined.)

Ever since I was six years old, I had dreamed of owning my own car. The day I got my driver's license was one of the happiest days of my life. All that was left, I thought, was having a car of my own. That day came, too, and it changed my life. <u>Owning my own car gave me freedom, cost me money, and made me a more careful driver.</u>

<u>The wonderful part of owning a car was the adult freedom it gave me.</u> First of all, I didn't have to beg my father for his truck anymore. Every time I asked him, he seemed reluctant to lend it to me. He was always worried that I would get the interior dirty. Second, I no longer had to get rides from my friends whenever I wanted to go somewhere. I was really tired of begging rides from my buddies, and I am sure they were sick of driving me around. With my own car, I could go to the city whenever I wanted. I could even ride around for fun.

On the more serious side, <u>I had to pay for the car and related expenses.</u> A car costs a lot to maintain. There are oil changes and tune-ups to keep the car in good running condition. Two months after I got my car, I had to buy four new and very expensive tires. Of course, I had monthly payments on my car loan. I also had to pay for car insurance, which, because of my young age, was unbelievably expensive. My insurance cost so much that I had to work overtime to pay it.

Now that I was paying for the car I drove, <u>I became a more careful driver.</u> I became worried about someone hitting the car; I could imagine my beautiful car dented and dinged. These thoughts made worry about bad drivers and become more nervous on the road. Parking lots made me nervous, too. To avoid the scratches cars can get in parking lots, I parked at the end of the row, away from other cars.

<u>Owning a car gave me adult freedom, but it gave me adult responsibilities and worries, too.</u> Even with the stress of car payments, insurance payments, and car maintenance, I would never give up my car. My fear of dents and scratches can't keep me from the joy of driving whenever and wherever I want. I'm happy to accept the responsibilities that come with being on the road in my own car.

 **Polishing and Proofreading: Effects Essay**

Following is the final version of the essay on owning a car. When you compare it to the draft on pages 318, you will notice some changes:

- Some of the word choice has been polished to replace a vague term like "costs a lot" with the more specific "costs hundreds of dollars" or to avoid repetition of words like "worry" and "expensive."
- Details have been added; for instance, in paragraph 2, there are new details about what makes a car dirty and about how friends feel ("acting like a taxi service") when they are constantly asked for rides.
- A sentence has been added to paragraph 4 to support the topic sentence. The focus of the paragraph is on careful driving, and the body of the paragraph gives many examples of the fears of a new-car owner, but it needed one more detail to show the change in the owner's driving.
- A title has been added.

A Final Version of an Effects Essay

(Changes from the draft are underlined.)

Owning a Car: My New Lease on Life

Ever since I was six years old, I had dreamed of owning my own car. The day I got my driver's license was one of the happiest days of my life. All that was left, I thought, was having a car of my own. That day came, too, and it changed my life. Owning my own car gave me freedom, cost me money, and made me a more careful driver.

The wonderful part of owning a car was the adult freedom it gave me. First of all, I didn't have to beg my father for his truck any more. Every time I asked him, he seemed reluctant to lend it to me. He was always worried that I would <u>dirty the interior with food wrappers and empty soda cans</u>. Second, I no longer had to get rides from my friends whenever I wanted to go somewhere. I was really tired of begging rides from my buddies, and I am sure they were sick of <u>acting like a taxi service</u>. With my own car, I could go to the city whenever I wanted. I could even ride around for fun.

On the more serious side, I had to pay for the car and related expenses. A car costs <u>hundreds of dollars</u> to maintain. There are oil changes and tune-ups to keep the car in good running condition. Two months after I got my car, I had to buy four new and very expensive tires. Of course, I had monthly payments on my car loan. I also had to pay for car insurance, which, because of my young age, was unbelievably <u>high</u>. My insurance cost so much that I had to work overtime to pay <u>the bill</u>.

Now that I was paying for the car I drove, I became a more careful driver. I became worried about someone hitting the car; I could imagine my beautiful car dented and dinged. These thoughts made me <u>fear</u> bad drivers and become more nervous on the road. <u>I began to drive more defensively, and instead of challenging aggressive drivers, I began to avoid them.</u> Parking lots made me nervous, too. To avoid the scratches cars can get in parking lots, I parked at the end of the row, away from other cars.

Owning a car gave me adult freedom, but it gave me adult responsibilities and worries, too. <u>Yet</u> even with the stress of car payments, insurance payments, and car maintenance, I would never give up my car. My fear of dents and scratches can't keep me from the joy of driving whenever and wherever I want. I'm happy to accept the responsibilities that come with being on the road, in my own car.

TOPICS FOR WRITING A CAUSE OR EFFECT ESSAY

When you write on any of these topics, work through the stages of the writing process in preparing your essay.

1. Think of a time when you had to make an important choice. Then write an essay explaining the reasons for your choice. Your essay can include an explanation of your options as well as the reasons for your choice.

2. Write an essay about the effects on you (or someone you know well) of one of the following:

learning to swim	learning to read
learning a new language	learning to use a computer
learning to dance	learning to sing
learning to play a new sport	learning to meditate
learning to play a musical instrument	

3. Write an essay on one of the following topics:

Why Some Students Are Nervous about Speaking in Class
Why Most Children No Longer Walk or Ride Bicycles to School
Why Many High School Students Have Part-Time Jobs
Why Many _____ (teens, young people, families, older people, Hispanics—you name the group) Like to Watch _____ (you name the television show)
Why College Students May Feel Lonely

4. Think of a singer, rapper, singing group, or musician who is popular with people of your age and background. Write an essay explaining that person's or group's popularity.

5. Explain why a certain kind of car has become much more popular than it used to be.

ARGUMENT

Hints for Writing an Argument Essay

1. **Pick a topic based on your own experience and observation.** Although you may not realize it, you have a wide range of experience because you play many roles: consumer, student, parent, child, husband or wife, parent, worker, driver, pet owner, athlete. These and many other roles may fit you. In each of your roles, you may have noticed or experienced something that can lead to a topic.

2. **Be sure to take a stand in your thesis.** That is, don't merely state a problem, but make a point about how to solve or eliminate it.

   not this: The potholes on Johnson Road are terrible.
   but this: The Department of Public Works must fix the potholes on Johnson Road immediately.

   not this: Skateboarders have nowhere to go in Mason Heights.
   but this: Mason Heights needs a skateboard park.

3. **Use the reasons in your argument as a way to focus your body paragraphs.** If you have three reasons, for instance, you can write three body paragraphs.

4. **Consider your audience's objections.** Always ask yourself who the audience is for your argument. If you are arguing that your office needs a new copier, you will probably be writing to your supervisor. If you are arguing for an after-school program at your child's elementary school, you will probably be writing to the school board. Think about why your audience should support your points and how they might object.

There are several ways to handle objections. If you can *refute* an objection, that is, prove that it isn't valid, you have removed a major obstacle. Sometimes you may have to admit the other side has a valid objection by *conceding* it. Even by conceding, however, you win confidence by showing that you know both sides of the argument and are open-minded enough to consider another point of view.

Another way to handle an objection is to *turn an objection into an advantage.* That is, you can admit the objection is valid but use it to reinforce your own point. If you are arguing for a new copier and your supervisor says it is too expensive, you can agree that it is expensive but that the office is losing time and money by constantly repairing the old copier. Turning an obstacle into an advantage shows that you are informed, open-minded, and quick-thinking.

Even if you do not openly refer to objections in your argument essay, being aware of possible objections helps you to frame your points effectively with your audience in mind.

WRITING THE ARGUMENT ESSAY IN STEPS

PREWRITING Gathering Ideas: Argument Essay

Imagine that your instructor has given you this assignment:

> Write a letter to the editor of your local newspaper.
> Argue for something in your town that needs to be changed.

One way to begin is to brainstorm for some specific issue that you can write about. You can ask questions such as these: Is there a part of town that needs to be cleaned up? Should something be changed at a school? What do I notice on my way to work or school that needs improvement? What could be improved in my neighborhood?

By answering these questions, you may come up with one topic, and then you can list ideas on it.

topic

Cleaning Up Roberts Park

ideas

dirty and overgrown
benches are all cracked and broken
full of trash

could be fixed up
people work nearby
they would use it

You can consider your audience and possible objections:

audience

local people of all ages who read the local paper

possible objections from this audience

would cost money
more important things to spend money on

answering objections

Money would be well spent to beautify the downtown.
City children could play there in the fresh air and in nature; workers could
   eat lunch there.

Once you have a list, you can start grouping the ideas on your list. Some of the objections you wrote down may actually lead you to reasons that support your argument. That is, by answering objections, you may come up with reasons that support your point. Following is a list with a point to argue, three supporting reasons, and some details about cleaning up Roberts Park.

A List for an Argument Essay

Topic: Cleaning Up a Park

point:	We should fix up Roberts Park.
reason:	Improving the park would make the downtown area more attractive to shoppers.
details:	Shoppers could stroll in the park or rest from their shopping.
	Friends could meet in the park for a day of shopping and lunch.
reason:	City children could play in the park.
details:	They could get fresh air.
	They could play in a natural setting.
reason:	Workers could get lunch outdoors.
details:	Several office complexes are nearby.
	Workers would take a break outdoors.

With your reasons and details, you can draft a thesis sentence:

Roberts Park should be cleaned up and improved.

With a thesis sentence, three reasons, and details, you are ready to move on to the planning stage of preparing an argument essay.

 **PLANNING** **Devising a Plan: Argument Essay**

Following is an outline for an argument essay on cleaning up a park.

An Outline for an Argument Essay

paragraph 1	I.	Thesis: Roberts Park should be cleaned up and improved.
paragraph 2 topic sentence and details	II.	Improving the park would make the downtown area more attractive to shoppers.
reason 1 a place for shoppers		A. If the city could clean, landscape, and refurbish the park, it would be a natural refuge for shoppers. B. It is located in the middle of the shopping district. C. Those who already shop in the city could stroll through the park or rest there after shopping. D. Soon, shoppers would tell their friends about the attractive, new-looking park. E. Eventually, friends could agree to meet at the park for a day of shopping and lunch. F. City shops and department stores would see business improve. G. Business would be good for restaurants, too.
paragraph 3 topic sentence and details	III.	Workers from nearby offices and stores could eat lunch outdoors.
reason 2 a place for workers		A. Several office buildings are nearby. B. During the lunch break, many people, even those who bring their lunch, want to get out of the office or store. C. Everyone wants to get up and forget the job for a little while. D. Some want fresh air. E. Others want to read a book or magazine while they eat. F. Others want to get some exercise by walking a little. G. Others just want to observe nature and people. H. An improved park could meet all these needs.
paragraph 4 topic sentence and details	IV.	City children could play there.
reason 3 a place for children		A. City children live in apartments. B. They don't have back yards to enjoy. C. They are reduced to playing in dangerous streets or on narrow sidewalks. D. Many aren't allowed outside at all. E. They go from sitting all day at school to sitting at home. F. In the park, children could interact rather than sit alone inside, watching television and playing video games. G. They could play on grass, not asphalt. H. They would not have to play near traffic.
paragraph 5 conclusion	V.	Roberts Park used to be the city's landmark, and it could be, once again.

The outline combined some of the details from the list with new details gathered during the outlining process. It focused each body paragraph on one reason to clean up the park. As you write and revise your draft, you can continue to add details to each reason. You can also combine sentences, add transitions, and work on word choice.

DRAFTING Drafting and Revising: Argument Essay

Following is a revised draft of the essay on cleaning up a park. As you read it, you'll notice many changes from the outline on page 323.

- An introduction has been added.
- Transitions have been added within and between paragraphs.
- Details have been added.
- A concluding paragraph has been added.

A Draft of an Argument Essay

(Thesis and topic sentences are underlined.)

Roberts Park was once a pretty little park with a fountain, dark wood benches, carefully landscaped paths, and lush trees and flowers. Today, however, the fountain is cracked and dry, the benches are faded and splintered, and the paths are overgrown. Trash fills the flowerbeds. <u>Roberts Park should be cleaned up and improved.</u>

There are several reasons why a better park would make a better city. <u>First, improving the park would make the downtown area more attractive to shoppers.</u> If the city could clean, landscape, and refurbish the park, it would be a natural refuge for shoppers. It is right in the middle of the shopping district, making it convenient for those who already shop in the city to stroll through the park or rest there. Soon, shoppers might tell their friends about the attractive, new-looking park. Eventually, friends could agree to meet at the park for a day of shopping and lunch. City shops and department stores would see an increase in business, and restaurants would benefit, too.

Those who do business in the city would appreciate a renovated park as well. <u>Workers from nearby offices and stores could eat lunch outdoors.</u> Several high-rise office buildings are nearby, full of office workers. During their lunch break, many people, even those who bring their lunch, want to get out of the office or store. Everyone wants to get up and forget the job for a little while. Some want fresh air while others want to read a book or magazine while they eat. The more ambitious want to get some exercise by walking a little; however, many people just want to observe nature and people. An improved park could meet all these needs.

The most important reason to clean up the park is to help children. <u>City children could play in Roberts Park.</u> City children, who live in apartments, don't have backyards to enjoy. If they go outside, they are reduced to playing in dangerous streets or on narrow sidewalks. Many aren't allowed outside at all. They go from sitting all day at school to sitting at home. In a restored park, children could interact rather than sit alone inside, watching television and playing video games. They could play on grass, not asphalt. Best of all, they would not have to play near traffic.

Today, the words "Roberts Park" describe a run-down, ragged plot of broken benches, weeds, and trash. But the place could be a haven for children, shoppers, and workers. Once the park was green, the fountain shimmered, and the benches shone. <u>Roberts Park used to be the city's landmark, and it could be, once again.</u>

 **Polishing and Proofreading:
Argument Essay**

Following is the final version of the essay on cleaning up a park. When you compare it to the draft on page 324, you will notice some changes:

- The introduction needed a transition from the description of the park to the thesis. A transition sentence has been added.
- One sentence in paragraph 2 has been revised to eliminate extra words.
- Also in paragraph 2, the words "shop," "shoppers," and "shopping" became repetitive, so one phrase, "these people," replaced one use of "shoppers."
- Some details have been added and word choice improved.
- A new sentence of details has been added to paragraph 4.
- A transition has been added to paragraph 4.
- A title has been added.

A Final Version of an Argument Essay

(Changes from the draft are underlined.)

The Case for Renovating Roberts Park

Roberts Park was once a pretty little park with a <u>bubbling</u> fountain, dark wood benches, carefully landscaped paths, and lush trees and flowers. Today, however, the fountain is cracked and dry, the benches are faded and splintered, and the paths are overgrown. Trash fills the flowerbeds. <u>It is time to make this place park-like again.</u> Roberts Park should be cleaned up and improved.

There are several reasons why a better park would make a better city. First, improving the park would make the downtown area more attractive to shoppers. If the city could clean, landscape, and refurbish the park, it would be a natural refuge for shoppers. <u>Because it is right in the middle of the shopping district, those who already shop in the city would be likely to stroll through the park or rest there.</u> Soon, <u>these people</u> might tell their friends about the attractive, new-looking park. Eventually, friends could agree to meet at the park for a day of shopping and lunch. City shops and department stores would see an increase in business, and restaurants would benefit, too.

Those who do business in the city would appreciate a renovated park as well. Workers from nearby offices and stores could eat lunch outdoors. Several high-rise office buildings are nearby, full of office workers. During their lunch break, many people, even those who bring their lunch, want to get out of the office or store. Everyone wants to get up and forget the job for a little while. Some want fresh air while others want to read a book or magazine while they eat. The more ambitious want to get some exercise by walking a little; however, many people just want to observe nature and people. An improved park could meet all these needs.

The most important reason to clean up the park is to help children. City children could play in Roberts Park. City children, who live in apartments, don't have backyards to enjoy. If they go outside, they are reduced to playing in dangerous streets or on narrow sidewalks. Many aren't allowed outside at all. They go from sitting all day at school to sitting at home. In a restored park, children could interact rather than sit alone inside, watching television and playing video games. <u>They would get some much-needed exercise.</u> <u>In addition</u>, they could play on grass, not asphalt. Best of all, they would not have to play near traffic.

Today, the words "Roberts Park" describe a run-down, ragged <u>site full of</u> broken benches, weeds, and trash. But the place could be a haven for children, shoppers, and workers. Once the park was green, the fountain shimmered, and the benches shone. Roberts Park used to be the city's landmark, and it could be, once again.

TOPICS FOR WRITING AN ARGUMENT ESSAY

When you write on any of these topics, work through the stages of the writing process in preparing your essay.

1. Write an essay for readers of your local newspaper, arguing for or against one of the following:

> a. a citywide curfew for every person under 18
> b. video surveillance cameras that record all activity in high-crime areas
> c. a ban on using a cell phone while driving
> d. an online traffic school

2. As a consumer, you purchase a number of products and services. Think of one product (like toothpaste, a calculator, or a pair of athletic shoes) or a service (like a flight on a plane, a car repair, or a meal in a restaurant) that you feel needs improvement. Write an essay in the form of a letter to the president of the company that produces the product or offers the service. Argue for the improvement you want. Be specific. For example, if you are dissatisfied with a brand of cereal, you might want less deceptive packaging, a lower price, or less sugar in the cereal.

3. Write to the president of a company whose advertising offends you. The advertising can be television or print advertising. In an essay in the form of a letter, argue for removing that advertising.

4. Argue for one of the following college issues. Your audience will be the president, vice presidents, and deans at your college.

> open parking (with the exception of handicapped spaces) at your college
> a laptop (at a minimal rental fee and with a security deposit) for each registered student
> a twenty-four-hour study area with computers available
> security escorts for all evening students who ask for them to get to their cars

5. If you are a parent, a husband or wife, a partner, an employee, an employer, a student, a pet lover, a driver, or a traveler, you have most likely noticed something (in one of your roles) that has irritated or upset you. Write an argument essay about how to change that place, rule, policy, procedure, situation, and so forth.

CHAPTER 13
Writing from Reading

WHAT IS WRITING FROM READING?

One way to find topics for writing is to draw on your ideas, memories, and observations. Another way is to write from reading you have done. You can *react* to it; you can *agree or disagree* with something you have read. In fact, many college assignments or tests ask you to write about an assigned reading: an essay, a chapter in a textbook, an article in a journal. This kind of writing requires an active, involved attitude toward your reading. Such reading is done in steps:

1. Preread
2. Read
3. Reread with a pen or pencil

After you have completed these three steps, you can write from your reading. You can write about what you have read, or you can react to what you have read.

AN APPROACH TO WRITING FROM READING

Attitude

Before you begin the first step of this reading process, you have to have a certain **attitude.** That attitude involves thinking of what you read as half of a conversation. The writer has opinions and ideas; he or she makes points, just like you do when you write or speak. The writer supports his or her points with specific details. If the writer were speaking to you in a conversation, you would respond to his or her opinions or ideas. You would agree, disagree, or question. You would jump into the conversation, linking or contrasting your ideas with those of the other speaker.

The right attitude toward reading demands that you read the way you converse: *you become involved.* In doing this, you "talk back" as you read, and later you react in your own writing. Reacting as you read keeps you focused on what you are reading. If you are focused, you will remember more of what you read. With an active, involved attitude, you can begin the step of prereading.

Prereading

Before you actually read an assigned essay, a chapter in a textbook, or an article in a journal, magazine, or newspaper, take a few minutes to look it over, and be ready to answer the following questions:

CHECKLIST: A Prereading Checklist

✔ How long is this reading?

✔ Will I be able to read it in one sitting, or will I have to schedule several time periods to finish it?

✔ Are there any subheadings in the reading? Do they give any hints about the reading?

✔ Are there any charts? Graphs? Boxed information?

✔ Are there any photographs or illustrations with captions? Do the photos or captions give me any hints about the reading?

✔ Is there any introductory material about the reading or its author? Does the introductory material give me any hints about the reading?

✔ What is the title of the reading? Does the title hint at the point of the reading?

✔ Are any parts of the reading underlined, italicized, or emphasized in some other way? Do the emphasized parts hint at the point of the reading?

Why Preread?

Prereading takes very little time, but it helps you immensely. Some students believe it is a waste of time to scan an assignment; they think they should jump right in and get the reading over with. However, spending just a few minutes on preliminaries can save hours later. Most importantly, prereading helps you to become a *focused reader.*

If you scan the length of an assignment, you can pace yourself. And if you know how long a reading is, you can alert yourself to its plan. A short reading, for example, has to come to its point fairly soon. A longer essay may take more time to develop its point and may use more details and examples.

Subheadings, charts, graphs, illustrations, boxed or other highlighted material are important enough that the author wants to emphasize them. Looking over that material *before* you read gives you an overview of the important points the reading will contain.

Introductory material or introductory questions also help you know what to look for as you read. Background on the author or on the subject may hint at ideas that will come up in the reading. Sometimes even the title of the reading will give you the main idea.

You should preread so that you can start reading the entire assignment with as much knowledge about the writer and the subject as you can get. When you then read the entire assignment, you will be reading *actively* for more knowledge.

Forming Questions Before You Read

If you want to read with a focus, it helps to ask questions before you read. Form questions by using the information you gained from prereading.

Start by noting the title and turning it into a question. If the title of your assigned reading is "Reasons for the Alien and Sedition Acts," you can turn that title into a question: "What were the reasons for the Alien and Sedition Acts?"

You can turn subheadings into questions. If you are reading an article on beach erosion, and one subheading is "Artificial Reefs," you can ask, "How are artificial reefs connected to beach erosion?"

You can form questions from graphs and illustrations. If a chapter in your history book includes a photograph of a Gothic cathedral, you can ask, "How are Gothic cathedrals connected to this period in history?" or "Why are Gothic cathedrals important?" or "What is Gothic architecture?"

You can write down these questions, but it's not necessary. Just forming questions and keeping them in the back of your mind helps you read actively and stay focused.

An Example of the Prereading Step

Take a look at the following article. Don't read it; *preread* it.

A Ridiculous Addiction

by Gwinn Owens

Gwinn Owens, a retired editor and columnist for the Baltimore Evening Sun, *writes this essay about his experiences in parking lots, noting that the American search for a good parking space "transcends logic and common sense."*

Words You May Need to Know (Corresponding paragraph numbers are in parentheses.)

preening (2): primping, making oneself appear elegant
perusing (2): reading
stymied (3): hindered, blocked, defeated
addiction (5): a compulsive habit
coveted (6): desired, eagerly wished for
transcends (6): rises above, goes beyond the limits of
atavistically (7): primitively

acrimonious (8): bitter, harsh
holy grail (8): a sacred object that the Knights of the Round Table (of Arthurian myth) devoted years to finding
antithesis (9): opposite
ensconced (10): securely sheltered
idiocy (11): foolish behavior
contempt (13): scorn, lack of respect
emporium (14): store

1   Let us follow my friend Frank Bogley as, on the way home from work, he swings into the shopping mall to pick up a liter of Johnny Walker, on sale at the Bottle and Cork. In the vast, herringboned parking area there are, literally, hundreds of empty spaces, but some are perhaps as much as a 40-second walk from the door of the liquor store. So Bogley, a typical American motorist, feels compelled to park as close as possible.

2   He eases down between the rows of parked cars until he notices a blue-haired matron getting into her Mercedes. This is a prime location, not more than 25 steps from the Bottle and Cork. Bogley stops to await her departure so as to slip quickly into the vacated slot. She shuts the door of her car as Bogley's engine surges nervously. But she does not move. She is, in fact, preening her hair and perusing a magazine she just bought.

3   The stymied Bogley is now tying up traffic in that lane. Two more cars with impatient drivers assemble behind him. One driver hits his horn lightly, then angrily. Bogley opens his window and gives him the finger, but reluctantly realizes that the Mercedes isn't about to leave. His arteries harden a little more as, exasperated, he gives up and starts circling the lot in search of another space, passing scores of empty ones which he deems too far from his destination. Predictably, he slips into the space for the handicapped. "Just for a moment," he says to his conscience.

4   The elapsed time of Bogley's search for a convenient parking space is seven minutes. Had he chosen one of the abundant spaces only a few steps farther away, he could have accomplished his mission in less than two minutes, without frazzled nerves or skyrocketing blood pressure—his as well as those who were backed up behind him. He could have enjoyed a little healthful walking to reduce the paunch that is gestating in his middle.

5   Frank Bogley suffers an acute case of parking addiction, which afflicts more Americans than the common cold. We are obsessed with the idea that it is our constitutional right not to have to park more than 10 steps from our destination.

6   Like all addictions, this quest for the coveted spot transcends logic and common sense. Motorists will pursue it without concern over the time it takes, as if a close-in parking space were its own sweet fulfillment. They will park in the fire lane, in the handicapped space or leave the car at the curb, where space is reserved for loading.

7   The quest atavistically transcends politeness and civility. My local paper recently carried a story about two motorists who, seeing a third car about to exit a spot, both lusted for the vacancy. As soon as the departing vehicle was gone, one of the standbys was a little faster and grabbed the coveted prize. The defeated motorist leaped from his car, threw open his rival's door and

punched him in the snoot. He was charged with assault. Hell hath no fury like a motorist who loses the battle for a close-in parking space.

8   The daily obsession to possess the coveted slot probably shortens the life of most Americans by at least 4.2 years. This acrimonious jockeying, waiting, backing, maneuvering for the holy grail of nearness jangles the nerves, constricts the arteries and turns puppylike personalities into snarling mad dogs.

9   I know a few Americans who have actually kicked the habit, and they are extraordinarily happy people. I am one, and I owe my cure to my friend Lou, who is the antithesis of Frank Bogley. One day I recognized Lou's red Escort in the wallflower space of the parking lot of our local supermarket. There was not another vehicle within 80 feet.

10   In the store I asked him why he had ensconced his car in lonely splendor. His answer made perfect sense: "I pull in and out quickly, nobody else's doors scratch my paint and I get a short walk, which I need." Lou, I might point out, is in his 60s and is built like 25—lean and fit.

11   These days, I do as Lou does, and a great weight has been lifted. Free of the hassle, I am suddenly aware of the collective idiocy of the parking obsession—angry people battling for what is utterly without value. I acquire what does have value: saving of time, fresh air, peace of mind, healthful exercise.

12   The only time I feel the stress now is when I am a passenger with a driver who has not yet taken the cure. On one recent occasion I accepted a ride with my friend Andy to a large banquet at which I was a head-table guest. The banquet hall had its own commodious parking lot, but Andy is another Frank Bogley.

13   He insisted on trying to park near the door "because it is late." He was right, it *was* late, and there being no slots near the door, he then proceeded to thread his way through the labyrinth of the close-in lot, as I pleaded that I didn't mind walking from out where there was plenty of space. He finally used five minutes jockeying his big Lincoln into a Honda-size niche. Thanks to Andy's addiction, I walked late into the banquet hall and stumbled into my conspicuous seat in the midst of the solemn convocation. My attitude toward him was a mixture of pity and contempt, like a recovering alcoholic must feel toward an incipient drunk.

14   These silly parking duels, fought over the right not to walk more than 15 steps, can be found almost anywhere in the fifty states. They reach their ultimate absurdity, however, at my local racquet and fitness club. The battle to park close to the door of the athletic emporium is fought as aggressively as at the shopping mall. Everyone who parks there is intending to engage in tennis, squash, aerobic dancing, muscle building or some other kind of

athletic constitutional. But to have to exercise ahead of time by walking from the lot to the door is clearly regarded by most Americans as unconstitutional.

The Results of Prereading By prereading the article, you might notice the following:

> The title is "A Ridiculous Addiction."
> The author is a former newspaper writer from Baltimore.
> There are many vocabulary words you may need to know.
> The essay is about parking lots.
> The introductory material says Americans' search for a desirable parking space goes beyond the limits of common sense.

You might begin reading the article with these questions in mind:

> What is the addiction?
> How can an addiction be ridiculous? An addiction is usually considered something very serious, like an addiction to drugs.
> What do parking spaces have to do with addiction?
> What is so illogical about looking for a good parking space?

Reading

The first time you read, try to get a sense of the whole piece you are reading. Reading with questions in mind can help you do this. If you find that you are confused by a certain part of the reading selection, go back and reread that part. If you do not know the meaning of a word, check the vocabulary list to see if the word is defined for you. If it is not defined, try to figure out the meaning from the way the word is used in the sentence.

If you find that you have to read more slowly than the way that you usually do, don't worry. People vary their reading speed according to what they read and why they are reading it. If you are reading for entertainment, for example, you can read quickly; if you are reading a chapter in a textbook, you must read more slowly. The more complicated the reading selection, the more slowly you will read it.

An Example of the Reading Step

Now read "A Ridiculous Addiction." When you've completed your first reading, you will probably have some answers to the prereading questions you formed, like those below.

Answers to Prereading Questions

> The author says that the ridiculous addiction is the need to find the best parking space.
> He means it's ridiculous because it makes parking a serious issue and because people do silly things to get good parking spots.
> People are illogical in getting parking because they'll even be late for an event in order to get a good space. Or they get upset.

Rereading with Pen or Pencil

The second reading is the crucial one. At this point, you begin to *think on paper* as you read. In this step, you make notes or write about what you read. Some students are reluctant to do this, for they are not sure *what* to note or write. Think of making these notes as a way of learning, thinking, reviewing, and reacting. Reading with a pen or pencil in your hand keeps you alert. With that pen or pencil, you can do the following:

Mark the main point of the reading.
Mark other points.
Define words you don't know.
Question parts of the reading you're not sure of.
Evaluate the writer's ideas.
React to the writer's opinions or examples.
Add ideas, opinions, or examples of your own.

There is no single system for marking or writing as you read. Some readers like to underline the main idea with two lines and to underline other important ideas with one line. Some students like to put an asterisk (a star) next to important ideas, while others like to circle key words.

Some people use the margins to write comments such as, "I agree!" or "Not true!" or "That's happened to me." Sometimes readers put questions in the margin; sometimes they summarize a point in the margin next to its location in the essay. Some people make notes in the white space above the reading and list important points, and others use the space at the end of the reading. Every reader who writes while he or she reads has a personal system; what these systems share is an attitude. *If you write as you read, you concentrate on the reading selection, get to know the writer's ideas, and develop ideas of your own.*

As you reread and write notes, don't worry too much about noticing the "right" ideas. Think of rereading as the time to jump into a conversation with the writer.

An Example of Rereading with Pen or Pencil

For "A Ridiculous Addiction," your marked article might look like the following.

A Ridiculous Addiction

Gwinn Owens

Let us follow my friend Frank Bogley as, on the way home from work, he swings into the shopping mall to pick up a liter of Johnny Walker, on sale at the Bottle and Cork. In the vast, herringboned parking area there are, literally, hundreds of empty spaces, but some are perhaps as much as a 40-second walk from the door of the liquor store. So Bogley, <u>a typical American motorist, feels compelled to park as close as possible.</u>

the bad habit

He eases down between the rows of parked cars until he notices a blue-haired matron getting into her Mercedes. This is a prime location, not more than 25 steps from the Bottle and Cork. Bogley stops to await her departure so as to slip quickly into the vacated slot. She shuts the door of her car as Bogley's engine surges nervously. But she does not move. She is, in fact, preening her hair and perusing a magazine she just bought.

The stymied Bogley is now tying up traffic in that lane. Two more cars with impatient drivers assemble behind him. One driver hits his horn lightly, then angrily. Bogley opens his window and gives him the finger, but reluctantly realizes that the Mercedes isn't about to leave. His arteries harden a little more as, exasperated, he gives up and starts circling the lot in search of another space, passing scores of empty ones which he deems too far from his destination. <u>Predictably, he slips into the space for the handicapped.</u> "Just for a moment," he says to his conscience.

I hate this!

<u>The elapsed time of Bogley's search for a convenient parking space is seven minutes.</u> Had he chosen one of the abundant spaces only a few steps farther away, <u>he could have accomplished his mission in less than two minutes, without frazzled nerves or skyrocketing blood pressure—his as well as those who were backed up behind him.</u> He could have enjoyed a little healthful walking to reduce the paunch that is gestating in his middle.

wasted time

irritation

Frank Bogley suffers an acute case of parking addiction, which afflicts more Americans than the common cold. <u>We are obsessed with the idea that it is our constitutional right not to have to park more than 10 steps from our destination.</u>

<u>Like all addictions, this quest for the coveted spot transcends logic and common sense.</u> Motorists will pursue it without concern over the time it takes, as if a close-in parking space were its own sweet fulfillment. <u>They will park in the fire lane, in the handicapped space or leave the car at the curb, where space is reserved for loading.</u>

The quest atavistically <u>transcends politeness and civility.</u> My local paper recently carried a story about two motorists who, seeing a third car about to exit a spot, both lusted for the vacancy. As soon as the departing vehicle was gone, one of the standbys was a little faster and grabbed the coveted prize. The defeated motorist leaped from his car, threw open his rival's door and punched him in the snoot. He was charged with assault. Hell hath no fury like a motorist who loses the battle for a close-in parking space.

example

The daily obsession to possess the coveted slot probably shortens the life of most Americans by at least 4.2 years. This acrimonious jockeying, waiting, backing, maneuvering for the holy grail of nearness <u>jangles the nerves, constricts the arteries and turns puppylike personalities into snarling mad dogs.</u>

I know a few Americans who have actually kicked the habit, and they are extraordinarily happy people. I am one, and I owe my cure to my friend Lou, who is the (antithesis) of Frank Bogley. One day I recognized Lou's red Escort in the wallflower space of the parking lot of our local supermarket. There was not another vehicle within 80 feet.

opposite

In the store I asked him why he had ensconced his car in lonely splendor. His answer made perfect sense: <u>"I pull in and out quickly, nobody else's doors scratch my paint and I get a short walk, which I need."</u> Lou, I might point out, is in his 60s and is built like 25—lean and fit.

breating the habit: the advantages

These days, I do as Lou does, and a great weight has been lifted. Free of the hassle, I am suddenly aware of the collective idiocy of the parking obsession—angry people battling for what is utterly without value. I acquire what does have value: <u>saving of time, fresh air, peace of mind, healthful exercise</u>.

more advantages

The only time I feel the stress now is when I am a passenger with a driver who has not yet taken the cure. On one recent occasion I accepted a ride with my friend Andy to a large banquet at which I was a head-table guest. The banquet hall had its own commodious parking lot, but Andy is another Frank Bogley.

back to bad habit

He insisted on trying to park near the door "because it is late." He was right, it *was* late, and there being no slots near the door, he then proceeded to thread his way through the labyrinth of the close-in lot, as I pleaded that I didn't mind walking from out where there was plenty of space. He finally <u>used five minutes jockeying his big Lincoln into a Honda-size niche</u>. Thanks to Andy's addiction, I walked late into the banquet hall and stumbled into my conspicuous seat in the midst of the solemn convocation. My attitude toward him was a mixture of pity and contempt, like a recovering alcoholic must feel toward an incipient drunk.

How true!

<u>These silly parking duels, fought over the right not to walk more than fifteen steps, can be found almost anywhere in the fifty states.</u> They reach their ultimate absurdity, however, at my local racquet and fitness club. The battle to park close to the door of the athletic emporium is fought as aggressively as at the shopping mall. Everyone who parks there is intending to engage in tennis, squash, aerobic dancing, muscle building or some other kind of athletic constitutional. But to have to exercise ahead of time by walking from the lot to the door is clearly regarded by most Americans as unconstitutional.

What the Notes Mean

In the preceding sample, the underlining indicates sentences or phrases that seem important. The words in the margin are often summaries of what is underlined. The words "wasted time," "irritation," and "effects," for instance, are like subtitles or labels in the margin.

Some words in the margin are reactions. When Owens describes a man who parked illegally in a handicapped spot, the reader notes, "I hate this!" When the writer talks about a Lincoln trying to fit into a Honda-sized spot, the reader writes, "How true!" One word in the margin is a definition. The word "antithesis" in the selection is defined as "opposite" in the margin.

The marked-up article is a flexible tool. You can go back and mark it further. You may change your mind about your notes and comments and find other, better, or more important points in the article.

You write as you read to involve yourself in the reading process. Marking what you read can help you in other ways, too. If you are to be tested on the reading selection or asked to discuss it, you can scan your markings and notations at a later time for a quick review.

Exercise 1 **Reading and Making Notes**

Following is the last paragraph of "A Ridiculous Addiction." First, read it. Then reread it and make notes on the following:

1. Underline the sentence that begins the long example in the paragraph.
2. Circle a word you don't know and define it in the margin.
3. In the margin, add your own example of a place where people fight for parking spaces.
4. At the end of the paragraph, summarize the point of the paragraph.

Paragraph from "A Ridiculous Addiction"

These silly parking duels, fought over the right not to walk more than fifteen steps, can be found almost anywhere in the fifty states. They reach their ultimate absurdity, however, at my local racquet and fitness club. The battle to park close to the door of the athletic emporium is fought as aggressively as at the shopping mall. Everyone who parks there is intending to engage in tennis, squash, aerobic dancing, muscle building, or some other kind of athletic constitutional. But to have to exercise ahead of time by walking from the lot to the door is clearly regarded by most Americans as unconstitutional.

Main point of the paragraph: _____

_____

WRITING A SUMMARY OF A READING

There are a number of ways you can write about what you've read. You may be asked for a summary of an article or chapter, or for a reaction to it, or to write about it on an essay test. For each of these, this chapter will give you guidelines so you can follow the stages of the writing process.

A **summary** of a reading tells the important ideas in brief form. It includes (1) the writer's main idea, (2) the ideas used to explain the main idea, and (3) some examples used to support the ideas.

When you preread, read, and make notes on the reading selection, you have already begun the prewriting stage for a summary. You can think further, on paper, by listing the points (words, phrases, sentences) you've already marked on the reading selection.

PREWRITING Gathering Ideas: Summary

Marking a List of Ideas

To find the main idea for your summary and the ideas and examples connected to the main idea, you can mark related items on your list. For example, the following expanded list was made from "A Ridiculous Addiction." Four symbols are used:

K   marks the **kinds** of close spots people will take.

X   marks all **examples** of what can happen when people want a good spot.

−   marks the **negative** effects of the close-parking habit.

+   marks the **advantages** of breaking the habit.

A List of Ideas for a Summary of "A Ridiculous Addiction"

K no close spots, takes handicapped

X seven minutes looking for close spot

− wasted time, could have found
   another in two minutes

X got mad

X made others wait

X they got angry
   Americans obsessed with right
   to good spot
   transcends logic
   no common sense

K park in fire lane

K leave car at curb

K loading zone

− impolite

X an assault over a spot

− jangles nerves, constricts
   arteries, and makes people mad dogs
   kicking the habit

+ get in and out fast

+ no scratched car doors

+ good exercise

+ saving time

+ fresh air

+ peace of mind

+ healthful exercise

X late for big dinner

X fitness clubs the silliest—won't walk

The marked list could be reorganized, like this:

kinds of close spots people will take

handicapped
fire lane
curb
loading zone

examples of what can happen when people want a good spot

seven minutes of wasted time
others, waiting behind, got angry
an assault over a spot
late for a big dinner
members of the fitness club won't walk

negative effects of the close-parking habit

wasted time
impolite
jangles nerves, constricts arteries
makes people mad dogs

advantages of breaking the habit

get in and out fast
no scratched car doors
good exercise
saving time
fresh air
peace of mind
healthful exercise

Selecting a Main Idea

The next step in the process is to select the idea you think is the writer's main point. If you look again at the list of ideas, you'll note a cluster of ideas that are unmarked:

1. Americans obsessed with the right to a good spot
2. transcends logic
3. no common sense

You might guess that they are unmarked because they are more general than the other ideas. In fact, these ideas are connected to the title of the essay: "A Ridiculous Addiction," and they are connected to some of the questions in the prereading step of reading: "What's the addiction?" and "How can an addiction be ridiculous?"

Linking the ideas may lead you to a main idea for the summary of the reading selection:

Americans' obsession with finding a good parking spot makes no sense.

Once you have a main idea, check that main idea to see if it fits with the other ideas in your organized list. *Do the ideas in the list connect to the main idea?* Yes. "Kinds of close spots people take" explains how silly it is to break the law. "Examples of what can happen" and "negative effects" show why the habit makes no sense, and "advantages of breaking the habit" shows the reasons to conquer the addiction.

Once you have a main point that fits an organized list, you can move to the planning stage of a summary.

(**Exercise 2**) **Marking a List of Ideas and Finding the Main Idea for a Summary**

Following is a list of ideas from an article called "How to Land the Job You Want." Read the list and then mark the items on the list with one of these symbols:

    X   **examples** of people looking for or getting jobs

    S   **steps** in getting a job

    A   **advice** from employers

After you've marked all the ideas, survey them and think of a main idea. Try to focus on an idea that connects to the title, "How to Land the Job You Want."

List of Ideas

_____ Laid-off engineer used his personality to get a sales job.

_____ Insurance company manager says applicants can walk in without appointment.

_____ Find the hidden job market.

_____ Unemployed teacher found a job through his insurance agent.

_____ Bank worker got a job through his club.

_____ Prepare specifically for each interview.

_____ Locate hidden openings.

_____ Company director says a good letter of application is crucial.

_____ Make résumé strong and polished.

_____ Put yourself in employer's place in writing a résumé.

_____ Cabinetmaker checked phone books of nine cities for companies in his field.

_____ Use the library to research job opportunities.

Main idea: _____

_____

PLANNING **Devising a Plan: Summary**

Below is a sample of the kind of outline you could do for a summary of "A Ridiculous Addiction." As you read it, you'll notice that the main idea of the prewriting stage has become the topic sentence of the outline, and the other ideas have become the details.

Outline for a Summary of "A Ridiculous Addiction"

topic sentence: Americans' obsession with finding a good parking spot makes no sense.

details:

examples Many bad or silly things can happen when people try for a good spot.
One person wasted seven minutes.
He made other drivers angry.
Someone else got involved in an assault.
Someone else was late for a big dinner.
Silly people, on their way to a fitness club, will avoid the walk in the fitness club parking lot.

negative effects Looking for a close spot can make people impolite or turn them into mad dogs.
It can jangle drivers' nerves or constrict arteries.
Some people will even break the law and take handicapped spots or park in a fire lane or loading zone.

advantages of kicking the habit If people can give up the habit, they can gain advantages.
A faraway spot is not popular, so they can get in and out of it fast.
Their cars won't be scratched.
They get exercise and fresh air by walking.

In the preceding outline, some ideas from the original list have been left out (they were repetitive), and the order of some points has been rearranged. That kind of selecting and rearranging is what you do in the planning stage of writing a summary.

DRAFTING Drafting and Revising: Summary

Attributing Ideas in a Summary

The draft of your summary paragraph is the place where you combine all the material into one paragraph. This draft is much like the draft of any other paragraph, with one exception: when you summarize another person's ideas, be sure to say whose ideas you are writing. That is, *attribute the ideas to the writer.* Let the reader of your paragraph know

1. the author of the selection you are summarizing, and
2. the title of the selection you are summarizing.

You may wish to do this by giving your summary paragraph a title like this:

A Summary of "A Ridiculous Addiction," by Gwinn Owens

(Note that you put the title of Owens' essay in quotation marks.)
On the other hand, you may want to put the title and author into the paragraph itself. Following is a draft of a summary of "A Ridiculous Addiction" with the title and author incorporated into the paragraph.

A Draft of a Summary of "A Ridiculous Addiction"

"A Ridiculous Addiction" by Gwinn Owens says that Americans' obsession with finding a good parking spot makes no sense. Many bad or silly things can happen when people try for a good spot. One person wasted seven minutes. He made other drivers angry. Someone else got involved in an assault. Someone else was late for a big dinner. Silly people, on their way to a fitness club, will avoid the walk in the club parking lot. Looking for a close spot can make people impolite or turn them into mad dogs. It can be stressful. Some people even break the law and take handicapped spots or park in a fire lane or loading zone. If people can give up the habit, they can gain advantages. A faraway spot is not popular, so they can get in and out of it fast. Their cars won't be scratched. They get exercise and fresh air by walking.

When you look this draft over and read it aloud, you may notice a few problems:

1. It is wordy.
2. In some places, the word choice could be better.
3. Some of the sentences are choppy.
4. It might be a good idea to mention that the examples in the summary were Gwinn Owens'.

Revising the draft means rewriting to eliminate some of the wordiness, to combine sentences or smooth out ideas, and to insert the point that the author, Gwinn Owens, gave the examples used in the summary. When you state that Owens created the examples, you are being clear in giving the author credit for his ideas. Giving credit is a way of attributing ideas to the author.

Note: When you refer to an author in something that you write, use the author's first and last name the first time you make a reference. For example, you write "Gwinn Owens" the first time you refer to this author. Later in the paragraph, if you want to refer to the same author, use only his or her last name. Thus, a second reference would be to "Owens."

POLISHING Polishing and Proofreading: Summary

Look carefully at the final version of the summary. Notice how the sentences have been changed and words added or taken out. "Owens" is used to show that the examples given came from the essay.

A Final Version of a Summary of "A Ridiculous Addiction"

"A Ridiculous Addiction" by Gwinn Owens says that Americans' obsession with finding a good parking spot makes no sense. Owens gives many examples of the unpleasant or silly things that can happen when people try for a good spot. One person wasted seven minutes and made the other drivers angry. Someone else got involved in an assault; another person was late for an important dinner. At fitness club parking lots, people coming for exercise are missing out on the exercise of walking through the parking lot. Looking for a good spot can turn polite people into impolite ones or even into mad dogs. The search is not only stressful; it can also lead people to break the law by taking handicapped, fire lane, or loading zone spots. If people broke the habit and took spots farther away from buildings, they would have several advantages. No one wants the faraway spots, so drivers can get in and out fast, without any scratches on their cars. In addition, people who break the habit get exercise and fresh air.

Writing summaries is good writing practice, and it helps you develop your reading skills. Even if your instructor does not require you to turn in a polished summary of an assigned reading, you may find it helpful to summarize what you have read. In many classes, midterms or other exams cover many assigned readings. If you make short summaries of each reading as it is assigned, you will have a helpful collection of focused, organized material to review.

WRITING A REACTION TO A READING

A summary is one kind of writing you can do after reading, but there are other kinds. You can react to a reading by writing on a topic related to the reading or by agreeing or disagreeing with some idea within the reading.

Writing on a Related Idea

Your instructor might ask you to react by writing about some idea connected to your reading. If you read "A Ridiculous Addiction," for example, your instructor might have asked you to react to it by writing about some practice or habit that irritates you. You can begin to gather ideas by freewriting.

PREWRITING Gathering Ideas: Reaction

Freewriting

You can freewrite in a reading journal if you wish. To freewrite, you can

- Write key points made by the author.
- Write about whatever you remember from the reading selection.

- Write down any of the author's ideas that you think you might want to write about someday.
- List questions raised by what you have read.
- Connect the reading selection to other things you have read or heard or experienced.
- Write any of the author's exact words that you might like to remember, putting them in quotation marks.

A freewriting that reacts to "A Ridiculous Addiction" might look like this:

Freewriting for a Reaction to a Reading

"A Ridiculous Addiction"—Gwinn Owens

People are silly in fighting for parking spaces. Owens says these are "silly parking duels." They get mean. Take handicapped spots. Angry. They fight over spots. Get angry when people sit in their cars and don't pull out of a spot. They jam big cars in small spaces, cars get damaged. They're "angry people battling for what is utterly without value." Why? To make a quick getaway?

Freewriting helps you review what you've read, and it can give you topics for a paragraph that is different from a summary.

Brainstorming

After you freewrite, you can brainstorm. You can ask yourself questions to lead you toward a topic for your own paragraph. For instance, brainstorming on the idea "angry people battling for what is utterly without value" could look like this:

Brainstorming After Freewriting

Owens says people fighting for spaces are "battling for what is utterly without value." So why do they do it? Is there any other time drivers battle for what has no value?
Sure. On the highway. All the time.

How?
They weave in and out. They cut me off. They tailgate. They speed.

What are they fighting for?
They want to gain a few minutes. They want to get ahead. Driving is some kind of contest to them.

Then don't they get some kind of satisfaction in the battle?
Not really. I often see them at the same red light I've stopped at. And their driving is very stressful for them. It raises their blood pressure, and it makes them angry and unhappy. They can't really win.

Could you write a paragraph on drivers who think of driving as a contest? If so, your brainstorming, based on your reading and freewriting, has led you to a topic.

Developing Points of Agreement or Disagreement

Another way to use a reading selection to lead you to a topic is to review the selection and jot down any statements that provoke a strong reaction in you. You are looking for sentences with which you can agree or disagree. If you already marked "A Ridiculous Addiction" as you read, you might list these statements as points of agreement or disagreement:

Points of Agreement or Disagreement

"Hell hath no fury like a motorist who loses the battle for a close-in parking space."—agree

"This quest for the coveted spot transcends logic and common sense."—disagree

---

Then you might pick one of the statements and agree or disagree with it in writing. If you disagreed with the second statement that "this quest for the coveted spot transcends logic and common sense," you might develop the prewriting part of writing by listing your own ideas. You might focus on why a close parking space is important to you. With a focus and a list of reasons, you could move to the planning part of writing from reading.

PLANNING Devising a Plan: Agree or Disagree

An outline might look like the one below. As you read it, notice that the topic sentence and ideas are your opinion, not the ideas of the author of "A Ridiculous Addiction." You used his ideas to come up with your own thoughts.

An Outline for an Agree or Disagree Paragraph

Topic sentence: Sometimes a close parking spot is important.
details:

convenience   { I may have heavy bags to carry from the store.

car safety   { Cars can be vandalized.
                     Vandalism and burglary are more likely if the car is
                     parked at a distance.

personal safety   { I can be attacked in a parking lot.
                     Attacks are more likely at night.
                     Muggings are more likely if I am parked far away.

DRAFTING Drafting and Revising: Agree or Disagree

If your outline gives you enough good points to develop, you are on your way to a paragraph. If you began with the ideas above, for example, you could develop them into a paragraph like this:

A Draft for an Agree or Disagree Paragraph

Sometimes a close parking spot is important. The short distance to a store can make a difference if I have heavy bags or boxes to carry from the store to my car. Convenience is one reason for parking close. A more important reason is safety. In my neighborhood, cars are often vandalized. Sometimes, cars get broken into. Cars are more likely to get vandalized or burglarized if they are parked far from stores. Most of all, I am afraid to park far from stores or restaurants because I am afraid of being attacked in a parking lot, especially at night. If I am far away from buildings and other people, I am more likely to be mugged.

POLISHING
Polishing and Proofreading: Agree or Disagree

When you read the paragraph above, you probably noticed some places where it could be revised:

- It could use more specific details.
- It should attribute the original idea about parking to Gwinn Owens, probably in the beginning.
- Some sentences could be combined.

Following is the final version of the same paragraph. As you read it, notice how a new beginning, added details, and combined sentences make it a smoother, clearer, and more developed paragraph.

Final Version for an Agree or Disagree Paragraph

Gwinn Owens says that people who look for close parking spaces are foolish, but I think that sometimes a close parking spot is important. The short distance to a store can make a difference if I have heavy bags or boxes to carry from the store to my car. Convenience is one reason for parking close, but the more important reason is safety. In my neighborhood, cars are often vandalized. Antennas get broken off; the paint jobs get deliberately scratched. Sometimes, cars get broken into. Radios and tape players are stolen. Cars are more likely to get vandalized or burglarized if they are parked far from stores. Most of all, I am afraid to park far from stores or restaurants because I am afraid of being attacked in a parking lot, especially at night. If I am far away from buildings or other people, I am more likely to be mugged.

Reading can give you many ideas for your own writing. Developing those ideas into a polished paragraph requires the same writing process as any good writing, a process that takes you through the stages of prewriting, planning, drafting, and polishing.

WRITING FOR AN ESSAY TEST

Most essay questions require a form of writing from reading. That is, your instructor asks you to write about an assigned reading. Usually, an essay test requires you to write from memory, not from an open book or notes. Such writing can be stressful, but breaking the task into steps can eliminate much of the stress.

Before the Test: The Steps of Reading

If you work through the steps of reading days before the test, you are halfway to your goal. Prereading helps to keep you focused, and your first reading will give you a sense of the whole selection. The third step, rereading with a pen or pencil, can be particularly helpful when you a preparing for a test. Most essay questions will ask you to summarize a reading selection or to react to it. In either case, you must be familiar with the reading's main idea, supporting ideas, examples, and details. If you note these by marking the selection, you are teaching yourself about the main point, supporting ideas, and structure of the reading selection.

Shortly before the test, review the marked reading assignment. Your notes will help you focus on the main point and the supporting ideas.

During the Test: The Stages of Writing

Answering an essay question for a test may seem very different from writing at home. After all, on a test, you must rely on your memory and write within a time limit, and these restrictions can make you feel anxious. However, by following the stages of the writing process, you can meet that challenge calmly and confidently.

Prewriting Before you begin to write, think about the question. Is the instructor asking for a summary of a reading selection? Or is he or she asking you to react to a specific idea in the reading by describing or developing that idea with examples or by agreeing or disagreeing? For example, if you were to answer an essay question about "A Ridiculous Addiction," you might be asked (1) to explain what Gwinn Owens thinks are the advantages and disadvantages of seeking a close parking space (a summary), or (2) to explain what he means when he says fighting for parking turns drivers into mad dogs (a reaction, where you develop and explain one part of the reading), or (3) to agree or disagree that close spaces are utterly without value (a reaction, where you have to be aware of what Owens said on this point).

Once you've thought about the question, list or freewrite your first ideas about the question. At this time, don't worry about how "right" or "wrong" your writing is—just write your first thoughts.

Planning Your writing will be clear if you follow a plan. Remember that your audience for this writing is your instructor and that he or she will be evaluating how well you stick to the subject, make a point, and support it. Your plan for making a point about the subject and supporting that point can be written in a brief outline.

First, reread the question. Next, survey your list or freewriting. Does it contain a main point that answers the question? Does it contain supporting ideas and details?

Next, write a main point; then list supporting ideas and details under the main point. Your main point will be the topic sentence of your answer. If you need more support, try brainstorming.

Drafting Write your point and supporting ideas in paragraph form. Remember to use effective transitions and to combine short sentences.

Polishing You will probably not have time to copy your answer, but you can review it, proofread it, and correct any errors in spelling, punctuation, and word choice. This final check can produce a more refined answer.

Organize Your Time

Some students skip steps: they immediately begin writing their answer to an essay question without thinking or planning. Sometimes they find themselves stuck in the middle of a paragraph, panicked because they have no more ideas. At other times, they find themselves writing in a circle, repeating the same point over and over. Occasionally, they even forget to include a main idea.

You can avoid these hazards by spending time on each of the stages. Planning is as important as writing. For example, if you have 30 minutes to write an essay, you can divide your time like this:

5 minutes: thinking, freewriting, listing
10 minutes: planning, outlining
10 minutes: drafting
5 minutes: reviewing and proofreading

Focusing on one step at a time can make you more confident and your task more manageable.

Lines of Detail: A Walk-Through Assignment

Here are two ideas from "A Ridiculous Addiction":

1. The typical American has a compulsion about finding a convenient parking space.

2. People who search for good parking spots become mean and nasty.

Pick one of the ideas with which you agree or disagree. Write a paragraph explaining why you agree or disagree. To write your paragraph, follow these steps:

Step 1: Begin by listing at least two reasons why you agree or disagree. Use your own experience with parking lots to come up with your reasons. For example, for statement 1, you could ask yourself these questions: Are all Americans concerned with parking spaces? How do you know? Is it a compulsion or just practical behavior? For statement 2, you might ask questions like these: Have you ever seen nastiness in parking lots? Have you ever experienced it? What actions were mean? Answering such questions can help you come up with your reasons for agreement or disagreement.

COLLABORATE ▶ **Step 2:** Read your list to a partner or group. With the help of your listener(s), you can add reasons or details to explain the reasons.

Step 3: Once you have enough ideas, transform the statement you agreed or disagreed with into a topic sentence.

Step 4: Write an outline by listing your reasons and details below the topic sentence. Check that your list is in a clear and logical order.

Step 5: Write a draft of your paragraph. Check that you have attributed Gwinn Owens' statement, that you have enough details, and that you have combined any choppy sentences. Revise your draft until the paragraph is smooth and clear.

Step 6: Before you prepare the final copy, check your last draft for errors in spelling, punctuation, and word choice.

Writing Your Own Paragraph

When you write on one of these topics, be sure to work through the stages of the writing process in preparing your paragraph.

1. Gwinn Owens writes about Americans' addiction to the close-in parking space. Write about another addiction that Americans have. Instead of writing about a topic like drug or alcohol addiction, follow Owens' example and write about a social habit that is hard to break. You might, for instance, write about one of these habits:

driving while talking on a phone	tailgating
weaving in and out of traffic	speeding
driving too slowly	pushing in line
running yellow traffic lights	littering
talking during a movie	arriving late

Once you've chosen a habit, brainstorm, alone or with a partner, for details. Think about details that could fit these categories: ◀ COLLABORATE 👥

why the habit is foolish	where and when people act this way
why the habit is dangerous	advantages of breaking the habit

Ask yourself questions, answer them, and let the answers lead to more questions. Once you've collected some good details, work through the stages of writing a paragraph.

2. Gwinn Owens writes about a great invention, the car, and about the parking problems caused by cars. Below are several other recent inventions that can cause problems. Your goal is to write a paragraph about *the problems one of these inventions can cause.*

   To start, pick two of the inventions below. Alone, or with a partner or group, brainstorm both topics: ask questions, answer them, add details, so that each topic can lead you to enough ideas for a paragraph.

   After you've brainstormed, pick the topic you like better and work through the stages of preparing a paragraph.

   Brainstorm on problems that could be caused by two of the following:

voice mail	lasers	passwords	cell phones
pagers	credit cards	e-mail	text messaging

3. Do some online research about one of the inventions listed in topic 2, and see if any current uses differ from the original ones. (For example, the Internet was originally intended for communication among scientists but is widely used by the general public today.) Write a paragraph about how this invention has developed various uses over the years.   ◀ COMPUTER 🖱️

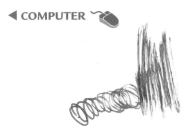

 COMPUTER ▶

4. Buying merchandise via Web sites or by phone has never been easier. Based on your observations or through personal experience, explain why shopping online or through television channels such as The Home Shopping Network and QVC can become as addictive as the parking obsession that Gwinn Owens describes. Examine the lure of this particular means of shopping, how or why the consumer may become hooked, and ways that one can recognize if he or she has become an obsessive online or cable television shopper.

Name: _____ Section: _____

PEER REVIEW FORM FOR WRITING FROM READING

After you've written a draft version of your paragraph, let a writing partner read it. When your partner has completed the form below, discuss the comments. Repeat the same process for your partner's paragraph.

This paragraph (1) summarizes, (2) agrees or disagrees with, or (3) discusses an idea connected to a reading selection (choose one).

I think this paragraph needs/does not need to include the title and author of the reading selection.

The topic sentence of this paragraph is _____

_____

_____

The best part of this paragraph started with the words _____

_____

One suggestion to improve this paragraph is _____

_____

_____

Other comments: _____

_____

_____

_____

_____

_____

_____

_____

_____

_____

_____

_____

_____

Reviewer's Name: _____

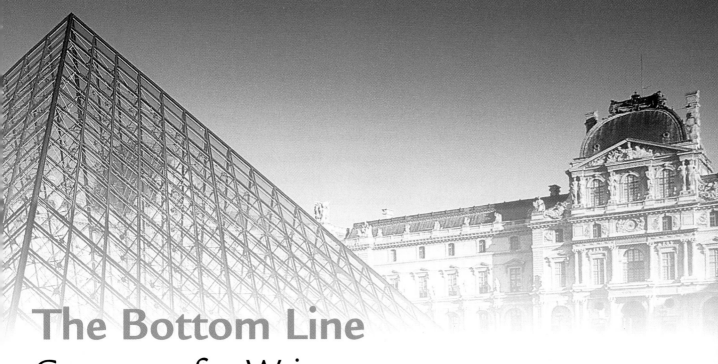

The Bottom Line
Grammar for Writers

INTRODUCTION

Overview

In this section, you'll be working with "The Bottom Line," the basics of grammar that you need to be a clear writer. If you are willing to memorize certain rules and work through the activities here, you will be able to apply grammatical rules automatically as you write.

Using "The Bottom Line"

Since this portion of the textbook is divided into self-contained segments, it does not have to be read in sequence. Your instructor may suggest you review specific rules and examples, or you may be assigned various segments as either a class or group assignment. Various approaches are possible, and thus you can regard this section as a "user-friendly" grammar handbook for quick reference. Mastering the practical parts of grammar will improve your writing; you will feel more sure of yourself because you will know the bottom line.

CONTENTS

Chapter 14   The Simple Sentence   353

Chapter 15   Beyond the Simple Sentence: Coordination   370

Chapter 16   Avoiding Run-On Sentences and Comma Splices   384

Chapter 17   Beyond the Simple Sentence: Subordination   393

Chapter 18   Avoiding Sentence Fragments   405

Chapter 19   Using Parallelism in Sentences   417

Chapter 20   Using Adjectives and Adverbs   427

Chapter 21   Correcting Problems with Modifiers   437

Chapter 22   Using Verbs Correctly   447

Chapter 23   More on Verbs: Consistency and Voice   461

Chapter 24   Making Subjects and Verbs Agree   474

Chapter 25   Using Pronouns Correctly: Agreement and Reference   491

Chapter 26   Using Pronouns Correctly: Consistency and Case   503

Chapter 27   Punctuation: The Period and the Question Mark   513

Chapter 28   Punctuation: The Comma   517

Chapter 29   Punctuation: The Semicolon and the Colon   526

Chapter 30   Punctuation: The Apostrophe   531

Chapter 31   Other Punctuation and Mechanics   536

Chapter 32   Spelling   546

Chapter 33   Words That Sound Alike/Look Alike   557

Chapter 34   Word Choice   572

Chapter 35   Sentence Variety   580

CHAPTER 14
The Simple Sentence

Identifying the crucial parts of a sentence is the first step in many writing decisions: how to punctuate, how to avoid sentence fragments, how to be sure that subjects and verbs "agree" (match). To move forward to these decisions requires a few steps back—to basics.

RECOGNIZING A SENTENCE

Let's start with a few basic definitions. A basic unit of language is a **word**.

> **examples:** *car, dog, sun*

A group of related words can be a **phrase**.

> **examples:** *shiny new car; snarling, angry dog; in the bright sun*

When the group of words contains a subject and a verb, it is called a **clause**. When the word group has a subject and a verb and makes sense by itself, it is called a **sentence** or an **independent clause.** When the word group has a subject and a verb but does not make sense by itself, it is called a **dependent clause.**

If you want to check whether you have written a sentence, and not just a group of related words, you first have to check for a subject and a verb. Locating the verbs first can be easier.

RECOGNIZING VERBS

Verbs are words that express some kind of action or being. Verbs about the five senses—sight, touch, smell, taste, sound—are part of the group called **being verbs.** Look at some examples of verbs as they work in sentences:

action verbs:
We *walk* to the store every day.
The children *ran* to the playground.

being verbs:
My mother *is* a good cook.
The family *seems* unhappy.
The soup *smells* delicious.

> **Exercise 1** **Recognizing Verbs**

Underline the verbs in each of the following sentences.

1. My sister called the police.
2. At night, the puppy sleeps in my bed.
3. Nelson sounds worried about the trip.
4. Marlon and Tommy were my closest friends on the team.
5. Jealousy ruined a good relationship.
6. The storm filled the air with a fresh green scent.
7. Many small children sleep with a special stuffed animal.
8. You are the kindest person in the family.
9. This blanket feels itchy.
10. A motorcycle roared across the intersection.

More on Verbs

The verb in a sentence can be more than one word. First of all, there can be **helping verbs** in front of the main verb, the action or being verb. Here is a list of some frequently used helping verbs: *is, am, are, was, were, do, must, might, have, has, shall, will, can, could, may, should, would.*

> I *was watching* the Super Bowl. (The helping verb is *was.*)
> You *should have called* me. (The helping verbs are *should* and *have.*)
> The president *can select* his assistants. (The helping verb is *can.*)
> Leroy *will graduate* in May. (The helping verb is *will.*)

Helping verbs can make the verb in a sentence more than one word long. But there can also be more than one main verb:

> Andrew *planned* and *practiced* his speech.
> I *stumbled* over the rug, *grabbed* a chair, and *fell* on my face.

COLLABORATE ▶

> **Exercise 2** **Writing Sentences with Helping Verbs**

Complete this exercise with a partner or a group. First, ask one person to add at least one helping verb to the verb given. Then work together to write two sentences using the main verb and the helping verb(s). As a final step, appoint one spokesperson for your group to read all your sentences to the class. Notice how many combinations of main verb and helping verb you hear.

The first one is done for you.

1. verb: named

verb with helping verb(s): was named

sentence 1: I was named after my father.

sentence 2: Washington, D.C. was named after the first president.

2. verb: smiling

verb with helping verb(s): *Was smiliy*

sentence 1: *I smiled when I got my pichur takun*

sentence 2: *She Smilives a lot.*

3. verb: explain

verb with helping verb(s): _____

sentence 1: _____

sentence 2: _____

4. verb: apologized

verb with helping verb(s): _____

sentence 1: _____

sentence 2: _____

5. verb: forgotten

verb with helping verb(s): _____

sentence 1: _____

sentence 2: _____

RECOGNIZING SUBJECTS

After you can recognize verbs, finding the subjects of sentences is easy because subjects and verbs are linked. If the verb is an action verb, for example, the subject will be the word or words that answer the question, Who or what is doing that action?

The truck stalled on the highway.

Step 1: Identify the verb: *stalled*
Step 2: Ask, "Who or what stalled?"
Step 3: The answer is the subject: The *truck* stalled on the highway. *Truck* is the subject.

If your verb expresses being, the same steps apply to finding the subject.

Spike was my best friend.

Step 1: Identify the verb: *was*
Step 2: Ask, "Who or what was my best friend?"
Step 3: The answer is the subject: *Spike* was my best friend. *Spike* is the subject.

Just as there can be more than one word to make up a verb, there can be more than one subject.

examples: *David* and *Leslie* planned the surprise party.
My *father* and *I* worked in the yard yesterday.

Exercise 3 **Recognizing the Subjects in Sentences**

Underline the subjects in the following sentences.

1. Alan might have taken the long way to work.
2. We will visit our cousins in the Dominican Republic.
3. With a smile, a man handed me a five-dollar bill.
4. On weekends, the road is less congested.
5. Optimism can make hard choices less stressful.
6. Banks are offering more credit cards to more age groups.
7. Sometimes listening to a friend's worries can be a great help.
8. Before the job interview, fear and misery filled my head.
9. Anything could be wrong with the plumbing.
10. Somebody has been stealing my magazines from the mailbox.

More About Recognizing Subjects and Verbs

When you look for the subject of a sentence, look for the core word or words; don't include descriptive words around the subject. The idea is to look for the subject, not for the words that describe it.

The dark blue *dress* looked lovely on Anita.
Dirty *streets* and grimy *houses* destroy a neighborhood.

The subjects are the core words *dress*, *streets*, and *houses*, not the descriptive words *dark blue*, *dirty*, and *grimy*.

PREPOSITIONS AND PREPOSITIONAL PHRASES

Prepositions are usually small words that often signal a kind of position or possession, as shown in the following list:

INFO BOX: Some Common Prepositions

about	before	beyond	inside	on	under
above	below	during	into	onto	up
across	behind	except	like	over	upon
after	beneath	for	near	through	with
among	beside	from	of	to	within
around	between	in	off	toward	without
at					

A prepositional phrase is made up of a preposition and its object. Here are some prepositional phrases. In each one, the first word is the preposition; the other words are the object of the preposition.

Prepositional Phrases

about the movie	of mice and men
around the corner	off the record
between two lanes	on the mark
during recess	up the wall
near my house	with my sister and brother

There is an old memory trick to help you remember prepositions. Think of a chair. Now, think of a series of words you can put *in front of* the chair:

around the chair	*with* the chair
behind the chair	*to* the chair
between the chairs	*near* the chair
by the chair	*under* the chair
of the chair	*on* the chair
off the chair	*from* the chair

Those words are prepositions.

You need to know about prepositions because they can help you identify the subject of a sentence. There is an important grammar rule about prepositions:

> **Nothing in a prepositional phrase can ever be the subject of the sentence.**

Prepositional phrases describe people, places, or things. They may describe the subject of a sentence, but they never include the subject. Whenever you are looking for the subject of a sentence, begin by putting parentheses around all the prepositional phrases.

> The restaurant (around the corner) makes the best fried chicken (in town).

The prepositional phrases are in parentheses. Because *nothing* in them can be the subject, once you have eliminated the prepositional phrases, you can follow the steps to find the subject of the sentence:

> What is the verb? *makes*
> Who or what makes the best fried chicken? The *restaurant.*
> *Restaurant* is the subject of the sentence.

By marking off the prepositional phrases, you are left with the *core* of the sentence. There is less to look at.

> (Behind the park), a *carousel* (with gilded horses) delighted children (from all the neighborhoods).
> subject: *carousel*

> The *dog* (with the ugliest face) was the winner (of the contest).
> subject: *dog*

Exercise 4   **Recognizing Prepositional Phrases, Subjects, and Verbs**

Put parentheses around all the prepositional phrases in the following sentences. Then underline the subject and verb and put an *S* above each subject and a *V* above each verb.

1. The story behind the theft of the ancient sword goes beyond any movie plot.

2. A few of the residents on my street complained about the constant noise from the construction site.

3. The little children with bad colds sneezed and coughed during the school play.

4. Before the wedding, the father of the bride wiped a few tears from his eyes and smiled at his daughter.

5. Nothing except a blizzard would keep me from a reunion with my old friends across the border.

6. Tamara climbed onto the windowsill and waved at her older brother on the street.

7. At the sound of the dog's barking, the frightened kitten skittered through the room and ran to the shelter of the closet.

8. Teenagers in our area are looking for jobs with salaries above the minimum wage.

9. A simple apology stood between me and my childhood friend.

10. I have been thinking about a trip to Malaysia after my graduation from nursing school.

 COLLABORATE ▶ (Exercise 5) **Writing Sentences with Prepositional Phrases**

Complete this exercise with a partner. First, add one prepositional phrase to the core sentence. Then ask your partner to add a second prepositional phrase to the same sentence. For the next sentence, switch places. Let your partner add the first phrase; you add the second. Keep reversing the process throughout the exercise. When you have completed the exercise, be ready to read the sentences with two prepositional phrases to the class. The first one has been done for you as a sample.

1. core sentence: Rain fell.

Add one prepositional phrase: _Rain fell on the mountains._

_____

Add another prepositional phrase: From a dark sky, rain fell
on the mountains.

2. **core sentence:** Shawn smiled.

Add one prepositional phrase: _____

_____

Add another prepositional phrase: _____

_____

3. **core sentence:** The soldier hid.

Add one prepositional phrase: _____

Add another prepositional phrase: _____

_____

4. **core sentence:** Students are pleased.

Add one prepositional phrase: _____

_____

Add another prepositional phrase: _____

_____

5. **core sentence:** A man handed me a small box.

Add one prepositional phrase: _____

_____

Add another prepositional phrase: _____

_____

WORD ORDER

When we speak, we often use a very simple word order: first, the subject; then, the verb. For example, someone would say, "I am going to the store." *I* is the subject that begins the sentence; *am going* is the verb that comes after the subject.

But not all sentences are in such a simple word order. Prepositional phrases, for example, can change the word order.

sentence: Among the contestants was an older man.

Step 1: Mark off the prepositional phrase(s) with parentheses: (Among the contestants) was an older man. Remember that nothing in a prepositional phrase can be the subject of a sentence.

Step 2: Find the verb: *was*

Step 3: Who or what was? An older *man* was. The subject of the sentence is *man*.

After you change the word order of this sentence, you can see the subject (S) and verb (V) more easily.

An older *man was* among the contestants.

Exercise 6 **Finding Prepositional Phrases, Subjects, and Verbs in Complicated Word Order**

Start by putting parentheses around the prepositional phrases in the following sentences. Then underline the subjects and verbs and put an *S* above each subject and a *V* above each verb.

1. In the back of my mind is a small ray of hope.

2. Behind the garage lies a flower bed with daisies and carnations.

3. Inside the toy chest are stuffed animals and wooden blocks from my father's childhood.

4. Among the actors on stage were a famous comedian from a late-night television show and a star of a soap opera.

5. Beyond the hills stands a famous old house with a history of mysterious crimes.

6. From the front of the lecture hall came the faint sound of someone with hiccups.

7. Between the end of December and the middle of January is a semester break.

8. In my wallet is a photograph of the two of us from our Little League days.

9. Under Dion's pillow is some money from the tooth fairy in exchange for Dion's baby tooth.

10. Among Tony's friends from school was a tall boy with an easy smile.

More on Word Order

The expected word order of subject first, then verb, changes when a sentence starts with *There is/are, There was/were, Here is/are, Here was/were.* In such cases, look for the subject after the verb.

             V   S   S
There *are* a *bakery* and a *pharmacy* down the street.

             V   S
Here *is* the *man* with the answers.

To understand this pattern, try changing the word order:

        S   S   V
A *bakery* and a *pharmacy* *are* there, down the street.

$$\overset{\text{S}}{} \qquad\qquad\qquad \overset{\text{V}}{}$$

The *man* with the answers *is* here.

You should also note that even if the subject comes after the verb, the verb has to "match" the subject. For instance, if the subject refers to more than one thing, the verb must also refer to more than one thing.

> There *are* a *bakery* and a *pharmacy* down the road. (Two things, a bakery and a pharmacy, *are* down the road.)

Word Order in Questions

Questions may have a different word order. The main verb and the helping verb may not be next to each other.

> **question:** Do you like pizza?
> **subject:**   *you*
> **verbs:**   *do, like*

To understand this concept, think of answering the question. If someone accused you of not liking pizza, you might say, "I *do like* it." You would use two words as verbs.

> **question:** Will he think about it?
> **subject:**   *he*
> **verbs:**   *will, think*

> **question:** Is Maria telling the truth?
> **subject:**   *Maria*
> **verbs:**   *is, telling*

Exercise 7   **Recognizing Subjects and Verbs in Complicated Word Order: A Comprehensive Exercise**

Underline the subjects and verbs, putting an *S* above the subjects and a *V* above the verbs.

1. Beneath my father's rough voice and tough appearance was

a man with a gentle heart.

2. Can you change your mind about the trip to Yucatan?

3. Near the end of the path were a small cabin and a couple of ponies.

4. Around the corner from the bank was a restaurant with a large

patio.

5. Here are the new neighbors with their cat and parrot.

6. Has Marie called you about a ride to work?

7. Is there anything about me in the newspaper?

8. From all our friends came letters of sympathy and support.

9. Will Alicia see the real story behind all the lies?

10. There was a look of fear in the old man's eyes.

Words That Cannot Be Verbs

Sometimes there are words that look like verbs in a sentence, but they are not verbs. Such words include adverbs (words like *always, often, nearly, rarely, never, ever*), which are placed close to the verb but are not verbs. Another word that is placed between a helping verb and a main verb is *not*. *Not* is not a verb.

When you are looking for verbs in a sentence, be careful to eliminate words such as *often* and *not*.

He *will* not *listen* to me. (The verbs are *will listen.*)
Althea *can* always *find* a bargain. (The verbs are *can find.*)

Be careful with contractions.

They *haven't raced* in years. (The verbs are *have raced. Not* is not a part of the verb, even in contractions.)
Don't you *come* from Arizona? (The verbs are *do come.*)
Won't he ever *learn?* (The verbs are *will learn. Won't* is a contraction for *will not.*)

Recognizing Main Verbs

If you are checking to see if a word is a main verb, try the *pronoun test.* Combine your word with this simple list of pronouns: *I, you, he, she, it, we, they.* A main verb is a word such as *drive* or *noticed* that can be combined with the words on this list. Now try the pronoun test.

For the word *drive:* I drive, you drive, he drives, she drives, it drives, we drive, they drive
For the word *noticed:* I noticed, you noticed, he noticed, she noticed, it noticed, we noticed, they noticed

But words such as *never* cannot be used, alone, with the pronouns:

~~I never, you never, he never, she never, it never, we never, they never~~ (Never did what?)

Never is not a verb. *Not* is not a verb either, as the pronoun test indicates:

~~I not, you not, he not, she not, it not, we not, they not~~ (These combinations do not make sense because *not* is not a verb.)

Verb Forms That Cannot Be Main Verbs

There are forms of verbs that cannot be main verbs by themselves either. **An *-ing* verb, by itself, cannot be the main verb,** as the pronoun test shows.

For the word *voting:* ~~I voting, you voting, he voting, she voting, we voting, they voting~~
If you see an *-ing* verb by itself, correct the sentence by adding a helping verb.

Scott ~~riding~~ his motorcycle. (*Riding*, by itself, cannot be a main verb.)
correction: Scott *was riding* his motorcycle.

Another verb form, called an infinitive, also cannot be a main verb. An **infinitive** is the form of the verb that has *to* placed in front of it.

INFO BOX: Some Common Infinitives

to care	to vote	to repeat
to feel	to play	to stumble
to need	to reject	to view

Try the pronoun test, and you'll see that infinitives cannot be main verbs:

For the infinitive *to vote:* ~~I to vote, you to vote, he to vote, she to vote, we to vote, they to vote~~

So if you see an infinitive being used as a verb, correct the sentence by adding a main verb.

We ~~to vote~~ in the election tomorrow. (There is no verb, just an infinitive.)

correction: We *are going* to vote in the election tomorrow. (Now there is a verb.)

The infinitives and the *-ing* verbs just do not work as main verbs. You must put a verb with them to make a correct sentence.

Exercise 8   **Correcting Problems with *-ing* or Infinitive Verb Forms**

Most—but not all—of the following sentences are faulty; an *-ing* verb or an infinitive may be taking the place of a main verb. Rewrite the sentences that contain errors.

1. A senator from our state to speak at the graduation ceremony next week.

rewritten: _____

_____

2. Brittany and Scott behaving like spoiled children at my surprise party for Simon.

rewritten: _____

_____

3. Without regrets, I said good-bye to my old school and started my first full-time job.

rewritten: _____

_____

4. A few of the salespeople at the hardware store need to sharpen their skills in customer relations.

rewritten: _____

_____

5. On rainy days, my dog to play fetch in the hallway at my house.

rewritten: _____

_____

6. In the most dramatic moment of his life, the famous movie star admitting his criminal record.

rewritten: _____

_____

7. A veteran of the war in Iraq to publish a book about her experiences in combat and at a military hospital.

rewritten: _____

_____

8. After an argument with the waiter, the angry customer storming out of the restaurant.

rewritten: _____

_____

9. In a few minutes, Mr. Duval is going to introduce the new members of the hockey team.

rewritten: _____

_____

10. Beneath the pile of sweaters and socks, Bobby's pet hamster dozing peacefully in a tightly curled ball.

rewritten: _____

_____

Exercise 9 **Finding Subjects and Verbs: A Comprehensive Exercise**

Underline the subjects and verbs in these sentences and put an *S* above each subject and a *V* above each verb.

1. Will you ever take me to a place with palm trees and sunshine?

2. After final exams, they're making plans for a wedding.

3. At the root of Maggie's problems are family pressures.

4. Keith needs to remember the reason for his commitment to Ella.

5. Won't you meet me for dinner at the barbecue place?

6. My father has rarely lost his temper with my brother.

7. Christina will never ask her sister for help with the bills.

8. At the end of the mall are a dollar store and a hair salon.

9. Ali might have been expecting a gift from his coworkers.

10. There were a banana, a tuna sandwich, and a bottle of orange

    juice in the lunch box.

Exercise 10   **Finding Subjects and Verbs: Another
Comprehensive Exercise**

Underline the subjects and verbs in these sentences and put an *S* above each
subject and a *V* above each verb.

1. Oliver shook my hand and offered me a seat in the front row.

2. Outside the door sat a large green frog with bulging eyes.

3. In the shadows, the trees and the path appeared mysterious and

    threatening.

4. Sam will often call and ask for advice.

5. Don't you ever regret your choice of a career?

6. You have rarely spoken with so much confidence.

7. We could never afford a house in this neighborhood.

8. Here is the beautiful woman from my night class at school.

9. In every relationship, there is a small amount of uncertainty at first.

10. Before the fancy dinner, my sister warned me about my table

    manners, smoothed my hair, and kissed me on the cheek.

Exercise 11   **Create Your Own Text**

◀ COLLABORATE

Complete this activity with two partners. Following is a list of rules you've
just studied. Each member of the group should write one example of each
rule. When your group has completed three examples for each rule, trade
your completed exercise with another group, and check their examples while
they check yours. The first rule has been done for you as a sample.

Rule 1: The verb in a sentence can express some kind of action.

examples:

   a. Wanda sleeps late on the weekends.

   b. On Monday, I found a wallet in the street.

   c. Melted snow covered the sidewalks and steps.

Rule 2: The verb in a sentence can express some state of being or one of the five senses.

examples:

   a. _____

   b. _____

   c. _____

Rule 3: The verb in a sentence can consist of more than one word.

examples:

   a. _____

   b. _____

   c. _____

Rule 4: There can be more than one subject of a sentence.

examples:

   a. _____

   b. _____

   c. _____

Rule 5: If you take out the prepositional phrases, it is easier to identify the subject of a sentence because nothing in a prepositional phrase can be the subject of a sentence. (Write sentences with at least one prepositional phrase and put parentheses around the prepositional phrases.)

examples:

   a. _____

   b. _____

   c. _____

Rule 6: Not all sentences have the simple word order of subject first, then verb. (Give examples of more complicated word order.)

examples:

   a. _____

   b. _____

   c. _____

Rule 7: Words such as *not, never, often, always,* and *ever* are not verbs. (Write sentences using those words, but underline the correct verb.)

examples:

a. _____

b. _____

c. _____

Rule 8: An *-ing* verb form by itself or an infinitive (*to* preceding the verb) cannot be a main verb. (Write sentences with *-ing* verb forms or infinitives, but underline the main verb.)

examples:

a. _____

b. _____

c. _____

Exercise 12   **Recognizing Subjects and Verbs in a Paragraph**

Underline the subjects and verbs in this paragraph and put an *S* above each subject and a *V* above each verb.   ◄ CONNECT ⚬⚬⚬

My father would have loved a job in education. He read everything in the house, from the newspapers to the back of cereal boxes. On Saturdays, he took me and my sisters to the library and always left with a stack of books. He helped us find books, too. My father didn't watch much television or care for movies. At night, he relaxed with his newest library book and read until late in the night. He never went to work without a book to read during his lunch break. During our family meals, he told us about his reading. From him we learned about history, science, medicine, and exploration. He made all these subjects interesting. Unfortunately, my father never had the chance to go to college. With a college degree and with his love of learning, he would have made a great teacher.

⫘ CONNECT ▶ **Exercise 13** **Recognizing Subjects and Verbs in a Paragraph**

Underline the subjects and verbs in this paragraph and put an *S* above each subject and a *V* above each verb.

A wait in the ticket line at the movies can be boring or entertaining. Guessing the movie choice of each person in line makes the visit enjoyable. The variety of movies at every theater helps make the game a challenge. Of course, some guesses are simple. Small children fidget and tug on their parents' hands on their way to a cartoon about adorable animals or funny monsters. Groups of teenage boys are harder to place. Are they going to a science fiction or fantasy film? Or are they waiting for a thrilling new martial arts film? Teenage girls may be headed for a romantic film or a comedy. Films with older actors on the posters usually attract older moviegoers. On the other hand, moviegoers of all ages will cross age barriers and choose a blockbuster film with universal appeal. At any local theater, there is a movie for everybody.

Chapter Test: The Simple Sentence

Underline the subjects and verbs in these sentences and put an *S* above each subject and a *V* above each verb.

1. The noise of the bulldozer across the street is giving me a terrible headache.

2. Professor Spinelli rarely asks a question about the assigned reading before discussing it in class.

3. Beyond the local mall there are a modern furniture store and a children's activity center.

4. Haven't you ever thought about a career in physical therapy?

5. The hole in my sock and the tear in my tee shirt created a bad impression of my style.

6. Mr. Zacaria always traveled with his dog and kept a pet carrier in his car.

7. The loose tile on the roof might have caused the leak in the bed-

room.

8. Among the most irritating people in my daily life are the constant

whiners.

9. My cat loves to look out the window at the birds in the trees.

10. A bad cold could not be the reason for his absence from

work.

CHAPTER 15
Beyond the Simple Sentence: Coordination

A group of words containing a subject and verb is called a **clause.** When that group makes sense by itself, it is called a sentence or an independent clause.

The kind of sentence that is one independent clause is called a **simple sentence.** If you rely too heavily on a sentence pattern of simple sentences, you risk writing paragraphs like this:

> I am a college student. I am also a salesperson in a mall. I am always busy. School is time-consuming. Studying is time-consuming. Working makes me tired. Balancing these activities is hard. I work too many hours. Work is important. It pays for school.

Here is a better version:

> I am a college student and a salesperson at a mall, so I am always busy. School and study are time-consuming, and working makes me tired. Balancing these activities is hard. I work too many hours, but that work is important. It pays for school.

OPTIONS FOR COMBINING SIMPLE SENTENCES

Good writing involves sentence variety; it means mixing a simple sentence with a more complicated one, a short sentence with a long one. Sentence variety is easier to achieve if you can combine related, short sentences into one.

Some students avoid such combining because they are not sure how to do it. They do not know how to punctuate the new combinations. It is true that punctuation involves memorizing a few rules, but once you know them, you will be able to use them automatically and write with more confidence. Here are three options for combining simple sentences and the punctuation rules to follow in each case.

OPTION 1: USING A COMMA WITH A COORDINATING CONJUNCTION

You can combine two simple sentences with a comma and a coordinating conjunction. The coordinating conjunctions are *for, and, nor, but, or, yet,* and *so.*

To coordinate means to join equals. When you join two simple sentences with a comma and a coordinating conjunction (CC), each half of the combination remains an independent clause with its own subject (S) and verb (V).

Here are two simple sentences:

  S   V   S   V
He cooked the dinner.   *She worked* late.

Here are the two simple sentences combined with a comma and with the word *for,* a coordinating conjunction (CC):

  S   V   , CC   S   V
He cooked the dinner, *for she worked* late.

The combined sentences keep the form they had as separate sentences; that is, they are still both independent clauses, with a subject and verb and with the ability to stand alone.

The word that joins them is the **coordinating conjunction.** It is used to join *equals.* Look at some more examples. These examples use a variety of coordinating conjunctions to join two simple sentences.

sentences combined with *and:*

     S   V   , CC   S   V
Jennifer likes Italian food, *and Mark prefers* Korean dishes.

sentences combined with *nor:*

  S   V   , CC V S V
I didn't like the book, *nor did I like* the movie made from the book. (Notice what happens to the word order when you use *nor.*)

sentences combined with *but:*

  S V   , CC S V
I rushed to the bank, *but I was* too late.

sentences combined with *or:*

  S   V   ,CC S   V
She can write a letter to Jim, *or she can call* him.

sentences combined with *yet:*

  S   V   ,CC S   V
Leo tried to please his sister, *yet she* never *seemed* appreciative of his efforts.

sentences combined with *so:*

> *I was* the first in line for the concert tickets, *so I got* the best seats in the stadium.

One easy way to remember the coordinating conjunctions is to call them, as a group, **fanboys** (**f**or, **a**nd, **n**or, **b**ut, **o**r, **y**et, **s**o).

Where Does the Comma Go?

Notice that the comma comes *before* the coordinating conjunction (*for, and, nor, but, or, yet, so*). It comes before the new idea, the second independent clause. It goes where the first independent clause ends. Try this punctuation check. After you've placed the comma, look at the combined sentences. For example:

> She joined the army, and she traveled overseas.

Then split it into two sentences at the comma:

> She joined the army. And she traveled overseas. (The split makes sense)

If you put the comma in the wrong place, after the coordinating conjunction, your split sentences would be:

> She joined the army and. She traveled overseas. (The split doesn't make sense)

This test helps you see whether the comma has been placed correctly—*where the first independent clause ends.* (Notice that you can begin a sentence with *and.* You can also begin a sentence with *but, or, nor, for, yet,* or *so*—as long as you're writing a complete sentence.)

Caution: Do *not* put a comma every time you use the words *and, but, or, nor, for, yet,* or *so;* put it only when the coordinating conjunction joins independent clauses. Do not put the comma when the coordinating conjunction joins words:

> blue and gold   tired but happy   hot or cold

Do not use a comma when the coordinating conjunction joins phrases:

> on the chair or under the table
> in the water and by the shore
> with a smile but without an apology

The comma is used when the coordinating conjunction joins two independent clauses. Another way to say the same rule is to say the comma is used when the coordinating conjunction joins two simple sentences.

Placing the Comma by Using Subject-Verb (S-V) Patterns

An independent clause, or simple sentence, follows one of these basic patterns:

> He ran.

or

> He and I ran.

or

    S   **V**   **V**
He ran and swam.

or

    S   **S V**   **V**
He and I ran and swam.

Study all four patterns for the simple sentence, and you will notice you can draw a line separating the subjects on one side and the verbs on the other:

S	V
SS	V
S	VV
SS	VV

So whether the sentence has one subject (or more than one) and one verb (or more than one) in the simple sentence, the pattern is subject(s) followed by verb(s)—one simple sentence.

When you combine two simple sentences, the pattern changes:

two simple sentences:

    S   **V**   **S V**
He swam. I ran.

two simple sentences combined:

    S   **V**   **S V**
He swam, but I ran.

In the new pattern, *SVSV*, you cannot draw a line separating all the subjects on one side and all the verbs on the other. This new pattern, with two simple sentences (or independent clauses) joined into one, is called a *compound sentence.*

Recognizing the *SVSV* pattern will help you place the comma for compound sentences.

Here is another way to remember this rule. If you have this pattern:

SV   SV

use a comma in front of the coordinating conjunction. Do not use a comma in front of the coordinating conjunction with these patterns:

S	V
SS	V
S	VV
SS	VV

For example, use a comma for this pattern:

    S   **V**   **,**   **S** **V**
Jane followed directions, but *I rushed* ahead.

Do not use a comma for this pattern:

    S   **V**   **V**
Carol cleans her kitchen every week but never *wipes* the top of the refrigerator.

You have just studied one way to combine simple sentences. If you are going to take advantage of this method, you have to memorize the coordinating conjunctions—*for, and, nor, but, or, yet,* and *so*—so that your use of them, with the correct punctuation, will become automatic.

> **Exercise 1**   **Recognizing Compound Sentences and Adding Commas**

Add commas only where they are needed in the following sentences. Do not add any words.

1. Hank fixed the refrigerator, but it still made a loud, whirring noise.

2. The woman behind the counter mixed the strawberries, bananas, and frozen yogurt in a blender and offered me a taste.

3. After dinner I took a walk around the block and I bought a newspaper at the drug store.

4. Soledad got a new television for her birthday so she gave her old one to me.

5. Andrew is quitting his job at the warehouse for he is tired of his forty-minute drive to work.

6. Heather spoke of her father with great affection yet she never visited him at his home in Tucson.

7. The car was five years old but rarely needed any repairs beyond regular maintenance.

8. The doctor at the clinic didn't write a prescription for me nor did she tell me to make a follow-up appointment.

9. Kids' Closet has the best prices for children's clothes so I buy my son's shorts and shirts there.

10. Walter is hoping for a raise next month or at least a bonus for working during the holidays.

> **Exercise 2**   **More on Recognizing Compound Sentences and Adding Commas**

Add commas only where they are needed in the following sentences. Do not add any words.

1. Yesterday Ronnie passed his driving test and today he is looking for a cheap car.

2. Two of my friends from my sociology class are meeting for lunch at school and asked me to join them.

3. Children need to spend part of each day in some type of physical activity or they risk becoming overweight.

4. Reality shows on television are hardly realistic yet they attract large audiences.

5. Teresa painted the bedroom and Aaron installed new shelves.

6. Teresa and Aaron painted the bedroom and installed new shelves.

7. Tom is always bragging about his money yet never offers to pick up the check at clubs or restaurants.

8. Tomorrow you can call me at the office or I will see you after work.

9. Doug is the perfect partner for someone with a sense of adventure and a love of travel.

10. The salesperson at the electronics store was neither helpful nor informed about the merchandise.

Exercise 3   **Combining Sentences Using Coordinating Conjunctions**

Combine each pair of sentences using a coordinating conjunction and the appropriate punctuation.

1. Leon brought me a warm-up jacket.
   It wasn't the right size.

   combined: _____

   _____

2. <u>The Revenge of the Shark People</u> does not have good actors.
   <u>The Revenge of the Shark People</u> does not have much suspense.

   combined: _____

   _____

3. It was snowing outside.
   Maria and I spent the day in front of the fireplace.

   combined: _____

   _____

4. My friend Ernesto was in love with my sister Rachel.
   He never gave her a hint of his feelings.

   combined: _____

   _____

5. I got the Camry for a reasonable price.
   The car dealer gave me a good trade-in price for my Hyundai.

   combined: _____

   _____

6. Chocolate frozen yogurt tastes fairly good.
   It is no substitute for chocolate ice cream.

   combined: _____

   _____

7. You can apologize to Levar right now.
   You can remain stubborn and end the friendship forever.

   combined: _____

   _____

8. Most people like to save money on their car insurance.
   Most people look around for the best deals before buying.

   combined: _____

   _____

9. Natalie got a haircut and a manicure.
   She wanted to make a good impression at the talent audition.

   combined: _____

   _____

10. The apartment had spacious rooms and a perfect location.
    It was too expensive for our budget.

    combined: _____

    _____

OPTION 2: USING A SEMICOLON BETWEEN TWO SIMPLE SENTENCES

Sometimes you may want to combine two simple sentences (independent clauses) without using a coordinating conjunction. If you want to join two simple sentences that are related in their ideas and you do not use a coordinating conjunction, you can combine them with a semicolon.

two simple sentences:

   S   **V**   **S**   **V**
I cooked the turkey. *She made* the stuffing.

two simple sentences combined with a semicolon:

   S   **V**   **; S**   **V**
I cooked the turkey; *she made* the stuffing.

Here's another example of this option in use:

   S   **V** **V**   **; S**   **V**
Rain can be dangerous; *it makes* the roads slippery.

Notice that when you join two simple sentences with a semicolon, the second sentence begins with a lowercase letter, not a capital letter.

You need to memorize the seven coordinating conjunctions so that you can make a decision about punctuating your combined sentences. Remember these rules:

- If a coordinating conjunction joins the combined sentences, put a comma in front of the coordinating conjunction.

     S **V**   **,**   **S**   **V**
  Tom had a barbecue in his back yard, and the *food was* delicious.

- If there is no coordinating conjunction, put a semicolon in front of the second independent clause.

     S **V**   **;**   **S**   **V**
  Tom had a barbecue in his back yard; the *food was* delicious.

OPTION 3: USING A SEMICOLON AND A CONJUNCTIVE ADVERB

Sometimes you want to join two simple sentences (independent clauses) with a connecting word called a **conjunctive adverb.** Here is a list of some conjunctive adverbs:

INFO BOX: Some Common Conjunctive Adverbs			
also	furthermore	likewise	otherwise
anyway	however	meanwhile	similarly
as a result	in addition	moreover	still
besides	in fact	nevertheless	then
certainly	incidentally	next	therefore
consequently	indeed	now	thus
finally	instead	on the other hand	undoubtedly

You can use a conjunctive adverb (CA) to join simple sentences, but when you do, you still need a semicolon in front of the adverb.

two simple sentences:

       S   **V**   **S V**

My *parents checked* my homework every night. *I did* well in math.

two simple sentences joined by a conjunctive adverb and a semicolon:

       S   **V**   **; CA S V**

My *parents checked* my homework every night; *thus I did* well in math.

  S **V**   **;**   **CA**   **S**   **V**

She gave me good advice; *moreover, she helped* me follow it.

Punctuating after a Conjunctive Adverb

Notice the comma after the conjunctive adverb in the preceding sentence. Here is the generally accepted rule:

> **Put a comma after the conjunctive adverb if the conjunctive adverb is more than one syllable long.**

For example, if the conjunctive adverb is a word like *consequently, furthermore,* or *moreover,* you use a comma. If the conjunctive adverb is one syllable, you do not have to put a comma after the conjunctive adverb. One-syllable conjunctive adverbs are words like *then* or *thus.*

> I saw her cruelty to her staff; *then* I lost respect for her.
> We worked on the project all weekend; *consequently,* we finished a week ahead of the deadline.

Exercise 4 **Combining Simple Sentences with Semicolons and Conjunctive Adverbs**

Some of the following sentences need a semicolon; others need a semicolon and a comma. Do not add, change, or delete any words; just add the correct punctuation.

1. A few of the children on the street played soccer they kicked the ball against a brick wall.

2. My aunt hated bad manners at the dinner table nevertheless she tolerated her little nephews' mashed-potato fights.

3. The gray poodle chased the orange cat across the room next the cat turned and hissed at the dog.

4. Anyone can make up a good excuse only a few people can get others to believe that excuse.

5. Eric apologized for forgetting my birthday furthermore he gave me a dozen roses.

6. The manager didn't call a meeting instead he sent an e-mail.

7. Your hair is thick and shiny mine is thin and brittle.

8. The old picnic area near the lake is becoming popular with families soon it will need more benches and picnic tables.

9. From the back of the classroom came a strange noise it was a muffled bark.

10. Crossroads Café has reasonable prices in fact it serves the cheapest dinners in town.

Exercise 5 **More on Combining Simple Sentences with Semicolons and Conjunctive Adverbs**

Following are pairs of simple sentences. Combine each pair into one sentence. You have two options: (1) use a semicolon, or (2) use a semicolon and a conjunctive adverb (with a comma if it is needed). Pick the option that makes the most sense for each sentence.

1. Jim constantly borrows my clothes without asking me.
   He's basically a good roommate.

   combined: _____

   _____

2. Lionel has to attend all his classes regularly.
   Lionel risks losing his financial aid.

   combined: _____

   _____

3. I was in a hurry yesterday.
   I forgot to lock the car doors.

   combined: _____

   _____

4. The sun streamed in the kitchen window.
The room seemed magical and bright.

combined: _____

_____

5. Damian cried with an outraged fury.
Damian beat the pillow with his tiny fists.

combined: _____

_____

6. The television is much too expensive.
It is too large for our living room.

combined: _____

_____

7. Sam spent three hours on the clogged drain.
He decided to call a plumber.

combined: _____

_____

8. Andre rushed to heat a bottle of baby formula.
Larry walked the screaming baby back and forth.

combined: _____

_____

9. The baseball game was a disaster for our team.
Fans began leaving before the end of the game.

combined: _____

_____

10. Our house was full of mosquitoes.
We spent the whole night slapping and swatting at the insects.

combined: _____

_____

Exercise 6 **Combining Simple Sentences Three Ways**

Add a comma, a semicolon, or a semicolon and a comma to the following sentences. Do not add, change, or delete any words; just add the correct punctuation.

1. My boyfriend loves pancakes in fact he has been known to drive thirty miles for his favorite blueberry pancakes.

2. My car has a rusty tailpipe and no air conditioning but it is good basic transportation.

3. Professor Silverman was a child movie star incidentally one of her movies is on television tomorrow night.

4. Yogurt used to be considered health food now yogurt drinks and desserts appeal to children and adults.

5. The landlord wouldn't return my security deposit nor would he give me back my first month's rent.

6. The mayor avoided any mention of the problems with the water treatment plant similarly the city manager refused to answer any questions on the subject.

7. The old oak table has been in my family for years yet it never seems to go out of style.

8. David works for a government agency thus he is able to get health insurance through his employer.

9. My nine-year-old niece wants a cell phone moreover she wants one with a digital camera.

10. Fifteen minutes passed no one spoke a word.

 COLLABORATE ▶   ⬭ Exercise 7 ⬭   **Using Three Options to Combine Simple Sentences**

Below are pairs of simple sentences. Working with a partner or partners, combine each pair into one sentence in two different ways. Remember, you have three options: (1) use a comma and a coordinating conjunction, (2) use a semicolon, or (3) use a semicolon and a conjunctive adverb (with a comma if it is needed). Pick the options that make the most sense for these sentences. The first one has been done for you.

1. Crystal ran out of money for her electric bill.
   I lent her enough to pay it.
   combinations:

   a. *Crystal ran out of money for her electric bill, so I lent her enough to pay it.*

   b. *Crystal ran out of money for her electric bill; therefore, I lent her enough to pay it.*

2. Botany is a fascinating class.
   It makes me think about the natural world.
   combinations:

   a. _____

   _____

   b. _____

   _____

3. Luisa crept into the closet.
   She found no safety in the dark space.
   combinations:

   a. _____

   _____

   b. _____

   _____

4. Armand won first prize in a college art contest.
   He decided to major in graphic design.
combinations:

   a. _____

   _____

   b. _____

   _____

5. The passengers waited in their seats for an hour.
   The pilot never announced the plane's departure.
combinations:

   a. _____

   _____

   b. _____

   _____

6. My brother rarely complained about his back-breaking job.
   He didn't mention his poor health.
combinations:

   a. _____

   _____

   b. _____

   _____

7. I'm not going to the store.
   I don't have time.
combinations:

   a. _____

   _____

   b. _____

   _____

8. You can rent a car for two weeks.
   You can borrow my car.
combinations:

   a. _____

   _____

   b. _____

   _____

9. Winter can be a depressing season.
   We can find ways to enjoy it.
combinations:

   a. _____

   _____

b. _____

_____

10. My girlfriend types my college papers.
I help her with her math homework.
combinations:

a. _____

_____

b. _____

_____

◯◖◯ CONNECT ▶   **Exercise 8**   **Editing a Paragraph for Errors in Coordination**

Edit the following paragraph for errors in coordination. You do not need to add or change words. Just add, delete, or change punctuation. There are seven errors in the paragraph.

The coffee shop around the corner from my college is an old-fashioned yet popular place. It doesn't offer fancy blends of coffee nor does it have an espresso machine. The plastic seats in the booths are torn the corners of the tables are chipped. Some people might call it a dump; nevertheless large numbers of students and faculty drop by every day. The shop is convenient, reliable, and cheap, therefore, it is always crowded. People can cross the street from college and find hot coffee, doughnuts, and bagels at a reasonable price. The place is open, for ten hours. The best part of the shop is the friendly atmosphere. Students are welcome to sit for hours over a cup of coffee; as a result campus romances often develop. Teachers grade papers meanwhile, campus police take a break.

◯◖◯ CONNECT ▶   **Exercise 9**   **Editing a Paragraph for Errors in Coordination**

Edit the following paragraph for errors in coordination. You do not need to add or change words. Just add, delete, or change punctuation. There are eight errors in the paragraph.

Losing one's voice can be a frustrating experience. Last year, I developed a bad case of laryngitis as a result, I struggled to speak for several days. Friends came up to me and talked in their ordinary tones. I tried to respond; but a weird croak came out of my throat. My friends looked shocked at first yet soon understood. Shock turned to sympathy and they would ask, "Have your lost your voice?" Then they kept on talking. I could only nod my head and listen. Trying to communicate with a stranger was worse. I struggled to whisper some words to a stranger with a question however he couldn't understand me. He just stared at me in surprise. I couldn't explain nor, could I apologize. After a few days, I got my voice back, and celebrated by talking nonstop.

Chapter Test: Beyond the Simple Sentence: Coordination

Add a comma, a semicolon, or a semicolon and a comma to the following sentences. Do not add, change, or delete any words; just add the correct punctuation.

1. Many retired people are moving to the city for they like the variety of activities and cultures there.

2. Hector was stuck in traffic for an hour meanwhile his wife waited for him at the bus station.

3. Nothing could be done with the shattered vase yet Emily carefully put the broken pieces in an envelope.

4. My aunt never buys tomatoes at the store instead she grows her own delicious ones in her backyard.

5. Our tour guide began with a history of the famous house next she led us from room to room.

6. The old dog never barked at visitors nor did it ever chew on the furniture.

7. I used to dream of going to college now I am making my dream into reality.

8. Canned peaches taste good still they are no substitute for fresh peaches.

9. The kindergarten class was restless yesterday so the teacher took the children outside for a brisk walk.

10. With a grin, the toddler threw his bowl of cereal to the floor oatmeal stuck to the table legs, the high chair, and the cat.

CHAPTER 16
Avoiding Run-On Sentences and Comma Splices

RUN-ON SENTENCES

Run-on sentences are independent clauses that have not been joined correctly. This error is also called a fused sentence.

> **run-on sentence error:**
> Carol cleans her kitchen every week she shines every pot and pan.

> **run-on sentence error corrected:**
> Carol cleans her kitchen every week; she shines every pot and pan.

> **run-on sentence error:**
> I studied for the test all weekend I am well prepared for it.

> **run-on sentence error corrected:**
> I studied for the test all weekend, so I am well prepared for it.

STEPS FOR CORRECTING RUN-ON SENTENCES

When you edit your writing, you can correct run-on sentences by following these steps:

> **Step 1:** Check for two independent clauses.
> **Step 2:** Check that the clauses are separated by either a coordinating conjunction and a comma or by a semicolon.

Follow the steps in checking this sentence:

> The meeting was a waste of time the club members argued about silly issues.

> **Step 1:** Check for two independent clauses. You can do this by checking for the subject-verb, subject-verb pattern that indicates two independent clauses:

> The *meeting was* a waste of time the club *members argued* about silly issues.

The pattern indicates that you have two independent clauses.

> **Step 2:** Check that the clauses are separated by either a coordinating conjunction (*for, and, nor, but, or, yet, so*) and a comma or by a semicolon.

There is no punctuation between the independent clauses, so you have a run-on sentence. You can correct it two ways:

> **run-on sentence corrected with a coordinating conjunction and a comma:**
> The meeting was a waste of time, *for* the club members argued about silly issues.

> **run-on sentence corrected with a semicolon:**
> The meeting was a waste of time; the club members argued about silly issues.

Follow the steps once more as you check this sentence:

> I had the flu I missed class last week.

> **Step 1:** Check for two independent clauses. Do this by checking the subject-verb, subject-verb pattern:

> *I had* the flu *I missed* class last week.

> **Step 2:** Check that the clauses are separated by either a coordinating conjunction (*for, and, nor, but, or, yet, so*) and a comma or by a semicolon.

There is no punctuation between the independent clauses, so you have a run-on sentence. You can correct the run-on sentence two ways:

> **run-on sentence corrected with a coordinating conjunction and a comma:**
> I had the flu, *so* I missed class last week.

> **run-on sentence corrected with a semicolon:**
> I had the flu; I missed class last week.

Using the steps to check for run-on sentences can also help you avoid unnecessary punctuation. Consider this sentence:

> The manager gave me my schedule for next week and told me about a special sales promotion.

> **Step 1: Check for two independent clauses. Do this by checking the subject-verb, subject-verb pattern:**

The *manager gave* me my schedule for next week and *told* me about a special sales promotion.

The pattern is *SVV*, not *SV, SV*. The sentence is not a run-on sentence. It does not need any additional punctuation.

Following the steps in correcting run-on sentences can help you avoid a major grammar error.

Exercise 1   Correcting Run-on (Fused) Sentences

Some of the sentences below are correctly punctuated. Some are run-on (fused) sentences; that is, they are two simple sentences run together without any punctuation. If the sentence is correctly punctuated, write *OK* in the space provided. If it is a run-on sentence, put an *X* in the space provided and correct the sentence above the lines.

1. _____ I have been feeling listless and groggy all day I couldn't get to sleep last night.

2. _____ The day began with fierce wind and heavy showers then the sun came out and dried up all the puddles.

3. _____ Below the cliff was the only survivor of the crash the man crawled away from the wreckage and looked up.

4. _____ Superstar athletes make enormous salaries but make even more money from product endorsements and personal appearances.

5. _____ Most candy is full of sugar and fat I have switched to fresh fruit for a snack.

6. _____ The local television news in my town often covers the same stories and uses the same film for two or three broadcasts.

7. _____ You can come to my house for Thanksgiving dinner you can stay home and watch all the football games.

8. _____ Mark always talks to me in class yet has never even asked me to have coffee.

9. _____ Andrea likes to be the center of attention she always wears exotic makeup and clothes.

10. _____ Occasionally, I take my daughter to the petting zoo and watch her enjoy the baby animals.

Exercise 2   More on Correcting Run-on (Fused) Sentences

Some of the following sentences are correctly punctuated. Some are run-on (fused) sentences; that is, they are two simple sentences run together without any punctuation. If the sentence is correctly punctuated, write *OK* in the space provided. If it is a run-on sentence, put an *X* in the space provided and correct the sentence above the lines.

1. _____ Victor works fifty hours a week thus he has little time for a social life.

2. _____ Mrs. Wong does not talk about the loss of her grandson she does not want to lose control of her emotions.

3. _____ Kindergartners and college freshmen experience a similar anxiety on the first day of school.

4. _____ The loss of my dog was a terrible experience for me her return home after six weeks turned misery into joy.

5. _____ Mr. and Mrs. Swenson opened a small restaurant in an old part of the city then they added a dance floor and band.

6. _____ A confident tone of voice impresses people and inspires faith in your ideas.

7. _____ This morning I locked my keys in the car next I couldn't get into my house.

8. _____ The construction crew arrived before dawn the workers drilled, pounded, and sawed for hours.

9. _____ Christina doesn't like salsa music I'm not taking her to the club on Saturday.

10. _____ Mel wants to go to a small college near his home instead of to a large and distant university with thousands of students.

COMMA SPLICES

A **comma splice** is an error that occurs when you punctuate with a comma but should use a semicolon instead. If you are joining two independent clauses without a coordinating conjunction (*for, an, nor, but, or, yet, so*), you must use a semicolon. A comma is not enough.

comma splice error:
The crowd pushed forward, people began to panic.

comma splice error corrected:
The crowd pushed forward; people began to panic.

comma splice error:
I forgot my glasses, thus I couldn't read the small print in the contract.

comma splice error corrected:
I forgot my glasses; thus I couldn't read the small print in the contract.

CORRECTING COMMA SPLICES

When you edit your writing, you can correct comma splices by following these steps:

Step 1: Check for two independent clauses.

Step 2: Check that the clauses are separated by a coordinating conjunction (*for, and, nor, but, or, yet, so*). If they are, then a comma in front of the coordinating conjunction is sufficient. If they are not separated by a coordinating conjunction, you have a comma splice. Correct it by changing the comma to a semicolon.

Follow the steps to check for a comma splice in this sentence:

I dropped the glass, it shattered on the tile floor.

Step 1: Check for two independent clauses. You can do this by checking for the subject-verb, subject-verb pattern that indicates two independent clauses.

I dropped the glass, *it shattered* on the tile floor.

The pattern indicates that you have two independent clauses.

Step 2: Check that the clauses are separated by a coordinating conjunction.

There is no coordinating conjunction. To correct the comma splice error, you must use a semicolon instead of a comma.

comma splice error corrected: I dropped the glass; it shattered on the tile floor.

Be careful not to mistake a short word like *then* or *thus* for a coordinating conjunction. Only the seven coordinating conjunctions (*for, and, nor, but, or, yet, so*) with a comma in front of them, can join independent clauses.

comma splice error: Susie watched television, then she went to bed.
comma splice error corrected: Susie watched television; then she went to bed.

Then is not a coordinating conjunction; it is a conjunctive adverb. When it joins two independent clauses, it needs a semicolon in front of it.

Also remember that conjunctive adverbs that are two or more syllables long (like *consequently, however, therefore*) need a comma after them as well as a semicolon in front of them when they join independent clauses:

Harry has been researching plane fares to New York; consequently, he knows how to spot a cheap flight.

(For a list of some common conjunctive adverbs, see Chapter 15.)

Sometimes writers see commas before and after a conjunctive adverb and think the commas are sufficient. Check this sentence for a comma splice by following the steps:

Jonathan loves his job, however, it pays very little.

Step 1: Check for two independent clauses by checking for the subject-verb, subject-verb pattern.

Jonathan loves his job, however, *it pays* very little.

The pattern indicates that you have two independent clauses.

Step 2: Check for a coordinating conjunction.

There is no coordinating conjunction. *However* is a conjunctive adverb, not a coordinating conjunction. Because there is no coordinating conjunction, you need a semicolon between the two independent clauses.

> **comma splice error corrected:**
> Jonathan loves his job; however, it pays very little.

Exercise 3 **Correcting Comma Splices**

Some of the sentences below are correctly punctuated. Some contain comma splices. If the sentence is correctly punctuated, write *OK* in the space provided. If it contains a comma splice, put an *X* in the space provided and correct the sentence above the lines. To correct a sentence, add the necessary punctuation. Do not add any words.

1. _____ Nick's truck was unreliable, it had bald tires and a leak in the radiator.

2. _____ Bridget needs a break, she has been studying for hours.

3. _____ A few of my friends got up early and watched the sun rise at the beach, then they had breakfast at a little beachfront restaurant.

4. _____ I always eat dinner at my folks' house, thus I don't have to buy many groceries for my apartment.

5. _____ My father hated the old sofa in the living room, but he refused to spend the money for a new sofa.

6. _____ New York City was loud, dirty, crowded, and expensive, nevertheless, it was exciting and fun.

7. _____ George has to get a full-time job, otherwise, he will not be able to pay his hospital bills.

8. _____ Lincoln River is not the prettiest town in America, yet most of the residents appreciate its good qualities.

9. _____ Latoya threw a rubber duck at her little brother, then she splashed him with the water in her tub.

10. _____ Learning a foreign language is not easy, however, it is definitely worth the work.

Exercise 4 **More on Correcting Comma Splices**

Some of the following sentences are correctly punctuated. Some contain comma splices. If the sentence is correctly punctuated, write *OK* in the space provided. If it contains a comma splice, put an *X* in the space provided and correct the sentence above the lines. To correct a sentence, do not add any words; just correct the punctuation.

1. _____ The woman in the blue suit is the best speaker on the debating team incidentally, she is my sister.

2. _____ Our local movie theater offers a discount on tickets for late afternoon movies, so we often go at 4:00 p.m.

3. _____ The house was crowded with guests, people pushed to get inside.

4. _____ My idea of a perfect home is a cabin in the woods, but I have never stayed in one.

5. _____ Some students carry backpacks, others come with small suitcases on wheels.

6. _____ My neighbor has a giant television, and I often watch the World Series at his house.

7. _____ You should have picked me up at the airport, anyway, you should have offered to do it.

8. _____ I lived in Venezuela for two years, so I have an advantage in my Spanish class.

9. _____ I lived in Venezuela for two years, therefore, I have an advantage in my Spanish class.

10. _____ There was no excuse, Sandra had to apologize.

COLLABORATE ▶ | Exercise 5 | **Completing Sentences**

With a partner or group, write the first part of each of the following incomplete sentences. Make your addition an independent clause. Be sure to punctuate your completed sentences correctly. The first one is done for you.

1. The driver ignored the railroad warning signals, and his car was hit by the train.

2. _____ then an upstairs window shattered.

3. _____ in addition, you have lied to me several times.

4. _____ or I will miss my favorite television show.

5. _____ now I have to start all over again.

6. _____ but no one was there.

7. _____ however, it made us

laugh.

8. _____ but I will never forget her.

9. _____ he was accused of

the murder.

10. _____ otherwise, we may owe more

money.

Exercise 6   **Editing a Paragraph for Run-on Sentences
and Comma Splices**

◀ CONNECT ⃝⃝⃝

Edit the following paragraph for run-on sentences and comma splices. There
are seven errors.

    Hair is always a topic of conversation in my family. My father has almost no
hair still he refuses to shave his tufts of frizz. My mother has thick, curly hair
down to her shoulders. We children often argue about our hair. My brother brags
about his hair he denies any fear of baldness. He enjoys teasing me he points to
my split ends and laughs. To him, those split ends are signs of hair loss. He threat-
ens me with looking like our father. My brother's constant teasing could be a sign
of his own fears. Maybe he is afraid of losing his own hair therefore he makes fun
of his male relatives' hair. My father feels insulted, meanwhile, my mother nags
my father about shaving his head. She encourages him with photographs of attractive bald men like Michael Jordan. Only my mother feels secure about her hair.
Maybe the men in the family should just shave our heads then we'd be happy.

Exercise 7   **Editing a Paragraph for Run-on Sentences
and Comma Splices**

◀ CONNECT ⃝⃝⃝

Edit the following paragraph for run-on sentences and comma splices. There
are seven errors.

    There was a small fire at the town hall last week, quick thinking saved the
building. The mayor's secretary was working late in her office. She smelled smoke
and followed the scent. She located the source of the fire in a nearby file room

immediately she called 911. The fire was burning near a wall and seemed to be caused by an electrical failure. The secretary should have left the building, instead she grabbed a small fire extinguisher and aimed it at the blaze. Minutes later, the fire department arrived. They rushed to the building. Soon they found the smoke and ashes however, the blaze had been extinguished. Fire officials called the secretary's action risky; on the other hand some people are grateful to her for saving the city's files and perhaps the building itself.

Chapter Test: Avoiding Run-on Sentences and Comma Splices

Some of the sentences below are correctly punctuated. Some are run-on sentences, and some contain comma splices. If a sentence is correctly punctuated, write *OK* in the space provided. If it is a run-on sentence or contains a comma splice, put an *X* in the space provided and correct the sentence above the lines. To correct a sentence, add the necessary punctuation. Do not add any words.

1. _____ One of the cashiers at Price-Mart always has a smile for his customers then he tells them a silly joke.

2. _____ I rarely check the air pressure in my car tires, as a result, my brother often scolds me for driving with underinflated tires.

3. _____ I took a big swig of the milk from the milk carton and immediately spit the milk into the sink.

4. _____ You can do the dishes, I did them yesterday.

5. _____ It's raining, so I can't take the dog for a walk.

6. _____ Tanika is an excellent tennis player in fact, she has already won several regional tournaments in her age group.

7. _____ George practiced his speech for hours; thus he gained confidence in his speaking ability.

8. _____ Elise can be irritating, nevertheless, she's a loyal friend.

9. _____ Mr. Paskowski could apply for the job in computer information systems at the college, or he could look into employment offerings at the rehabilitation center.

10. _____ The check was supposed to arrive on Monday finally it came in the mail on Thursday.

CHAPTER 17
Beyond the Simple Sentence: Subordination

MORE ON COMBINING SIMPLE SENTENCES

Before you go any further, look back. Review the following:

- A clause has a subject and a verb.
- An independent clause is a simple sentence; it is a group of words, with a subject and verb, that makes sense by itself.

There is another kind of clause called a **dependent clause.** It has a subject and a verb, but it does not make sense by itself. It cannot stand alone. It is not complete by itself. That is, it *depends* on the rest of the sentence to give it meaning. You can use a dependent clause in another option for combining simple sentences.

OPTION 4: USING A DEPENDENT CLAUSE TO BEGIN A SENTENCE

Often, you can combine simple sentences by changing an independent clause from one sentence into a dependent clause and placing it at the beginning of the new sentence.

two simple sentences:

S V   S V

I was late for work. My *car had* a flat tire.

changing one simple sentence into a beginning dependent clause:

Because my *car had* a flat tire, *I was* late for work.

OPTION 5: USING A DEPENDENT CLAUSE TO END A SENTENCE

You can also combine simple sentences by changing an independent clause from one sentence into a dependent clause and placing it at the end of the new sentence:

S V   S V
I was late for work because my *car had* a flat tire.

Notice how one simple sentence can be changed into a dependent clause in two ways:

two simple sentences:
    S   S   V   S V
Mother and *Dad wrapped* my presents. *I slept.*

changing one simple sentence into a dependent clause:
    S   S   V   S V
Mother and *Dad wrapped* my presents while *I slept.*

or

             S V   S   S
While *I slept, Mother* and *Dad wrapped* my presents.

Using Subordinating Conjunctions

Changing an independent clause to a dependent one is called **subordinating.** How do you do it? You add a subordinating word, called a **subordinating conjunction,** to an independent clause, making it dependent—less "important," or subordinate—in the new sentence.

Keep in mind that the subordinate clause is still a clause; it has a subject and a verb, but it does not make sense by itself. For example, let's start with an independent clause:

Caroline studies.

Somebody (Caroline) does something (studies). The statement makes sense by itself. But if you add a subordinating conjunction to the independent clause, the clause becomes dependent, incomplete, unfinished, like this:

When Caroline studies (When she studies, what happens?)
Unless Caroline studies (Unless she studies, what will happen?)
If Caroline studies (If Caroline studies, what will happen?)

Now, each dependent clause needs an independent clause to finish the idea:

    dependent clause   **independent clause**
When Caroline studies, she gets good grades.

    dependent clause   **independent clause**
Unless Caroline studies, she forgets key ideas.

    dependent clause   **independent clause**
If Caroline studies, she will pass the course.

There are many subordinating conjunctions. When you put any of these words in front of an independent clause, you make that clause dependent. Here is a list of some subordinating conjunctions.

INFO BOX: Subordinating Conjunctions

after	before	so that	whenever
although	even though	though	where
as	if	unless	whereas
as if	in order that	until	whether
because	since	when	while

If you pick the right subordinating conjunction, you can effectively combine simple sentences (independent clauses) into a more sophisticated sentence pattern. Such combining helps you add sentence variety to your writing and helps explain relationships between ideas.

simple sentences:

S   V   V   S   V

Leo could not *read* music. His *performance was* exciting.

new combination:

dependent clause   independent clause

Although Leo could not read music, his performance was exciting.

simple sentences:

S   V   S   V

I caught a bad cold last night. *I forgot* to bring a sweater to the baseball game.

new combination:

independent clause   dependent clause

I caught a bad cold last night because I forgot to bring a sweater to the baseball game.

Punctuating Complex Sentences

A sentence that has one independent clause and one or more dependent clauses is called a **complex sentence.** Complex sentences are very easy to punctuate. See if you can figure out the rule for punctuating by yourself. Look at the following examples. All are punctuated correctly.

dependent clause   independent clause

Whenever the baby smiles, his mother is delighted.

independent clause   dependent clause

His mother is delighted whenever the baby smiles.

dependent clause   independent clause

While you were away, I saved your mail for you.

independent clause   dependent clause

I saved your mail for you while you were away.

In the examples above, look at the sentences that have a comma. Look at the ones that do not have a comma. Both kinds of sentences are punctuated correctly. Do you see the rule?

If the dependent clause comes at the beginning of the sentence, put a comma after the dependent clause. If the dependent clause comes at the end of the sentence, do not put a comma in front of the dependent clause.

Although we played well, we lost the game.
We lost the game although we played well.

Until he called, I had no date for the dance.
I had no date for the dance until he called.

Exercise 1 Punctuating Complex Sentences

All the sentences below are complex sentences; that is, they have one independent and one or more dependent clauses. Add a comma to each sentence that needs one.

1. Before I met my husband I had never known anyone from China.

2. If Wayne needs help with his garden he can ask his brothers.

3. I climbed into bed and snuggled against the pillows while the snowstorm raged outside my windows.

4. French fries don't taste right unless they are covered with ketchup.

5. Because my roommate borrows my clothes without asking I lock my bedroom door.

6. My son always protests when I try to wake him up in the morning.

7. Antonio started training for a paramedic's position after he finished high school in San Diego.

8. After Antonio finished high school in San Diego he started training for a paramedic's position.

9. Let me know when you need a ride to work.

10. Until you learn to say "no" to your children they will continue to manipulate you.

Exercise 2 More on Punctuating Complex Sentences

All the following sentences are complex sentences; that is, they have one independent clause and one or more dependent clauses. Add a comma to each sentence that needs one.

1. As the children sang and danced on the school stage their proud parents took dozens of photographs.

2. Although the suit cost me too much it will give me confidence at the job interview.

3. Norman is determined to lose weight even if he has to give up pizza and beer.

4. When I see Halloween decorations and candy in the stores in early September I lose all sense of time.

5. Before our street was widened there wasn't much traffic.

6. While the police interviewed the witnesses to the accident a crowd formed at the scene.

7. Kelly doesn't expect a gift from her brother because they have not spoken in six months.

8. Whether you want a used car or a new one you should consider the cost of car insurance.

9. The house was designed so that the kitchen and dining room are one open space.

10. The well-dressed traveler tried to talk on his cell phone as the noise of the airport boomed around him.

INFO BOX: OPTIONS FOR COMBINING SENTENCES

Coordination

Option 1
Independent clause

{ , for
, and
, nor
, but
, or
, yet
, so }

independent clause

Option 2
Independent clause   ;   independent clause

Option 3
Independent clause

{ ; also
; anyway,
; as a result,
; besides,
; certainly,
; consequently,
; finally,
; furthermore,
; however,
; incidentally,
; in addition,
; in fact,
; indeed,
; instead,
; likewise,
; meanwhile,
; moreover,
; nevertheless,
; next
; now
; on the other hand,
; otherwise,
; similarly,
; still
; then
; therefore,
; thus
; undoubtedly, }

independent clause

Subordination

Option 4 Dependent clause (Put a comma at the end of the dependent clause.)	After Although As As if Because Before Even though If In order that Since So that Though Unless Until When Whenever Where Whereas Whether While	independent clause
Option 5 Independent clause	after although as as if because before even though if in order that since so that though unless until when whenever where whereas whether while	dependent clause

Note: In Option 4, words are capitalized because the dependent clause will begin your complete sentence.

Exercise 3 **Using the Five Options for Combining Sentences**

Add the necessary commas and/or semicolons to the following sentences. Some are correct as they are.

  1. You can get a good seat at the music festival if you get to the outdoor theater early.

2. The copier at our office is old and slow so we do not expect much from it.

3. Our two-bedroom house became too small for our growing family consequently we moved to a larger home.

4. Tell me the truth you owe it to me.

5. Unless we get some rain soon my flowers will all die.

6. Whenever I hear the sound of an ambulance on the street I think about the people caught in that emergency situation.

7. My cat has a sneaky side even though he seems submissive and sweet.

8. The small computer business expanded and eventually became an international success.

9. One person at the end of the line began pushing ahead then all the others in line reacted with anger and threats.

10. After the little boy took one step into the street his father pulled him to safety.

Exercise 4   **More on Using the Five Options for Combining Sentences**

Add the necessary commas and/or semicolons to the following sentences. Some are correct as they are.

1. One of the teachers at my old school wrote me a letter of recommendation I can use it to apply for a scholarship.

2. The Mediterranean Grill offers good food at reasonable prices however it is not the place for a quiet dinner.

3. Alicia set the table for dinner while Derek grilled some fish outdoors.

4. Although Miriam seems to act too good for the neighborhood she is actually shy and eager to make friends.

5. Levon was thrilled when his daughter was born.

6. My uncle was once a taxi driver in New York and all kinds of celebrities and sports stars rode in his cab.

7. I rarely eat meals at home instead I grab something to eat at a fast-food place and eat it in the car.

8. My brother is not particularly handsome but he is extremely popular.

9. Because you know the way to Melissa's house you can drive us to her party.

10. All the clothes in the washer came out with purple stains I had left a ballpoint pen in the pocket of my jeans.

COLLABORATE ▶   Exercise 4   **Combining Sentences**

Do this exercise with a partner or a group. Following are pairs of sentences. Combine each pair of sentences into one clear, smooth sentence in two different ways. You can add words as well as punctuation. The first pair of sentences is done for you.

1. We always go to Country Ice Cream for a treat.
   The store has the best hot fudge sundaes in the world.

   combination 1: We always go to Country Ice Cream for a treat because the store has the best hot fudge sundaes in the world.

   combination 2: We always go to Country Ice Cream for a treat; the store has the best hot fudge sundaes in the world.

2. Henry was lonely.
   He started visiting online chat rooms.

   combination 1: _____

   _____

   combination 2: _____

   _____

3. My brother wrecked my car.
   I had to take the bus to work.

   combination 1: _____

   _____

   combination 2: _____

   _____

4. Zack had always loved Lynette.
   Zack married Dana.

   combination 1: _____

   _____

   combination 2: _____

   _____

5. Everyone warned me about my spending habits.
   I ended up deeply in debt.

   combination 1: _____

   _____

   combination 2: _____

   _____

6. Keith always dresses well.
   He wants to impress the women at work.

   combination 1: _____

   _____

combination 2: _____

_____

7. Forked lightning struck the forest.
A huge tree split in half.

combination 1: _____

_____

combination 2: _____

_____

8. The rappers didn't perform any of their old hits.
They didn't pay attention to the audience's requests.

combination 1: _____

_____

combination 2: _____

_____

9. My brother was showing us his new haircut.
My sister was laughing hysterically.

combination 1: _____

_____

combination 2: _____

_____

10. My small chihuahua doesn't like to play with other dogs.
She prefers to associate with cats.

combination 1: _____

_____

combination 2: _____

_____

Exercise 5   **Create Your Own Text on Combining Sentences**   ◀ COLLABORATE 👥

Following is a list of rules for coordinating and subordinating sentences.
Working with a group, write two examples for each rule.

Option 1: You can join two simple sentences (two independent
clauses) into a compound sentence with a coordinating
conjunction and a comma in front of it.

(The coordinating conjunctions are *for, and, nor, but, or,
yet, so.*)

example 1: _____

_____

example 2: _____

_____

Option 2: You can combine two simple sentences (two independent clauses) into a compound sentence with a semicolon between independent clauses.

example 1: _____

_____

example 2: _____

_____

Option 3: You can combine two simple sentences (two independent clauses) into a compound sentence with a semicolon and a conjunctive adverb between independent clauses. (Some conjunctive adverbs are *also, anyway, as a result, besides, certainly, consequently, finally, furthermore, however, incidentally, in addition, indeed, in fact, instead, likewise, meanwhile, moreover, nevertheless, next, now, on the other hand, otherwise, similarly, still, then, therefore, thus,* and *undoubtedly.*)

example 1: _____

_____

example 2: _____

_____

Option 4: You can combine two simple sentences (two independent clauses) into a complex sentence by making one clause dependent. The dependent clause starts with a subordinating conjunction. Then, if the dependent clause begins the sentence, the clause ends with a comma. (Some common subordinating conjunctions are *after, although, as, as if, because, before, even though, if, in order that, since, so that, though, unless, until, when, whenever, where, whereas, whether, while.*)

example 1: _____

_____

example 2: _____

_____

Option 5: You can combine two simple sentences (two independent clauses) into a complex sentence by making one clause dependent. Then, if the dependent clause comes after the independent clause, no comma is needed.

example 1: _____

_____

example 2: _____

Exercise 6   **Editing a Paragraph for Errors in Coordination and Subordination**

◀ CONNECT ⬤⬤⬤

Edit the following paragraph for errors in coordination and subordination. You do not have to add words to the paragraph; just add, delete, or change punctuation. There are six errors.

Calico Hills used to be an attractive neighborhood now it looks like the victim of many bad storms. Although Calico Hills has never been an expensive part of town it used to be a clean, bright area of single-family homes. Recently it has shown signs of deterioration moreover, the residents seem to have given up on maintaining the neighborhood. Unless those residents take action Calico Hills will continue its slide toward decay. Many of the changes in the neighborhood wouldn't take much money to reverse. Residents could work together to remove the curbside trash, weed the front yards, and trim the ragged bushes. If the residents united they could also petition the city to fill in the potholes and repair the sidewalks. These changes would improve the appearance of the area and boost the residents' morale then Calico Hills would be moving in the right direction.

Exercise 7   **Editing a Paragraph for Errors in Coordination and Subordination**

◀ CONNECT ⬤⬤⬤

Edit the following paragraph for errors in coordination and subordination. You do not have to add words to the paragraph; just add, delete, or change punctuation. There are seven errors.

Large-screen televisions are wonderful but they pose several problems. They are particularly troublesome, when viewers sit too close to the screen. Insufficient distance between the viewer and the screen results in a distorted picture consequently, the viewer is likely to see an enormous nose instead of an actor's entire face on the screen. Another problem can arise, if a huge television is placed in a small room. The television is likely to cover most of one wall; as a result, the other furniture in the room may have to be rearranged. The large television may look monstrous, when the rest of the furniture is small. When the rest of the furniture is large, the room may look overcrowded. A large television can transform a living room into a home theater and the entertainment value can be

great. Some people may welcome a large new addition to their home others may

prefer their entertainment on a smaller scale.

Chapter Test: Coordination and Subordination

Add missing commas and/or semicolons to the following sentences. Some sentences are correct. Write *X* next to incorrect sentences and correct them above the lines.

1. _____ Nancy took three advanced mathematics classes in high school she also participated in a math and science summer program at a local community college.

2. _____ The teacher smiled at the children as if she had a wonderful secret to share with them.

3. _____ The argument between my parents stretched through the night finally someone slammed a door and walked into the darkness.

4. _____ Fred entered the room with a giant bag of popcorn and a can of lemonade in his hands for he was settling down to watch his favorite television show.

5. _____ Because Monday is a holiday I will have a long weekend and a chance to catch up on my studying.

6. _____ Reducing my hours at work will give me more time with my family on the other hand it will cut my salary in half.

7. _____ After the snow had transformed the streets into crisp white hills the neighborhood children skidded down the slopes on homemade sleds.

8. _____ My dog looks at me with longing in his eyes and then focuses his gaze on his empty bowl whenever he wants a treat.

9. _____ The birthday party began with children's games and songs next the children were treated to chocolate birthday cake and ice cream.

10. _____ My years of work on the night shift have been long and hard yet they have taught me about teamwork and a positive attitude.

CHAPTER 18
Avoiding Sentence Fragments

A **sentence fragment** is a group of words that looks like a sentence, is punctuated like a sentence, but is not a sentence. Writing a sentence fragment is a major error in grammar because it reveals that the writer is not sure what a sentence is.

The following groups of words are all fragments:

Because customers are often in a hurry and have little time to look for bargains.
My job being very stressful and fast-paced.
For example, the introduction of salads into fast-food restaurants.

There are two easy steps that can help you check your writing for sentence fragments.

INFO BOX: Two Steps in Recognizing Sentence Fragments

Step 1: Check each group of words punctuated like a sentence, looking for a subject and a verb.

Step 2: If you find a subject and a verb, check that the group of words makes a complete statement.

RECOGNIZING FRAGMENTS: STEP 1

Step 1: Check for a subject and a verb. Some groups of words that look like sentences may actually have a subject but no verb, or they may have a verb but no subject, or they may have no subject *or* verb.

> The puppy in the pet store window. (*Puppy* could be the subject of a sentence, but there's no verb.)
> Doesn't matter to me one way or the other. (There is a verb, *does matter*, but there is no subject.)
> In the back of my mind. (There are two prepositional phrases, *in the back*, and *of my mind*, but there are no subject and verb.)

Remember that an *-ing* verb by itself cannot be the main verb in a sentence. Therefore, groups of words like the ones below may look like sentences, but they lack a verb and are really fragments:

> Your sister having all the skills required of a good salesperson.
> The two top tennis players struggling with exhaustion and the stress of a highly competitive tournament.
> Jack being the only one in the room with a piece of paper.

An infinitive (*to* plus a verb) cannot be a main verb in a sentence, either. The following groups of words are also fragments:

> The manager of the store to attend the meeting of regional managers next month in Philadelphia.
> The purpose to explain the fine points of the game to new players.

Groups of words beginning with words like *also, especially, except, for example, in addition,* and *such as* need subjects and verbs, too. Without subjects and verbs, these groups can be fragments, like the ones below:

> Also a good place to grow up.
> Especially the youngest member of the family.
> For example, a person without a high school diploma.

(**Exercise 1**) **Checking Groups of Words for Subjects and Verbs**

Some of the following groups of words have subjects and verbs; these are sentences. Some are missing subjects, verbs, or both; these are fragments. Put an *S* by each sentence and an *F* by each fragment.

1. _____ On the top of the restaurant was a giant plastic hot dog in a plastic bun.

2. _____ The kind man expecting no reward for changing my tire.

3. _____ In addition, the rent is high.

4. _____ In a confrontation with the owner of the property and the property manager.

5. _____ Selena has no interest in moving to Malaysia.

6. _____ Especially a husband with good looks and a sense of humor.

7. _____ Hasn't even visited his cousin in the rehabilitation center.

8. _____ My former girlfriend walking directly in front of me, a huge sneer on her face.

9. _____ For instance, two kittens in a white straw basket.

10. _____ For example, a hot temper can cause problems.

> **Exercise 2**   **More on Checking Groups of Words for Subjects and Verbs**

Some of the following groups of words have subjects and verbs; these are sentences. Some are missing subjects, verbs, or both; these are fragments. Put an *S* by each sentence, and put an *F* by each fragment.

1. _____ Would like to find a college with a good physical therapy program.

2. _____ At the window was a red bird.

3. _____ The reason for her success being a strong desire to escape poverty.

4. _____ Except the boxes with pots, pans, and dishes in them.

5. _____ Could have answered the question with more sympathy.

6. _____ The glasses in the cupboard should be handled with care.

7. _____ Two men in dark clothing and baseball caps leaving the building last night.

8. _____ My grandmother bringing me her famous chicken soup and my sister offering to do my laundry.

9. _____ Someone from the sheriff's office is asking questions.

10. _____ Will announce the winner of the lottery tomorrow night on television.

RECOGNIZING FRAGMENTS: STEP 2

Step 2: If a group of words has both a subject and a verb, check that it makes a complete statement. Many groups of words that have both a subject and a verb do not make sense by themselves. They are **dependent clauses.** How can you tell if a clause is dependent? After you have checked each group of words for a subject and verb, check to see if it begins with one of the subordinating conjunctions that start dependent clauses. (Here are some common subordinating words: *after, although, as, as if, because, before, even though, if, in order that, since, so that, though, unless, until, when, whenever, where, whereas, whether, while.*)

A clause that begins with a subordinating conjunction is a dependent clause. When you punctuate a dependent clause as if it were a sentence, you have a kind of fragment called a **dependent-clause fragment.**

After I woke up this morning.
Because he liked football better than soccer.
Unless it stops raining by lunchtime.

It is important to remember both steps in checking for fragments:

Step 1: Check for a subject and a verb.

Step 2: If you find a subject and a verb, check that the group of words makes a complete statement.

Exercise 3   **Checking for Dependent-Clause Fragments**

Some of the following groups of words are sentences. Some are dependent clauses punctuated like sentences: these are sentence fragments. Put an *S* by each sentence and an *F* by each fragment.

1. _____ When the days get shorter and the nights require a blanket on my bed.

2. _____ Since the room was not big enough for a sofa and a bed.

3. _____ If our state government could provide an after-school program for children in low-income families.

4. _____ Yet most parents would welcome more time at home with their children.

5. _____ While Maggie worked on a quilt for her nephew's crib.

6. _____ Most of the radio stations play the same music.

7. _____ Although our house was old and ready to fall into pieces.

8. _____ Because of the lack of interest in physical education programs and the cost of a new gym.

9. _____ Around the fountain was a border of flowers.

10. _____ As we drove through miles of trees blazing with red and yellow leaves.

Exercise 4   **More on Checking for Dependent-Clause Fragments**

Some of the following groups of words are sentences. Some are dependent clauses punctuated like sentences; these are sentence fragments. Put an *S* by each sentence and an *F* by each fragment.

1. _____ Whenever you need a place to stay in Orlando.

2. _____ Unless the restaurant can attract more customers in the next few weeks.

3. _____ Before Richard could think of an answer to the man's question.

4. _____ Until Lori makes up her mind about painting the house.

5. _____ Because you might have warned me about the prices at that store.

6. _____ Then the smoke detector began to beep.

7. _____ Near the gas station is a tire store.

8. _____ Since we worked together at the movie theater.

9. _____ With a smile on his face, he handed me the check.

10. _____ After a long talk with my family and my boss.

Exercise 5   **Using Two Steps to Recognize Sentence Fragments**

Some of the following are complete sentences; some are fragments. To recognize the fragments, check each group of words by using the two-step process:

> **Step 1:** Check for a subject and a verb.
> **Step 2:** If you find a subject and verb, check that the group of words makes a complete statement.

Then put an _S_ by each sentence and an _F_ by each fragment.

1. _____ Africa fascinating him as a part of his heritage.

2. _____ For example, a long walk in the mountains on a sunny day.

3. _____ Although Rachel often wondered about the reason for her boyfriend's bad behavior.

4. _____ Two famous country and western singers to appear at the state fair on Friday evening.

5. _____ The company's president promising all the salespeople a bonus within six months.

6. _____ While the baby sat happily in his crib and played with his toes.

7. _____ From the end of the dark tunnel came a cry for help.

8. _____ Because of the long delay in sending you the information about applying for financial aid.

9. _____ Then a line of ducks and their babies walked solemnly across the lawn.

10. _____ Behind David's clownish behavior were a deep insecurity and a longing for popularity.

Exercise 6   **More on Using Two Steps to Recognize Sentence Fragments**

Some of the following are complete sentences; some are fragments. To recognize the fragments, check each group of words by using the two-step process:

> **Step 1:** Check for a subject and a verb.
> **Step 2:** If you find a subject and verb, check that the group of words makes a complete statement.

Then put an _S_ by each sentence and an _F_ by each fragment.

1. _____ The reason being a manufacturing defect in the car's electrical system.

2. _____ As I studied the priceless painting at the museum.

3. _____ Your little girl is being careful about selecting her favorite toy.

4. _____ Whenever he offers me a cup of his disgusting homemade tea.

5. _____ Without a thought for the many people waiting for him to appear on stage.

6. _____ Around his waist was an expensive leather belt with a gold buckle.

7. _____ Without calling first, Terry appeared at my door.

8. _____ Several local organizations to sponsor a community food drive before Thanksgiving.

9. _____ Popularity was the only desire of the troubled teen.

10. _____ If I can get my boss to let me out of work early on Saturday.

CORRECTING FRAGMENTS

You can correct fragments easily if you follow the two steps for identifying them.

Step 1: Check for a subject and a verb. If a group of words is a fragment because it lacks a subject or a verb, or both, *add what is missing.*

> **fragment:** My father being a very strong person. (This fragment lacks a main verb.)
> **corrected:** My father *is* a very strong person. (The verb *is* replaces *being*, which is not a main verb.)
>
> **fragment:** Doesn't care about the party. (This fragment lacks a subject.)
> **corrected:** *Alicia* doesn't care about the party. (A subject, *Alicia*, is added.)
>
> **fragment:** Especially on dark winter days. (This fragment has neither a subject nor a verb.)
> **corrected:** *I love* a bonfire, especially on dark winter days. (A subject, *I*, and a verb, *love*, are added.)

Step 2: If you find a subject and a verb, check that the group of words makes a complete statement. To correct the fragment, you can turn a dependent clause into an independent one by removing the subordinating conjunction, *or* you can add an independent clause to the dependent one to create a sentence.

> **fragment:** When the rain beat against the windows. (The statement does not make sense by itself. The subordinating conjunction *when* leads the reader to ask, "What happened when the rain beat against the windows?" The subordinating conjunction makes this a dependent clause, not a sentence.)
> **corrected:** The rain beat against the windows. (Removing the subordinating conjunction makes this an independent clause, a sentence.)

corrected: When the rain beat against the windows, *I reconsidered my plans for the picnic.* (Adding an independent clause turns this into a sentence.)

Note: Sometimes you can correct a fragment by linking it to the sentence before it or after it.

fragment (underlined): I have always enjoyed outdoor concerts. <u>Like the ones at Pioneer Park.</u>
corrected: I have always enjoyed outdoor concerts *like the ones at Pioneer Park.*

fragment (underlined): <u>Even if she apologizes for that nasty remark.</u> I will never trust her again.
corrected: *Even if she apologizes for that nasty remark,* I will never trust her again.

You have several choices for correcting fragments: you can add words, phrases, or clauses; you can take words out or combine independent and dependent clauses. You can transform fragments into simple sentences or create compound or complex sentences. To punctuate your new sentences, remember the rules for combining sentences.

Exercise 7 **Correcting Fragments**

Correct each sentence fragment in the most appropriate way.

1. If I have a few extra dollars in my pocket, I buy my son a treat. Such as his favorite ice cream or candy.

corrected: _____

_____

2. When you start a regular exercise routine. You will begin to feel more fit and energetic.

corrected: _____

_____

3. Making everyone at the party feel uncomfortable. Jennifer started a nasty argument with her brother-in-law.

corrected: _____

_____

4. The comedian delivered ninety minutes of jokes and delighted everyone. Especially his most devoted fans.

corrected: _____

_____

5. The reason for Jessica's sudden interest in vitamins and herbs being her struggle with pneumonia.

   corrected: _____

   _____

6. Then broke into the car and stole Damon's wallet and cell phone.

   corrected: _____

   _____

7. Because the library closes at 11:00 p.m. We went to Nora's house to study all night.

   corrected: _____

   _____

8. A car made a sudden turn in front of me. As I approached the intersection.

   corrected: _____

   _____

9. Lisa spent four years in the military. To earn enough money for a college education.

   corrected: _____

   _____

10. I can drive us to Detroit. Unless you want to take us in your van.

   corrected: _____

   _____

COLLABORATE ▶   **Exercise 8** **Correcting Fragments Two Ways**

Working with a partner or group, correct each fragment in two ways. The first one is done for you.

1. Whenever I am waiting for an important phone call.

   corrected: *I am waiting for an important phone call.*

   _____

   corrected: *Whenever I am waiting for an important phone call, I am*

   extremely impatient and nervous.

2. Yolanda had never tasted sushi. Until her sister took her to a Japanese restaurant.

corrected: _____

_____

corrected: _____

_____

3. Unless Sam gets eight hours sleep at night. He falls asleep at his desk in the late afternoon.

corrected: _____

_____

corrected: _____

_____

4. Lewis knowing more about cooking than his mother does.

corrected: _____

corrected: _____

_____

5. After he smiled at his mother in the back row of the school auditorium. The child recited his poem.

corrected: _____

_____

corrected: _____

_____

6. Although you would like me to study accounting in college.

corrected: _____

_____

corrected: _____

7. In front of the hotel, where the fans gathered.

corrected: _____

_____

corrected: _____

_____

8. I will not go to my sister's wedding with you. If you wear that ugly jacket.

corrected: _____

_____

corrected: _____

_____

9. Which is the best car on the road today.

corrected: _____

_____

corrected: _____

_____

10. Except a man like my father.

corrected: _____

_____

corrected: _____

CONNECT ▶ Exercise 9 **Editing a Paragraph for Sentence Fragments**

Correct the sentence fragments in the following paragraph. There are four fragments.

Summer is a perfect time for most people. When they can wear fewer clothes, enjoy longer days, and soak up more sunshine. Even an ordinary trip to work or to the store can be a pleasure. If people do not have to pile on heavy coats, gloves, scarves, and hats just to get out the door. In addition, a long day at college or work can seem shorter in the summer since the sun doesn't set until 8:00 or 9:00 p.m. The long days leave time on the weekdays for many outdoor activities. Including evening softball games, long walks, and bike rides. Finally, summer weekends mean that winter's indoor activities can move outside. For exam-

ple, people can cook, eat, read, play cards, listen to music, and even sleep out-

doors under the sun. Summer days an invitation to relax and enjoy simple

pleasures.

Exercise 10   **Editing a Paragraph for Sentence Fragments**   ◀ CONNECT

Correct the sentence fragments in the following paragraph. There are six
fragments.

I do not want to be a multimillionaire. Although I would like to have enough

money to pay all my bills regularly. Worrying about credit card payments and my

car loan. These concerns can keep me up at night. As the bills pile up on my

kitchen table. I wonder how to economize. Maybe I could sell my car and take

public transportation to work and school. Or find a find a better-paying job. My

needs do not require millions of dollars. In fact, I would never want to be rich.

Rich people have their own problems. Such as making the right investments and

finding trustworthy advisors. My financial goal is more limited. Having enough

money to sleep soundly at night.

Chapter Test: Avoiding Sentence Fragments

Some of the following are complete sentences; some are sentence fragments.
Put an *S* by each sentence and an *F* by each fragment.

1. _____   Under the table, with a shoe in his mouth, a brown dog
   looking at me with guilt in his eyes.

2. _____   Next to the cereal on the top shelf of the cabinet is a box of
   chocolate chip cookies.

3. _____   In order that the students will have enough seats in the
   back of the crowded auditorium.

4. _____   When the neighbors show a lack of consideration for the
   people around them by blasting their music all night.

5. _____   Then two squealing children ran into their father's open
   arms.

6. _____   The identity of the murderer being a mystery to all the detectives assigned to the case.

7. _____   Except for Julie, nobody wanted to drive fifty miles to hear
   last year's teen idol perform.

8. _____ Even though the roof has a small leak in it and the kitchen needs a new floor.

9. _____ Until I was sixteen and visited my aunt in Montana, I had never seen snow.

10. _____ A representative from the local animal shelter to talk about training therapy dogs.

CHAPTER 19
Using Parallelism in Sentences

Parallelism means balance in a sentence. To create sentences with parallelism, remember this rule:

Similar points should get a similar structure.

Often, you will include two or three (or more) related ideas, examples, or details in one sentence. If you express these ideas in a parallel structure, they will be clearer, smoother, and more convincing.

Here are some pairs of sentences with and without parallelism:

not parallel: Of all the sports I've played, I prefer tennis, handball, and playing golf.

parallel: Of all the sports I've played, I prefer *tennis, handball,* and *golf.* (Three words are parallel.)

not parallel: If you're looking for the car keys, you should look under the table, the kitchen counter, and behind the refrigerator.

parallel: If you're looking for the car keys, you should look *under the table, on the kitchen counter,* and *behind the refrigerator.* (Three prepositional phrases are parallel.)

not parallel: He is a good choice for manager because he works hard, he keeps calm, and well-liked.

parallel: He is a good choice for manager because *he works hard, he keeps calm,* and *he is well-liked.* (Three clauses are parallel.)

From these examples, you can see that parallelism involves matching the structures of parts of your sentence. There are two steps that can help you check your writing for parallelism.

INFO BOX: **Two Steps in Checking a Sentence for Parallel Structure**

Step 1: Look for the list in the sentence.

Step 2: Put the parts of the list into a similar structure. (You may have to change or add something to get a parallel structure.)

ACHIEVING PARALLELISM

Let's correct the parallelism of the following sentence:

> **sample sentence:** The committee for neighborhood safety met to set up a schedule for patrols, coordinating teams of volunteers, and also for the purpose of creating new rules.

To correct this sentence, we'll follow the steps.

> **Step 1:** Look for the list. The committee met to do three things. Here's the list:
> 1. to set up a schedule for patrols
> 2. coordinating teams of volunteers
> 3. for the purpose of creating new rules

> **Step 2:** Put the parts of the list into a similar structure:
> 1. *to set up* a schedule for patrols
> 2. *to coordinate* teams of volunteers
> 3. *to create* new rules

Now revise to get a parallel sentence.

> **parallel:** The committee for neighborhood safety met *to set up* a schedule for patrols, *to coordinate* teams of volunteers, and *to create* new rules.

If you follow Steps 1 and 2, you can also write the sentence like this:

> **parallel:** The committee for neighborhood safety met to *set up* a schedule for patrols, *coordinate* teams of volunteers, and *create* new rules.

But you cannot write a sentence like this:

> **not parallel:** The committee for neighborhood safety met *to set up* a schedule for patrols, *coordinate* teams, and *to create* new rules.

Think of the list again. You can have

> The committee met
> 1. to set up
> 2. to coordinate   } parallel
> 3. to create

Or you can have

> The committee met to
> 1. set up
> 2. coordinate   } parallel
> 3. create

But your list cannot be

> The committee met to
> 1. set up
> 2. coordinate   } not parallel
> 3. to create

In other words, use the *to* once (if it fits every part of the list), or use it with every part of the list.

Caution: Sometimes making ideas parallel means adding something to a sentence because all the parts of the list cannot match exactly.

> **sample sentence:** In his pocket the little boy had a ruler, rubber band, baseball card, and apple.

> **Step 1:** Look for the list. In his pocket the little boy had a
> 1. ruler
> 2. rubber band
> 3. baseball card
> 4. apple

As the sentence is written, the *a* goes with *a ruler, a rubber band, a baseball card*, and *a apple*. But *a* isn't the right word to put in front of *apple*. Words beginning with vowels (*a, e, i, o, u,*) need *an* in front of them: *an apple*. So to make the sentence parallel, you have to change something in the sentence.

> **Step 2:** Put the parts of the list into a parallel structure.

> **parallel:** In his pocket the little boy had *a ruler, a rubber band, a baseball card*, and *an apple*.

Here's another example:

> **sample sentence:** She was amused and interested in the silly plot of the movie.

> **Step 1:** Look for the list. She was
> 1. amused
> 2. interested in
> the silly plot of the movie.

Check the sense of that sentence by looking at each part of the list and how it works in the sentence: "She was *interested in* the silly plot of the movie." That part of the list seems clear. But "She was *amused* the silly plot of the movie"? Or "She was *amused in* the silly plot of the movie"? Neither sentence is right. People are not *amused in*.

> **Step 2:** The sentence needs a word added to make the structure parallel.

> **parallel:** She was *amused by* and *interested in* the silly plot of the movie.

When you follow the two steps to check for parallelism, you can write clear sentences and improve your style.

(Exercise 1) **Revising Sentences for Parallelism**

Some of the following sentences need to be revised so that they have parallel structures. Revise the ones that need parallelism.

1. My day began at 6:00 a.m.; midnight is when it ended.

revised: _____

_____

2. Annette is smart, strong, and has a great deal of ambition.

revised: _____

_____

3. Whenever I visit my sister, I get so angry that I have to keep my mouth shut, nodding my head at her stupid remarks, and find an excuse to leave the room.

revised: _____

_____

_____

4. I can make the cake with or without pineapple.

revised: _____

_____

5. After you finish dinner, be sure to clean the plates, stack them in the sink, wipe off the table, and to put the leftovers in the refrigerator.

revised: _____

_____

_____

6. On my first day at work, my boss spent an hour explaining my responsibilities, introducing me to my coworkers, and my workspace was shown to me also.

revised: _____

_____

_____

7. The apartment's layout, size, and where it was made it attractive to the young couple.

revised: _____

_____

8. In my family, dinner without dessert is like when you have a birthday but don't get presents.

revised: _____

_____

9. The movie was the longest I have ever seen, also the most boring and the silliest of all.

revised: _____

_____

10. My doctor says it is better to establish long-term, healthy eating habits than relying on quick weight-loss diets.

revised: _____

_____

Exercise 2   **Writing Sentences With Parallelism**   ◄ COLLABORATE 👥

Complete this exercise with a partner or a group. First, brainstorm a draft list; then revise the list for parallelism. Finally, complete the sentence in parallel structure. You may want to assign one step (brainstorming a draft list, revising it, etc.) to each group member, then switch steps on the next sentence. The first one is done for you, as an example.

1. Three habits I'd like to break are

draft list	revised list
a. worry too much	a. worrying too much
b. talking on the phone for hours	b. talking on the phone for hours
c. lose my temper	c. losing my temper

sentence: Three habits I'd like to break are worrying too much, talking on the phone for hours, and losing my temper.

2. Three ways to stay healthy are

draft list	revised list
a. _____	a. _____
b. _____	b. _____
c. _____	c. _____

sentence: _____

_____

3. Two reasons why people choose not to marry are

draft list	revised list
a. _____	a. _____
b. _____	b. _____

sentence: _____

_____

4. Three gifts that money cannot buy are

draft list   revised list

a. _____   a. _____

b. _____   b. _____

c. _____   c. _____

sentence: _____

_____

5. Saving money is important because it (add three reasons)

draft list   revised list

a. _____   a. _____

b. _____   b. _____

c. _____   c. _____

sentence: _____

_____

6. Starting a new job can be stressful because (add three reasons)

draft list   revised list

a. _____   a. _____

b. _____   b. _____

c. _____   c. _____

sentence: _____

_____

7. When I finish college, I want to (add two goals)

draft list   revised list

a. _____   a. _____

b. _____   b. _____

sentence: _____

_____

8. People seem to get angry when (add two times or occasions)

draft list   revised list

a. _____   a. _____

b. _____   b. _____

sentence: _____

_____

9. Three characteristics of a good friend are

draft list   revised list

a. _____   a. _____

b. _____   b. _____

c. _____   c. _____

sentence: _____

_____

10. Two household chores most people dislike are

draft list   revised list

a. _____   a. _____

b. _____   b. _____

sentence: _____

_____

Exercise 3   **Combining Sentences and Creating a Parallel Structure**

Combine each cluster of sentences into one clear, smooth sentence that includes some parallel structure. The first one is done for you.

1. Before you buy a used car, you should research what similar models are selling for.
It would be a good idea to have a mechanic examine the car.
Also, how much mileage it has racked up is a consideration.

combination: Before you buy a used car, you should compare prices of

similar models, get a mechanic to examine the car, and think carefully

about the mileage.

2. Inspect the house for water damage.
You can also investigate any chipped woodwork.
Check for cracked windows.

combination: _____

_____

3. When you visit, we'll go to my favorite restaurant.
Swimming in the ocean is something else we'll do.
In addition, the two of us can shop at the discount mall that is nearby.

combination: _____

_____

4. If I feel depressed, I talk to Algeron, who is a positive person.
Algeron has kindness.
Thoughtfulness is another one of his good qualities.

combination: _____

_____

5. The dog was trained.
It had a sleek black coat.
Its eyes were deep and brown.
Its expression was alert.
It was a search-and-rescue dog.

combination: _____

_____

6. High schools educate teenagers.
They offer adult education classes.
Student theater productions are shown to the community.
High schools involve local businesses in sports.
They serve many parts of the community by doing all these things.

combination: _____

_____

_____

7. My brother started as a grocery bagger at Miro Foods.
Then he worked his way up to produce manager.
Eventually my brother became the assistant manager.

combination: _____

_____

_____

8. At the entrance to the store, hundreds of people waited for the
doors to open.
They were hoping to find bargains at the special sale.
Their other goal was to be one of the first fifty shoppers inside and
win a DVD player.

combination: _____

_____

_____

9. Mr. McManus was the toughest teacher I ever had.
He was more interesting than any other teacher I had.
His generosity was the best, too.

combination: _____

_____

10. The training for the position includes handling online sales.
Trainees also have to learn how to deal with complaints.
Another part of the training is taking orders quickly.

combination: _____

_____

⊂◼◻⊃ CONNECT ▶   (Exercise 4) **Editing a Paragraph for Errors in Parallelism**

Correct any errors in parallelism in the following paragraph. There are four
errors.

Family gatherings at my parents' house always follow the same routine. As

soon as we arrive at the house, my husband joins the men in front of the televi-

sion, my children racing outdoors, and I go to the kitchen. In the kitchen, my mother and sister struggle to fry chicken, to mash potatoes, and bake cornbread while I set the table. Meanwhile, my children, nieces, and nephews run through my parents' big yard, playing with my father's old dog, Sally. When the women have placed huge platters of food on the table, everyone sits down to dinner. As always, we eat until we are stuffed, laugh until we are breathless, and make ourselves speechless by arguing. At the end of dinner, the men in the family clear the table and do the dishes. The females in the family, including the dog, Sally, take a nap in the living room. The children play with old toys that once belonged to their parents. This family ritual may be repetitive and boring, but it is also a comfort and relaxing.

Exercise 5 **Editing a Paragraph for Errors in Parallelism**   ◄ CONNECT ⚬⚬⚬

Correct any errors in parallelism in the following paragraph. There are five errors.

When I was a child, physical education class used to fill me with dread. First, I was smaller and less coordinated than most children my age. If the teacher called on two students to serve as captains and to pick the rest of the class as team members, I was always the last to be chosen. The captain of each team would look around me, beside me, or look past me to find anybody except me. I feared the gym teacher, who was always loud, with a cheerful attitude, aggressive, and energetic. I used to suffer through each class, terrified that the teacher would make some comment about my awkwardness or to criticize my team spirit. Now that I am an adult, I find basketball, baseball games, football, and soccer exciting to watch. On weekends, I play basketball with some friends. However, whenever I think of my old gym classes, I feel twinges of anxiety, being afraid, and insecurity return.

Chapter Test: Using Parallelism in Sentences

Some of the following sentences have errors in parallelism; some are correct. Put an *X* by the sentences with errors in parallelism.

1. _____ In high school, I spent most of my time working at my job, socializing with my friends, trying to fall in love, and at the movies.

2. _____ If you don't have ambition, a sense of confidence, energy, and courage, you will never reach your goals or satisfy your longings.

3. _____ Umberto looked in his wallet, on his desk, between the sofa cushions, and under the table, but he could not find the tickets.

4. _____ An understanding friend can offer sympathy, support, share ideas, and propose solutions when you have a problem.

5. _____ Getting my grandfather a dog was a great idea because the dog keeps him company, gives him a reason to exercise, and makes him laugh.

6. _____ If my class gets out early and you are still in class, I will sit outside your classroom, to study for my math test, and wait for you.

7. _____ When I finally cleaned the area under my bed, I found an old tee shirt, a hundred dust bunnies, a moldy doughnut, hairbrush, and a pencil.

8. _____ The scientist was fascinated by and jealous of his rival's discovery.

9. _____ Imelda is a loyal daughter, a friend who was generous, a loving wife, and a dynamic attorney.

10. _____ The agenda for the council meeting includes selection of a staff attorney, assessment of the safety program, revision of the park improvement program, and discuss the landscaping project.

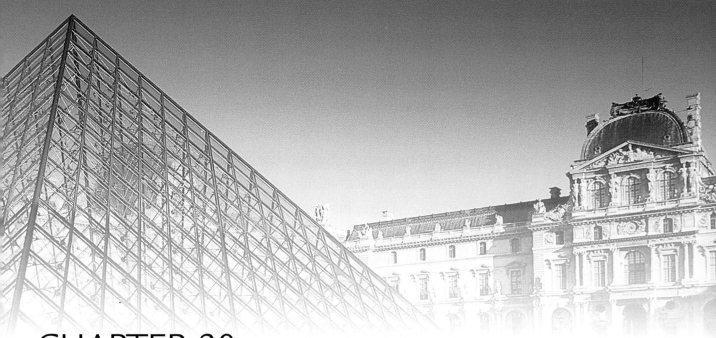

CHAPTER 20
Using Adjectives and Adverbs

WHAT ARE ADJECTIVES?

Adjectives describe nouns (persons, places, or things) or pronouns (words that substitute for nouns).

adjectives:
She stood in a *dark* corner. (*Dark* describes the noun *corner.*)
I need a *little* help. (*Little* describes the noun *help.*)
She looked *happy.* (*Happy* describes the pronoun *she.*)

An adjective usually comes before the word it describes.

He gave me a *beautiful* ring. (*Beautiful* describes *ring.*)
A *small* horse pulled the cart. (*Small* describes *horse.*)

Sometimes it comes after a being verb, a verb that tells what something is. Being verbs are words like *is, are, was, am,* and *has been.* Words like *feels, looks, seems, smells, sounds,* and *tastes* are part of the group called being verbs.

He seems *unhappy.* (*Unhappy* describes *he* and follows the being verb *seems.*)
Alan was *confident.* (*Confident* describes *Alan* and follows the being verb *was.*)

Exercise 1 **Recognizing Adjectives**

Circle the adjective in each of the following sentences.

1. Wilder Woods is a strange place.

2. My brothers are great athletes.

3. Micah wanted a reliable car.

4. The custard at the restaurant tastes delicious.

5. An ugly bug crawled across the sheet.

6. A shiny bracelet circled her wrist.

7. The mayor seems unhappy in his position.

8. The large truck skidded on the highway.

9. Tina and Michelle were good friends in college.

10. Kevin hurried through the dark streets.

ADJECTIVES: COMPARATIVE AND SUPERLATIVE FORMS

The **comparative** form of an adjective compares two persons or things. The **superlative** form compares three or more persons or things.

comparative: Your car is *cleaner* than mine.
superlative: Your car is the *cleanest* one in the parking lot.

comparative: Hamburger is *cheaper* than steak.
superlative: Hamburger is the *cheapest* meat on the menu.

comparative: Lisa is *friendlier* than her sister.
superlative: Lisa is the *friendliest* of the three sisters.

For most adjectives of one syllable, add -*er* to form the comparative and add -*est* to form the superlative:

The weather is *colder* than it was yesterday, but Friday was the *coldest* day of the year.
Orange juice is *sweeter* than grapefruit juice, but the *sweetest* juice is grape juice.

For longer adjectives, use *more* to form the comparative and *most* to form the superlative:

I thought algebra was *more difficult* than composition; however, physics was the *most difficult* course I ever took.
My brother is *more outgoing* than my sister, but my father is the *most outgoing* member of the family.

The three forms of adjectives usually look like this:

Adjective	Comparative	Superlative
	(two)	(three or more)
sweet	sweeter	sweetest

fast	faster	fastest
short	shorter	shortest
quick	quicker	quickest
old	older	oldest

They may look like this instead:

Adjective	**Comparative**	**Superlative**
	(two)	(three or more)
confused	more confused	most confused
specific	more specific	most specific
dangerous	more dangerous	most dangerous
confident	more confident	most confident
beautiful	more beautiful	most beautiful

However, there are some irregular forms of adjectives:

Adjective	**Comparative**	**Superlative**
	(two)	(three or more)
good	better	best
bad	worse	worst
little	less	least
many, much	more	most

Exercise 2   **Selecting the Correct Adjective Form**

Write the correct form of the adjective in each of the following sentences:

1. I like both jackets, but I think the black one is a _____ (good) buy than the blue one.

2. Spiderman, The Lord of the Rings, and I, Robot were all popular movies, but I think I, Robot was the _____(good) of the three films.

3. Finding a few true friends is _____ (tough) than collecting many superficial friends, but maintaining a long friendship is the _____ (challenging) part of all friendships.

4. Of the two cousins, Tony is _____ (old).

5. I attended three weddings last month, and my cousin's wedding was the_____ (bad) of the three.

6. Doing all my school work at the last minute was _____ (good) enough to get me through high school; however, a few months in college taught me that working consistently every day is _____ (good) than procrastinating.

7. Which one of these four cards is the_____ (appropriate) for an elderly person?

8. The menu at the banquet offered a choice of fish or steak; I chose the fish because it had _____ (little) fat than the steak.

9. Last year I spent_____(many) hours taking care of my nephew, but my mother spent _____ (many) time than I did.

10. A constant cough is _____ (bad) than constant sniffles.

 **COLLABORATE** ▶   [Exercise 3] **Writing Sentences with Adjectives**

Working with a partner or group, write a sentence that correctly uses each of the following adjectives. Be prepared to share your answers with another group or with the class.

1. oldest _____

2. more useful _____

3. richest _____

4. least _____

_____

5. most foolish _____

_____

6. stronger _____

7. longer _____

8. more alert _____

9. worse _____

10. much _____

WHAT ARE ADVERBS?

Adverbs describe verbs, adjectives, or other adverbs.

adverbs:
As she spoke, Steve listened *thoughtfully.* (*Thoughtfully* describes the verb *listened.*)
I said I was *really* sorry for my error. (*Really* describes the adjective *sorry.*)
The cook worked *very* quickly. (*Very* describes the adverb *quickly.*)

Adverbs answer questions like How? How much? How often? When? Why? and Where?

[Exercise 4] **Recognizing Adverbs**

Circle the adverbs in the following sentences.

1. Sherry smiled confidently as she approached the stage.

2. We can expect a really busy day at the store tomorrow.

3. Lennie's carefully planned surprise went badly.

4. My neighbor's cat often comes to my window and stares at my indoor cat.

5. The price of the house was ridiculously low.

6. The company can hardly give raises in bad economic times.

7. My boyfriend handed me a neatly folded letter.

8. Yesterday, Danielle had a very frightening encounter with a snake.

9. When Dr. Gonzalez works late at the office, he sometimes falls asleep at his desk.

10. At work, the computers are usually reliable, but occasionally they shut down without any warning.

Exercise 5   **Writing Sentences with Adverbs**   ◀ COLLABORATE 👥

Working with a partner or group, write a sentence that correctly uses each of the following adverbs. Be prepared to share your answers with another group or with the class.

1. rarely   _____

2. completely   _____

3. never   _____

4. sadly   _____

5. slowly   _____

6. sweetly   _____

7. viciously   _____

8. truly   _____

9. always   _____

10. really   _____

HINTS ABOUT ADJECTIVES AND ADVERBS

Do not use an adjective when you need an adverb. Some writers make the mistake of using an adjective when they need an adverb.

not this: Talk to me ~~honest~~.
but this: Talk to me *honestly*.

not this: You can say it ~~simple~~.
but this: You can say it *simply*.

not this: He was breathing ~~deep~~.
but this: He was breathing *deeply*.

Exercise 6   **Changing Adjectives to Adverbs**

In each pair of sentences, change the underlined adjective in the first sentence to an adverb in the second sentence. The first one is done for you.

1. a. She is a <u>graceful</u> dancer.

   b. She dances *gracefully*_____.

2. a. Her answer was <u>direct</u>.

   b. She answered _____.

3. a. The manager's decision seemed <u>unfair</u>.

    b. The manager decided _____

4. a. Jonelle made a <u>bold</u> move toward the gunman.

    b. Jonelle moved _____ toward the gunman.

5. a. General Armstrong had a <u>poor</u> plan for defending the fort.

    b. General Armstrong's defense of the fort was _____ planned.

6. a. Just give a <u>simple</u> explanation of the concept.

    b. Explain the concept _____.

7. a. When the brothers argue, they become <u>loud</u>.

    b. The brothers argue _____.

8. a. Once the tennis star changed coaches, her playing was <u>superb</u>.

    b. Once the tennis star changed coached, she played _____.

9. a. The woman was <u>impatient</u> as she waited in line for her flu shot.

    b. The woman in line for her flu shot waited _____.

10. a. Mr. Friedman was a <u>frequent</u> volunteer at the homeless shelter.

    b. Mr. Friedman _____ volunteered at the homeless shelter.

Don't Confuse *Good* and *Well* or *Bad* and *Badly*

Remember that *good* is an adjective; it describes nouns. *Well* is an adverb; it describes verbs. (The only time *well* can be used as an adjective is when it means "healthy": "I feel well today.")

> **not this:** You ran that race ~~good~~.
> **but this:** You ran that race *well*.

> **not this:** I cook eggs ~~good~~.
> **but this:** I cook eggs *well*.

> **not this:** How ~~good~~ do you understand grammar?
> **but this:** How *well* do you understand grammar?

Bad is an adjective; it describes nouns. It also follows being verbs like *is, are, was, am, has been*. Words like *feels, looks, seems, smells, sounds*, and *tastes* are part of the group called being verbs. *Badly* is an adverb; it describes action verbs.

> **not this:** He feels ~~badly~~ about his mistake.
> **but this:** He feels *bad* about his mistake. (*Feels* is a being verb; it is described by the adjective *bad*.)

> **not this:** That soup smells ~~badly~~.
> **but this:** That soup smells *bad*. (*Smells* is a being verb; it is described by the adjective *bad*.)

> **not this:** He dances ~~bad~~.
> **but this:** He dances *badly*.

Exercise 7   Using *Good* and *Well* or *Bad* and *Badly*

Write the appropriate word in the following sentences.

1. I have never been a _____ (good, well) cook, but my cousin cooks _____ (good, well).

2. Because Leonard wasn't feeling _____ (good, well), he missed another_____ party.

3. I couldn't see the exit because the room was _____(bad, badly) lit.

4. Even though Dave had a sore arm, he did _____(good, well) in the last moments of the game.

5. That new jacket looks _____ (bad, badly) on you.

6. Brianna shouldn't feel_____ (bad, badly) about losing a promotion.

7. Mrs. Woo wasn't _____ (bad, badly) hurt in the car accident.

8. When I play the CD in my car, the music sounds _____(bad, badly), but when I play it at home, the music sounds _____ (good, well).

9. After a week in the hospital, Jose might not feel _____(good, well) enough to drive a car.

10. Henry lent money to his best friend Karram, who needed it_____ (bad, badly).

Not *More* + *-er* or *Most* + *-est*

Be careful. Never write both an *-er* ending and *more* or an *-est* ending and *most*.

not this: I want to work with someone ~~more smarter~~.
but this: I want to work with someone *smarter*.

not this: Alan is the ~~most richest~~ man in town.
but this: Alan is the *richest* man in town.

Use *Than*, not *Then*, in Comparisons

When you compare things, use *than*. *Then* means "at a later time."

not this: You are taller ~~then~~ I am.
but this: You are taller *than* I am.

not this: I'd like a car that is faster ~~then~~ my old one.
but this: I'd like a car that is faster *than* my old one.

When Do I Need a Comma Between Adjectives?

Sometimes you use more than one adjective to describe a noun.

I visited a cold, dark cave.
The cat had pale blue eyes.

If you look at the preceding examples, one uses a comma between the adjectives *cold* and *dark*, but the other does not have a comma between the adjectives *pale* and *blue*. Both sentences are correctly punctuated. To decide whether you need a comma, try one of these tests:

Test 1: Try to put *and* between the adjectives. If the sentence still makes sense, put a comma between the adjectives.

> **check for comma:** I visited a cold, dark cave. (Do you need the comma? Add *and* between the adjectives.)
> **add *and*:** I visited a cold *and* dark cave. (Does the sentence still make sense? Yes. You need the comma.)
> **correct sentence:** I visited a cold, dark cave.

> **check for comma:** The cat had pale blue eyes. (Do you need a comma? Add *and* between the adjectives.)
> **add *and*:** The cat had pale *and* blue eyes. (Does the sentence still make sense? No. You do not need a comma.)
> **correct sentence:** The cat had pale blue eyes.

Test 2: Try to reverse the order of the adjectives. If the sentence still makes sense, put a comma between the adjectives.

> **check for comma:** I visited a cold, dark cave. (Do you need the comma? Reverse the order of the adjectives.)
> **reverse order:** I visited a dark, cold cave. (Does the sentence still make sense? Yes. You need the comma.)
> **correct sentence:** I visited a cold, dark cave.

> **check for comma:** The cat had pale blue eyes. (Do you need a comma? Reverse the order of the adjectives.)
> **reverse order:** The cat had blue pale eyes. (Does the sentence still make sense? No. You don't need a comma.)
> **correct sentence:** The cat had pale blue eyes.

You can use test 1 or test 2 to determine whether you need a comma between adjectives.

CONNECT ▶ **Exercise 8** **Editing for Errors in Adjectives and Adverbs**

Edit the following paragraph, correcting all the errors in the use of adjectives and adverbs. Write your corrections above the errors. There are six errors.

I used to envy my cousin Annette, but I have grown out of that silly emotion. As a child, I used to look at Annette's shiny, black curls and compare them to my dull straight hair. In addition, Annette had long legs and a trim body. She was taller then I was and slimmer, too. My feelings of inferiority did not change as Annette and I grew oldest. I wanted so bad to be her. Then, last year, a funny incident changed my mind. Annette and I were both bridesmaids in our aunt's wedding. As we dressed for the ceremony, Annette said, "You know, I always wanted to look like you." I laughed bitterly because I believed she was just trying to be kindly. "No, I mean it," she insisted. "I always felt like a string bean next you," she added, "a string bean with frizzy hair." It was time for me to confess my

own envy of Annette. After I told her that I had always wanted to be her, we both

laughed and completed our makeup. Ready for the ceremony, we smiled at each

other in the mirror and said, "Don't we look well?"

Exercise 9   **Editing for Errors in Adjectives and Adverbs**   ◀ CONNECT ○○○

Edit the following paragraph, correcting all the errors in the use of adjectives
and adverbs. Write your corrections above the errors. There are seven errors.

Taking my driving test was the more frightening experience in my life. As

soon as I saw the examiner, I knew this process would not be easily. The man

never smiled or said hello; he just hung on to his clipboard and directed me to the

driver's seat. As I started the car, he gave me his first command. One after another,

the directions continued. After I performed each task, the examiner wrote some-

thing on his clipboard. After ten minutes of this treatment, I was real scared. I

was desperately to get a look at his writing, but I couldn't see it. I couldn't under-

stand why this man couldn't be more kinder. Finally, he stopped giving orders,

and we returned to the license bureau's parking lot. As I sat in the car, facing

front, my eyes filled with panic. "You don't have to worry," the examiner said. "You

did good. You'll get your license." Suddenly I felt that this flinty-eyed man was

most compassionate than anyone else in the world. I wanted to hug him, but his

clipboard was in the way.

Chapter Test: Using Adjectives and Adverbs

Some of the following sentences have errors in the use of adjectives and adverbs. Some are correct. Put an *X* by each sentence with an error.

1. _____ Karen and Nelson were both struggling in their biology
class, but Nelson was the more confused.

2. _____ All three of the Martinez brothers were known for their violent behavior; Andy Martinez was the worse.

3. _____ I like all kinds of chocolate, but white chocolate is the more
appealing to me.

4. _____ We looked at two apartments; unfortunately, the one we
could afford is the least attractive.

5. _____ Both Lake College and City College of Technology are good schools; you must choose the one that is better for you.

6. _____ Eric had a dirty, green sweater with holes at the elbows.

7. _____ I bought a watch that is less expensive than the one I lost last month.

8. _____ If we lie and tell Michael that the fish tastes good, he won't feel badly about his cooking.

9. _____ No one understood the man because he was talking too quick.

10. _____ Mrs. Masih has three daughters; Adrienne is the oldest.

CHAPTER 21
Correcting Problems with Modifiers

Modifiers are words, phrases, or clauses that describe (modify) something in a sentence. All the italicized words, phrases, and clauses below are modifiers.

the *blue* van (word)
the van *in the garage* (phrase)
the van *that she bought* (clause)

foreign tourists (word)
tourists *coming to Florida* (phrase)
tourists *who visit the state* (clause)

Sometimes modifiers limit another word. They make another word (or words) more specific.

the girl *in the corner* (tells exactly which girl)
fifty acres (tells exactly how many acres)
the movie *that I liked best* (tells which movie)
He *never* calls. (tells how often)

Exercise 1 **Recognizing Modifiers**

In each sentence following, underline the modifiers (words, phrases, or clauses) that describe the italicized word or phrase.

    1. *The house* with the red roof belongs to Captain O'Hara.

    2. Tiffany couldn't stop staring at *the man* holding a baby.

3. I felt sorry for *the student* locked out of his car.

4. *The people* sitting in the back row couldn't hear the speaker.

5. My aunt sent me and Jennifer *a* wedding *present.*

6. Andrew borrowed *an* expensive *camera* and never returned it.

7. Carrying his leash in his mouth, *my dog* insisted on a walk.

8. *The* antique *painting* framed in gold contained a secret.

9. Surrounded by bodyguards, *the actor* never talked to his fans.

10. *A* tiny green *lizard* with a curious expression stared at me.

CORRECTING MODIFIER PROBLEMS

Modifiers can make your writing more specific and more concrete. Used effectively and correctly, modifiers give the reader a clear, exact picture of what you want to say, and they help you to say it precisely. But modifiers have to be used correctly. You can check for errors with modifiers as you revise your sentences.

INFO BOX: Three Steps in Checking for Sentence Errors with Modifiers

Step 1: Find the modifier.

Step 2: Ask, "Does the modifier have something to modify?"

Step 3: Ask, "Is the modifier in the right place, as close as possible to the word, phrase, or clause it modifies?"

If you answer no in either step 2 or step 3, you need to revise your sentence. Let's use the steps in the following example.

> **sample sentence:** I saw a girl driving a Mazda wearing a bikini.

> **Step 1:** Find the modifier. The modifiers are *driving a Mazda* and *wearing a bikini.*
>
> **Step 2:** Ask, "Does the modifier have something to modify?" The answer is yes. The girl is driving a Mazda. The girl is wearing a bikini. Both modifiers go with *a girl.*
>
> **Step 3:** Ask, "Is the modifier in the right place?"

The answer is yes and no. One modifier is in the right place:

> I saw a *girl driving a Mazda*

The other modifier is *not* in the right place

> a *Mazda wearing a bikini*

The Mazda is not wearing a bikini.

> **revised:** I saw a girl *wearing a bikini* and *driving a Mazda.*

Let's work through the steps once more:

> **sample sentence:** Scampering through the forest, the hunters saw two rabbits.

Step 1: Find the modifier. The modifiers are *scampering through the forest* and *two*.

Step 2: Ask, "Does the modifier have something to modify?" The answer is yes. There are *two rabbits*. The *rabbits* are *scampering through the forest.*

Step 3: Ask, "Is the modifier in the right place?"

The answer is yes and no. The word *two* is in the right place:

> *two* rabbits

But *scampering through the forest* is in the wrong place:

> *Scampering through the forest*, the hunters

The hunters are not scampering through the forest. The rabbits are.

> **revised:** The hunters saw two rabbits *scampering through the forest.*

Caution: Be sure to put words like *almost, even, exactly, hardly, just, merely, nearly, only, scarcely,* and *simply* as close as possible to what they modify. If you put them in the wrong place, you may write a confusing sentence.

> **sample sentence:** Etienne only wants to grow carrots and zucchini. (The modifier that creates confusion here is *only*. Does Etienne have only one goal in life—to grow carrots and zucchini? Or are these the only vegetables he wants to grow? To create a clearer sentence, move the modifier.)
>
> **revised:** Etienne wants to grow *only* carrots and zucchini.

The examples you have just worked with show one common error in using modifiers. This error involves **misplaced modifiers,** words that describe something but are not where they should be in the sentence. Here is the rule to remember:

> **Put a modifier as close as possible to the word, phrase, or clause it modifies.**

> **Exercise 2** **Correcting Sentences with Misplaced Modifiers**

Some of the following sentences contain misplaced modifiers. Revise any sentence that has a misplaced modifier by putting the modifier as close as possible to whatever it modifies.

1. Skittering under a crack in the baseboards, I noticed a huge cockroach.

revised: _____

_____

2. Marcia nearly slept for ten hours last night.

revised: _____

_____

3. Whenever my brother goes to that restaurant, he only eats fajitas.

revised: _____

_____

4. Hot off the grill, David served the steaks.

revised: _____

_____

5. Tucked under the warm blankets, the children looked like angels.

revised: _____

_____

6. Waiting in the dentist's office, Sylvia read nearly every magazine in the room.

revised: _____

_____

7. Coated with green mold, he scrubbed at the filthy shower stall.

revised: _____

_____

8. Tony and Martha saw several chipmunks biking on the nature path.

revised: _____

_____

9. Tommy gave all the books to a friend that he didn't need anymore.

revised: _____

_____

10. The town is famous for its pig farms where my parents were married.

revised: _____

_____

Correcting Dangling Modifiers

The three steps for correcting modifier problems can help you recognize another kind of error. Let's use the steps to check the following sentence.

> **sample sentence:** Strolling through the tropical paradise, many colorful birds could be seen.

> **Step 1:** Find the modifier. The modifiers are *Strolling through the tropical paradise* and *many colorful.*
> **Step 2:** Ask, "Does the modifier have something to modify?" The answer is yes and no. The words *many* and *colorful* modify birds. But who or what is *strolling through the tropical paradise?* There is no person mentioned in this sentence. The birds are not strolling.

This kind of error is called a **dangling modifier.** It means that the modifier does not have anything to modify; it just dangles in the sentence. To correct this kind of error, you cannot just move the modifier:

still incorrect: Many colorful birds could be seen strolling through the tropical paradise. (There is still no person strolling.)

The way to correct this kind of error is to add something to the sentence. If you gave the modifier something to modify, you might come up with several different revised sentences:

revised sentences: *As I strolled through the tropical paradise, I saw* many colorful birds.

or

Many colorful birds could be seen *when we were strolling through the tropical paradise.*

or

While the tourists strolled through the tropical paradise, they saw many colorful birds.

Try the process for correcting dangling modifiers once more:

sample sentence: Ascending in the glass elevator, the hotel lobby glittered in the light.

Step 1: Find the modifier. The modifiers are *Ascending in the glass elevator* and *hotel.*

Step 2: Ask, "Does the modifier have anything to modify?" The answer is yes and no. The word *hotel* modifies lobby, but *ascending in the glass elevator* doesn't modify anything. Who is ascending in the elevator? There is nobody mentioned in the sentence.

To revise this sentence, put somebody or something in it for the modifier to describe:

As the guests ascended in the glass elevator, the hotel lobby glittered in the light.

or

Ascending in the glass elevator, she saw the hotel lobby glitter in the light.

Remember that you cannot correct a dangling modifier just by moving the modifier. You have to give the modifier something to modify; you have to add something to the sentence.

Exercise 3 **Correcting Sentences with Dangling Modifiers**

Some of the following sentences use modifiers correctly. Some sentences have dangling modifiers. Revise the sentences with dangling modifiers. To revise, you will have to add words and change words.

1. Lingering alone in the twilight, the memories of the girl returned.

revised: _____

_____

2. While discussing the problem, a simple solution was found.

revised: _____

3. At the age of six, my family moved to Sacramento.

revised: _____

_____

4. With study skills and the ability to organize, success in college becomes more likely.

revised: _____

_____

5. Sitting by his father's hospital bed, hope filled Ivan's heart.

revised: _____

_____

6. Trapped by the flood waters, the residents climbed to the roofs of their houses.

revised: _____

_____

7. Having lied on his application, Tim's career in the police force ended before it began.

revised: _____

_____

8. To be accepted into that program, three letters of recommendation are required.

revised: _____

_____

9. Working long hours and gradually accepting more responsibility, Andrea was promoted several times.

revised: _____

_____

10. When tempted by the power of a credit card, foolish purchases can be made.

revised: _____

_____

REVIEWING THE STEPS AND THE SOLUTIONS

It is important to recognize problems with modifiers and to correct these problems. Modifier problems can result in confusing or even silly sentences. And when you confuse or unintentionally amuse your reader, you are not making your point.

Remember to check for modifier problems in three steps and to correct each kind of problem in the appropriate way.

INFO BOX: **A Summary of Modifier Problems**

Checking for Modifier Problems

Step 1: Find the modifier.
Step 2: Ask, "Does the modifier have something to modify?"
Step 3: Ask, "Is the modifier in the right place?"

Correcting Modifier Problems
If the modifier is in the wrong place (a misplaced modifier), put it as close as possible to the word, phrase, or clause it modifies.
If the modifier has nothing to modify (a dangling modifier), add or change words so that it has something to modify.

Exercise 4   **Revising Sentences with Modifier Problems**   ◀ COLLABORATE

All of the following sentences have modifier problems. Working with a partner or group, write a new, correct sentence for each incorrect one. You may move words, add words, change words, or remove words. The first one is done for you.

1. Written in stone, the archaeologist could not understand the ancient message.

   revised: <u>The archaeologist could not understand the ancient message</u>

   <u>written in stone.</u>

2. To design an effective safety plan, the participation of all the residents of the city is essential.

   revised: _____

   _____

3. Caught sneaking into an R-rated movie, the theater manager warned the young teens.

   revised: _____

   _____

4. A beautiful woman entered the ballroom wearing a bright silk gown.

   revised: _____

   _____

5. Tired of all the arguing, Sean only agreed to talk for a few minutes.

   revised: _____

   _____

6. After leaving muddy paw prints all over the kitchen, Aaron wiped his dog's feet with a towel.

   revised: _____

   _____

7. Because my mother was in the Navy during most of my childhood, she almost missed all of my birthdays.

revised: _____

_____

8. Before deciding on a divorce, counseling for both partners should be tried.

revised: _____

_____

9. Without a valid driver's license, test driving a car at a car dealership is not possible.

revised: _____

_____

10. Trying to lose weight, patience with the process and realistic goals can be the keys to success.

revised: _____

_____

○○○ CONNECT ▶   (Exercise 5) **Editing a Paragraph for Modifier Problems**

Correct any errors with modifiers in the following paragraph. There are four errors. Write your corrections above the line.

Movies about college often show carefree students celebrating at fraternity parties or socializing between classes on wide green campus lawns. However, college is always not like that. Many students attend commuter colleges, which do not have fraternity or sorority houses and may not feature green lawns. Other students attend more traditional colleges with residence halls, football teams, and lovely surroundings, but the students live off campus. In addition, most students today work part time or full time, so they do not have time for a traditional college experience. Rushing to class between work and family obligations, it can be hard to feel part of college. Most colleges offer clubs and activities, but many students are busy in the late afternoons, in the evenings, and on the weekends when student activities take place. Fortunately, busy students still find ways to make friends. Waiting for their instructor to arrive, students lean across their desks and talk about the course, the assignments, and the next test. Motivated by a desire to succeed, alliances are formed between students. Some stay after class to share class notes, others come early to review for a test. To make connections, today's students rely on cell phones, e-mail, and quick conversations instead of parties

and clubs. Late-night study groups meet off campus. Later, alliances become true

friendships that extend through the semesters. Designed for a new kind of college

life, students are creating their own traditions.

Exercise 6   **Editing a Paragraph for Modifier Problems**   ◄ CONNECT

Correct any errors with modifiers in the following paragraph. There are five
errors. Write your corrections above the line.

Stuffed animals used to just be for children, but they are nearly universal

figures today. Teenage girls can be seen carrying their teddy bears or Disney fig-

ures on airplanes. In the rear windows of their cars, drivers in their twenties, thir-

ties, or forties place stuffed mascots. Many adults have small plush toys in their

cubicles at work. When unable to decide on a gift, stuffed animals become the an-

swer. Patients in hospitals get them instead of flowers, wives and girlfriends love

them on Valentine's Day, and a huge plush snake, alligator, or lizard will amuse a

grown man. Some stuffed animals have become collectibles. A few years ago,

thousands of people fought to own the latest Beanie Baby. Today, many expensive

department stores offer a new version of the stores' teddy bear each year. Funny-

looking, soft, and huggable, the appeal of stuffed animals is irresistible. In every

adult, they comfort the child.

Chapter Test: Correcting Problems with Modifiers

Some of the sentences below have problems with modifiers; some are correct. Put an *X* by each sentence with a modifier problem.

1. _____   Stretched out on the top of the tall bookcase, I found my
cat.

2. _____   At age five, my father and mother got a divorce.

3. _____   Trapped by a sudden snowstorm, the mountain climbers
struggled to survive.

4. _____   In order to find the solution to the problem, creativity and
determination are required.

5. _____   I dropped the folder, and the wind blew away almost all the
pages of my research paper.

6. _____ Crusted with years of dirt, Robert tried to clean the old candlesticks.

7. _____ Grinning like a fool, my brother pranced around in his Halloween costume.

8. _____ Sitting on the back porch on a summer night, hundreds of fireflies danced in the dark.

9. _____ Before ending a relationship, partners should talk honestly and calmly.

10. _____ When asked to speak before a large group, preparation and organization can lead to a confident presentation.

CHAPTER 22
Using Verbs Correctly

Verbs are words that show some kind of action or being. These verbs show action or being:

> **verb**
> He *runs* to the park.

> **verb**
> Melanie *is* my best friend.

> **verb**
> The pizza *tastes* delicious.

Verbs also tell about time.

> He *will run* to the park. (The time is future.)
> Melanie *was* my best friend. (The time is past.)
> The pizza *tastes* delicious. (The time is present.)

The time of a verb is called its *tense*. You can say a verb is in the *present tense, future tense,* or many other tenses.

Using verbs correctly involves knowing which form of the verb to use, choosing the right verb tense, and being consistent in verb tense.

USING STANDARD VERB FORMS

Many people use nonstandard verb forms in everyday conversation. But everyone who wants to write and speak effectively should know different levels of language, from the slang and dialect of everyday conversation to the **standard English** of college, business, and professional environments.

In everyday conversation, you may use **nonstandard forms** like these:

I goes	he don't	we was
you was	it don't	she smile
you be	I be	they walks

But these are not correct forms in standard English.

THE PRESENT TENSE

Look at the standard verb forms for the present tense of the word *listen:*

verb: listen

I listen	we listen
you listen	you listen
he, she, it listens	they listen

Take a closer look at the standard verb forms. Only one form is different:

he, she, it *listens*

This is the only form that ends in *s* in the present tense.

INFO BOX: **In the present tense, use an -s or -es ending on the verb only when the subject is *he, she,* or *it,* or the equivalent.**

He calls his mother every day.
She chases the cat away from the bird cage.
It runs like a new car.

Jim calls his mother every day.
Samantha chases the cat away from the bird cage.
The jalopy runs like a new car.

Take another look at the present tense. If the verb is a standard verb, it will follow this form in the present tense.

I attend every lecture.
You care about the truth.
He visits his grandfather regularly.
She drives a new car.
The new *album sounds* great.
We follow that team.
You work well together.
They buy the store brand of cereal.

Exercise 1   **Picking the Correct Verb in the Present Tense**

Underline the subject and circle the correct verb form in parentheses in each sentence below.

1. The salsa in the green jar (taste, tastes) better than the salsa in the red jar.

2. On Saturdays, the people across the street (ride, rides) their bikes to town.

3. Deciding on the right answers to your questions (take, takes)time.

4. After a long day, you always (fall, falls) asleep on the sofa.

5. In the snow, the house and the trees (look, looks) like a postcard of a winter scene.

6. Lisa (need, needs) new clothes for school.

7. On the roof of the apartment building (live, lives) two hawks.

8. Without much money, my brothers (manage, manages) to have a good time.

9. Sometimes, my newborn baby (resemble, resembles) my great uncle Morris.

10. Patience (allow, allows) a person to relax in frustrating circumstances.

Exercise 2 **More on Picking the Correct Verb in the Present Tense**

Underline the subject and circle the correct verb form in parentheses in each sentence below.

1. At large parties, you (act, acts) silly.

2. My large brown dog (snore, snores) at night.

3. With my loud voice, I (make, makes) too much noise in a crowd.

4. A small house (require, requires) less furniture than a large one.

5. Behind the stone wall (live, lives) a beautiful woman and her child.

6. The men in the coffee shop (spend, spends) hours together.

7. Every Saturday morning, my mother (hunt, hunts) for bargains at local garage sales.

8. Tolerance (turn, turns) suspicion and fear into acceptance.

9. Someone from the jury (serve, serves) as the jury chairperson.

10. The chairs with the leather seats (seem, seems) perfect for our living room.

THE PAST TENSE

The past tense of most verbs is formed by adding -*d* or -*ed* to the verb.

verb: listen

I listened	we listened
you listened	you listened
he, she, it listened	they listened

Add -*ed* to *listen* to form the past tense. For some other verbs, you may add -*d*.

The sun *faded* from the sky.
He *quaked* with fear.
She *crumpled* the paper into a ball.

Exercise 3 **Writing the Correct Verb Forms of Past Tense**

Write the correct past tense form of each verb in parentheses in each sentence below.

    1. The handsome boy _____ (smile) at me last night.

    2. As a child, I _____ (need) constant reassurance from my parents.

    3. The frightened kitten _____ (climb) up the tree.

    4. In his twenties, my father _____ (travel) around the country.

    5. Isabel _____ (struggle) to get to America for three years.

    6. Yesterday, the city council _____ (change) its policy on parking tickets.

    7. The police officer _____ (look) everywhere for the suspect.

    8. Two months ago, a judge _____ (suspend) my driver's license.

    9. In kindergarten, Ashley _____ (enjoy) singing with the rest of the children.

    10. You _____ (cover) up the real reasons for your decision.

THE FOUR MAIN FORMS OF A VERB: PRESENT, PAST, PRESENT PARTICIPLE, PAST PARTICIPLE

When you are deciding what form of a verb to use, you will probably rely on one of four forms: the present tense, the past tense, the present participle, and the past participle. Most of the time, you will use one of these forms or add a helping verb to it. As an example, look at the four main forms of the verb *listen*.

Present	Past	Present Participle	Past Participle
listen	listened	listening	listened

You use the four verb forms—present, past, present participle, past participle—alone or with helping verbs, to express time (tense). Forms of regular verbs like *listen* are very easy to remember. Use the present form for the present tense:

We *listen* to the news on the radio.

The past form expresses past tense:

I *listened* to language tapes for three hours yesterday.

The present participle, or *-ing* form, is used with helping verbs:

He *was listening* to me.
I *am listening* to you.
You *should have been listening* more carefully.

The past participle is the form used with the helping verbs *have, has,* or *had:*

I *have listened* for hours.
She *has listened* to the tape.
We *had listened* to the tape before we bought it.

Of course, you can add many helping verbs to the present tense:

present tense:
We *listen* to the news on the car radio.

add helping verbs:
We *will* listen to the news on the car radio.
We *should* listen to the news on the car radio.
We *can* listen to the news on the car radio.

When a verb is regular, the past form is created by adding *-d* or *-ed* to the present form. The present participle is formed by adding *-ing* to the present form, and the past participle form is the same as the past form.

IRREGULAR VERBS

Irregular verbs do not follow the same rules for creating verb forms that regular verbs do. Three verbs that we use all the time—*be, have, do*—are irregular verbs. You need to study them closely. Look at the present tense forms for all three, and compare the standard, present tense forms with the nonstandard ones. *Remember to use the standard forms for college or professional writing.*

verb: be

Nonstandard	Standard
~~I be~~ or ~~I is~~	I am
~~you be~~	you are
~~he, she, it be~~	he, she, it is
~~we be~~	we are
~~you be~~	you are
~~they be~~	they are

verb: have

Nonstandard	Standard
~~I has~~	I have
~~you has~~	you have
~~he, she, it have~~	he, she, it has
~~we has~~	we have
~~you has~~	you have
~~they has~~	they have

verb: do

Nonstandard	Standard
~~I does~~	I do
~~you does~~	you do
~~he, she, it do~~	he, she, it does
~~we does~~	we do
~~you does~~	you do
~~they does~~	they do

Caution: Be careful when you add *not* to *does*. If you are writing a contraction of *does not*, be sure you write *doesn't*, not *don't*.

not this: ~~The light don't work.~~
but this: The light doesn't work.

Exercise 4   **Choosing the Correct Form of *be, have,* or *do* in the Present Tense**

Circle the correct form of the verb in parentheses in each sentence below.

1. On weekdays, I (be, am) awake by 6:00 a.m.

2. With his education, William (has, have) a good chance of finding a job in information technology.

3. Our supermarket (don't, doesn't) offer coupons each week.

4. During a conversation, it (be, is) important to maintain eye contact.

5. On her trips to Grand Bahama, Sylvia (has, have) many relatives to visit.

6. Ruben and Tara (do, does) everything for their parents.

7. People in stressful jobs (has, have) to make time for rest and relaxation.

8. During the winter, we (be, are) ready for days without heat or electricity.

9. At night, you (do, does) your best thinking.

10. The complaints about our prices (be, are) coming from a small group of customers.

Exercise 5   **More on Choosing the Correct Form of *be, have,* or *do* in the Present Tense**

Circle the correct form of the verb in parentheses in each sentence below.

1. Unfortunately, the manager (do, does) not care about the tenant's problems.

2. Today I (be, am) the first member of my family to own a house.

3. Dion (has, have) a plan for improving the office telephone system.

4. You may not believe me, but chicken soup (do, does) soothe a cold.

5. When you have an assignment, you (do, does) too much procrastinating before you get started.

6. In our family, sending a card (doesn't, don't) mean as much as making a visit.

7. Rick and I love Indian food; we (has, have) curry for dinner two or three times a week.

8. Those earrings (be, are) pretty; they match your eyes.

9. The carrot cake (has, have) walnuts in it.

10. When you (has, have) a driver's license, you can use it as an ID card.

The Past Tense of *be, have, do*

The past forms of these irregular verbs can be confusing. Again, compare the nonstandard forms to the standard forms. *Remember to use the standard forms for college or professional writing.*

verb: be

Nonstandard	Standard
~~I were~~	I was
~~you was~~	you were
~~he, she, it were~~	he, she, it was
~~we was~~	we were
~~you was~~	you were
~~they was~~	they were

verb: have

Nonstandard	Standard
~~I has~~	I had
~~you has~~	you had
~~he, she, it have~~	he, she, it had
~~we has~~	we had
~~you has~~	you had
~~they has~~	they had

verb: do

Nonstandard	Standard
~~I done~~	I did
~~you done~~	you did
~~he, she, it done~~	he, she, it did
~~we done~~	we did
~~you done~~	you did
~~they done~~	they did

Exercise 6   **Choosing the Correct Form of *be, have,* or *do* in the Past Tense**

Circle the correct verb form in parentheses in each sentence below.

1. The hole in the wall (was, were) large and deep.

2. Without much luck, Danny Shapiro (done, did) his best to score points for his team.

3. Children loved to visit Tyler Park because it (have, had) a huge playground.

4. Last weekend, we (was, were) in Detroit for a family reunion.

5. A week ago, I (has, had) a strange phone call from Kelly.

6. At sixteen, my father (was, were) supporting his mother and his sister.

7. By taking my car keys, my parents (done, did) their best to prevent an accident.

8. Last semester, I (was, were) sharing an apartment with two friends from my old neighborhood.

9. In kindergarten, you (was, were) my secret love.

10. The doctor (done, did) a thorough examination of my throat.

Exercise 7 **More on Choosing the Correct Form of *be*, *have*, or *do* in the Past Tense**

Circle the correct verb form in parentheses in each sentence below.

1. Ray and Jack (was, were) once partners in a small plumbing supply business.

2. When my mother got married, she (have, had) never been away from her family for more than a week.

3. Colin visited me every day when I (was, were) in the hospital.

4. Eric planned the program, but Julian (done, did) most of the work.

5. We (was, were) in shock after the tornado hit our town.

6. Last week, a detective from the local police department (have, had) a talk with the parents of the suspect.

7. After a long day at school, you and I (was, were) always ready to play.

8. Yesterday, Chantel (have, had) to find a babysitter for her little boy.

9. I need a good night's sleep because I (done, did) nothing but listen to customers' complaints all day.

10. When I was growing up, the hamburger place at the end of my block (have, had) the best French fries in town.

More Irregular Verb Forms

Be, *have*, and *do* are not the only verbs with irregular forms. There are many such verbs, and everybody who writes uses some form of an irregular verb. When you write and you are not certain if you are using the correct form of a verb, check the list of irregular verbs on pages 455 and 456.

For each irregular verb listed below, the *present*, the *past*, and the *past participle* forms are given. The present participle isn't included because it is always formed by adding *-ing* to the present form.

Irregular Verb Forms

Present	Past	Past Participle
(Today I *arise*.)	(Yesterday I *arose*.)	(I have/had *arisen*.)
arise	arose	arisen
awake	awoke, awaked	awoken, awaked
bear	bore	born, borne
beat	beat	beaten
become	became	become
begin	began	begun
bend	bent	bent
bite	bit	bitten
bleed	bled	bled
blow	blew	blown
break	broke	broken
bring	brought	brought
build	built	built
burst	burst	burst
buy	bought	bought
catch	caught	caught
choose	chose	chosen
come	came	come
cling	clung	clung
cost	cost	cost
creep	crept	crept
cut	cut	cut
deal	dealt	dealt
draw	drew	drawn
dream	dreamed, dreamt	dreamed, dreamt
drink	drank	drunk
drive	drove	driven
eat	ate	eaten
fall	fell	fallen
feed	fed	fed
feel	felt	felt
fight	fought	fought
find	found	found
fling	flung	flung
fly	flew	flown
freeze	froze	frozen
get	got	got, gotten
give	gave	given
go	went	gone
grow	grew	grown
hear	heard	heard
hide	hid	hidden
hit	hit	hit
hold	held	held
hurt	hurt	hurt

Present	Past	Past Participle
keep	kept	kept
know	knew	known
lay (means to put)	laid	laid
lead	led	led
leave	left	left
lend	lent	lent
let	let	let
lie (means to recline)	lay	lain
light	lit, lighted	lit, lighted
lose	lost	lost
make	made	made
mean	meant	meant
meet	met	met
pay	paid	paid
ride	rode	ridden
ring	rang	rung
rise	rose	risen
run	ran	run
say	said	said
see	saw	seen
sell	sold	sold
send	sent	sent
sew	sewed	sewn, sewed
shake	shook	shaken
shine	shone, shined	shone, shined
shrink	shrank	shrunk
shut	shut	shut
sing	sang	sung
sit	sat	sat
sleep	slept	slept
slide	slid	slid
sling	slung	slung
speak	spoke	spoken
spend	spent	spent
stand	stood	stood
steal	stole	stolen
stick	stuck	stuck
sting	stung	stung
stink	stank, stunk	stunk
string	strung	strung
swear	swore	sworn
swim	swam	swum
teach	taught	taught
tear	tore	torn
tell	told	told
think	thought	thought
throw	threw	thrown
wake	woke, waked	woken, waked
wear	wore	worn
win	won	won
write	wrote	written

Exercise 8   **Choosing the Correct Form of Irregular Verbs**

Write the correct form of the verb in parentheses in each sentence below. Be sure to check the list of irregular verbs.

1. Someone had _____ (draw) a picture of a cat on the playroom wall.

2. Louisa is thoughtful; last week she_____ (bring) flowers to her elderly neighbor.

3. I'm not afraid of horses because I have _____ (ride) them since I was a child.

4. He _____ (sling) the heavy sack over his shoulder as if it contained marshmallows, not stones.

5. Jerome is acting strangely; maybe he has _____ (fall) in love.

6. A year ago, Sammy _____ (lend) us the money to pay our baby's medical bills.

7. When I have a day off, I like to _____ (lie) in the sun and listen to music.

8. My dog has _____ (sleep) on my bed ever since he was big enough to jump up to it.

9. I don't know how Mario _____ (bear) the pain of arthritis for so many years.

10. The last of the fireworks had _____ (burst) into the sky before I reached the fairgrounds.

Exercise 9   **Choosing the Correct Form of Irregular Verbs**

Write the correct form of the verb in parentheses in each sentence below. Be sure to check the list of irregular verbs.

1. When I asked about the turquoise jewelry, Adam _____ (lay) all the necklaces on the counter so that I could choose.

2. For days, the smell lingered and the kitchen _____ (stink) of fish.

3. Getting arrested last year _____ (teach) me a hard lesson.

4. Lea has always _____ (dream) of visiting Africa.

5. A helpful stranger_____ (lead) us to a waiting area filled with people of all ages.

6. The soldier has _____ (swear) an oath to protect the weak and helpless.

7. Before Keith went to work, he _____ (shut) the back door and closed all the windows.

8. Even when she was struggling to make a living as a seamstress, Dina _____ (cling) to her dream of becoming a famous designer.

9. The supervisor has _____ (tell) us the new rules on overtime pay, and we have to accept them.

10. I have never _____ (speak) to anyone about my fear of heights.

COLLABORATE ▶ **Exercise 10**   **Writing Sentences with Correct Verb Forms**

With a partner or a group, write two sentences that correctly use each of the verb forms below. In writing these sentences, you may add helping verbs to the verb forms, but do not change the verb form itself. The first one is done for you.

1. sent

a. He sent her a dozen roses on Valentine's Day. _____

b. I have sent him all the information he needs. _____

2. swam

a. _____

b. _____

3. shrank

a. _____

b. _____

4. meant

a. _____

b. _____

5. paid

a. _____

b. _____

6. lain

a. _____

b. _____

7. shined

a. _____

b. _____

8. seen

a. _____

b. _____

9. chose

    a. _____

    b. _____

10. dealt

    a. _____

    b. _____

Exercise 11   **Editing a Paragraph for Correct Verb Forms**   ◀ CONNECT ⬤⬤⬤

Correct the errors in verb forms in the following paragraph. There are twelve errors.

The house I love most is my grandparents' home in the Dominican Republic. It is not a fancy house; in fact, it have no air conditioning, expensive furniture, or elaborate entertainment system. I loves it because it is filled with a family's warmth and surrounded by natural beauty. When I was a child, I spended my summer vacations at this house. Every morning I awoken with the sun and ran outdoors. For breakfast, my grandmother feeded me fruit from her own trees. I could hear the ocean, which was only a short distance away, as I sat on the porch. For the rest of the day, the neighborhood children and I swum in the blue-green water, played on the pale sand, and laid under the shady trees. In the evening, my grandparents' house was full of people: my aunts, uncles, and cousins shared dinner. Everyone brung food or helped to cook it. After dinner, the adults sat outside and told old stories while the children creeped closer. These tales of local ghosts and legends was more exciting than television. Even as my eyes began to close, I fighted to hear more. The long summer days and nights at my grandparents' house become to be the happiest times of my childhood.

Exercise 12   **Editing a Paragraph for Correct Verb Forms**   ◀ CONNECT ⬤⬤⬤

Correct the errors in verb forms in the following paragraph. There are ten errors.

Unless you be shy, you cannot understand a shy person. Shy people are often considered snobs because they don't talk to strangers, even in familiar situations. For example, I have often sat in the same seat in the same classroom for ten weeks and not sayed a word. The teacher and the students probably thought I

was arrogant, but I were just scared. In addition, some shy people are considered

dependent or possessive. Shy people gets these labels because they finds it hard

to make friends. Once they do make a friend, some shy people clings to that per-

son out of fear of losing him or her. If you are not shy yourself, remember that

what be so easy for you feel nearly impossible for a shy person. Then be patient

as the fearful person find his or her way.

Chapter Test: Using Verbs Correctly

Some of the sentences below use verbs correctly; others do not. Put an *X* by
each sentence with an error in using verbs correctly.

1. _____ Carly had a headache, so I told her to lie on the sofa for a few minutes.

2. _____ Craig is an intelligent man, but he have no desire to continue his education.

3. _____ At family gatherings, my son gets all the attention from his grandfather, but his sisters never attracts much notice.

4. _____ Our car was ready two hours before we was supposed to pick it up at the repair shop.

5. _____ The witness swore to tell everything he had seen during the robbery.

6. _____ Last night at the store, I dealt with three nasty customers; one threw her money at me.

7. _____ The firefighters done everything they could to save the historic building, but they got to the scene too late.

8. _____ Luther froze with fear when the large bird rose from the branch of the tree and flew toward Luther's face.

9. _____ A week ago, I finally payed all my bills; now I feel wonderful.

10. _____ A small boy who rode a Shetland pony led the parade of local schoolchildren.

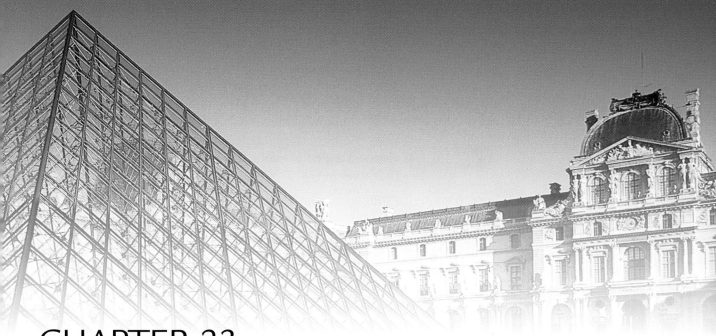

CHAPTER 23
More on Verbs: Consistency and Voice

Remember that your choice of verb form indicates the time (tense) of your statements. Be careful not to shift from one tense to another unless you have a reason to change the time.

CONSISTENT VERB TENSES

Staying in one tense (unless you have a reason to change tenses) is called **consistency of verb tense.**

incorrect shifts in tense:
The waitress *ran* to the kitchen with the order in her hand, *raced*
    back to her customers with glasses of water, and *smiles* calmly.
He *grins* at me from the ticket booth and *closed* the ticket window.

You can correct these errors by putting all the verbs in the same tense.

consistent present tense:
The waitress *runs* to the kitchen with the order in her hand, *races*
    back to her customers with glasses of water, and *smiles* calmly.
He *grins* at me from the ticket booth and *closes* the ticket window.

consistent past tense:
The waitress *ran* to the kitchen with the order in her hand, *raced*
    back to her customers with glasses of water, and *smiled* calmly.
He *grinned* at me from the ticket booth and *closed* the ticket window.

Whether you correct by changing all the verbs to the present tense or by changing them to the past tense, you are making the tenses consistent. Consistency of tense is important in the events you are describing because it helps the reader understand what happened and when it happened.

Exercise 1 **Correcting Sentences That Are Inconsistent in Tense**

In each sentence following, one verb is inconsistent in tense. Cross it out and write the correct tense above it.

1. On Mondays, I start the day with my 8:00 a.m. class; then I drove to work and stay there until 5:30 p.m., when I grab a sandwich before my evening class.

2. At the city council meeting, the council discussed the plans for the new apartment complex and explained the economic benefits to the city, but no one brings up the potential parking problems.

3. Whenever my boyfriend has a free weekend, he drives to the mountains and goes hiking on the trails, for he loved the fresh air and enjoys the scenery.

4. Sometimes I eat three meals a day at regular hours, but at other times, my schedule gets so hectic that I skipped meals and wind up eating dinner at midnight.

5. Last week, one of the soccer players was in a car accident; as a result, the team loses its best player and did poorly at yesterday's match.

6. Harry slapped the giant ants with his sneaker as they crawled across the kitchen floor; meanwhile, Tommy searches desperately for the can of insect spray.

7. As soon as the days start to get longer, I sit outdoors as often as I could and use my backyard grill on the weekends.

8. Because the best store bargains were available as soon as the doors opened, people begin to line up outside the store at dawn.

9. Getting to class on time is difficult for Peter because he doesn't have his own car and had to depend on his brother, who is unreliable, for rides.

10. Although I listen to everything the instructor says, I needed to take bet-

ter notes as she explains new ideas.

◀ CONNECT ⟨⟩⟨⟩⟨⟩

Exercise 2 **Editing a Paragraph for Consistency of Tenses**

Read the following paragraph. Then cross out any verbs that are inconsistent in tense and write the corrections above. There are seven errors.

Waiting for my final examination grade in my Introduction to Algebra class made me very tense. After I finished the examination, I asked my instructor when I would know my grade. She says the grade would be posted on her office door as soon as she scores all the examinations in my class. She told me to check the door in two days. I knew that if I fail this test, I could not pass the course. I did not sleep for two days. Early in the morning of the third day, I went to my instructor's door, but she hasn't put the grades up. Worse, she is not in her office. Throughout the day, I checked her door so many times that I felt like I was haunting the office. Finally, at 6:00 p.m., I see a list on the door. I search for my name and found my passing grade. The tension left my body, and I breathed freely again.

◀ CONNECT ⟨⟩⟨⟩⟨⟩

Exercise 3 **Editing a Paragraph for Consistency of Tenses**

Read the following paragraph. Then cross out any verbs that are inconsistent in tense and write the corrections above. There are five errors.

Dave does not have an easy life, but his sense of humor helps him survive. Dave drives an old, rusted car, but instead of complaining, he calls it the Clunkmobile and laughs at its defects. He says he was so used to it breaking down that he is slightly disappointed when the car takes him where he wants to go. If the car performs perfectly, Dave says it wasn't meeting his expectations. Dave had a humorous attitude toward work, too. He loses jobs regularly, so he kept a chart listing his job losses and asks his friends to guess the date of his next layoff, downsizing, or termination. Dave is not lazy or stupid, and his misfortunes are mainly the result of bad luck. Dave's humor was his way of coping with disappointment and not feeling sorry for himself.

 COLLABORATE ▶ (Exercise 4) **Writing a Paragraph with Consistent Verb Tenses**

The following paragraph has many inconsistencies in verb tenses; it shifts between past and present tenses. Working with a group, write two versions of the paragraph: write it once in the present tense, then a second time in the past tense. Split your activity; half the group can write it in one tense while the other half can write it in the other tense.

After both rewrites are complete, read the new paragraph aloud to both parts of the team, as a final check.

> My best friend took me for a ride in the country and tells me some bad news. He says that in two weeks he was moving to another state. This news is very sudden and shocks me to my core. My friend is more than a friend; he was a brother, a partner in pranks, a teammate in games, and a keeper of secrets. After he told me, we walk in the woods together. We find it hard to say much because we each knew what the other is feeling. After what seems like hours, he stops walking and faces me. He says the move wasn't what he wanted, but he added that his family needs him. I see sadness in his eyes, and I knew he saw the sorrow in mine.

Paragraph Revised for Consistent Tenses:

_____

_____

_____

_____

_____

_____

_____

_____

_____

_____

_____

_____

_____

_____

_____

_____

_____

_____

THE PRESENT PERFECT TENSE

When you are choosing the right verb tense, you should know about two verb tenses, the present perfect and the past perfect, that can make your meaning clear.

The **present perfect tense** is made up of the past participle form of the verb plus *have* or *has* as a helping verb. Use this tense to show an action that started in the past but is still going on in the present.

> **past tense:** My father *drove* a truck for five months. (He doesn't drive a truck anymore, but he did drive one in the past.)
>
> **present perfect tense:** My father *has driven* a truck for five months. (He started driving a truck five months ago; he is still driving a truck.)
>
> **past tense:** For years, I *studied* ballet. (I don't study ballet now; I used to.)
>
> **present perfect tense:** For years, I *have studied* ballet. (I still study ballet.)

Remember, use the present perfect tense to show that an action started in the past and is still going on.

Exercise 5   **Distinguishing Between the Past and the Present Perfect Tense**

Circle the correct verb in parentheses in each sentence below. Be sure to look carefully at the meaning of the sentences.

1. Last week Kenny (asked, has asked) me about my new friend.

2. Sally and George (worked, have worked) at the West End Clinic for several years now.

3. Brad (was, has been) spending too much money on his car, but he won't take my advice.

4. Yesterday my parents finally traveled to their native country and (made, have made) a dream come true.

5. Carly (was, has been) on the phone for twenty minutes and is still trying to get someone at the electric company to answer her question.

6. One of the women in my class (was, has been) a fashion model but is now studying fashion design.

7. The clothing store (advertised, has advertised) its going-out-of-business sale for a year now.

8. After Jack returned from Portland, he (renewed, has renewed) his friendship with Alicia.

9. Kelly (investigated, has investigated) three recent burglaries in the neighborhood and discovered a pattern to the crimes.

10. Manny (lost, has lost) his wallet and credit cards last night.

THE PAST PERFECT TENSE

The **past perfect tense** is made up of the past participle form of the verb and *had* as a helping verb. You can use the past perfect tense to show more than one event in the past—that is, when two or more things thing happened in the past but at different times.

past tense: He *washed* the dishes.

past perfect tense: He *had washed* the dishes by the time I came home. (He washed the dishes *before* I came home. Both actions happened in the past, but one happened earlier than the other.)

past tense: Susan *waited* for an hour.

past perfect tense: Susan *had waited* for an hour when she gave up on him. (Waiting came first; giving up came second. Both actions are in the past.)

The past perfect tense is especially useful because you write most of your essays in the past tense, and you often need to get further back into the past. Remember, to form the past perfect tense, use *had* with the past participle of the verb.

Exercise 6 **Distinguishing Between the Past and the Past Perfect Tense**

Circle the correct verb in parentheses in each sentence below. Be sure to look carefully at the meaning of the sentences.

1. By the time my girlfriend arrived, I (hid, had hidden) her birthday gift.

2. My car suddenly died on the highway because I (forgot, had forgotten) to fill the gas tank the night before.

3. Yesterday I bought a pair of shoes I (saw, had seen) in a newspaper advertisement last week.

4. The scientists studied medicines that ancient civilizations (used, had used) to treat infections.

5. Elena wondered whether her father (heard, had heard) the rumors yet.

6. As the children (filed, had filed) slowly into the classroom, they longed for the freedom of the final school bell.

7. By the time I got to the airport, my plane (left, had left) the runway.

8. On Saturday, the children (baked, had baked) sugar cookies and covered them with pink icing.

9. Bob questioned whether the plumber (did, had done) the job right earlier that afternoon.

10. Most of the students (finished, had finished) the test before the instructor began collecting the papers.

PASSIVE AND ACTIVE VOICE

Verbs not only have tenses, but they also have voices. When the subject in the sentence is doing something, the verb is in the **active voice.** When something is done to the subject, when it receives the action of the verb, the verb is in the **passive voice.**

active voice:

I painted the house. (*I*, the subject, did it.)

The people on the corner made a donation to the emergency fund. (The *people*, the subject, did it.)

passive voice:

The house was painted by me. (The *house*, the subject, didn't do anything. It received the action—it was painted.)

A donation to the emergency fund was made by the people on the corner. (The *donation*, the subject, didn't do anything. It received the action—it was given.)

Notice what happens when you use the passive voice instead of the active:

active voice: I painted the house.

passive voice: The house was painted by me.

The sentence in the passive voice is two words longer than the one in the active voice. Yet the sentence that uses the passive voice does not say anything different, and it does not say it more clearly than the one in the active voice.

Using the passive voice can make your sentences wordy, it can slow them down, and it can make them boring. The passive voice can also confuse readers. When the subject of the sentence is not doing anything, readers may have to look carefully to see who or what *is* doing something. Look at this sentence, for example:

A decision to fire you was reached.

Who decided to fire you? In this sentence, it is hard to find the answer to that question.

Of course, there will be times when you have to use the passive voice. For example, you may have to use it when you do not know who did something, as in these sentences:

Our house was broken into last night.

A leather jacket was left behind in the classroom.

But in general, you should avoid using the passive voice and rewrite sentences so they are in the active voice.

<hr>

Exercise 7 **Rewriting Sentences, Changing the Passive Voice to the Active Voice**

In the following sentences, change the passive voice to the active voice. If the original sentence does not tell you who or what performed the action, add words that tell who or what did it. An example is done for you.

example: Sandy Adams was appointed chief negotiator last night.

rewritten: The union leaders appointed Sandy Adams chief negotiator last night.

1. The mayor of Mid River was arrested for speeding last night.

rewritten: _____

_____

2. An agreement has been reached between the rival teams.

rewritten: _____

_____

3. An attempt to reach the landlord was made yesterday.

rewritten: _____

_____

4. Finally, the food was brought to the table by our server.

rewritten: _____

_____

5. These policies have been designed for our guests' safety.

rewritten: _____

_____

6. At last, the results of the talent contest were announced by a panel of judges.

rewritten: _____

_____

7. Every week, the residents of the nursing home are visited by a beautiful therapy dog and its owner.

rewritten: _____

_____

8. The poems were written by schoolchildren in South Africa.

rewritten: _____

_____

9. The real story of Jessica's battle with cancer is not known by Raymond.

rewritten: _____

_____

10. This murder is being investigated by the FBI.

rewritten: _____

_____

Avoiding Unnecessary Shifts in Voice

Just as you should be consistent in the tense of verbs, you should be consistent in the voice of verbs. Do not shift from active voice to passive voice, or vice versa, without some good reason to do so.

                   active   **passive**

       shift: *I designed* the decorations for the dance; *they were put up* by Chuck.

active   **active**
rewritten: *I designed* the decorations for the dance; *Chuck put* them *up*.

passive
shift: Many *problems were discussed* by the council members,

active
but *they found* no easy answers.

active
rewritten: The council *members discussed* many problems, but

active
they found no easy answers.

Being consistent in voice can help you to write clearly and smoothly.

Exercise 8   **Rewriting Sentences to Correct Shifts in Voice**

Rewrite the sentences below so that all the verbs are in the active voice. You may change the wording to make the sentences clear, smooth, and consistent in voice.

1. The sisters decided to buy their mother a new television, but no decision about the kind of television was made.

rewritten: _____

_____

2. A plan for the renewal of the harbor district is being designed by a team of architects; the team is also working on a plan for the neighboring park.

rewritten: _____

_____

3. Because you have known Bruno for years, he can be persuaded by you.

rewritten: _____

_____

4. Hallways were crowded by photographers as the celebrity couple left the courtroom.

rewritten: _____

_____

5. It was announced by the state legislature that college tuition would increase next year.

rewritten: _____

_____

6. A resourceful child was featured on the local television news; the child called 911 and saved his mother's life.

rewritten: _____

_____

7. My uncle is a fanatic about UFOs; stories about strange lights in the night sky and alien creatures are loved by him.

rewritten: _____

_____

8. Keisha cried with joy when her brother was given a medal.

rewritten: _____

_____

9. If a lease was signed by my husband, he never showed me the document.

rewritten: _____

_____

10. Most of the people at the club kept dancing until they found glass had been smashed on the floor by some careless person.

rewritten: _____

_____

A Few Tips About Verbs

There are a few errors that people tend to make with verbs. If you are aware of these errors, you'll be on the lookout for them as you edit your writing.

Used to: Be careful when you write that someone *used to* do, say, or feel something. It is incorrect to write *use to*.

> **not this:** Janine ~~use to~~ visit her mother every week.
> They ~~use to~~ like Thai food.
> **but this:** Janine *used to* visit her mother every week.
> They *used to* like Thai food.

Could Have, Should Have, Would Have: Using *of* instead of *have* is another error with verbs.

> **not this:** I ~~could of~~ done better on the test.
> **but this:** I *could have* done better on the test.

> **not this:** He ~~should of~~ been paying attention.
> **but this:** He *should have* been paying attention.

> **not this:** The girls ~~would of~~ liked to visit Washington.
> **but this:** The girls *would have* liked to visit Washington.

Would Have/Had: If you are writing about something that might have been possible, but that did not happen, use *had* as the helping verb.

> **not this:** If I ~~would have~~ taken a foreign language in high school, I wouldn't have to take one now.
> **but this:** If I *had* taken a foreign language in high school, I wouldn't have to take one now.

not this: I wish they ~~would have~~ won the game.
but this: I wish they *had* won the game.

not this: If she ~~would have~~ been smart, she would have called a
plumber.
but this: If she *had* been smart, she would have called a plumber.

Exercise 9   **Writing Sentences with the Correct Verb Forms**   ◀ COLLABORATE

Do this exercise with a partner or a group. Follow the directions to write or
complete each sentence below.

1. Complete this sentence and add a verb in the correct tense: My dog
   had chewed my best pair of shoes before

   _____

   _____

2. Write a sentence that is more than eight words long and that uses
   the words *would have been happier* in the middle of the sentence.

   _____

   _____

3. Write a sentence that uses the past tense form of these words: *act*
   and *lose.*

   _____

   _____

4. Write a sentence in the passive voice.

   _____

   _____

5. Write a sentence in the active voice.

   _____

   _____

6. Write a sentence that uses *would have* and *had.*

   _____

   _____

7. Write a sentence that is more than six words long and that uses the
   words *had decided* and *before.*

   _____

   _____

8. Write a sentence of more than six words that uses the words *used to.*

   _____

   _____

9. Write a sentence that contains two verbs in the same tense.

_____

_____

10. Write a sentence that uses the words *should have*.

_____

_____

CONNECT ▶   **Exercise 10**   **Editing a Paragraph for Errors in Verbs: Consistency, Correct Tense, and Voice**

Edit the following paragraph for errors in verb consistency, tense, or voice. There are seven errors.

Yesterday, I finally decided to buy an alarm for my car. Several incidents convince me that I needed one. The street where I live was considered a high-crime area for years, yet I never thought about protecting my car until recent events changed my mind. A month ago, thieves stole two cars off the street in broad daylight, and another car's windshield was smashed. Suddenly, I became nervous; still I avoided taking any precautions. I assumed that my car was too old to steal and that it would be overlooked by greedy thieves. Unfortunately, I woke up early yesterday, looked out my apartment window, and saw my car windshield smashed into a thousand pieces. Running downstairs to the curb, I saw a huge hole where my car radio use to be. Later that day, I took my car to be repaired and bought a car alarm. Maybe if I would have bought the alarm sooner, I would have saved the money for my new car radio.

CONNECT ▶   **Exercise 11**   **Editing a Paragraph for Errors in Verbs: Consistency, Correct Tense, and Voice**

Edit the following paragraph for errors in verb consistency, tense, or voice. There are six errors.

My mother sings every day. She use to sing professionally, at weddings and other celebrations, and with a band. Now that she is the mother of four children and a full-time employee at a hotel restaurant, she didn't have much time to entertain the public. Instead, her family is entertained by her, and she is likely to sing at the most unexpected moments. Many people sing in the shower, but my mother sings in the kitchen, at the ironing board, or on the stairs. On the phone, she sings a lullaby to her baby grandchild. She did this spontaneous entertaining for years, and most of the time her singing is great. However, there is one time when I cannot stand the sound of my mother's cheery voice. "Wake up!" she sings every morning at 7:00 a.m. "Rise and shine! Oh, what a beautiful morning!" she called to me. Every morning, I wish I would have been born to a less musical mother.

Chapter Test: More on Verbs: Consistency and Voice

Some of the sentences below are correct; others have errors in verb consistency, correct tense, and voice. Put an *X* next to the sentences with errors.

1. _____ When Felice asked me to lend her my camera, I should of refused.

2. _____ Ben wrote the letter; it was mailed by Gustavo.

3. _____ By the time I finished high school, I had taken three math courses.

4. _____ Last week, Keith visited Aunt Nora, Mario sends her a card, and Lisa called her several times.

5. _____ Caitlin has known Lewis for two years.

6. _____ Two of my neighbors have been employed at the tire plant but left to join the National Guard.

7. _____ I had managed to hide Luisa's surprise birthday present before she came through the door.

8. _____ A choice among the candidates for assistant manager was made, and you are our choice.

9. _____ Every night, my girlfriend sits in front of the television, manicures her nails, and answered her constantly ringing phone.

10. _____ My brothers would have appreciated a few words of praise from my father.

CHAPTER 24
Making Subjects and Verbs Agree

Subjects and verbs have to agree in number. That means a singular subject must be matched to a singular verb form; a plural subject must be matched to a plural verb form.

singular subject, singular verb:
My *sister walks* to work every morning.

plural subject, plural verb:
Mary, David, and *Sam believe* in ghosts.

singular subject, singular verb:
That *movie is* too violent for me.

plural subject, plural verb:
Bulky *packages are* difficult to carry.

Caution: Remember that a regular verb has an *s* ending in one singular form in the present tense—the form that goes with *he, she, it,* or their equivalents:

He *makes* me feel confident.
She *appreciates* intelligent conversation.
It *seems* like a good buy.
Bo *runs* every day.
That girl *swims* well.
That machine *breaks* down too often.

Exercise 1   **Subject-Verb Agreement: Selecting the Correct Verb Form**

Select the correct form of the verb in each sentence below.

1. It (take, takes) too long to drive from here to Omaha.

2. If it is cold outside, my sister (struggle, struggles) to get out of her warm bed.

3. Thoughtfulness (smooth, smoothes) some awkward situations.

4. Petty arguments always (begin, begins) when my children are overtired.

5. When our dogs (sleep, sleeps) on our bed, it is covered in long red hair.

6. Jack's hair and his clothes (smell, smells) like cigarette smoke.

7. I like Ted's new car; it (look, looks) a little like an expensive Italian sports car.

8. My brother and I often (feel, feels) homesick during the holidays.

9. The movie theater sometimes (show, shows) movies from Mexico and China.

10. You (is, are) the oldest and most respected member of the family.

Exercise 2   **Correcting Errors in Subject-Verb Agreement in a Paragraph**   ◀ CONNECT ⬤⬤⬤

There are errors in subject-verb agreement in the paragraph below. If a verb does not agree with its subject, change the verb form. Cross out the incorrect verb form and write the correct one above. There are six errors in agreement in the paragraph.

Every Sunday afternoon, the lady next door bakes cookies. She bakes pans of ginger cookies, oatmeal cookies, and chocolate chip cookies. I can smell the cookies as they bake, and the smell tempt me to run to her door and beg for a taste. The lady bake the cookies for her niece and nephew, who visit each week. They stays for an hour or two. Then their aunt kisses them good-bye and hand each child a tin of the fresh-baked cookies. From my window, I can see them leave, and each time I wishes for a cookie-baking aunt. However, I do not have to wish too hard because every Sunday, after the children leaves, their aunt rings my doorbell. Like a good neighbor, she hands me a small package of my own fresh-baked cookies.

PRONOUNS AS SUBJECTS

Pronouns can be used as subjects. Pronouns are words that take the place of nouns. **When pronouns are used as subjects, they must agree in number with verbs.**

Here is a list of the subject pronouns and the regular verb forms that agree with them in the present tense:

INFO BOX: Subjective Pronouns and a Present Tense Verb

pronoun	verb	
I	listen	
you	listen	all singular forms
he, she, it	listens	
we	listen	
you	listen	all plural forms
they	listen	

In all the sentences below, the pronoun used as the subject of the sentence agrees in number with the verb:

> **singular pronoun, singular verb:**
> I *make* the best omelet in town.

> **singular pronoun, singular verb:**
> You *dance* very well.

> **singular pronoun, singular verb:**
> She *performs* like a trained athlete.

> **plural pronoun, plural verb:**
> *We need* a new refrigerator.

> **plural pronoun, plural verb:**
> *They understand* the situation.

SPECIAL PROBLEMS WITH AGREEMENT

Agreement seems fairly simple: if a subject is singular, you use a singular verb form, and if a subject is plural, you use a plural verb form. However, there are special problems with agreement that will come up in your writing. Sometimes, it is hard to find the subject of a sentence; at other times, it is hard to determine if a subject is singular or plural.

Finding the Subject

When you are checking for subject-verb agreement, you can find the real subject of the sentence by first eliminating the prepositional phrases. To find the real subject, put parentheses around the prepositional phrases. Then it is easy to find the subject because nothing in a prepositional phrase is the subject of a sentence.

prepositional phrases in parentheses:

> S   V
> *One* (of my oldest friends) *is* a social worker.

>   S   V
> A *student* (from one)(of the nearby school districts) *is* the winner.

>   S   V
> The *store* (across the street) (from my house) *is* open all night.

> S   V
> *Jim*, (with all his silly jokes), *is* a nice person.

Note: Words and phrases such as *along with, as well as, except, in addition to, including, plus,* and *together with* introduce prepositional phrases. The words that follow them are part of the prepositional phrase and cannot be part of the subject.

>   S   V   V
> My *sister*, (along with her husband), *is planning* a trip to Bolivia.

>   S   V
> Tom's *house*, (as well as his apartment), *is* part of a family inheritance.

Exercise 3   **Finding the Real Subject by Recognizing Prepositional Phrases**

Put parentheses around all the prepositional phrases in the following sentences. Put an *S* above each subject and a *V* above each verb.

1. Two of the people in the car are members of a national racing team.

2. Alberto, along with his parents, is moving to a small town in Nebraska.

3. One of the stars of the popular television series comes from a neighborhood near the old train station.

4. The best of the new employees arrives at the office with an alert look in his eyes.

5. A lawyer for the hospital, in addition to a group of doctors, is meeting about the need for more staff in the emergency room.

6. The story behind my grandfather's escape from Haiti is a tale with many twists and surprises.

7. At night, a security guard with a large German shepherd patrols the area around the secret laboratories.

8. With a superior attitude, the millionaire complains to his driver about the unavoidable traffic delays.

9. Marisol, plus her sister, is renting an apartment near the college.

10. Sugar, as well as caffeine, keeps me awake at night.

Exercise 4 **Selecting the Correct Verb Form by Identifying Prepositional Phrases**

Put parentheses around all the prepositional phrases in the following sentences. Then circle the verb that agrees with the subject.

1. A spokesperson from Volunteers for Animals (is, are) showing a film at the council meeting on Tuesday.

2. Several of the professional football players, plus their coach, (is, are) signing autographs at the Children's Sports Club.

3. One of the women in my music class (has, have) been accepted into a well-known summer program for music students.

4. The runners at the state semifinals (train, trains) for hours in all kinds of weather in hopes of making a name for themselves.

5. A college student with too many credit cards (is, are) taking a chance on his or her financial future.

6. Without a good reason for leaving, my brother, together with his girlfriend, (is, are) moving to Montana.

7. One of the older ladies in the lawn chairs (is, are) a famous soap opera star from Mexico.

8. Associating with constant complainers (turn, turns) even the happiest person into a bundle of gloom.

9. Bill's extensive training, in addition to his kind and sympathetic nature, (make, makes) him the most valued member of the emergency team.

10. A counseling center with family therapists, financial advisors, and employment services (is, are) open to all residents of Cedar Hills.

Changed Word Order

You are probably used to looking for the subject of a sentence in front of the verb, but not all sentences follow this pattern. Questions, sentences beginning with words like *here* or *there*, and other sentences change the word order. So you have to look carefully to check for subject-verb agreement.

         V   S
Where *are* my *friends*?

       V S   V
When *is he going* to work?

                    V   S
Behind the elm trees *stands* a huge *statue*.

       V   S
There *are potholes* in the road.

       V   S
There *is* a *reason* for his impatience.

Exercise 5 **Making Subjects and Verbs Agree in Sentences with Changed Word Order**

In each of the sentences below, underline the subject; then circle the correct verb in parentheses.

1. Here (is, are) an old photograph of your mother and a birthday card from 1999.

2. Where (is, are) my notes from last week's psychology class?

3. Under the trees near my bedroom (was, were) an old wooden bench with peeling paint.

4. There (was, were) moments of anxiety during the plane's emergency landing.

5. Beyond all the family arguments (is, are) fiercely loyal and loving people with hot tempers.

6. There (is, are) a group of investors with an interest in the lakefront property.

7. Here (is, are) the man from the financial aid office and the student activities director.

8. Along the banks of the river (was, were) people with fishing gear and picnicking families.

9. Among the guests at the wedding (was, were) the groom's great uncle from Egypt.

10. Below my apartment (is, are) a basement area with a laundry section and a storage room.

Exercise 6 **More on Making Subjects and Verbs Agree in Sentences With Changed Word Order**

In each sentence below, underline the subject and circle the correct verb in parentheses.

1. Near the old market (is, are) several antique shops and a vegetarian restaurant.

2. After the blizzard, there (was, were) many reports of power outages in the suburbs.

3. Between the supermarket and the drug store (is, are) a new dollar store with many bargains.

4. Inside the package from my sister in Minneapolis (was, were) a box of clothes for my new baby.

5. Where in the world (is, are) my extra set of car keys?

6. Crouched in the high branches of the apple tree (was, were) my adventurous cat.

7. About ten minutes ago, there (was, were) a strange woman and two angry-looking teens near the playground.

8. Beneath Joey's loud and often obnoxious behavior (is, are) a basic shyness and a fear of being found out.

9. Across the street from the apartments (is, are) an old stone house with a crumbling wall.

10. Apart from Alexander's medal for bravery, there (is, are) his athletic and public service awards.

COMPOUND SUBJECTS

A **compound subject** is two or more subjects joined by *and*, *or*, or *nor*. When subjects are joined by *and*, they are usually plural.

S   S V
Jermaine and *Lisa are* bargain hunters.

S   S V
The *house* and the *garden need* attention.

       S   S   V

A *bakery* and a *pharmacy are* down the street.

Caution: Be careful to check for a compound subject when the word order changes.

         V   S   S

There *are* a *bakery* and a *pharmacy* down the street. (Two things, a
    bakery and a *pharmacy, are* down the street.)

         V   S   S

Here *are* a *picture* of your father and a *copy* of his birth certificate. (A
    picture and a *copy,* two things, *are* here.)

When subjects are joined by *or, either . . . or, neither . . . nor, not only . . . but
also,* the verb form agrees with the subject closer to the verb.

                singular S   **plural S, plural V**

Not only the restaurant *manager* but also the *waiters were* pleased
    with the new policy.

             plural S   **singular S, singular V**

Not only the *waiters* but also the restaurant *manager was* pleased
    with the new policy.

          plural S   **singular S, singular V**

Either the *parents* or the *boy walks* the dog every morning.

        singular S   **plural S, plural V**

Either the *boy* or the *parents walk* the dog every morning.

         plural S   **singular S, singular V**

Neither the *tenants* nor the *landlord cares* about the parking
    situation.

        singular S   **plural S, plural V**

Neither the *landlord* nor the *tenants care* about the parking situation.

Exercise 7 **Making Subjects and Verbs Agree: Compound
Subjects**

Circle the correct form of the verb in parentheses in each sentence below.

    1. Jonelle's sense of humor and her ability to forgive (is, are) her
        best qualities.

    2. Not only the kitchen but also the bathrooms (need, needs) remod-
        eling.

    3. Either Christina or Heather (was, were) supposed to call me.

    4. In the back of the bedroom closet there (is, are) a suitcase and an
        overnight bag.

    5. In the morning, either the children or their mother (walk, walks)
        the dog.

    6. Not only the manager but also the employees (was, were) given a
        small bonus.

7. Here (is, are) the lost ticket and the directions to the airport.

8. Neither the old man nor his companions (was, were) able to help us.

9. Either the casserole in the freezer or the leftovers in the refrigerator (is, are) easy to reheat for dinner.

10. Neither a job at a restaurant nor one in a department store (was, were) suitable for a person with a low energy level.

Exercise 8 **More on Making Subjects and Verbs Agree: Compound Subjects**

Circle the correct form of the verb in parentheses in each sentence below.

1. On Tuesdays, neither a party nor other invitations from friends (keep, keeps) me from watching my favorite televsion show.

2. Within days after Hilary's graduation from high school, there (was, were) a death in her family and a crisis at work.

3. Either the people at the front of the line or the man with the tickets (is, are) holding up the process.

4. Here (is, are) a cup of coffee and a bag of doughnuts from the shop on Balsam Street.

5. Perseverance and patience (help, helps) my brother reach his goals.

6. Whenever I cut my hair, neither my mother nor my friends (notice, notices) the difference in my appearance.

7. There (is, are) a cat and three kittens curled up on the front porch.

8. Hours after Thanksgiving dinner, either my brothers or my son (starts, start) checking the refrigerator for the leftovers.

9. Usually, Jim Chang or Terry Lopez (invite, invites) the neighbors to watch the fireworks on the Fourth of July.

10. Not only Mr. Horowitz but also his daughters (love, loves) to walk on the beach.

INDEFINITE PRONOUNS

Certain pronouns that come from a group called **indefinite pronouns** always take a singular verb.

INFO BOX: Indefinite Pronouns

one	nobody	nothing	each
anyone	anybody	anything	either
someone	somebody	something	neither
everyone	everybody	everything	

If you want to write clearly and correctly, you must memorize these words and remember that they always take a singular verb. Using your common sense is not enough because some of these words seem plural: for example, *everybody* seems to mean more than one person, but in grammatically correct English, it takes a singular verb. Here are some examples of the pronouns used with singular verbs:

singular S   **singular V**
Everyone in town *is talking* about the scandal.

singular S   **singular V**
Each of the boys *is* talented.

singular S   **singular V**
One of their biggest concerns *is* crime in the streets.

singular S   **singular V**
Neither of the cats *is* mine.

Hint: You can memorize the indefinite pronouns as the *-one*, *-thing*, and *-body* words (every*one*, every*thing*, every*body*, and so forth) plus *each*, *either*, and *neither*.

Exercise 9   **Making Subjects and Verbs Agree: Using Indefinite Pronouns**

Circle the correct verb in parentheses in each sentence below.

1. Here (is, are) everybody from the citizens' safety committee.

2. One of the most expensive items in the display case (was, were) a diamond bracelet.

3. Anything from the top shelves (need, needs) to be dusted and polished.

4. Nobody in my college classes (bring, brings) a laptop computer to class.

5. (Has, Have) everybody at the store been notified of the new closing hours?

6. Anyone with good mechanical skills (know, knows) how to assemble this bicycle in minutes.

7. Everything in my personal life and at work (seem, seems) to be falling apart at the same time.

8. Somebody (is, are) calling me at all hours of the night.

9. Nothing in that shoe store (cost, costs) less than a hundred dollars.

10. Anybody except a few lucky people at the front of the line (was, were) likely to be denied admission.

Exercise 10   **More on Making Subjects and Verbs Agree: Using Indefinite Pronouns**

Circle the correct verb in parentheses in each sentence below.

1. Everything about science fiction films (fascinate, fascinates) Ian.

2. During the candidate's speech, (was, were) anyone applauding?

3. Behind the bags of garbage, there (was, were) nothing but a rusty old lawn chair.

4. Something about the stranger's explanations (cause, causes) me to doubt her.

5. On Labor Day, everyone in my family (gather, gathers) at my sister's house for the last barbecue of the summer.

6. Neither of Frank's children (has, have) ever been in trouble.

7. Each of Professor Malloy's assignments (require, requires) some research.

8. (Is, Are) someone with problems asking for advice?

9. Either of the digital cameras (meet, meets) your needs.

10. (Was, Were) anybody at the mall last night?

COLLECTIVE NOUNS

Collective nouns refer to more than one person or thing:

team	company	council
class	corporation	government
committee	family	group
audience	jury	crowd

Most of the time, collective nouns take a singular verb.

> **singular S, singular V**
> The *committee is sponsoring* a fundraiser.

> **singular S, singular V**
> The *audience was* impatient.

> **singular S, singular V**
> The *jury has reached* a verdict.

The singular verb is used because the group is sponsoring, or getting impatient, or reaching a verdict, *as one unit.*

Collective nouns take a plural verb only when the members of the group are acting individually, not as a unit.

> The sophomore *class are fighting* among themselves. (The phrase *among themselves* shows that the class is not acting as one unit.)

Exercise 11 **Making Subjects and Verbs Agree: Using Collective Nouns**

Circle the correct verb in parentheses in each sentence below.

1. Every season, the drama club (present, presents) a new play.

2. The board of directors (is, are) studying the plan for expanding the office park.

   3. The audience of proud parents (was, were) thrilled by the graduation ceremonies.

   4. Even when it rains, the loyal crowd at the home games (remain,
   remains) in the stands.

   5. The group from Australia (was, were) touring the Rocky Mountains.

   6. The Recreational Council (approve, approves) next year's budget
   tomorrow.

   7. My botany class (require, requires) work in a campus garden.

   8. An air transport company from Ohio (is, are) opening an office in
   our town.

   9. The family (is, are) moving to a farm near the county line.

   10. The Flower Corporation (offer, offers) health insurance to all full-
   time employees.

MAKING SUBJECTS AND VERBS AGREE: THE BOTTOM LINE

As you have probably realized, making subjects and verbs agree is not as
simple as it first appears. But if you can remember the basic ideas in this
section, you will be able to apply them automatically as you edit your own
writing. Below is a quick summary of subject-verb agreement.

INFO BOX: Making Subjects and Verbs Agree: A Summary

1. Subjects and verbs should agree in number: singular subjects get singular
   verb forms; plural subjects get plural verb forms.

2. When pronouns are used as subjects, they must agree in number with verbs.

3. Nothing in a prepositional phrase can be the subject of the sentence.

4. Questions, sentences beginning with *here* or *there*, and other sentences can
   change word order, making subjects harder to find.

5. Compound subjects joined by *and* are usually plural.

6. When subjects are joined by *or, either . . . or, neither . . . nor*, or *not only
   . . . but also*, the verb form agrees with the subject closest to the verb.

7. Indefinite pronouns always take singular verbs.

8. Collective nouns usually take singular verbs.

Exercise 12   **A Comprehensive Exercise on Subject-Verb
Agreement**

Circle the correct verb form in parentheses in each sentence below.

   1. Not only the clothes in my closet but also my carpet (was, were)
   damaged by the roof leak.

2. Every month, one of the student organizations (sponsor, sponsors) a campus event.

3. Nothing except a box of cookies (was, were) left on the shelf.

4. Sometimes, humility and openness (lead, leads) people to new answers to old questions.

5. Neither the warden nor the prisoners (want, wants) the change in prison policies.

6. Within the city limits (is, are) an all-night restaurant.

7. Each of the witnesses to the accident (tell, tells) a different story.

8. When (was, were) the packages supposed to arrive?

9. Anybody with allergies (know, knows) about sneezing and stuffy noses.

10. One of the cats in the neighborhood (is, are) leaving dead mice on my doorstep.

Exercise 13 **Another Comprehensive Exercise on Subject-Verb Agreement**

Circle the correct verb form in parentheses in each sentence below.

1. Mr. Lee, as well as Sergeant Simms, (belong, belongs) to a motorcycle club.

2. Either my husband or my sisters (has, have) planned a surprise party for my thirty-fifth birthday.

3. Neither of my parents (like, likes) to go out often.

4. When the trees turn red, yellow, and orange, someone (has, have) to rake the leaves.

5. A comfortable routine and a sense of belonging (make, makes) troubled children feel safe.

6. My phone company (is, are) raising my long-distance rates.

7. Whenever a famous case is tried, the jury (is, are) the focus of much television coverage.

8. Around the back of the old shed (is, are) a rusted hoe and an old wheelbarrow.

9. A week ago, there (was, were) a Lexus and a Cadillac parked in front of the abandoned building.

10. Everything at the garage sale (look, looks) fresh, new, and attractive.

 COLLABORATE ▶ **Exercise 14** **Writing Sentences with Subject-Verb Agreement**

With a partner or a group, turn each of the following phrases into a sentence—twice. That is, write two sentences for each phrase. Use a verb that fits, and put the verb in the present tense. Be sure that the verb agrees with the subject.

1. A large bag of rocks _____

_____

A large bag of rocks _____

_____

2. Either cake or ice cream _____

_____

Either cake or ice cream _____

_____

3. The company _____

_____

The company _____

_____

4. Mickey and Minnie _____

_____

Mickey and Minnie _____

_____

5. Everything on the menu _____

_____

Everything on the menu _____

_____

6. Someone on the Crime Prevention Committee _____

_____

Someone on the Crime Prevention Committee _____

_____

7. Not only my friends but also my brother _____

_____

Not only my friends but also my brother _____

_____

8. Anybody from this state _____

_____

Anybody from this state _____

_____

9. One of children's greatest fears _____

_____

One of children's greatest fears _____

_____

10. Neither broccoli nor other green vegetables _____

_____

Neither broccoli nor other green vegetables _____

_____

COLLABORATE ▶   **Exercise 15**   **Create Your Own Text on Subject-Verb Agreement**

Working with a partner or a group, create your own grammar handbook.
Below is a list of rules on subject-verb agreement. Write one sentence that
is an example of each rule. The first one is done for you.

Rule 1: Subjects and verbs should agree in number: singular subjects
get singular verb forms; plural subjects get plural verb forms.

example: A battered old car stands in the front yard. _____

_____

Rule 2: When pronouns are used as subjects, they must agree in number with verbs.

example: _____

_____

Rule 3: Nothing in a prepositional phrase can be the subject of the
sentence.

example: _____

_____

Rule 4: Questions, sentences beginning with *here* or *there*, and other
sentences can change word order, making subjects harder to
find.

example: _____

_____

Rule 5: When subjects are joined by *and*, they are usually plural.

example: _____

_____

Rule 6: When subjects are joined by *or, either . . . or, neither . . . nor,*
or *not only . . . but also*, the verb form agrees with the subject
closest to the verb.

example: _____

_____

Rule 7: Indefinite pronouns always take singular verbs.

example: _____

_____

Rule 8: Collective nouns usually take singular verbs.

example: _____

Exercise 16   **Editing a Paragraph for Errors in Subject-Verb**   ◀ CONNECT ⬭⬭⬭
                 Agreement

Edit the following paragraph by correcting any verbs that do not agree with
their subjects. Write your corrections above the lines. There are eight errors.

There is two keys to understanding my father. As children, neither my sisters

nor I were aware of how much my father's background influenced his beliefs and

behavior. My father's family were from China, and he came to this country as a lit-

tle boy. His parents were strong believers in family unity, so my father was raised

to believe that adult children lived at home until they married. He still cannot be-

lieve that today nearly everyone want to leave home and live independently

before marriage. In addition, my father's family was poor and had to struggle to

make a living. An understanding of those struggles help me to accept the way my

father treats money. Everyone tease him about his obsession with saving and his

love of bargains, but these values comes from his parents. Each time my father

warns me about spending too much money or cautions me about the dangers of

living on my own, he is repeating the lessons his parents taught him. Yet I am from

another generation and another country, so something about my attitudes are

bound to disturb him. As I grow older, I hope my father and I will grow in under-

standing.

Exercise 17   **Editing a Paragraph for Errors in Subject-Verb**   ◀ CONNECT ⬭⬭⬭
                 Agreement

Edit the following paragraph by correcting any verbs that do not agree with
their subjects. Write your corrections above the lines. There are four errors.

Everything in my dresser drawers are such a mess that I can't find the sim-

plest item. For instance, I can't find a pair of socks in my top drawer because it is

too crammed with tee shirts and DVDs. I have no idea how DVDs managed to find

their way to my top drawer, but I am too lazy to move them. My second drawer is

filled with sweaters, photo albums, a broken clock, a softball, several old and

shabby sweat pants, and a pair of scissors. There is a hair dryer and empty boxes

in the third drawer. The bottom drawer looks a little like a medicine cabinet: it is filled with aspirin, shaving cream, ratty old hairbrushes, a box of tissues, and half-empty shampoo bottles. This drawer would seem to be logically organized, but the group of drug store items share the space. As if to trick me, underwear and sneakers have also stashed themselves in that drawer. Either a team of clever objects are sneaking into my dresser at night, or I am an extremely disorganized person.

Chapter Test: Making Subjects and Verbs Agree

Some of the sentences below are correct; others have errors in making subjects and verbs agree. Put an *X* next to the sentences with errors.

1. _____ Each of the puppies in the basket have a different kind of bark.

2. _____ After the movie started, the audience was fascinated by the mysterious events on the screen.

3. _____ Where is your friends when you are in trouble?

4. _____ Either my salary or your overtime payments has to be used to cover the cost of our hospital bills.

5. _____ At the end of the road by the big palm trees is a house with a red roof.

6. _____ Not only the living room walls but also the front door needs a fresh coat of paint.

7. _____ Everyone in Mrs. Collins' classes are hoping for her speedy recovery from pneumonia.

8. _____ After Lewis returned home from Iraq, there was a block party in his neighborhood and a celebration at the veterans' hall.

9. _____ I have to take my car to an auto mechanic; something seems to be wrong with the brakes.

10. _____ Neither of the new discount stores have fashionable clothes for big and tall men.

CHAPTER 25
Using Pronouns Correctly: Agreement and Reference

NOUNS AND PRONOUNS

Nouns are the names of persons, places, or things.

> *Jack* is a good friend. (*Jack* is the name of a person.)
> The band is from *Orlando*. (*Orlando* is the name of a place.)
> I hated the *movie*. (*Movie* is the name of a thing.)

Pronouns are words that substitute for nouns. A pronoun's **antecedent** is the word or word it replaces.

>   **antecedent**   **pronoun**
> *Jack* is a good friend; *he* is very loyal.

>   **antecedent**   **pronoun**
> I hated *the movie* because *it was* too violent.

>   **antecedent**   **pronoun**
> *Playing tennis* was fun, but *it* started to take up too much of my time.

>   **antecedent**   **pronoun**
> *Mike and Michelle* are sure *they* are in love.

>   **antecedent**   **pronoun**
> *Sharon* gave away *her* old clothes.

>   **antecedent** **pronoun**
> *The dog* rattled *its* dish, begging for dinner.

Exercise 1 **Identifying the Antecedents of Pronouns**

Underline the word or words that are the antecedent of the italicized pronoun in each sentence below.

1. Tommy and I will buy some new clothes when *we* go to the mall.

2. Taking a short nap can be good for you; *it* renews your energy for the rest of the day.

3. Your brothers have finally cleaned *their* bedroom.

4. The restaurant raised *its* prices during the summer.

5. Lisa, do *you* want to go to the basketball game?

6. Gregory won't get anywhere without finishing *his* education.

7. My mother loves dancing, but my father hates *it*.

8. I went to see a counselor before I registered for classes, and *she* helped me plan my schedule.

9. My nephews are going to the zoo tomorrow; *they* are very excited.

10. A healthy breakfast is important for weight watchers because *it* can prevent a craving for mid-morning doughnuts and other unhealthy snacks.

AGREEMENT OF A PRONOUN AND ITS ANTECEDENT

A pronoun must agree in number with its antecedent. If the antecedent is singular, the pronoun must be singular. If the antecedent is plural, then the pronoun must be plural.

singular antecedent   **singular pronoun**
Susan tried to arrive on time, but *she* got caught in traffic.

plural antecedent   **plural pronoun**
Susan and Ray tried to arrive on time, but *they* got caught in traffic.

plural antecedent   **plural pronoun**
The visitors tried to arrive on time, but *they* got caught in traffic.

Agreement of pronoun and antecedent seems fairly simple. If an antecedent is singular, use a singular pronoun. If an antecedent is plural, use a plural pronoun. There are, however, some special problems with agreement of pronouns, and these problems will come up in your writing. If you become familiar with the explanations, examples, and exercises that follow, you will be ready to handle the special problems.

INDEFINITE PRONOUNS

Certain words called **indefinite pronouns** always take a singular verb. Therefore, if one of these indefinite pronouns is the antecedent, the pronoun that replaces it must be singular. Here are the indefinite pronouns:

> **INFOBOX: Indefinite Pronouns**
>
> | | | | |
> |---|---|---|---|
> | one | nobody | nothing | each |
> | anyone | anybody | anything | either |
> | someone | somebody | something | neither |
> | everyone | everybody | everything | |

You may think that *everybody* is plural, but in grammatically correct English, it is a singular word. Therefore, if you want to write clearly and correctly, memorize these words as the *-one*, *-thing*, and *-body* words: every*one*, every*thing*, every*body*, and so on, plus *each*, *either*, and *neither*. If any of these words is an antecedent, the pronoun that refers to it is singular.

singular antecedent   **singular pronoun**
Each of the Boy Scouts received *his* merit badge.

singular antecedent   **singular pronoun**
Everyone in the sorority donated *her* time to the project.

Avoiding Sexism

Consider this sentence:

Everybody in the math class brought _____ own calculator.

How do you choose the correct pronoun to fill in the blank? If everybody in the class is male, you can write

Everybody in the math class brought *his* own calculator.

Or if everybody in the class is female, you can write

Everybody in the math class brought *her* own calculator.

Or if the class has students of both sexes, you can write

Everybody in the math class brought *his or her* own calculator.

In the past, most writers used the pronoun *his* to refer to both men and women. Today, many writers try to use *his or her* to avoid sexual bias. If you find using *his or her* is getting awkward or repetitive, you can rewrite the sentence and make the antecedent plural:

correct: *The students* in the math class brought *their* own calculators.

But you cannot shift from singular to plural:

incorrect: ~~Everybody in the math class brought their own calculators.~~

Exercise 2   **Making Pronouns and Antecedents Agree**

Write the appropriate pronoun in the blank in each sentence below. Look carefully for the antecedent before you choose the pronoun.

1. Adnan bought a new car; _____ is a Ford Mustang.

2. Each of the brothers brought _____ wife to the family reunion.

3. Everyone chosen for the Girls' Chorus has earned _____ place through years of training and performing.

4. Either of the men from the antiques exhibit will give _____ honest appraisal of your grandmother's china vase.

5. A young girl with an unhappy home life may rely on _____ friends for guidance and comfort.

6. Once my little nephew began to talk, _____ never stopped.

7. All of the students in my night class rush to school from _____ daytime jobs.

8. I don't know whether the woman sitting on the stairs is catching _____ breath or needs help.

9. The residents of Pine View apartments have experienced many problems with mold and mildew;_____ are taking legal action against the building's owners.

10. The sweater was warm and comfortable, so I bought _____ .

Exercise 3 **More on Making Pronouns and Antecedents Agree**

Write the appropriate pronoun in the blank in each sentence below. Look carefully for the antecedent before you choose the pronoun.

1. Either of the women can use _____ knowledge of Portuguese to translate the document.

2. Nothing in the jewelry display case looked as if _____ would please my girlfriend.

3. Maybe somebody from the boys' team lost _____catcher's mitt.

4. After I argued with my best friend, everything at the fancy dinner

   lost _____ magic.

5. All the children demanded _____ surprise after they had behaved so well during dinner.

6. One of the climbing roses grew so high that _____ reached the roof.

7. In the summer, Al and Doug spend _____ weekends working in the yard.

8. Everyone in the Women's Action League gives hours of _____ time to helping the homeless.

9. During the men's soccer game, one of the most popular players lost _____ temper and shouted at one of the referees.

10. For Hank's birthday, you can give him anything connected to cars; he will love _____ .

COLLECTIVE NOUNS

Collective nouns refer to more than one person or thing:

team	company	council
class	corporation	government
committee	family	group
audience	jury	crowd

Most of the time, collective nouns take a singular pronoun.

collective noun   singular pronoun
The *team* that was ahead in the playoffs lost *its* home game.

collective noun   singular pronoun
The *corporation* changed *its* policy on parental leave.

Collective nouns are usually singular because the group is losing a game or changing a policy as one, as a unit. Collective nouns take a plural pronoun only when the members of the group are acting individually, not as a unit.

The *class* picked up *their* class rings this morning. (The members of the class pick up their rings individually.)

Exercise 4   **Making Pronouns and Antecedents Agree: Collective Nouns**

Circle the correct pronoun in each sentence below.

1. The chief executive office was confident that the company could maintain (its, their) reputation for quality products.

2. When the star player lost another opportunity to score, the crowd expressed (its, their) displeasure.

3. The rebel army started to fall apart when the leaders argued among (itself, themselves).

4. Several of the teams held a news conference about (its, their) new drug policy.

5. Ryan is cancelling his contract with the Wireless Connection Corporation because of (its, their) hidden fees.

6. Whenever the club meets, one of (its, their) members brings coffee and cake.

7. Yesterday, a family in my neighborhood found (its, their) dog after the animal had been lost for a month.

8. When the judge called for silence, the jury announced (its, their) verdict.

9. The gang of friends from middle school lost contact when (its, their) hangout, the old pizza parlor, was destroyed in a fire.

10. Sometimes I think the leaders of our local government lost (its, their) common sense a long time ago.

 COLLABORATE ▶   Exercise 5   **Writing Sentences with Pronoun-Antecedent Agreement**

With a partner or a group, write a sentence for each pair of words below, using each pair as a pronoun and its antecedent. The first pair is done for you.

1. women . . . their

     sentence: <u>Women who work outside the home have to plan their time</u>

     <u>carefully.</u>

2. family . . . its

     sentence: _____

     _____

3. anybody . . . his or her

     sentence: _____

     _____

4. drivers . . . they

     sentence: _____

     _____

5. security . . . it

     sentence: _____

     _____

6. either . . . her

     sentence: _____

     _____

7. everybody . . . his or her

     sentence: _____

     _____

8. America . . . it

     sentence: _____

     _____

9. music videos . . . they

sentence: _____

_____

10. Identity theft . . . it

sentence: _____

_____

Exercise 6 **Editing a Paragraph for Errors in Pronoun-Antecedent Agreement** ◀ CONNECT ⬭⬭

Read the following paragraph carefully, looking for errors in agreement of pronouns and their antecedents. Cross out each pronoun that does not agree with its antecedent and write the correct pronoun above it. There are seven pronouns that need correcting.

What began with a simple question has turned into a long battle with the Family Pharmacy Company. It started when my grandmother received a bill from the company. The mail-order prescription service told her that she owed them for two months' worth of her heart medication. Since I take care of my grandmother and help her pay her bills, I knew that she had sent the company a check when she had sent them her order. My grandmother was very upset about this bill because it included a warning that the company would drop her from their mail-order service if she didn't pay her bills on time. Of course, I called the Family Pharmacy Company, and a representative calmed me down. He told me that he couldn't explain the bill but said I should wait a few days until the accounting department could investigate. I waited a few days and called again. Another representative told me to wait because he was sure the company would update their accounts soon. A week later, my grandmother received another incorrect bill. After five calls to the company, I still cannot get a straight answer. I am not sure whether they lost my grandmother's file or they lost their integrity. Either way, my grandmother has lost a way to buy prescription drugs at a discount.

☐☐☐ CONNECT ▶ (Exercise 7) **Editing a Paragraph for Errors in Pronoun-Antecedent Agreement**

Read the following paragraph carefully, looking for errors in agreement of pronouns and their antecedents. Cross out each pronoun that does not agree with its antecedent and write the correct pronoun above it. There are six pronouns that need correcting.

My English class had an adventure yesterday. As the students sat, quietly working on revising their drafts, one girl shrieked with terror. "A mouse!" she cried. "It's under my desk!" Immediately, everybody in the room jumped on their chair. Soon somebody in the back of the room swore they saw a large mouse, maybe even a rat, running along the baseboard. This new sighting brought more excitement. "Does anybody have a box or a book bag?" asked one resourceful student. "Somebody could empty the box or bag. Then they could use it to trap the mouse." Just as this suggestion was made, the mouse decided to make another dash around the room. Now everybody snatched their belongings off the floor so the rodent would not hide in them. Nobody knew what to do. Even our instructor was left without a way to restore order. Let's finish class early today," he said. We all filed cautiously out of the room. No one considered the class that comes after ours. They would have to deal with the mouse on their own.

PRONOUNS AND THEIR ANTECEDENTS: BEING CLEAR

Remember that pronouns are words that replace or refer to other words, and the words that are replaced or referred to are antecedents.

Make sure that a pronoun has one clear antecedent. Your writing will be vague and confusing if a pronoun appears to refer to more than one antecedent or if it doesn't have any specific antecedent to refer to. In grammar, such confusing language is called a problem with *reference of pronouns.*

When a pronoun refers to more than one thing, the sentence becomes confusing or silly. The following are examples of unclear reference:

Jim told Leonard his bike had been stolen. (Whose bike was stolen? Jim's? Leonard's?)
She put the cake on the table, took off her apron, pulled up a chair, and began to eat it. (What did she eat? The cake? The table? Her apron? The chair?)

If there is no one clear antecedent, you must rewrite the sentence to make the reference clear. Sometimes the rewritten sentence may seem repetitive, but a little repetition is better than a lot of confusion.

> **unclear:** Jim told Leonard his bike had been stolen.
> **clear:** Jim told Leonard Jim's bike had been stolen.
> **clear:** Jim told Leonard, "My bike has been stolen."
> **clear:** Jim told Leonard Leonard's bike had been stolen.
> **clear:** Jim told Leonard, "Your bike has been stolen."

> **unclear:** She put the cake on the table, took off her apron, pulled up a chair, and began to eat it.
> **clear:** She put the cake on the table, took off her apron, pulled up a chair, and began to eat the cake.

Sometimes the problem is a little more tricky. Can you spot what's wrong with this sentence?

> **unclear:** Bill decided to take a part-time job which worried his parents. (What worried Bill's parents? His decision to work part-time? Or the job itself?)

Be very careful with the pronoun *which*. If there is any chance that using *which* will confuse the reader, rewrite the sentence and get rid of *which*.

> **clear:** Bill's parents were worried about the kind of part-time job he chose.
> **clear:** Bill's decision to work part-time worried his parents.

Sometimes, a pronoun has nothing to refer to; it has no antecedent.

> **no antecedent:** When Bill got to the train station, they said the train was going to be late. (Who said the train was going to be late? The ticket agents? Strangers Bill met on the tracks?)
> **no antecedent:** Maria has always loved medicine and has decided that's what she wants to be. (What does "that" refer to? The only word it could refer to is "medicine," but Maria certainly doesn't want to be a medicine. She doesn't want to be an aspirin or a cough drop.)

If a pronoun lacks an antecedent, add an antecedent or get rid of the pronoun.

> **add an antecedent:** When Bill got to the train station and asked the ticket agents about the schedule, they said the train was going to be late. ("They" refers to the ticket agents.)
> **drop the pronoun:** Maria has always loved medicine and has decided she wants to be a physician.

Note: To check for clear reference of pronouns, underline any pronoun that may not be clear. Then try to draw a line from that pronoun to its antecedent. Are there two or more possible antecedents? Is there no antecedent? In either case, you need to rewrite.

(**Exercise 8**)   **Rewriting Sentences for Clear Reference of Pronouns**

Rewrite the following sentences so that the pronouns have clear references. You may add, take out, or change words.

1. Suzanne complained to Maggie about her money problems.

2. I love eating breakfast at Montana's; they have the best omelets.

3. After the wedding, Harry heard some gossip which amazed him.

4. Sometimes, older children may resent younger ones because they want all the attention.

5. Patrick has watched stock car racing since he was four years old, and that's what he wants to be.

6. I would never want to live in Diamond Hills; all they care about is money.

7. Mrs. Chang told Mrs. O'Brien that her dog was digging in the flower beds.

8. Nick's car hit a tree, but it wasn't badly damaged.

9. When I was little, they always told me to eat everything on my plate at dinner.

10. Yasmin regretted her choice of a career, which was foolish.

 CONNECT ▶   **Exercise 9**   **Editing a Paragraph for Errors in Pronoun Agreement and Reference**

Correct any errors in pronoun agreement or reference in the following paragraph. There are seven errors. Write your corrections above the line.

    After I took my six-year-old cousin to the movies, I realized that his age group and mine are similar in their reactions to a film and their behavior in the theater. One Saturday, I was asked to babysit my cousin Luke, so I took him to one of those popular, computer-animated films full of action figures. The place was full of children, and whenever one action figure aimed a laser gun at another, everybody screamed their approval. At other times, one of the smaller and sweeter action figures were in great danger, and I could hear crying among the smaller children. Although the movie was filled with excitement, the children became bored. They climbed on and over their seats, talked to one another, and even ran up and down the aisles. By the end of the afternoon, I longed to be in a theater with people of my own age, young adults. Then I began to realize that my own age group exhibits their own version of childhood behavior in a movie theater. Young adults have been known to cheer at exciting scenes. In addition, neither the child group nor the young adult group can control their emotions during a sad or suspenseful moment. Just like children, adults can become bored. Nobody in a young adult audience climbs over their chair, but young adults have been known to put their feet on the chairs in front of them when they are uncomfortable. Like children, young adults make noise during movies. They laugh loudly and even carry on conversations. They walk up and down the aisles to find their friends or to escape a boring part of the movie. A group of young adults in front of a movie screen soon loses their adult status.

Exercise 10   **Editing a Paragraph for Errors in Pronoun Agreement and Reference**   ◀ CONNECT ⊂⊃⊃

Correct any errors in pronoun agreement or reference in the following paragraph. There are seven errors. Write your corrections above the line.

My first day at a new school began as a frightening experience for an eight-year-old. My family had just moved from the city to the suburbs, and I faced the challenge of being the new student at mid-year when all the other students had made friends. As soon as my new teacher brought me into the classroom, they stared at me blankly. I sat at an empty desk, and nobody on either side of me turned their head to smile. I felt that everybody had already formed their opinion of me and saw me as uninteresting. Possibly, nobody cared enough to waste their time looking at me. At lunch, my teacher was kind enough to lead me to a table full of classmates, but I was too shy to start a conversation. The group at the table went on with their lunchtime rituals of laughing and joking. When the bell rang and we filed back into the classroom, I wondered if anybody would ever want me for their friend. Suddenly, someone behind me pushed me hard. It was a boy with curly black hair and a wide grin. I saw it and pushed him back. At that moment, a friendship began.

Chapter Test: Using Pronouns Correctly: Agreement and Reference

Some of the sentences below are correct; others have errors in pronoun agreement or reference. Put an X next to the sentences with errors.

1. _____ I love going to Hawaii; they are so friendly and warm.

2. _____ Has somebody in our health class lost their wallet?

3. _____ Nothing in the men's clothing stores looked as if it would fit my husband.

4. _____ Sunshine Airlines is changing its policy on carry-on luggage.

5. _____ Neither of my friends attended their high school graduation ceremony.

6. _____ Yesterday I finished a project which my supervisor liked.

7. _____ Everything about the mountains lost its meaning for me after the tragic accident.

8. _____ Julio has always enjoyed helping train dogs, and now he is going to be one.

9. _____ Anyone in my family can recall his or her first visit to Uncle Samuel's farm.

10. _____ A woman on the bus told Tara she had just missed her stop.

CHAPTER 26
Using Pronouns Correctly: Consistency and Case

When you write, you write from a point of view, and each point of view gets its own form. If you write from the first-person point of view, your pronouns are in the *I* (singular) or *we* (plural) forms. If you write from the second-person point of view, your pronouns are in the *you* form, whether they are singular or plural. If you write from the third-person point of view, your pronouns are in the *he, she,* or *it* (singular) or *they* (plural) forms.

Different kinds of writing may require different points of view. When you are writing a set of directions, for example, you may use the second-person (*you*) point of view. An essay about your childhood may use the first-person (*I*) point of view.

Whatever point of view you use, be consistent in using pronouns. That is, you should not shift the form of your pronouns without some good reason.

not consistent: Every time *I* go to that mall, the parking lot is so crowded *you* have to drive around for hours, looking for a parking space.

consistent: Every time *I* go to that mall, the parking lot is so crowded *I* have to drive around for hours, looking for a parking space.

Exercise 1   **Consistency in Pronouns**

Correct any inconsistency in point of view in the sentences below. Cross out the incorrect pronoun and write the correct one above it.

1. The first time I met Lila, I recognized her as the kind of person who can be trusted to respect ~~your~~ deepest beliefs and support my most difficult decisions.

2. When my brother and I flew to Houston last week, we were surprised when the flight attendants served us soft drinks but didn't offer ~~you~~ anything to eat, not even a tiny bag of pretzels.

3. After I get my hair cut at Hair Designs, I can see the difference a good haircut makes in ~~your~~ appearance.

4. Randall is always going on a diet and complaining about his weight, but he fails to realize that ~~you~~ should exercise as well as diet in order to stay fit.

5. My sisters rarely ask my mother for a favor, because she won't agree to help without giving ~~you~~ a lecture about personal responsibility.

6. Andrew likes to eat at Caribbean Kitchen because ~~you~~ can always get fresh fish there.

7. Teenagers starting their first job should be careful about punctuality; if a supervisor sees ~~you~~ come in late, they will be regarded as unreliable.

8. I sometimes struggle to control my temper and remain calm when I have to deal with the kind of customer who criticizes everything ~~you~~ do.

9. After hundreds of elderly people have waited outside for an hour or more, someone with a clipboard announces that ~~you~~ will have to return another day when more flu vaccine becomes available.

10. Running has become a passion for me; it can give ~~you~~ a kind of exhilaration that I can't find anywhere else.

Exercise 2 **Correcting Sentences with Consistency Problems**

Rewrite the following sentences, correcting any errors in consistency of pronouns. To make the corrections, you may have to change, add, or take out words.

1. If a grandparent wants to get closer to a grandchild, you shouldn't be overly critical of the child.

   rewrite: _____

   _____

2. My favorite class in high school was studio art; you could work on your own without having to listen to a teacher.

   rewrite: _____

   _____

3. Some people can sell almost anything if you know how to appeal to a customer's emotional needs.

   rewrite: _____

   _____

4. I won't let Aunt Olivia cook dinner for me anymore because she always feeds you some food I can't identify.

   rewrite: _____

   _____

5. Al enjoys being in a crowd; he likes the noise of excited people, the press of people pushing you forward, and the sense of belonging to something powerful.

   rewrite: _____

   _____

   _____

6. Residents who have never visited the museum should go; you will be impressed by the modern photography exhibits.

   rewrite: _____

   _____

7. Raymond and I have no influence with our mother; once she's made up her mind, you can't convince her to change it.

   rewrite: _____

   _____

8. Children applying for admission to the Lincoln Child Care Center will be considered only if you are a resident of Owen County.

   rewrite: _____

   _____

9. You can see the kindness in Dr. Noda's eyes whenever he tutors us in biology.

   rewrite: _____

   _____

10. Unless a young person is willing to work at two jobs and keep to a tight budget, you will never be able to buy your own home in this area.

    rewrite: _____

    _____

    _____

CHOOSING THE CASE OF PRONOUNS

Pronouns have forms that show number and person, and they also have forms that show **case.**

Singular Pronouns	Subjective Case	Objective Case	Possessive Case
1st person	I	me	my
2nd person	you	you	your
3rd person	he, she, it	him, her, it	his, her, its
	who, whoever	whom, whomever	whose
Plural Pronouns			
1st person	we	us	our
2nd person	you	you	your
3rd person	they	them	their
	who, whoever	whom, whomever	whose

The rules for choosing the case of pronouns are simple:

1. When a pronoun is used as a subject, use the subjective case.
2. When a pronoun is used as the object of a verb or the object of a preposition, use the objective case.
3. When a pronoun is used to show ownership, use the possessive case.

   pronouns used as subjects:
   He practices his pitching every day.
   Bill painted the walls, and *we* polished the floors.
   Who is making that noise?

   pronouns used as objects:
   Ernestine called *him* yesterday.
   He gave all his money to *me.*
   With *whom* did you argue?

   pronouns used to show possession:
   I am worried about *my* grade in Spanish.
   The nightclub has lost *its* popularity.
   I wonder *whose* dog this is.

Pronoun Case in a Related Group of Words

You need to be careful in choosing case when the pronoun is part of a related group of words. If the pronoun is part of a related group of words, isolate the pronoun. Next, try out the pronoun choices. Then decide which pronoun is correct and write the correct sentence. For example, which of these sentences is correct?

> Aunt Sophie planned a big dinner for Tom and *I*.

> or

> Aunt Sophie planned a big dinner for Tom and *me*.

Step 1: Isolate the pronoun. Eliminate the related words *Tom and*.
Step 2: Try each case:

> Aunt Sophie planned a big dinner for *I*.

> or

> Aunt Sophie planned a big dinner for *me*.

Step 3: The correct sentence is

> Aunt Sophie planned a big dinner for Tom and me.

The pronoun acts as an object, so it takes the objective case.

Try working through the steps once more to be sure that you understand this principle. Which of the following sentences is correct?

> Last week, *me* and my friend took a ride on the new commuter train.

> or

> Last week, *I* and my friend took a ride on the new commuter train.

Step 1: Isolate the pronoun. Eliminate the related words *and my friend*.
Step 2: Try each case:

> Last week, *me* took a ride on the new commuter train.

> or

> Last week, *I* took a ride on the new commuter train.

Step 3: The correct sentence is

> Last week, I and my friend took a ride on the new commuter train.

The pronoun acts as a subject, so it takes the subjective case.

Note: You can also write it this way:

Last week my friend and I took a ride on the new commuter train.

COMMON ERRORS WITH CASE OF PRONOUNS

Be careful to avoid these common errors:

1. *Between* is a preposition, so the pronouns that follow it are objects of the preposition: between *us*, between *them*, between *you and me*. It is never correct to write *between you and I*.

not this: ~~The plans for the surprise party must be kept a secret between you and I.~~
but this: The plans for the surprise party must be kept a secret between you and me.

2. Never use *myself* as a replacement for *I* or *me*.

not this: ~~My father and myself want to thank you for this honor.~~
but this: My father and I want to thank you for this honor.

not this: ~~She thought the prize should be awarded to Arthur and myself.~~
but this: She thought the prize should be awarded to Arthur and me.

3. The possessive pronoun *its* has no apostrophe.

not this: ~~The car held it's value.~~
but this: The car held its value.

not this: ~~The baby bird had fallen from it's nest.~~
but this: The baby bird had fallen from its nest.

4. Pronouns that complete comparisons can be in the subjective, objective, or possessive case.

subjective: Christa speaks better than *I*.
objective: The storm hurt Manny more than *her*.
possessive: My car is as fast as *his*.

Note: To decide on the correct pronoun, add the words that complete the comparison and say them aloud:

Christa speaks better than I *speak*.
The storm hurt Manny more than *the storm hurt* her.
My car is as fast as his *car*.

5. *Who* and *whoever* are in the subjective case. *Whom* and *whomever* are in the objective case.

subjective: *Who* came to the house?
subjective: *Whoever* wants the books can take them.
objective: *Whom* did Larry bring to the house?
objective: You can bring *whomever* you like to the house.

Note: If you have trouble choosing between *who* and *whom*, or *whoever* and *whomever*, substitute *he* for *who* and *whoever*, and substitute *him* for *whom* and *whomever* to check the correctness of your choice.
Check this sentence:

Who made the cake?

Is it correct? Change the sentence, substituting *he* in one version, and *him* in another version. To make your choice easier, write the sentence as a statement, not a question:

He made the cake.
Him made the cake.

If *he* is correct, then *who* is correct.

Check another sentence:

With whom are you arguing?

Is it correct? Change the sentence, substituting *he* in one version and *him* in another version. To make your choice simpler, write the sentence as a statement, not a question:

You are arguing with *he*.
You are arguing with *him*.

If *him* is correct, then *whom* is correct.

Exercise 3   **Choosing the Right Case of Pronoun**

Circle the correct pronoun in parentheses in each of the following sentences.

1. Another customer and (we, us) reached for the last sale-priced computer at the same time.

2. The vice president of the eastern branch of the insurance company praised the assistant manager and (me, myself) for our productivity.

3. Even with new owners, the restaurant can't get rid of (its, it's) reputation for bad food at expensive prices.

4. (Who, Whom) in the world is sending Casey flowers?

5. Just remember that you have to keep this information strictly between you and (I, me), or we'll both be in trouble.

6. After the snow fell, Tony and (he, him) ran outside to make snowballs.

7. Graham makes a good living, but his sister is better at managing her money than (he, him).

8. Lou has an elegant new apartment, but your apartment is more comfortable than (him, his, he).

9. I will be happy with (whoever, whomever) you choose for the job.

10. My cousins and (I, myself) are exploring the possibility of opening a small restaurant near campus.

Exercise 4   **More on Choosing the Right Case of Pronoun**

Circle the correct pronoun in parentheses in each of the following sentences.

1. (I, Me) and my brother never wake up early on the weekends.

2. (Who, Whom) were you talking about when I came in the door?

3. Yesterday I spent three hours working on a class project with Bobby and (she, her); today they are going to finish it.

4. A strange cat has found (its, it's) way into my garage and is sleeping on a pile of old towels.

5. The price of admission to the new club was a shock to my friends and (I, me).

6. You and Jerry may be brothers, but your sense of humor is different from (him, his).

7. Lieutenant James Okara has excellent leadership skills, but Lieutenant Jan Van Devere inspires just as much loyalty as (he, him).

8. Once I found a job and was able to afford my own place, life began to look brighter for my baby son and (I, me).

9. When my parents sold their house, they divided their old furniture between my brother and (me, myself).

10. (He, Him) and Dr. Lindstrom are advising my mother to have the heart surgery as soon as possible.

 COLLABORATE ▶   **Exercise 5**   **Write Your Own Text on Pronoun Case**

With a partner or with a group, write two sentences that could be used as examples for each of the following rules. The first one is done for you.

Rule 1: When a pronoun is used as a subject, use the subjective case.

examples: He complained about the noise in the street.

Tired and hungry, they stopped for lunch.

Rule 2: When a pronoun is used as the object of a verb or the object of a preposition, use the objective case.

examples: _____

_____

Rule 3: When a pronoun is used to show ownership, use the possessive case.

examples: _____

_____

Rule 4: When a pronoun is part of a related group of words, isolate the pronoun to choose the case. (For examples, write two sentences in which the pronoun is part of a related group of words.)

examples: _____

_____

 CONNECT ▶   **Exercise 6**   **Editing a Paragraph for Errors in Pronoun Consistency and Case**

In the following paragraph, correct any errors in pronoun consistency and case. There are seven errors. Write your corrections above the line.

Malcolm loves movies, but lately he has been having a hard time finding a place to see them. Malcolm stopped going to the Palace Theater because every time he goes there, you can't find a seat anywhere except the first two rows. Sometimes he goes to the Movie Six Theater near the mall; it's part of a discount movie chain, so the tickets are cheap. However, Malcolm doesn't really like that theater because they show only second-run movies, movies that have already played at more expensive theaters. Malcolm likes the low price, but he also likes to see movies as soon as they come out, so he goes to the Movie Six only as a last resort. He misses the old Starburst Theater that was near his house. It had the latest films and was rarely crowded. Unfortunately, it closed it's doors last month. Malcolm lost his favorite movie house, but I am luckier than him. I live close to a small theater that shows first-run films and has plenty of empty seats. I am going to start inviting Malcolm to the movies near my house. There will be plenty of good seats for myself and him. In addition, me and him can enjoy the newest films together.

> **Exercise 7**   **Editing a Paragraph for Errors in Pronoun Consistency and Case**   ◀ CONNECT ⬤⬤⬤

In the following paragraph, correct any errors in pronoun consistency and case. There are seven errors. Write your corrections above the line.

Last month, the vice president of the Volunteers for Safe Streets Club asked Arthur Sansovino and myself to prepare a report on the group's financial assets and on it's future needs. The work of the report was divided between Arthur and I so that both aspects of the report are covered adequately. Arthur's most important finding is that this year's financial statement is better than last year. This year, Volunteers for Safe Streets has a balance of $1,250 in the treasury, with no bills left to be paid. However, my research uncovered a need for more money, especially if the club wants to expand its education program for children and expand the nighttime patrols. Clearly, us members of the club know that working for safe streets is a continuing challenge. In studying the club's future needs, I have learned that it is difficult for an organization to collect donations when people

don't know you. Therefore, I believe that next year the club should work on be-

coming better known in the community. To end this summary, I want to say that

Arthur and me welcome any questions and will be distributing copies of our com-

plete report.

Chapter Test: Using Pronouns Correctly: Consistency and Case

Some of the sentences below are correct; others have errors in pronoun consistency or case. Put an *X* next to the sentences with errors.

1. _____ I was not my father's favorite child; he always praised my sister Denise more than I.

2. _____ After the storm, volunteer emergency workers gave food and water to my son and me.

3. _____ Cameron has stopped going to the gym because they don't keep it clean.

4. _____ For Gregory and I, learning to scuba dive was a new experience.

5. _____ On behalf of my parents and myself, I want to thank everybody who planned this special dinner.

6. _____ You can go to the game with whoever you want; I don't care.

7. _____ Nobody's excuse for missing class is more ridiculous than his.

8. _____ In the winter in Minnesota, the snowstorms can be so fierce that you can't see anything in front of your face.

9. _____ I and the police officers ran toward the car that had flipped into the canal.

10. _____ Whom did you ask to make the transportation arrangements?

CHAPTER 27
Punctuation: The Period and the Question Mark

THE PERIOD

Periods are used two ways.

1. Use a period to mark the end of a sentence that makes a statement.

   We invited him to dinner at our house.
   When Richard spoke, no one paid attention.

2. Use a period after abbreviations.

   Mr. Ryan
   James Wing, Sr.
   10:00 P.M.

Note: If a sentence ends with a period marking an abbreviation, do not add a second period.

Exercise 1 **Using Periods**

Add periods where they are needed in each of the following sentences.

1. Oscar bought about fifteen lbs of special food for his sick terrier

2. When the elementary schoolchildren went on field trips, they were nervous around people like Mr Carlson, the principal

3. Isaac wants to get a BS degree in biology, and his friend, Dr Hamilton, told him to prepare by taking many science classes in high school

4. Tell Ms Marko or Mr Scanlon about the parking problems in the gymnasium parking lot.

5. Last night I studied for my social sciences test until nearly 2:00 AM

6. Nicholas Anderson, Sr, is a better businessman than his son

7. Someday, I want to be known as Cecilia Knowles, RN, so I am going to college to study nursing.

8. We had a traditional Thanksgiving dinner with turkey, stuffing, cranberry sauce, pumpkin pie, etc, at my mother's house

9. After Sgt Albury left the scene, people crowded around the yellow tape to see what was left of the burned car.

10. You could have asked Aunt Maya to visit us next September

THE QUESTION MARK

Use a question mark after a direct question.

Isn't she adorable?
Do you have car insurance?

If a question is not a direct question, it does not get a question mark.

They asked if I thought their grandchild was adorable.
She questioned whether I had car insurance.

Exercise 2 **Punctuating with Periods and Question Marks**

Add any missing periods and question marks to each sentence below.

1. Fred asked me if I would drive to St Louis with him

2. Have the painters finished the bathroom walls yet

3. Leonard wanted to find out whether his old girlfriend was still single

4. Is it possible that the people in the house next door have gone away for good

5. Maybe you can tell me when Mr Lynch is arriving at the airport

6. If Javier goes to Dr Nair for the surgery, Javier will be in the hands of an experienced surgeon

7. Wasn't that a terrible experience

8. Annabel wanted to know why the cat loved to scratch the rough wood of the picnic table

9. Can anyone tell me where Ms Harris meets her 2:00 PM class

10. There is some question about the exact time of the incident

Exercise 3   **More on Punctuating with Periods
and Question Marks**

Add any missing periods or question marks to each sentence below.

1. Are the people upstairs moving out of their apartment

2. Have you ever thought about getting a B A in graphic design

3. Two of my friends have been asking me about my plans for semester break

4. Were there any good-looking men sitting in the food court

5. I'm not certain that the meeting will take place as scheduled

6. How has the old school changed since you graduated ten years ago

7. Don't you think 6:00 A M is a little early to start driving to Tallahassee

8. Is it possible that Mrs Mikulski forgot to lock the front door

9. I wonder why you never call me on Saturdays

10. The supervisors questioned whether Miss Chen would want to leave a secure, high-level position for a potentially better but risky one

Exercise 4   **Editing a Paragraph for Errors in Periods
and Question Marks**   ◀ CONNECT ⬤⬤⬤

In the following paragraph, correct errors related to punctuating with periods and question marks. The errors may involve missing or incorrect punctuation. There are ten errors.

When I saw Mr Pollack for the first time, I wondered what kind of boss he would be? Would he be easygoing or mean, understanding or inflexible After a week of working with him, I realized that he was a mix of all these qualities. On the first day that he worked at the store, Mr. Pollack seemed to be inflexible. In his first words to his new employees, he stressed the rules He warned us about lateness, inappropriate dress, absences, etc, and he said that he would enforce the rules without exceptions Every day of the first week, Mr. Pollack was at the store before the start of the 5:00 AM shift. In fact, some of the staff were not sure whether he spent the night in the storeroom. He seemed to be watching all his employees, sneaking behind their backs and spying. Quickly, Mr. Pollack became unpopular. Then, after six days of his supervision, an accident happened. Mrs Lerner, an older woman who has been with the store for years, slipped and fell on a wet patch of the newly mopped floor. Mr. Pollack stayed by her side, comforting her until the ambulance came. He told her not to worry about hospital bills or missed days at work. He assured her that no matter how long it took for her to get well, she would have a job waiting for her. On that day, I first saw the human side of Mr Pollack

CHAPTER 28
Punctuation: The Comma

There are four main ways to use a comma, as well as other, less important ways. *Memorize the four main ways.* If you can learn and understand these four rules, you will be more confident and correct in your punctuation. That is, you will use a comma only when you have a reason to do so; you will not be scattering commas in your sentences simply because you think a comma might fit, as many writers do.

The four main ways to use a comma are as a lister, a linker, an introducer, and an inserter (use two commas).

USE A COMMA AS A LISTER

Commas support items in a series. These items can be words, phrases, or clauses.

> **comma between words in a list:** Her bedroom was decorated in shades of blue, green, and gold.
>
> **comma between phrases in a list:** I looked for my ring under the coffee table, between the sofa cushions, and behind the chairs.
>
> **comma between clauses in a list:** Last week he graduated from college, he found the woman of his dreams, and he won the lottery.

Note: In a list, the comma before *and* is optional, but most writers use it.

Exercise 1 **Using a Comma as a Lister**

Add commas only where they are needed in the following sentences. Do not add any other punctuation or change existing punctuation.

1. Meat fish cheese beans and dairy products are sources of protein.

2. Nicole can do the laundry Mike can vacuum the house and I can clean the kitchen.

3. The thief caught with the money was silent snarling and slippery.

4. Bargain prices for DVD players satellite radios and flat-screen televisions drew shoppers to the electronics store.

5. I will wash dry and fold your dirty clothes when you take them off the floor and put them in the laundry basket.

6. My aunt knew she was spending too much time and money on television shopping channels when boxes of glittering jewelry expensive makeup and household gadgets started piling up in her house.

7. Eric is self-centered he lacks any sense of responsibility and he lies to his friends.

8. Sweaters pajamas and scarves are the only gifts my aunt ever gave me.

9. I misplaced my backpack with my chemistry workbook cell phone and student ID card in it.

10. There are certain creatures I hope never to see in my house; these include rats mice snakes and lizards.

USE A COMMA AS A LINKER

A comma and a coordinating conjunction link two independent clauses. The coordinating conjunctions are *for, and, nor, but, or, yet, so.* The comma goes in front of the coordinating conjunction:

> I have to get to work on time, or I'll get into trouble with my boss.
> My mother gave me a beautiful card, and she wrote a note on it.

Exercise 2 **Using a Comma as a Linker**

Add commas only where they are needed in the following sentences. Some sentences do not need commas. Do not change words or add any other punctuation.

1. Dr. Pinsky used to clean my teeth and he would give me a new toothbrush afterward.

2. My daughter can spend the weekend with her father or she can stay at her grandmother's house.

3. A day with my best friend lets me escape from my worries and act like a child again.

4. Todd wouldn't talk to his wife nor would he listen to his friends' advice.

5. Sophie must be sick for she has missed every class this week.

6. George had planned a perfect holiday party but something went wrong.

7. Jerry has tried several diets and exercise plans yet can't seem to lose weight.

8. Lisa's cousin Lev is quiet and rarely goes out to the movies or sports events.

9. My dog missed me so he went to sleep with an old sock of mine in his mouth.

10. Tim does all his assignments at the last minute yet he always manages to turn them in on time.

USE A COMMA AS AN INTRODUCER

Put a comma after introductory words, phrases, or clauses in a sentence.

a comma after an introductory word:
Yes, I agree with you on that issue.
Dad, give me some help with the dishes.

a comma after an introductory phrase:
In the long run, you'll be better off without him.
Before the anniversary party, my father bought my mother a necklace.

a comma after an introductory clause:
If you call home, your parents will be pleased.
When the phone rings, I am always in the shower.

> **Exercise 3** **Using a Comma as an Introducer**

Add commas only where they are needed in the following sentences. Some sentences do not need commas. Do not change words or add any other punctuation.

1. In the back of the dark room stood a man from my past.

2. Unless the weather improves we won't be able to hunt tomorrow.

3. Sure I can take care of your cat while you are away.

4. Courtney do you have an extra pencil or pen?

5. On my little brother's birthday I took him to a water park.

6. While Bernard grills the fish you can make the rice and beans.

7. Behind the curtains are two children playing hide-and-seek.

8. After a few days Luisa got used to the noisy city streets.

9. If he calls tell him I went away for the weekend.

10. Under the circumstances you should be the one to apologize for the misunderstanding.

USE A COMMA AS AN INSERTER

When words or phrases that are *not* necessary are inserted into a sentence, put a comma on *both* sides of the inserted material:

> The game, unfortunately, was rained out.
> My test score, believe it or not, was the highest in the class.
> Potato chips, my favorite snack food, are better tasting when they're fresh.
> James, caught in the middle of the argument, tried to keep the peace.

Using commas as inserters requires that you decide what is essential to the meaning of the sentence and what is nonessential.

> **If you do not need material in a sentence, put commas around the material. If you need material in a sentence, do not put commas around the material.**

For example, consider this sentence:

> The girl who called me was selling magazine subscriptions.

Do you need the words "who called me" to understand the meaning of the sentence? To answer that question, write the sentence without those words:

> The girl was selling magazine subscriptions.

Reading the shorter sentence, you might ask, "Which girl?" The words *who called me* are essential to the sentence. Therefore, you do not put commas around them.

> **correct:** The girl who called me was selling magazine subscriptions.

Remember that the proper name of a person, place, or thing is always sufficient to identify it. Therefore, any information that follows a proper name is inserted material; it gets commas on both sides.

> Video Views, which is nearby, has the best prices for video and DVD rentals.
> Sam Harris, the man who won the marathon, lives on my block.

Note: Sometimes the material that is needed in a sentence is called *essential* (or *restrictive*), and the material that is not needed is called *nonessential* (or *nonrestrictive*).

> **Exercise 4** **Using Commas as Inserters**

Add commas only where they are needed in the following sentences. Some sentences do not need commas.

1. A house full of toys will not always make a troubled child happy.

2. My best friend his eyes red and swollen mourned the loss of his cousin.

3. Mr. Murdock could of course decide to raise the phone rates.

4. Drivers who take the shortcut to the airport can save at least ten minutes and avoid the congestion at the toll plaza.

5. Our neighbor an enthusiastic gardener has transformed his yard into a small park.

6. <u>The Polar Express</u> which both children and adults enjoy was created with an experimental animation process.

7. The little girl at the end of the line has dropped the ice cream out of her cone.

8. Ultimate Books the bookstore in the Midland Mall has the biggest collection of fantasy books and magazines.

9. The woman in the gray suit introduced the guest of honor at the luncheon.

10. Baltimore where I was born has changed a great deal since I was a child.

Remember the four main ways to use a comma—as a lister, a linker, an introducer, and an inserter—and you'll solve many of your problems with punctuation.

Exercise 5 **Punctuating with Commas: The Four Main Ways**

Add commas only where they are needed in the following sentences. Do not add any other punctuation, and do not change any existing punctuation. Some sentences do not need commas.

1. Until I get a good job I have to watch my spending use public transportation and take advantage of free entertainment.

2. Byron's house is near the campus so he can ride his bike to his classes.

3. Shakira will never be lonely for she has a group of loving long-time and loyal friends.

4. No we can't get the car repaired until we find a mechanic who works on Saturdays.

5. Shocked and happy Lena reread the winning numbers and her grip on the lottery ticket tightened.

6. The puppy with the white face is the smartest-looking one in the litter.

7. Ruben stood at the side of the road and waited for Diego to catch up with him.

8. Patrick asked me to return his electric drill paint brushes and paint scraper before the weekend.

9. If you want a good used car go to Edward Motors the car lot next to the flea market.

10. The Egg Palace the old place on Route 4 has the cheapest breakfast the best coffee and the nicest staff in town.

Exercise 6 **More on Punctuating with Commas: The Four Main Ways**

Add commas only where they are needed in the following sentences. Do not add any other punctuation, and do not change any existing punctuation. Some sentences do not need commas.

1. As Philip turned the key in the front door he heard a strange noise coming from the second floor.

2. The giant shrimp the best item on the buffet table disappeared in about five minutes.

3. Anyone who loves a bargain will want to visit the new outlet mall on Gibbons Road.

4. I had to work overtime at the hospital of course and couldn't go to the lake with Martin.

5. A house with a fireplace seems more appealing to me than a house with a pool.

6. Well you can do whatever you want and I'll just stay home and watch television.

7. Because we bought an old house we spent a year painting the exterior refinishing the wooden floors repairing the plumbing and remodeling the kitchen.

8. Shelley would you like a mango cake from the Cuban bakery for your birthday?

9. Dealing with frazzled travelers and enforcing airline rules was too much for me so I quit my job at Dynamic Airlines.

10. It will take me hours but I'll fix your computer.

Other Ways to Use a Comma

There are other places to use a comma. Reviewing these uses will help you feel more confident as a writer.

1. Use commas with quotations. Use a comma to set off a direct quotation from the rest of the sentence.

> My father told me, "Money doesn't grow on trees."
> "Let's split the bill," Raymond said.

Note that the comma that introduces the quotation goes before the quotation marks. But once the quotation has begun, commas or periods go inside the quotation marks.

2. Use commas with dates and addresses. Use commas between the items in dates and addresses.

> August 5, 1980, is Chip's date of birth.
> We lived at 133 Emerson Road, Lake Park, Pennsylvania, before we moved to Florida.

Notice the comma after the year in the date, and the comma after the state in the address. These commas are needed when you write a date or address within a sentence.

3. Use commas in numbers. Use commas in numbers of one thousand or larger.

> The price of equipment was $1,293.

4. Use commas for clarity. Put a comma when you need it to make something clear.

Whoever it is, is about to be punished.
While hunting, the eagle is swift and strong.
I don't like to dress up, but in this job I have to, to get ahead.

Exercise 7   **Punctuation: Other Ways to Use a Comma**

Add commas wherever they are needed in the following sentences. Do not add any other punctuation, and do not change any existing punctuation.

1. "There isn't any milk in the refrigerator " my little boy complained.

2. On January 1 2002 Suzanne and Colin moved into a small house in Clifton New Jersey.

3. Be sure that anything you do you do for the right reasons.

4. The electric bill at my father's restaurant can run as high as $1 500 a month.

5. "I have lived at 535 Orchid Place Denver Colorado for more than six years " Alex told me.

6. Kevin graduated from high school on June 15 2003 and soon started work as a landscaper in Mobile Alabama.

7. Melissa stood in front of the clothes in her closet and muttered "I have got to clean out this mess."

8. "Let's talk this over like adults " my cousin pleaded.

9. "It's going to be twins " my wife said on March 22 1999.

10. The car salesman said "The sticker price for that car is only $26299."

Exercise 8   **Punctuating with Commas: A Comprehensive Exercise**

Add commas only where they are needed in the following sentences. Do not add any other punctuation, and do not change any existing punctuation. Some of the sentences do not need commas.

1. Fortunately I made it to work on time and avoided another lecture from my supervisor.

2. "Never promise more than you can deliver " my father used to say.

3. As I tucked my daughter into bed she held her teddy bear close to her heart.

4. The man who got arrested was from my neighborhood.

5. It took me a whole day to sort through my bills finish my math assignment and study for my accounting test.

6. My sister the first member of our family to go to college is a pediatrician.

7. Isaac always complained about his high school science classes but wound up becoming a science teacher.

8. All I can say Mario is that you have done me a great favor.

9. Frank was awarded a Purple Heart on May 12 2003 at a special ceremony.

10. China silver and glassware are the specialties of the store so I am going there to look for a wedding gift.

Exercise 9 **Punctuating with Commas: Another Comprehensive Exercise**

Add commas only where they are needed in the following sentences. Do not add any other punctuation, and do not change any existing punctuation. Some of the sentences do not need commas.

1. The spoiled little boy refused to eat any of his chicken nuggets nor would he touch his French fries.

2. Whenever I start to worry about the future my boyfriend shrugs his shoulders and says "Whatever happens happens and there is nothing you can do about it."

3. My old sneakers are in bad shape yet they are more comfortable than any other shoes I own.

4. Cough syrup in tasty flavors should be kept out of children's reach.

5. Island Treats the most popular restaurant in town is opening another restaurant in Maybrook Georgia.

6. People who walk in after a movie has started should stay in one place until their eyes adjust to the darkness.

7. Tim can meet me at the coffee shop or call me when he gets home.

8. Running as fast as he could the officer shouted "Get out of the building!"

9. Dr. Liu the famous psychiatrist has written a book about depression and teenagers.

10. My mother cautioned me threatened me and even begged me but I would not give up the woman whom my family disliked.

CONNECT ▶ Exercise 10 **Editing a Paragraph for Errors in Commas**

In the following paragraph, correct any errors related to punctuating with commas. The errors may involve missing or incorrect use of commas. There are eleven errors.

My brother is in general a good person but he has one major flaw. He refuses to lend me his car. I have asked to borrow his car to go to a movie to get to school on time to go out on Saturday night, and even to go to work. In every case, he has refused. I am not sure why he is so selfish about his car. It isn't a magnificent car. It's a dented old KIA and has 70533 miles on it. I have tried to reason with my brother about his selfishness. Unfortunately my brother makes the same comment each time, that I mention the car. "Think about the dent in the car" he says. He gives me a phony smile, and adds "Remember how the dent got there." Well, I guess he has a point. I'm the one who dented the car. It happened on the one and only time he let me borrow it.

CHAPTER 29
Punctuation: The Semicolon and the Colon

THE SEMICOLON

There are two ways to use semicolons:

1. Use a semicolon to join two independent clauses:

Michael loved his old Camaro; he worked on it every weekend.

The situation was hopeless; I couldn't do anything.

Note: If the independent clauses are joined by a conjunctive adverb, you will still need a semicolon. You will also need a comma after any conjunctive adverb that is more than one syllable long.

njunctive adverb
He was fluent in Spanish; *consequently*, he was the perfect companion for our trip to Venezuela.

conjunctive adverb
I called the hotline for twenty minutes; *then* I called another number.

A list of common conjunctive adverbs is on page 377.

Independent clauses joined by coordinating conjunctions (the words *for*, *and*, *nor*, *but*, *or*, *yet*, and *so*) do not need semicolons. Use a comma in front of the coordinating conjunction:

coordinating conjunction
Michael loved his old Camaro, *and* he worked on it every weekend.

coordinating conjunction

He was fluent in Spanish, *so* he was the perfect companion for our trip to Venezuela.

2. Use semicolons to separate the items on a list that contains commas. Adding semicolons will make the list easier to read:

The contestants came from Rochester, New York; Pittsburgh, Pennsylvania; Trenton, New Jersey; and Boston, Massachusetts. (The semicolons show that Rochester is a city in the state of New York, Pittsburgh is a city in the state of Pennsylvania, and so forth.)

The new officers of the club will be Althea Bethell, president; Francois Riviere, vice president; Ricardo Perez, secretary; and Lou Phillips, treasurer. (The semicolons link the person, Althea Bethell, with the office, president, and so forth.)

Exercise 1 **Punctuating with Semicolons**

Add any missing semicolons to the following sentences. In some sentences, you may have to change commas to semicolons.

1. The noise of construction workers outside the building grew louder meanwhile, I was trying to conduct a serious conversation on the telephone.

2. Two years ago, I was terrified of water, now I love to jump into the deep end of the pool.

3. My aunt took me to a fancy restaurant for dinner in addition, she bought me two new CDs at a music store.

4. Stacey is smart, attractive, and outgoing, yet she longs to be more like her younger sister.

5. Mario, my father, Mark, my older brother, Michael, my younger brother, and Michelle, my sister, all have first names that begin with *M*.

6. Gene is upset about something you need to talk to him.

7. Arthur was wearing a new jacket and had just gotten a haircut in fact, he looked quite handsome.

8. I studied hard for my grammar test, thus I didn't think it was too difficult.

9. Sarah will call the cable company or stop by its office for an explanation of the latest bill.

10. I have to pack my suitcase tonight otherwise, I might forget something in the morning rush to the airport.

THE COLON

A colon is used at the end of a complete statement. It introduces a list or an explanation:

colon introduces a list: When I went grocery shopping, I picked up a few things: milk, eggs, and coffee.

colon introduces an explanation: The room was a mess: dirty clothes were piled on the chairs, wet towels were thrown on the floor, and an empty pizza box was tossed in the closet.

Remember that the colon comes after a complete statement. What comes after the colon explains or describes what came before the colon. Look once more at the two examples, and you'll see the point.

When I went grocery shopping, I picked up a few things: milk, eggs, and coffee. (The words after the colon—*milk, eggs, and coffee*—explain what few things I picked up.)

The room was a mess: dirty clothes were piled on the chairs, wet towels were thrown on the floor, and an empty pizza box was tossed in the closet. (In this sentence, all the words after the colon describe what the mess was like.)

Some people put a colon every time they put a list in a sentence, but this is not a good rule to follow. Instead, remember that a colon, even one that introduces a list, must come after a complete statement.

not this: ~~When I go to the beach, I always bring: suntan lotion, a big towel, and a cooler with iced tea.~~

but this: When I go to the beach, I always bring my supplies: suntan lotion, a big towel, and a cooler with iced tea.

A colon may also introduce long quotations.

On December 8, 1941, the day after the Japanese attacked Pearl Harbor, President Franklin Delano Roosevelt summed up the situation: "Hostilities exist. There is no blinking at the fact that our people, our territory, and our interests are in grave danger." (Note that what comes after the colon explains what came before it.)

(Exercise 2)   **Punctuating with Colons**

Add colons where they are needed in the following sentences. Some sentences do not need a colon.

1. When you go to the cabin for the weekend, be sure to fill your car with groceries, extra blankets, insect repellent, books, binoculars, and fishing gear.

2. My husband did a superb job of cleaning the bathroom a shining bathtub, a spotless mirror, a gleaming toilet, a sink without toothpaste stuck on it, and even a floor free of footprints.

3. Since I had twenty dollars left over at the end of the week, I bought some small surprises for my husband a can of cashews, a bottle of wine, and his favorite magazine.

4. Until we cleaned out the garage, we had a collection of tools, ladders, empty boxes, lawn chairs, broken appliances, and rags crowded into the space.

5. My cat brings me what he thinks are trophies a dead lizard, a mouse, even a small snake.

6. Our neighborhood has several Fourth of July traditions flags flying in people's yards, a parade of small children on their bikes or in strollers, and a community barbecue on a dead-end street.

7. If you want to contribute to the food drive for victims of the storm, you can bring canned food, bread and rolls, bottled water, and paper plates and towels.

8. My grandmother believes that there are two kinds of children the ones who behave and the ones who don't.

9. The bridesmaids had their choice of three colors for their dresses pink, yellow, or lavender.

10. The men looked like hip-hop celebrities lots of jewelry, designer clothes, and shoes that cost more than my monthly salary.

Exercise 3 **Using Semicolons and Colons**

Add semicolons and colons where they are needed in the following sentences. You might have to change a comma to a semicolon.

1. I will never go to a sushi restaurant the idea of eating raw fish makes me sick.

2. You need floor mats for your car, and be sure to look for the usual auto supplies motor oil, car wax, and windshield wiper fluid.

3. Leroy sent me a get-well card he's always thoughtful.

4. If you go to the drug store, get me some toothpaste, hair gel, and aspirin.

5. Arthur seems like a trustworthy employee, on the other hand, I don't know that much about him.

6. There has been a shake-up in the managerial staff of Tompkins Motors, so the new leaders are Karen Killian, manager, Pierre LaValle, assistant manager, Ron Jessup, service manager, and Lorena Robles, business manager.

7. After my father got a job with a hotel, he took classes in accounting, customer relations, restaurant management, and business law.

8. Your parents love Luisa, also, she is fond of them.

9. Every time I take my father to a good restaurant, he orders the same thing a salad with thousand island dressing, a steak, and a baked potato.

10. Marianne skipped dinner last night then she left the house at 10:00 A.M.

⊂⊃◯⊃ CONNECT ▶

Exercise 4 **Editing a Paragraph for Errors in Semicolons and Colons**

In the following paragraph, correct any errors related to punctuating with semicolons or colons. The errors may involve missing or incorrect use of semicolons or colons. There are seven errors.

Miscommunication can lead to a pleasant surprise. My surprise began yesterday when I asked my husband to pick up a few items at the supermarket. He was on his way out the door at the last minute, he asked, "Do you need anything?" "Get something for lunch," I called. I told him to buy: some turkey sandwiches, potato salad, and apples. He came back with all the wrong items a frozen turkey instead of turkey sandwiches, sweet potatoes instead of potato salad, and an apple pie instead of apples. He claimed that these items were exactly what I had ordered. My husband has always loved the turkey, sweet potatoes, and apple pie we eat at Thanksgiving, and I suspected he had grabbed the chance to buy the ingredients for his favorite meal. At first, I was angry then I calmed down. We couldn't eat a frozen turkey for lunch; so I'd have to adapt. He had brought me food for dinner as a result, we'd have a lovely dinner. Late that night, after the turkey had baked for many hours and the sweet potatoes had become candied yams, we had a delicious, Thanksgiving-style dinner in June. In addition, I learned a new lesson make the most of any surprise that comes your way.

CHAPTER 30
Punctuation:
The Apostrophe

Use the apostrophe in the following ways:

1. Use an apostrophe in contractions to show that letters have been omitted.

do not	=	don't
I will	=	I'll
is not	=	isn't
she would	=	she'd
will not	=	won't

Also use the apostrophe to show that numbers have been omitted:

the summer of 1998 = the summer of '98

Exercise 1 **Using Apostrophes in Contractions**

Add apostrophes where they are necessary in each sentence below.

1. Dr. Fanelli is a great veterinarian; shell tell you whats wrong with your potbellied pig.

2. My grandfather never stops talking about the blizzard of 84 and how he didnt think hed live through it.

3. The cruise wasnt what Id expected, but Ill never forget it.

4. Hows your new baby doing?

5. Terry wont tell you that theres a problem with the financing for the car.

6. Henry and Lori couldn't make the trip this week; theyll come next month when theyve got more time.

7. I havent seen Monica lately; I hear shes got a new job.

8. If youre sick, youd better stay home from work today.

9. Its wonderful to see dolphins in their natural habitat.

10. Parents shouldnt argue in front of their small children; the children dont know how to cope with family conflict.

2. Use an apostrophe to show possession. If a word does not end in *s*, show ownership by adding an apostrophe and *s*.

the ring belongs to Jill   = Jill's ring
the wallet belongs to somebody   = somebody's wallet
the books are owned by my father = my father's books

If two people jointly own something, put the *'s* on the last person's name.

Ann and Mike own a house = Ann and Mike's house

If a word already ends in *s* and you want to show ownership, just add an apostrophe.

the ring belongs to Frances   = Frances' ring
two boys own a dog   = the boys' dog
the house belongs to Ms. Jones = Ms. Jones' house

Caution: Be careful with apostrophes. These words, the possessive pronouns, do not take apostrophes: *his, hers, theirs, ours, yours, its.*

not this: ~~The pencils were their's.~~
but this: The pencils were theirs.

not this: ~~The steak lost it's flavor.~~
but this: The steak lost its flavor.

(**Exercise 2**) **Using Apostrophes to Show Possession**

Add apostrophes where they are needed in the following sentences. Some sentences do not need apostrophes.

1. Mrs. Noriko promised to improve the companys marketing division and expand its overseas office.

2. I went to Charles and Agnes wedding yesterday, and I thought their wedding cake tasted better than yours.

3. I tried to put the dinner dishes, pots, and pans away quietly, but I dropped one pots lid against the stoves hood, creating a horrible clanking sound.

4. Catherine and Anthony are creative people, and the credit for renovating the pediatric wing of the hospital is all theirs.

5. I hope that, when I mentioned the changes at the womens club, I did not hurt anyones feelings.

6. Be careful when you pack my aunts photograph albums; her whole life is contained in them.

7. I miss San Diegos weather, but I love Bostons college life and its sense of history.

8. My sister Allisons musical ability is all hers; no one else in the family can sing, play an instrument, or read music.

9. I had to describe the lost suitcase to the airport cargo manager so that he could be sure the bag was ours.

10. In a week or two, the beautiful tree will have lost all its gold and scarlet leaves.

3. **Use the apostrophe for special uses of time, and to create a plural of numbers mentioned as numbers, letters mentioned as letters, and words that normally do not have plurals.**

special uses of time: It will take a *week's* work.
numbers mentioned as numbers: Take out the 5's.
letters mentioned as letters: Cross your *t*'s.
words that normally do not have plurals: I want no more "maybe's."

Caution: Do not add an apostrophe to a simple plural.

not this: ~~He lost three suitcase's.~~
but this: He lost three suitcases.

Exercise 3 **Special Uses of Apostrophes**

Add apostrophes where they are needed in the following sentences. Some sentences do not need apostrophes. Do not change or add any words.

1. I have *B*s on all my science quizzes, so I feel confident about the test.

2. Alice is going to New Zealand for three weeks; she will stay with relatives who live there.

3. Jennifer deserves a days pay for all the time she spent on cleaning up your office.

4. There are two *e*s in the word "coffee."

5. The winner of the lottery won an amount of money with six 0s at the end, so it has to be at least one million dollars.

6. It will be several months before I can save up enough vacation days for a trip to Wyoming.

7. My mother writes very fancy capital *A*s because she used to study calligraphy.

8. The down payment on my new house is less than a years worth of rent on my old one.

9. Don wants to spend hundreds of dollars on an anniversary party for our parents, but I think we can give them a memorable day for less money.

10. Don't forget your "excuse mes" and "pleases" when you visit Aunt Claudia.

Exercise 4 Using Apostrophes: A Comprehensive Exercise

Add apostrophes where they are needed in the following sentences. Some sentences do not need apostrophes. Do not change or add any words.

1. I forgot the books title and had to ask my friend for the information.

2. Don't get involved in the childrens project; let the experience be all theirs.

3. Ill never forget Texas storms and its blistering summer heat.

4. You pronounce your *r*s differently than I pronounce mine.

5. Professor Harris tests are always challenging, so Ill have to study hard for his final exam.

6. Wont you tell me whos been asking questions about me?

7. Some of the mail is hers, and the rest of it is yours.

8. Nothings worse than having a neighbors dog barking all night.

9. The club I belong to has an annual awards banquet for its members.

10. It cost me a months worth of overtime to pay for my daughters dental work, but her smile is my reward.

Exercise 5 Another Comprehensive Exercise in Using Apostrophes

Circle the correct form in parentheses in each sentence below.

1. I think the notebook belongs to (Carlos, Carlos').

2. Could the white rabbit in our yard be (someones, someone's) pet?

3. (Theres, There's) nothing wrong with your computer.

4. A new (mens, men's) store just opened in the Palms Plaza.

5. The mail carrier delivered the package to our neighbors, but it was (ours, our's).

6. I fell in love for the first time in the spring of (95, '95).

7. My brother was in Korea for two (years, year's).

8. Tell me if you like (Laura's and Kim's, Laura and Kim's) new roommate.

9. Lamont's answers to my requests are too full of ("nos," "no's").

10. Staying out late began to lose (its, it's) appeal for me when I became a father.

Exercise 6   **Editing a Paragraph for Errors in Apostrophes**   ◀ CONNECT ⊂⊃⊂⊃

In the following paragraph, correct any errors related to punctuating with apostrophes. The errors may involve missing or incorrect use of apostrophes. There are ten errors.

My friend Ryan visited me last week, and because of the weather, I saw a years worth of movies in a week. Ryan came from Florida to visit, expecting to see snow and enjoy such winter sports as ice-skating and sledding. However, the weather didnt cooperate with Ryan's plan's. It rained heavily for seven day's. As a result, I had to find activities that interested my friend. Since Ryan love's films, it wasnt too difficult to amuse him. We went to every movie in town. For me, the week was unusual since I rarely go to the movies; in fact, its possible for me to spend twelve months without visiting the neighborhood multiplex. Before Ryans visit, the last film I remember seeing was in the fall of 04 when my sister dragged me to see <u>SpongeBob SquarePants.</u> Last week, the weather arranged things so that Id see many movies. Ryan and I saw two action movies, a horror film, a cartoon adventure, and two comedies. Ryan couldn't have been happier, and I am now an expert on early-bird ticket prices and rocking-chair seating.

CHAPTER 31
Other Punctuation and Mechanics

THE EXCLAMATION MARK

The exclamation mark is used at the end of sentences that express strong emotion:

> **appropriate:** You've won the lottery!
> **inappropriate:** We had a great time! (*Great* already implies excitement.)

Be careful not to overuse the exclamation mark. If your choice of words is descriptive, you should not have to rely on the exclamation point for emphasis. Use it sparingly, for it is easy to rely on exclamations instead of using better vocabulary.

THE DASH

Use a dash to interrupt a sentence. It usually indicates a dramatic shift in tone or thought.

> I picked up the crystal bowl carefully, cradled it in my arms, walked softy—and tripped, sending the bowl flying.

Two dashes set off dramatic words that interrupt a sentence.

> Ramon took the life preserver—our only one—and tossed it far out to sea.

Because dashes are somewhat dramatic, use them sparingly.

PARENTHESES

Use parentheses to enclose extra material and afterthoughts.

> I was sure that Ridgefield (the town I'd just visited) was not the place for me.
> Her name (which I have just remembered) was Celestine.

Note: Commas in pairs, dashes in pairs, and parentheses are all used as inserters. They set off material that interrupts the flow of the sentence. The least dramatic and smoothest way to insert material is to use commas.

THE HYPHEN

A hyphen joins two or more descriptive words that act as a single word.

> The old car had a souped-up engine.
> Bill was a smooth-talking charmer.

 Punctuating with Exclamation Marks, Dashes, Parentheses, and Hyphens

Add any exclamation marks, dashes, parentheses, and hyphens that are needed in the sentences below.

1. Larry took the airline ticket my last chance at freedom and threw it into the incinerator.

2. There's someone hiding in the closet

3. Lenny Montalbano the boy who used to live next door grew up to start his own medical research company.

4. Mr. Okada is a caring, competent, and good natured supervisor.

5. Mr. Thompson is known for his eccentric ways; one day he came to work in a handsome blue blazer, striped silk tie, gray flannel slacks and bright orange sneakers.

6. Get off the train tracks

7. The salesperson said the radio was a top of the line product.

8. The Aces Club where my cousin said all the single people met turned out to be a loud, dirty bar and grill.

9. The killer drew a breath his last one and fell to the ground.

10. Amanda married a battle weary veteran of the war in Iraq.

QUOTATION MARKS

Use quotation marks for direct quotations, for the titles of short works, and for other special uses.

1. Put quotation marks around direct quotations, a speaker or writer's exact words:

   My mother told me, "There are plenty of fish in the sea."
   "I'm never going there again," said Irene.

"I'd like to buy you dinner," Peter said, "but I'm out of cash."
My best friend warned me, "Stay away from that guy. He will break your heart."

Look carefully at the preceding examples. Notice that a comma is used to introduce a direct quotation and that at the end of the quotation, the comma or period goes inside the quotation marks:

My mother told me, "There are plenty of fish in the sea."

Notice how direct quotations of more than one sentence are punctuated. If the quotation is written in one unit, quotation marks go before the first quoted word and after the last quoted word:

My best friend warned me, "Stay away from that guy. He will break your heart."

But if the quotation is not written as one unit, the punctuation changes:

"Stay away from that guy," my best friend warned me. "He will break your heart."

Caution: Do *not* put quotation marks around indirect quotations:

indirect quotation: He asked if he could come with us.
direct quotation: He asked, "Can I come with you?"

indirect quotation: She said that she wanted more time.
direct quotation: "I want more time," she said.

2. Put quotation marks around the titles of short works. If you are writing the title of a short work like a short story, an essay, a newspaper or magazine article, a poem, or a song, put quotation marks around the title:

In middle school, we read Robert Frost's poem "The Road Not Taken."
My little sister has learned to sing "Itsby Bitsy Spider."

If you are writing the title of a longer work like a book, movie, magazine, play, television show, or CD, underline the title:

Last night I saw an old movie, <u>Stand By Me</u>.
I read an article called "Campus Crime" in <u>Newsweek</u>.

In printed publications such as books or magazines, titles of long works are put in italics. But when you are handwriting, typing, or using a word processor, underline the titles of long works.

3. There are other, special uses of quotation marks. You use quotation marks around words mentioned as words in a sentence.

When you said "never," did you mean it?
People from the Midwest pronounce "water" differently than I do.

If you are using a quotation within a quotation, use single quotation marks.

My brother complained, "Every time we get in trouble, Mom has to say 'I told you so.'"
Kyle said, "Linda has a way of saying 'Excuse me' that is really very rude."

CAPITAL LETTERS

There are ten main situations in which you capitalize:

1. Capitalize the first word of every sentence:

    Yesterday we saw our first soccer game.

2. Capitalize the first word in a direct quotation if the word begins a sentence:

    My aunt said, "This is a gift for your birthday."
    "Have some birthday cake," my aunt said, "and have some more ice cream." (Notice that the second section of this quotation does not begin with a capital letter because it does not begin a sentence.)

3. Capitalize the names of persons:

    Nancy Perez and Frank Murray came to see me at the store.
    I asked Mother to feed my cat.

Do not capitalize words like *mother*, *father*, or *aunt* if you put a possessive in front of them.

    I asked my mother to feed my cat.

4. Capitalize the titles of persons:

    I spoke with Dr. Wilson.
    He has to see Dean Johnston.

Do not capitalize when the title is not connected to a name:

    I spoke with that doctor.
    He has to see the dean.

5. Always capitalize countries, cities, languages, nationalities, religions, races, months, days of the week, documents, organizations, holidays, and historical events or periods:

    In high school, we never studied the Vietnam War.
    The Polish-American Club will hold a picnic on Labor Day.

Use small letters for the seasons:

    I love fall because I love to watch the leaves change color.

6. Capitalize the names of particular places:

    We used to hold our annual meetings at Northside Auditorium in Springfield, Iowa, but this year we are meeting at Riverview Theater in Langton, Missouri.

Use small letters if a particular place is not given:

    We are looking for an auditorium we can rent for our meeting.

7. Use capital letters for geographic locations:

    Jim was determined to find a good job in the West.

But use small letters for geographic directions:

    To get to my house, you have to drive west on the turnpike.

8. Capitalize the names of specific products:

   I always drink Diet Pepsi for breakfast.

But use small letters for a kind of product:

   I always drink a diet cola for breakfast.

9. Capitalize the names of specific school courses:

   I have to take Child Psychology next term.

But use small letters for a general academic subject:

   My advisor told me to take a psychology course.

10. Capitalize the first and last words in the titles of long or short works, and capitalize all other significant words in the titles:

    I've always wanted to read <u>The Old Man and the Sea</u>.
    Whenever we go to see the team play, my uncle sings "Take Me Out to the Ballgame."

(Remember that the titles of long works, like books, are underlined; the titles of short ones, like songs, are quoted.)

> **Exercise 2** Using Quotation Marks, Underlining, and Capital Letters

Add any missing quotation marks, underlining, and capital letters to the sentences below.

1. When I was growing up, uncle Richard was my favorite relative, but I later discovered my uncle had a dangerous temper.

2. When Melanie signed up for her winter term at college, she registered for classes in social science, writing, and music.

3. I can't stand it, my girlfriend said, when you say maybe instead of giving me a definite answer.

4. I finally found a good preschool for my son; it's the madison school for early childhood education, and dr. Howard of Miller university is the director.

5. One night, my brother Jason was watching a television show called Fear Factor; I watched it for a minute and said, Ugh! Turn off that disgusting program."

6. David is looking for a job in the midwest because he wants to be near his parents, who live north of Chicago.

7. Whenever Mimi says the word love, she means the word infatuation.

8. Gerry, stop complaining, his father said. It doesn't do any good to complain.

9. I took my little cousins to see The Polar Express; afterward, they said it was the best movie in the world.

10. There is nothing funnier than listening to my husband sing Marvin Gaye's song, I heard it Through the Grapevine.

NUMBERS

Spell out numbers that take one or two words:

> Alice mailed two hundred brochures.
> I spent ninety dollars on car repairs.

Use the numbers themselves if it takes more than two words to spell them out.

> We looked through 243 old photographs.
> The sticker price was $10,397.99.

Also use numbers to write dates, times, addresses, and parts of a book.

> We live at 24 Cambridge Street.
> They were married on April 3, 1993.
> Chapter 3 had difficult maps to read, especially the one on page 181.

ABBREVIATIONS

Although you should spell out most words rather than abbreviate them, you may abbreviate *Mr.*, *Mrs.*, *Ms.*, *Jr.*, *Sr.*, and *Dr.* when they are used with a proper name. You should abbreviate references to time and to organizations widely known by initials.

> The moderator asked Ms. Steinem to comment.
> The bus left at 5:00 P.M., and the trip took two hours.
> He works for the FBI.

You should spell out the names of places, months, days of the week, courses of study, and words referring to parts of a book, such as "chapter" and "section."

> **not this:** I missed the last class, so I never got the notes for Chap. 3.
> **but this:** I missed the last class, so I never got the notes for Chapter 3.

> **not this:** He lives on Chestnut Street in Boston, Mass.
> **but this:** He lives on Chestnut Street in Boston, Massachusetts.

not this: ~~Pete missed his trig. test.~~
but this: Pete missed his trigonometry test.

> **Exercise 3**   **Using Numbers and Abbreviations**

Correct any errors in the use of numbers or abbreviations in the following sentences. Some sentences may not need corrections.

1. Ellen came into our soc. class last Mon., carrying her research paper, which looked about three in. thick.

2. Mr. and Mrs. Chang sent one hundred fifty-five invitations to their daughter's wedding in Minneapolis, Minn.

3. My parents' apartment on Sunset Ave. had 4 rooms.

4. Matthew left Fla. on Mar. third, 2004, to begin a job with the Abraham and Braun Co. in N. Dakota.

5. My psych. prof starts class promptly at 8:30 A.M. every Fri.

6. It took me two hrs. to finish Chap. 3 of my sociology textbook.

7. Gregory charges twenty-five dollars to help people with their computer problems.

8. Charles Woods, Jr., was an executive with the NFL for ten years before he took a job with ABC Sports.

9. My father and his 3 brothers arrived in New York on a cold Feb. day in 1975.

10. Dr. Hoffman used to live on 5723 Elm Street, Boston, Mass., until he took a job at the Univ. of Wisconsin in Madison.

> **Exercise 4**   **A Comprehensive Exercise on Punctuation and Mechanics**

Add any missing punctuation to the following sentences. Also, correct any errors in capitalization and in use of numbers or abbreviations.

1. We had a second rate meal at Frank and Maries house of Ribs last Sat. night we can't recommend the place to you.

2. I'm looking for a book called the rule of four my friend recommended it.

3. The five year old boy began to pour chocolate syrup on the kitchen floor meanwhile the babysitter dozed on the living room couch.

4. Lance took 2 spanish courses at National H.S. so he does not have to take a foreign language at Centenary college.

5. The star athlete wanted to know if she could miss a days practice.

6. The star athlete asked Can I miss a days practice

7. I love Its a whole new world, the song from the movie Aladdin.

8. Now that we live in Buffalo N.Y. I need some warm clothes sweaters, gloves, hats, and a coat with a heavy lining.

9. Ill keep your secret Bill as long as your secret doesnt hurt anyone elses chance at happiness.

10. An old man with a cane walked slowly down the sidewalk for the ice made the pavement treacherous.

(**Exercise 5**)   **A Comprehensive Exercise on Punctuation and Mechanics**

Add any missing punctuation to the following sentences. Also, correct any errors in capitalization and in use of numbers or abbreviations.

1. Tonya Brillstein my best friend told me she is sick of Lance and Agnes teasing.

2. The oral surgery will cost me $2321 nevertheless I intend to have it as soon as possible.

3. All I can say, dad is that youve hurt Nicoles feelings.

4. Let me see your license, the officer said and give me your registration too.

5. A man with bright red hair was seen leaving the scene of the crime but witnesses could not identify him.

6. The teenagers wonder whether their favorite teacher will ever return to the classroom at Penn. State University.

7. The movie Friday Night Lights was based on a book about a real High school football team in Texas.

8. When Vincent takes a trip with his Great Danes, he packs his van full of the animals possessions two large dog beds giant bags of dog food special spill proof water bowls and at least a dozen dog toys.

9. Theres a red Mustang in the parking lot with its lights on maybe the car is yours.

10. No don't buy me that book called The 7 Habits of Highly Effective People I have to break my bad habits before I can start developing good ones.

 CONNECT ▶   **Exercise 6**   **Editing a Paragraph for Errors in Punctuation and Mechanics**

In the following paragraph, correct any errors related to punctuation or mechanics. The errors may involve missing or incorrect punctuation, capitalization, use of numbers, or abbreviations. There are twenty-two errors.

Babies can be hard to figure out. I made this discovery, when my neighbor Rosanna asked me for a favor. When she knocked on my door she looked like she had just climbed out of bed her eyes half-open, her hair flat and matted, and her clothes rumpled. In reality she wasnt waking up she was desperate for sleep. Can you do me a big favor? she asked I wouldnt ask you but its an emergency". Rosanna explained that she had been up all night, walking her baby Marcus, singing to him, and rocking him. Nothing would put Marcus to sleep. "I've got to get a couple of hours sleep" she explained "before I go to work. All I need is for you to watch the baby until my husband comes home from his job in two hours. Then, she said, her husband could take over and she could go to her job. I felt sorry for her so I agreed. The strangest part of the story is a happy ending. As

soon as I had Marcus in my arms he fell asleep. Babies certainly seem to live by

their own strange schedule's.

Exercise 7 **Editing a Paragraph for Errors in Punctuation
and Mechanics**

◀ CONNECT ⬤⬤⬤

In the following paragraph, correct any errors related to punctuation or mechanics. The errors may involve missing or incorrect punctuation, capitalization, use of numbers, or abbreviations. There are twenty-three errors.

In my first year of high school, I signed up for a music class called Introduction to choral music. I had no idea the class would involve so much singing and even worse so much practice. During one class, we sang the first notes of the song Summertime at least 30 times before our teacher let us move on. In the early weeks of the semester I became impatient with all the emphasis on perfection. I was happy on the one day when our teacher was sick because, his absence meant we didnt have to sing. Instead we watched an old movie called Mr Holland's opus. After about a months worth of practice, my attitude began to change. The students including me began to form into a group. The groups singing improved meanwhile our teacher prepared us to face an audience. By the end, of the year, I was a proud member of the Eleanor Roosevelt H.S. Chorus. Every time I sang for students, parent's, or community members, I felt the power of music. In addition, I understood how those hard hours of practice can lead to a special kind of accomplishment.

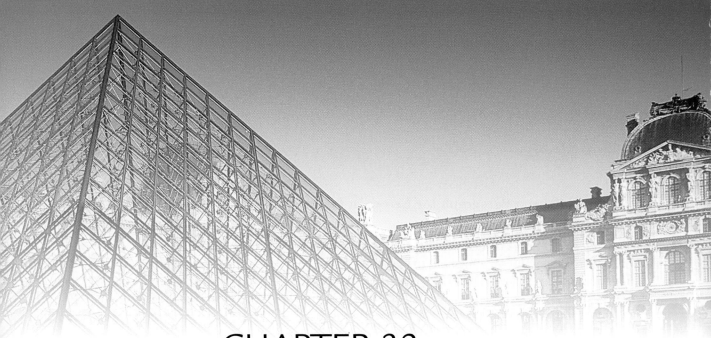

CHAPTER 32
Spelling

No one is a perfect speller, but there are ways to become a better speller. If you can learn a few spelling rules, you can answer many of your spelling questions.

VOWELS AND CONSONANTS

To understand the spelling rules, you need to know the difference between vowels and consonants. **Vowels** are the letters *a, e, i, o, u,* and sometimes *y*. **Consonants** are all the other letters.

> The letter *y* is a vowel when it has a vowel sound.
> silly (The *y* sounds like *ee*, a vowel sound.)
> cry (The *y* sounds like *i*, a vowel sound.)

> The letter *y* is a consonant when it has a consonant sound.
> yellow (The *y* has a consonant sound.)
> yesterday (The *y* has a consonant sound.)

SPELLING RULE 1: DOUBLING A FINAL CONSONANT

Double the final consonant of a word if all three of the following are true:

1. The word is one syllable, or the accent is on the last syllable,
2. The word ends in a single consonant preceded by a single vowel, and
3. The ending you are adding starts with a vowel.

begin	+	ing	=	beginning
shop	+	er	=	shopper
stir	+	ed	=	stirred
occur	+	ed	=	occurred
fat	+	est	=	fattest
pin	+	ing	=	pinning

Exercise 1   **Doubling a Final Consonant**

Add -*ed* to the following words by applying the rules for double consonants.

1. hammer _____   **6.** repel _____

2. swat   _____   **7.** uncoil _____

3. trick   _____   **8.** stop   _____

4. order   _____   **9.** excel _____

5. admit   _____   **10.** defer _____

SPELLING RULE 2: DROPPING THE FINAL *e*

Drop the final *e* before you add an ending that starts with a vowel.

observe	+	ing	=	observing
excite	+	able	=	excitable
fame	+	ous	=	famous
create	+	ive	=	creative

Keep the final *e* before an ending that starts with a consonant.

love	+	ly	=	lovely
hope	+	ful	=	hopeful
excite	+	ment	=	excitement
life	+	less	=	lifeless

Exercise 2   **Dropping the Final *e***

Combine the following words and endings by following the rule for dropping the final *e*.

1. imagine   +   able   _____

2. care   +   less   _____

3. arrange   +   ment   _____

4. resource +   ful   _____

5. behave   +   ing   _____

6. home + less _____

7. expense + ive _____

8. intense + ly _____

9. adore + able _____

10. refuse + ing _____

SPELLING RULE 3: CHANGING THE FINAL y TO i

When a word ends in a consonant plus y, change the y to i when you add an ending:

try	+	es	=	tries
silly	+	er	=	sillier
rely	+	ance	=	reliance
tardy	+	ness	=	tardiness

Note: When you add *-ing* to words ending in y, always keep the y.

cry	+	ing	=	crying
rely	+	ing	=	relying

Exercise 3   **Changing the Final y to i**

Combine the following words and endings by applying the rule for changing the final y to i.

1. happy + er _____

2. apply + ing _____

3. convey + er _____

4. penny + less _____

5. marry + ed _____

6. deny + es _____

7. ally + ance _____

8. comply + ant _____

9. ready + ness _____

10. imply + ing _____

SPELLING RULE 4: ADDING -s OR -es

Add -es instead of -s to a word if the word ends in ch, sh, ss, x, or z. The es adds an extra syllable to the word.

box	+	es	=	boxes
witch	+	es	=	witches
class	+	es	=	classes
clash	+	es	=	clashes

Exercise 4 **Adding -s or -es**

Apply the rule for adding -s or -es to the following words.

1. polish _____   6. fix _____

2. defeat _____   7. pass _____

3. march _____   8. smash _____

4. stock _____   9. back _____

5. distress _____   10. tax _____

SPELLING RULE 5: USING ie OR ei

Use i before e, except after c, or when the sound is like a, as in neighbor and weigh.

i before e:
relief   convenience   friend   piece

e before i:
conceive   sleigh   weight   receive

Exercise 5 **Using ie or ei**

Add ie or ei to the following words by applying the rule for using ie or ei.

1. dec _ _t   6. ch _ _ f

2. fr _ _ght   7. n _ _ ce

3. conc _ _t   8. f _ _ ld

4. bel _ _f   9. ingred _ _ nt

5. perc _ _ve   10. sh _ _ ld

Exercise 6 **Spelling Rules: A Comprehensive Exercise**

Combine the following words and endings by applying the spelling rules.

1. blur   +   ed   _____

2. carry   +   ed   _____

3. fizz   +   s or es   _____

4. tidy   +   er   _____

5. perch   +   s or es   _____

6. harass   +   s or es   _____

7. plan   +   ed   _____

8. steady   +   ness   _____

9. ply   +   able   _____

10. concur   +   ed   _____

11. unhappy   +   est   _____

12. observe   +   ant   _____

13. spite   +   ful   _____

14. impulse   +   ive   _____

15. confine   +   ment   _____

16. rely   +   es   _____

17. apply   +   ance   _____

18. catch   +   s or es   _____

19. offer   +   ed   _____

20. suffer   +   ing   _____

⊂○○⊃ CONNECT ▶   **Exercise 7** **Editing a Paragraph for Spelling**

Correct the spelling errors in the following paragraph. Write your corrections above each error. There are ten errors.

      Driveing above the speed limit is so common that I became angry when I

recieved a speeding ticket yesterday. I was ziping down the highway on my way home until a police officer turned on her flashing light and stoped me. She claimmed I had been going twenty miles above the speed limit. What irritates me is that the traffic situation on that highway encourages defyance of the rules. Everyone speeds on that road, and there has been no enforcment of the rules for years. I exceed the speed limit for two reasons: because everyone disobeys the rules and gets away with it and because it's safer to speed than to follow the rules. If I slow down, I risk an accident as the cars around me tailgate my car, cut me off, or run me off the road. On a crowded highway, people who observe the speed limit risk crashs. I know the police officer was doing her job, but I beleive I was doing mine by keeping up with the flow of traffic. I realize that driving at high speeds in heavy traffic is crazy, but unfortunately, trying to slow down can be crazyer.

DO YOU SPELL IT AS ONE WORD OR TWO?

Sometimes you can be confused about certain words. You are not sure whether to combine them to make one word or to spell them as two words. The lists below show some commonly confused words.

Words That Should Not Be Combined

a lot	each other	high school	every time
even though	good night	all right	no one
living room	dining room	in front	

Words That Should Be Combined

another	newspapers	bathroom
bedroom	playroom	good-bye, goodbye, or good-by
bookkeeper	roommate	cannot
schoolteacher	downstairs	southeast, northwest, etc.
grandmother	throughout	nearby
worthwhile	nevertheless	yourself, himself, myself, etc.

Words Whose Spelling Depends on Their Meaning

one word: *Already* means "before."

He offered to do the dishes, but I had *already* done them.

two words: *All ready* means "ready."

My dog was *all ready* to play Frisbee.

one word: *Altogether* means "entirely."
That movie was *altogether* too confusing.
two words: *All together* means "in a group."
My sisters were *all together* in the kitchen.

one word: *Always* means "every time."
My grandfather is *always* right about baseball statistics.
two words: *All ways* means "every path" or "every aspect."
We tried *all ways* to get to the beach house.
He is a gentleman in *all ways*.

one word: *Anymore* means "any longer."
I do not want to exercise *anymore*.
two words: *Any more* means "additional."
Are there *any more* pickles?

one word: *Anyone* means "any person at all."
Is *anyone* home?
two words: *Any one* means "one person or thing in a special group."
I'll take *any one* of the chairs on sale.

one word: *Apart* means "separate."
Liam stood *apart* from his friends.
two words: *A part* is "a piece or section."
I read *a part* of the chapter.

one word: *Everyday* means "ordinary."
Tim was wearing his *everyday* clothes.
two words: *Every day* means "each day."
Sam jogs *every day*.

one word: *Everyone* means "all the people."
Everyone has bad days.
two words: *Every one* means "all the people or things in a specific group."
My father asked *every one* of the neighbors for a donation to the Red Cross.

(Exercise 8) **Do You Spell It as One Word or Two?**

Circle the correct choice in parentheses in each sentence below.

1. Jason apologized to me yesterday; he said he wanted to make

    everything (all right, allright) between us.

2. Terry would be happy to own (any one, anyone) of the beautiful

    houses being built on Pinewood Avenue.

3. If you have (all ready, already) seen the new Jamie Fox movie,

    let's go see the one with Brad Pitt and Drew Barrymore.

4. Robin is thinking of moving back to the (North East, Northeast);

    she misses her friends in Vermont.

5. Being snowed in at the airport was an (all together, altogether)

horrible experience.

6. My father sold insurance, and my mother was a (school teacher,

schoolteacher) in an elementary school.

7. (Every time, Everytime) I hear that song, I think of Luis.

8. My math professor says he doesn't want to hear (any more, any-

more) complaints about the homework.

9. Lynn told me to return (every one, everyone) of the CDs I bor-

rowed from her.

10. Tom will have to get a new (room mate, roommate) if Bernard

leaves town.

Exercise 9   **Do You Spell It as One Word or Two? Correcting**   ◀ CONNECT
Errors in a Paragraph

The following paragraph contains errors in word combinations. Correct the
errors in the space above each line. There are nine errors.

Even in my first year of highschool, I was all ready certain that I wanted to

attend college and earn a degree. Seven years later, I am starting to make my dream

come true. Alot happened in those seven years. First, I struggled through out my

teens, dropping out of high school in my junior year. At that time, I was having a

hard time coping with my parents' divorce. The divorce caused my mother to

lose much of the family income, and I was angry at my father and at much of the

world. I also hated being the student without money in a school where every one

else had new clothes, expensive jewelry, and the latest in cell phones. I worked at

a series of jobs to help support my mother, and I fell into a routine of meaning-

less work, bursts of rage, and a sense of hopelessness. Suddenly, two years ago,

hope returned in the form of a new friend. She urged me to take steps, even if

they were small ones, to change my life. It was hard to change my life all together,

but small steps led me to earn my G.E.D. Next month, I will begin my first class

at a near by college. I can say good by to a dead-end life. I will be working hard and taking a big chance; never the less, I will be moving toward my seven-year-

old dream.

A LIST OF COMMONLY MISSPELLED WORDS

Following is a list of words you use often in your writing. Study this list and use it as a reference.

1. absence	**41.** behavior	**81.** competition
2. absent	**42.** belief	**82.** conscience
3. accept	**43.** believe	**83.** convenient
4. achieve	**44.** benefit	**84.** conversation
5. ache	**45.** bicycle	**85.** copy
6. acquire	**46.** bought	**86.** cough
7. across	**47.** breakfast	**87.** cousin
8. actually	**48.** breathe	**88.** criticism
9. advertise	**49.** brilliant	**89.** criticize
10. again	**50.** brother	**90.** crowded
11. a lot	**51.** brought	**91.** daily
12. all right	**52.** bruise	**92.** daughter
13. almost	**53.** build	**93.** deceive
14. always	**54.** bulletin	**94.** decide
15. amateur	**55.** bureau	**95.** definite
16. American	**56.** buried	**96.** dentist
17. answer	**57.** business	**97.** dependent
18. anxious	**58.** busy	**98.** deposit
19. apparent	**59.** calendar	**99.** describe
20. appetite	**60.** cannot	**100.** desperate
21. apology	**61.** career	**101.** development
22. appreciate	**62.** careful	**102.** different
23. argue	**63.** catch	**103.** dilemma
24. argument	**64.** category	**104.** dining
25. asked	**65.** caught	**105.** direction
26. athlete	**66.** cemetery	**106.** disappearance
27. attempt	**67.** cereal	**107.** disappoint
28. August	**68.** certain	**108.** discipline
29. aunt	**69.** chair	**109.** disease
30. author	**70.** cheat	**110.** divide
31. automobile	**71.** chief	**111.** doctor
32. autumn	**72.** chicken	**112.** doesn't
33. avenue	**73.** children	**113.** don't
34. awful	**74.** cigarette	**114.** doubt
35. awkward	**75.** citizen	**115.** during
36. balance	**76.** city	**116.** dying
37. basically	**77.** college	**117.** early
38. because	**78.** color	**118.** earth
39. becoming	**79.** comfortable	**119.** eighth
40. beginning	**80.** committee	**120.** eligible

121. embarrass
122. encouragement
123. enough
124. environment
125. especially
126. etc.
127. every
128. exact
129. exaggeration
130. excellent
131. except
132. exercise
133. excite
134. existence
135. expect
136. experience
137. explanation
138. factory
139. familiar
140. family
141. fascinating
142. February
143. finally
144. forehead
145. foreign
146. forty
147. fourteen
148. friend
149. fundamental
150. general
151. generally
152. goes
153. going
154. government
155. grammar
156. grateful
157. grocery
158. guarantee
159. guard
160. guess
161. guidance
162. guide
163. half
164. happiness
165. handkerchief
166. heavy
167. height
168. heroes
169. holiday
170. hospital
171. humorous
172. identity

173. illegal
174. imaginary
175. immediately
176. important
177. independent
178. integration
179. intelligent
180. interest
181. interfere
182. interpretation
183. interrupt
184. irrelevant
185. irritable
186. iron
187. island
188. January
189. jewelry
190. judgment
191. kindergarten
192. kitchen
193. knowledge
194. laboratory
195. language
196. laugh
197. leisure
198. length
199. library
200. loneliness
201. listen
202. lying
203. maintain
204. maintenance
205. marriage
206. mathematics
207. meant
208. measure
209. medicine
210. million
211. miniature
212. minute
213. muscle
214. mysterious
215. naturally
216. necessary
217. neighbor
218. nervous
219. nickel
220. niece
221. ninety
222. ninth
223. occasion
224. o'clock

225. often
226. omission
227. once
228. operate
229. opinion
230. optimist
231. original
232. parallel
233. particular
234. peculiar
235. perform
236. perhaps
237. permanent
238. persevere
239. personnel
240. persuade
241. physically
242. pleasant
243. possess
244. possible
245. potato
246. practical
247. prefer
248. prejudice
249. prescription
250. presence
251. president
252. privilege
253. probably
254. professor
255. psychology
256. punctuation
257. pursue
258. quart
259. really
260. receipt
261. receive
262. recognize
263. recommend
264. reference
265. religious
266. reluctantly
267. remember
268. resource
269. restaurant
270. ridiculous
271. right
272. rhythm
273. sandwich
274. Saturday
275. scene
276. schedule

277. scissors
278. secretary
279. seize
280. several
281. severely
282. significant
283. similar
284. since
285. sincerely
286. soldier
287. sophomore
288. strength
289. studying
290. success

291. surely
292. surprise
293. taught
294. temperature
295. theater
296. thorough
297. thousand
298. tied
299. tomorrow
300. tongue
301. tragedy
302. trouble
303. truly
304. twelfth

305. unfortunately
306. unknown
307. until
308. unusual
309. using
310. variety
311. vegetable
312. Wednesday
313. weird
314. which
315. writing
316. written
317. yesterday

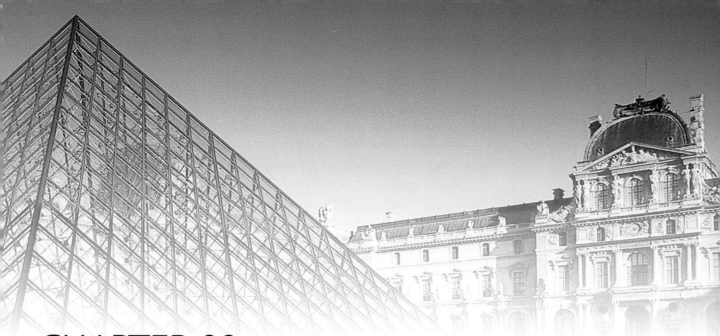

CHAPTER 33
Words That Sound Alike/Look Alike

WORDS THAT SOUND ALIKE/LOOK ALIKE

Words that sound alike or look alike can be confusing. Here is a list of some of the confusing words. Study this list, and make a note of any words that give you trouble.

a/an/and *A* is used before a word beginning with a consonant or a consonant sound:

   Jason bought *a* car.

An is used before a word beginning with a vowel or vowel sound:

   Nancy took *an* apple to work.

And joins words or ideas:

   Pudding *and* cake are my favorite desserts.
   Fresh vegetables taste delicious, *and* they are nutritious.

accept/except *Accept* means "to receive":

   I *accept* your apology.

Except means "excluding":

   I'll give you all my books *except* my dictionary.

addition/edition An *addition* is something that is added:

   My father built an *addition* to our house in the form of a porch.

An *edition* is an issue of a newspaper or one of a series of printings of a book:

   I checked the latest *edition* of the <u>Daily News</u> to see if my advertisement is in it.

advice/advise *Advice* is an opinion offered as a guide; it is what you give someone:

Betty asked for my *advice* about finding a job.

Advise is what you do when you give an opinion offered as a guide:

I couldn't *advise* Betty about finding a job.

affect/effect *Affect* means "to influence something":

Getting a bad grade will *affect* my chances for a scholarship.

Effect means "a result" or "to cause something to happen":

Your kindness had a great *effect* on me.

The committee struggled to *effect* a compromise.

allowed/aloud *Allowed* means "permitted":

I'm not *allowed* to skateboard on those steps.

Aloud means "out loud":

The teacher read the story *aloud*.

all ready/already *All ready* means "ready":

The dog was *all ready* to go for a walk.

Already means "before":

David had *already* made the salad.

altar/alter An *altar* is a table or place in a church:

They were married in front of the *altar*.

Alter means "to change":

My plane was delayed, so I had to *alter* my plans for the evening.

angel/angle An *angel* is a heavenly being:

That night, I felt an *angel* guiding me.

An *angle* is the space within two intersecting lines:

The road turned at a sharp *angle*.

are/our *Are* is a verb, the plural of *is:*

We *are* friends of the mayor.

Our means "belonging to us":

We have *our* family quarrels.

beside/besides *Beside* means "next to":

He sat *beside* me at the concert.

Besides means "in addition":

I would never lie to you; *besides*, I have no reason to lie.

brake/break *Brake* means "to stop" or "a device for stopping":

That truck *brakes* at railroad crossings.

When he saw the animal on the road, he hit the *brakes*.

Break means "to come apart" or "to make something come apart":

The eggs are likely to *break*.

I can *break* the seal on that package.

breath/breathe *Breath* is the air you take in, and it rhymes with *death:*

I was running so fast, I lost my *breath*.

Breathe means "to take in air":

He found it hard to *breathe* in high altitudes.

buy/by *Buy* means "to purchase something":

Sylvia wants to *buy* a shovel.

By means "near," "by means of," or "before":
>   He sat *by* his sister.
>   I learn *by* taking good notes in class.
>   *By* ten o'clock, Nick was tired.

capital/capitol *Capital* means "city" or "wealth":
>   Albany is the *capital* of New York.
>   Jack invested his *capital* in real estate.

A *capitol* is a building where a legislature meets:
>   The city has a famous *capitol* building.

cereal/serial *Cereal* is a breakfast food or type of grain:
>   My favorite *cereal* is Cheerios.

Serial means "in a series":
>   Look for the *serial* number on the appliance.

choose/chose *Choose* means "to select." It rhymes with *snooze:*
>   Today I am going to *choose* a new sofa.

Chose is the past tense of *choose:*
>   Yesterday I *chose* a new rug.

close/clothes/cloths *Close* means "near" or "intimate." It can also mean "to end or shut something":
>   We live *close* to the train station.
>   James and Margie are *close* friends.
>   Noreen wants to *close* her eyes for ten minutes.

Clothes are wearing apparel:
>   Eduardo has new *clothes.*

Cloths are pieces of fabric:
>   I clean the silver with damp *cloths* and a special polish.

coarse/course *Coarse* means "rough" or "crude":
>   The top of the table had a *coarse* texture.
>   His language was *coarse.*

A *course* is a direction or path. It is also a subject in school:
>   The hurricane took a northern *course.*
>   In my freshman year, I took a *course* in drama.

complement/compliment *Complement* means "complete" or "make better":
>   The colors in that room *complement* the style of the furniture.

A *compliment* is praise:
>   Trevor gave me a *compliment* about my cooking.

conscience/conscious Your *conscience* is your inner, moral guide:
>   His *conscience* bothered him when he told a lie.

Conscious means "aware" or "awake":
>   The accident victim was not fully conscious.

council/counsel A *council* is a group of people:
>   The city *council* meets tonight.

Counsel means "advice" or "to give advice":
>   I need your *counsel* about my investments.
>   My father always *counsels* me about my career.

decent/descent *Decent* means "suitable" or "proper":
>   I hope Mike gets a *decent* job.

Descent means "going down, falling, or sinking":
>The plane began its *descent* to the airport.

desert/dessert A *desert* is dry land. To *desert* means "to abandon":
>To survive a trip across the *desert*, people need water.
>He will never *desert* a friend.

Dessert is the sweet food we eat at the end of a meal.
>I want ice cream for *dessert*.

do/due *Do* means "perform":
>I have to stop complaining; I *do* it constantly.

Due means "owing" or "because of":
>The rent is *due* tomorrow.
>The game was canceled *due* to rain.

does/dose *Does* is a form of *do:*
>My father *does* the laundry.

A *dose* is a quantity of medicine.
>Whenever I had a cold, my mother gave me a *dose* of cough syrup.

fair/fare *Fair* means "unbiased." It can also mean "promising" or "good":
>The judge's decision was *fair.*
>Jose has a *fair* chance of winning the title.

A *fare* is the amount of money a passenger must pay.
>I couldn't afford the plane *fare* to Miami.

farther/further *Farther* means "a greater physical distance":
>His house is a few blocks *farther* down the street.

Further means "greater" or "additional." Use it when you are not describing a physical distance:
>My second French class gave me *further* training in French conversation.

flour/flower *Flour* is ground-up grain, an ingredient used in cooking:
>I use whole-wheat *flour* in my muffins.

A *flower* is a blossom:
>She wore a *flower* in her hair.

forth/fourth *Forth* means "forward":
>The pendulum on the clock swung back and *forth.*

Fourth means "number four in a sequence":
>I was *fourth* in line for tickets.

hear/here *Hear* means "to receive sounds in the ear":
>I can *hear* the music.

Here is a place:
>We can have the meeting *here.*

heard/herd *Heard* is the past tense of *hear:*
>I *heard* you talk in your sleep last night.

A *herd* is a group of animals:
>The farmer has a fine *herd* of cows.

hole/whole A *hole* is an empty place or opening:
>I see a *hole* in the wall.

Whole means "complete" or "entire":
>Silvio gave me the *whole* steak.

isle/aisle An *isle* is an island:
   We visited the *isle* of Capri.
An *aisle* is a passageway between sections of seats:
   The flight attendant came down the *aisle* and offered us coffee.

its/it's *Its* means "belonging to it":
   The car lost *its* rear bumper.
It's is a shortened form of *it is* or *it has:*
   It's a beautiful day.
   It's been a pleasure to meet you.

knew/new *Knew* is the past tense of *know:*
   I *knew* Teresa in high school.
New means "fresh, recent, not old":
   I want some *new* shoes.

know/no *Know* means "to understand":
   They *know* how to play soccer.
No is a negative:
   Carla has *no* fear of heights.

Exercise 1   **Words That Sound Alike/Look Alike**

Circle the correct words in parentheses in each sentence below.

1. I need to look (farther, further) into the circumstances of the crime before I can (advice, advise) you about possible suspects.

2. The rich investment banker collects first (additions, editions) of famous books; he has an expert tell him which ones to (buy, by).

3. Edward must have no (conscience, conscious), for he was willing to (desert, dessert) his children in order to satisfy his own desires.

4. Whenever Kim (complements, compliments) me, I (hear, here) a hint of insincerity in her voice.

5. Eric needs a (does, dose) of reality before he makes plans to walk to the (altar, alter) with Sabrina.

6. I spent a (hole, whole) lot of money on dresses and other (close, clothes, cloths) last month, and now payment is (do, due).

7. When I had to speak in front of the town (council, counsel), I was so nervous I could hardly (breath, breathe).

8. One of (are, our) trees was struck by lightning; a huge branch fell at a crazy (angel, angle).

9. A large man crowded in (beside, besides) me on the bus right before I tried to reach the (isle, aisle).

10. I'm lazy, and I don't know how to cook, so I live on (cereal, serial) and Pop Tarts unless someone cooks me a (decent, descent) meal.

COLLABORATE ▶   **Exercise 2**   **Words That Sound Alike/Look Alike**

Working with a partner or group, write one sentence for each word below.

1. a. its   _____

   b. it's   _____

2. a. coarse   _____

   b. course   _____

3. a. fair   _____

   b. fare   _____

4. a. forth   _____

   b. fourth   _____

5. a. capital   _____

   b. capitol   _____

6. a. accept   _____

   b. except   _____

7. a. brake   _____

   b. break   _____

8. a. affect   _____

   b. effect   _____

9. a. know   _____

   b. no   _____

10. a. flour   _____

   b. flower   _____

CONNECT ▶   **Exercise 3**   **Editing a Paragraph for Words That Sound Alike/Look Alike**

The following paragraph has errors in words that sound alike/look alike. Correct each error in the space above it. There are twelve errors.

The secret to losing weight is a healthy diet. I used to believe the advise I

herd on television: try this quick weight-loss product, or take these pills and

watch the pounds melt away. I also convinced myself that I really didn't eat

much, anyway, so I had no reason to change my diet. I would skip meals and live on snacks from the vending machine at my workplace. In edition, I would by desert foods like cake and cookies to reward myself after a long day. I justified these treats by telling myself I had barely eaten all day, so I could afford the calories. Meanwhile, my cloths were getting tight, and I was constantly tired. Deep down, I new I was not living a healthy life. Eventually, I excepted the fact that I had to make a conscience choice to change my eating habits. Today, when I walk down the supermarket isle, I chose carefully. I plan my meals so that I do not have to resort to chips and candy bars for energy. I do not focus on shedding pounds but concentrate on a hole new approach to food.

MORE WORDS THAT SOUND ALIKE/LOOK ALIKE

lead/led When *lead* rhymes with *need*, it means "to give directions, to take charge." If *lead* rhymes with *bed*, it is a metal:
> The marching band will *lead* the parade.
> Your bookbag is as heavy as *lead*.
Led is the past form of *lead* when it means "to give directions, to take charge":
> The cheerleaders *led* the parade last year.

loan/lone A *loan* is something you give on the condition that it be returned:
> When I was broke, I got a *loan* of fifty dollars from my aunt.
Lone means "solitary, alone":
> A *lone* shopper stood in the checkout line.

loose/lose *Loose* means "not tight":
> In the summer, *loose* clothing keeps me cool.
To *lose* something means "to be unable to keep it":
> I'm afraid I will *lose* my car keys.

moral/morale *Moral* means "upright, honorable, connected to ethical standards":
> I have a *moral* obligation to care for my children.
Morale is confidence or spirit:
> After the game, the team's *morale* was low.

pain/pane *Pain* means "suffering":
> I had very little *pain* after the surgery.
A *pane* is a piece of glass:
> The girl's wild throw broke a window *pane*.

pair/pear A *pair* is a set of two:
> Mark has a *pair* of antique swords.

A *pear* is a fruit:

In the autumn, I like a *pear* for a snack.

passed/past *Passed* means "went by." It can also mean "handed to":

The happy days *passed* too quickly.

Janice *passed* me the mustard.

Past means "the time that has gone by":

Let's leave the *past* behind us.

patience/patients *Patience* is calm endurance:

When I am caught in a traffic jam, I should have more *patience*.

Patients are people under medical care:

There are too many *patients* in the doctor's waiting room.

peace/piece *Peace* is calmness:

Looking at the ocean brings me a sense of *peace*.

A *piece* is a part of something:

Norman took a *piece* of coconut cake.

personal/personnel *Personal* means "connected to a person." It can also mean "intimate":

Whether to lease or own a car is a *personal* choice.

That information is too *personal* to share.

Personnel are the staff in an office:

The Digby Electronics Company is developing a new health plan for its *personnel*.

plain/plane *Plain* means "simple, clear, or ordinary." It can also mean "flat land":

The restaurant serves *plain* but tasty food.

Her house was in the center of a windy *plain*.

A *plane* is an aircraft:

We took a small *plane* to the island.

presence/presents Your *presence* is your attendance, your being somewhere:

We request your *presence* at our wedding.

Presents are gifts:

My daughter got too many birthday *presents*.

principal/principle *Principal* means "most important." It also means "the head of a school":

My *principal* reason for quitting is the low salary.

The *principal* of Crestview Elementary School is popular with students.

A *principle* is a guiding rule:

Betraying a friend is against my *principles*.

quiet/quit/quite *Quiet* means "without noise":

The library has many *quiet* corners.

Quit means "stop":

Will you *quit* complaining?

Quite means "truly" or "exactly":

Victor's speech was *quite* convincing.

rain/reign/rein *Rain* is wet weather:

We have had a week of *rain*.

To *reign* is to rule; *reign* is royal rule:
>King Arthur's *reign* in Camelot is the subject of many poems.

A *rein* is a leather strap in an animal's harness:
>When Charlie got on the horse, he held the *reins* very tight.

right/rite/write   *Right* is a direction (the opposite of left). It can also mean "correct":
>To get to the gas station, turn *right* at the corner.

>On my sociology test, I got nineteen out of twenty questions *right*.

A *rite* is a ceremony:
>I am interested in the funeral *rites* of other cultures.

To *write* is to set down in words:
>Brian has to *write* a book report.

sight/site/cite   A *sight* is something you can see:
>The truck stop was a welcome *sight*.

A *site* is a location:
>The city is building a courthouse on the *site* of my old school.

Cite means "to quote an authority." It can also mean "to give an example":
>In her term paper, Christina wanted to *cite* several computer experts.

>When my father lectured me on speeding, he *cited* the story of my best friend's car accident.

sole/soul   A *sole* is the bottom of a foot or shoe. It can also mean "the only one":
>My left boot needs a new *sole*.

>My father was the *sole* man at dinner.

A *soul* is the spiritual part of a person:
>Some people say meditation is good for the *soul*.

stair/stare   A *stair* is a step:
>The toddler carefully climbed each *stair*.

A *stare* is a long, fixed look:
>I wish that woman wouldn't *stare* at me.

stake/steak   A *stake* is a stick driven into the ground:
>The gardener put *stakes* around the tomato plants.

A *steak* is a piece of meat or fish:
>I like my *steak* cooked medium rare.

stationary/stationery   *Stationary* means "standing still":
>As the speaker presented his speech, he remained *stationary*.

Stationery is writing paper:
>For my birthday, my uncle gave me some *stationery* with my name printed on it.

steal/steel   To *steal* means "to take someone else's property without permission or right":
>Last night, someone tried to *steal* my car.

Steel is a form of iron:
>The door is made of *steel*.

than/then   *Than* is used to compare things:
>My dog is more intelligent *than* many people.

Then means "at that time":
>I lived in Buffalo for two years; *then* I moved to Albany.

their/there/they're *Their* means "belonging to them":

My grandparents donated *their* old television to a women's shelter.

There means "at that place." It can also be used as an introductory word:

Sit *there*, next to Simone.

There is a reason for his happiness.

They're is a contraction of *they are:*

Jaime and Sandra are visiting; *they're* my cousins.

thorough/through/threw *Thorough* means "complete":

I did a *thorough* cleaning of my closet.

Through means "from one side to the other." It can also mean "finished":

We drove *through* Greenview on our way to Lake Western.

I'm *through* with my studies.

Threw is the past tense of *throw:*

I *threw* the ball to him.

to/too/two *To* means "in a direction toward." It is also a word that can go in front of a verb:

I am driving *to* Miami.

Selena loves *to* write poems.

Too means "also." It also means "very":

Anita played great golf; Adam did well, *too*.

It is *too* kind of you to visit.

Two is the number:

Mr. Almeida owns *two* clothing stores.

vain/vane/vein *Vain* means "conceited." It also means "unsuccessful":

Victor is *vain* about his dark, curly hair.

The doctor made a *vain* attempt to revive the patient.

A *vane* is a device that moves to indicate the direction of the wind:

There was an old weather *vane* on the barn roof.

A *vein* is a blood vessel:

I could see the *veins* in his hands.

waist/waste The *waist* is the middle part of the body:

He had a leather belt around his *waist*.

Waste means "to use carelessly." It also means "thrown away because it is useless":

I can't *waste* my time watching trashy television shows.

That manufacturing plant has many *waste* products.

wait/weight *Wait* means "to hold yourself ready for something":

I can't *wait* until my check arrives.

Weight means "heaviness":

He tested the *weight* of the bat.

weather/whether *Weather* refers to conditions outside.

If the *weather* is warm, I'll go swimming.

Whether means "if":

Whether you help me or not, I'll paint the hallway.

were/we're/where *Were* is the past form of *are:*

Only last year, we *were* scared freshmen.

We're is the contraction of *we are:*

Today, *we're* confident sophomores.

Where refers to a place:
> Show me *where* you used to play basketball.

whined/wind/wined *Whined* means "complained":
> Polly *whined* about the weather because the rain kept her indoors.

Wind (if it rhymes with *find*) means "to coil or wrap something" or "to turn a key":
> *Wind* that extension cord, or you'll trip on it.

Wind (if it rhymes with *sinned*) is air in motion:
> The *wind* blew my cap off.

If someone *wined* you, he or she treated you to some wine:
> My brother *wined* and dined his boss.

who's/whose *Who's* is a contraction of *who is* or *who has:*
> *Who's* driving?

Whose means "belonging to whom":
> I wonder *whose* dog this is.

woman/women *Woman* means "one adult female person":
> A *woman* in the supermarket gave me her extra coupons.

Women means "more than one woman":
> Three *women* from Missouri joined the management team.

wood/would *Wood* is a hard substance made from trees:
> I have a table made of a polished *wood.*

Would is the past form of *will:*
> Albert said he *would* think about the offer.

your/you're *Your* means "belonging to you":
> I think you dropped *your* wallet.

You're is the short form of *you are:*
> *You're* not telling the truth.

(**Exercise 4**) **More Words That Sound Alike/Look Alike**

Circle the correct words in each sentence below.

1. During the (rain, reign, rein) of King George III of England, the American colonies lost (patience, patients) with the king's restrictive laws and fought for (their, there, they're) freedom.

2. (Moral, Morale) at the fraternity has declined since the group was criticized for its reckless initiation (rights, rites, writes).

3. In these negotiations, the ambassador's (principal, principle) goal is to maintain the (peace, piece) and not (loose, lose) the support of our allies.

4. It was (quiet, quit, quite) noisy in the library today until the librarian asked the three elderly men to (quiet, quit, quite) laughing and chatting at the computers.

5. We thought we were lost at first, but eventually Diane's directions (lead, led) us to a large red barn with a (weather, whether) (vain, vane, vein).

6. The (whined, wind, wined) swept the rain against the car with such force that we hardly knew (were, we're, where) we (were, we're, where) going.

7. I want to know (who's, whose) responsible for making that (woman, women) wait for an hour and (than, then) giving her the wrong prescription.

8. If (your, you're) looking for a (loan, lone) to start your business, you will have to (site, site, cite) other, similar projects that have been successful.

9. Edward knew he (wood, would) be (to, too, two) busy to stop for a meal, so he put a (pair, pear), a bottle of water, and a granola bar in his briefcase.

10. It will take time to lessen the (pain, pane) of Rick's loss, but eventually he will find (peace, piece).

 COLLABORATE ▶ (Exercise 5) **More Words That Sound Alike/Look Alike**

Working with a partner or group, write one sentence for each of the words below.

1. a. loose   _____

  b. lose   _____

2. a. stationary _____

  b. stationery _____

3. a. wander   _____

  b. wonder   _____

4. a. passed   _____

  b. past   _____

5. a. plain   _____

  b. plane   _____

6. a. thorough _____

  b. through   _____

  c. threw   _____

7. a. sole   _____

  b. soul   _____

8. a. stake   _____

  b. steak   _____

9. a. wait   _____

  b. weight   _____

10. a. stair   _____

     b. stare   _____

Exercise 6   **Editing a Paragraph for Errors in More Words**   ◀ CONNECT ⊂⊃⊂⊃
           That Sound Alike/Look Alike

The following paragraph has errors in words that sound alike or look alike.
Correct each error in the space above it. There are eleven errors.

    For months, I envied my roommate's remarkable luck in college. Tony is

one of those students who never seems to study until the last minute and yet

always seems to have the rite answers on a test. I, on the other hand, study regu-

larly and steadily for all my tests and quizzes. Yet Tony always got better grades

then I did. Sometimes I wandered if he had managed to steel a copy of the test,

but I realized he had two talents: a knack for memorizing facts quickly and nerves

of steal that allowed him to remain cool under pressure. I used to wind to my sis-

ter that it wasn't fair. Than, one day, Tony and I, who were in the same history

class, took our final exam. My preparation for the test had been through; Tony

hadn't had the patients to do anything but skim the textbook. As I worked on my

exam, I saw Tony stair blankly. Later, he began to fidget. After the exam, Tony

asked me, "Wasn't that a terrible test?" "No," I answered, "I thought it was quiet

easy." When our instructor posted the results of the exam, I stopped envying Tony.

Exercise 7   **Words That Sound Alike/Look Alike:**
           A Comprehensive Exercise

Circle the correct words in parentheses in each sentence below.

    1. As the officer began to (advice, advise) Lucy of her (rights, rites,
        writes), Lucy remained (stationary, stationery).

    2. Mrs. Kowalski is such a good (sole, soul) that I sometimes feel
        she is an (angel, angle) (hear, here) on earth.

    3. (Its, It's) a sad day when a Tom Cruise movie loses (its, it's)
        power to entertain me, but this movie is a (waist, waste) of my
        time.

    4. Liam's shirt (complements, compliments) the color of his eyes,
        and that color (wood, would) look good on you, (to, too,
        two).

5. I was not (conscience, conscious) of Anita's bad temper until she jerked hard on her horse's (rains, reigns, reins) and (than, then) kicked the poor animal.

6. It was so cold that I could see my (breath, breathe) on the window (pane, pain), and I (knew, new) that winter had arrived.

7. Bart was not willing to (accept, except) his brother's (council, counsel) about applying for financial aid.

8. (Your, You're) behavior in court can (affect, effect) the outcome of the trial, no matter how (fair, fare) the jury tries to be.

9. As I walked down the (isle, aisle) with my bride, I suddenly realized that we were about to go (forth, fourth) into a (knew, new) life.

10. My doctor is encouraging his (patience, patients) to try a (does, dose) of an over-the-counter cold medicine instead of overusing antibiotics.

11. My brother's class is taking a trip to Tallahassee, the (capital, capitol) of Florida, as part of a (coarse, course) in political science.

12. I hope that the loss of his home will have no (farther, further) (affect, effect) on the (all ready, already) unhappy child.

13. Larry doesn't follow fashion trends; when he needs (close, clothes, cloths), he buys (plain, plane) old jeans and flannel shirts from discount stores.

14. My first goal is to find a (decent, descent) apartment; (then, than) I want to meet someone (who's, whose) (principals, principles) are the same as mine.

15. I (wander, wonder) if I should go to the (personal, personnel) department of Satellite Services and apply for a job; I've (heard, herd) that (moral, morale) is high among the staff.

16. The actress is so (vain, vane, vein) that she expects fresh (flours, flowers) in her dressing room every night.

17. I want to take my toddler to Felipe's wedding, but I don't (know, no) (weather, whether) children are (aloud, allowed) at the ceremony.

18. Residents of the area are nervous about the rumors of a (cereal, serial) killer; (their, there, they're) locking (their, there, they're) doors at night.

19. It was difficult for the employees at the plant to (wait, weight) for a decision from the company president when so many jobs (were, we're, where) at (stake, steak).

20. The famous athlete's (presence, presents) at the local basketball game caused many people to (stair, stare.)

◀ CONNECT ◯◯◯

Exercise 8   **Editing a Paragraph for Errors in Words That Sound Alike/Look Alike: A Comprehensive Exercise**

The following paragraph has errors in words that sound alike or look alike. Correct each error in the space above it. There are nineteen errors.

There are a rite way and a wrong way to make important decisions. The wrong way is to act on impulse and to chose immediately. Decisions made this way can prove to be the correct ones, but more frequently they lead to pane and regret. A better way to decide is to use patients and be true to personnel principals. It takes time to reach a conclusion, and some of that time can be spent seeking advise from people who's knowledge, experience, or morales you respect. Another step in decision-making is to look farther than the immediate affects of a choice. Getting married on a whim, for example, can bring instant happiness. However, once the joyful trip down the isle is complete and a blissful period has past, there are problems like money and education to consider. Beside, any life-changing decision deserves to be looked at from all the angels. Its better to consider your options carefully then to spend years wandering how your life wood have been different if you'd made another choice.

CHAPTER 34
Word Choice

One way to improve your writing is to pay attention to your choice of words. As you revise and edit, be careful to use precise language and to avoid wordiness and cliches.

PRECISE LANGUAGE

Try to be as specific as you can in explaining or describing. Replace vague, general words or phrases with more precise language.

not this: Last night, I made a lot of money in tips.
but this: Last night, I made *fifty dollars* in tips.

not this: He gave me a nice smile.
but this: He gave me a *friendly* smile.
or this: He gave me a *reassuring* smile.
or this: He gave me a *welcoming* smile.

not this: Maggie is a good friend.
but this: Maggie is a *loyal* friend.
or this: Maggie is a *devoted* friend.

> **Exercise 1**   **Using Precise Language**

In the following sentences, replace each italicized word or phrase with a more precise word or phrase. Write your revisions above the lines.

1. I had a *nice* weekend with my folks.

2. You need to buy *a lot* of potato chips for the party.

3. I think about you *often*.

4. Take Mr. Benson for English; he's *nice*.

5. Mitchell had another *bad* day at work.

6. This time, let's go to an *interesting* movie.

7. I am going to need *a lot* of help with this course.

8. I tried to practice my speech, but it sounds *stupid*.

9. What's wrong? You sound *funny* today.

10. You will make a *great* father someday.

WORDINESS

As you revise and edit your work, check for *wordiness*, the use of extra words. If you can say the same thing in fewer words, do so. You can be precise *and* direct.

> **not this:** After the accident, ~~I thought in my mind that~~ I was to blame.
> **but this:** After the accident, *I thought* I was to blame.

> **not this:** ~~In my opinion,~~ I think children should exercise daily.
> **but this:** *I think* children should exercise daily.

> **not this:** Jorge bought a CD ~~for the price of~~ $10.95.
> **but this:** Jorge bought a CD *for* $10.95.

Here is a list of some wordy expressions and possible substitutes:

Wordy Expressions	Possible Substitutes
asset group	assets
attach together	attach
at a later date and time	later
at a future date	later
at that time	then
at the present moment	now, presently
at the present time	now, presently
at this point in time	now, today
basic essentials	essentials
blend together	blend
by means of	by
by the fact that	because
combine together	combine

day in and day out	daily
deep down inside he believed	he believed
due to the fact that	because
each and every one	each one
end result	result
for the reason that	because
gather together	gather
have a need for	need
have a realization of	realize
I felt inside	I felt
I personally feel	I feel
I thought in my head	I thought
I thought to myself	I thought
in the field of art (music, etc.)	in art (music, etc.)
in the near future	soon
in this day and age	today
in this modern world	today
in my mind, I think	I think
in my opinion, I think	I think
in order to	to
in today's society	today
join together	join
maximum amount	maximum
mix together	mix
of a remarkable kind	remarkable
on a daily basis	daily
on a regular basis	regularly
past experience	experience
point in time	time
reached a decision	decided
really and truly	really
refer back	refer
repeat again	repeat
share in common	share
short in stature	short
small in size	small
skills set	skills
the reason being	because
top priority	priority
true facts	facts
two different kinds	two kinds
unite together	unite
very unique	unique

Exercise 2   **Revising for Wordiness**

Revise the following sentences, eliminating the wordiness. Write your revisions in the space above the lines.

1. At this point in time, I personally feel that better office technology

should be the company's top priority.

2. I cannot approve a promotion for Walter Ford because in my opinion I think that his skills set would not be adequate in the new position.

3. By means of researching the alternatives, our committee has reached a decision to continue the office's contract with the Info-Fix computer maintenance company due to the fact that Info-Fix offers us the maximum amount of service at a reasonable price.

4. In this day and age, consumers are willing to spend their money on some computer products of a remarkable kind.

5. I thought to myself that I had better start studying on a regular basis if I really and truly wanted to finish college.

6. Todd asked me to repeat my refusal again because deep down inside he believed that I would never say "no" to him.

7. Christina is small in size and short in stature, yet she has a powerful personality and a very unique ability to motivate others.

8. Past experience has taught me that in today's society we can blend together two different kinds of music and create a popular and profitable sound.

9. By the fact that I plan to be an artist, I would rather not take a course in the field of mathematics, but I have to learn the basic essentials as a college requirement.

10. I want to know the true facts of the store's bankruptcy, but you just refer back to gossip and rumors.

CLICHÉS

Clichés are worn-out expressions. Once they were a new way of making a point, but now they are old and tired. You should avoid them in your writing.

> **not this:** I know that Monica will always ~~be there for me~~.
> **but this:** I know that Monica will always support me.

> **not this:** Alan experienced the ~~trials and tribulations~~ of late registration.
> **but this:** Alan experienced the difficulties of late registration.

Following are some common clichés. If you spot clichés in your writing, replace them with more direct or thoughtful statements of your own.

Some Common Clichés

all in all	in the final analysis
at the end of the day	hustle and bustle
beat around the bush	I wouldn't be where I am today
between a rock and a hard place	information superhighway
break the ice	last but not least
break new ground	let bygones be bygones
climb the ladder of success	light as a feather
cry my eyes out	live life to the fullest
cutting edge	make ends meet
dead as a doornail	one day at a time
down in the dumps	on top of the world
down on his luck	quick as a wink
a drop in the bucket	shoulder to cry on
few and far between	sick as a dog
free as a bird	state of the art
first and foremost	through thick and thin
give it your best shot	tried and true
go the distance	up at the crack of dawn
grass is always greener	when all is said and done
hard as a rock	without a shadow of a doubt
he (she) is always there for me	worked and slaved
hit the nail on the head	work like a dog

COLLABORATE ▶ | Exercise 3 | **Revising Clichés**

The following sentences contain clichés (italicized). Working with a partner or a group, rewrite the sentences, replacing the clichés with more direct or thoughtful words or phrases. Write in the space above the lines.

1. When I lost my best friend, I was ready to *cry my eyes out.*

2. Kind neighbors are *few and far between.*

3. *I wouldn't be where I am today* without Professor Miyori's

inspiring classes.

4. Since I lost my weekend job at the hospital, I am struggling to

make ends meet.

5. Hank has a *tried and true* method of repairing leaky

windows.

6. When I take my dog for a walk, she acts like she is *on top of the*

world.

7. If you want to be on our management team, you have to be able to

go the distance.

8. Tanika has been *down in the dumps* ever since she had

an argument with her sister.

9. If I am not qualified for the job, *don't beat around the bush*

about the situation.

10. Some people might have envied my family, but that's only because

they believed *the grass is always greener* in

somebody else's home.

Exercise 4   **Identifying Clichés**   ◀ CONNECT ⬤⬤⬤

Underline all the clichés in the following paragraph. There are nine clichés.

> Last month my husband faced so many problems that he had no choice but to take things one day at a time. First, Geraldo was as sick as a dog with the flu for ten days, but that illness proved to be a drop in the bucket compared to his other difficulties. His truck broke down just when Geraldo was most needed at work, and he had already missed several work days because of the flu. His boss told him to show up for work or lose his job, putting Geraldo between a rock and a hard place. To repair the truck, Geraldo got a loan from his brother and returned to work. He worked like a slave, getting up at the crack of dawn and working until late in the evening to make up for the days he had missed. Last but not least, Geraldo learned that his niece had been injured in a car accident in Miami. All in all, it was a tough time for Geraldo, but he proved that he knows how to cope through thick and thin.

Exercise 5   **Editing for Precise Language, Wordiness,**
                and Clichés

Edit the following paragraph for precise language, wordiness, and clichés.   ◀ CONNECT ⬤⬤⬤
Write your revisions above the lines. There are twelve places that need editing.

When Nina finished high school, she expected to find a job at a nice clothing store and quickly climb the ladder of success. Deep down inside, Nina believed that because she had a lot of good ideas about fashion, she could really and truly become a famous designer in two or three years. She felt that her designs would be very unique, and without a shadow of a doubt, she would soon be a star in the fashion world. Once she landed a job in a clothing store at the mall, however, Nina learned that anyone who wants to learn how to create fashion first has to learn how to sell fashion. Day in and day out, she worked and slaved until she became an assistant manager. Once her salary was enough to allow her to make ends meet, Nina made an important decision. She enrolled in college, where she is taking classes in the fields of fashion design and business. Although she can afford only part-time attendance, she is giving her best shot to an education that can lead her closer to her dreams.

SLANG

Slang is an informal vocabulary used by a specific group such as teenagers, musicians, or sports fans. Those who are not a part of the group may not understand its slang, and slang changes quickly. "Cool" and "hot" sometimes mean "popular," and "bad" as a slang term can mean "good." Slang is not standard English, and you should avoid it in your academic writing.

> **slang:** No problem.
> **standard English:** You're welcome. (After "Thank you.")

> **slang:** I got your back.
> **standard English:** I'll protect you.

> **slang:** Give it up for
> **standard English:** welcome; applaud for

> **slang:** back in the day
> **standard English:** in the past; when I was younger

> **slang:** creeps me out
> **standard English:** makes me uneasy

> **slang:** my bad
> **standard English:** my fault; my mistake

> **slang:** They got served.
> **standard English:** They were soundly defeated.

Exercise 6 **Identifying Slang**   ◀ COLLABORATE 👥

Working with a partner or group, write five examples of slang that you and your friends use today. After each example of slang, write its meaning in standard English.

1. slang: _____

standard English: _____

2. slang: _____

standard English: _____

3. slang: _____

standard English: _____

4. slang: _____

standard English: _____

5. slang: _____

standard English: _____

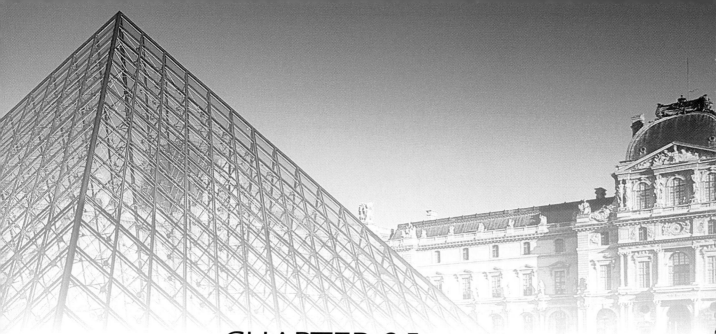

CHAPTER 35
Sentence Variety

One way to polish your writing is to work on *sentence variety*, the use of different lengths and kinds of sentences. You can become skilled in sentence variety by (1) revising your writing for a balance of short and long sentences and for a mix of sentence types and (2) being aware of the kinds of sentences you can use.

BALANCING LONG AND SHORT SENTENCES

There are no grammar errors in the following paragraph, but it needs revision for sentence variety.

> I have a routine for waking up. First, I grab a can of Diet Pepsi. I gulp it down. I turn on the TV at the same time. I watch cartoons. I sit for about half an hour. Then the caffeine in the Pepsi starts working. I move to the shower. I make the water temperature very hot. Steam fills the bathroom. My muscles come alive. I begin to feel fully awake.

The paragraph is filled with short sentences. Read it aloud, and you will notice the choppy, boring style of the writing. Compare it with the following revised paragraph, which contains a variety of short and long sentences:

> I have a routine for waking up. First, I grab a can of Diet Pepsi and gulp it down while I turn on the TV. Then I watch cartoons for about half an hour. When the caffeine in the Pepsi starts working, I move to the shower. I make the water tempera-

ture so hot that steam fills the bathroom. My muscles come alive as I begin to feel fully awake.

The revised paragraph balances short and long sentences. Read it aloud, and you will notice the way the varied lengths create a more flowing, interesting style.

Some writers rely too heavily on short sentences; others use too many long sentences. The following paragraph contains too many long sentences.

Randall wanted to make new friends because his old friends had become a bad influence. Randall loved his old friends, especially Michael, but they had begun to be involved in some dangerous activities, and Randall didn't want to be part of these crimes because Randall wanted to apply to the police academy, and he knew that having a record would destroy his chances of admission. Consequently, Randall was honest with Michael, and Randall told him that Randall couldn't risk his future by mixing with people who liked to joyride in stolen cars or steal from neighborhood stores. Soon Randall's friends stopped asking him out, and, for a while Randall felt lonely and isolated, but eventually, Randall formed some new friendships, and he was happy to be part of a new group and happy it was one that didn't break the law.

Read the previous paragraph aloud, and you will notice that the sentences are so long and complicated that part of their meaning is lost. Piling on one long sentence after another can make a paragraph boring and difficult to follow. Compare the previous paragraph with the following revised version.

Randall wanted to make new friends because his old friends had become a bad influence. Randall loved his old friends, especially Michael. However, they had begun to be involved in some dangerous activities, and Randall didn't want to be a part of these crimes. He wanted to apply to the police academy and knew that having a record would destroy his chances of admission. Consequently, Randall spoke honestly to Michael. Randall explained that he couldn't risk his future by mixing with people who liked to joyride in stolen cars or steal from neighborhood stores. Soon Randall's friends stopped asking him out, and, for a while, Randall felt lonely and isolated. Eventually, Randall formed some new friendships and was happy to be part of a new, law-abiding group.

Read the revised paragraph aloud, and you will notice the combination of long and short sentences makes the paragraph clearer and smoother. Careful revision helps you achieve such a mix.

Exercise 1   **Revising Short Sentences**

The following paragraph is composed entirely of short sentences. Rewrite it so that it contains a mix of short and long sentences. Write your revisions above the lines.

My great aunt leads an active life for a woman of seventy-five. She works at a

drug store. She has worked there for thirty years. She works five days a week.

Every Friday night she meets her friends. They drink coffee and play cards. They also gossip about their neighbors. Each weekend, she sings in a choir. Afterwards, the members of the choir go out for brunch. My great aunt also keeps up with the latest fashions. She is well known for her style. It is clearly expressed in her elaborate hats. She is a young woman of seventy-five. I'd like to be like her someday.

Exercise 2 **Revising Long Sentences**

The following paragraph is composed entirely of long sentences. Rewrite it so that it contains a mix of short and long sentences. Write your revisions above the lines.

Yesterday, I heard a conversation that hurt me deeply. I am still upset about it because I cannot figure out why people would be so unkind about me when they hardly know me or have any right to assess me so negatively. It all began at work as I was about to enter the break room and I heard two people I considered to be my friends talking. All I heard was my name, and then someone laughed as if I were a joke of some kind, and by this point I decided to stay outside the door and listen. Soon I heard one of my so-called friends say, "Jerome? He's not invited." I decided to walk away from the room so the two wouldn't notice me outside and since I couldn't walk in without them wondering what I might have heard. I have spent hours trying to understand why they laughed at me and, even worse, why I'm being left out of some party or other event. I know I'm being silly, and I tell myself I heard only part of a conversation that could be interpreted in a different way, but I still feel that hearing others discuss me was a terrible experience.

USING DIFFERENT WAYS TO BEGIN SENTENCES

Most of the time, writers begin sentences with the subject. However, if you change the word order, you can break the monotony of using the same pattern over and over.

Begin With an Adverb

One way to change the word order is to begin with an **adverb,** a word that describes verbs, adjectives, or other adverbs. (For more on adverbs, see Chapter 20.) You can move adverbs from the middle to the beginning of the sentence as long as the meaning is clear.

> **adverb in middle:** Ricky opened the package *carefully* and checked the contents.
>
> **adverb at beginning:** *Carefully*, Ricky opened the package and checked the contents.
>
> **adverb in middle:** The policewoman *calmly* issued a ticket to the aggressive driver.
>
> **adverb at beginning:** *Calmly*, the policewoman issued a ticket to the aggressive driver.

Exercise 3 **Writing Sentences That Begin with an Adverb**

Rewrite each sentence so that it begins with an adverb. Write your revisions above the lines.

1. Isabel smiled slyly at the unsuspecting new team member.

2. Emilio searched frantically for his lost concert tickets.

3. The big dog barked angrily at the strange man in the yard.

4. Ernie stroked the horse rhythmically to calm it.

5. My mother frequently spends her Saturdays at garage sales.

6. Amber walked carefully between the shelves filled with antiques.

7. The evil scientist in the film laughed cruelly at his victim.

8. Andrew thoughtlessly revealed his sister's infatuation with his new friend.

9. Charlie silently accepted the blame for the incident.

10. The little boy slept blissfully in his father's arms.

Begin With a Prepositional Phrase

A **prepositional phrase** contains a preposition and its object. (For more on prepositions, see Chapter 14.) You can change the usual word order of a sentence by moving a prepositional phrase from the end of a sentence to the beginning. You can do this as long as the meaning of the sentence remains clear.

> **prepositional phrase at the end:** A gleaming silver convertible suddenly passed me *in the left lane.*
> **prepositional phrase at the beginning:** *In the left lane,* a gleaming silver convertible suddenly passed me.
> **prepositional phrase at the end:** The bulldog growled and snarled *with fierce intensity.*
> **prepositional phrase at the beginning:** *With fierce intensity,* the bulldog growled and snarled.

Note: Most of the time, you put a comma after a prepositional phrase that begins a sentence. However, you do not need a comma if the prepositional phrase is short.

Exercise 4 Writing Sentences That Begin with a Prepositional Phrase

Rewrite the following sentences, moving a prepositional phrase to the beginning of the sentence. Write your revisions above the lines.

1. Oscar was in bed with the flu during most of spring break.

2. The white van with a dented rear panel remained in the alley.

3. Daniel felt most lonely on the weekends.

4. You can get homemade lemon cake at the Superior Bakery.

5. Ardeese can't write a letter or an essay without her dictionary.

6. I'll do the laundry before I go to work.

7. The heroic soldier received letters and gifts from hundreds of strangers.

8. An old letter was concealed inside a dusty leather book.

9. There is a kind person underneath Vinnie's rough exterior.

10. We swam in the ice-cold lake after the rain stopped.

Exercise 5 Creating Sentences That Begin With Prepositional Phrases   ◀ COLLABORATE 👥

Working with a partner or group, write sentences that begin with the following prepositional phrases.

1. In a year _____

2. On long weekends _____

3. After the accident _____

4. For amusement _____

5. Under too much pressure _____

6. Between us _____

7. Near my house _____

8. With no regret _____

9. Before you go _____

10. At the end of class _____

USING DIFFERENT WAYS TO JOIN IDEAS

Another way to create sentence variety is to try different methods of combining ideas. Among these methods are (1) using an *-ing* modifier, (2) using an *-ed* modifier, (3) using an appositive, and (4) using a *who*, *which*, or *that* clause.

Use an *-ing* Modifier

You can avoid short, choppy sentences by using an *-ing* modifier. This way, one of the short sentences becomes a phrase. (For more on modifiers, see Chapter 21.)

two short sentences: Sarah was talking on her cell phone. She drove into a tree.
combined with an *-ing* modifier: *Talking on her cell phone*, Sarah drove into a tree.

two short sentences: Mr. Martinez loves to read travel books. He plans his next vacation.
combined with an *-ing* modifier: *Planning his next vacation*, Mr. Martinez loves to read travel books.

Note: If the modifier begins the sentence, be sure that the next word is the one the modifier describes.

Exercise 6 Using *-ing* Modifiers

Following are pairs of sentences. Combine each pair by using an *-ing* modifier.

1. A fat black cat sat by the window. It was licking its paws.

combined: _____

2. The earrings gleamed in the velvet box. They invited me to try them on.

combined: _____

_____

3. Tonya wiped her little boy's tears. She struggled to comfort the child.

combined: _____

_____

4. My neighbor's television blasted through my apartment walls. It irritated me all weekend.

combined: _____

_____

5. One of my friends hoped to get good tips. She took a job at a popular restaurant.

combined: _____

_____

6. Aggressive drivers tailgate at high speeds. They risk their own and others' lives.

combined: _____

_____

7. My mother worried about my first job away from home. She called me three times a day.

combined: _____

_____

8. Philip Delgado needed a favor. He showed up at my house last night.

combined: _____

_____

9. Carrie Swenson dreamed of a career as a dancer. She enrolled in a high school dedicated to the arts.

combined: _____

_____

10. The bride wore a black dress. She shocked all the wedding guests.

combined: _____

_____

Use an *-ed* Modifier

You can also avoid short, choppy sentences by using an *-ed* modifier. This way, one of the short sentences becomes a phrase. (For more on modifiers, see Chapter 21.)

two short sentences: The fish was broiled with lemon and butter. The fish was delicious.
combined with an *-ed* modifier: *Broiled with lemon and butter,* the fish was delicious.

Note: If the modifier begins the sentence, be sure that the next word is the one the modifier describes.

two short sentences: Sam gave me a jewelry box. It was painted with silver and blue flowers.
combined with an *-ed* modifier: Sam gave me a jewelry box *painted with silver and blue flowers.*

Exercise 7 Using *-ed* Modifiers

Following are pairs of sentences. Combine each pair, using an *-ed* modifier.

1. The chicken was stuffed with herb dressing. The chicken was tasty.

combined: _____

_____

2. Armand's boat was a total loss. Armand's boat was wrecked in a fierce storm.

combined: _____

3. Alan followed every rule. Alan was motivated by fear of his supervisor.

combined: _____

_____

4. I lost a beautiful bracelet. The bracelet was studded with coral beads.

combined: _____

_____

5. My new belt had a large silver buckle. The buckle was engraved with an elaborate design.

combined: _____

_____

6. Sergeant Thomas Levy was named Officer of the Year. He risked his life to save a woman drowning in a canal.

combined: _____

_____

7. The old house was designed for a large family. It was converted into three spacious apartments.

   combined: _____

   _____

8. Patrick is inspired by his famous mother. He is studying to become a child psychologist.

   combined: _____

   _____

9. Samantha was married at eighteen. She has never experienced living on her own.

   combined: _____

   _____

10. Now that I have my own place, I miss my mother's kitchen. It was stocked with snacks and treats.

    combined: _____

    _____

👥 COLLABORATE ▶   (Exercise 8) **Completing Sentences with *-ing* or *-ed* Modifiers**

Working with a partner or group, complete each sentence below.

1. Stranded in the airport _____

   _____

2. Looking for trouble _____

3. Taking the wrong turn_____

4. Suspected of murder _____

5. Deprived of sleep _____

6. Smiling at me _____

7. Trapped in the cave_____

8. Dropping the ball _____

9. Excited by the news _____

10. Trusting his friend_____

Use an Appositive

Another way to combine short, choppy sentences is to use an appositive. An **appositive** is a phrase that renames or describes a noun. Appositives can go in the beginning, middle, or end of a sentence. Use commas to set off the appositive.

> **two short sentences:** Chocolate milk contains calcium and vitamins. It is a favorite of children.
> **combined with an appositive:** *A favorite of children*, chocolate milk contains calcium and vitamins.

> **two short sentences:** Richard is my best friend. He has been a wrestler for several years.
> **combined with an appositive:** Richard, *my best friend*, has been a wrestler for several years.

> **two short sentences:** I am looking forward to Thanksgiving. It is my favorite holiday.
> **combined with an appositive:** I am looking forward to Thanksgiving, *my favorite holiday*.

Exercise 9   **Using Appositives**

Following are pairs of sentences. Combine each pair by using an appositive.

1. Inez is an accountant. She is helping me with my taxes.

   combined: _____

   _____

2. Island Theaters is an old movie house. It is being sold to a restaurant chain.

   combined: _____

   _____

3. I want to take you to Electronics Unlimited. It is the cheapest computer store in the area.

   combined: _____

   _____

4. My new boyfriend took me to dinner at Sunflower. It is the fanciest restaurant in the city.

   combined: _____

   _____

5. Kima is a warm-hearted person. She adopted a shelter cat last week.

   combined: _____

   _____

6. Arrogance and impatience are my brother's worst qualities. They show up whenever he is under stress.

   combined: _____

   _____

7. Yesterday, I heard the buzz of a mosquito. It is a sure sign of summer.

combined: _____

_____

8. Dr. Harjo dresses like a college student. He is a world-renowned scientist.

combined: _____

_____

9. Chicken nuggets and French fries are full of fat. They are my son's favorite foods.

combined: _____

_____

10. Lucille Okara is a respected negotiator. She is heading an international peace conference in Guatemala.

combined: _____

_____

Use a *Who, Which,* or *That* Clause

Clauses beginning with *who, which,* or *that* can combine short sentences.

two short sentences: Jacob is my favorite cousin. He won the golf tournament.
combined with a *who* clause: Jacob, *who is my favorite cousin,* won the golf tournament.

two short sentences: Good running shoes can be expensive. They make running easier.
combined with a *which* clause: Good running shoes, *which can be expensive,* make running easier.

two short sentences: The cinnamon buns were delicious. I tasted them.
combined with a *that* clause: The cinnamon buns *that I tasted* were delicious.

Punctuating *who, which,* or *that* clauses requires some thought. Decide whether the information in the clause is *essential* or *nonessential.* If the information is essential, do not put commas around it:

essential clause: Students *who like history* will love the movie. (Without the clause *who like history,* the sentence would not have the same meaning. Therefore, the clause is essential and is not set off by commas.)
nonessential clause: Mel, *who has been singing for years,* deserves to win. (The clause *who has been singing for years* is not essential to the meaning of the sentence. Therefore, it is set off by commas.)

If you have to choose between *which* and *that, which* usually begins a nonessential clause, and *that* usually begins an essential clause.

essential clause: The car *that he was driving* is expensive.
nonessential clause: The car, *which I've had for years*, needs a new muffler.

Note: Essential and nonessential clauses are also referred to as "restrictive" and "nonrestrictive" clauses.

Exercise 10   Using *Who, Which,* or *That* Clauses

Following are pairs of sentences. Combine each pair by using a *who, which,* or *that* clause.

1. Sharon told me a secret. The secret shocked me.

combined: _____

_____

2. Belgian chocolate is available in the United States. Some consider it the best chocolate in the world.

combined: _____

_____

3. Clara works with a young man. The young man teaches yoga in the evening.

combined: _____

_____

4. Tyler Nelson is married to my sister. He used to play baseball on a minor league team.

combined: _____

_____

5. People love their pets. They will spend a great deal of money to keep their animals healthy and happy.

combined: _____

_____

6. Pocket scooters are popular with children. The scooters can be dangerous on public roads.

combined: _____

_____

7. Joanna bought a new coffeemaker. The coffeemaker brews one cup of coffee at a time.

combined: _____

_____

8. Selena wants to go back to Albuquerque. Albuquerque is her favorite vacation spot.

combined: _____

_____

9. I need to thank my father. He worked at two jobs to help me finish college.

combined: _____

_____

10. Talking to strangers once made me nervous. Talking to strangers is now an important part of my job.

combined: _____

_____

○○○ CONNECT ▶   ⬭ Exercise 11 ⬭   **Revising for Sentence Variety: A Comprehensive Exercise**

Rewrite the following paragraph, combining each pair of underlined sentences using one of the following: an -*ing* modifier, an -*ed* modifier, an appositive, or a *who*, *which*, or *that* clause. Write your revisions in the spaces above the lines.

Jealousy is like a poison. <u>My last girlfriend was a beautiful woman. She swore she had not a drop of jealous blood.</u> At first, she was understanding and tolerant of the time I spent without her. Then I noticed a slight change. <u>She would check my eyes carefully. She tried to detect any lies about my social activities.</u> This subtle surveillance made me somewhat uneasy. <u>Antonio was my best friend. He advised me to break off the relationship.</u> Antonio said I would soon see my girlfriend become more possessive. <u>I was blinded by my infatuation. I hoped that my girlfriend would change.</u> She did, but the change made me jealous. She left me when she found someone she liked better.

Readings
to Accompany
the Writing Chapters

WRITING FROM READING:
THE WRITING PROCESS

Sticky Stuff

Kendall Hamilton and Tessa Namuth

This article is a tribute to three modern products that hold our lives together. One got its start when its creator was walking his dog, another changed its original purpose, and the third was the result of a boring sermon.

Words You May Need to Know (Corresponding paragraph numbers are in parentheses.)

bounty (1): a generous number
ingenious (1): clever
amalgam (1): combination
marveled (2): wondered
burrs (2): the rough, prickly case around the seeds of certain plants
spawn (2): produce
dubbed (2): named
velours (2): velvet

crochet (2): small hook
arthritic (2): people with arthritis, an inflammation of the joints
invective (3): angry, abusive language
sought (3): searched
rendered (3): became
obsolete (3): out of date, no longer useful

debuted (3): was introduced
ironically (3): unexpectedly
Great Depression (3): a period in the United States, beginning in 1929 and continuing through the 1930s, when business, employment, and stock market values were low and poverty was widespread

improvised (4): created on the spot, without planning
hymnal (4): a book of hymns, religious songs
colleague (4): a fellow worker
voila! (4): French for "there it was!"
ubiquitous (4): everywhere

1   Never before in the history of humankind has it been so easy to attach one thing to another. Over the past century, inventive minds have brought us a bounty of products designed to keep our daily lives—and who knows, maybe even the universe—together. The paper clip, for instance, is not only an ingenious amalgam of form and function, but it's also a powerful force for order. Below are a few more of the finest products.

2   Anybody who's ever struggled with a stuck zipper or stubborn button owes a debt of gratitude to Georges de Mestral, the Swiss engineer who gave us all an alternative. After a walk in the woods with his dog one day in 1948, de Mestral marveled at the ability of burrs to fasten themselves to his dog's coat and to his own wool clothing. De Mestral shoved a bit of burr under a microscope and saw that its barbed, hooklike seed pods meshed beautifully with the looped fibers in his clothes. Realizing that his discovery could spawn a fastening system to compete with, not replace, the zipper, he devised a way to reproduce the hooks in woven nylon, and dubbed the result Velcro, from the French words *velours* and *crochet*. Today Velcro-brand hook-and-loop fasteners (which is how trademark attorneys insist we refer to the stuff) not only save the arthritic, fumble-fingered or just plain lazy among us untold aggravation with our clothing, they secure gear—and astronauts—aboard the space shuttle, speed diaper changes, and help turn the machine-gun turrets in the M1A1 tank. Velcro U.S.A., Inc., engineers have even used the product to assemble an automobile. Try doing that with zippers.

3   Some theorize that the world is held together by Scotch tape. If that's not true, it could be: 3M, the company behind the brand, makes enough tape each day to circle the earth almost three times. This was certainly not fore-seen by a young 3M engineer named Richard Drew when he invented the tape in 1930. Drew, who'd come up with the first masking tape after over-hearing a burst of frustrated invective in an auto-body painting shop, sought to create a product to seal the cellophane that food producers were start-ing to use to wrap everything from bread to candy. Why not coat strips of cellophane itself with adhesive, Drew wondered, and Scotch tape was born. It was also soon rendered obsolete for its original purpose, as a process to heat-seal cellophane packaging debuted. Ironically, the Great Depression

came to the rescue: consumers took to the tape as a dollar-stretcher to keep worn items in service. Ever since, it's just kind of stuck.

4   The Post-it note not only keeps information right where we want it, but it may also be the best thing ever to come out of a dull sermon. Art Fry, a chemical engineer for 3M who was active in his church choir, was suffering through just such a sermon one day back in 1974 when he got to thinking about a problem he'd been having with improvised bookmarks falling out of his hymnal. "I realized what I really needed was a bookmark that would attach and detach lightly, wouldn't fall off and wouldn't hurt the hymnal," recalls Fry, now 66 and retired from 3M. Fry called to mind a weak adhesive developed by his colleague, Spencer Silver. Fry slathered a little of the adhesive on the edge of a piece of paper, and *voila!* He wrote a report about his invention and forwarded it to his boss, also jotting a question on one of his new bookmarks and pressing it down in the middle of one page. His boss scribbled an answer on the note and sent it back to Fry, attached to some other paperwork. Later, over coffee, the two men realized Fry had invented a new communications tool. Today Post-its are ubiquitous—available in eighteen colors, twenty-seven sizes and fifty-six shapes. Some even contain fragrances that smell like pizza, pickles, or chocolate. Soon, perhaps, we'll have our notes and eat them, too.

Comprehension Check

1. What gave Georges de Mestral the idea for his invention, Velcro?

2. Who invented Scotch tape, and what was the tape's original purpose?

3. How did Scotch tape become a "dollar-stretcher"?

4. How do hymnal bookmarks play a role in the invention of the Post-it note?

5. How did Art Fry and Spencer Silver find a new way to use their adhesive?

Discussion Prompts/Writing Options

If you write on any of the following topics, work through the stages of the writing process in preparing your work.

1. "Sticky Stuff" describes how three products, all used to attach one thing to another, were invented. Write a summary of the article. Describe the inventor of each product, how he came up with the idea for the product, and how the product was developed and used.

2. Describe one item in modern technology you just cannot live without. Using as many specific details as possible, explain why this invention is essential in your daily life.

3. "Sticky Stuff" is about three inventions that hold things together. For an assignment or class discussion, select one such item (for instance, Scotch tape, duct tape, masking tape, paper clips, or superglue), and describe ways to use it creatively or in an emergency.

 **COMPUTER ▶**

With instructor approval, you may want to conduct a Google search on the Internet to learn a few interesting facts about the item's history, such as where, when, and how it was invented, original uses, and so forth.

4. Think of some item that many children take for granted today but that you did not have when you were growing up. For example, you could write about portable CD players, DVDs, or cable or satellite television. Describe the item, what it does, and how children take it for granted. Then explain how you amused yourself without this item.

5. Post-it notes are such a small convenience that people may not notice how useful they are. Describe one other small convenience (in the office, the car, or the kitchen) that is extremely useful. Explain how it works and consider how people coped before this item was created.

WRITING FROM READING: ILLUSTRATION

Spanglish

Janice Castro, with Dan Cook and Cristina Garcia

The authors of this article discuss the "free-form blend of Spanish and English" that has developed from a mix of cultures. They explain this blend by using many examples.

Words You May Need to Know (Corresponding paragraph numbers are in parentheses.)

bemused (1): confused
Quiero un **(1):** I want a . . . .
cerveza **(1):** beer
linguistic currency (2): way of speaking
syntax (3): word order
patter (3): quick talk
Anglo (3): native-born Americans
ir al **(4):** go to the

counterparts (5): duplicates
phenomena (5): remarkable things
implicit (5): contained
languorous (5): lacking energy
almuerzo **(5):** lunch
hybrids (6): blends
wielded (9): used
gaffes (9): social mistakes

1   In Manhattan a first-grader greets her visiting grandparents, happily exclaiming, "Come here, *sientate!*" Her bemused grandfather, who does not speak Spanish, nevertheless knows she is asking him to sit down. A Miami personnel officer understands what a job applicant means when he says, "Quiero un part time." Nor do drivers miss a beat reading a billboard alongside a Los Angeles street advertising *CERVEZA*—SIX-PACK!

2   This free-form blend of Spanish and English, known as Spanglish, is common linguistic currency wherever concentrations of Hispanic Americans are found in the U.S. In Los Angeles, where fifty-five percent of the city's three million inhabitants speak Spanish, Spanglish is as much a part of daily life as sunglasses. Unlike the broken-English efforts of earlier immigrants from Europe, Asia, and other regions, Spanglish has become a widely accepted conversational mode used casually—even playfully—by Spanish-speaking immigrants and native-born Americans alike.

3   Consisting of one part Hispanicized English, one part Americanized Spanish and more than a little fractured syntax, Spanglish is a bit like a Robin Williams comedy routine: a crackling line of cross-cultural patter straight from the melting pot. Often it enters Anglo homes and families through the children, who pick it up at school or at play with their young Hispanic contemporaries. In other cases, it comes from watching TV; many an Anglo child has learned *uno dos tres* almost as quickly as one two three.

4   Spanglish takes a variety of forms, from the Southern California Anglos who bid farewell with the utterly silly "*hasta la* bye-bye" to the Cuban-American drivers in Miami who *parquean* their *carros* (park their cars). Some Spanglish sentences are mostly Spanish, with a quick detour for an English word or two. A Latino friend may cut short a conversation by glancing at his watch and excusing himself with the explanation that he must "*ir al* supermarket."

5   Many of the English words transplanted this way are simply handier than their Spanish counterparts. No matter how distasteful the subject, for example, it is still easier to say "income tax" than *impuesto sobre la renta.* At the same time, many Spanish-speaking immigrants have adopted such terms as VCR, microwave, and dishwasher for what they view as largely American phenomena. Still other English words convey a cultural context that is not implicit in the Spanish. A friend who invites you to *lonche* most likely has in mind the brisk American custom of "doing lunch" rather than the languorous afternoon break traditionally implied by *almuerzo.*

6   Mainstream Americans exposed to similar hybrids of German, Chinese, or Hindi might be mystified. But even Anglos who speak little or no Spanish are somewhat familiar with Spanglish. Living among them, for one thing, are nineteen million Hispanics. In addition, more American high school and university students sign up for Spanish than for any other foreign language.

7   Only in the past ten years, though, has Spanish begun to turn into a national slang. Its popularity has grown with the explosive increases in U.S. immigration from Latin American countries. English has increasingly collided with Spanish in retail stores, offices and classrooms, in pop music and on street corners. Anglos whose ancestors picked up such Spanish words

as *rancho*, *bronco*, *tornado*, and *incommunicado*, for instance, now freely use such Spanish words as *gracias*, *bueno*, *amigo*, and *por favor*.

8   Among Latinos, Spanglish conversations often flow easily from Spanish into several sentences of English and back. Spanglish is a sort of code for Latinos: the speakers know Spanish, but their hybrid language reflects the American culture in which they live. Many lean to shorter, clipped phrases in place of the longer, more graceful expressions their parents used. Says Leonel de la Cuesta, an assistant professor of modern languages at Florida International University in Miami: "In the U.S., time is money, and that is showing up in Spanglish as an economy of language." Conversational examples: *taipiar* (type) and *winshi-wiper* (windshield wiper) replace *escribir a maquina* and *limpiaparabrisas*.

9   Major advertisers, eager to tap the estimated $134 billion in spending power wielded by Spanish-speaking Americans, have ventured into Spanish to promote their products. In some cases, attempts to sprinkle Spanish through commercials have produced embarrassing gaffes. A Braniff Airlines ad that sought to tell Spanish-speaking audiences they could settle back *en* (in) luxuriant *cuero* (leather) seats, for example, inadvertently said they could fly without clothes (*encuero*). A fractured translation of the Miller Lite slogan told readers the beer was "Filling, and less delicious." Similar blunders are often made by Anglos trying to impress Spanish-speaking pals. But if Latinos are amused by mangled Spanish, they also recognize these goofs as a sort of friendly acceptance. As they might put it, *no problema*.

Comprehension Check

1. Define "Spanglish" and describe how it becomes commonly used in both Anglo and Hispanic homes.

2. What do you think is the most interesting Spanglish word or phrase in the essay? Why?

3. According to the professor quoted in the article, how does Spanglish reflect the idea that "time is money"?

4. Give some humorous examples from the essay of how major advertisers have made mistakes in trying to reach Spanish-speaking audiences.

Discussion Prompts/Writing Options

If you write on any of the following topics, work through the stages of the writing process in preparing your illustration assignment.

1. "Spanglish" gives several reasons for the growth of this blend of languages. In a paragraph, explain how and why Spanglish has become so widespread.

2. Groups often share their own special language. Computer users, for example, use many terms that a non-user would not

understand. Police officers, health-care workers, restaurant workers, musicians, bloggers, and others all use words or terms that are understood only by their groups. For a writing assignment, describe four key words or phrases used by a specific group. Focus it with a topic sentence like the following:

> There are four key terms in the language of _____ (name the group.)

You can write from your own experience, brainstorm with classmates, or interview a member of a specific group.

3. Describe the blending of two languages in your daily life. You can discuss the language of two cultures or countries (like English and Creole, or English and Portuguese), or of two parts of your life (like the formal language you use at work and the informal language you use at home). Give several specific examples of each language.

4. For class discussion or for a writing assignment, describe how two cultures can blend in a person's choice of clothing, music, or family rituals.

5. The authors of "Spanglish" say that "English has increasingly collided with Spanish in retail stores, offices and classrooms, in pop music and on street corners." Working with a partner or group, brainstorm examples to support that statement. For example, ask and answer such questions as "Where and how does Spanish appear in music popular with both Anglos and Hispanics?" and "How is Spanish appearing in offices?" When you have at least five examples, work individually on a writing assignment that is based on the authors' statement.

◀ COLLABORATE 👥

6. If English is not your native language, describe the problems you have learning English. Give specific examples of each problem.

7. Write about one of the following main ideas:

> What we think of as "American" food really includes food from many cultures.
>
> or
>
> Americans regularly use words or phrases from other languages. (If you use this idea, avoid using the examples given in "Spanglish.")

To support your main idea, be sure to use as many specific examples as you can.

WRITING FROM READING: DESCRIPTION

A Present for Popo

Elizabeth Wong

The child of Chinese immigrants, Elizabeth Wong was born in Los Angeles, California. She has a Master of Fine Arts degree and has worked as a writer for newspapers and television. She has also written several plays. In "A Present for Popo," Wong describes a beloved grandmother.

Words You May Need to Know (Corresponding paragraph numbers are in parentheses.)

nimbly (1): quickly, gracefully
problematic (2): difficult, or leading to problems
vain (2): proud of your appearance
co-opted (3): taken over
niggling (4): unimportant
dim sum **(6):** a light meal

terrarium (7): a small container where plants and small creatures are kept alive under conditions imitating their natural environment
tenuous (12): weak, or fragile
cohesive (12): binding

1   When my Popo opened a Christmas gift, she would shake it, smell it, listen to it. She would size it up. She would open it nimbly, with all enthusiasm and delight, and even though the mittens were ugly or the blouse too small or the card obviously homemade, she would coo over it as if it were the baby Jesus.

2   Despite that, buying a gift for my grandmother was always problematic. Being in her late 80s, Popo didn't seem to need any more sweaters or handbags. No books certainly, as she knew only six words of English. Cosmetics might be a good idea, as she was just a wee bit vain.

3   But ultimately, nothing worked. "No place to put anything anyway," she used to tell me in Chinese. For in the last few years of her life, Popo had a bed in a room in a house in San Gabriel owned by one of her sons. All her belongings, her money, her very life was now co-opted and controlled by her sons and their wives. Popo's daughters had little power in this matter. This was a traditional Chinese family.

4   For you see, Popo had begun to forget things. Ask her about something that happened twenty years ago, and she could recount the details in the heartbeat of a New York minute. But it was those niggling everyday matters that became so troubling. She would forget to take her heart medicine. She would forget where she put her handbag. She would forget she talked to you just minutes before. She would count the few dollars in her billfold, over and over again. She would ask me for the millionth time, "So when are you going to get married?" For her own good, the family decided she should give up her beloved one-room Chinatown flat. Popo herself recognized she might be a danger to herself. "I think your grandmother is going crazy," she would say.

5   That little flat was a bothersome place, but Popo loved it. Her window had a view of several import-export shops below, not to mention the grotesque plastic hanging lanterns and that nasty loudspeaker serenading tourists with eighteen hours of top-40 popular hits.

6   My brother Will and I used to stand under her balcony on Mei Ling Way, shouting up, "Grandmother on the Third Floor! Grandmother on the Third Floor!" Simultaneously, the wrinkled faces of a half-dozen grannies would peek cautiously out their windows. Popo would come to the balcony and proudly claim us. "These are my grandchildren coming to take me to *dim sum*." Her neighbors would cluck and sigh, "You have such good grandchildren. Not like mine."

7   In that cramped room of Popo's, I could see past Christmas presents. One was a full-wall collage of family photos that my mother and I made together and presented one year with lots of fanfare. Popo had attached additional snapshots by way of paper clips and Scotch tape. And there, on the window sill, sat a little terrarium to which Popo had tied a small red ribbon. "For good luck," as she gleefully pointed out the sprouting buds. "See, it's having babies."

8   Also, there were the utility shelves on the wall, groaning from a wide assortment of junk, stuff, and whatnot. Popo was fond of salvaging discarded things. After my brother had installed the shelving, she did a little jig, then took a whisk broom and lightly swept away any naughty spirits that might be lurking on the walls. "Shoo, shoo, shoo, away with you, Mischievous Ones!" That apartment was her independence, and her pioneer spirit was everywhere in it.

9   Popo was my mother's mother, but she was also a second mother to me. Her death was a great blow. The last time I saw her was Christmas 1990, when she looked hale and hearty. I thought she would live forever. Last October, at ninety-one, she had her final heart attack. The next time I saw her, it was at her funeral.

10   There she was in an open casket, with a shiny new penny poised between her lips, a silenced warrior woman. Her sons and daughters placed colorful pieces of cloth in her casket. They burned incense and paper money. A small marching band led a New Orleans–like procession through the streets of Chinatown. Popo's picture, larger than life, stood in a flatbed truck to survey the world of her adopted country.

11   This little four-foot, nine-inch woman had been the glue of our family. She wasn't perfect, she wasn't always even nice, but she learned from her mistakes, and, ultimately, she forgave herself for being human. It is a lesson of forgiveness that seems to have eluded her own sons and daughters.

12   And now she is gone. And with her—the tenuous, cohesive ties of blood and duty that bound us to family. My mother predicted that once the distribution of what was left of Popo's estate took place, no further words would be exchanged between Popo's children. She was right.

13   But this year, six of the twenty-seven grandchildren and two of the eighteen great-grandchildren came together for a holiday feast of honey-

baked ham and mashed potatoes. Not a gigantic family reunion. But I think, for now, it's the one yuletide present my grandmother might have truly enjoyed.

Comprehension Check

1. Despite Popo's excitement at Christmas, what was "problematic" for the narrator?

2. Where did Popo live, and who was in charge of her life?

3. What were three indications of Popo's forgetfulness?

4. What do you think is the most descriptive sentence in the essay? Why?

5. What did Popo do with a small red ribbon? Why?

6. What superstitious act did Popo perform after her son installed shelving?

7. Describe what you feel is the most intriguing part of Popo's funeral ritual.

8. What passage suggests that Popo's children were not close to each other?

Discussion Prompts/Writing Options

If you write on any of the following topics, work through the stages of the writing process in preparing your descriptive paragraph.

1. Elizabeth Wong uses many details about her grandmother's apartment to describe the woman. With as many details as possible, describe how a person's environment (for example, her office, his apartment) reflects that person.

2. Wong's essay includes a description of a funeral in a Chinese-American family. Write a description of some custom or ritual in your family. You could write, for instance, about a wedding, funeral, celebration of a holiday, or religious occasion.

3. "A Present for Popo" is a tribute to a beloved person. Write a description of someone who holds a special place in your life.

4. The grandmother in Wong's essay is an immigrant, a Chinese woman who moved to America. Describe an immigrant whom you know. Focus on how the person reflects a combination of two countries or cultures.

5. Describe an elderly person you know well. In your description, you can use details of appearance and behavior. Focus on how these details reveal personality.

6. Describe yourself at age ninety. Use your imagination to give details of your appearance, behavior, and family relationships at that stage of your life.

WRITING FROM READING: NARRATION

The Good Father

Alisa Valdes-Rodriguez

In this essay, best-selling author Alisa Valdes-Rodriguez writes about her father. He was orphaned, shipped to one foster home after another, and later abandoned by his wife to raise their children alone. Yet, despite it all, this Latino father maintained an open heart and became his only daughter's hero and best friend.

Words You May Need to Know (Corresponding paragraph numbers are in parentheses.)

elitist (2): people who believe they belong to a superior group and deserve special treatment

tantamount (2): equal to

scarlet letter (2): a sign of shame; the term comes from Nathaniel Hawthorne's novel about a woman forced to wear the letter as punishment for committing adultery

transplanted (4): moved or relocated from one place to another

confronted (4): stood in front of, faced

***arroz con pollo* (6):** chicken with rice

1 For years I have sent my father a Mother's Day card. I'm not trying to insult him, and I'm not trying to make a joke. Rather, I am acknowledging the fact that from the time I was eleven, when my parents divorced and my mother left us, my father served as both a mother and a father to me. A single father raising a daughter through her adolescence is unusual. But that my Cuban dad raised me to be strong, confident, and brave is all the more remarkable considering the details of his early life.

2 The story begins in Santa Clara, Cuba, in the 1940s. My grandmother Eugenia Leyba was a beautiful teenager, the maid in the home of a wealthy family. The family had two sons. The sons made a bet, each thinking that he would be the first to sleep with the maid. My grandfather Ricardo Hernandez "won" that bet (no one knows whether by force or through charm). What we do know is that my father, Nelson, was the product of this unhappy union, and Ricardo, now living in Miami, never claimed him. When Ricardo's parents discovered that the maid was pregnant by their son, they did what most class- and color-conscious elitists would have done at the time: they fired Eugenia and spread rumors about her around town, rumors that made it impossible for her to find work. Being a single mother—and a single teen mother from the working class—is difficult anywhere in Latin America, even today; in the 1940s it was tantamount to wearing a scarlet letter.

3 The young Eugenia gave birth to my father on the kitchen table in her mother's house. She then moved to Havana, shamed, and took jobs as a domestic servant. When my father was seven, his mother married. The

man's name was Elpidio Valdes. In those days it was scandalous for a man to marry a woman who had a child, so Eugenia and Elpidio pretended that he was my dad's father, even changing my dad's last name to Valdes. When my dad was nine, Eugenia died of leukemia. No one told him she was dead until the funeral. Elpidio stood at the grave with my father as the casket was lowered and said simply, "That's your mother. Men don't cry." My father didn't cry.

4   When my dad was fifteen, Elpidio heard about Operation Pedro Pan, a U.S.-based program that arranged for children to be taken out of the newly communist Cuba, and thought it was a marvelous idea. He sent my father, alone, to the United States. (Ultimately the program transplanted 14,000 children.) Unlike many of the other kids, however, my father never saw his family again. Elpidio did not come after him or even try to reach him. At fifteen my father was on his own in a new country, placed in the fourth grade because he spoke no English, and shuffled from one foster home to another until he was eighteen. Then he fell in love with a tall American woman, married, and had a son. He took a job as a janitor at the University of New Mexico at Albuquerque and started reading student papers he found on teachers' desks. He thought the papers in the sociology department were particularly interesting and confronted the head of the department, saying that he, the lowly janitor, could do a better job than the students.

5   The department head took my father under his wing, and within six years, during which time I was born, my dad had a Ph.D. in sociology. He eventually became a professor at the same university where he had once cleaned toilets. My mother, a woman with a history of picking low-life men to scandalize her parents and to match her terrible self-esteem, did not have as much interest in a successful academic as she'd had in an immigrant janitor with limited English. She moved out of the state with scarcely a second thought—leaving behind my brother, Ricardo, and me.

6   My father, despite his own troubled history, embraced the opportunity to raise me. He taught himself to cook, and some of my fondest memories are of him whipping up *arroz con pollo* in the kitchen of our house near the university. And when I was twelve and got my period, my dad—an orphan boy from the mean streets of Havana—celebrated by buying me flowers and having a female friend of his take me out for ice cream.

7   When I wanted to be a jazz saxophonist, my father bought me the most expensive tenor sax he could find. He listened as I practiced and came to my room with tears in his eyes to tell me how talented I was. When I decided that I wanted to be a journalist, my dad told me to apply to Columbia University, which had the best graduate school for journalism in the nation. I was afraid I wouldn't get in, but Dad told me I would. He was right. When I decided to leave newspapers—and my steady salary—to write nov-

els, my dad opened his home to me and told me to stay as long as I needed to. I was thirty-two years old, married, with a baby. My dad did not care; he knew I could do it. He read pages of what I'd written and told me it was great. As always, my father believed in me before I believed in myself, and helped guide me toward publication of my first novel and a whole new career as an author.

8   I hear so many Latinas bashing our men as if somehow this will help move us toward equality. And I know that many men are rotten to women. But many are not. Many are like my father: wonderful, sensitive human beings who stand behind their daughters. Papi, I love you. Happy Father's Day.

Comprehension Check

1. According to the author, what was remarkable about the way her father, Nelson Valdes, raised her?

2. What job did Valdes-Rodriguez's grandmother hold as a teenager, and how did she become a victim of a cruel bet?

3. Whom did Eugenia marry, and what did her husband do to avoid the appearance of a scandal?

4. What sad event happened when Nelson was nine, and what so-called advice did his stepfather give him at this time?

5. What was Operation Pedro Pan, and how did the program change Nelson's life when he was fifteen?

6. What was Nelson's first job at the University of New Mexico, and who became a mentor for him?

7. What does Valdes-Rodriguez suggest was the reason her mother abandoned the family?

8. Nelson supported his daughter's various career goals and provided much encouragement. Describe three specific examples of such encouragement.

Discussion Prompts/Writing Options

If you write on any of the following topics, be sure to work through the stages of the writing process in preparing your narrative assignment.

1. One of the author's fondest childhood memories is of her father "whipping up *arroz con pollo,*" a chicken and rice dish. What is one of your fondest memories of a family ritual? If you write a narrative of this memory, be sure to arrange specific details in a clear, logical order.

2. When he was a janitor at a university, Nelson Valdes was brave enough to confront the head of the sociology department. Write a

narrative about the first time you tried to conquer a particular fear, such as speaking in front of an audience, flying for the first time, asking someone out on a first date, and so forth.

3. When Nelson Valdes was only fifteen years old, he was sent to the United States all alone and was placed in the fourth grade because he could not speak English. His life, however, turned out to be positive and productive. Write about an experience that seemed negative for you at the time but that proved to be a positive turning point in your life. Although you will be writing your narrative in time order, try to use a variety of transitional words and phrases. (Avoid repetitive use of *then* and *next*.)

4. Nelson Valdes supported his daughter's changing career goals even when she had to give up a steady salary and move back home with a husband and baby. Recall the first time you realized that a friend or family member would accept you, no matter how risky your choices may have seemed.

WRITING FROM READING: PROCESS

How to Write a Personal Letter

Garrison Keillor

Garrison Keillor is best known as host of the radio show A Prairie Home Companion, *where his stories of the fictional town of Lake Wobegone and its inhabitants made him famous. He is also a popular writer with a comfortable, friendly style. In this essay, he explains how people, especially shy ones, can write what he calls the "gift" of a personal letter "to be our own sweet selves and express the music of our souls."*

Words You May Need to Know (Corresponding paragraph numbers are in parentheses.)

trudges (2): walks with weariness
wahoos (2): a version of the word
  yahoo, meaning a coarse and
  ignorant person
despite (4): in spite of
anonymity (4): being unknown,
  namelessness
obligatory (5): required
pulsating (5): vibrating, quivering
sensate (5): felt by the senses
sensuous (6): appealing to the
  senses

declarative (7): making a
  statement
episode (9): incident, topic
urinary tract (9): all the organs
  and ducts involved in the release
  of urine
indebtedness (9): owing money
  or being under some obligation
sibling (9): brother or sister
relic (11): an object that has
  survived for many years

1   We shy people need to write a letter now and then, or else we'll dry up and blow away. It's true. And I speak as one who loves to reach for the phone, dial the number, and talk. The telephone is to shyness what Hawaii is to February; it's a way out of the woods. *And yet:* a letter is better.

2   Such a sweet gift—a piece of handmade writing, in an envelope that is not a bill, sitting in our friend's path when she trudges home from a long day spent among savages and wahoos, a day our words will help repair. They don't need to be immortal, just sincere. She can read them twice and again tomorrow: "You're someone I care about, Corinne, and think of often, and every time I do, you make me smile."

3   We need to write; otherwise, nobody will know who we are. They will have only a vague impression of us as "A Nice Person" because, frankly, we don't shine at conversation, we lack the confidence to thrust our faces forward and say, "Hi, I'm Heather Hooten; let me tell you about my week." Mostly we say "Uh-huh" and "Oh really." People smile and look over our shoulder, looking for someone else to meet.

4   So a shy person sits down and writes a letter. To be known by another person—to meet and talk freely on the page—to be close despite distance. To escape from anonymity and be our own sweet selves and express the music of our souls. The same thing that moves a giant rock star to sing his heart out in front of 123,000 people moves us to take ballpoint in hand and write a few lines to our dear Aunt Eleanor. *We want to be known.* We want her to know that we have fallen in love, that we have quit our job, that we're moving to New York, and we want to say a few things that might not get said in casual conversation: "Thank you for what you've meant to me. I am very happy right now."

5   The first step in writing letters is to get over the guilt of *not* writing. You don't "owe" anybody a letter. Letters are a gift. The burning shame you feel when you see unanswered mail makes it harder to pick up a pen and makes for a cheerless letter when you finally do. "I feel bad about not writing, but I've been so busy," etc. Skip this. Few letters are obligatory and they are "Thanks for the wonderful gift" and "I am terribly sorry to hear about George's death" and "Yes, you're welcome to stay with us next month." Write these promptly if you want to keep your friends. Don't worry about other letters, except love letters, of course. When your true love writes, "Dear Light of My Life, Joy of My Heart, O Lovely Pulsating Core of My Sensate Life," some response is called for.

6   Some of the best letters are tossed off in a burst of inspiration, so keep your writing stuff in one place where you can sit down for a few minutes, and—"Dear Roy, I am in the middle of an essay but thought I'd drop you a line. Hi to your sweetie too"—dash off a note to a pal. Envelopes, stamps, address book, everything in a drawer so you can write fast when the pen is hot. A blank white 8″ × 11″ sheet can look as big as Montana if the pen's not so hot; try a smaller page and write boldly. Get a pen that makes a sensuous line, get a comfortable typewriter, a friendly word processor—whichever feels easy to the hand.

7   Sit for a few minutes with the blank sheet of paper in front of you, and meditate on the person you will write to; let your friend come to mind until you can almost see him or her in the room with you. Remember the last time you saw each other and how your friend looked and what you said and what perhaps was unsaid between you, and when your friend becomes real to you, start to write. Write the salutation, "Dear You," and take a deep breath and plunge in. A simple declarative sentence will do, followed by another and another. Talk about what you're doing and tell it like you were talking to us. Don't think about grammar, don't think about style, don't try to write dramatically, just give us your news. Where did you go, who did you see, what did they say, what do you think?

8   If you don't know where to begin, start with the present: "I'm sitting at the kitchen table on a rainy Saturday morning. Everyone is gone, and the house is quiet." Let your description of the present moment lead to something else; let the letter drift gently along. The toughest letter to crank out is one that is meant to impress, as we all know from writing job applications; if it's hard work to write a letter to a friend, maybe you're trying too hard to be terrific. A letter is only a report to someone who already likes you for reasons other than your brilliance. Take it easy.

9   Don't worry about form. It's not a term paper. When you come to the end of one episode, just start a new paragraph. You can go from a few lines about the sad state of pro football to the fight with your mother to your cat's urinary tract infection to a few thoughts on personal indebtedness and on to the kitchen sink and what's in it. The more you write, the easier it gets, and when you have a true friend to write to, a *compadre*, a soul sibling, then it's like driving a car; you just press on the gas.

10   Don't tear up the page and start over when you write a bad line; try to write your way out of it. Make mistakes and plunge on. Let the letter cook along and let yourself be bold. Outrage, confusion, love—whatever is in your mind, let it find a way to the page. Writing is a means of discovery, always, and when you come to the end and write "Yours ever" or "Hugs and Kisses," you'll know something that you didn't when you wrote "Dear Pal."

11   Probably your friend will put your letter away, and it'll be read again a few years from now, and it will improve with age. And forty years from now, your friend's grandkids will dig it out of the attic and read it, a sweet and precious relic that gives them a sudden clear glimpse of you and her and the world we old-timers knew. Your simple lines about where you went, who you saw, what they said, will speak to those children, and they will feel in their hearts the humanity of our times.

12   You can't pick up a phone and call the future and tell them about our times. You have to pick up a piece of paper.

Comprehension Check

1. Why does Garrison Keillor feel that writing a letter is better than making a telephone call, especially for shy people?

2. What does Keillor say is "the first step in writing letters," and which type of letters are the ones that need to be written promptly?

3. How are some of the best letters written, and where should all of "your writing stuff" be kept? What are the items he suggests you have on hand?

4. If you don't know how to start a letter, what is Keillor's advice?

5. What does Keillor mean when he states that your letter "will improve with age"?

Discussion Prompts/Writing Options

If you write on any of the following topics, work through the stages of the writing process in preparing your process assignment.

1. While Garrison Keillor does not list the steps to follow in writing a personal letter, he does describe the process in sequence. Summarize the steps he uses. Explain each step by giving an example.

2. A personal letter is written to one special person. Keillor describes it as a gift that says, "You're someone I care about." Write a process paragraph or short essay about how to give another kind of special gift to someone special. The gift can be an object or an experience (for example, a visit to a special place or event, a meal, a party).

3. The telephone is a more popular form of personal communication than the letter, but talking on the phone presents certain problems. One of them is the caller who talks on and on when you want to end the call. Provide some advice on how to end an endless conversation without being rude or unkind. Be sure that your advice involves steps.

4. Imagine that a close relative has sent your friend a gift that he or she hates. Teach your friend how to write that relative a kind and tactful "thank you" for the awful gift.

5. Keillor says a letter is a way for shy people to open up. If you consider yourself shy, what advice would you give to outgoing people about talking to a shy person who is reluctant to speak?

6. If you are an outgoing person, think about the process you follow when you meet someone new. You may want to list the steps of this initial conversation, including what you say first, second, and so forth; the kinds of questions you ask; and the kind of information you volunteer to keep the conversation going. Then, in a

paragraph, explain the steps you follow in your first encounter with a new person.

 COMPUTER ▶

7. Keillor's article was published in the 1980s, well before e-mail became so common. Do you think that writing an e-mail to a friend can be as effective as mailing a handwritten letter? If so, describe the steps you take to be sure that your e-mail will be appreciated.

8. Keillor believes that "writing is a means of discovery." Have you ever learned anything about yourself unexpectedly while writing alone or with others? If so, how did you make this discovery? Based on your recollection, summarize the steps involved in reaching this new awareness about yourself.

WRITING FROM READING: COMPARISON OR CONTRAST

Beautiful Daughter

Carolyn Mason

In Carolyn Mason's contrast of two teenage girls and their mothers, she explores the power of beauty and the powerlessness of mothers who try to protect their children from life's lessons.

Words You May Need to Know (Corresponding paragraph numbers are in parentheses.)

preening (1): taking pride in dressing up
willowy (1): slender and graceful
muted (1): soft
swirl (1): twist or whirl
oblivious (1): unaware
concoction (2): combination
bolster (2): support, cushion
avert (4): turn away

ill-gotten gain (4): an advantage or benefit obtained unfairly or dishonestly
rant (5): speak loudly or violently
fleeting (6): temporary
fickle (6): unreliable, unpredictable
wax (7): talk for a long time

1 We are preening in front of the three-way mirror in the dressing room of an upscale clothing store when I spot them staring at us. I am modeling a business suit, all gray flannel and boring, pretending to be a lawyer on my way to court. My 16-year-old daughter is twirling in a thousand-dollar, glittery evening gown. She's tall and willowy, and she spins around with moves perfected by years of dance lessons. The muted light of the dressing room shows off her stunning beauty—a beauty she is just beginning to notice. Heads swirl across crowded malls, and middle-aged men stare a second or two longer than they should. Grocery store bag boys grin foolishly as they stack cans upon loaves of bread. Once oblivious, she is becoming more aware and increasingly intrigued by the attention.

She twirls back for another look in the mirror and smiles at visions of her long black hair and olive skin set off by the sparkling fabric of the dress.

2   They are also a mother and daughter, and they stare at our reflections with frozen smiles. The teenage girl, plump, short, and splashed with acne, is squeezed into a horrible, frothy, pink concoction of lace and ribbons unkindly wrapping her. The girl's mother puts her arm around her shoulder, as if to bolster her from the shock of the contrast between the two girls.

3   I try to stop my daughter, to pull her from the mirror where she's dancing in her pretend dress, and she looks at me curiously. *Why do we have to stop? We like to do this. Try on clothes for the fun of it.* It's innocent amusement, but today I feel the familiar pain that comes when I see the naked longing my daughter's beauty stirs. The mother, with the fine cheekbones and luxurious hair of a still-beautiful woman, locks eyes with me, and we pass between us a deeply painful knowledge.

4   And that's why I avert my eyes first, my cheeks flaming. I know it's ill-gotten gain. Beauty, born not earned, is unfairly distributed among the daughters of the world. I duck my head and lead my daughter to the dressing stall, where we change silently into our everyday clothes. I know the research. My daughter gets called on more often by her teachers, has better social skills and is more likely to be hired for the job. Her daughter's self-image is clouded by what she sees in the mirror. Even after the teenage years she may find it hard to escape those negative emotions.

5   I like to picture a different ending. I like to imagine that I reached out my hand and stopped them from leaving the dressing room. Then two mothers, strangers to each other, would tell each of our daughters the truths we know. I'll bet her mother would tell her that physical beauty is not all it's cracked up to be. She would point out the girls they know who seem to have it all, but lack a kind heart or a giving spirit. I think she'd try to convince her daughter that achievements in school and on the field are more important than a pretty face. She'd rant against the fashion and beauty industry and warn about disorders of every kind.

6   I figure she knows what I tell my own daughter. Don't put all your eggs in one beauty basket. Life has a cruel way of knocking you around. Physical beauty is too fleeting to count on and too fickle to stay for long. The march of time evens out the early advantages, and a once-beautiful teenager is not always the most beautiful woman. There are other disadvantages to physical attractiveness. You're never sure if the guy chooses you for you or for how great you look next to him. You have to spend all kinds of time and money to maintain your natural resources. Finally, you might never value your inner beauty because you are so distracted by its cover.

7   We would both wax on about the danger of judging anything by its cover.

8   That's not going to happen, though. I've said those very words for 16 years, but as any mother of a teenage girl will agree, I might as well save my breath. We can tell our daughters what we know, but lessons like these have to be lived to be learned. Too bad, because we could save them a lot of pain.

Comprehension Check

1. Explain the contrast in the clothing the two girls try on in the store.

2. Two of the four females in this essay are described as beautiful. Who are they?

3. The mother who narrates this essay says, "I know the research." What research is she talking about, and what does it indicate?

4. The narrator imagines the mother of the less-attractive daughter giving the young woman advice. What would that advice be?

5. What advice would the narrator give her own daughter regarding life's "cruel way"?

6. The narrator imagines both mothers giving their daughters the same piece of advice. What is that advice?

Discussion Prompts/Writing Options

If you write on any of the following topics, be sure to work through the stages of the writing process in preparing your comparison or contrast assignment.

1. Carolyn Mason warns about "the danger of judging anything by its cover." Write about a time when your first judgment of a person, thing, or situation was different from your later judgment. The change may have been from a bad first impression to a positive one, or from a positive impression to a negative one.

2. "Beautiful Daughter" focuses on the early advantages of good-looking teenage girls. Do you believe looks are as important in boys' teen years, or are other qualities admired? Contrast how any of the following pairs are treated:

   handsome vs. ordinary-looking teenage boys
   athletic vs. non-athletic teenage boys
   "cool" vs. "non-cool" teenage boys

3. Mason's article contains advice she and another mother would like to give their daughters, but the author knows that the girls would not accept or understand it until they grew older. Compare or contrast how you responded to a piece of advice given to you when you were younger with how you feel about that advice now.

4. Write a letter to someone younger than you. Use the benefit of your experience to warn him or her that some youthful belief or expectation may be unrealistic or untrue. Your letter should

contrast what you once believed or expected with what you later learned. For instance, you may have a new perspective on the power of love, or the importance of money, or the need to be popular, and so forth.

5. Contrast how an asset in high school or early adulthood can become a drawback later in life. For example, some young people may be admired for their recklessness, for their many romantic encounters, or for their ability to talk their way out of any unpleasant situation. Write about how such a trait can be enviable in one's youth but destructive in later years.

6. Contrast an unpopular trait in high school or early adulthood with its potential for helping a person experience fulfillment or success later. For example, the loner may develop inner strength or creativity, while a person considered unattractive may cope with social rejection by striving hard in a career. Write about how the "loser" in the early years can become the "winner" in later years.

WRITING FROM READING: CLASSIFICATION

Three Disciplines for Children

John Holt

John Holt is an educator and activist who believes our system of education needs a major overhaul. In this essay, he classifies the ways children learn from their disciplines, and he warns against overusing one kind of discipline.

Words You May Need to Know (Corresponding paragraph numbers are in parentheses.)

discipline (1): the training effect of experience

impersonal (2): without personal or human connection

impartial (2): fair

indifferent (2): not biased, not prejudiced

wheedled (2): persuaded by flattery or coaxing

ritual (3): an established procedure, a ceremony

yield (5): give in to, submit

impotent (5): powerless

1   A child, in growing up, may meet and learn from three different kinds of disciplines. The first and most important is what we might call the Discipline of Nature (or of Reality). When he is trying to do something real, if he does the wrong thing or doesn't do the right one, he doesn't get the results he wants. If he doesn't pile one block right on top of another, or tries to build on a slanting surface, his tower falls down. If he hits the wrong key, he hears the wrong note. If he doesn't hit the nail squarely on the head, it bends, and he has to pull it out and start with another. If he doesn't measure properly what he is trying to build, it won't open, close, fit, stand up, fly, float, whistle, or do whatever he wants it to do. If he closes his eyes when he swings, he won't hit the ball. A child meets

this kind of discipline every time he tries to *do* something, which is why it is so important in school to give children more chances to do things, instead of just reading or listening to someone talk (or pretending to).

2   This discipline is a great teacher. The learner never has to wait long for his answer; it usually comes quickly, often instantly. Also it is clear, and very often points to the needed correction; from what happened he cannot only see what he did was wrong, but also why, and what he needs to do instead. Finally, and most important, the giver of the answer, call it Nature, is impersonal, impartial, and indifferent. She does not give opinions or make judgments; she cannot be wheedled, bullied, or fooled; she does not get angry or disappointed; she does not praise or blame; she does not remember past failures or hold grudges. With her one always gets a fresh start; this time is the one that counts.

3   The next discipline we might call the Discipline of Culture, of Society, of What People Really Do. Man is a social, cultural animal. Children sense around them this culture, this network of agreements, customs, habits, and rules binding the adults together. They want to understand it and be a part of it. They watch very carefully what people around them are doing and want to do the same. They want to do right, unless they become convinced they can't do right. Thus children rarely misbehave seriously in church, but sit as quietly as they can. The example of all those grown-ups is contagious. Some mysterious ritual is going on, and children, who like rituals, want to be part of it. In the same way, the little children I see at concerts or operas, though they may fidget a little or perhaps take a nap now and then, rarely make any disturbance. With all those grownups sitting there, neither moving nor talking, it is the most natural thing in the world to imitate them. Children who live among adults who are habitually courteous to each other, and to them, will soon learn to be courteous. Children who live surrounded by people who speak a certain way will speak that way, however much we may try to tell them that speaking that way is bad or wrong.

4   The third discipline is the one that most people mean when they speak of discipline—the Discipline of Superior Force, of sergeant to private, of "you do what I tell you, or I'll make you wish you had." There is bound to be some of this in a child's life. Living as we do surrounded by things that can hurt children, or that children can hurt, we cannot avoid it. We can't afford to let a small child find out from experience the danger of playing in a busy street, or of fooling with the pots on top of a stove, or of eating up the pills in the medicine cabinet. So, along with other precautions, we say to him, "Don't play in the street, or touch things on the stove, or go into the medicine cabinet, or I'll punish you." Between him and the danger too great for him to imagine we put a lesser danger, but one he can imagine and

maybe therefore want to avoid. He can have no idea of what it would be like to be hit by a car, but he can imagine being shouted at, or spanked, or sent to his room. He avoids these substitutes for the greater danger until he can understand it and avoid it for its own sake.

5   However, we ought to use this discipline only when it is necessary to protect the life, health, safety, or well-being of people or other living creatures, or to prevent destruction of things that people care about. We ought not to assume too long, as we usually do, that a child cannot understand the real nature of the danger from which we want to protect him. The sooner he avoids the danger, not to escape our punishment, but as a matter of good sense, the better. He can learn that faster than we think. In Mexico, for example, where people drive their cars with a good deal of spirit, I saw many children no older than five or four walking unattended on the streets. They understood about cars; they knew what to do. A child whose life is full of the threat and fear of punishment is locked into babyhood. There is no way for him to grow up, to learn to take responsibility for his life and acts. Most important of all, we should not assume that having to yield to the threat of our superior force is good for the child's character. It is never good for anyone's character. To bow to superior force makes us feel impotent and cowardly for not having had the strength or courage to resist. Worse, it makes us resentful and vengeful. We can hardly wait to make someone pay for our humiliation, yield to us as we were once made to yield. No, if we cannot always avoid using the Discipline of Superior Force, we should at least use it as seldom as we can.

Comprehension Check

1. According to Holt's "Discipline of Nature (or of Reality)," why should schools give children more "chances to do things"?

2. Why is the Discipline of Nature such a great teacher?

3. What does Holt feel is most important about the Discipline of Nature?

4. Holt states that the Discipline of Culture involves children imitating adults because children want to understand this world and "be a part of it." What are three specific examples Holt gives of this type of discipline?

5. How would an adult use the Discipline of Superior Force to protect a child from a greater danger? Give some specific examples.

6. What does Holt say that adults "should not assume for too long" regarding children's understanding of danger?

Discussion Prompts/Writing Options

If you write on any of the topics below, be sure to work through the stages of the writing process in preparing your classification assignment.

1. John Holt writes a very clear classification with a clear purpose: he is trying to explain how children should learn. Write a summary of the types of discipline Holt explains. In your summary, include definitions and examples for each type of discipline. Your examples can come from Holt's article as well as from your own experiences.

COLLABORATE ▶

2. Holt says that it is very important "in school to give children more chances to do things, instead of just reading or listening to someone talk."

   Classify your elementary or high school classes according to how much they allowed you to do. Include your opinion of each category.

   If your instructor agrees, begin this assignment with an interview. Ask a writing partner to interview you about your learning experiences as a way of gathering ideas for this topic. Then do the same for your partner. Before any interviewing begins, write at least seven questions to ask your partner.

COLLABORATE ▶

3. Holt says children want to understand society and to be a part of it. "They watch very carefully what people around them are doing and want to do the same."

   Classify children according to the behavior they have learned from their parents. If your instructor agrees, freewrite on this topic, and then share your freewriting with a writing partner or group, for reaction and further ideas.

4. Classify the types of school discipline you experienced on the basis of how effective each type was in changing your behavior or attitude.

COMPUTER ▶

5. Visit *http://www.home-school.com/group* to gain some knowledge about the growing trend of home-schooling. Classify types of home-schooling programs according to one of the following bases: accreditation standards, innovative curricula, or interactive activities offered by state or local home-schooling clubs and organizations.

WRITING FROM READING: DEFINITION

Breaking the Bonds of Hate

Virak Khiev

Khiev, who immigrated to America at age ten, wrote this essay when he was a nineteen-year-old senior at the Blake School in Minneapolis, Minnesota. As you read his essay, you will notice how he defines The American Dream and two kinds of war.

Words You May Need to Know (Corresponding paragraph numbers are in parentheses.)

carrion (4): dead flesh
stereotype (5): an established image of someone or something, believed in by many people
unscrupulous (5): without a conscience
mentality (6): attitude, way of thinking

adversaries (7): enemies
immortalized (9): given the ability to live forever
"the melting pot" (10): an image of America in which all the races and ethnic groups blend in harmony
mind-set (10): attitude

1   Ever since I can remember, I wanted the ideal life: a big house, lots of money, cars. I wanted to find the perfect happiness that so many people have longed for. I wanted more than life in the jungle of Cambodia. America was the place, the land of tall skyscrapers, televisions, cars and airplanes.

2   In the jungles of Cambodia I lived in a refugee camp. We didn't have good sanitation or modern conveniences. For example, there were no inside bathrooms—only ones made from palm-tree leaves, surrounded by millions of flies. When walking down the street, I could smell the aroma of the outhouse; in the afternoon, the five- and six-year-olds played with the dirt in front of it. It was the only thing they had to play with, and the "fragrance" never seemed to bother them, and it never bothered me. Because I smelled it every day, I was used to it.

3   The only thing that bothered me was the war. I have spent half of my life in war. The killing is still implanted in my mind. I hate Cambodia. When I came to America nine years ago at the age of ten, I thought I was being born into a new life. No more being hungry, no more fighting, no more killing. I thought I had escaped the war.

4   In America, there are more kinds of material things than Cambodians could ever want. And here we don't have to live in the jungle like monkeys, we don't have to hide from mortar bombing and we don't have to smell the rotten human carrion. But for the immigrant, America presents a different type of jungle, a different type of war and a smell as bad as the waste of Cambodia.

5   Most Americans believe the stereotype that immigrants work hard, get a good education and have a very good life. Maybe it used to be like that, but not anymore. You have to be deceptive and unscrupulous in order to make it. If you are not, then you will end up like most immigrants I've known: living in the ghetto in a cockroach-infested house, working on the assembly line or in the chicken factory to support your family, getting up at three o'clock in the morning to take the bus to work and not getting home until 5:00 p.m.

6   If you're a kid my age, you drop out of school to work because your parents don't have enough money to buy you clothes for school. You may end

up selling drugs because you want cars, money and parties, as all teenagers do. You have to depend on your peers for emotional support because your parents are too busy working in the factory trying to make money to pay the bills. You don't get along with your parents because they have a different mentality: you are an American, and they are Cambodian. You hate them because they are never there for you, so you join a gang as I did.

7   You spend your time drinking, doing drugs and fighting. You beat up people for pleasure. You don't care about anything except your drugs, your beers and your revenge against adversaries. You shoot at people because they've insulted your pride. You shoot at the police because they are always bothering you. They shoot back, and then you're dead like my best friend Sinerth.

8   Sinerth robbed a gas station. He was shot in the head by the police. I'd known him since the sixth grade from my first school in Minneapolis. I can still remember his voice calling me from California. "Virak, come down here, man," he said. "We need you. There are lots of pretty girls down here." I promised him that I would be there to see him. The following year he was dead. I felt sorry for him. But as I thought it over, maybe it is better for him to be dead than to continue with the cycle of violence, to live with hate. I thought, "It is better to die than live like an angry young fool, thinking that everybody is out to get you."

9   When I was like Sinerth, I didn't care about dying. I thought that I was on top of the world, being immortalized by drugs. I could see that my future would be spent working on the assembly line like most of my friends, spending all my paycheck on the weekend and being broke again on Monday morning. I hated going to school because I couldn't see a way to get out of the endless cycle. My philosophy was "Live hard and die young."

10   I hated America because, to me, it was not the place of opportunities or the land of "the melting pot," as I had been told. All I had seen were broken beer bottles on the street and homeless people and drunks using the sky as their roof. I couldn't walk down the street without someone yelling out, "You gook" from his car. Once again I was caught in the web of hatred. I'd become a mad dog with the mind-set of the past: "When trapped in the corner, just bite." The war mentality of Cambodia came back: get what you can and leave. I thought I came to America to escape war, poverty, fighting, to escape the violence, but I wasn't escaping; I was being introduced to a newer version of war—the war of hatred.

11   I was lucky. In Minneapolis, I dropped out of school in the ninth grade to join a gang. Then I moved to Louisiana, where I continued my life of "immortality" as a member of another gang. It came to an abrupt halt when I crashed a car. I wasn't badly injured, but I was underage, and the fine took all my money. I called a good friend of the Cambodian community in Min-

neapolis for advice (she'd tried to help me earlier). I didn't know where to go or whom to turn to. I saw friends landing in jail, and I didn't want that. She promised to help me get back in school. And she did.

12   Since then I've been given a lot of encouragement and caring by American friends and teachers who've helped me turn my life around. They opened my eyes to a kind of education that frees us all from ignorance and slavery. I could have failed so many times except for those people who believed in me and gave me another chance. Individuals who were willing to help me have taught me that I can help myself. I'm now a twelfth grader and have been at my school for three years; I plan to attend college in the fall. I am struggling to believe I can reach the other side of the mountain.

Comprehension Check

1. Describe the conditions of the refugee camp where Khiev once lived.

2. Khiev states that for an immigrant, "America presents a different type of jungle, a different type of war, and a smell as bad as the waste of Cambodia." What are some examples Khiev gives of trying to survive this new jungle?

3. How was Khiev once like his friend Sinerth, and what happened to his friend?

4. What was Khiev's stereotype of America before he arrived in the United States, and how did this image differ from the "newer version of war" he experienced in his new country?

5. What was a major turning point for Khiev, and to whom did he turn for help?

6. What does Khiev say "frees us all from ignorance and slavery"?

Discussion Prompts/Writing Options

If you write on any of these topics, be sure to work through the stages of the writing process in preparing your assignment.

1. Trace the turning points in Virak Khiev's life. Consider all the changes in his life and whether they made his life better or worse.

2. Khiev defines "the bonds of hate," a hate that kept him from achieving a good life. He says that he was a prisoner of his hatred for the country that denied him what he hoped for and of his hatred for his parents. He hated the endless cycle of poverty and struggle he found in the ghetto.

   Define the term "bonds of hate" by providing examples you have observed (or experienced) of the kind of hatred that can keep a person in chains.

3. By explaining what a gang does and why he joined one, Khiev defines the term "gang." Write your own definition of a gang.

When you brainstorm about this word, remember that "gang" can have both positive and negative associations. For example, the actor Paul Newman has established a camp called "The Hole-in-the-Wall Gang" for children with cancer, so he used the word in a positive way. On the other hand, a "gang" of thieves has a negative association.

4. Write your personal definition of The American Dream. Use examples from your life or from the lives of others you know well.

5. Khiev says, "for the immigrant, America presents a different type of jungle, a different type of war, and a smell as bad as the waste of Cambodia."

   Define "The Immigrant's Experience of America." Define the term using the experiences of one or more immigrants as examples. Your definition does not have to be similar to Khiev's. If you are an immigrant to America, you can use your own experiences as examples. If you are not an immigrant, interview one or more immigrants, taking notes and/or taping the interviews to gather details. Your classmates or teachers may include people to interview. Before you interview, have at least six questions to ask.

6. Khiev defines the luck in his life as the help of other people, particularly one woman who was a friend to the Cambodian community. Define the luck in your life.

WRITING FROM READING: CAUSE AND EFFECT

Students in Shock

John Kellmayer

In this 1989 essay, John Kellmayer, an educator, explores the reasons why college students are stressed beyond their limits. He also discusses how colleges are reacting to student problems.

Words You May Need to Know (Corresponding paragraph numbers are in parentheses.)

warrant(6): demand, call for, require

magnitude (9): great importance

biofeedback (10): a method of monitoring your blood pressure, heart rate, etc., as a way of monitoring and controlling stress

1   If you feel overwhelmed by your college experiences, you are not alone—many of today's college students are suffering from a form of shock. Going to college has always had its ups and downs, but today the "downs" of the college experience are more numerous and difficult, a fact that schools are responding to with increased support services.

2   Lisa is a good example of a student in shock. She is an attractive, intelligent twenty-year-old college junior at a state university. Having been a straight-A student in high school and a member of the basketball and soft-

ball teams there, she remembers her high school days with fondness. Lisa was popular then and had a steady boyfriend for the last two years of school.

3   Now, only three years later, Lisa is miserable. She has changed her major four times already and is forced to hold down two part-time jobs in order to pay her tuition. She suffers from sleeping and eating disorders and believes she has no close friends. Sometimes she bursts out crying for no apparent reason. On more than one occasion, she has considered taking her own life.

4   Dan, too, suffers from student shock. He is nineteen and a freshman at a local community college. He began college as an accounting major but hated that field. So he switched to computer programming because he heard the job prospects were excellent in that area. Unfortunately, he discovered that he had little aptitude for programming and changed majors again, this time to psychology. He likes psychology but has heard horror stories about the difficulty of finding a job in that field without a graduate degree. Now he's considering switching majors again. To help pay for school, Dan works nights and weekends as a sales clerk at K-Mart. Dan feels he has no choice except to stay on the job. A few months ago, his girlfriend of a year and a half broke up with him.

5   Not surprisingly, Dan has started to suffer from depression and migraine headaches. He believes that in spite of all his hard work, he just isn't getting anywhere. He can't remember ever being this unhappy. A few times he considered talking to somebody in the college psychological counseling center. He rejected that idea, though, because he didn't want people to think there was something wrong with him.

6   What is happening to Lisa and Dan happens to millions of college students each year. As a result, one-quarter of the student population at any time will suffer from symptoms of depression. Of that group, almost half will experience depression intense enough to warrant professional help. At schools across the country, psychological counselors are booked up months in advance. Stress-related problems such as anxiety, migraine headaches, insomnia, anorexia, and bulimia are epidemic on college campuses. Suicide rates and self-inflicted injuries among college students are higher now than at any other time in history. The suicide rate among college youth is fifty percent higher than among non-students of the same age. It is estimated that each year more than five hundred college students take their own lives. College health officials believe these reported problems represent only the tip of the iceberg. They fear that most students, like Lisa and Dan, suffer in silence.

7   There are three reasons today's college students are suffering more than in earlier generations. First is a weakening family support structure. The transition from high school to college has always been difficult, but in the past,

there was more family support to help get through it. Today, with divorce rates at a historical high and many parents experiencing their own psychological difficulties, the traditional family is not always available for guidance and support. And when students who do not find stability at home are bombarded with new and stressful experiences, the results can be devastating.

8   Another problem college students face is financial pressure. In the last decade tuition costs have skyrocketed—up about sixty-six percent at public colleges and ninety percent at private schools. And at the same time that tuition costs have been rising dramatically, there has been a cutback in federal aid to students. College loans are now much harder to obtain and are available only at near-market interest rates. Consequently, most college students must work at least part-time. And for some students, the pressure to do well while holding down a job is too much to handle.

9   A final cause of student shock is the large selection of majors available. Because of the magnitude and difficulty of choosing a major, college can prove a time of great indecision. Many students switch majors, some a number of times. As a result, it is becoming commonplace to take five or six years to get a degree. It can be depressing to students not only to have taken courses that don't count toward a degree but also to be faced with the added tuition costs. In some cases, these costs become so high that they force students to drop out of college.

10   While there is no magic cure for all student shock, colleges have begun to recognize the problem and are trying in a number of ways to help students cope with the pressures they face. First of all, many colleges are upgrading their psychological counseling centers to handle the greater demand for services. Additional staff is being hired, and experts are doing research to learn more about the psychological problems of college students. Some schools even advertise these services in student newspapers and on campus radio stations. Also, third- and fourth-year students are being trained as peer counselors. These peer counselors may be able to act as a first line of defense in the battle for students' well-being by spotting and helping to solve problems before they become too big for students to handle. In addition, stress management workshops have become common on college campuses. At these workshops, instructors teach students various techniques for dealing with stress, including biofeedback, meditation, and exercise.

11   Finally, many schools are improving their vocational counseling services. By giving students more relevant information about possible majors and career choices, colleges can lessen the anxiety and indecision often associated with choosing a major.

12   If you ever feel that you're "in shock," remember that your experience is not unique. Try to put things in perspective. Certainly, the end of a

romance or failing an exam is not an event to look forward to. But realize that rejection and failure happen to everyone sooner or later. And don't be reluctant to talk to somebody about your problems. The useful services available on campus won't help you if you don't take advantage of them.

Comprehension Check

1. How did Lisa's high school experience differ from her college experience?

2. What are some of the pressures facing Dan, and why did he keep changing his major?

3. Why did Dan decide against getting some psychological counseling at his college?

4. What are some common "stress-related problems" facing college students?

5. What three reasons does the author give for students "suffering more than earlier generations"?

6. Describe some financial pressures students face.

7. Even though colleges offer students a wide choice of majors, what problems do some students experience regarding their choice of majors?

8. What are some of the steps colleges have taken to help students who feel overwhelmed by college pressures? What is the role of "peer counselors"?

Discussion Prompts/Writing Options

If you write on any of the following topics, work through the stages of the writing process in preparing your cause or effect assignment.

1. Based on "Students in Shock," write a summary of the three significant reasons college students are in distress, and then give an overview of how colleges are reacting to student stress. Remember to use logical and effective transitions throughout your summary.

2. Make a list of all the reasons this 1989 article gives for college students feeling "in shock." Working with a group or on your own, list some pressures that the article does not mention. Then, working alone, select one of these pressures and describe its effects.

3. For discussion or for a paragraph or short essay, describe either the positive or negative effects of your college experience thus far. Be sure you have at least three effects.

4. Write a letter to your college instructors. Your letter will be a paragraph giving at least three reasons why students seem tired in class.

5. Stress has different effects on different people. Freewrite about the effects of college stress on you and people you know. Use

your freewriting to plan and write a paragraph or short essay on the effects of college stress. Use your and your friends' experiences as examples of the different effects of college stress.

6. If your campus offers peer counseling, contact your counseling department to learn more about the program. See if you can interview a peer counselor and find out what some of the positive effects have been for him or her and the students who seek help. Bring your notes to class for discussion, or write an essay that explains the program's goals, and then, based on your interview, describe some of the positive effects of this program.

WRITING FROM READING: ARGUMENT

"Why Is Geezer-Bashing Acceptable?"

Abigail Trafford

Abigail Trafford says that we casually and openly discriminate against one group of Americans: the old. Many people who see themselves as fair and open-minded find it socially acceptable and even amusing to stereotype anybody "over a certain age." To remedy the situation, Trafford advises, "Society needs a reality check on what it means to grow old."

Words You May Need to Know (Corresponding paragraph numbers are in parentheses.)

condescending (1): showing a superior attitude
mirth (1): amusement or laughter
ageism (2): discrimination based on age
generalization (2): a vague statement about a large group based on little evidence
disparages (2): belittles, makes small or unimportant
fueling (2): stimulating
geezer (3): an old person, or a strange old person
bashing (3): criticizing harshly
doddering (3): shaking or trembling with age
chronological diversity (3): variety of age groups

myopia (4): a lack of perspective in thinking or planning
demographic (4): related to populations
endemic (4): widespread in a particular region
marginalizing (4): banishing to the edges of society
internalize (4): to make a part of one's attitudes or beliefs
longevity (5): length of life
proxy (5): a substitute
Indian summer (5): a pleasant, peaceful, or thriving time that occurs near the end of something
ageist (5): discriminatory based on age

1   "Oh, my God, they're sooooo slow." These words, quoted in a newspaper article, come from a 20-year-old woman in Florida. The subject of her condescending mirth: older drivers. Florida is full of them—whitehairs in big cars, poking along . . . chuckle, chuckle.

2   But what if the "they" in such a quote were black postal workers? Or girls in algebra class? Oh my God. . . . Instead of chuckles there would be

outrage and charges of racism and sexism. Where's the outrage at ageism? The statement about older drivers is a sweeping generalization that disparages a whole group of citizens—reinforcing stereotypes that the old are incompetent, while fueling prejudice against anyone who is not young.

3   Geezer-bashing is socially acceptable. What's the harm in making fun of the Doddering Class? Anybody over a certain age is fair game for stereotyping. Chronological diversity is not regarded as part of cultural diversity.

4   This social myopia is a prescription for demographic tragedy. The country—indeed, the world—is aging. Over the next 25 years, an increasing proportion of the population will be "old." Yet the social virus of ageism is endemic. It harms older Americans by unfairly portraying them with negative characteristics and marginalizing them in society. Many older men and women internalize these negative messages and lose confidence in themselves—at work, at home, and in the community.

5   Society needs a reality check on what it means to grow old. And here's the surprise: The decades after 50 have been transformed into a period of vitality and productivity, thanks to gains in health and longevity. To be sure, there are losses and hardships at this stage. A significant part of the older population is frail. The fear of aging is often proxy for the fear of dying, and mortality is ever-present in the lives of older people. Yet for many, these years are an Indian summer of contentment and personal development—of exploring new avenues of meaningful activity and significant relationships. They do not fit the ageist stereotypes of decline and incompetence.

6   The stereotypes take us back to older drivers. As a group, they are competent behind the wheel. They have a better safety record than those the age of the woman who was complaining about geezer drivers in Florida. According to statistics from the National Highway Traffic Safety Administration, crash rates for people older than 65 are about 30 per 100,000 licensed drivers. This compares with 119 crashes per 100,000 licensed drivers aged 16 to 24. Young people also have a higher death rate in traffic: about 29 deaths per 1,000 people compared with 22 deaths per 1,000 75 and older.

7   Older drivers deserve more respect. Meanwhile, it would be nice if some of those 20-year-old drivers would slow down.

Comprehension Check

   1. When a 20-year-old woman in Florida complains that "they're sooooo slow," who are "they"?

   2. What does Abigail Trafford mean by the "Doddering Class?"

   3. What is ageism, and how does it harm older Americans?

4. What does Abigail Trafford mean by saying that the years after 50 can be an Indian summer?

5. Trafford uses statistics to reveal a mistaken belief about older people. What is that belief?

Discussion Prompts/Writing Options

If you write on any of the following topics, be sure to work through the stages of the writing process in preparing your argument assignment.

1. Abigail Trafford's article argues that one group unfairly stereotyped is the elderly, and that many people are not aware of the prejudice involved in "geezer bashing." Consider other groups that many people feel free to stereotype. Such groups may be fat people, teenagers, or smokers. Argue for more understanding of one such group by (1) showing the cruelty of such stereotyping, and (2) attacking the truth of the stereotypes.

 COLLABORATE ▶

2. Working with a partner or a group, consider these questions: How old is old? What characteristics are associated with being old? Appearance? Bad health? Being a grandparent? Being retired? Are old people ridiculed for being cranky and mean? Romanticized as wise and benevolent or pitied as mentally incompetent and physically helpless? Once you have discussed these questions, split up, and write an argument using the following statement as your main point: There is no single image of an old person that applies to all people in the group. To support your point, you can use the ideas you gathered in your group discussion as well as in your own relationships with older people.

3. Consider how old people are portrayed on television. For example, how often do you see an older character in a television drama or comedy, and what role does he or she play? Is the character a fool? A victim of crime? A crabby old lady or nasty old man? Also, think about television commercials and the products linked to older people. (Older actors, for example, are often seen in commercials for arthritis medicine or hemorrhoid creams.) What image of the old is created by television programming and commercials? Once you have thought about these questions, you can argue that television stereotypes old people in unflattering (or unrealistic) ways.

4. Stereotypes are easy, thoughtless ways to categorize and dehumanize others. If you have ever felt that you were a victim of stereotyping, argue that the stereotype assigned to you was hurtful and unrealistic.

 COLLABORATE ▶

5. Working with a group, make a list of the casual, frequent statements or assumptions that reveal prejudice. For instance, some people believe that anyone who has reached 30 (or 35 or 40) and who has not married must have some deep flaws, and others believe that parents who have more than four (or five) children are irresponsible. Others assume that people who receive government aid are lazy. Once you have a list of such assumptions, pick one and argue that it is foolish, cruel, or unfair.

WRITING FROM READING: ARGUMENT

A Cell Phone? Never for Me.

Robert J. Samuelson

Robert J. Samuelson, a former reporter, is a columnist for Newsweek *and the* Washington Post *Writers' Group. His syndicated columns appear regularly in newspapers throughout the United States and abroad. Samuelson often challenges popular opinion, and in the following article, he argues that cell phones can be a nuisance, a danger, and a thief of our freedom.*

Words You May Need to Know (Corresponding paragraph numbers are in parentheses.)

aggravate (1): make worse
basket case (1): a person in a hopeless condition
milestone (2): turning point
underclass (2): the lowest class in society
orneriness (3): disagreeableness or meanness
immunize (3): create a resistance to
godsend (4): something wanted or needed that comes unexpectedly
murky (4): unclear

gab (7): talk endlessly or talk about trivia
keep tabs on (8): observe carefully
monitor (8): check
spawn (8): produce
gallows humor (8): humor about a serious situation
constitute (9): compose
factoids (9): inaccurate information that is presented as fact
rendezvous (9) a meeting at a prearranged time and place

1   Someday soon, I may be the last man in America without a cell phone. To those who see cell phones as progress, I say: they aggravate noise pollution and threaten our solitude. The central idea of cell phones is that you should be connected to almost everyone and everything at all times. The trouble is that cell phones assault your peace of mind no matter what you do. If you turn them off, why have one? You just irritate anyone who might call. If they're on and no one calls, you're a basket case.

2   I'm a dropout and aim to stay that way. I admit this will be increasingly difficult because cell phones are now passing a historical milestone. As with other triumphs of the mass market, they've reached a point when people forget what it was like before they existed. No one remembers life before cars, TVs, air conditioners, jets, credit cards, microwave ovens, and ATM cards. So, too, now with cell phones. Anyone without one will soon be classified as a crank or member of the (deep) underclass.

3   Look at the numbers. In 1985 there were 340,213 cell-phone users. By year-end 2003 there were 159 million. (These figures come from the Cellular Telecommunications & Internet Association, or CTIA.) I had once assumed that age, orneriness, or hearing loss would immunize most of the over-60 population against cell phones. Wrong. Among those 60 to 69, cell

phone ownership (60 percent) is almost as high as among 18- to 24-year-olds (66 percent), though lower than among 30- to 49-year-olds (76 percent), according to a recent survey from the Pew Research Center. Even among those 80 and older, ownership is 32 percent.

4   Of course, cell phones have productive uses. For those constantly on the road (salespeople, real-estate agents, repair technicians, some managers, and reporters), they're a godsend. The same is true for critical workers (doctors, oil-rig firefighters) needed at a moment's notice. Otherwise, benefits seem murky.

5   They make driving more dangerous, though how much so is unclear. The Insurance Information Institute recently summarized some studies: the Harvard Center for Risk Analysis blamed cell phones for 6 percent of auto accidents each year, involving 2,600 deaths (but admitted that estimates are difficult); the AAA Foundation for Traffic Safety studied videotapes of 70 drivers and concluded that cell phones are distracting, though less so than many other activities (say, stretching for an item in the glove compartment).

6   Then there's sheer nuisance. Private conversations have gone public. We've all been subjected to someone else's sales meeting, dinner reservation, family feud, and dating problem. In 2003, cell-phone conversations totaled 830 billion minutes, reckons CTIA. That's about 75 times greater than in 1991 and almost 50 hours for every man, woman, and child in America. How valuable is all this chitchat? The average conversation lasts two-and-a-half to three minutes. Surely many could be postponed or forgotten.

7   It's true that many people like to gab. Cell phones keep them company. Count that as a plus. But it's also true that many people dislike being bothered. These are folks who have cell phones but often wish they didn't. A recent poll, sponsored by the Lemelson-MIT program, asked which invention people hated most but couldn't live without. Cell phones won, chosen by 30 percent of respondents.

8   Some benefits may be oversold. Cell phones for teens were sold as a way for parents to keep tabs on children. That works—up to a point. The point is when your kids switch off the phones. Two of my teens have cell phones (that was Mom's idea; she has one, too). Whenever I want them most, their phones are off. Hmm. Similar advantages are claimed for older people. They have cell phones to allow their children to monitor their health. This may spawn gallows humor on voice-mail messages. (For example: "Hi Sonny. If you get this, I'm dead.")

9   Cell phones—and, indeed, all wireless devices—constitute another chapter in the ongoing breakdown between work and everything else. They pretend to increase your freedom while actually stealing it. People are supposed to be always capable of participating in the next meeting, responding to their e-mails, or retrieving factoids from the Internet. People so devoted

to staying interconnected are kept in a perpetual state of anxiety because they may have missed some significant memo, rendezvous, bit of news or gossip. They may be more plugged in and less thoughtful.

10   All this is the wave of the future or, more precisely, the present. According to another survey, two thirds of Americans would choose a cell phone over a traditional land line. Land lines have already dropped from 189.5 million in 1999 to 181.4 million at the end of 2003, says the Federal Communications Commission. Cell phones, an irresistible force, will soon pull ahead. But I vow to resist just as I've resisted ATM cards, laptops, and digital cameras. I agree increasingly with the poet Ogden Nash, who wrote, "Progress might have been all right once, but it's gone on too long."

Comprehension Check

1. What does Samuelson state is the "central idea of cell phones"?

2. Samuelson notes that he was wrong about the "over-60 population" and their attitudes about cell phones. What did he assume about this age group, and what statistic proved him wrong?

3. According to the Samuelson, there are a few "productive uses" of cell phones. What are they?

4. What did the AAA Foundation for Traffic Safety conclude about cell phones?

5. Samuelson says that two of his teenagers have cell phones but that the phones are not really a good way for him to keep in touch with his children. Why?

6. Why does Samuelson believe that "people so devoted to staying interconnected are kept in a perpetual state of anxiety"?

7. What other products associated with technology has Samuelson avoided?

Discussion Prompts/Writing Options

If you write on any of the following topics, work through the stages of the writing process in preparing your argument assignment.

1. Samuelson argues that many cell-phone conversations "could be postponed or forgotten." In a short essay, argue that many people waste time and money making unnecessary cell-phone calls.

2. Write a short paragraph or argument essay using this thesis statement:

    My school's (or classroom's) policy on cell-phone use is
    _____. (Fill in the blank with an appropriate adjective, such as "beneficial," "unfair," "illogical," "practical," or "positive.")

3. Based on your own experience with cell-phone companies, argue that the billing practices of your provider are fair or unfair.

4. Samuelson vows to resist using cell phones just as he resisted using "ATM cards, laptops, and digital cameras." Write a paragraph or short essay convincing a non-user of one of these items to become a user, or, if you know someone who has become obsessive about one of these items, persuade him or her to stop using this product.

WRITING FROM READING: THE ESSAY

Eleven

Sandra Cisneros

Sandra Cisneros, the child of a Mexican father and a Mexican-American mother, grew up in Chicago. She has worked as a teacher to high school dropouts and in other areas of education and the arts. A poet and writer of short stories, Cisneros incorporates her ethnic background into her writing. Her story "Eleven" is about a birthday gone wrong.

1   What they don't understand about birthdays and what they never tell you is that when you're eleven, you're also ten, and nine, and eight, and seven, and six, and five, and four, and three, and two, and one. And when you wake up on your eleventh birthday, you expect to feel eleven, but you don't. You open your eyes and everything's just like yesterday, only it's today. And you don't feel eleven at all. You feel like you're still ten. And you are—underneath the year that makes you eleven.

2   Like some days you might say something stupid, and that's the part of you that's still ten. Or maybe some days you might need to sit on your mama's lap because you're scared, and that's the part of you that's five. And maybe one day when you're all grown up you may need to cry like if you're still three, and that's okay. That's what I tell Mama when she's sad and needs to cry. Maybe she's feeling three.

3   Because the way you grow old is kind of like an onion or like the rings inside a tree trunk or like my little wooden dolls that fit one inside the other, each year inside the next one. That's how being eleven years old is.

4   You don't feel eleven. Not right away. It takes a few days, weeks even, sometimes even months before you say "Eleven" when they ask you. And you don't feel smart eleven, not until you're almost twelve. That's the way it is.

5   Only today I wish I didn't have only eleven years rattling around inside me like pennies in a tin Band-Aid box. Today I wish I was one hundred and two instead of eleven because if I was one hundred and two, I would have known what to say when Mrs. Price put the red sweater on my desk. I would've known how to tell her it wasn't mine instead of just sitting there with that look on my face and nothing coming out of my mouth.

6   "Whose is this?" Mrs. Price says, and she holds the red sweater up in the air for all the class to see. "Whose? It's been sitting in the coatroom for a month."

7   "Not mine," says everybody. "Not me."

8   "It has to belong to somebody," Mrs. Price keeps saying, but nobody can remember. It's an ugly sweater with red plastic buttons and a collar and sleeves all stretched out like you could use it for a jump rope. It's maybe a thousand years old and even if it belonged to me, I wouldn't say so.

9   Maybe because I'm skinny, maybe because she doesn't like me, that stupid Sylvia Saldivar says, "I think it belongs to Rachel." An ugly sweater like that, all raggedy and old, but Mrs. Price believes her. Mrs. Price takes the sweater and puts it right on my desk, but when I open my mouth nothing comes out.

10   "That's not. I don't, you're not. . . . Not mine," I finally say in a little voice that was maybe me when I was four.

11   "Of course it's yours," Mrs. Price says. "I remember you wearing it once." Because she's older and the teacher, she's right and I'm not.

12   Not mine, not mine, but Mrs. Price is already turning to page thirty-two, and math problem number four. I don't know why, but all of a sudden, I'm feeling sick inside, like the part of me that's three wants to come out of my eyes, only I squeeze them shut tight and bite down on my teeth real hard and try to remember today I am eleven. Mama is making a cake for me tonight, and when Papa comes home everybody will sing Happy birthday, happy birthday to you.

13   But when the sick feeling goes away and I open my eyes, the red sweater's still sitting there like a big red mountain. I move the red sweater to the corner of my desk with my ruler. I move my pencil and books and eraser as far from it as possible. I even move my chair a little to the right. Not mine, not mine, not mine.

14   In my head I'm thinking how long till lunchtime, how long till I can take the red sweater and throw it over the schoolyard fence, or leave it hanging on a parking meter, or bunch it up into a little ball and toss it into the alley. Except when the math period ends Mrs. Price says loud and in front of everybody, "Now, Rachel, that's enough," because she sees I've shoved the red sweater to the tippy-tip corner of my desk and it's hanging all over the edge like a waterfall, but I don't care.

15   "Rachel," Mrs. Price says. She says it like she's getting mad. "You put that sweater on right now and no more nonsense."

16   "But it's not—"

17   "Now!" Mrs. Price says.

18   This is when I wish I wasn't eleven, because all the years inside me—ten, nine, eight, seven, six, five, four, three, two, and one—are pushing at

the back of my eyes when I put one arm through one sleeve of the sweater that smells like cottage cheese, and then the other arm through the other and stand there with my arms apart like if the sweater hurts me and it does, all itchy and full of germs that aren't even mine.

19   That's when everything I've been holding in since this morning, since when Mrs. Price put the sweater on my desk, finally lets go, and all of a sudden I'm crying in front of everybody. I wish I was invisible but I'm not. I'm eleven and it's my birthday today and I'm crying like I'm three in front of everybody. I put my head down on my desk and bury my face in my stupid clown-sweater arms. My face all hot and spit coming out of my mouth because I can't stop the little animal noises from coming out of me, until there aren't any more tears left in my eyes, and it's just my body shaking like when you have the hiccups, and my whole head hurts like when you drink milk too fast.

20   But the worst part is right before the bell rings for lunch. That stupid Phyllis Lopez, who is even dumber than Sylvia Saldivar, says she remembers the red sweater is hers! I take it off right away and give it to her, only Mrs. Price pretends like everything's okay.

21   Today I'm eleven. There's a cake Mama's making for me tonight, and when Papa comes home from work we'll eat it. There'll be candles and presents and everybody will sing Happy birthday, happy birthday to you, Rachel, only it's too late.

22   I'm eleven today. I'm eleven, ten, nine, eight, seven, six, five, four, three, two, and one, but I wish I was one hundred and two. I wish I was anything but eleven, because today I want to be far away already, far away like a runaway balloon, like a tiny *o* in the sky, so tiny-tiny you have to close your eyes to see it.

Comprehension Check

1. What does the narrator of this story say she tells "Mama" when her mother is sad and needs to cry?

2. Who is Mrs. Price, and what did she put on the narrator's school desk? Why could anyone "use it as a jump rope"?

3. What does Sylvia tell the teacher about Rachel, the narrator of this story?

4. What image does Rachel focus on in order to block out the fact that the teacher is making a false assumption about her?

5. Why does Rachel start "crying in front of everybody"?

6. What does Phyllis Lopez, Rachel's classmate, remember?

7. Read the story again. This time, write down descriptive phrases that capture images or emotions clearly.

Discussion Prompts/Writing Options

If you write on any of the following topics, work through the stages of the writing process in preparing your essay.

1. Describe two emotions that Rachel, the girl in "Eleven," feels. Use details from "Eleven" to describe and explain these emotions.

2. Write about a time when you didn't feel your age. You can call the essay "Seventeen" or "Eleven," or whatever your chronological age was, but write about why you felt you were a different age.

3. Write about a time, or several times, when an older person was wrong, and you were right. Include how you reacted to this dilemma at the time.

4. Write about a teacher who taught you an important lesson. The teacher does not have to be a formal classroom teacher.

5. Write an essay about three common fears of children.

6. You may have heard the saying, "You're only as old as you feel." Interview three people. Ask them their age; ask them how old they feel and why. Use the information you gather to write an essay about people and their views about age.

7. Cisneros writes that "the way you grow old is kind of like an onion or like the rings inside a tree trunk." Write an essay about three memorable "rings," three experiences, when you grew in some significant way.

8. If you feel "Eleven" is an effective story because it is written from the viewpoint of a little girl, explain why this approach works better than a more formal style.

WRITING FROM READING: THE ESSAY

A Brother's Murder

Brent Staples

In 1984, writer Brent Staples received news of his younger brother's murder. In this essay, he explores how two black men growing up in poverty and pain can take such different paths. As he traces his escape from anger and desperation, he grieves the loss of the brother he could not rescue.

Words You May Need to Know (Corresponding paragraph numbers are in parentheses.)

emerged (1): came out of
massive (1): large
inseparable (1): very close

escalated (1): increased
posturing (1): trying to look tough

assailant (1): attacker
wrenched (2): suddenly pulled
light-years (2): a long way
mortality (2): death
brash (2): fast-moving, impulsive
donned (2): put on
noncommissioned officer (3): an enlisted member of the armed forces appointed to lead other enlisted men and women
affluent (3): prosperous
paranoia (3): extreme irrational distrust of others
machismo (3): a strong sense of manhood that includes aggressiveness, domination of women, and physical courage
incursions (3): attacks, violations

upwardly mobile (4): likely to move up in wealth and status
ensconced (4): securely settled
grim (4): gloomy
umbilical (4): a connection between family members
desolate (5): deserted, lifeless
idle (5): unemployed, inactive
embittered (5): made bitter
forays (5): trips, ventures
terrain (5): ground
dive (6): a rundown bar or nightclub
affected (6): imitated, put on
alarm (7): sudden fear
earnestly (8): seriously
recurrent (8): occurring repeatedly

1   It has been more than two years since my telephone rang with the news that my younger brother Blake—just twenty-two years old—had been murdered. The young man who killed him was only twenty-four. Wearing a ski mask, he emerged from a car, fired six times at close range with a massive .44 Magnum, then fled. The two had once been inseparable friends. A senseless rivalry—beginning, I think, with an argument over a girl-friend—escalated from posturing to threats, to violence, to murder. The way the two were living, death could have come to either of them from anywhere. In fact, the assailant had already survived multiple gunshot wounds from an incident much like the one in which my brother lost his life.

2   As I wept for Blake, I felt wrenched backwards into events and circumstances that had seemed light-years gone. Though a decade apart, we both were raised in Chester, Pennsylvania, an angry, heavily black, heavily poor, industrial city southwest of Philadelphia. There, in the 1960s, I was introduced to mortality, not by the old and failing, but by beautiful young men who lay wrecked after sudden explosions of violence. The first, I remembered from my fourteenth year—Johnny, brash lover of fast cars, stabbed to death two doors from my house in a fight over a pool game. The next year, my teenage cousin, Wesley, whom I loved very much, was shot dead. The summers blur. Milton, an angry neighbor, shot a crosstown rival, wounding him badly. William, another teenage neighbor, took a shotgun blast to the shoulder in some urban drama and displayed his bandages proudly. His brother, Leonard, severely beaten, lost an eye and donned a black patch. It went on.

3   I recall not long before I left for college, two local Vietnam veterans—one from the Marines, one from the Army—arguing fiercely, nearly at blows

about which outfit had done the most in the war. The most killing, they meant. Not much later, I read a magazine article that set that dispute in a context. In the story, a noncommissioned officer—a sergeant, I believe—said he would pass up any number of affluent, suburban-born recruits to get hard-core soldiers from the inner city. They jumped into rice paddies with "their manhood on their sleeves," I believe he said. These two items—the veterans arguing and the sergeant's words—still characterize for me the circumstances under which black men in their teens and twenties kill one another with such frequency. With a touchy paranoia born of living battered lives, they are desperate to be *real* men. Killing is only machismo taken to the extreme. Incursions to be punished by death were many and minor, and they remain so: they include stepping on the wrong toe, literally; cheating in a drug deal; simply saying "I dare you" to someone holding a gun; crossing territorial lines in a gang dispute. My brother grew up to wear his manhood on his sleeve. And when he died he was in that group—black, male, and in its teens and early twenties—that is far and away the most likely to murder or be murdered.

4   I left the East Coast after college, spent the mid- and late 1970s in Chicago as a graduate student, taught for a time, then became a journalist. Within ten years of leaving my hometown, I was overeducated and "upwardly mobile," ensconced on a quiet, tree-lined street where voices raised in anger were scarcely ever heard. The telephone, like some grim umbilical, kept me connected to the old world with news of deaths, imprisonings, and misfortune. I felt emotionally beaten up. Perhaps to protect myself, I added a psychological dimension to the physical distance I had already achieved. I rarely visited my hometown. I shut it out.

5   As I fled the past, so Blake embraced it. On Christmas of 1983, I traveled from Chicago to a black section of Roanoke, Virginia, where he then lived. The desolate public housing projects, the hopeless, idle young men crashing against one another—these reminded me of the embittered town we'd grown up in. It was a place where once I would have been comfortable, or at least sure of myself. Now, hearing of my brother's forays into crime, his scrapes with police and street thugs, I was scared, unsteady on foreign terrain.

6   I saw that Blake's romance with the street life and the hustler image had flowered dangerously. One evening that late December, standing in some Roanoke dive among drug dealers and grim, hair-trigger losers, I told him I feared for his life. He had affected the image of the tough he wanted to be. But behind the dark glasses and the swagger, I glimpsed the baby-faced toddler I'd once watched over. I nearly wept. I wanted desperately for him to live. The young think themselves immortal, and a dangerous light shone in his eyes as he spoke laughingly of making fools of the policemen

who had raided his apartment looking for drugs. He cried out as I took his right hand. A line of stitches lay between the thumb and index finger. Kickback from a shotgun, he explained, nothing serious. Gunplay had become part of his life.

7   I lacked the language simply to say: Thousands have lived this for you and died. I fought the urge to lift him bodily and shake him. This place and the way you are living smells of death to me, I said. Take some time away, I said. Let's go downtown tomorrow and buy a plane ticket anywhere, take a bus trip, anything to get away and cool things off. He took my alarm casually. We arranged to meet the following night—an appointment he would not keep. We embraced as though through glass. I drove away.

8   As I stood in my apartment in Chicago holding the receiver that evening in February 1984, I felt as though part of my soul had been cut away. I questioned myself then, and I still do. Did I not reach back soon enough or earnestly enough for him? For weeks I awoke crying from a recurrent dream in which I chased him, urgently trying to get him to read a document I had, as though reading it would protect him from what had happened in waking life. His eyes shining like black diamonds, he smiled and danced just beyond my grasp. When I reached for him, I caught only the space where he had been.

Comprehension Check

1. Brent Staples says that his brother's murder was a result of a senseless rivalry. Who killed his brother, and what was the reason behind the rivalry?

2. How old was the author when he was "introduced to mortality"? Describe some of the fatal shootings of teenagers whom Staples knew.

3. Describe the type of recruit the noncommissioned officer was seeking, and explain why many of the teenagers Staples grew up with were perfect recruits.

4. Staples believes that angry inner city teens like his brother possess a "touch of paranoia born of living battered lives," and are "desperate to be *real* men." What are some of the seemingly simple acts that can lead to killing among this group of young men?

5. During Staples' ten-year absence from his hometown, he became "upwardly mobile" but felt "emotionally beaten up." How did he try to cope with the distance he had put between himself and his roots?

6. How did Blake's path differ from his brother's, and why did Brent fear for his brother's life?

7. Describe Staples' recurrent dream after his brother was murdered.

8. What do you think is the most effective description (phrase or sentence) in this article? Be prepared to explain your choice.

Discussion Prompts/Writing Options

If you write on any of the following topics, work through the stages of the writing process in preparing your assignment.

1. Brent Staples tried to connect emotionally with his brother. He warned Blake about the dangers of staying on a violent path. Do you think Staples did everything he could to save his brother? Use specific details from the article to support your point of view.

2. If you have witnessed or experienced a particularly disturbing or violent event in your neighborhood, describe the event and its consequences. You can include its immediate impact on you and your neighbors as well as its lasting effects.

3. Although "A Brother's Murder" was first published in 1986, some of Staples' descriptions, such as "idle young men crashing against one another," can apply to some violent and angry young males today. Select three or four descriptions or statements from the article that are still relevant and accurate. Be sure to include specific connections to senseless violence today.

4. Imagine all that could have happened in Staples' recurrent dream: What was the chase like? Why is he "urgently" trying to get his brother to read a document? What did the document say? How did his brother react? and so forth. Focus on creating a clear picture of what each man sees and feels.

WRITING FROM READING: THE ESSAY

Navajo Code Talkers: The Century's Best Kept Secret

Jack Hitt

In this essay, Jack Hitt talks of the secret heroism of a group of Native Americans during World War II. By using the language of their tribe, the Navajo Code Talkers made an "incredible contribution" to "winning history's biggest war."

Words You May Need to Know (Corresponding paragraph numbers are in parentheses.)

decisive (1): unmistakable
Iwo Jima (1): a Japanese Island in the Pacific
momentous (1): important
guttural (1): harsh, grating
intonations (1): tones
baffled (1): confused
infuriated (1): made angry

conformed (1): followed the rules of
linguistic (1): language
cryptographers (1): people who study secret codes
decipher (1): solve or decode
clandestine (1): secret
cryptographic (2): secret code

intercepted (2): stopped, interrupted, or turned aside
proficient (2): expert
sabotage (2): destroy
the Pentagon (2): the United States military establishment
gambits (2): maneuvers
virtually (3): practically
artillery (3): weapons

coined (3): created
neologisms (3): new words
pyrotechnic (4): resembling fireworks
elite (5): high status
solemnly (5): gravely
messaging apparatus (6): means for sending messages

1   During World War II, on the dramatic day when Marines raised the American flag to signal a key and decisive victory at Iwo Jima, the first word of this momentous news crackled over the radio in odd guttural noises and complex intonations. Throughout the war, the Japanese were repeatedly baffled and infuriated by these seemingly inhuman sounds. They conformed to no linguistic system known to the Japanese. The curious sounds were the military's one form of conveying tactics and strategy that the master cryptographers in Tokyo were unable to decipher. This perfect code was the language of the Navajo tribe. Its application in World War II as a clandestine system of communications was one of the twentieth century's best-kept secrets.

2   After a string of cryptographic failures, the military in 1942 was desperate for a way to open clear lines of communication that would not be intercepted by the enemy. In the 1940s, there was no such thing as a "secure line." All talk had to go out onto the public airwaves. Standard codes were an option, but the cryptographers in Japan could quickly crack them. And there was another problem: the Japanese were proficient at intercepting short-distance communications, on walkie-talkies for example, and then having well-trained English-speaking soldiers either sabotage the message or send out false commands to set up an ambush. That was the situation in 1942 when the Pentagon authorized one of the boldest gambits of the war.

3   The solution was conceived by the son of missionaries to the Navajos, a former Marine named Philip Johnston. His idea: station a native Navajo speaker at every radio station. Since Navajo had never been written down or translated into any other language, it was an entirely self-contained human communication system restricted to Navajos alone; it was virtually indecipherable without Navajo help. Without some key or way into a language, translation is virtually impossible. Not long after the bombing of Pearl Harbor, the military dispatched twenty-nine Navajos to Camp Elliott and Camp Pendleton in California to begin a test program. These first recruits had to develop a Navajo alphabet since none existed. And because Navajo lacked technical terms of military artillery, the men coined a number of neologisms specific to their task and war.

4   According to Chester Nez, one of the original code talkers, "Everything we used in the code was what we lived with on the reservation every day, like the ants, the birds, bears." Thus, the term for a tank was "turtle," a tank destroyer was "tortoise killer." A battleship was "whale." A hand grenade was "potato," and plain old bombs were "eggs." A fighter plane was "hummingbird," and a torpedo plane "swallow." A sniper was "pick 'em off." Pyrotechnic was "fancy fire."

5   It didn't take long for the original twenty-nine recruits to expand to an elite corps of Marines, numbering at its height 425 Navajo Code Talkers, all from the American Southwest. Each Talker was so valuable, he traveled everywhere with a personal bodyguard. In the event of capture, the Talkers had solemnly agreed to commit suicide rather than allow America's most valuable war code to fall into the hands of the enemy. If a captured Navajo did not follow that grim instruction, the bodyguard's instructions were understood: shoot and kill the Code Talker.

6   The language of the Code Talkers, their mission, and every detail of their messaging apparatus were secrets they were all ordered to keep, even from their own families. They did. It wasn't until 1968, when the military felt convinced that the Code Talkers would not be needed for any future wars, that America learned of the incredible contribution a handful of Native Americans made to winning history's biggest war. The Navajo Code Talkers, sending and receiving as many as 800 errorless messages at fast speed during "the fog of battle," are widely credited with giving U.S. troops the decisive edge at Guadalcanal, Tarawa, Saipan, Iwo Jima, and Okinawa.

Comprehension Check

1. Why was the Navajo tribe's language considered a "perfect code" for the United States to use for conveying "tactics and strategy" during World War II?

2. Before the United States started using the Navajo language as a secret code of communication, why were standard codes ineffective?

3. Who was Philip Johnston, what was his idea concerning Navajo speakers, and why was the Navajo language such a perfect choice for secret communication?

4. What did the first group of Navajo recruits have to develop in order to use their language as code?

5. The Navajo Code Talkers became "an elite corps of Marines." How many recruits did this corps have at its height, and where were they all from?

6. What were some indications that each Talker was extremely valuable to the United States?

7. If the Navajo Code Talkers were captured by the enemy, what were they expected to do?

8. When did America finally learn about "the incredible contribution a handful of Native Americans made to winning history's biggest war"?

Discussion Prompts/Writing Options

If you write on any of the following topics, work through the stages of the writing process in preparing your assignment.

1. The language of the Navajo tribe was the perfect language to use for secret code. Are you familiar with any regional language or slang that would be hard to decipher by anyone unfamiliar with this form of communication? If so, describe where this language developed, how often it is used, and why it would be so difficult to decipher or translate.

2. The Navajo Code Talkers could be considered unsung heroes because their heroic contributions during World War II went unrecognized for so many years. Write a short essay about whom you regard as an unsung hero in your school, community, city, or state.

 COMPUTER ▶

3. Jack Hitt, author of "Navajo Code Talkers," states that the Talkers "are widely credited with giving U.S. troops the decisive edge at Guadalcanal, Tarawa, Saipan, Iwo Jima, and Okinawa." Conduct an online search for information about one or more of these battles, and see if the contributions of the Navajo Code Talkers are mentioned. If so, summarize the specific contributions of the Talkers. If not, summarize the main points of the article(s); you may want to include details about the purpose of the battle, the length of the battle, the number of casualties, and the degree of success.

Note: If you choose to summarize one article, refer to "Writing a Summary of a Reading," on pp. 336–341 in Chapter 13.

WRITING FROM READING

My Daughter Smokes

Alice Walker

Alice Walker, the award-winning writer of fiction and non-fiction, is best known for her novel The Color Purple. *In this essay, she describes a family habit that has passed through the generations. She also connects that habit to poverty and oppression through the years.*

Words You May Need to Know (Corresponding paragraph numbers are in parentheses.)

Queen Victoria (2): queen of England from 1837 to 1901
consort (2): the husband or wife of a royal person; Prince

Albert was Queen Victoria's husband
pungent (2): sharp smelling or tasting

coupled with (3): joined with
dapper (3): neat and trim
perennially (5): continually
toxic (11): poisoned or poisonous
chronic (11): constant
bronchitis (12): an inflammation
of the membrane lining of the air
passages beyond the windpipe
that lead to the lungs
emphysema (12): a defect in the
lung system
emaciated (12): thin and wasted
away
eradicating (13): destroying,
exterminating
futility (14): uselessness

empathy (15): identification with
and understanding of another's
situation
venerated (15): treated with
reverence
denatured (15): deprived of its
natural character or traits
mono-cropping (15): growing a
single crop on a farm or in a
region
kin (16): relatives, things of a
similar kind
cajole (18): to persuade by
flattery or promise, to coax
literally (18): actually, truly

1   My daughter smokes. While she is doing her homework, her feet on the bench in front of her and her calculator clicking out answers to her algebra problems, I am looking at the half-empty package of Camels tossed carelessly close at hand. Camels. I pick them up, take them into the kitchen, where the light is better, and study them—they're filtered, for which I am grateful. My heart feels terrible. I want to weep. In fact, I do weep a little, standing there by the stove holding one of the instruments, so white, so precisely rolled, that could cause my daughter's death. When she smoked Marlboros and Players, I hardened myself against feeling so bad; nobody I knew ever smoked these brands.

2   She doesn't know this, but it was Camels that my father, her grandfather, smoked. But before he smoked "ready-mades"—when he was very young and very poor, with eyes like lanterns—he smoked Prince Albert tobacco in cigarettes he rolled himself. I remember the bright-red tobacco tin, with a picture of Queen Victoria's consort, Prince Albert, dressed in a black frock coat and carrying a cane. The tobacco was dark brown, pungent, slightly bitter. I tasted it more than once as a child, and the discarded tins could be used for a number of things: to keep buttons and shoelaces in, to store seeds, and best of all, to hold worms for the rare times my father took us fishing.

3   By the late forties and fifties no one rolled his own any more (and few women smoked) in my hometown, Eatontown, Georgia. The tobacco industry, coupled with Hollywood movies in which both hero and heroine smoked like chimneys, won over completely people like my father, who were hopelessly addicted to cigarettes. He never looked as dapper as Prince Albert, though; he continued to look like a poor, overweight, overworked colored man with too large a family; black, with a very white cigarette stuck in his mouth.

4   I do not remember when he started to cough. Perhaps it was unnoticeable at first. A little hacking in the morning as he lit his first cigarette

upon getting out of bed. By the time I was my daughter's age, his breath was a wheeze, embarrassing to hear; he could not climb stairs without resting every third or fourth step. It was not unusual for him to cough for an hour.

5   It is hard to believe there was a time when people did not understand that cigarette smoking is an addiction. I wondered aloud once to my sister—who is perennially trying to quit—whether our father realized this. I wondered how she, a smoker since high school, viewed her own habit.

6   It was our father who gave her her first cigarette, one day when she had taken water to him in the fields.

7   "I always wondered why he did that," she said, puzzled, and with some bitterness.

8   "What did he say?" I asked.

9   "That he didn't want me to go to anyone else for them," she said, "which never really crossed my mind."

10   So he was aware it was addictive, I thought, though as annoyed as she that he assumed she would be interested.

11   I began smoking in eleventh grade, also the year I drank numerous bottles of terrible sweet, very cheap wine. My friends and I, all boys for this venture, bought our supplies from a man who ran a segregated bar and liquor store on the outskirts of town. Over the entrance there was a large sign that said COLORED. We were not permitted to drink there, only to buy. I smoked Kools because my sister did. By then I thought her toxic darkened lips and gums glamorous. However, my body simply would not tolerate smoke. After six months, I had a chronic sore throat. I gave up smoking, gladly. Because it was a ritual with my buddies—Murl, Leon, and "Dog" Farley—I continued to drink wine.

12   My father died from "the poor man's friend," pneumonia, one hard winter when his bronchitis and emphysema had left him low. I doubt he had much lung left at all, after coughing for so many years. He had so little breath that, during his last years, he was always leaning on something. I remember once, at a family reunion, when my daughter was two, that my father picked her up for a minute—long enough for me to photograph them—but the effort was obvious. Near the very end of his life, and largely because he had no more lungs, he quit smoking. He gained a couple of pounds, but by then he was so emaciated no one noticed.

13   When I travel to Third World countries, I see many people like my father and daughter. There are large billboards directed at them both: the tough, "take-charge," or dapper older man, the glamorous, "worldly" young woman, both puffing away. In these poor countries, as in American ghettos and on reservations, money that should be spent for food goes instead to the tobacco companies; over time, people starve themselves of both food and air, effectively weakening and addicting their children, eventually eradicat-

ing themselves. I read in the newspaper and in my gardening magazine that cigarette butts are so toxic that if a baby swallows one, it is likely to die, and that the boiled water from a bunch of them makes an effective insecticide.

14   My daughter would like to quit, she says. We both know the statistics are against her; most people who try to quit smoking do not succeed. There is a deep hurt that I feel as a mother. Some days it is a feeling of futility. I remember how carefully I ate when I was pregnant, how patiently I taught my daughter how to cross a street safely. For what, I sometimes wonder; so that she can wheeze through most of her life feeling half her strength, and then die of self-poisoning, as her grandfather did?

15   But, finally, one must feel empathy for the tobacco plant itself. For thousands of years, it has been venerated by Native Americans as a sacred medicine. They have used it extensively—its juice, its leaves, its roots, its (holy) smoke—to heal wounds and cure diseases, and in ceremonies of prayer and peace. And though the plant as most of us know it has been poisoned by chemicals and denatured by intensive mono-cropping and is therefore hardly the plant it was, still, to some modern Indians it remains a plant of positive power. I learned this when my Native American friends, Bill Wahpepah and his family, visited with me for a few days and the first thing he did was sow a few tobacco seeds in my garden.

16   Perhaps we can liberate tobacco from those who have captured and abused it, enslaving the plant on large plantations, keeping it from freedom and its kin, and forcing it to enslave the world. Its true nature suppressed, no wonder it has become deadly. Maybe by sowing a few seeds of tobacco in our gardens and treating the plant with the reverence it deserves, we can redeem tobacco's soul and self-respect.

17   Besides, how grim, if one is a smoker, to realize one is smoking a slave.

18   There is a slogan from a battered women's shelter that I especially like: "Peace on earth begins at home." I believe everything does. I think of a slogan for people trying to stop smoking: "Every home a smoke-free zone." Smoking is a form of self-battering that also batters those who must sit by, occasionally cajole or complain, and helplessly watch. I realize now that as a child I sat by, through the years, and literally watched my father kill himself; surely one such victory in my family, for the rich white men who own the tobacco companies, is enough.

Note: Three months after reading this essay, Alice Walker's daughter stopped smoking.

Comprehension Check

    1. Alice Walker's daughter is unaware that she has something in common with her grandfather. What is it?

2. What does Alice Walker say was the best use of the discarded Prince Albert tobacco tins?

3. Walker says that the tobacco industry and Hollywood "won over completely people like my father." How were these forces so persuasive?

4. Why was Walker's sister, "a smoker since high school," both puzzled and bitter that their father gave her "her first cigarette"?

5. When did Walker begin smoking, and what did she find "glamorous" about her sister?

6. When did Walker give up smoking? Why?

7. According to Walker, why did her father quit smoking, and what was sad about the last years of his life?

8. Walker states, "When I travel to Third World countries, I see many people like my father and daughter." Explain how large billboard advertising is aimed at attracting such people in these countries.

9. What are some of the Native American traditions that treat the tobacco plant with respect and as a source of "positive power"?

10. What is Walker's suggestion for redeeming tobacco's "soul and self-respect"?

Discussion Prompts/Writing Options

If you write on any of the topics below, be sure to work through the stages of the writing process in preparing your assignment.

1. Write a summary of Alice Walker's essay. Be sure to include (a) her description of her daughter's habit, (b) the story of her father's decline, and (c) her point about the misuse of the tobacco plant.

   For tips on summarizing this essay, refer to "Writing a Summary of a Reading," on pp. 336–341 in Chapter 13.

2. Walker writes of addicted smokers as people who end up "eradicating themselves" by spending the money that should go for food on tobacco. Describe how some people end up destroying themselves by depriving themselves of what they need. You might want to consider another serious addiction or such conditions as anorexia, bulimia, obsession with fitness, and so forth.

 COLLABORATE ▶

3. Working with a partner or a group, brainstorm a list of behaviors that people your age might laugh about or justify with a joke but which are dangerous. Then write individual paragraphs on one of those behaviors and how and why its risks are often ignored.

4. Imagine that your father is Alice Walker's father. Write him a letter about his smoking. Include all the feelings about his smoking that you never expressed when he was alive.

5. Pick one of the statements below (both are from "My Daughter Smokes") and use it to write an agree or disagree paragraph.

> "Smoking is a form of self-battering that also batters those who must sit by, occasionally cajole and complain, and help-lessly watch."
> "Peace on earth begins at home."

6. If you have a habit that you (or others) feel you should break, write about that habit. You can consider why you don't want to or can't break it, its dangers, and its satisfactions.

7. Based on your observations, is smoking still common among teens and young children in your community? Explain why the smoking habit has either declined, remained the same, or increased among these age groups.

WRITING FROM READING

Parental Discretion

Dennis Hevesi

Dennis Hevesi is a writer for The New York Times. *In this essay, he writes about how the family structure changes when a parent goes back to school.*

Words You May Need To Know (Corresponding paragraph numbers are in parentheses.)

discretion (title): the right to make your own decision
wrought (4): created
havoc (4): disorder, confusion
diehard (4): stubbornly committed, dedicated
feminists (4): people who fight for women's rights
genes (8): a unit in the body that controls the development of hereditary traits

maternal (14): motherly
anthropology (16): a study of the origins and physical and cultural development of mankind
Renaissance (17): a period of European history, roughly from the late 1300s to 1600

1 When the letter came saying that Pamela Stafford, after all her part-time study at night, had been accepted at the age of thirty four as a full-time student by the University of California at Berkeley, her two teenage sons leaped into the air, slapped palms in a high five, and

2 shouted: "We did it! We did it!"

3 "I'm not sure they included me," she said.

Several months ago, when Gary Hatfield, also thirty four, and a sopho-more at the Ohio State University in Columbus, was telling his son Seth, eleven, why he was spending so much time studying, "He patted me on the shoulder and said, 'Dad, I understand. You want to finish school,'" Mr. Hat-field recalled, adding, "Blessed is the child's forgiving nature."

4   In hundreds of homes throughout the nation, as the rolls of those signing up for continuing education courses grow, getting mom or pop off to school has often wrought a kind of joyous havoc on family life and forced the sort of realignment of expectations that would warm the hearts of diehard feminists.

5   Dads or children are doing the shopping, the cooking, the cleaning, the laundry. Teenagers have become the family chauffeur, or at least make sure the car is available when a parent has to get to class. Schedules have been turned on end. Children have even adopted parental roles—nagging when homework hasn't been done.

6   Mr. Hatfield, an English major, wants to teach high school or college English. "I'll sometimes get jabbed if I make a spelling or grammatical mistake," he said. "Seth will say, 'Hey, English teacher . . .'"

7   What can come through the difficulties and the role reversals is a shared commitment, a strengthened bond, and a deepened appreciation for education. "When I went back to school, my older son went from being a C and D student to making the honor roll," said Ms. Stafford, who is divorced and lives near the university. "The younger guy, well, not as much improvement. But he did develop a more serious attitude towards school. Now it's sort of a given that what you really do in life is finish school first."

8   And when the boys—Joseph, 18, and Christopher, 14—run into what Ms. Stafford called "the geek mentality" of friends who think doing well in school is totally lame, they are equipped to respond. "Joseph once told his friend," Ms. Stafford said, "'Hey, my mom is smart. It's in the genes. I can't help being smart.'"

9   Mom is indeed smart. Out of a possible 4.0, Ms. Stafford is maintaining a 3.9 grade-point average as an English major at Berkeley, where she is also on staff as an administrative assistant.

10   "I felt really guilty about taking night courses," she said. "Then, at the end of that first semester, I got an A in ancient Mediterranean literature, and my sons developed an investment in my education. They sort of fired me as a mother and recreated me as a student."

11   Joseph, now a freshman at St. Mary's College in nearby Moraga, said, "I had to cook, wash dishes, pretty much take care of myself and my brother, too. There were times when I wished she was around, when things would happen that I couldn't handle."

12   Joseph said Christopher "was always a hyper kid. So I just had to be real patient. I talked to him about girls, about drugs. He doesn't do the silly stuff he used to do to get attention, like kitchen gymnastics—you know, dancing and flipping around the house like an idiot. Sometimes we fought. But he and I loved each other enough to punch each other and then hug."

13   During midterms and finals, Ms. Stafford said, the boys "would mysteriously disappear" so that she could study. "I like to deejay," Joseph said,

"you know, sound-mixing in my room. I had to do this with the headphones the entire time. There could be no noise."

14   Between classes, Ms. Stafford would call home "and try to at least bring a maternal presence into the conversation: 'Have you done your homework? Have you done your chores?' But they would say, 'Hey, we don't need you. Goodness, the things we go through putting a parent through school.'"

15   Sometimes it seemed that Seth Hatfield wasn't so much putting his father through school as accompanying him. "Last quarter, I was taking an anthropology course," Mr. Hatfield said, "and one of the evenings I would take Seth to that class. He would sit and do his homework at the table with me. And the teacher was so nearsighted that she would walk by and give him handouts, just like one of the students."

16   Mr. Hatfield, who is divorced and lives in Columbus, has worked as a landscaper, a salesman, a counselor to juvenile delinquents, and a social worker at a home for the mentally retarded. With a part-time job, a little money in the bank, and a grant from Ohio State, he returned to college and is maintaining a grade-point average of 3.2.

17   "I get hit with anxiety attacks," he said, "because here I am plowing through Renaissance literature and wishing I was sitting with my son playing a game."

18   But Seth doesn't complain, and his exposure to college has had benefits. "I found out from his teachers that he speaks proudly of going to Ohio State with his dad," Mr. Hatfield said. "Just walking across campus, with him wearing his Ohio State sweatshirt, gives me the opportunity to familiarize him with what the place really is. We go plunder through the library. He knows the computer catalogue search system can lead him to information on Superman."

19   "I might go there when I grow up," Seth said. "When my dad gets his education, if he becomes a teacher, he'll have a larger income, and I might even have him as a teacher. Maybe I'll borrow money from him for lunch."

20   Mr. Hatfield realizes that Seth, who lives with his mother about a mile away, is his first priority. "I will cut class to go to his band concert," he said. "Those things are too precious. I can take an incomplete in a course and make it up. I can't take an incomplete as a parent and ever make that up."

Comprehension Check

1. When the University of California at Berkeley accepted Pamela Stafford, how did her teenage sons react?

2. What are some examples of role reversals in families in which the parents are attending college, and what benefits did the Stafford family experience?

3. Explain what is meant by "geek mentality" and how Joseph Stafford was "equipped to respond" to it?

4. How did Joseph Stafford adapt to his mother's new role as a student, and how did he handle his younger brother, Christopher?

5. Explain what the author means when he states that "it seemed like Seth Hatfield wasn't so much putting his father through school as accompanying him"?

6. How has Seth's exposure to college been beneficial?

7. What is the reason Seth's father will cut class?

Discussion Prompts/Writing Options

If you write on any of the following topics, be sure to work through the stages of the writing process in preparing your assignment.

1. Write a summary paragraph of Hevesi's article. Be sure to include Hevesi's points about the good and bad effects of parents' returning to college.

   For tips on summarizing this essay, refer to "Writing a Summary of a Reading," on pp. 336–341 in Chapter 13.

 COLLABORATE ▶

2. No matter how old you are, attending college presents certain challenges. If you are the "traditional" college age of eighteen or nineteen, you may face the challenge of adjusting to a place that is not like high school. If you are in your twenties, you may be facing other challenges: earning money for college, living at home and going to college, balancing the demands of a family, work, and school. Students in their thirties, forties, fifties, sixties, and seventies all have different problems when they go to college. Write a short essay about the problems one age group faces in attending college. You may use a topic sentence like this one:

   > It's not easy being eighteen (or twenty-five, or thirty, or sixty—you fill in the age) and going to college.

   If your instructor agrees, you might interview a writing partner about the difficulties his or her age group faces in going to college. Then your partner can interview you. By interviewing, each of you can help the other gather details.

3. As an alternative to activity 2, choose a topic sentence that is closer to your experience, such as one of the following:

   > Working full time and going to college is not easy.
   > Being in a wheelchair and going to college is not easy.
   > Being a single parent and going to college is not easy.

4. Begin this assignment by working with a group. Plan a paragraph or essay with this main idea: ◀ COLLABORATE

> Today, the term "college student" can include many kinds of people.

In your group, have each member support this main idea by talking about himself or herself. You might mention age, reason for going to college, ethnic background, college major, hobbies, special talents, family background, and so on. As each member describes himself or herself, write down the details. Ask follow-up questions and write down the answers. After you have gathered enough specific examples, write your paragraph.

5. Visit your school's counseling center and ask about where to find statistics about the age range of the student population on your campus: the average age of entering freshmen; the percentage of students in their teens, twenties, and so forth; and the average age of day versus evening and weekend students. You may also want to investigate the ages of students enrolled in online courses.

Once you have gathered the statistics, summarize your findings about the diversity of ages on your campus. Show how these findings were either surprising to you or confirmed what you had already assumed about the age range on campus.

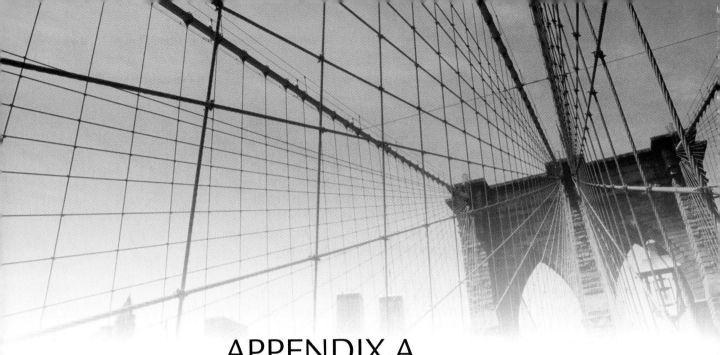

APPENDIX A
Grammar Practice
for ESL Students

NOUNS AND ARTICLES

A **noun** names a person, place, or thing. There are count nouns and noncount nouns.

> **Count nouns** refer to persons, places, or things that can be counted: three *doughnuts*, two *kittens*, five *pencils*.
>
> **Noncount nouns** refer to things that can't be counted: *medicine, housework, mail.*

Here are some more examples of count and noncount nouns.

count	noncount
rumor	gossip
violin	music
school	intelligence
suitcase	luggage

One way to remember the difference between count and noncount nouns is to put the word *much* in front of the noun. For example, if you can say *much luggage*, then *luggage* is a noncount noun.

Exercise 1   **Identifying Count and Noncount Nouns**

Write *count* or *noncount* next to each word below.

1. _____ gift

6. _____ safety

2. _____ fence

7. _____ ice cream

3. _____ gossip

8. _____ money

4. _____ toothpaste

9. _____ toothbrush

5. _____ coin

10. _____ cookie

Using Articles with Nouns

Articles point out nouns. Articles are either **indefinite** (*a, an*) or **definite** (*the*). There are several rules for using these articles.

1. Use *a* in front of consonant sounds, and use *an* before vowel sounds:

a card   an orange
a radio   an answer
a button   an entrance
a thread   an invitation
a nightmare   an uncle

2. Use *a* or *an* in front of singular count nouns (*a* or *an* mean "any one"):

I ate *an* egg.
James planted *a* tree.

3. Do not use *a* or *an* with noncount nouns:

not this: Selena filled the tank with ~~a~~ gasoline.
but this: Selena filled the tank with gasoline.

not this: I am studying ~~an~~ algebra.
but this: I am studying algebra.

4. Use *the* before both singular and plural count nouns whose specific identify is known to the reader:

The dress with the sequins on it is my party dress.
Most of *the* movies I rent are science fiction films.

5. Use *the* before noncount nouns only when they are specifically identified.

not this: I need ~~the~~ help. (Whose help? What help? The noncount noun *help* is not specifically identified.)
but this: I need *the help* of a good plumber. (Now *help* is specifically identified.)

not this: ~~Kindness~~ of the people who took me in was remarkable. (The nouncount noun *kindness* is specifically identifed, so you need *the*.)
but this: *The kindness* of the people who took me in was remarkable.

Exercise 2 **Using *a* or *an***

Put *a* or *an* in the spaces where it is needed. Some sentences are correct as they are.

1. Mr. Kaminsky lent us _____ flashlight.

2. Kelly received _____ criticism for her behavior.

3. The lake near my house has _____ alligator in it.

4. Tamsin drew _____ picture of _____ elephant.

5. He admires _____ honesty in his friends.

6. Nina should take _____ class in _____ biology if she wants to become _____ nurse.

7. We visited _____ island with _____ reputation for beautiful beaches.

8. What Brian needs is _____ ambition and _____ set of goals.

9. The swimmer got caught in _____ undertow and called for _____ lifeguard.

10. Tommy was lucky to have had _____ aunt with _____ appetite for _____ fun.

Exercise 3 **Using *the***

Put *the* in the spaces where it is needed. Some sentences are correct as they are.

1. Ryan dreamed of _____ adventures of his teen years.

2. If you stay focused, you will find _____ strength to finish _____ college.

3. Arthur never listened to _____ advice or bothered to consider _____ consequences of his actions.

4. Charlene is interested in _____ art, but she has no interest in _____ business of selling art.

5. My parents have never attended _____ concerts at the town hall, yet they love _____ music.

6. Tests show that my six-year-old has _____ intelligence of a much older child.

7. Thanks to _____ dedication of _____ people at _____ Family Harvest Food Bank, we have been able to serve 1,200 more Thanksgiving dinners to _____needy parents and children of our community.

8. Finding the right career takes _____ insight to know your strengths and weaknesses and _____ careful investigation.

9. Whenever Ian feels overcome by _____ stress, he watches _____ soccer on _____ television.

10. An over-the-counter cream from _____ drugstore took _____ sting out of _____ ant bites I got in _____ back yard.

Exercise 4   **Correcting a Paragraph with Errors in Articles**   ◀ CONNECT 🔗

Correct the errors with *a*, *an*, or *the* in the following paragraph. You may need to add, change, or eliminate articles. Write the corrections in the space above the errors. There are fourteen errors.

My older brother Sam has the ability to assess the people after only one meeting. He can recognize who is telling the lies and who is shy but good-hearted. Sam has gift; he can read body language of strangers who are trying to present the good image. This talent is useful to him when he has to deal with salespeople or others trying to get a money from him. Sometimes, his talent helps me. When Sam met my new boyfriend, he warned me that the man was the manipulator. I was fooled because my boyfriend had a charm of the movie star. Weeks later, I saw truth of Sam's warning and felt like a idiot to be so trusting. It took me few months to realize that I don't have Sam's rare gift and must rely on the experience, not the insight, in order to choose my friends.

NOUNS OR PRONOUNS USED AS SUBJECTS

A noun or a pronoun (a word that takes the place of a noun) is the subject of each sentence or dependent clause. Be sure that all sentences or dependent clauses have a subject.

> **not this:** Drives to work every day.
> **but this:** *He* drives to work every day.

> **not this:** My sister is pleased when gets a compliment.
> **but this:** My sister is pleased when *she* gets a compliment.

Be careful not to *repeat* the subject.

> **not this:** The police officer ~~she~~ said I was speeding.
> **but this:** The police officer said I was speeding.

> **not this:** The car that I needed ~~it~~ was a sportscar.
> **but this:** The car that I needed was a sportscar.

Exercise 5 **Correcting Errors with Subjects**

Correct any errors with subjects in the sentences below. Write your corrections above the errors.

1. Danielle she never calls me unless gets in trouble.

2. When it rains, my hair it often gets frizzy.

3. In December, small oranges from Spain they are a delicious gift.

4. In a strange city, is easy to get lost.

5. Cotton clothes are cool in the summer; also let your skin breathe.

6. Your brother Raoul he gave me a ride to work yesterday.

7. Last year Michelle and I we drove to Nashville, Tennessee.

8. Rarely mentions his childhood and avoids talking about his family.

9. Every time gets a test back in math class, she reviews her

   mistakes.

10. The happiest day of my life it was when you were born.

VERBS

Necessary Verbs

Be sure that a main verb isn't missing from your sentences or dependent clauses.

> **not this:** My boyfriend very ambitious.
> **but this:** My boyfriend *is* very ambitious.

> **not this:** Sylvia cried when the hero in the movie.
> **but this:** Sylvia cried when the hero in the movie died.

-s Endings

Be sure to put the -s on present tense verbs in the third-person singular:

> **not this:** He ~~run~~ in the park every morning.
> **but this:** He *runs* in the park every morning.

not this: The concert ~~start~~ at 9:00 P.M.
but this: The concert *starts* at 9:00 P.M.

-ed Endings

Be sure to put -*ed* endings on the past participle form of a verb. There are three main forms of a verb:

present: Today I walk.

past: Yesterday I walked.

past participle: I *have* walked. He *has* walked.

The past participle form is also used after *were, was, had,* and *has.*

not this: He has ~~call~~ me every day this week.
but this: He has *called* me every day this week.

not this: My neighbor was ~~surprise~~ by the sudden storm.
but this: My neighbor was *surprised* by the sudden storm.

Do not add -*ed* endings to infinitives. An infinitive is the verb form that uses *to* plus the present form of the verb:

infinitives: to consider, to obey

not this: Dean wanted me to ~~considered~~ the proposal.
but this: Dean wanted me to *consider* the proposal.

not this: I taught my dog to ~~obeyed~~ commands.
but this: I taught my dog to *obey* commands.

Exercise 6   **Correcting Errors in Verbs: Necessary Verbs, Third-Person Present Tense, Past Participles, and Infinitives**

Correct any errors in verbs in the sentences below. Write your corrections in the space above the lines. Some sentences do not need any corrections.

1. After Ellen start to cooked, she concentrate on the food and pay no

   attention to her family's conversation.

2. Obsessive jealousy a sign of danger in any romantic relationship.

3. Before Roy was introduce to Joanne, he had never meet a woman

   from Australia.

4. Every morning, my dog kisses my face and begs for a walk.

5. Three of the smartest babies at the daycare center Jonelle,

   Hedrick, and Tyrese, my niece and nephews.

6. Lucy was flatter by the attention she received at Wynona's wedding

   reception.

7. Monique urged Roberto to refused the offer from his father.

8. Will had expected a very different gift from the one his family gave

him.

9. Once I got my driver's license, I wanted to explored new places

every weekend.

10. Parts of the movie were film at an amusement park where my

friend sell souvenirs.

 CONNECT ▶   (Exercise 7)   **Correcting a Paragraph with Errors in Necessary Verbs, Third-Person Present Tense, Past Participles, and Infinitives**

Correct the verb errors in the following paragraph. Write your corrections above the lines. There are thirteen errors.

My dog very old, yet he still likes to walked every morning. At 7:00 A.M., he wake me up by kissing me. He sleep at the foot of my bed, but he is too elderly to jumped off the high bed, so he must wait until I can help him. I remember when my dog was a puppy; then he could jump a foot off the floor. Now that he is older, he has lose some of his strength but none of his spirit. As soon as he hear the jingle of his leash, he wag his tail with joy. Although he is a senior dog, he loves to pulled on his leash and to dragged me to his favorite spots. Because he mean so much to me, I happy to followed my dog on his morning adventures.

Two-Word Verbs

Two-word verbs contain a verb plus another word: a preposition or adverb. The meaning of each word by itself is different from the meaning the two words have when they are together. Look at this example:

Sometimes Consuelo *runs across* her sister at the park.

You might check *run* in the dictionary and find that it means "to move quickly." *Across* means "from one side to the other." But *run across* means something different:

not this: Sometimes Consuelo ~~moves quickly from one side to the other of~~ her sister at the park.
but this: Sometimes Consuela *encounters* her sister at the park.

Sometimes a word or words come between the words of a two-word verb:

> On Friday night, I *put* the garbage *out;* the Sanitation Department collects it early Saturday morning.

Here are some common two-word verbs:

ask out:	Jamal wants to *ask* Teresa *out* for dinner.
break down:	I hope my car doesn't *break down.*
bring in:	Advertising will *bring in* more customers.
bring up:	Don't *bring up* Carmella's divorce.
call off:	You can *call* the party *off.*
call on:	I need to *call on* you for help.
call up:	Jim will *call* Ken *up* tomorrow.
come across:	I often *come across* bargains at thrift shops.
drop in:	Let's *drop in* on Claude.
drop off:	My father will *drop* the package *off.*
fill in:	You can *fill in* your name.
fill out:	Danny has to *fill out* a complaint form.
get up:	Gill has to *get up* early tomorrow.
give in:	Zack won't *give in* to Leo's demands.
give up:	Keith won't *give up* on getting a promotion.
hand in:	We have to *hand in* our assignments.
hand out:	I hope the theater *hands out* free passes.
hang up:	Just *hang up* the telephone.
keep on:	You must *keep on* practicing your speech.
keep up:	Gary can't *keep up* with the math assignments.
let out:	My brother *let* the secret *out.*
look into:	Jonelle will *look into* the situation.
look over:	Jake needs to *look* the plans *over.*
make up:	Can I *make up* the test I missed?
look up:	I had to *look* the word *up* in the dictionary.
open up:	Elaine began to *open up* to me about her problem.
pack up:	Rick is going to *pack up* his old clothes.
pick up:	Tomorrow I *pick up* my first paycheck.
put down:	I want to *put* this box *down.*
put on:	Wait until I *put on* a coat.
quiet down:	The teacher told the class to *quiet down.*
run into:	Nancy will *run into* Alan at the gym.
run out:	The family has *run out* of money.
send off:	Chris can *send* Mike *off* to get pizza.
take down:	Ted will *take down* the old window shades.
take off:	It's time to *take off* that silly hat.
take out:	I have to *take out* the garbage.
think over:	I like your idea; let me *think* it *over.*
think through:	We have to *think through* this problem.
throw out:	It's time to *throw out* these old magazines.
try on:	Before you buy the shirt, *try* it *on.*
try out:	She wants to *try* the lawnmower *out.*
turn down:	Sal thinks Wayne should *turn* the job *down.*
turn off:	I forgot to *turn* the oven *off.*
turn on:	*Turn* the television *on.*
turn out:	I wonder how this story will *turn out.*

| turn up: | Nick is sure to *turn up* at the party. |
| write down: | You can *write down* your address. |

Exercise 8 **Writing Sentences with Two-Word Verbs**

Write a sentence for each of the following two-word verbs. Use the examples above as a guide, but consult a dictionary if you are not sure what the verbs mean.

1. take out _____

2. turn on _____

3. keep up _____

4. fill in _____

5. hand in _____

6. turn out _____

7. write down _____

8. think over _____

9. break down _____

10. put on _____

Contractions and Verbs

Contractions often contain verbs you may not recognize in their shortened forms.

contraction: *I'm* losing weight.
long form: *I am* losing weight.

contraction: *She's* been my best friend for years.
long form: *She has* been my best friend for years.

contraction: *He's* leaving tomorrow.
long form: *He is* leaving tomorrow.

contraction: *They'll* never know.
long form: *They will* never know.

contraction: The *truck's* in the garage.
long form: The *truck is* in the garage.

Exercise 9 **Contractions and Verbs**

In the space above each contraction, write its long form. The first one is done for you.

You would
1. *You'd* be unhappy in a place with constant rain.

2. *We've* never been to a Greek restaurant.

3. *We're* going to a Greek restaurant.

4. *She'll* be home by nine or ten.

5. The *dog's* sleeping on your bed.

6. The *day's* had some surprises for me.

7. *They'll* find a cheaper apartment near the turnpike.

8. I am sure *she'd* quit her job.

9. Robert *won't* sell his motorcycle.

10. You *could've* called me this morning.

PREPOSITIONS

Prepositions are little words such as *with, for, of, around,* and *near.* Some prepositions can be confusing; these are the ones that show time and place.

Prepositions That Show Time

1. Use *at* to show a specific or precise time:

> I will call you *at* 7:30 P.M.
> The movie starts *at* midnight.

2. Use *on* with a specific day or date:

> The meeting is *on* Friday.
> Frances begins basic training *on* June 23.

3. Use *by* when you mean "no later than that time":

> Jean has to be at work *by* 8:00 A.M.
> We should be finished with the cleaning *by* 5:00 P.M.

4. Use *until* when you mean "continuing up to a time":

> Yesterday I slept *until* 10:00 A.M.
> The dentist cannot see me *until* tomorrow.

5. Use *in* when you refer to a specific time period (minutes, hours, days, months, years):

> I'll be with you *in* a minute.
> Nikela works *in* the morning. (You can also say *in* the afternoon, or *in* the morning, or *in* the evening, but *at* night.)

6. Use *during* when you refer to a continuing time period or within the time period:

> I fell asleep *during* his speech.
> My sister will study management *during* the summer.

7. Use *for* to tell the length of a period of time:

We have been married *for* two years.
Wanda and Max cleaned the attic *for* three hours.

8. Use *since* to tell the starting time of an action:

He has been calling *since* 9:00 A.M.
We have been best friends *since* third grade.

Prepositions That Show Place

1. Use *in* to refer to a country, area, state, city, or neighborhood:

He studied *in* Ecuador.
Mr. Etienne lives *in* Houston.

2. Use *in* to refer to an enclosed space:

He put the money *in* his wallet.
Delia waited for me *in* the dining room.

3. Use *at* to refer to a specific address:

The repair shop is *at* 7330 Glades Road.
I live *at* 7520 Maple Lane.

4. Use *at* to refer to a corner or intersection:

We went to a garage sale *at* the corner of Spring Street and Lincoln Avenue.
The accident occurred *at* the intersection of Madison Boulevard and Temple Road.

5. Use *on* to refer to a street or a block:

Dr. Lopez lives *on* Hawthorne Street.
Malcolm bought the biggest house *on* the block.

6. Use *on* to refer to a surface:

Put the sandwiches *on* the table.
There was a bright rug *on* the floor.

7. Use *off* to refer to a surface:

Take the sandwiches *off* the table.
She wiped the mud *off* the floor.

8. Use *into* and *out of* for small vehicles such as cars:

Our dog leaped *into* the convertible.
The children climbed *out of* the car.

9. Use *on* and *off* for large vehicles like planes, trains, buses, and boats:

I was so seasick, I couldn't wait to get *off* the ship.
I like to ride *on* the bus.

Exercise 10   **Correcting Errors in Prepositions**

Correct any errors in prepositions in the following sentences. Write your corrections above the lines.

1. We used to live on 770 Third Avenue, but now we live on

   Appleton Way.

2. Lisa found her kitten on the kitchen, sleeping at a shelf.

3. Our flight was so bumpy, I couldn't wait to get out of the plane.

4. Pierre lived at Haiti until he was a teenager.

5. The restaurant on the intersection of Lincoln Road and Green

   Street has been in business until 1991.

6. Clean out the mess on your closet and put your dirty clothes at

   the washing machine during 6:00 P.M.

7. The surprise birthday party is at Saturday night; you have to

   arrive during 7:30 P.M.

8. I had to scrub in an hour to get the tomato sauce stains in

   the floor.

9. Sean helped his mother on the car and put her suitcase at

   the trunk.

10. James took the twenty-dollar bill off the table and put the money

    on his wallet.

APPENDIX B
The Research Process

RESEARCH IN DAILY LIFE

During your college experience, you will no doubt use research techniques in your coursework as well as in your daily life. Even if you have not yet written a formal paper involving research, you probably have already employed various research techniques to solve problems or make crucial decisions. For example, deciding about what college or technical school to attend and learning about financial aid opportunities may have involved contacting professionals and taking careful notes. Similarly, if you are a parent who has investigated community day-care options or family insurance plans, you are well aware of the importance of thorough research. Asking key questions and organizing your findings are research skills that can serve you well in college and in life.

USING RESEARCH TO STRENGTHEN ESSAYS

Most of the writing assignments you have completed thus far have probably been based on your own experiences, observations, or opinions. By writing regularly, you now know the importance of purpose, audience, organization, supporting details, and revision in producing a polished, final version of an essay. By appreciating the basics of effective writing, you can also recognize how essays can be strengthened through research. This appendix introduces you to the research process and explains how a stu-

dent writer can strengthen his or her original essay by smoothly incorporating supporting material from outside sources.

AN EXAMPLE OF AN ESSAY WITHOUT RESEARCH

The following outline and short essay about dog-rescue groups are based solely on the writer's own experience and knowledge about dog-rescue operations. The writer's thesis is that such groups perform a humane service by rescuing homeless dogs and carefully matching potential adopters with suitable pets. (Later you will see how the writer smoothly incorporated information from five sources into an outline, draft, and final version of the essay.)

An Outline Without Research

Here is the outline of an essay without research. You may notice that it is in the same form as the outlines you viewed in Chapter 11, "Writing an Essay."

An Outline for an Essay Without Research

I.   Dog-rescue organizations perform a humane service by saving homeless dogs and matching responsible adopters with a devoted new family member.

II. Dog-rescue volunteers play several roles.
    A. Some volunteers are "spotters" who look for specific breeds at local shelters.
    B. Experienced rescue volunteers may become coordinators and arrange assistance from various sources.
    C. Volunteers work with national organizations such as Save-A-Pet, which maintains a database of adoptable dogs from rescue groups throughout the U.S. and Canada.
    D. Volunteers assist at rescue-dog "Adoption Days" hosted by pet supply chains such as Petco and PetSmart.

III. Rescue groups provide important information and benefits for prospective adopters.
    A. By viewing a rescue group's Web site, potential adopters can read about a dog's age, temperament, adoption fee, and any special medical conditions.
    B. If a potential adopter does not find a suitable dog, he or she can still complete an online application.
    C. On an application, a potential adopter can list his or her preferences for the age, sex, and size of the dog.
    D. Although some dogs are puppies rescued from abusive situations, most are adult dogs already socialized and housebroken.

IV. Careful screening often results in a successful adoption.
    A. Rescue groups routinely conduct home visits to check the living conditions and the neighborhood.

  B. The applicant must have access to veterinary care.
  C. The applicant must agree to return the dog to the rescue organization if he or she can no longer care for the animal.
  D. A foster parent can fully inform the adoptive parent about potential adjustment problems.
  E. Careful attention to such details leads to a winning adoption process.

V. Rescue groups not only provide care for homeless dogs; they also remind us of the joy made possible by compassionate adoption.

An Essay Without Research

The following essay, written from the outline you have just reviewed, contains no research from outside sources; it is based solely on the writer's own knowledge and experience. As you read it, you will notice how the points in the outline have been developed through the use of specific details, effective sentence combining, and key transitions. You may also notice that some of the original words and phrases in the outline have been changed for better style.

The Humane Work of Dog-Rescue Groups

Although the United States is generally regarded as a country that loves and pampers its pets, animal shelters are often filled to capacity with dogs that have been abandoned, abused, or surrendered by their owners. Sadly, some shelters routinely euthanize healthy dogs if no one claims or adopts them after a grace period ranging from just days to a few weeks. Fortunately, however, many shelters work closely with dog-rescue organizations that find loving, temporary homes where foster parents can provide care and, if necessary, rehabilitation. Staffed by dedicated volunteers, rescue groups perform a humane service by saving homeless dogs and enabling responsible adopters to gain a devoted new family member.

From rescuing retired greyhounds to saving mini "mutts," dog-rescue volunteers play several roles. For example, they often serve as "spotters" at local shelters, looking for specific dogs that can be fostered by individuals who specialize in specific breeds such as boxers and golden retrievers. Experienced volunteers may become coordinators who arrange for assistance from a variety of sources, including local veterinarians, groomers, transporters, and Web site designers. Many rescue groups work closely with national organizations such as Save-A-Pet, whose Web site publishes a comprehensive list of adoptable rescue dogs throughout the United States and Canada. On weekends, rescue volunteers can be seen helping out during "Adoption Days" sponsored by national chains, including Petco and PetSmart.

Rescue groups provide both crucial information and welcome benefits for potential adopters. When one becomes interested in

a specific dog on a rescue group's Web site, he or she
can read about the animal's medical needs, age, temperament, and adoption fee. Even if he or she does not spot
a suitable dog but remains interested in adopting one
from rescue, he or she can fill out an application and
list preferences regarding a dog's age, sex, and size.
Although rescue groups occasionally receive puppies and
young dogs that have been picked up during police raids
of abusive puppy mills and backyard breeders, the majority of dogs available for adoption are older ones. Any
pet owner who has experienced the aggravation of sleepless nights and numerous housetraining "accidents" can
appreciate the benefits of adopting an older, socialized, and housebroken dog.

　　Although the adoption process may take several weeks
or even months to find the best match, careful screening
improves the chances for a successful adoption. Rescue
groups routinely conduct home visits of prospective dog
owners to see if both the living conditions and the
neighborhood will be suitable for the dog's size, temperament, and exercise needs. In addition, the applicant
must have access to veterinary care and agree to return
the dog to the rescue organization if he or she can no
longer properly care for it. A foster parent can fully
inform the adoptive parent about a dog's potential adjustment problems because the animal's behavior has been
observed over a period of weeks—if not months—in a home
setting. Careful attention to such details leads to a
winning adoption process.

　　However a dog finds its way to a rescue group—by an
owner surrender, a good Samaritan, or even by a police
raid of an illegal breeding operation—it will have an
opportunity to live out the rest of its life free from
harm and neglect. Rescue groups not only provide care
for homeless dogs; they also remind us of the joy made
possible by compassion, commitment, and unconditional
love.

FINDING RESEARCH TO STRENGTHEN ESSAYS

Locating Material in Your College Library

The Online Catalog If you decide to use research to strengthen an essay,
you can take advantage of a number of options. Your college library probably
has an online catalog system that lists all of the library's books and major hold-
ings. You can search the online catalog by a keyword related to your subject,
or, if you already have information about authors who deal with your subject,
you can search by the author's last name or the title of an author's book. An online catalog can provide you with a list of sources, the call number of each
source (the number that will help you find the book on the library shelves), and
information regarding the availability of the source. If your college has more

than one campus, the online catalog can tell you which campus has a copy of the book you want. Be sure to take advantage of any "Help" menu the system provides as well as any library orientation offered on your campus.

Popular Periodical Indexes College libraries commonly subscribe to several index services that provide access to complete articles (called "full-text" articles) from periodicals (magazines, journals, and newspapers). Some of the most widely used periodical indexes include the following: *EBSCOhost, InfoTrac, LexisNexis, NewsBank, Reader's Guide to Periodical Literature,* and *WilsonWeb.*

Always preview articles carefully to see if they contain useful information for your research essay. Scan articles online, and print copies of the pages that will be useful for highlighting and note-taking later. Also copy the first and last page of the article, which include information you will need for giving credit to the author and the source of the article. Be sure to ask your instructor if he or she will require copies of entire articles or just the pages you used in your essay.

Internet Search Engines The World Wide Web is the largest component of the Internet, and every Web site has an address, or URL (uniform resource locator). Many students now use search engines, which help users locate specific Web sites and potential sources if they do not know URL addresses. Here are some of the more popular search engines, along with their URLs:

AltaVista	http://www.altavista.com
Google	http://www.google.com
HotBot	http://www.hotbot.com
Yahoo!	http://www.yahoo.com

Unfortunately, some links posted on Web sites may be unavailable, and students will have to conduct searches carefully. Also, outdated information may remain posted on a Web site indefinitely, so students need to be cautious about using statistics or expert opinions that are several years old.

Checking for Validity of Sources

The writer of the dog-rescue essay decided to strengthen his paper by adding material from outside sources. The instructor required students to incorporate information from at least one print publication (magazine, newspaper, or book) and two valid electronic (online) sources. While a traditional research paper involves a more comprehensive use of outside sources and a lengthier planning and research process, a short essay can often be enhanced by adding relevant material from experts. Regardless of the scope of any research assignment, the sources used must be valid.

The student began his Internet search by typing the key phrase "dog rescue organizations" into the Google search function. This initial search resulted in a list of several hundred potential sources. After consulting with his instructor about the validity of his sources, the student was able to narrow his list to several dozen suitable sources.

Although the Internet and popular search engines are valuable tools to use for research, students are often tempted to use information from a Web site without checking for accuracy or validity. Students should check the author's credentials, such as educational background and professional experience, and other significant connections. In addition, students should locate any information about the background of the company or individuals responsible for a Web site. For example, if a student is investigating dog-rescue groups, the words of a veterinarian or background information from a nonprofit organization such as the Humane Society of the United States can generally be considered reliable. Because the veterinarian and the non-profit group are experienced and have no financial ties to the selling of dogs, their information is more valid than opinions from a pet shop owner, who makes money selling pets, or from a chat room popular with pet own-ers, who may know very little about dog rescue groups.

Similarly, print sources need to be evaluated just as carefully. For example, a brochure advertising quick or foolproof dog training programs would not be as reliable as an article from a magazine endorsed by the American Society for the Prevention of Cruelty to Animals (ASPCA). Many colleges offer library orientations that include suggestions for determining the validity of a Web site's information and of a print source's reliability.

If you have any doubt about a source's validity, check with your instructor or seek advice from a campus librarian. At the very least, see if an article lists the title or credentials of the author. If you have found an unsigned article, see if the organization responsible for the material lists its history and/or purpose. Also check for the publication date of the article, the original place of publication, the tone of the article (i.e., Does it avoid slang? Does it appear serious?), and the proper use of statistics and expert opinion. Using valid sources will lend credibility to your work.

INCORPORATING AND ACKNOWLEDGING YOUR SOURCES

Gathering and Organizing Sources

Once you have previewed your potential sources and have selected the ones best suited for your topic, you will need printouts of any online article (or at least the necessary pages) for highlighting and note-taking. If you are using a book or a magazine in its original form, you need to photocopy the relevant pages. To keep track of all the sources you are using, you should staple or paper clip the pages of each source and label each one clearly.

If you have narrowed your search to several sources (for example, three magazine articles, two newspaper articles, and one book), you could organize your sources alphabetically by the authors' last names. If an arti-cle does not list its author, you can use the first major word of the title in place of the author's last name. Then you can label your sources as Source #1, Source #2, and so forth. This type of labeling will be useful for you later as you develop an outline that includes references to your sources.

Your instructor may want to see a preliminary list of your potential sources, and he or she may also require that your notes from sources be written on lined 4″ × 6″ note cards. Be sure you follow your instructor's specific guidelines and directions.

Taking Notes and Acknowledging Your Sources

When you take notes from one of your sources and use the information in your paper, you must acknowledge the source. This acknowledgment is called **documentation** because you are documenting, or giving credit to, the author and the work that provided the information. When you provide documentation within a research essay, you are using what is called

internal citation. "Citation" means "giving credit," and "internal" means "inside," or "within," the paper. At the end of your essay, you list all the sources you cited within the paper. This list is called the **Works Cited.** The list of works cited is on a separate page from the rest of the essay, and it is the last numbered page of the essay.

Avoiding Plagiarism

Plagiarism occurs when you use a source's words or ideas and fail to give proper credit to the author and/or source of the work. Even if you **paraphrase** (state someone's else's ideas in your own wording), you must give credit to the original source.

Whether you summarize material from an outside source, quote directly from it, or even paraphrase from it, you must acknowledge the source. Failure to do so is a form of academic theft. Depending on departmental or college policy, the penalties for plagiarism can be severe, ranging from receiving a failing grade on the plagiarized paper or failing a course, to expulsion. Some departments now use special software programs to check all student papers for plagiarism, and it is simply not worth the risk to submit research assignments without proper documentation.

Options for Acknowledging Your Sources

The Modern Language Association (MLA) System of Documentation The Modern Language Association (MLA) system of documentation is preferred by English instructors, and you may find that humanities instructors on your campus also want you to follow MLA guidelines. In other departments, such as psychology and social sciences, instructors may ask you to follow the American Psychological Association (APA) system of documentation. Be sure to follow your instructor's directions regarding documentation requirements for your research assignments. There are many handbooks available that contain both MLA and APA styles of documentation, and most freshman composition courses require that students purchase a handbook. You may want to check with your instructor to see which handbook is used for freshman composition on your campus.

Over the next several pages, you will see how MLA documentation is used for summarizing, paraphrasing, and directly quoting information from sources. You will also see how books, periodicals, and electronic sources should be listed on a Works Cited page that conforms to MLA guidelines.

MLA Internal ("In-Text") Citation When using internal citation, you have several options for incorporating and giving credit to the source of your information. If you use a combination of techniques, your paper will read more smoothly. The following examples of summarizing, directly quoting, paraphrasing, and combining a direct quote and paraphrasing will provide you with sufficient documentation options as you draft your essay. Notice that authors and/or page numbers appear in parentheses, and this form is called **parenthetical documentation.**

A Summary of an Entire Book

One at a Time: A Week in an American Animal Shelter describes the fate of seventy-five animals who passed through a local shelter in Northern California over a seven-day period (Leigh and Geyer).

Note: No page numbers are included in the summary because the *entire* work is summarized.

A Direct Quotation

According to Leigh and Geyer, "The safest and most reliable identification is provided by a combination of an ID tag, which is easily visible, and a microchip, which is permanent" (2).

Note: If you do not introduce the author before you quote from his or her work, you must put the author's name in parentheses at the end of the quoted material. In this case, there are two authors. Both of their names could be placed in parentheses, as follows: (Leigh and Geyer 2). Notice that the period goes after the parentheses.

A Paraphrase

A clearly marked ID tag, along with a permanent microchip, provides an animal with the best and safest means of identification (Leigh and Geyer 2).

A Source Quoted in Another Author's Work

Kathy Nicklas-Varraso, author of <u>What to Expect from Breed Rescue</u>, notes that adopters will "most often get an adult whose chewing phase, housebreaking phase, and general puppy wildness are gone" (qtd. in Mohr).

Note: Nicklas-Varraso is the author being quoted; her comment was found in an online magazine article by Mohr. Mohr is the source that the student writer found. Therefore, Mohr is the source cited in parentheses. No page numbers are cited when the article comes from an online magazine.

A Combination of a Direct Quotation and a Paraphrase

Leigh and Geyer emphasize that the best means of identification for an animal is "provided by a combination of an ID tag, which is easily visible, and a microchip, which is permanent" (2).

Signal Phrases

In three of the above examples, **signal phrases** are used to introduce quoted or paraphrased material. Signal phrases such as "Leigh and Geyer emphasize," "According to Leigh and Geyer," and "Kathy Nicklas-Varraso notes" are phrases that enable you to lead smoothly into documented information. Here are some of the more commonly used signal phrases, using Smith as the author:

According to Smith,	Smith reports that
As Smith notes,	Smith claims that
Smith suggests that	Smith points out that
Smith emphasizes that	Smith contends that

Documenting Information from a Source with an Unknown Author

If there is no author listed for a source, you can introduce the full title of the work after a signal phrase or place an abbreviation of the title in parentheses at the end of the information cited. For example, you can choose either of the following forms:

As the article "The Rules of Local Zoning Boards" notes, many counties prohibit businesses from operating out of garages in residential communities (C1).

or

Many counties prohibit businesses from operating out of garages in residential communities ("Rules" C1).

Note: When your source is a newspaper article, as in the examples above, give the section of the newspaper and the page number, as in C1, which stands for section C, page 1. Article titles are placed within quotation marks; book titles are underlined.

Works Cited Entries: MLA Format

The **Works Cited** list of sources contains only the works you cited in your paper. This alphabetized list starts on a separately numbered page after the essay itself. The following sample entries represent some of the most commonly used sources. **On the Works Cited page, entries should be double-spaced, and the second and subsequent lines of each entry should be indented five spaces. Double-spacing should also be used between each entry.**

Books

Book by One Author

Stevens, Paul Drew. <u>Real Animal Heroes</u>. New York: Signet, 1997.

Note: New York is the place of publication, Signet is the publisher, and 1997 is the year of publication. Short forms of the publisher's name should be used, so "Inc.," "Co.," and "Press" can be omitted.

Book by Two Authors

Leigh, Diane, and Marilee Geyer. <u>One at a Time: A Week in an American Animal Shelter</u>. Santa Cruz: No Voice Unheard, 2003.

Note: When two or three authors are listed, the name of the first author is listed last name first, and the other authors are listed in regular order. If there are more than three authors, the name of the first author is listed last name first and followed by the Latin phrase *et al.*, which means "and others."

Short Work in an Anthology

Wong, Edward. "A Long Overdue Apology." <u>Tales from the Times</u>. Ed. Lisa

Belkin. New York: St. Martin's Griffin, 2004. 29-34.

Note: An anthology is a book-length collection of short works such as articles, essays, poems, or short stories. It usually has at least one editor who compiles and organizes all of the short works, which are by different authors. When you are citing from an anthology, begin with the author of the short work and its title; then list the name of the anthology and its editor. Continue with the place of publication, the publisher, and the year of publication. At the end of the entry, list the page numbers of the short work.

Introduction from a Book

Curtis, Jamie Lee. Foreword. <u>Second Chances: More Tales of Found Dogs</u>. By

Elise Lufkin. Guilford: Lyons, 2003. ix-x.

Note: Sometimes a book will contain either an introduction, preface, or foreword written by someone other than the author of the book. When citing from such introductory material, begin with the author of this material, followed by the word "Introduction" (or "Preface" or "Foreword"), the name of the book, the author of the book, place of publication, publisher, date of publication, and page numbers of the introduction, which will be in small Roman numerals.

Dictionary or Encyclopedia

"Luxate." <u>The American Heritage College Dictionary</u>. Third Edition. New York:

Houghton Mifflin, 1993.

Note: "Luxate" is the word you defined by using this dictionary.

Periodicals

Periodicals are newspapers, magazines, and scholarly journals. In Works Cited listings, all months except May, June, and July are abbreviated.

Newspaper Article

Caldwell, Tanya. "Boca Names Its New Dog Park." <u>South Florida Sun-Sentinel</u>

10 Aug. 2005: B1.

Note: B1 refers to the section (B) and page number (1) of the article.

Newspaper Editorial

"Disaster Aid." Editorial. <u>South Florida Sun-Sentinel</u> 9 Aug. 2005: A10.

Note: Newspaper editorials do not list an author.

Magazine Article (From a Monthly or Bimonthly Publication)

Richard, Julie. "The Lost Tigers of China." <u>Best Friends</u> Mar. 2005: 27-29.

Magazine Article (From a Weekly Publication)

Boks, Ed. "The Dirty Little Secret in Your Community." <u>Newsweek</u> 27 June 2005:

15.

Journal Article

Newkirk, Thomas. "The Dogma of Transformation." <u>College Composition and</u>

<u>Communication</u> 56.2 (2004): 251-71.

Note: The number 56 is the volume number, 2 is the issue number, and 2004
is the year of publication.

Electronic Sources

Electronic sources can include professional Web sites, online periodicals,
works from subscription services (such as NewsBank), and even e-mails.

When you list a Web site as one of your sources, you should include as
many of the following items as you can find on the site:

1. Author or group author's name
2. Title of the site
3. Date of publication or date of latest update
4. The company or organization that sponsors the Web site (if it is different from the group author)
5. Date you accessed the Web site
6. URL (list it with angle brackets)

Entire Web Site

Humane Society of the United States. <u>Pet Adoption Information</u>. 30 May 2005.

June 20 2005. <http://www.hsus.org/pets/issues.html>.

Note: In this example, the sponsoring organization, the Humane Society of
the United States, is also the group author of the site. Occasionally,
the URL address will appear on its own line because word process-
ing programs will not split the site's address when slashes are used.

Article or Short Work from a Web Site

Mohr, Lori. "Adopting from a Breed Rescue Group." <u>Animal Forum</u>. 23 June

2005. <http://www.animalforum.com/dbreedrescue.htm>.

Note: In this example, no date of publication was available, so the only date given in this listing is the date the article was accessed by the student writer. Page numbers are not listed for online articles because different printers will affect the page numbering of the printed article. However, the exception to this rule is that if an article is contained within a PDF file, the page numbers can be listed because the numbers will be consistent regardless of the system used.

Article from an Online Magazine

Woolf, Norma Bennett. "Getting Involved in Purebred Rescue." <u>Dog Owner's</u>

<u>Guide</u> 18 May 2005. 20 June 2005 <http://www.canismajor.com/dog/rescinv

.html>.

Article from an Online Subscription Service

Foss, Brad. "No Braking for Higher Prices." <u>South Florida Sun Sentinel</u> 11 Aug.

2005: D1. <u>NewsBank</u>. Broward County Lib., Fort Lauderdale, Fl. 16 Aug.

2005 <http://www.newsbank.com>.

Note: If you use one of your library's online subscription services, you can first follow the same format as a print periodical, but you will need to add the name of the subscription service, the library you used, the date you accessed the article, and the URL address (if available).

E-mail

Brown, Vernon. "Re: Answers to Your Questions." E-mail to the author. 15 July

2005.

Other Sources: Non-Print

Personal Interview

Carter, Michael. Personal interview. 17 Mar. 2005.

Radio or Television Program

"Babies Having Babies." <u>Live on Five Series</u>. Narr. Harry Anderson. NBC.

WPTV, West Palm Beach. 6 Aug. 2004.

Note: In this listing, "Narr." refers to the narrator of the program, "NBC" refers to the network, and "WPTV" refers to the local channel that broadcast the program. The date is the date of the broadcast.

Incorporating Research into Your Outline

After you have compiled all of your notes from your sources, you need to determine what information you will use and where it best fits into your essay. The best way to do this is to work with your original outline before you draft a research version of your essay. Here again is the outline for the dog-rescue essay, but it is a bit different from the outline on pages 663 to 664. This version now includes references to sources; key information from these sources will be the research that strengthens the essay.

Notice that the headings "Introduction" and "Conclusion" have been added to the outline. In this version, the writer wanted to include some relevant research in both the introductory and concluding paragraphs as well as in the body paragraphs, so he expanded his outline. By placing research references in the outline, the student writer will know where the new information will be included when he prepares the drafts and final version of his research essay.

Note: The references to the added research appear in bold print so that you can compare this outline with the previous one without research on page 663.

An Outline for an Essay with Research

I. Introduction
   A. Six to eight million dogs and cats are placed in shelters each year; three to four million are euthanized. **See Humane Society, source #2.**
   B. Some shelters euthanize animals routinely. **See Leigh and Geyer, source #3.**
   C. Some shelters work with rescue groups.

   Thesis Statement: Dog-rescue organizations perform a humane service by saving homeless dogs and matching responsible adopters with a devoted new family member.

II. Dog-rescue volunteers play several roles.
   A. Some volunteers are "spotters" who look for specific breeds at local shelters.
   B. Experienced rescue volunteers may become coordinators and arrange assistance from various sources. **See Woolfe, source #5.**
   C. Volunteers work with national organizations such as Save-A-Pet, which maintains a database of adoptable dogs from rescue groups throughout the U.S. and Canada.
   D. Volunteers assist at rescue-dog "Adoption Days" hosted by pet supply chains such as Petco and PetSmart.

III. Rescue groups provide important information and benefits for prospective adopters.
   A. By viewing a rescue group's Web site, potential adopters can read about a dog's age, temperament, adoption fee, and any special medical conditions.
   B. If a potential adopter does not find a suitable dog, he or she can still complete an online application.
   C. On an application, a potential adopter can list his or her preferences for the age, sex, and size of the dog.

D. Although some dogs are puppies rescued from abusive situations, most are adult dogs already socialized and housebroken. **See Nicklas-Varrraso in Mohr, source #4.**

IV. Careful screening often results in a successful adoption.
   A. Rescue groups routinely conduct home visits to check the living conditions and the neighborhood.
   B. The applicant must have access to veterinary care.
   C. The applicant must agree to return the dog to the rescue organization if he or she can no longer care for the animal.
   D. A foster parent can fully inform the adoptive parent about potential adjustment problems.
   E. Careful attention to such details leads to a winning adoption process.

V. Conclusion
   A. Rescue groups provide an opportunity for a dog to live out the rest of its life free from harm and neglect.
   B. We should "embrace non-lethal strategies" to show we are a humane society. **See Bok, source #1.**

Concluding Statement: Rescue groups not only provide care for homeless dogs; they also remind us of the joy made possible by compassionate adoption.

A Draft of an Essay with Research

The following is a rough version of the original essay on dog-rescue groups; it has been strengthened with some material from outside sources. (The material is underlined so that you can spot it easily.) The marginal annotations will alert you to (1) places where the information is directly quoted or paraphrased, and (2) places where revisions are necessary to achieve a better style.

The Humane Work of Dog-Rescue Groups

Although the United States is generally regarded as a country that loves and pampers its pets, animal shelters are often filled to capacity with dogs that have been abandoned, abused, or surrendered by their owners. <u>Each year, six to eight million dogs and cats are placed in shelters, and three to four million of them are euthanized (Humane Society).</u> Sadly, some shelters routinely euthanize healthy dogs if no one claims or adopts them after a grace period ranging from just days to a few weeks. <u>These dogs have only "about a fifty percent chance of getting out alive" (Leigh and Geyer viii).</u> Fortunately, however, many shelters work closely with dog-rescue organizations that find loving, temporary homes where foster parents can provide care and, if necessary, rehabilitation. Staffed by dedicated volunteers, rescue groups perform a humane service

statistic and paraphrased statement from online source as part of introduction

direct quotation from the preface of a book with two authors

by saving homeless dogs and enabling responsible adopters to gain a devoted new family member.

From rescuing retired greyhounds to saving mini "mutts," dog-rescue volunteers play several roles. For example, they often serve as "spotters" at local shelters, looking for specific dogs that can be fostered by individuals who specialize in specific breeds such as boxers and golden retrievers. Experienced volunteers may become coordinators who arrange for assistance from a variety of sources, including local veterinarians, groomers, transporters, and Web site designers. <u>Norma Bennett Woolf writes for the online magazine, Dog Owner's Guide. Woolf states, "There's always room for more foster homes, fund-raisers, dog spotters, kennels, public relations workers, and trainers."</u> Many rescue groups work closely with national organizations such as Save-A-Pet, whose Web site publishes a comprehensive list of adoptable rescue dogs throughout the United States and Canada. On weekends, rescue volunteers can be seen helping out during "Adoption Days" sponsored by national chains, including Petco and PetSmart.

Rescue groups provide both crucial information and welcome benefits for potential adopters. When one becomes interested in a specific dog on a rescue group's Web site, he or she can read about the animal's medical needs, age, temperament, and adoption fee. Even if he or she does not spot a suitable dog but remains interested in adopting one from rescue, he or she can fill out an application and list preferences regarding a dog's age, sex, and size. Although rescue groups occasionally receive puppies and young dogs that have been picked up during police raids of abusive puppy mills and backyard breeders, the majority of dogs available for adoption are older ones. Kathy Nicklas-Varraso wrote <u>What to Expect from Breed Rescue. This writer says, "You'll most often get an adult whose chewing phase, housebreaking phase, and general puppy wildness are gone" (qtd. in Mohr).</u> Any pet owner who has experienced the aggravation of sleepless nights and numerous housetraining "accidents" can appreciate the benefits of adopting an older, socialized, and housebroken dog.

Although the adoption process may take several weeks or even months to find the best match, careful screening improves the chances for a successful adoption. Rescue groups routinely conduct home visits of prospective dog owners to see if both the living conditions and the neighborhood will be suitable for the dog's size, temperament, and exercise needs. In addition, the applicant must have access

---

direct quotation from an online magazine; sentence combining needed

a source quoted in another author's work; needs to be more smoothly blended

to veterinary care and agree to return the dog to the rescue organization if he or she can no longer properly care for it. A foster parent can fully inform the adoptive parent about a dog's potential adjustment problems because the animal's behavior has been observed over a period of weeks—if not months—in a home setting. <u>Nicklas-Varraso states, "Borderline pets are offered for adoption within strict guidelines, such as no other pets or fenced yards only"</u> (qtd. in Mohr). Careful attention to such details leads to a winning adoption process.

direct quote; needs a transition

However a dog finds its way to a rescue group—by an owner surrender, a good Samaritan, or even by a police raid of an illegal breeding operation—it will have an opportunity to live out the rest of its life free from harm and neglect. <u>Ed Bok is the director of Animal Care and Control for New York City. He believes that we should "embrace preventive, non-lethal strategies that reveal that at our core we truly are a humane society"</u> (15). Rescue groups not only follow Bok's advice by providing care for homeless dogs; they also remind us of the joy made possible by compassion, commitment, and unconditional love.

print source is a magazine; sentence combining needed; put Bok's name in a signal phrase

Note: A Works Cited page will be included in the final version of this essay.

PREPARING THE FINAL VERSION OF AN ESSAY WITH RESEARCH

Making Final Changes and Refinements

The final version of the research essay includes the refinements suggested in the margins of the previous draft. You will notice that the final essay reflects proper MLA documentation and page numbering format. Other improvements relate to the style of the essay. Changes from the previous draft include the following:

- The title has been changed to be more descriptive and appealing.
- Information from sources has been more smoothly blended by sentence combining and the use of signal phrases.
- An awkward repetition of "he or she" has been changed to the more specific term "a potential adopter" in the third paragraph.
- The word "humane" has been added in the last paragraph to reinforce the idea of compassionate care for animals.
- To conform to MLA format, the writer has placed his name, his instructor's name, the course title, and the date in the upper left-hand corner of the first page.
- Again following MLA guidelines, the writer has placed his last name and page number in the upper right-hand corner of each page of the essay.
- A Works Cited page, in proper MLA format, is included and appears as the last page of the essay.

Roberts 1

Jason Roberts

Professor Alvarez

English 100

7 December 2005

Crusading for Canines: Dog-Rescue Groups
and Winning Adoptions

Although the United States is generally regarded
as a country that loves and pampers its pets, animal shelters are often filled to capacity with dogs
that have been abandoned, abused, or surrendered by
their owners. Each year, six to eight million dogs
are placed in shelters, and three to four million
of them are euthanized (Humane Society). Sadly,
some shelters routinely euthanize healthy dogs if
no one claims or adopts them after a grace period
ranging from just days to a few weeks. These dogs
have only "about a fifty percent chance of getting
out alive" (Leigh and Geyer viii). Fortunately,
however, many shelters work closely with dog-rescue
organizations that find loving, temporary homes
where foster parents can provide care and, if necessary, rehabilitation. Staffed by dedicated volunteers, rescue groups perform a humane service by
saving homeless dogs and enabling responsible
adopters to gain a devoted new family member.

From rescuing retired greyhounds to saving mini
"mutts," dog-rescue volunteers play several roles.
For example, they often serve as "spotters" at
local shelters, looking for specific dogs that can
be fostered by individuals who specialize in specific breeds such as boxers and golden retrievers.
Experienced volunteers may become coordinators who
arrange for assistance from a variety of sources,

Roberts 2

including local veterinarians, groomers, transporters, and Web site designers. As Norma Bennett
Woolf suggests in the online magazine, <u>Dog Owner's
Guide</u>, "There's always room for more foster homes,
fund-raisers, dog-spotters, kennels, public relations
workers, and trainers." Many rescue groups work
closely with national organizations such as Save-A-
Pet, whose Web site publishes a comprehensive list of
adoptable rescue dogs throughout the United States
and Canada. On weekends, rescue volunteers can be
seen helping out during "Adoption Days" sponsored by
national chains, including Petco and PetSmart.

Rescue groups provide both crucial information and
welcome benefits for potential adopters. When one becomes interested in a specific dog on a rescue
group's Web site, he or she can read about the animal's medical needs, age, temperament, and adoption
fee. Even if a potential adopter does not spot a
suitable dog but remains interested in adopting one
from rescue, he or she can fill out an application
and list preferences regarding a dog's age, sex, and
size. Although rescue groups occasionally receive
puppies and young dogs that have been picked up during police raids of abusive puppy mills and backyard
breeders, the majority of dogs available for adoption
are older ones. Kathy Nicklas-Varraso, author of <u>What
to Expect from Breed Rescue</u>, notes that adopters will
"most often get an adult whose chewing phase, housebreaking phase, and general puppy wildness are gone"
(qtd. in Mohr). Any pet owner who has experienced the
aggravation of sleepless nights and numerous housetraining "accidents" can appreciate the benefits of
adopting an older, socialized, and housebroken
dog.

Although the adoption process may take several weeks or even months to find the best match, careful screening improves the chances for a successful adoption. Rescue groups routinely conduct home visits of prospective dog owners to see if both the living conditions and the neighborhood will be suitable for the dog's size, temperament, and exercise needs. In addition, the applicant must have access to veterinary care and agree to return the dog to the rescue organization if he or she can no longer properly care for it. A foster parent can fully inform the adoptive parent about a dog's potential adjustment problems because the animal's behavior has been observed over a period of weeks—if not months—in a home setting. Nicklas-Varraso stresses that the "borderline pets are offered for adoption within strict guidelines, such as no other pets or fenced yards only" (qtd. in Mohr). Careful attention to such details leads to a winning adoption process.

However a dog finds its way to a rescue group—by an owner surrender, a good Samaritan, or even by a police raid of an illegal breeding operation—it will have an opportunity to live out the rest of its life free from harm and neglect. Ed Boks, director of Animal Care and Control for New York City, urges us to "embrace preventive, non-lethal strategies that reveal that at our core, we truly are a humane society" (15). Rescue groups not only provide humane care for homeless dogs; they also remind us of the joy made possible by compassion, commitment, and unconditional love.

Roberts 4

Works Cited

Boks, Ed. "The Dirty Little Secret in Your Community." <u>Newsweek</u> 27 June 2005: 15.

Humane Society of the United States. "HSUS Pet
Overpopulation Estimates." 2005. 30 April 2005
<http://www.hsus.org/pets.html>.

Leigh, Diane, and Marilee Geyer. Preface. <u>One at a
Time: A Week in an American Animal Shelter</u>.
Santa Cruz: No Voice Unheard, 2003. vii-viii.

Mohr, Lori. "Adopting from a Breed Rescue Group."
<u>Animal Forum</u>. 23 June 2005. <http://www
.animalforum.com/dbreedrescue.htm>.

Woolf, Norma Bennett. "Getting Involved in Purebred Rescue." <u>Dog Owner's Guide</u> 18 May 2005. 20
June 2005 <http://www.canismajor.com/dog/
rescinv.html>.

Text Credits

Page 333: "A Ridiculous Addiction" by Gwinn Owens. Originally appeared in *Newsweek*, December 4, 1989, My Turn, p. 17. Reprinted by permission of the author.

Page 593: "Sticky Stuff" by Kendall Hamilton and Tessa Namuth. From *Newsweek*, Winter 1997/1998. © 1997/1998 Newsweek, Inc. All rights reserved. Reprinted by permission.

Page 596: "Spanglish" by Janice Castro. Copyright © Time Inc. Reprinted with permission.

Page 599: "A Present for Popo" by Elizabeth Wong. Published by permission of the author Elizabeth Wong, www.elizabethwong.net.

Page 603: "The Good Father" by Alisa Valdes-Rodriguez, *Latina*, June 2004, pp. 79-80. Reprinted by permission of the author.

Page 606: "How to Write a Personal Letter" by Garrison Keilor. Copyright © 1987 by International Paper Company. Reprinted by permission of Garrison Keillor.

Page 610: "Beautiful Daughter" by Carolyn Magner Mason. Carolyn Magner Mason is a freelance writer with articles appearing in publications such as *Family Circle*, *Runner's World*, *Health.com*, *WebMD*, *Salon.com* and national and regional newspapers. Her email address is cmagner@randallpub.com.

Page 613: "Three Disciplines for Children" by John Holt. Reprinted by permission from *Freedom and Beyond* by John Holt. Copyright © 1995, 1972 by Holt Associates. Published by Heinemann, a division of Reed Elsevier, Inc., Portsmouth, NH. All rights reserved.

Page 616: "Breaking the Bonds of Hate" by Virak Khiev, *Newsweek*, April 27, 1992. From *Newsweek*, April 1992. © 1992 Newsweek, Inc. All rights reserved. Reprinted by permission.

Page 620: "Students in Shock" by John Kellmayer. Reprinted by permission of Townsend Press.

Page 624: "Why Is Geezer-Bashing Acceptable?" by Abigail Trafford. Copyright © 2005, The Washington Post, reprinted with permission.

Page 627: "A Cell Phone? Never for Me" by Robert J. Samuelson, *Newsweek*, August 23, 2004. Copyright © 2004, Newsweek. Reprinted with permission.

Page 630: "Eleven" by Sandra Cisneros, From *Woman Hollering Creek*. Copyright © 1991 by Sandra Cisneros. Published by Vintage Books, a division of Random House Inc., and originally in hardcover by Random House Inc. Reprinted by permission of Susan Begholz Literary Services, New York. All rights reserved.

Page 633: "A Brother's Murder" by Brent Staples, *The New York Times*, March 30, 1986. Copyright © 1986, The New York Times. Reprinted by permission.

Page 637: "Navajo Code Talkers: The Century's Best Kept Secret" by Jack Hitt. From *American Greats* by Robert Wilson. Copyright © 1999 by Robert Wilson. Reprinted by permission of Public Affairs, a member of Perseus Books, L.L.C.

Page 640: "My Daughter Smokes," from *Living by the Word: Selected Writings 1973–1987*, copyright 1987 by Alice Walker, reprinted by permission of Harcourt, Inc.

Page 645: "Parental Discretion" by Dennis Hevesi, *The New York Times*, April 8, 1990. Copyright © 1990 by The New York Times Co. Reprinted with permission.

Photograph Credits

Page 1: Getty Images, Inc.; **Page 3:** Getty Images, Inc.; **Page 36 (top):** Michael Newman/PhotoEdit Inc.; **Page 36 (bottom):** Bill Bachmann/PhotoEdit Inc.; **Page 37:** Meredith Parmelee/Getty Images Inc.—Stone Allstock; **Page 39:** Getty Images, Inc.; **Page 56:** Laima Druskis/Pearson Education/PH College; **Page 57:** David Young-Wolff/PhotoEdit Inc.; **Page 59:** Getty Images, Inc.; **Page 79:** Ryan McVay/Getty Images, Inc.—Photodisc.; **Page 80:** Geri Engberg/Geri Engberg Photography; **Page 82:** Getty Images, Inc.; **Page 105:** Stockbyte; **Page 106:** AP Wide World Photos; **Page 108:** Getty Images, Inc.; **Page 126:** Photolibrary.Com; **Page 127:** Jeff Gross/Getty Images, Inc.; **Page 129:** Getty Images, Inc.; **Page 154:** Peter Wilson/Dorling Kindersley Media Library/Peter Wilson © Dorling Kindersley; **Page 155:** Joseph Sohm/Corbis/Bettmann/ © Joseph Sohm; ChromoSohm Inc./Corbis; **Page 157:** Getty Images, Inc.; **Page 173:** Gary Conner/PhotoEdit Inc.; **Page 175:** Getty Images, Inc.; **Page 194:** Stockbyte; **Page 196:** Getty Images, Inc.; **Page 216:** China Tourism Press.Xie, Guang Hui/Getty Images Inc.—Image Bank; **Page 217:** Jose Luis Pelaez/Corbis/Bettmann; **Page 219:** Getty Images, Inc.; **Page 238 (top):** Bill Bachmann/Photo Researchers, Inc.; **Page 238 (bottom):** Alex L. Fradkin/Getty Images, Inc.—Photodisc.; **Page 240:** Getty Images, Inc.; **Page 274:** Michael Newman/PhotoEdit Inc.; **Page 275:** Getty Images, Inc.—Photodisc; **Pages 277, 327, 351, 353, 370, 384, 393, 405, 417, 427, 437, 447, 461, 474, 491, 503, 513, 517, 526, 531, 536, 546, 557, 572, 580:** Getty Images, Inc.; **Page 593:** Simon Evanst Alamy Images. **Pages 650 & 662:** Getty Images, Inc.

Index

Note: Readings are listed under "reading selections" on page 691.

A

a/an/and, 557
a/an (indefinite articles), 651
abbreviations, 513, 541–42
accept/except, 557
acronyms, 541
action verbs, 354–55
  with adverbs, 432
active voice, 466–70
addition/edition, 557
adjectives, 427–30
  adverbs vs., 431–32
  commas with, 433–34
  comparative forms of, 428–29,
    433
  good/bad, 432–33
  superlative forms of, 428–29
  with *than*, 433
adverbs, 362, 430–32
  adjectives vs., 431–32
  beginning sentences, 583
  conjunctive, 377–78, 388–89,
    526
  placement, 438–40
  well/badly, 432–33
advice/advise, 558
affect/effect, 558
agreement
  of pronouns, 491–502
  between subject and verb,
    474–90
agreement/disagreement writing,
    341–44
  brainstorming, 342
  drafting, 343–44
  freewriting, 341–42
  planning for, 343
  polishing, 344
  proofreading, 344
  revising, 343–44
allowed/aloud, 558
all right, 551
a lot, 551
already/all ready, 551, 558
altar/alter, 558
altogether/all together, 552
always/all ways, 552
angel/angle, 558
antecedents, 491–502
anymore/any more, 552

anyone/any one, 552
apart/a part, 552
apostrophes, 531–35
  in contractions, 531–32
  indicating possession, 532
  in *its/it's*, 508
  with letters, 533
  with numbers, 531, 533
  with plural forms, 533
  in time expressions, 533
appositives, 588–90
are/our, 558
argument essays, 320–26
  drafting, 324
  planning for, 322–24
  polishing, 325–26
  prewriting, 321–22
  proofreading, 325–26
  revising, 324
  thesis for, 320
  writing from reading, 624–30
argument paragraphs, 219–39
  audience for, 220
  drafting, 230–31
  grouping ideas in, 223–24
  peer review form for, 239
  planning for, 226–30
  polishing, 234
  prewriting, 223–26
  proofreading, 234
  revising, 226, 230–32
  sequencing, 226–28
  topic sentences in, 219–20
  transitions in, 231
articles, 651–53
ask out, 657
at, 659
attitude, 327–28
audience, 4
  for argument essays, 321
  for argument paragraphs, 220

B

bad/badly, 432–33
being verbs, 354–55
  with adjectives, 427, 432
beside/besides, 558
between, 507–8
books, documentation of as
    research sources, 670–71

brainstorming, 4–5
  adding details with, 9–11
  for classification paragraphs,
    160–61
  for reaction writing, 342
brake/break, 558
break down, 657
breath/breathe, 558
but also, 481
buy/by, 558–59
by, 558–59, 659

C

call off/on/up, 657
capital/capitol, 559
capitalization, 539–41
  of course names, 540
  of names of persons, 539
  of place names, 539
  of product names, 540
  in quotations, 539
  semicolons with, 376
  of titles of persons, 539
cause and effect essays, 315–20
  drafting, 318
  planning for, 317–18
  polishing, 318
  prewriting, 315–17
  proofreading, 318
  thesis in, 317
  writing from reading, 620–24
cause and effect paragraphs,
    196–218
  drafting, 207–8
  freewriting, 199–201
  linking, 208
  peer review form for, 218
  planning for, 204–7
  polishing, 212–13
  prewriting, 199–201
  proofreading, 212–13
  revising, 204, 207–9
  sequencing, 204–5
  topic sentences in, 197–98,
    201
cereal/serial, 559
checklists
  argument paragraph, 226, 230
  basic paragraph, 22
  cause and effect, 204, 208

checklists (*cont.*)
   classification paragraph, 165,
      167
   comparison and contrast para-
      graph, 147
   definition paragraph, 183, 187
   descriptive paragraph, 72
   essay, 251, 257, 261
   illustration paragraph, 51
   narrative paragraph, 96
   prereading, 328
   process paragraph, 114, 120
   revising drafts, 27
   topic sentence, 257
choose/chose, 559
classification essays, 304–9
   drafting, 306–7
   planning for, 305–6
   polishing, 307–8
   prewriting, 304–5
   proofreading, 307–8
   revising, 306–7
   sequencing, 304
   theses in, 305
   writing from reading, 613–16
classification paragraphs, 157–74
   brainstorming, 160–61
   drafting, 166
   explanation of, 157–58
   peer review form for, 174
   planning for, 163–64
   polishing, 169–70
   prewriting, 160–61
   proofreading, 169–70
   revising, 166–67
   sequencing, 164–65
   topic sentences in, 162
   transitions in, 166
clauses. *See also* sentences
   definition of, 353
   dependent, 393–404, 407–10,
      653–54
   punctuation with, 590–91
   that modify, 437
   using *who/which/that*, 590–92
clichés, 575–77
close/clothes/cloths, 559
coarse/course, 559
coherence, 22–26
collective nouns, 484–85,
   495–96
colons, 527–29
   in introductions, 527–28
combining sentences, 397–98. *See
   also* complex sentences;
   compound sentences; run-on
   sentences

come across, 657
commas
   in addresses, 522
   between adjectives, 433–34
   with coordinating conjunctions,
      371–76, 518–19
   in dates, 522
   with insertions, 520, 538
   with introductions, 519
   as links, 518–19
   in lists, 517–18, 527
   in numbers, 522
   with proper names, 520
   in quotations, 522, 538
   splices, 387–89
commonly misspelled words,
   554–56
comparative forms, 428–29, 433
   of pronouns, 508
   with *than*, 433
comparison and contrast essays,
   297–304
   drafting, 301–2
   planning for, 299–300
   point-by-point organization of,
      297–98
   polishing, 302–3
   prewriting, 298–99
   proofreading, 302–3
   revising, 301–2
   sequencing, 297–98
   theses in, 297
   writing from reading, 610–13
comparison and contrast paragraphs, 129–56
   adding details in, 139–41
   drafting, 146–49
   peer review form for, 156
   planning for, 141–46
   point-by-point organization of,
      133–35, 149–50
   polishing, 149–53
   prewriting, 137–41
   proofreading, 149–53
   revising, 146–49
   subject-by-subject organization
      of, 131–33, 150–51
   topic selection for, 129–30
   topic sentences in, 130–31
   transitions in, 135–37
complement/compliment, 559
complex sentences, 393–404
   punctuation of, 395–96
   using dependent clauses,
      393–404
   using subordinating conjunc-
      tions, 394–95, 397, 407–8

compound sentences, 370–83
   using conjunctive adverbs,
      377–78, 526
   using coordinating conjunc-
      tions, 371–76
   using semicolons, 376–79,
      527
compound subjects, 480–82
conclusions
   in essays, 259–60
   in illustration paragraphs,
      53–54
conjunctions
   adverbial, 377–78, 388–89
   coordinating, 371–76, 384, 388,
      397
   in run-on sentences, 385
   subordinating, 394–95, 397,
      407–8
conscience/conscious, 559
consonants, 546
contractions, 362, 452, 531–32,
   658–59
contrast. *See* comparison and
   contrast essays; comparison
   and contrast paragraphs
coordinating conjunctions,
   371–76, 385, 388, 397
could have, 470
council/counsel, 559
count nouns, 650

D

dashes, 536
decent/descent, 559–60
definite articles, 651
definition essays, 309–15
   drafting, 312–13
   planning for, 311–12
   polishing, 313–14
   prewriting, 310–11
   proofreading, 313–14
   revising, 312–13
   theses for, 310
   writing from reading, 616–20
definition paragraphs, 175–95
   drafting, 185–87
   peer review form for, 195
   planning for, 183–84
   polishing, 190–91
   prewriting, 180–81
   proofreading, 190–91
   revising, 183–87, 187
   topic sentences in, 176, 181
   transitions in, 186
   using examples in, 176–77

dependent clauses, 393–404,
   407–10, 653–54
description essays, 283–87
   drafting, 285
   planning for, 284
   polishing, 285–86
   prewriting, 283
   proofreading, 285–86
   revising, 285
   sequencing, 283
   using details in, 283
description paragraphs, 59–81
   choosing a dominant impres-
      sion for, 65–67
   choosing specific words for,
      59–65, 63–65
   colons in, 527–28
   drafting, 72
   peer review form for, 81
   planning for, 67–72
   polishing, 76–77
   prewriting, 65
   proofreading, 76–77
   revising, 72–73
   sequencing, 67–72
   topic sentences in, 66, 67–68
   transitions in, 74–76
   writing from reading, 599–602
descriptive words, 59–65, 63–65,
   427–36
desert/dessert, 560
details, 9–12, 19–22
   in comparison and contrast
      paragraphs, 139–41
   in definition paragraphs,
      180–81
   in description essays, 283
   in essays, 250
   in illustration paragraphs,
      43–44
   in narrative paragraphs, 93–96
   sequencing, 22–26
   using questions, 180–81
differences. *See* comparison and
   contrast essays; comparison
   and contrast paragraphs
dining room, 551
directional writing, 108, 118, 292.
   See also process paragraphs
documentation of sources, 667–75
   books, 670–71
   electronic, 672–73
   non-print, 673
   periodicals, 671–72
   with unknown authors, 670
do/due, 560
does/dose, 560

drafting, 2, 26–29, 254–68
   agreement/disagreement writ-
      ing, 343–44
   argument essays, 324
   argument paragraphs, 230–31
   cause and effect essays, 318
   cause and effect paragraphs,
      207–8
   classification essays, 306–7
   classification paragraphs, 166
   comparison and contrast
      essays, 301–2
   comparison and contrast para-
      graphs, 146–49
   definition essays, 312–13
   definition paragraphs, 185–87
   description essays, 285
   description paragraphs, 72
   essays, 254–68
   illustration essays, 280–81
   illustration paragraphs, 51–53
   narrative essays, 289–90
   narrative paragraphs, 96
   process essays, 294–95
   process paragraphs, 118–21,
      121–22
   reaction writing, 343–44
   summaries, 340–41
   transitions, 51
drop in/off, 657
during, 659

E

each other, 551
editing, 27. *See also* revising
either, 481, 482
electronic sources, 672–73
e-mail, documenting as research
   source, 672–73
emphatic order, 22, 204–5, 226–27
English as a second language
   (ESL), 650–61
essays, 3, 240–76
   argument, 320–26
   body of, 242, 250, 257–59
   cause and effect, 315–20
   classification, 304–9
   clustering ideas in, 246–47
   comparison and contrast,
      297–304
   conclusions in, 242, 259–60
   definition, 309–15
   description, 283–87
   details in, 250
   documenting sources in,
      668–79

drafting, 254–68
   illustration, 277–83
   introductions in, 242, 254–56
   lists in, 245–46
   narrative, 287–92
   peer review form for, 276
   planning for, 248–54
   polishing, 268–71
   prewriting, 245–48, 251
   process, 292–97
   proofreading, 268–71
   reading steps for, 345
   repetition in, 262–63
   revising, 251, 260–63
   single paragraphs vs., 240–42
   strengthening through
      research, 662–63
   subpoints of, 240, 243
   theses in, 242–45, 254, 259
   titles of, 268
   topic sentences in, 240–41,
      249–50, 257
   transitions in, 261–63
   without research, 663–65
   writing from reading, 630–49
essay tests, 344–47
essential clauses, 590–91
essential phrases, 520
even though, 551
every day/everyday, 552
every one/everyone, 552
every time, 551
examples
   in definition paragraphs,
      176–77
   in illustration essays, 277–78
exclamation marks, 536

F

fair/fare, 560
farther/further, 560
fill in/out, 657
Florida Exit Test competencies
   capitalization, 376, 539–40
   effectively using coordination,
      370–74, 376–77
   effectively using semicolons,
      376–77, 526–27
   effectively using subordination,
      393–404, 407–9
   effectively using transitions, 27,
      51–52, 75–76, 101, 119–20,
      135–36, 166, 186, 231, 261–62
   effectively using verb tense,
      461, 464
   parallelism, 417–26

Florida Exit Test competencies
(*cont.*)
pronoun case, 506–9
pronoun consistency, 503
pronoun reference, 491–502
recognizing comma splices,
387–90
recognizing fused sentences,
384–89
recognizing misplaced modifiers, 438–46
recognizing sentence fragments, 405–16
recognizing unclear pronoun
reference, 491–502
spelling, 546–56
subject-verb agreement, 474–90
understanding
adjectives/adverbs, 378,
427–36, 526, 583
understanding
apostrophes/possessives,
531–32
understanding
comparatives/superlatives,
428–29, 433
understanding homonyms,
557–71
understanding topic sentences,
13–15, 23, 44, 68, 83–85, 97–98,
109, 112, 130, 162, 176, 181,
197–98, 201, 220–21, 240–50
understanding word
choice/vocabulary, 572–79
flour/flower, 560
focusing ideas, 12–22
in descriptive paragraphs, 65–66
in lists, 12, 15
in maps, 13
in topic sentences, 13–22
for, 660
formal outlines, 248–49
forth/fourth, 560
fragments, 405–16
freewriting, 4
cause and effect writing,
199–201
narrative writing, 90
reaction writing, 341–42
topic selection and, 9
fused sentences, 384–92

G

general statements, 277
good night, 551
good/well, 432–33

grammar for ESL students
articles, 651–53
contractions, 658–59
idiomatic expressions, 657–58
necessary verbs, 654
nouns, 650–51, 653–54
prepositions, 659–61
pronouns, 653–54
subjects of sentences, 653–54
two-word verbs, 656–58
grammatical person, 118–19
grouping ideas, 223–24

H

hand in/out, 657
heard/herd, 560
hear/here, 560
helping verbs, 354–55, 450–51
have and *had*, 470–71
with past participles, 655
past perfect tense, 465–66
present perfect tense, 464–65
using *of*, 470
here is/are/was/were, 360–61
here/there
compound subjects, 481
subject-verb agreement, 481
high school, 551
himself/herself, 551
hole/whole, 560
homonyms, 557–71. *See also
specific word pairs*
hyphens, 537

I

idiomatic expressions, 656–58
illustration essays, 277–83
drafting, 280–81
planning for, 279–80
polishing, 281–82
prewriting, 278–79
proofreading, 281–82
revising, 280–81
theses in, 279
illustration paragraphs, 39–58
adding details in, 43–44
concluding sentences in, 53–54
drafting, 51–53
gathering ideas for, 43–44
general statements in, 39–42
peer review form for, 58
planning for, 48–50
polishing, 53–54
proofreading, 53–54
revising, 52–53

specific statements in, 39–42
topic sentences in, 44
transitions in, 51
writing from reading, 596–99
in, 660
indefinite articles, 651
indefinite pronouns, 482–84,
492–93
independent clauses. *See* sentences
infinitives, 363, 655
informational writing, 108, 118,
292. *See also* process paragraphs
in front, 551
internal citations, 667–68
Internet search engines, 666
in-text citations, 668–69
into/out of, 660
in topic sentences
focusing ideas, 13–22
introductions
in essays, 242, 254–56
punctuation of, 519, 527–28
irregular verbs, 451–58
list of, 455–56
isle/aisle, 561
italic print, 538
its/it's, 508, 561

J

journals, documentation of as
research sources, 671–72
journal writing, 4, 5

K

keep on, 657
knew/new, 561
know/no, 561

L

lead/led, 563
lessen/lesson, 563
letters. *See* spelling
library research materials, 665–66
linking cause and effect, 208–9
lists, 11–12, 15
colons in, 527
of essay ideas, 245–46
semicolons in, 527
living room, 551
loan/lone, 563
look into/over/up, 657
loose/lose, 563

M

magazines, documentation of as research sources, 671–72
main ideas, 338–39
mapping, 13
Modern Language Association (MLA) documentation system, 668–79
  for books, 670–71
  for electronic sources, 672–73
  electronic sources in, 672–73
  in-text citations, 668–69
  for non-print sources, 673
  for periodicals, 671–72
  unknown authors in, 670
  Works Cited entries, 670–73
modifiers, 437–46. *See also* adjectives; adverbs
  dangling, 440–42
  -ed, 587–88
  -ing, 585–86
  misplaced, 438–40
  phrases as, 437
moral/morale, 563
more/most, 433

N

narrative essays, 287–92
  drafting, 289–90
  planning for, 288–89
  polishing, 290–91
  prewriting, 288
  proofreading, 290–91
  revising, 289–90
  sequencing, 288
narrative paragraphs, 82–107
  clarity and interest in, 86–87
  detail selection for, 93–96, 97
  drafting, 96
  freewriting, 90
  having a point, 82–83, 88, 91
  peer review form for, 107
  planning for, 93–94
  polishing, 102–3
  prewriting, 89–93
  proofreading, 102–3
  quotations in, 88
  relevance of, 93
  sequencing, 87, 93–94, 101–2
  topic selection for, 90–93
  topic sentences in, 82–86, 91–93, 97–98
  transitions in, 101–2
  writing from reading, 603–6

neither, 481, 482
newspapers, documentation of as research sources, 671–72
noncount nouns, 650–51
nonessential clauses, 590–91
nonessential phrases, 520
non-print sources, 673
nonrestrictive clauses, 590–91
nonrestrictive phrases, 520
nonstandard English, 447–48
no one, 551
not, 362
note taking, 332–36, 667–68
not only, 481
nouns, 491
  appositives, 588–90
  articles with, 651–53
  collective, 484–85, 495–96
  contractions, 658–59
  proper names, 520
numbers, 531, 533, 541

O

off, 660
on, 659
one, 493
online catalogs, 665
or, 481
order. *See* sequencing
organization abbreviations, 541
outlines, 1, 19–26, 248–54
  argument essay, 322–24
  argument paragraph, 226–30
  cause and effect essay, 317–18
  cause and effect paragraph, 204–7
  classification essay, 305–6
  classification paragraph, 164–66
  comparison and contrast essay, 299–300
  comparison and contrast paragraph, 141–46
  definition essay, 311–12
  definition paragraph, 183–84
  description essay, 284
  description paragraph, 67–72
  essay test, 345
  illustration essay, 279–80
  illustration paragraph, 93–94
  incorporating research into, 673–75
  process essay, 293–94
  process paragraph, 113–17
  reaction writing, 343
  summary, 339
  without research, 663–64

P

pain/pane, 563
pair/pear, 563–64
paragraphs, basic, 3–48. *See also specific types of paragraphs*
  coherence in, 22–26
  details in, 9–12, 19–22
  drafting, 26–29
  essays vs., 240–42
  focusing ideas for, 12–22
  generating ideas for, 4–7
  length of, 3
  peer review form for, 38
  planning, 19–26
  polishing, 29–30
  prewriting techniques for, 4–7
  proofreading, 30
  revising, 27–29
  sequencing ideas in, 22–23
  titles for, 30
  topic selection for, 7
  topic sentences in, 13–22
  transitions in, 27
  unity in, 3
  writing from reading, 40–41
parallelism in sentences, 417–26
paraphrases, 668–69
  signal phrases indicating, 669–70
parentheses, 537
parenthetical documentation, 668–69
passed/past, 564
passive voice, 466–70
past participles, 450–51, 464–65, 655
past perfect tense, 465–66
past tense, 449–50, 464–65
patience/patients, 564
peace/piece, 564
peer review forms
  argument paragraph, 239
  basic paragraph, 38
  cause and effect, 218
  classification paragraphs, 174
  comparison and contrast, 156
  definition paragraph, 195
  description paragraph, 81
  essay, 276
  illustration paragraph, 58
  narrative paragraph, 107
  process paragraph, 128
  writing from reading, 349
periodical indexes, 665–66
periodicals, documentation of as research sources, 671–72

periods, 538

person, shifts in, 118–19

personal/personnel, 564

pick up, 657

plagiarism, 668

plain/plane, 564

plural verbs. *See* subject-verb
   agreement

point-by-point organization,
   133–35, 149–50, 297–98

polishing, 2, 29–37, 268–71
   argument essay, 325–26
   argument paragraph, 234
   cause and effect essay, 318
   cause and effect paragraph,
      212–13
   classification essay, 307–8
   classification paragraph,
      169–70
   comparison and contrast essay,
      302–3
   comparison and contrast para-
      graph, 149–53
   definition essay, 313–14
   definition paragraph, 190–91
   description essay, 285–86
   description paragraph, 76–77
   essay test, 346
   illustration essay, 281–82
   illustration paragraph, 53–54
   narrative essay, 290–91
   narrative paragraph, 122–24
   reaction writing, 344
   summary, 341

possessive forms
   apostrophes in, 532
   of pronouns, 506–9, 532

precise language, 572–73

prepositional phrases, 356–59
   between in, 507–8
   beginning sentences with,
      584–85
   not the subject of a sentence,
      476–77
   pronouns case in, 507–8
   showing place, 660
   showing time, 659–60

prereading, 328–32

presence/presents, 564

present participles, 362, 406,
   450–51

present perfect tense, 464–65

present tense, 448–49, 450–51
   -s endings and, 654–55

prewriting, 1, 4–22, 245–48, 251
   argument essays, 321–22
   argument paragraphs, 223–26

cause and effect essays, 315–17

cause and effect paragraphs,
   199–201

classification essays, 304–5

classification paragraphs,
   160–61

comparison and contrast
   essays, 298–99

comparison and contrast paragraphs, 137–41

definition essays, 310–11

definition paragraphs, 180–83

description essays, 283

description paragraphs, 65

essay tests, 345

focusing ideas, 12–22

illustration essays, 278–79

illustration paragraphs, 42–48

narrative essays, 288

narrative paragraphs, 89–93

process essays, 292–93

process paragraphs, 111–13

summaries, 336–39

principal/principle, 564

process essays, 292–97
   drafting, 294–95
   planning for, 293–94
   polishing, 295–96
   prewriting, 292–93
   proofreading, 295–96
   revising, 294–95
   sequencing, 292
   theses in, 292

process paragraphs, 108–28
   drafting, 118–21, 121–22
   grammatical person in, 118–19
   peer review form for, 128
   planning for, 113–17
   polishing, 122–24
   prewriting, 111–13
   proofreading, 122–23
   sequencing, 108–11, 119
   topic selection for, 109, 111
   topic sentences in, 112
   transitions in, 119
   writing from reading, 606–10

pronouns
   antecedents of, 491–502
   apostrophes with, 532
   avoiding sexism and, 493
   case of, 506–9
   for collective nouns, 495–96
   comparative forms of, 508
   consistency of, 503–12
   contractions and, 658–59
   indefinite, 482–84, 492–93
   myself, 508

noun agreement with, 491–502

objective case, 506–9

points of view and, 503

possessive case of, 506–9, 532

in prepositional phrases, 507–8

punctuation of, 508

spelled as one word, 551

subjective case of, 506–9

subject-verb agreement and,
   476

they/their, 493, 499

proofreading, 2, 29–30, 268–71
   argument essays, 325–26
   argument paragraphs, 234
   basic essays, 268–71
   basic paragraphs, 29–30
   cause and effect essays, 318
   cause and effect paragraphs,
      212–13
   classification essays, 307–8
   classification paragraphs,
      169–70
   comparison and contrast
      essays, 302–3
   comparison and contrast para-
      graphs, 149–53
   definition essays, 313–14
   definition paragraphs, 190–91
   description essays, 285–86
   descriptive paragraphs, 76–77
   illustration essays, 281–82
   illustration paragraphs, 53–54
   narrative essays, 290–91
   narrative paragraphs, 102–3
   process essays, 295–96
   process paragraphs, 122–23
   reaction writing, 344
   summaries, 341

proper names, 520

punctuation
   of addresses, 522
   after conjunctive adverbs, 377
   apostrophes, 531–35
   capitalization, 539–41
   colons, 527–29
   commas, 387–89, 433–34,
      517–25, 538
   in complex sentences, 395–96
   in compound sentences, 371–76
   dashes, 536
   of dates, 522
   exclamation marks, 536
   hyphens, 537
   inserters, 536–37
   of numbers, 522
   or possessive pronouns, 508
   parentheses, 537

periods, 513–14, 538
question marks, 514–15
quotation marks, 537–38
of quotations, 522, 528, 537–38
in run-on sentences, 385–86
semicolons, 376–79, 387–89, 526–27
in titles of works, 538
underlining, 538
in *who/which/that* clauses, 590–91
purpose of writing, 4

Q

questions
for identifying details, 180–81
punctuation of, 514–15
for reading, 329, 332
subject-verb agreement in, 479
word order of, 361
quiet down, 657
quiet/quit/quite, 564
quotation marks, 537–38
quotations
capitalization in, 539
indirect, 538
in narrative writing, 88
within other quotations, 538
punctuation of, 522, 528, 537–38
signal phrases to indicate, 669–70

R

rain/reign/rein, 564–65
reaction writing, 341–44
brainstorming for, 342
drafting, 343–44
freewriting, 341–42
planning for, 343
points of agreement/disagreement in, 343
polishing, 344
proofreading, 344
revising, 343–44
reading selections
"A Brother's Murder" (Staples), 633–37
"A Cell Phone? Never for Me" (Samuelson), 627–30
"A Present for Popo" (Wong), 599–602
"Beautiful Daughter" (Mason), 610–13

"Breaking the Bonds of Hate" (Khiev), 616–20
"Eleven" (Cisneros), 630–33
"How to Write a Personal Letter" (Keillor), 606–10
"My Daughter Smokes" (Walker), 640–45
"Navajo Code Talkers: The Century's Best Kept Secret" (Hitt), 637–40
"Parental Discretion" (Hevesi), 645–49
"Spanglish" (Castro, Cook, and Garcia), 596–99
"Sticky Stuff" (Hamilton and Namuth), 593–96
"Students in Shock" (Kellmayer), 620–24
"The Good Father" (Valdes-Rodriguez), 603–6
"Three Disciplines for Children" (Holt), 613–16
"Why Is Geezer-Bashing Acceptable?" (Trafford), 624–26
reading steps, 328–36, 345
reasons. *See* cause and effect paragraphs
relevance, 93
repetition, 262–63
rereading, 332–36
research process, 662–81
checking validity of sources in, 666–67
in daily life, 662
final version of essays using, 677–80
incorporating and acknowledging sources in, 666–77
locating material in, 665–66
outlines and, 674–75
plagiarism and, 668
signal phrases and, 669–70
strengthening essays through, 662–81
restating an idea, 262
restrictive clauses, 590–91
restrictive phrases, 520
results. *See* cause and effect paragraphs
reviewing. *See* polishing
revising, 2, 27–29, 251, 260–63. *See also* checklists
argument essays, 324
argument paragraphs, 226, 230–32
cause and effect essays, 318

cause and effect paragraphs, 204, 207–9
classification essays, 306–7
classification paragraphs, 165, 166–68
comparison and contrast essays, 301–2
comparison and contrast paragraphs, 146–49
definition essays, 312–13
definition paragraphs, 183–87, 187
description essays, 285
descriptive paragraphs, 72–73
illustration essays, 280–81
illustration paragraphs, 52–53
narrative essays, 289–90
narrative paragraphs, 97
process essays, 294–95
process paragraphs, 122–24
reaction writing, 343–44
summaries, 340–41
right/rite/write, 565
run into/out, 657
run-on sentences, 384–87

S

search engines, 666
semicolons, 376–79, 387–89, 526–27
sense words, 63–65
sentences. *See also* punctuation
balancing length of, 580–82
beginning with an adverb, 583
beginning with a prepositional phrase, 584–85
combining, 28–29, 370–83, 526–27
complex, 393–404
compound, 371–76, 526–27
with compound subjects, 480–82
definition of, 353
fragments, 405–16
fused, 384–92
joining ideas, 585–88
parallelism in, 417–26
prepositional phrases in, 356–59
recognizing subjects of, 355–56
recognizing verbs in, 354–55, 356
run-on, 384–87
simple, 353–69, 373
subordination in, 393–404
using adverbs, 362

sentences (*cont.*)
  using appositives, 588–90
  using -*ed* modifiers, 587–88
  using *here is/are/was/were*,
    360–61
  using -*ing* modifiers, 585–86
  using semicolons, 526–27
  using *there is/are was/were*,
    360–61
  using *who/which/that* clauses,
    590–92
  variety in, 580–92
  word order in, 359–62, 479–80,
    582–85
sequencing, 22–23. *See also* word
  order
  adverbs, 438–40
  argument paragraphs, 226–28
  cause and effect paragraphs,
    204–5
  classification essays, 304
  classification paragraphs,
    164–65
  comparison and contrast
    essays, 297–98
  description essays, 283
  description paragraphs, 67–72
  emphatic order, 204–5, 226–27
  ideas in paragraphs, 22–23
  logical order, 22–23, 204–5,
    220–21
  modifiers, 438–40
  narrative essays, 288
  narrative paragraphs, 87, 93–94,
    101–2
  point-by-point organization,
    133–35, 149–50, 297–98
  process essays, 292
  process paragraphs, 108–11,
    119
  subject-by-subject organization,
    131–33, 150–51
  time order, 204–5
sexism in writing, 493
shifts in person, 118–19
should have, 470
sight/site/cite, 465
signal phrases, 669–70
similarities. *See* comparison and
  contrast essays; comparison
  and contrast paragraphs
simple sentences, 353–69, 373
since, 660
singular verbs. *See* subject-verb
  agreement
slang, 578–79

sole/soul, 565
sound alike/look alike words,
  557–71. *See also specific*
  words
sources
  acknowledging, 667–75
  checking validity of, 666–67
  gathering and organizing, 667
  taking notes on, 667–68
space/spatial order, 22, 68
specific words and phrases,
  39–42, 59–65, 63–65, 277–78
spelling, 546–79
  adding -*s* or -*es*, 549
  changing final *y* to *i*, 548
  combining words, 551–52
  commonly misspelled words,
    554–56
  doubling final consonants,
    546–47
  dropping final *e*, 547–48
  sound alike/look alike words,
    557–71
  using *ie* or *ei*, 549
stair/stare, 565
stake/steak, 565
standard English forms, 447–48,
  451, 453
  slang and, 578–79
stationary/stationery, 565
steal/steel, 565
story telling. *See* narrative essays;
  narrative paragraphs
subject-by-subject organization,
  131–33, 150–51
subject of a sentence, 355–56,
  360–61, 653–54
  collective nouns as, 484–85
  compound, 480–82
  hard-to-find, 476–77
  reverse word order of, 479–80
  in sentence fragments, 410
subject pronouns, 476, 653–54
subject-verb agreement, 474–90
  collective nouns and, 484–85
  compound subjects and, 480–82
  hard-to-find subjects and,
    476–77
  indefinite pronouns and, 482–84
  number and, 474–75
  reverse word order and, 479–80
subordinating conjunctions,
  394–95, 397, 407–8
subpoints of essays, 240, 243
summaries, 336–41
  drafting, 340–41

  planning for, 339
  polishing, 341
  prewriting, 336–39
  proofreading, 341
  revising, 340–41
superlative adjectives, 428–29,
  433
support, 22
synonyms
  in comparison and contrast
    writing, 149
  for essay transitions, 262–63

T

tense, 447. *See also* verbs
  consistency in, 462–64
  past, 449–50, 465
  past perfect, 465–66
  present, 448–49, 450–51,
    654–55
  present perfect, 464–65
Texas Higher Education
  Assessment Test objectives
  adjectives and adverbs, 362,
    377–78, 388–89, 427–36, 526,
    583
  appropriateness, 4, 220, 321
  comparatives/superlatives,
    428–29, 433, 508
  concrete examples, 176–77,
    277–78
  development, 1, 4–22 (*See also*
    prewriting)
  introductions and conclusions,
    53–54, 242, 254–56, 259–60,
    519, 527–28
  organization, 1, 27–29 (*See also*
    drafting)
  prewriting skills, 1, 4–22 (*See*
    also prewriting)
  recognizing dangling modifiers,
    440–42
  recognizing effective organiza-
    tion, 27–37 (*See also* polish-
    ing)
  recognizing effective sentences,
    353–69
  recognizing fragments, 405–16
  recognizing ineffective word
    choice, 572–79
  recognizing purpose and audi-
    ence, 4, 220, 321
  recognizing run-on sentences,
    384–92

recognizing standard American English, 447–48, 451, 453

recognizing unity, focus, and development, 4–22, 30–37 (*See also* polishing)

rough outline of essay, 19–26, 248–54 (*See also* outlines)

subject-verb agreement, 474–90

thesis statements, 240, 242–45, 254, 259, 279, 292, 297, 305, 317, 320

timing, 345–47

unity and focus, 12–22

verb forms, 447–60, 461–64, 464–65, 468–69

than, 433

than/then, 565

that clauses, 590–92

the (definite article), 651

their/there/they're, 566

then, 388, 433

there is/are was/were, 360–61

thesis of an essay, 240, 242–45, 254, 259

  argument, 320

  cause and effect, 317

  classification, 305

  comparison and contrast, 297

  definition, 310

  illustration, 279

  process, 292

they/their, 493, 499

think over, 657

thorough/through/threw, 566

time abbreviations, 541

time order, 22, 68, 204–5

titles, 30

  abbreviations of, 541

  capitalization of, 540

  of essays, 268

  italic print for, 538

  of persons, 539, 541

  punctuation of, 537, 538

to be, 451, 453

to do, 452, 453

to have, 451, 453

topic sentences, 13–22

  argument paragraphs, 219–20

  checklist for, 257

  classification paragraphs, 162

  comparison and contrast paragraphs, 130–31

  definition paragraphs, 176, 181

  description paragraphs, 66, 67–68

  essay, 240, 242–45, 249–50, 257

illustration paragraphs, 44

location of, 23, 83–84

narrative paragraphs, 82–86, 91–93, 97–98

process paragraphs, 112

staying on one point, 250–51

supporting details and, 19–22

to/too/two, 566

to with verbs, 363, 406

transitions, 27, 261–63

  argument paragraphs, 231

  cause and effect paragraphs, 208

  classification paragraphs, 166

  comparison and contrast paragraphs, 135–37

  definition paragraphs, 186

  description paragraphs, 74–76

  essays, 261–63

  illustration paragraphs, 51

  narrative paragraphs, 101–2

  between paragraphs, 262–63

  within paragraphs, 261

  process paragraphs, 119

  restating an idea, 262

  using synonyms, 262–63

try on/out, 657

turn on/down/up, 657–58

two-word verbs, 656–58

U

underlining, 538

unity, 22

until, 659

used to, 470

V

vain/vane/vein, 566

verbs, 447–60. *See also* subject-verb agreement

  active voice, 466–70

  with adverbs, 656–58

  consistency in, 461–64, 466–70

  contractions, 362, 658–59

  -d or *-ed* endings, 449–50, 451

  -ed endings, 449–50, 655

  for ESL students, 654–59

  helping, 354–55, 450–51, 464–65, 470–71, 655

  infinitives, 363, 406, 655

  -ing, 362, 406, 450–51

  irregular, 451–58

  passive voice, 466–70

past participles, 450–51, 464–65, 655

past perfect tense, 465–66

past tense, 449–50, 465

  with prepositions, 656–58

present participles, 362, 406, 450–51

present perfect tense, 464–65

present tense, 448–49, 450–51, 654–55

  pronoun test and, 362

  -s endings, 448, 654–55

  sentence fragments, 410

  in simple sentences, 354–55, 356

  -s or *-es* endings, 448

  standard English forms, 448, 451

  tense of, 447, 461–64

  used to, 470

  using *have* and *had*, 470–71

  using *of*, 470

  voice of, 466–70

voice, 466–70

vowels, 546

W

waist/waste, 566

wait/weight, 566

wander/wonder, 567

weather/whether, 566

Web sites, documenting as research sources, 671–72

well/badly, 432–33

were/we're/where, 566–67

whined/wind/wined, 567

who clauses, 590–92

who's/whose, 567

woman/women, 567

wood/would, 567

word choice, 572–79

  clichés, 575–77

  precision in, 572–73

  slang, 578–79

  wordiness and, 573–75

word order

  in questions, 361

  in sentences, 359–62, 582–85

Works Cited lists, 667–68

  books in, 670–71

  electronic sources in, 672–73

  non-print sources in, 673

  periodicals in, 671–72

would have, 470–71

write down, 658

writing from reading, 327–49
   prereading, 328–29
   reading and rereading, 330–35
   writing a reaction, 341–44
   writing a summary, 336–41
   writing for an essay test,
     345–46
writing from reading, selections/
   writing topics from, 593–649

argument, 624–30
cause and effect, 620–24
classification, 613–16
comparison and contrast,
  610–13
definition, 616–20
description, 599–602
illustration, 596–99
narration, 603–6

process, 606–10
the essay, 630–49
the writing process,
  593–95

Y

y (letter), 546
yourself, 551
your/you're, 567